SSC CGL, CPO, CHSL,Bank, CUET, UPSC, NDA, CDS,
Other Entrance & Competitive Exams

COMPLETE ENGLISH

VOCABULARY

UNDERSTAND ! PRACTICE ! REVISE !

Satender Singh

Published By

Invincible Publication Pvt. Ltd.

Published by

Invincible Publication Pvt. Ltd.

201A, SAS Tower, Sector 38, Gurugram – 122003

Phone: +91-124-4034247, +91 9599066061

www.invinciblepublishers.com

Sales: Office No. 4760-61/23 Basement, Pratap Street,

Ansari Road Daryaganj, New Delhi. 110002

Phone: +91-11-40198405

Email: invinciblepublishers@gmail.com

First edition – 2023

ISBN: 978-93-58867-65-7

About the Book

Vocabulary of any language is a fundamental aspect that should be mastered for further advancement in the subject. Therefore, 'Vocab power' has been specially curated in alliance to the readers' needs and aspirations. In addition to 15,000+ words, the book lays an emphasis on homonyms, proverbs, idioms, palindromes, etc. The simple format of the book has been specially designed to simplify the learning process, as well as increase the proficiency of the readers. The book is a must-read for SSC, CGL, CHSL, BANK, CTET, DSSSB, CUET, NDA, UPSC and Defence aspirants. The author, with more than 10 years of experience in education field, has encapsulated his years of experience and knowledge in this book with an aim to simplify the learning for all.

Contents

One Word Substitutions

Synonyms, Antonyms, Acronyms, Paronyms, Contronyms, Hetronyms and Homonyms

Defining Words (A to Z Words)

Idioms and Phrases

Spellings and Formation of Words

UNIT 1

Vocabulary: One-Word Substitutions asked in Various Competitive Exams

One word substitution is the use of one word in place of a wordy phrase in order to make the sentence structure clearer. The meaning, with the replacement of the phrase remains identical while the sentence becomes shorter

S.N.	Phrases	One Word	PoS	Hindi
1.	Acutely distressing	Harrowing	(Adj.)	ख़ौफनाक
2.	Irritating inconvenience	Hassle	(V.)	परेशान करना
3.	A transport vehicle for conveying the coffin at a funeral	**Hearse**	(N.)	शवयान
4.	In an enthusiastic way		(Adv.)	उत्साह से
5.	Making one feel very sad	Heartily, Heart-Wrenching	(Adj.)	दुखी करने वाला
6.	Interrupt (a public speaker) with derisive or aggressive comments or abuse	Heckle	(V.)	प्रश्नों से तंग करना
7.	One who believes that gaining pleasure is the most important thing in life	Hedonist	(N.)	सुखवादी
8.	Pay attention	Heed	(V.)	सावधान रहना
9.	Person who is the natural successor to ancestral property	Heir	(N.)	वारिस
10.	Preferring or attracted to sunlight	Heliophilous	(Adj.)	सूर्यभिमुख
11.	The therapeutic use of sunlight	Heliotherapy	(N.)	सूर्य चिकित्सा
12.	A seven-sided figure	**Heptagon**	(N.)	सप्तभुज
13.	Place for collection of dried plant specimens	**Herbarium**	(N.)	वनस्पति संग्रहालय
14.	Animal that feeds on plants	Herbivorous	(N.)	शाकाहारी
15.	A group of cattle	Herd	(N.)	झुंड
16.	A belief or an opinion that is against the principle of a particular religion. Opinion contrary to accepted doctrines	Heresy	(N.)	विधर्म
17.	Things of different nature	Heterogeneous	(Adj.)	विविध
18.	A geometrical figure with six sides	Hexagon	(N.)	षट्भुज
19.	To spend winter in a dormant state	Hibernate	(V.)	शीतनिद्रा में होना
20.	Condition of sleep during certain parts of the year	Hibernation	(N.)	शीतनिद्रा

S.N.	Phrases	One Word	PoS	Hindi
21.	A person claiming to be superior in culture and intellect to others	Highbrow	(Adj.)	बुद्धिमान
22.	An act of violence to take control of a plane	**Hijack**	(V.)	विमान का अपहरण
23.	Parts of a country behind the coast or a river bank.	Hinterland	(N.)	आंतरिक इलाके
24.	The sound made by a snake	Hiss	(N.)	सांप की फुफकारी आवाज़
25.	Very dramatic	Histrionic	(Adj.)	नाटकीय
26.	To secretly store more than what is allowed	Hoard	(V.)	खजाना
27.	Destruction or slaughter on a mass scale	Holocaust	(N.)	विध्वंस
28.	Murder of a man	Homicide	(N.)	मानव हत्या
29.	All (things or people) of the same or similar kind or nature	Homogeneous	(Adj.)	सजातीय
30.	Things which are of the same kind and of the same dimensions	Homogenous	(Adj.)	एक समान
31.	A mass of wax cells built by honey bees to store honey	Honeycomb	(N.)	शहद का छत्ता
32.	A payment given for professional services that are rendered nominally without charge	Honorarium	(N.)	मानदेय
33.	Holding an office without receiving a pay	Honorary	(Adj.)	माननीय
34.	The cry of an owl	**Hoot**	(N.)	उल्लू की बोली
35.	A large group of people	Horde	(N.)	भीड़
36.	The line where the land and sky seems to meet	Horizon	(N.)	क्षितिज
37.	Something that is extremely unpleasant	**Horrendous**	(Adj.)	भयानक
38.	The study of growing garden plants	Horticulture	(N.)	उद्यान-विज्ञान
39.	One who studies the art of gardening	**Horticulturist**	(N.)	बाग़बानी करनेवाला
40.	Friendly and welcoming to visitors.	Hospitable	(Adj.)	सत्कार करने वाला
41.	Receiving guests warmly	Hospitality	(N.)	अतिथि सत्कार
42.	Someone taken a prisoner to fulfil demands	Hostage	(N.)	बंधक
43.	A woman who entertains guests	Hostess	(N.)	सत्कारिणी
44.	One who loses temper very soon	**Hot-Headed**	(Adj.)	उग्र स्वभाव का
45.	Annoyed or irritated and quick to take offence at petty things	Huffy	(Adj.)	झुंझलाया हुआ
46.	The organic component of soil, formed by the decomposition of leaves and other plant material	Humus	(N.)	सड़ी पत्तियों की मिट्टी

S.N.	Phrases	One Word	PoS	Hindi
47.	Assembly or parliament in which no party has got clear majority.	Hung	(Adj.)	लटका हुआ
48.	A box or cage for rabbits or small animals	Hutch	(N.)	छोटे जानवरों के रहने का घर
49.	The science of surveying and charting bodies of water	Hydrography	(N.)	जलराशि विज्ञान
50.	Extreme fear of water	Hydrophobia	(N.)	पानी से भय
51.	A song or music in praise of God	**Hymn**	(N.)	स्तुति का गीत
52.	Excessive preoccupation with one's health	Hypochondria	(N.)	रोगभ्रम
53.	A person who suffers from an imaginary illness / A person who is abnormally anxious about his health	Hypochondriac	(N.)	रोगभ्रमी
54.	A person pretending to be somebody he isn't	Hypocrite	(N.)	पाखंडी
55.	A tentative theory about the natural world	Hypothesis	(N.)	परिकल्पना
56.	One who destroys images or attacks popular beliefs	Iconoclast	(N.)	मूर्ति तोड़ने वाला
57.	A person's peculiar habit	Idiosyncrasy	(N.)	अनोखापन
58.	A mode of behavior or way of thought peculiar to an individual (not sub- or abnormal in any way)	**Idiosyncratic**	(Adj.)	विशेष स्वभाव का
59.	The practice of worshipping statues as gods	**Idolatry**	(N.)	मूर्ति पूजा
60.	Extremely happy, peaceful, or picturesque	**Idyllic**	(Adj.)	शांतिपूर्ण
61.	A small round house / shelter built from blocks of hard snow by the inuit people of northern n.merica	**Igloo**	(N.)	हिम-कुटी
62.	Not to pay attention to someone or something	Ignore	(N.)	नज़रअंदाज़ करना
63.	Handwriting which is difficult or impossible to read	Illegible	(Adj.)	अपठनीय
64.	That which is unlawful	Illicit	(Adj.)	अवैध
65.	A person who cannot read or write	Illiterate	(Adj.)	निरक्षर
66.	To brighten up with lights	**Illuminate**	(V.)	प्रकाश करना
67.	Pictures given in a book for the purpose of explaining things	Illustration	(N.)	चित्रण
68.	Existing only in the mind	Imaginary	(Adj.)	
69.	A foreigner who settles in a country. / A person coming to a foreign land to settle there.	Immigrant	(N.)	काल्पनिक
70.	That which cannot be moved	Immobile	(Adj.)	अचल
71.	Matter which is against moral values	Immoral	(Adj.)	अनैतिक

S.N.	Phrases	One Word	PoS	Hindi
72.	Resistant to a particular infection	Immune	(Adj.)	प्रतिरक्षित
73.	Protection or exemption from something, especially an obligation or penalty	Immunity	(N.)	प्रतिरोधक क्षमता
74.	Transfix or pierce with a sharp instrument	Impale	(V.)	छेदना
75.	Not supporting any side in an argument	Impartial	(Adj.)	निष्पक्ष
76.	The policy of extending a country's empire and influence	Imperialism	(N.)	साम्राज्यवाद
77.	Not allowing fluid to pass-through. A person who remains unmoved and unaffected by othe people's opinions, suggestions	Impervious	(Adj.)	अभेद्य
78.	A person who dishonestly pretends to be somebody else	Imposter	(N.)	बहुरूपिया
79.	Strong and impossible to defeat, change, that which cannot be taken by force	Impregnable	(Adj.)	अभेद्य
80.	Made or done without previous preparation	Impromptu	(Adj.)	बिना तैयारी के
81.	Make better	Improve	(V.)	बेहतर बनाना
82.	One who is too careless to plan for the future	Improvident	(Adj.)	लापरवाह
83.	Shamelessly rude	Impudent	(Adj.)	बेहूदा
84.	Without risk of punishment	Impunity	(N.)	दण्ड मुक्ति
85.	Incapable of being approached	Inaccessible	(Adj.)	दुर्गम
86.	Not endowed with life / lifeless objects	Inanimate	(Adj.)	अचेतन
87.	Something that cannot be heard	Inaudible	(Adj.)	अश्राव्य
88.	A deity or spirit embodied in human form	Incarnate	(Adj.)	अवतार लिया हुआ
89.	Motive or incitement to action	Incentive	(N.)	प्रोत्साहन
90.	Lack of civic-mindedness or of patriotism	Incivism	(N.)	देशद्रोह
91.	Travelling under a name other than one's own	Incognito	(Adj.)	गुप्त रूप से
92.	Something that is expressed in a confusing way	Incoherent	(Adj.)	असंगत
93.	Something that is difficult to understand	Incompre-hensible	(Adj.)	समझ से बाहर
94.	One who cannot be corrected, One who is beyond reform	Incorrigible	(Adj.)	असंशोधनीय
95.	That which cannot be believed	Incredible	(Adj.)	अविश्सनीय
96.	Owing money to someone	Indebted	(Adj.)	ऋणी
97.	Incapable of feeling tired or exhausted	Indefatigable	(Adj.)	न थकनेवाला
98.	That which cannot be effaced	Indelible	(Adj.)	स्थायी
99.	Extreme or indefinite to be adequately described.	Indescribable	(Adj.)	अवर्णनीय

S.N.	Phrases	One Word	PoS	Hindi
100.	Originating or occurring naturally in the place or country where found/ native	Indigenous	(Adj.)	स्वदेशी
101.	Anger about an unfair situation or about someone's unfair behaviour	Indignation	(N.)	अन्याय देखकर
102.	A person who is absolutely necessary for someone or something	Indispensable	(Adj.)	अपरिहार्य
103.	One who works very hard	Industrious	(Adj.)	मेहनती
104.	Not suitable for eating	Inedible	(Adj.)	अखाद्य
105.	That cannot be expressed in words	Ineffable	(Adj.)	अवर्णनीय
106.	Someone not fit to be chosen	Ineligible	(Adj.)	अयोग्य
107.	showing a lack of skill	Ineptness	(Adj.)	अयोग्यता
108.	Unable to act	Inert	(Adj.)	अक्रिय
109.	Something that cannot be avoided	Inevitable	(Adj.)	अटल
110.	Not to be moved by entreaty	Inexorable	(Adj.)	हठी
111.	That which cannot be put out	Inextinguishable	(Adj.)	जिसे बुझाया न
112.	One who cannot make mistake	Infallible	(Adj.)	अचूक
113.	The crime of killing a baby	Infanticide	(N.)	शिशु हत्या
114.	Not limited by number	Infinite	(Adj.)	अनंत
115.	A place in a large institution for the care of those who are ill.	Infirmary	(N.)	अस्पताल
116.	That can burn / catches fire easily	Inflammable	(Adj.)	ज्वलनशील
117.	A cluster of flowers on a branch	Inflorescence	(N.)	पुष्पगुच्छ
118.	The money, property, etc. that you receive from somebody when he dies	Inheritance	(N.)	विरासत
119.	Causing no harm	Innocuous	(Adj.)	अहानिकर
120.	An indirect reference	Innuendo	(N.)	इशारा (गलत भावना से)
121.	That which cannot be satisfied	Insatiable	(Adj.)	लालची
122.	Write or carve words on stone or paper	Inscribe	(V.)	अंकित करना
123.	Words carved on a stone or monument	Inscription	(N.)	शिलालेख
124.	Being unable to pay one's debt	Insolvent	(Adj.)	दिवालिया
124.	The condition of being unable to sleep over a period of tim	Insomnia	(N.)	अनिद्रा
126.	Covered with a material or substance in order to top heat, sound etc. From entering or escaping	Insulated	(Adj.)	विद्युत-रोधित
127.	Rebellious or opposing the authority	Insurgent	(N.)	विद्रोही
128.	That which cannot be perceived by touch	Intangible	(Adj.)	अस्पृश्य

S.N.	Phrases	One Word	PoS	Hindi
129.	Combine to form a whole	Integrate	(V.)	संघटित करना
130.	The quality of being honest and having strong moral principles.	Integrity	(N.)	अखंडता
131.	One who interferes in the affairs of others, often for selfish reason	Interloper	(N.)	घुसपैठिया
132.	Interval between two events	Interlude	(N.)	मध्यांतर कार्यक्रम
133.	One who intervenes between two or more parties to settle differences	Intermediary	(Adj.)	मध्यस्थ
134.	The act of burying a dead person	Interment	(N.)	दफ़न
135.	Continuing for a very long time	Interminable	(Adj.)	अनंतकालीन
136.	The act of confining someone in a prison	Internment	(N.)	नजरबंदी
137.	Estimate the value of	Interpolate	(V.)	अनुमान लगाना
138.	Place or insert between one thing and another	Interpose	(V.)	घुसाना
139.	The period between two reigns	Interregnum	(N.)	दो शासनों के बीच का काल
140.	To prevent or alter a result or course of events	Intervene	(V.)	हस्तक्षेप करना
141.	One who dies without a will	**Intestate**	(Adj.)	बिन वसीयत मरा मरा हुआ
142.	Force someone through fear to do or not to do something	Intimidate	(V.)	धमकाना
143.	The action of looking within or into one's own mind	Introspection	(N.)	आत्म निरीक्षण
144.	A quiet person who is more interested in his own thoughts and feelings than in spending time with other people	**Introvert**	(N.)	अन्तर्मुखी व्यक्ति
145.	A person who enters without any invitation	Intruder	(N.)	घुसपैठिया
146.	Overflow or fill an area with excess water, as in a flood	Inundate	(V.)	डुबोना
147.	A person weak and disabled by illness	Invalid	(N.)	लंबे समय से बीमार व्यक्ति
148.	A detailed list of things in a place	Inventory	(N.)	वस्तु सूची
149.	An animal lacking a backbone	Invertebrates	(N.)	अकशेरुकी
150.	An official examination of the facts about a situation, crime, etc.	Investigation	(N.)	जाँच पड़ताल
151.	A person who supervises during an examination	Invigilator	(N.)	निरीक्षक
152.	Refresh and revive	Invigorate	(V.)	बलवर्धन करना
153.	That which cannot be conquered	Invincible	(Adj.)	अजेय

S.N.	Phrases	One Word	PoS	Hindi
154.	Call upon God or any other power (like law) etc. for help or protection	Invocation	(N.)	आह्वान
155.	A statement which cannot be contradicted	Irrefutable	(Adj.)	अखंडनीय
156.	Showing a lack of respect for people or things that are generally taken seriously	Irreverent	(Adj.)	अपमान जनक
157.	That which cannot be called back	Irrevocable	(Adj.)	अटल
158.	To supply land with water by artificial means	Irrigate	(V.)	सींचना
159.	A piece of land entirely surrounded by water	Island	(N.)	द्वीप
160.	Far away from other places	Isolated	(Adj.)	अलग किया हुआ
161.	A narrow stretch of land connecting two large bodies of land	Isthmus	(N.)	भूमि की एक संकरी पट्टी जो दो बड़े भूभागों को जोड़ती है
162.	Travelling from place to place, especially to find work	Itinerant	(Adj.)	भ्रमणकारी
163.	A plan of a journey, including the route and the places that you visi	Itinerary	(N.)	यात्रा कार्यक्रम
164.	One who takes care of a building	Janitor	(N.)	चौकीदार
165.	Special words and phrases used by particular groups of people, especially in their work	Jargon	(N.)	विशिष्ट शब्दावली
166.	A short journey that you make for pleasure	Jaunt	(N.)	मनोरंजन की यात्रा
167.	Having or expressing a lively, cheerful, and self confident manner	Jauntily	(Adj.)	मनोरंजन से
168.	To cross streets on foot carelessly	Jaywalk	(N.)	रास्ता पार करने में लापरवाह होना
169.	A person or thing that brings bad luck	Jinx	(N.)	मनहूस
170.	Something which brings bad luck	Jinxed	(V.)	मनहूस
171.	A person who rides in horse races, especially as a profession	**Jockey**	(N.)	घुड़दौड़ का घुड़सवार
172.	The work of collecting and writing news, stories for newspapers, magazines, radio or television	Journalism	(N.)	पत्रकारिता
173.	A person who writes for newspapers and magazines	Journalist	(N.)	पत्रकार
174.	The act of traveling from one place to another	Journey	(N.)	यात्रा
175.	A person in a court who has the authority to decide how criminals should be punished or to make legal decisions	Judge	(N.)	न्यायाधीश

S.N.	Phrases	One Word	PoS	Hindi
176.	The part of a country's government responsible for its legal system	Judiciary	(N.)	न्यायतंत्र
177.	A military or political group that rules a country after taking power by force	Junta	(N.)	सत्ताधारी सेना
178.	The science or philosophy of law	Jurisprudence	(N.)	न्यायशास्त्र
179.	A group of members of the public who listen to the facts of a case in a court and decide whether or not somebody is guilty of a crime	**Jury**	(N.)	न्यायपीठ
180.	Connected with young people who are not yet adults	Juvenile	(Adj.)	किशोर
181.	Placing different things in order to create an interesting effect	Juxtapose	(V.)	पास-पास रखना
182.	Soft, inner part of a nut or fruit-stone	Kernel	(N.)	गिरी/दाना
183.	A person with strong desire to steal.	**Kleptomania**	(N.)	चोरी करने की बीमारी
184.	A natural skill at doing something	**Knack**	(N.)	कौशल
185.	The sound of the funeral bell	Knell	(N.)	शोक सूचक घंटे की ध्वनि
186.	A deep cut or tear in skin or flesh	Laceration	(N.)	घाव
187.	Two lengths of rope, bamboo or wood with rungs used for climbing up and down walls, sides of ships etc.	Ladder	(N.)	सीढ़ी
188.	A place where wild animals live	Lair	(N.)	माँद
189.	Worthy of high praise	Laudable	(Adj.)	प्रशंसनीय
190.	A place where clothes are washed and pressed	Laundry	(N.)	धोभीघर
191.	A medicine that softens the bowels	Laxative	(Adj.)	पेट साफ करने वाली
192.	Unwilling to work or use energy	Lazy	(Adj.)	आलसी
193.	A legal agreement that allows someone to use a building or land for a period of time, usually in return for rent	Lease	(N.)	पट्टा
194.	A sly look that is lustful	Leer	(N.)	बुरी नज़र से देखना
195.	That which is lawful	Legal	(Adj.)	कानूनी
196.	A person who writes and edits dictionaries	**Lexicographer**	(N.)	शब्दकोश के लेखक

S.N.	Phrases	One Word	PoS	Hindi
197.	A list of words on a particular subject or in a language in alphabetical order	Lexicon	(N.)	शब्दकोश
198.	Responsible according to law	Liable	(Adj.)	उत्तरदायी
199.	A person who strongly believes that people should have the freedom to do and think as they like	Libertarian	(N.)	मुक्तिवादी
200.	A strong band of tissues in the body that connects bones and supports organs and keeps them in position	**Ligaments**	(N.)	जोड़
201.	Eating mud	**Limivorous**	(Adj.)	मिट्टी खाने वाला
202.	A person who knows several foreign languages well / a person who studies languages	Linguist	(N.)	बहुभाषाविद्
203.	One who talks a lot	**Loquacious**	(Adj.)	बतूनी
204.	A soft gentle song sung to make a child go to sleep	**Lullaby**	(N.)	निद्रा गीत
205.	Related to the moon	**Lunar**	(Adj.)	चन्द्र संबंधी
206.	One who is mentally not sound	Lunatic	(Adj.)	पागल
207.	A girl or young woman, especially an unmarried one	Maiden	(N.)	अविवाहित
208.	The first public speech delivered by a person	**Maiden-speech**	(N.)	प्रथम भाषण
209.	Usage of an incorrect word in place of the one which is similar in pronunciation	Malapropism	(N.)	ध्वनि में समानता
210.	Easy to shape in any desired form	Malleable	(Adj.)	लचीला
211.	Insufficient feeding or nourishing	Malnutrition	(N.)	कुपोषण
212.	Animals which suckle their young	Mammals	(N.)	स्तनपायी
213.	In a way that is clear or obvious to the eye or mind	Manifestly	(Adv.)	साफ़ तौर पर
214.	A written statement in which a group of people, especially a political party, explains their beliefs and says what they will do if they win an election	Manifesto	(N.)	घोषणा पत्र
215.	A dummy used to display clothes in a shop window	Mannequin	(N.)	पुतला
216.	An underhand device resorted to in order to justify misconduct	Manoeuvre	(N.)	पैंतरेबाज़ी
217.	An instrument used for measuring the pressure of liquids and gases	Manometer	(N.)	दबाव नापने का
218.	A large impressive house	Mansion	(N.)	हवेली
219.	A copy of a book, piece of music, etc. before it has been printed	Manuscript	(N.)	हस्तलिपि

S.N.	Phrases	One Word	PoS	Hindi
220.	Animals living in the sea only	Marine	(N.)	समुद्री
221.	Relating to soldiers or war	Martial	(Adj.)	युद्ध संबंधी
222.	Someone who is killed fighting for the cause of religion or faith.	Martyr	(N.)	शहीद
223.	Someone who obtains pleasure from receiving punishment	Masochist	(N.)	पीड़ा सुखभोगी
224.	A person skilled in cutting, dressing, and laying stone in buildings.	**Mason**	(N.)	राजमिस्त्री
225.	One for whom money is the most important thing	Materialistic	(Adj.)	भौतिकवादी
226.	A cinema show held in the afternoon	Matinee	(N.)	अपराह्न का फिल्म
227.	Woman who is the head of the family	Matriarch	(N.)	मातृ सत्ता
228.	The killing of one's mother	Matricide	(N.)	मातृहत्या
229.	The state of being married.	Matrimohy	(N.)	विवाह
230.	A stately or impressive building housing a tomb or group of tombs	Mausoleum	(N.)	मकबरा
231.	An established principle of practical wisdom / a short statement of a general truth or rule of conduct	**Maxim**	(N.)	कहावत
232.	An area of grassland where animals graze	Meadow	(N.)	चारागाह
233.	To try to settle a dispute between two other parties	Mediate	(V.)	मध्यस्थता करना
234.	Belonging to the middle ages	Medieval	(Adj.)	मध्यकालीन
235.	Of only average standard	Mediocre	(Adj.)	औसत दर्जे का
236.	A musical composition made up of a series of songs or short pieces	Medley	(N.)	गीत समूह
237.	Feeling or expressing pensive sadness	Melancholic	(Adj.)	उदासी की अवस्था
238.	Pleasant-sounding	Melodious	(Adj.)	मधुर
239.	Something that serves as a reminder	Memento	(N.)	यादगार निशानी
240.	A person or thing that is likely to cause harm	Menace	(N.)	हानिकारक
241.	A soldier who will fight for any country / group that offers payment	**Mercenary**	(N.)	किराये का सैनिक
242.	The scientific study of metals and their uses	Metallurgy	(N.)	धातु विज्ञान
243.	A change in the form or nature of something	Metamorphosis	(N.)	कायांतरण
244.	Paying careful attention to every detail	Meticulous	(Adj.)	अतिसावधान
245.	Fear of small things	Microphobia	(N.)	छोटी चीजों से डर

S.N.	Phrases	One Word	PoS	Hindi
246.	An instrument used in scientific study for making very small things look larger so that you may examine them carefully	Microscope	(N.)	सूक्ष्मदर्शी
247.	A traveller who moves from one region or country to another	Migrant	(N.)	प्रवासी
248.	Movement of people or animals from one area to another	Migration	(N.)	प्रवास
249.	A period of one thousand years	Millennium	(N.)	हज़ार वर्ष
250.	Imitate someone's action or words in order to entertain or ridicule	Mimic	(V.)	नकल उतारना
251.	A place where money is coined by authority of the government	Mint	(N.)	टकसाल
252.	A person who hates and avoids other people	**Misanthrope**	(N.)	मानवद्वेषी
253.	A person who loves money and hates spending it	Miser	(N.)	कंजूस
254.	An unforseen happening which creates some damage	Mishap	(N.)	दुर्घटना
255.	A person who dislikes women	Misogynist	(N.)	स्त्री द्वेषी
256.	One who hates reason, argument, or enlightenment	Misologist	(N.)	तर्क वितर्क से
257.	A hater of new things	Misoneist		नई चीजों से नफ़रत करने वाला
258.	Helping you to remember something	Mnemonic	(Adj.)	स्मृति सहायक
259.	A large crowd of people, especially one that may become violent / cause trouble	Mob	(N.)	भीड़
260.	A particular method of working	Modus operandi	(N.)	कार्य-प्रणाली
261.	Lasting for a very short time	Momentary	(Adj.)	क्षणिक
262.	Very important or serious	**Momentous**	(Adj.)	सबसे अहम
263.	A supreme ruler	Monarch	(N.)	सम्राट
264.	A system of government by a king / a queen	**Monarchy**	(N.)	राज-तंत्र
265.	A building where monks live as a community	Monastery	(N.)	मठ
266.	A warning of impending danger	Monition	(N.)	चेतावनी
267.	A person who practices one spouse at a time	Monogamist	(N.)	एक विवाहवादी
268.	The practice of marrying one person at a time	Monogamy	(N.)	एक विवाह प्रथा
269.	Obsession with one particular thing	Monomania	(N.)	एक ही बात की धुन

S.N.	Phrases	One Word	PoS	Hindi
270.	The complete control of trade in particular goods or the supply of a particular service	Monopoly	(N.)	एकाधिकार
271.	A person who believes that there is only one god	Monotheist	(N.)	एकेश्वरवादी
272.	Lacking in variety and interest	Monotonous	(Adj.)	नीरस
273.	A building which is constructed to keep alive one's memory	Monument	(N.)	स्मारक
274.	To secure a boat by attaching it to an anchor	Moor	(V.)	लंगर डालना
275.	Customs and habits of a particular group	Mores	(N.)	रीति रिवाज
276.	The state of being subject to death	Mortality	(N.)	नश्वरता
277.	A legal agreement by which a bank lends you money to buy a house	Mortgage	(N.)	गिरवी
278.	A place for keeping dead bodies before burial or cremation	Mortuary	(N.)	शवगृह
279.	Art consisting of a design made of small pieces of coloured stone / glass	Mosaic	(N.)	रंगीन पत्थर या कांच के टुकड़े से बना कलात्मक रचना
280.	Wrap or cover for warmth	Muffle	(V.)	ओढ़ना
281.	Consisting of many things or parts	Multitudinous	(Adj.)	बहुसंख्यक
282.	A body of a human/ an animal that has been preserved by treating it with special oils and wrapping it in cloth	Mummy	(N.)	पुराना परिरक्षित शव
283.	Ordinary and dull	Mundane	(Adj.)	साधारण
284.	A place where antiques are kept	Museum	(N.)	संग्रहालय
285.	The act of refusing to obey the orders of somebody in authority, especially by soldiers sailors	Mutiny	(N.)	बगावत करना
286.	Lacking foresight or intellectual insight	Myopic	(Adj.)	अदूरदर्शी
287.	Something that is hidden	Mystery	(N.)	रहस्य
288.	Fear of telling lies	Mythophobia	(N.)	झूठ बोलने का डर
289.	A person or thing that has the same name as another	**Namesake**	(N.)	हमनाम
290.	The habit of admiring yourself too much, especially your appearance	Narcissism	(N.)	अहंकार
291.	A person who admires himself/herself too much,	Narcissist	(N.)	आत्ममोही
292.	Connected with the place you were born/ a person, animal or plant belonging originally to a place	**Native**	(Adj.)	मूल निवासी

S.N.	Phrases	One Word	PoS	Hindi
293.	Guide the course of a ship especially by using instruments or maps	Navigate	(V.)	मार्ग निर्देशन करना
294.	Fluid secreted by flowers which is collected by bees for making honey	Nectar	(N.)	पुष्प रस
295.	So small or unimportant as to be not worth considering	Negligible	(N.)	नगण्य
296.	Sound of horses	**Neigh**	(N.)	हिनहिनाहट
297.	Group of people living together in the same locality	Neighbourhood	(N.)	अड़ोस-पड़ोस
298.	Deserved and unavoidable punishment for wrong doing // Downfall that satisfies natural justice	**Nemesis**	(N.)	अपरिहार्य दंड
299.	A new word coined by an author	Neologism	(N.)	नवनिर्मित शब्द
300.	A person who has recently started an activity	Neophyte	(N.)	नौसिखिया
301.	Giving undue favours to one's own kith and kin.	**Nepotism**	(N.)	भाई-भतीजावाद
302	A doctor who studies and treats diseases of nerves	Neurologist	(N.)	स्नायु विज्ञानी
303.	The study of nerves	Neurology	(N.)	स्नायु विज्ञान
304.	Scientific study of the nervous system and brain	Neuroscience	(N.)	तंत्रिका विज्ञान
305.	A hollow space in a wall for a statue or ornament	Niche	(N.)	दीवार पर छोटी सी गुफा
306.	The rejection of all religious and moral principles, in the belief that life is meaningless	Nihilism	(N.)	शून्यवाद
307.	A transcendent state in which there is neither suffering, desire, nor sense of self	Nirvana	(N.)	मोक्ष
308.	Occurring at night	Nocturnal	(Adj.)	रात में होने वाली
309.	People of no fixed abode	**Nomads**	(N.)	खानाबदोश
310.	A system of naming things	Nomenclature	(N.)	नाम पद्धति
311.	An unimportant person	Nonentity	(N.)	तुच्छ व्यक्ति
312.	Delusion of suffering from a disease	Nosomania	(N.)	बीमारी से पीड़ित होने का भ्रम
313.	Sentimental longing for a period in the past	**Nostalgia**	(N.)	अतीत की घटनाओं की याद
1229.	Well-known for being bad / A person of evil reputation	**Notorious**	(Adj.)	कुख्यात
1230.	A person who is new to a profession without training or experience in a skill or subject	**Novice**	(N.)	नौसिखिया

S.N.	Phrases	One Word	PoS	Hindi
316.	To reduce to nothing	Null	(V.)	शून्य
317.	One who studies the occult meanings of numbers and their supposed influence on human life	Numerologist	(N.)	अंक ज्योतिषि
318.	The study or collection of coins	Numismatics	(N.)	मुद्राशास्त्र
319.	A person who collects coins	**Numismatist**	(N.)	मुद्राशास्त्री
320.	A place where young plants / trees are grown for sale / for planting somewhere else	Nursery	(N.)	पौधा-घर
321.	An extreme fear of darkness	Nyctophobia	(N.)	अँधेरे का डर
322.	A fertile tract in a desert (where the water table approaches the surface)	Oasis	(N.)	मरुस्थल के
323.	A notice of a person's death	Obituary	(N.)	शोक सन्देश
324.	Not clear	Obscure	(Adj.)	अस्पष्ट
325.	A place where astronomical observations are made	Observatory	(N.)	वेधशाला
326.	Passing out of use	Obsolescent	(Adj.)	अप्रचलित
327.	Something no longer in use	**Obsolete**	(Adj.)	अप्रचलित
328.	Relating to the countries of the west	**Occidental**	(Adj.)	पश्चिमवासी
329.	A geometrical figure with eight sides	**Octagon**	(N.)	अष्टभुज
330.	One who is eighty years old	Octogenarian	(N.)	अस्सी साल का का बुढ़ा
331.	Eight armed sea creature	Octopus	(N.)	अष्टभुज समुद्रीय जीव
332.	A person who examines or treats people's eyes	Oculist	(N.)	नेत्र-विशेषज्ञ
333.	Obsession for wine	**Oenomania**	(N.)	मादक पेय के लिए एक असामान्य और अतृप्त लालसा
334.	Government or rule by a small group of people	**Oligarchy**	(N.)	अल्पतंत्र
335.	Suggesting that something unpleasant is likely to happen	Ominous	(Adj.)	अशुभसूचक
336.	A volume containing several books previously published separately	Omnibus	(N.)	बहुग्रंथ
337.	One who is all powerful	Omnipotent	(Adj.)	सर्वसक्तिमान
338.	Present everywhere	Omnipresent	(Adj.)	सर्वव्यापक
339.	One who knows everything	Omniscient	(Adj.)	सर्वज्ञानी

S.N.	Phrases	One Word	PoS	Hindi
340.	One who eats both vegetables and meat	Omnivorous	(N.)	सर्व-भक्षक
331.	That through which light cannot pass	Opaque	(Adj.)	अपारदर्शी
342.	Study of snakes	Ophiology	(N.)	सांपो का अध्ययन
343.	Fear of snakes	Ophiophobia	(N.)	सांप का डर
344.	A doctor who specializes in the diseases of the eyes	**Ophthalmologist**	(N.)	नेत्र-विशेषज्ञ
345.	To be dogmatic in one's opinions.	Opinionated	(Adj.)	हठधर्मी
346.	Public disgrace arising from shameful conduct	Opprobrium	(N.)	अपमान
347.	One who see bright side of things	Optimist	(N.)	आशावादी
348.	A musical work that has been created / An artistic work, especially one on a large scale	Opus	(N.)	संगीत रचना
349.	A formal speech, especially one given on a ceremonial occasion	Oration	(N.)	भाषण
350.	A proficient public speaker	**Orator**	(N.)	वक्ता
351.	A piece of land / garden, in which fruit trees are grown	**Orchard**	(N.)	फलोद्यान
352.	A large body of people playing various musical instruments.	Orchestra	(N.)	वादक समूह
353.	The arrangement or disposition of people or things in relation to each other according to a particular sequence, pattern, or method	Order	(N.)	क्रम
354.	Something like an opening, particularly one in the body such as a nostril	Orifice	(N.)	छिद्र
355.	A person who studies birds	**Ornithologist**	(N.)	पक्षी विज्ञानी
356.	The scientific study of birds	Ornithology	(N.)	पक्षी विज्ञान
357.	A child whose parents are dead	Orphan	(N.)	अनाथ
358.	A public institution for the care and protection of children without parents.	**Orphanage**	(N.)	अनाथालय
359.	One who holds established opinions	Orthodox	(Adj.)	रूढ़िवादी
360.	The area of medicine that treats illnesses of bones	Orthopaedics	(N.)	हड्डी रोग
361.	Doctor who deals with bone problems	Orthopaedist	(N.)	हड्डियों का डॉक्टर
362.	A person who looks after horses at an inn	Ostler	(N.)	घोड़ी की देखभाल करने वाला
363.	To banish or turn out of society and fellowship	Ostracise	(V.)	निष्कासित करना
364.	Be more successful than someone	Outdo	(V.)	आगे बढ़ना

S.N.	Phrases	One Word	PoS	Hindi
365.	A person who has broken the law, especially one who remains at large or is a fugitive	Outlaw	(N.)	नियमविरोधी
366.	Pertaining to sheep	Ovine	(N.)	भेड़ के समान
367.	Belief that war and violence are unjustified	**Pacifism**	(N.)	शांतिवाद
368.	A person who opposes war or use of military force.	**Pacifist**	(N.)	शांतिवाद
369.	A group of wolves	Pack	(N.)	भेड़ियों का झुंड
370.	A set of 52 playing cards	Pack	(N.)	ताश की गड्डी
371.	A doctor who treats children diseases	**Paediatrician**	(N.)	बच्चों का चिकित्सक
372.	A word that reads the same backwards as forwards	Palindrome	(N.)	ऐसा शब्द जो आगे और पीछे दोनों तरफ सेएक जैसा हो
373.	Make something less severe.	Palliation	(N.)	कम गंभीर बनना
374.	Thing that can be felt or touched	Palpable	(Adj.)	स्पर्शनीय
375.	A solution for all difficulties or diseases	Panacea	(N.)	रामबाण इलाज
376.	Wild and noisy disorder	Pandemonium	(N.)	कोलाहल
377.	Gratify an immoral or distasteful desire	Pander	(V.)	नीच कार्य में सहायता देने वाला
378.	Sudden uncontrollable fear or anxiety, often causing wildly unthinking behaviour	Panic	(N.)	आतंक, भगदड़
379.	Wide, uninterrupted view	Panorama	(N.)	चित्रमाला
380.	Breathe hard and with difficulty	Pant	(V.)	हाँफना
381.	The belief that God is in everything, including nature	Pantheism	(N.)	सर्वेश्वरवाद
382.	A temple dedicated to all the gods	Pantheon	(N.)	सर्वदेवालय
383.	A small room in a big house, hotel, ship etc. where glasses, dishes, spoons, food etc. are kept.	Pantry	(N.)	रसोई भंडार
384.	Story told to illustrate a moral or spiritual truth	Parable	(N.)	नीति कथा
385.	One who lives/survives on others/other lives.	Parasite	(N.)	परजीवी
386.	A method of boiling briefly to cook food slightly	Parboil	(V.)	अधूरा पकाना
387.	Having a limited or narrow outlook or scope	Parochial	(Adj.)	सीमित
388.	Permission that is given to a prisoner to leave prison before the end of his sentence on condition that he behaves well	Parole	(N.)	पैरोल

S.N.	Phrases	One Word	PoS	Hindi
389.	The crime of killing your father, mother or a close relative	Parricide	(N.)	पितृघातक
390.	One who has suddenly gained new wealth, power or prestige	Parvenu	(N.)	नयी नयी दौलत
391.	Sole right to make and sell some invention	Patent	(N.)	एकस्व अधिकार
392.	The scientific study of diseases	Pathology	(N.)	रोग विज्ञान
393.	A system of society or government in which men hold the power and women are largely excluded from it	Patriarchy	(N.)	पितृसत्ता
394.	Murdering his own father	Patricide	(N.)	पितृहत्या
395.	used to describe the relationship between father and child that continues in a family with each generation; something based on this relationship	Patrilineal	(Adj.)	पितृवंशीय
396.	Property that is given to somebody when his father dies	Patrimony	(N.)	पैतृक संपत्ति
397.	A person who loves, supports and defends his country	Patriot	(N.)	देश-भक्त
398.	To go around an area to keep a watch	Patrol	(V.)	गश्त लगाना
399.	One who has no money	Pauper	(N.)	कंगाल
400.	The method and practice of teaching	Pedagogy	(N.)	शिक्षा शास्त्र
401.	A person who insists on adherence to formal rules or literary meaning	Pedant	(N.)	रूढ़िवादी
402.	A style in which a writer makes display of his knowledge	Pedantic	(Adj.)	रूढ़िवादी
402.	A person who walks on foot and not travelling in a vehicle	Pedestrian	(N.)	पैदल यात्री
403.	Branch of medicine concerned with children and their illness	Pediatrics	(N.)	बाल चिकित्सा
404.	A punishment imposed for breaking a law, rule, or contract.	Penalty	(N.)	जुर्माना
405.	A special fondness or liking for	Penchant	(N.)	विशेष रुचि
406.	A small ornament which hangs down especially from a necklace	Pendant	(N.)	लटकन
407.	A large mass of land projecting into a body of water	Peninsula	(N.)	प्रायद्वीप
408.	Deep in thought	Pensive	(Adj.)	चिंताग्रस्त
409.	Continuing for a long period of time without interruption	Perpetual	(Adj.)	लगातार

S.N.	Phrases	One Word	PoS	Hindi
410.	An incidental benefit awarded for certain types of employment	Perquisite	(N.)	रिआयत
411.	Subject someone to hostility and ill-treatment, especially because of their race or political or religious beliefs	Persecute	(N.)	अत्याचार करना
412.	Constant effort to achieve something.	Perseverance	(N.)	दृढ़ता
413.	A person employed in armed forces	Personnel	(N.)	कार्मिक
414.	A person who always expects bad things to happen or something not to be successful	Pessimist	(N.)	निराशावादी
415.	Killing of pests	Pesticide	(N.)	कीटनाशक
416.	That which is morally dangerous	Pestiferous	(Adj.)	विनाशक
417.	Stick with a thick end used in a mortar for pounding	Pestle	(N.)	मूसल
418.	Decrease or fade gradually before coming to an end	Peter	(V.)	धीरे-धीरे समाप्त हो जाना
419.	A person who always runs after women	Philanderer	(N.)	इश्कबाज
420.	One who loves all mankind // Someone who freely gives money and help to people who need it	Philanthropist	(N.)	जन हितैषी
421.	A person who collects or studies stamps	Philatelist	(N.)	डाक के टिकट का संग्रहक
422.	One who does not care for literature or art.	Philistine	(N.)	अशिक्षित
423.	Intense and unreasoned fear or dislike	Phobia	(N.)	भय
424.	The study and classification of sounds	Phonetics	(N.)	ध्वनि-विज्ञान
425.	A doctor, who is a specialist in general medicine and not surgery	Physician		चिकित्सक
426.	A study of the human body	Physiology	(N.)	शरीरविज्ञान
427.	Treatment by means of exercise and massage.	Physiotherapy	(N.)	भौतिक चिकित्सा
428.	A large number of things placed one on top of another	Pile	(Adj.)	ढेर
429.	The act of stealing something in small quantities	Pilferage	(N.)	छोटी चोरी
430.	One who does something for the first time	Pioneer	(N.)	प्रथम अन्वेषक
431.	A person who attacks and robs ships at sea	Pirate	(N.)	समुद्री डाकू
432.	Persons who rob ships	Pirates	(N.)	समुद्री डाकू
433.	One who lives on fish	Piscivorous	(Adj.)	मत्स्यभक्षी
434.	Make someone less angry or hostile	Placate	(V.)	शांत करना
435.	Not easily excited or upset	Placid	(Adj.)	शांत

S.N.	Phrases	One Word	PoS	Hindi
436.	Stealing of ideas or writings of someone else	Plagiarism	(N.)	साहित्यिक चोरी
437.	One who copies from other writers	Plagiarist	(N.)	साहित्यिक चोर
438.	Person who files a suit.	Plaintiff	(N.)	अर्जीदार
439.	Flat metal or Porcelain plate fixed on a wall as an ornament or memorial.	Plaque	(N.)	प्लेट को दीवार
440.	Seeming reasonable	Plausible	(Adj.)	संभाव्य
441.	A decision made by public voting.	Plebiscite	(N.)	जनमत-संग्रह
442.	A solemn promise or undertaking	Pledge	(N.)	प्रतिज्ञा करना
443.	One who repairs leaking water pipes	Plumber	(N.)	नलसाज
444.	Government by the richest people of a country	Plutocracy	(N.)	धनिक तन्त्र
445.	A speaker's platform	Podium	(N.)	मंच
446.	The custom of having more than one husband at the same time	Polyandry	(N.)	बहुपतित्व प्रथा
447.	A person having more than one wife at the same time	Polygamist	(N.)	बहुपत्नीवादी
448.	The custom of having more than one husband or wife at the same time	Polygamy	(N.)	बहुविवाह
449.	A person who knows and is able to use several languages.	Polyglot	(N.)	बहुभाषी
450.	A flat shape with at least three straight sides and three angles, and usually five or more	Polygon	(N.)	बहुभुज
451.	One who believes in a plurality of gods	Polytheist	(N.)	बहुदेववादी
452.	A place where ships load and unload goods	Port	(N.)	बंदरगाह
453.	Something that can be carried easily	Portable	(N.)	आसानी से साथ ले जाने योग्य
454.	A collection of drawings, documents, etc. That represent a person's, especially an artist's, wor	Portfolio	(N.)	पेटिका
455.	Occurring or coming into existence after a person's death	Posthumous	(Adj.)	मरणोपरांत
456.	A child born after the death of its father	Posthumous child	(N.)	पिता के मरणोपरांत पैदा हुआ बच्चा
457.	A medical examination of a dead body	Postmortem		शव परीक्षा
458.	An examination of a dead body to determine the cause of death	Post-Mortem	(N.)	शव परीक्षा
459.	Delay an event to a later date or time	Postpone	(N.)	स्थगित करना

S.N.	Phrases	One Word	PoS	Hindi
460.	A note appended to a letter after the signature	Postscript	(N.)	उपसंहार
461.	Safe to drink (water)	Potable	(Adj.)	पीने योग्य
462.	A liquid with healing, magical, or poisonous properties	Potion	(N.)	पेय औषधि
463.	A mixture of dried flowers and leaves used for making a room smell	Potpourri	(N.)	सुगंधित मिश्रण
464.	One who values practicality	Pragmatist	(N.)	व्यवहारवादी
465.	A previous case that might serve as an example or guide in subsequent situations	Precedent	(N.)	मिसाल
466.	A very steep or overhanging rock face or cliff on a mountain	Precipice	(N.)	खड़ी चट्टान
467.	An animal that lives by killing and eating other animals	Predator	(N.)	परजीवी
468.	Something that precedes and indicates the approach of something / someone	Predecessor	(N.)	पूर्वज
469.	We are expecting a good monsoon this year	Predicting	(N.)	पूर्वानुमान करना
470.	An introduction to a book, especially one that explains the author's aims	Preface	(N.)	प्रस्तावना
471.	To be biased against	Prejudiced	(Adj.)	पक्षपातपूर्ण
472.	An action or event that happens before another important one and forms an introduction to it	Prelude	(N.)	प्रस्तावना
473.	The first public performance of a musical or theatrical work or the first showing of a film	Premiere	(N.)	प्रथम प्रदर्शन
474.	A strong feeling that something is about to happen, especially something unpleasant	Premonition	(N.)	पूर्वाभास
475.	To get ready	Prepare	(V.)	तैयार करना
476.	Feint	Pretended attack	(V.)	छल, भुलावा
477.	To meke avasive or misleading statement	Prevaricate	(V.)	छल कपट करना
478.	A grup of lions	Pride	(N.)	शेरों का समूह
479	Right or advantage available to a person	Privilege	(N.)	विशेषाधिकार
480.	A person working on a trial period	Probationer	(N.)	काम सीखने के लिए नियुक्त
481.	Put off for a future time	Procrastinate	(V.)	टालना
482.	The art of delaying	Procrastination	(N.)	टालमटोल
483.	A person, especially a young one, with exceptional abilities	Prodigy	(N.)	विलक्षण प्रतिभा संपन्न व्यक्ति
484.	A high degree of skill	Proficiency	(N.)	निपुणता

S.N.	Phrases	One Word	PoS	Hindi
485.	General view of a person's character	Profile	(N.)	बाह्य रूपरेखा
486.	Recklessly extravagant or wasteful in the use of resources	Profligate	(Adj.)	अतिअपव्ययी
487.	Working-class people regarded collectively	Proletariat	(N.)	श्रमिक वर्ग
488.	Rapid increase in the number or amount of something	Proliferation	(N.)	प्रसार, फैलाव
489.	An introduction to a literary work	Prologue	(N.)	प्रस्तावना
490.	Continuing for a long time	Prolonged	(V.)	दीर्घकालीन
491.	A piece of wood, metal, etc. used for supporting something or keeping it in position	Prop	(N.)	टेक, सहारा
492.	A person sent by god to teach the people and give them messages from god	Prophet	(N.)	पैगम्बर (ईश्वरदूत)
493.	The action of driving or pushing forwards	Propulsion	(N.)	संचालक शक्ति
494.	A person who has been converted to another religious or political belief	Proselyte	(N.)	धर्मांतरित व्यक्ति
495.	Central character in a story or play	Protagonist	(N.)	नायक
496.	A system of fixed rules and formal behaviour used at official meetings	Protocol	(N.)	नियमों की प्रणाली
497.	The first design of something from which other forms are copied or developed	Prototype	(N.)	नमूना
498.	Food for farm animals	Provender	(N.)	चारा
499.	Concern for one's own area or region at the expense of national or supranational unity	Provincialism	(N.)	प्रांतीयता
500.	A person who moves stealthily about or loiters near a place with a view to committing a crime	Prowler	(N.)	शिकार की खोज में घूमने वाला
501.	One who studies election trends by means of opinion polls.	Psephologist	(N.)	चुनाव विश्लेषण
502.	The study of how people vote in elections	Psephology	(N.)	चुनाव विश्लेषण
503.	A fictitious name especially one assumed by an author	Pseudonym	(N.)	उपनाम
504.	A scientist who studies the mind and the way that people behave	Psychologist	(N.)	मनोविज्ञानी
505.	To come to an end	Expire	(V.)	समाप्त होना
506.	To remove an objectionable part from a book.	Expurgate	(V.)	छाँटना
507.	A speech or a presentation made without previous preparation.	Extempore	(Adj.)	बिना तैयारी के
508.	Stop something from burning	Extinguish	(V.)	बुझाना

S.N.	Phrases	One Word	PoS	Hindi
509.	To send back a criminal or an unwanted person to the country of his/her origin	Extradite	(V.)	भागे हुए सौंपना
510.	A person who wastes his money on luxury	Extravagant	(Adj.)	फ़िज़ूल ख़र्च
511.	A lively and confident person who enjoys being with other people // one who is outgoing	Extrovert	(N.)	बहिर्मुखी
512.	A short story with a moral, usually with animals as characters	Fable	(N.)	कल्पित कहानी
513.	Performing adroitly and without effort	Facile	(Adj.)	सहज
514.	An exact copy of handwriting or a picture produced by a machine	Facsimile	(N.)	प्रतिच्छाया
515.	A thing that is not genuine	Fake	(Adj.)	नकली
516.	One who is subject to failure or to committing mistake	Fallible	(Adj.)	पतनशील
517.	Farmland ploughed and harrowed but left for a period without being sown in order to restore its fertility	Fallow	(N.)	परतीभूमि
518.	A lack of food during a long period of time in a region	Famine	(N.)	अकाल
519.	A person motivated by irrational enthusiasm	Fanatic	(N.)	कट्टरपंथी
520.	Marked by extreme enthusiasm	Fanatical	(Adj.)	कट्टरता
521.	A pleasant situation that you imagine but that is unlikely to happen	Fantasy	(V.)	कोरी कल्पना
522.	One who is difficult to please	Fastidious	(Adj.)	ढीठ, हठी
523.	Causing or ending in death	Fatal	(Adj.)	घातक
524.	The belief that events are decided by fate and that you cannot control them	Fatalism	(N.)	भाग्यवाद
525.	Someone who believes that people cannot change the way events will happen	Fatalist	(N.)	भाग्यवादी
526.	The animals living in an area or in a particular period of history	Fauna	(N.)	पशुवर्ग
527.	That is possible and likely to be achieved	Feasible	(Adj.)	संभव
528.	Well chosen or suited to the circumstances	Felicitous	(Adj.)	परम सुखी
529.	Relating to or involved in crime	Felonious	(Adj.)	अपराधी
530.	One who believes in giving equal opportunity to women in all fields	Feminist	(N.)	नारीवाद
531.	A boat or ship for conveying passengers and goods, especially over a relatively short distance and as a regular service	Ferry	(N.)	नौका

S.N.	Phrases	One Word	PoS	Hindi
532.	Relating to a festival	Festal	(Adj.)	उत्सव संबंधी
533.	Bitter quarrel over a long period of time	Feud	(N.)	शत्रुता
534.	As opposed to reality imagined not real	Fictitious	(Adj.)	काल्पनिक
535.	Something that is imagined but does not exist	Figment	(N.)	मनगढ़ंत
536.	Killing of one's own child	Filicide	(N.)	पुत्र-हत्या
537.	A strong interest in something or someone	Fixation	(N.)	किसी से गहरा लगाव
538.	A person who attracts attention with a flashy style	Flamboyant	(N.)	भड़कीला
539.	A group of ships sailing together	Fleet	(N.)	जहाजों का बेड़ा
540.	Which can easily be carved without breaking	Flexible	(Adj.)	लचीला
541.	A quick, sudden movement	Flick	(N.)	झटका
542.	Shine with a bright but brief or irregular light	Flicker	(V.)	झिलमिलाना
543.	Unwelcome aspect of a situation	Flip side	(N.)	अवांछित पहलू
544.	A group of birds of one kind	Flock	(N.)	झुण्ड
545.	The plants and vegetation of a region	Flora	(N.)	वनस्पति
546.	A person who sells and arranges cut flowers	Florist	(N.)	फूलवाला
547.	To struggle helplessly	Flounder	(V.)	घबरा जाना
548.	Accidental good fortune	Fluke	(N.)	अकस्मात सफलता
549.	Continuous movement and change	Flux	(N.)	प्रवाह
550.	Go or come after a person or thing proceeding ahead	Follow	(V.)	पीछा करना
551.	Chief of a group of workmen	Foreman	(N.)	अधिकर्मी
552.	Ability to see what might happen in the future	Foresight	(N.)	दूरदर्शिता
553.	Be deprived of property or a right or privilege as a penalty for wrongdoing	Forfeited	(Adj.)	जब्त कर लिया
554.	Move ahead or forward steadily and gradually	Forge	(V.)	लगातार आगे बढ़ना
555.	Falsification of documents etc.	Forgery	(N.)	जालसाजी
556.	A period of two weeks	Fortnight	(N.)	दो सप्ताह
557.	Something that is to your advantage but happened by chance	Fortuitous	(Adj.)	भाग्यशाली
558.	The hard remains of a prehistoric animal or planet that are found inside a rock	Fossil	(Adj.)	जीवावशेष
559.	An abandoned child of unknown parents who is found by some- body.	Foundling	(N.)	परित्यक्त शिशु

S.N.	Phrases	One Word	PoS	Hindi
560.	An entrance hall in a building used by the public, especially a hotel or theatre	Foyer	(N.)	बरामदा
561.	Something which gets broken easily	Fragile	(Adj.)	भंगुर
562.	Constitutional right to cast vote	Franchise	(N.)	मताधिकार
563.	An act of murdering one's brother	Fratricide	(N.)	भ्रातृहत्या
564.	An act of deceiving somebody in order to make money	Fraud	(N.)	धोखा
565.	The feeling of being upset or annoyed as a result of being unable to change or achieve something	Frustration	(N.)	निराश
566.	One who runs away from justice or the law	Fugitive	(N.)	भगोड़ा
567.	Doing something awkwardly or in a clumsy manner	Fumbling	(Adj.)	गड़बड़ करना
568.	One who walks on ropes	Funambulist	(N.)	रस्सी पर चलने वाला नट
569.	Simple, fast-spreading plant without flowers or leaves, which can often cause disease	Fungus	(N.)	फफूंदी
570.	Hair of animals, which is soft and used for making wool	Fur	(N.)	रोआं
571.	The main body of an aircraft	Fuselage	(N.)	हवाई जहाज का ढांचा
572.	A brave, nobleminded or chivalrous man	Gallant	(Adj.)	वीर
573.	Causing annoyance or resentment	Galling	(Adj.)	कष्टकार
574.	To express in an unclear way	Garbled	(Adj.)	अस्पष्ट
575.	Talks a lot to explain something very trivial	Garrulous	(Adj.)	बातूनी
576.	The art and practice of cooking and eating good food	Gastronomy	(N.)	पाक करना
577.	Chief or Commander of army	General	(N.)	सेनाध्यक्ष
578.	Science of heredity	Genetics	(N.)	आनुवंशिकी
579.	The murder of a whole race or a group of people	Genocide	(N.)	जातिसंहार
580.	A person who studies the structure of the earth	Geologist	(N.)	भूवैज्ञानिक
581.	The study of earth, including the origin and history of the rocks and soil of which the earth is made	Geology	(N.)	भूगर्भशास्त्र
582.	The branch of medical science which deals with the problems of the old	Geriatrics	(N.)	वृद्धावस्था चिकित्साशास्त्र
583.	A state governed by old people	Gerontocracy	(N.)	वृद्ध-शासन

S.N.	Phrases	One Word	PoS	Hindi
584.	A movement of part of the body to express an idea or feeling	Gesture	(N.)	इशारा
585.	In a threatening manner	Ghastly	(Adj.)	खौफ़नाक रूप से
586.	A part of the city especially the slum area	Ghetto	(N.)	बस्ती
587.	Inflammation of gums	Gingivitis	(N.)	मसूड़े की सूजन
588.	An extremely large mass of ice which moves very slowly, often down a mountain valley	Glacier	(N.)	हिमनदी
589.	A person who repairs broken window-glasses	Glazier	(N.)	कांच का काम करनेवाला
590.	A list of technical / special words, especially those in a particular text, explaining their meanings	Glossary	(N.)	शब्दकोश
591.	To look at someone in an angry or threatening way	Glower	(V.)	घूर कर देखना
592.	One who eats too much	Glutton	(N.)	खाऊ, पेटू
593.	To bite like a rat	Gnaw	(V.)	कुतरना
594.	One who has keen interest in good food	Gourmet	(N.)	खाद्य पारखी
595.	Writing or drawings scribbled, scratched, or sprayed illicitly on a wall or other surface in a public place	Graffiti	(N.)	दीवार चित्रण
596.	A building where grain is stored	Granary	(N.)	धान्यगार
597.	Costing nothing.	Gratis	(Adv.)	निशुल्क
698.	A room or building, for the preservation of plants	Green house	(N.)	पौधा-घर
699.	An animal that lives in groups // Tending to associate with others of one's kind	Gregarious	(Adj.)	झुण्ड में रहने वाला
600.	The sound a bear makes	Growl	(N.)	भालू के गुर्राने की आवाज
601.	One who is easily deceived	Gullible	(Adj.)	आसानी से धोखा खाने वाला
602.	Eat or drink food quickly and in large amounts	Gulp	(V.)	निगल जाना
603.	A strong blast of wind.	Gust	(N.)	हवा का झोंका
604.	One who treats female ailments	Gynaecologist	(N.)	स्त्रीरोग विशेषज्ञ
605.	Science of blood	Haematology	(N.)	रुधिर विज्ञान
606.	A perception without objective reality	Hallucination	(N.)	माया
607.	A drug which makes one see things that are not really there.	Hallucinogen	(N.)	विभ्रामक दवा
608.	A very small village	Hamlet	(N.)	छोटा गांव

S.N.	Phrases	One Word	PoS	Hindi
609.	Come in the way of	Hamper	(V.)	रोकना
610.	Activities such as sewing and making cloth that use skill with your hands and artistic ability to make things	Handicraft	(N.)	हस्तशिल्प
611.	A building in which aircraft are housed	Hangar	(N.)	विमानशाला
612.	A lengthy and aggressive speech addressed to a large assembly.	Harangue	(N.)	प्रभावशाली भाषण
613.	Trouble and annoy continually	Harass	(V.)	परेशान करना
614.	Somebody that foretells the coming of something	Harbinger	(N.)	सन्देश वाहक
615.	A place of shelter for ships	Harbour	(N.)	बंदरगाह
616.	a strong feeling of anger and of not liking somebody/something	Animosity	(N.)	घृणा
617.	to destroy or defeat somebody/something completely	Annihilate	(V.)	विनाश करना
618.	The date on which an even happened in some previous year	**Anniversary**		सालगिरह
619.	With a name that is not known / that is not made public	Anonymous	(ADJ.)	बेनाम
620.	Obessive desire to lose witht by refusing to eat	Anorexia	(N.)	वजन कम करने के लिए भोजन त्याग
621.	A collection of poems, stories, etc. that have been written by different people and published together in a book/ a collection of poems	Anthology	(N.)	पद्य संग्रह
622.	The study of human race, especially of its origin, development, customs and beliefs	**Anthropology**	(N.)	मानव विज्ञान
623.	Look forward to	Anticipate	(V.)	आशा रखना
624.	A medicine to nullify the effect of poison	**Antidote**	(N.)	विषहर औषध
625.	Strong dislike between two persons/ A deep-seated feeling of aversion	**Antipathy**	(N.)	घृणा, चिढ़
626	One who studies antique things	Antiquarian	(N.)	पुरातात्विक
627.	The exact opposite	Antithesis	(N.)	प्रतिवाद

S.N.	Phrases	One Word	PoS	Hindi
628.	A word that means the opposite of another word	Antonym	(N.)	विलोम शब्द
629.	A policy that segregates people on the basis of race	Apartheid	(N.)	रंगभेद
630.	A set of rooms forming one residence in a building	Apartment	(N.)	किसी इमारत में कमरों का समूह (फ़्लैट)
631.	Showing or feeling no interest, enthusiasm, or concern	Apathetic	(Adj.)	उदासीन
632.	The feeling of not being interested in or enthusiastic about anything	**Apathy**		उदासीनता
633.	Loss of speech due to mnedical problem	Aphasia	(N.)	बोली बंद होना
634.	A place where bees are kept	Apiary	(N.)	मधुमक्खियों के पालने का स्थान
635.	To Express regret for something that one has done wrong	Apologize	(V.)	क्षमा मांगना
636.	The state of having rejected your religious beliefs or your political part or a caus	Apostasy	(N.)	स्वधर्म त्याग
637.	A pioneer of a reform movement	Apostle	(N.)	प्रचारक
638.	Causing shock or dismay	Appalling	(Adj.)	भयावह
639.	Be appropriate of applicable	Appertain	(V.)	संबंध रखना
640.	a person who formally requests something, especially a jo	Applicant	(N.)	आवेदक
641.	Estimation of a thing's worth	Appraisal	(N.)	मूल्यांकन
642.	To rise in value	Appreciate	(V.)	मूल्य बढ़ाना
643.	A person who works for an expert to learn a trade	**Apprentice**	(N.)	शिक्षार्थी
644.	Being afraid of water or being near water	Aquaphobia	(N.)	जल का भय
645.	A glass tank where fish and water plants are kept	**Aquarium**	(N.)	मछलीघर
646.	Animals and plants growing or living in, or near water	**Aquatic**	(Adj.)	जलीय
647.	Suitable for growing crops	Arable	(Adj.)	कृषि योग्य
648.	Based on chance rather than on reason or a plan	Arbitrary	(Adj.)	मनमाना
649.	A person who is chosen to settle a disagreement / a person appointe by two parties to resolve a dispute	**Arbitrator**	(N.)	पंच
650.	One who studies human antiquities	Archaeologist	(N.)	पुरातत्व विज्ञानी
651.	The study of human history and prehistory through the exacavation of sites	**Archaeology**	(N.)	पुरातत्व

S.N.	Phrases	One Word	PoS	Hindi
652.	A large body of water with may islands	Archipelago	(N.)	द्वीप समूह
653.	The place where public, government or historical records are kept	Archives	(N.)	अभिलेखागार
654.	A place where fights take place / A place or scene of activity, debate, or conflict.	Arena	(N.)	अखाड़ा
655.	A government by the nobles / government by person of higherst social order	Aristocracy	(N.)	श्रेष्ठ जनों के द्वारा राज्य शासन
656.	a building where military weapons and explosives are made or stored	Arsenal	(N.)	शास्त्रागार
657.	Intentionally starting a fire to damage something	Arson	(N.)	आग लगाना
658.	A criminal who illegally sets fire to property	Arsonist	(N.)	आगजनी करने वाला
659.	Fear of fire	Arsonphobia	(N.)	आग से डर
660.	Good at expressing ideas / feelings clearly in words	Articulate	(Adj.)	सुस्पष्ट
661.	One who practice one of the fine arts	Artist	(N.)	कलाकार
662.	One who denies oneself ordinary bodialy pleasures	Ascetic	(N.)	तपस्वी
663.	Regard something as being due to a cause	Ascribe	(V.)	श्रेय देना
664.	Nation that do not trust each other / look upon each other.	Askance	(Adj.)	संदेह करना
665.	Become less intense or widespread	Abate	(V.)	रोक-थाम करना
666.	A Place where animals are slaughtered or consumption as food	Abattoir	(N.)	कसाईखाना
667.	The superior of a monastery	Abbort	(N.)	मठगुरु
668.	To reduce to a shorter from intended to stand for the whole	Abbreviation	(N.)	संक्षेपण
669.	To give up one's authority or throne	Abdicate	(V.)	पद त्यागना
670.	Act of giving up the throne	Abdication	(N.)	पद त्याग
671.	Deviation from the right course	Aberration	(N.)	असामान्य
672.	Formally put an end to a system, practice, or institution	Abolish	(N.)	समाप्त करना
673.	The original inhabitants of a country	Aborigines	(N.)	मुलनिवासी
674.	To shorten a piece of writing without losing the sense	Abridge	(V.)	संक्षिप्त करना
675.	Wildly unreasonable, illogical or ridiculous	Absurd	(Adj.)	बेतुका

S.N.	Phrases	One Word	PoS	Hindi
676.	To increase the speed	Accelerate	(V.)	गति बढ़ाना
677.	A person who helps another to commit a crime crime or to do something morally wrong/ A partner in crime	Accomplice	(N.)	सह अपराधी
678.	Be harmonious or consistent with	Accord	(N.)	समझौता
679.	A person whose profession is to keep accounts	Accountant	(N.)	मुनीम
680.	Study of sound	Acoustics	(N.)	ध्वनि-विज्ञान
681.	To decide and state officially in court that somebody is not guilty of a crime	Acquit	(V.)	बरी करना
682.	One who performs daring gymnastic feats / A person who entertains people by doing difficult feats	Acrobat	(N.)	कलाबाज
683.	A word formed from the first letters of the words that make up the name of something	Acronym	(N.)	शब्दों के पहले अक्षरों से बना एक शब्द
684.	Fear of great heights	Acrophobia	(N.)	ऊँचाई का डर
685.	To do something / to behave in a particular way / to perform a part in a play / film / function	Act	(V.)	कार्य करना
686.	Make a machine active or operative	Activate	(V.)	सक्रिय करना
687.	The ability to make good judgments and take quick decisions	Acumen	(N.)	कुशाग्र बुद्धि
688.	A person who is physically dependent on a substance / harmful drugs	Addict	(N.)	लत, नशेबाज
689.	Believe in and follow the practices of	Adhere	(V.)	पालन करना
690.	The period between the beginning of puberty and adulthood	Adolescence	(N.)	किशोरावस्था
691.	An extremely young man	Adonis	(N.)	खूबसूरत नौजवान
692.	Make impure by adding inferior substances	Adulterate	(V.)	मिलावट करना
693.	A person who supports or speaks in favour of something	Advocate	(N.)	वकील
694.	Growing/ existing / living in air	Aerial	(Adj.)	हवाई
695.	Concerned with beauty or the appreciation of beauty	Aesthetic	(Adj.)	सौन्दर्यबोधी
696.	A list of items to be discussed at a meeting	Agenda	(N.)	कार्यसूची
697.	Always ready to attack or quarrel	Aggressive	(Adj.)	अक्रामक
698.	Extreme mental or physical suffering	Agony	(N.)	कष्ट

S.N.	Phrases	One Word	PoS	Hindi
699.	Fear of pain	Algophobia	(N.)	शरीर में कष्ट होने का डर
700.	A person belonging to a foreign country	Alien	(N.)	अजनबी
701.	An allowance made to a wife by her husband, when they are legally separated.	Alimony	(N.)	परित्क्ता पत्नी के लिये निर्वाह निधि
702.	A story, play, picture, etc. in which each character / event is a symbol representing an idea / a quality, such as truth, evil, death, etc.	Allegory	(N.)	निति कथा
703.	Commencement of adjacent words with the same letter // Repetition of an initial sound in two or more words of a line	Alliteration	(N.)	अनुप्रास अलंकार
704.	The school or college in which one has been educated	Alma Mater	(N.)	जहां शिक्षा पाई वह संस्था
705.	Mountain climbing	Alpinism	(N.)	पर्वतारोहण
706.	A table or flat surface where offerings are made to a deity	Altar	(N.)	बलिदेवी
707.	Instrument that measures the altitude of the land surface	Altimeter	(N.)	ऊंचाई नापने का यंत्र
708.	The height above sea level	Altitude	(N.)	ऊंचाई
709.	Someone who makes charitable donations intended to increase human wellbeing	Altruist	(N.)	परोपकारी
710.	A former student of a school, college or university	Alumnus	(N.)	भूतपूर्व छात्र
711.	One who plays for pleasure rather than as a profession / A person who is neither well experienced nor professional experienced nor professional	Amateur	(N.)	शौकीन व्यक्ति
712.	Fear of riding in a car	Amaxophobia	(N.)	वाहनों का डर
713.	A diplomatic representative in another country	Ambasador	(N.)	दूत
714.	Able to use the left hand and right hand equally well	Ambidextrous	(N.)	उभयहस्त
715.	Capable of being understood in either of two or more possible senses, and therefore not definite.	Ambiguous	(Adj.)	अनेकार्थी
716.	Having or showing both good and bad feelings	Ambivalent	(Adj.)	उभयभावी
717.	Readily reacting to suggestions and influences / willing to be guided or controlled	Amenable	(Adj.)	आज्ञाकारी
718.	A partial or total loss of memory	Amnesia	(N.)	भूलने की बीमारी

S.N.	Phrases	One Word	PoS	Hindi
719.	An official pardon // the formal act of liberating someone	Amnesty	(N.)	राज-क्षमा
720.	Not following any moral rules and not caring about right / wrong	Amoral	(Adj.)	नीतिहीन
721.	Animal that can live both on land and in water	Amphibian	(N.)	उभयचर
722.	Animals that can live on land and water	Amphibians	(N.)	उभयचर जन्तु
723.	A person who has had one or more limbs removed	Amputee	(N.)	अपंग, छिन्नांग
724.	Comparison between things that have similar features	Analogy	(N.)	समानता
725.	Detailed examination of something complex	Analysis	(N.)	विश्लेषण
726.	A person who believes that laws and governments are not necessary	Anarchist	(N.)	अराजकतावादी
727.	A situation in a country, an organization, etc. in which there is no government, order / control	Anarchy	(N.)	अराजकता
728.	The branch of science concerned with the bodily structure of humans, animals, and other living organisms	Anatomy	(N.)	शरीर रचना विज्ञान
729.	A person who presents a radio / television programme	Anchor	(N.)	समाचार उद्घोषक
730.	Belonging to long past	Ancient	(Adj.)	प्राचीन
731.	A short, interesting or amusing story about a real person or an event	Anecdote	(N.)	लघुकथा
732.	A medical specialist who administers drugs for relieving pain during surgery	Anesthetist	(N.)	बेहोशी लाने वाला
733.	Like a weak old woman	Anile	(N.)	कमजोर बुढ़िया जैसा
734.	A person who physically attacks another	Assailant	(N.)	आक्रमणकारी
735.	To agree to a request / an idea / a suggestion	Assent	(V.)	स्वीकृति
736.	The quality of being politely firm and demanding	Assertive	(Adj.)	दबंग, हठ धर्मी
737.	One who tells future from the stars	Astrologer	(N.)	ज्योतिषी
738.	A person who is trained to travel in space	Astronaut	(N.)	अंतरिक्ष यात्री
739.	The scientific study of celestial bodies like sun, moon, stars, planets, etc.	Astronomy	(N.)	खगोल शास्त्र
740.	Place that provides refuge/ a hospital where people who were mentally ill could be cared for, often for a long time	Asylum	(N.)	शरणस्थल, अस्पताल
741.	A person who does not believe in God	Atheist	(N.)	नास्तिक

S.N.	Phrases	One Word	PoS	Hindi
742.	That can be heard clearly	Audible	(Adj.)	श्रवण योग्य
743.	One who makes an official examination of accounts/financial records	Auditor	(N.)	लेखा परीक्षक
744.	A building where an audience sits	Auditorium	(N.)	सभागार
745.	Made or done in the traditional or original way // Something that is genuine	Authentic	(Adj.)	प्रामाणिक
746.	An account of a person's life written by self	Autobiography	(N.)	आत्मकथा
747.	A system of government of a country in which one person has complete power	Autocracy	(N.)	तानाशाही
748.	A ruler who has complete power	Autocrat	(N.)	तानाशाह
749.	A self-governing country or region	Autonomy	(N.)	स्वशासन
750.	An official examination of a dead body by a doctor in order to discover the cause of death	Autopsy	(Adj.)	शव परीक्षण
751.	The group, especeally in the arts, regarded as being the most experimental	Avant-garde	(Adj.)	अपने क्षेत्र में अग्रणी
752.	Insatiable desire for wealth	Avarice	(N.)	लोभ
753.	Having an extreme desire for wealth	Avaricious	(Adj.)	लालची
754.	A place where birds are kept	Aviary	(N.)	पक्षीशाल
755.	Killing of birds	Avicide	(N.)	पक्षियों को मारना
756.	Keen interest or enthusiasm	Avidity	(N.)	उत्सुकता
757.	To keep away from	Avoid	(V.)	दूर रहना
758.	a rule or principle that most people believe to be true	Axiom	(N.)	सिद्धांत
759.	A man who has never been married	Bachelor	(N.)	अविवाहित
760.	A man having no hair on the scalp	Bald	(Adj.)	गंजा
761.	Senseless talk or writing	Balderdash	(N.)	बकवास
762.	A large bundle bound for storage or transport	Bale	(N.)	गट्ठा
763.	Poem in short stanzas narrating a popular story	Ballad	(N.)	गाथागति
764.	Without enough money to pay what you own	Bankrupt	(N.)	दिवालिया
765.	An instrument used for measuring atmospheric pressure	Barometer	(N.)	वायु-दाब-मापक
766.	Place given to soldiers to live in	Barracks	(N.)	सैनिकों के लिए बने घर
767.	A wooden drum in which beer or oil is stored	Barrel	(N.)	पीपा
768.	Revel in and make the most of something pleasing	Bask	(V.)	मजा लेना

S.N.	Phrases	One Word	PoS	Hindi
769.	A person who is fond of fighting	Bellicose	(Adj.)	लड़ाकू
770.	The sound made by a crocodile	Bellow	(V.)	मगरमच्छ की आवाज
771.	One who helps people by giving them money or other aid	Benefactor	(N.)	दान देने वाला
772.	A person who gains as a results of something	Beneficiary	(N.)	लाभार्थी
773.	Deprived of or lacking of something	Bereft	(Adj.)	अभाव से दुःखी
774.	Any soft drink except water	Beverage	(N.)	पेय पदार्थ
775.	A group of girls / boys / birds etc	**Bevy**	(N.)	झुंड
776.	A list of the books referred to in a scholarly work	**Bibliography**	(N.)	ग्रंथसूची
777.	Preoccupation with the acquisition and possession of books	Bibliomania	(N.)	किताबों के लिए पागलपन
778.	One who is a great lover of books	Bibliophile	(N.)	पुस्तक प्रेमी
779.	200th anniversary.	Bicentennial	(N.)	दो सौ साल का
780.	Happening every second year	Biennial	(N.)	द्विवार्षिक
781.	A person is intolerant towards those holding different opinions	Bigot	(N.)	कट्टर व्यक्ति
782.	A person who can speak only two languages	Bilingual	(Adj.)	द्विभाषिक
783.	Twice a month	Bimonthly	(Adj.)	द्वैमाषिक
784.	Capable of being decomposed by biological agents, especially bacteria	Biodegradable	(Adj.)	प्राकृतिक तरीके से सड़नशील
785.	The story of a person's life written by somebody else	Biography	(N.)	जीवनी
786.	Study of living organisms	Biology	(N.)	जीव विज्ञान
787.	The removal of tissue from the body of somebody who is ill and its examination in order to find out more about the disease	Biopsy	(N.)	जीव ऊतकों की जांच
788.	Very strange or unusual	Bizarre	(Adj.)	विचित्र
789.	Words uttered impiously about God/ The act of speaking irreverently about sacred things.	Blasphemy	(N.)	ईश्वर की निंदा
790.	The cry of a goat	Bleat	(V.)	मिमियाना
791.	A person of South African Dutch descent	Boer	(N.)	डच या डच वंशीय
792.	One who does not follow the usual rules of social life	Bohemian	(Adj.)	रूढ़िमुक्त

S.N.	Phrases	One Word	PoS	Hindi
793.	Subject (someone) to a continuous flow of questions, criticisms or information	Bombard	(V.)	बौछार करना
794.	Using high-sounding words but with little meaning	Bombastic	(Adj.)	बड़े बड़े शब्दों वाला
795.	Dwarf varieties of trees and shrubs grown in pots	Bonsai	(N.)	उथले बर्तन में उगी झाड़ी का किस्म
796.	A sum of money added to a person's wages as a reward for good performance.	Bonus	(N.)	अधिलाभ
797.	An avid book reader // One who reads a lot	Bookworm	(N.)	किताबी कीड़ा
798.	A hunting weapon which comes back, used by Australian Aborigines	Boomerang	(N.)	एक किस्म का जो फेंकने वाले के पास लौट आता है
799.	To take something on loan with the intention of returning it	Borrow	(V.)	उधार लेना
800.	The study of plant life	Botany	(N.)	वनस्पति विज्ञान
801.	A narrow or busy section of road where the traffic often gets slower and stops	Bottleneck	(N.)	संकीर्ण भाग
802.	A broad road bordered with trees	Boulevard	(N.)	मुख्य मार्ग
803.	An arrangement of flowers that is usually given as a present	Bouquet	(N.)	गुलदस्ता
804.	Belonging to middle class.	Bourgeois	(N.)	मध्य वर्ग
805.	A shop that sells women's clothes and jewellery	Boutique	(N.)	महिलाओं का वस्त्रालय
806.	Affecting or relating to cows / Pertaining to cattle	Bovine	(Adj.)	गोजातीय
807.	A shady place under trees	Bower	(N.)	पेड़ों के नीचे का छायादार स्थान
808.	An act of breaking or failing to observe a law	Breach	(V.)	नियम तोड़ना
809.	A factory where beer is made	Brewery	(N.)	शराब की भट्ठी
810.	Leather straps put around a horse's head to control it	Bridle	(N.)	लगाम
811.	Member of a band of robbers	Brigand	(N.)	डाकू
812.	Hard but easily broken / liable to break easily	Brittle	(Adj.)	भंगुर
813.	The young of an animal cared for at one time/ A family of young birds	Brood	(N.)	किसी जीव का बच्चा

S.N.	Phrases	One Word	PoS	Hindi
814.	A woman with dark brown hair	Brunette	(N.)	गहरे भूरे बालों वाली स्त्री
815.	To plan carefully how much money to spend on something	Budgeting	(N.)	बजट
816.	Gold and silver before using for manufacturing ornaments	Bullion	(N.)	सोने चांदी की ईंट
817.	A collection of sticks.	Bundle	(N.)	गट्ठा
818.	Carry out a task clumsily or incompetently	Bungle	(V.)	गड़बड़ करना
819.	A government run by officials in a state	Bureaucracy	(N.)	नौकरशाही
820.	A person who enters a building illegally in order to steal	Burglar	(N.)	सेंधमार
821.	Hole excavated by an animal as dwelling	Burrow	(N.)	बिल
822.	The sound made by bees	Buzz	(V.)	भनभनाहट
823.	Place where cows are sheltered	Byre	(N.)	गोशाला
824.	a mixture of loud, unpleasant sounds; noise	Cacophony	(N.)	कोलाहल
825.	A person who practises calligraphy, the art of writing beautifully with a special pen or brush.	Calligrapher	(N.)	सुलेखक
826.	Beautiful handwriting that you do with a pen / special brush.	Calligraphy	(N.)	सुलेख
827.	A man devoid of kind feeling and sympathy.	Callous	(Adj.)	कठोर हृदय
828.	materials or colours that soldiers use to make themselves and their equipment difficult to see	Camouflage	(N.)	छलावरण
829.	A person who eats human flesh	Cannibal	(N.)	नरभक्षक
830.	Love for dogs	Canophilia	(N.)	कुत्ते से प्यार
831.	House or shelter of a gipsy / A group of people travelling together, especially in a desert	Caravan	(N.)	काफिला
832.	The dead body of an animal	Carcass	(N.)	पशु शव
833.	Something which is considered to be very important	Cardinal	(N.)	प्रमुख
834.	A doctor who specializes in the study or treatment of heart diseases	Cardiologist	(N.)	हृदय रोग विशेषज्ञ
835.	A picture of a person or a thing drawn in such a highly exaggerated manner as to cause laughter	Caricature	(N.)	व्यंग्य-चित्र
836.	Animals that eat meat	Carnivorous	(N.)	मांसभक्षी
837.	Song which is sung in a church by a group of singers	Carol	(N.)	ईसाइयों का भजन
838.	A person who draws or makes maps	Cartographer	(N.)	मानचित्रकार

S.N.	Phrases	One Word	PoS	Hindi
839.	The art or process of drawing or making maps	Cartography	(N.)	मानचित्रकार
840.	An amusing drawing about politics / events in the news	Cartoon	(N.)	व्यंगचित्र
841.	A place where gambling games are played	Casino	(N.)	जुआखाना
842.	A large, deep pot used both in the oven and as a serving vessel.	Casserole	(N.)	हाँडी (एक तरह का बरतन)
843.	A complete list of books	Catalogue	(N.)	सूची
844.	An event causing great and sudden damage or suffering	Catastrophe	(V.)	तबाही
845.	Causing great damage or suffering	Catastrophic	(Adj.)	विनाशकारी
846.	A large, deep, metal pot used for cooking over open fire	Cauldron	(N.)	हंडा, कड़ाही
847.	Soldiers who fight on horseback	Cavalry	(N.)	घुड़सवार सेना
848.	The sound of a crow	Caw	(N.)	कौवे की कांव-कांव
849.	A time when enemies agree to stop fighting	Ceasefire	(N.)	संघर्ष विराम
850.	The state of living / remaining unmarried	Celibacy	(N.)	ब्रह्मचर्य
851.	Underground place for storing wine or other provisions	Cellar	(N.)	तहख़ाना
852.	A large burial ground	Cemetery	(N.)	कब्रिस्तान
853.	A person who is a 100 years old or more	Centenarian	(N.)	सौ वर्ष की अवस्थ
854	The 100th anniversary of an event	Centennial	(N.)	शताब्दी
855.	Anything tending to move away from centre	Centrifugal	(Adj.)	केन्द्रत्यागी
856.	Art of designing or writing on wax	Cerography	(N.)	मोम पर नक्काशी का काम करना
857.	Rub a part of the body to restore warmth or sensation	Chafe	(V.)	रगड़कर गरमाना
858.	Vexation for humiliation or disappointment	Chagrin	(V.)	झुंझलाहट
859.	A child who is believed to have been secretly left in exchange for another	Changeling	(N.)	बदला हुआ बच्चा
860.	A small building / room used for christian worship in a school, prison, large private house, etc.	Chapel	(N.)	छोटा गिरजा घर
861.	Compelling attractiveness or charm that can inspire or influence others	Charisma	(N.)	आकर्षण

S.N.	Phrases	One Word	PoS	Hindi
862.	Exercising a compelling charm which inspires devotion in others.	Charismatic	(Adj.)	आकर्षक
863.	A person falsely claiming to have a special knowledge or skill	Charlatan	(N.)	ढोंगी
864.	Run after in order to catch or catch up with	Chase	(N.)	पीछा करना
865.	A deep fissure in the earth's surface	Chasm	(N.)	खाई
866.	The base frame of car or other wheel vehicle	Chassis	(N.)	ढाँचा
867.	A person employed to drive a private or hired car	Chauffeur	(N.)	मोटर-चालक
868.	Palm reading	Chiromancy	(N.)	हस्तरेखा विद्या
869.	A group of singers in a church	Choir	(N.)	गायक-मंडली
870.	A routine task, especially a household one	Chore	(N.)	दैनिक काम
871.	One who plans the steps and moves in a dance	Choreographer	(N.)	नृत्य-निर्देशक
872.	A factual written account of important or historical events in the order of their occurrence.	Chronicle	(N.)	कालक्रम से अभिलेखन
873.	An arrangement of events or dates in the order of their occurrence	Chronology	(N.)	कालक्रम
874.	An instrument for measuring time accurately in spite of motion or variations in temperature, humidity, and air pressure.	Chronometer	(N.)	बिलकुल ठीक
875.	Rude in a mean-spirited and surly way	Churlish	(Adj.)	अभद्र
876.	Extreme self-confidence or audacity	Chutzpah	(N.)	दुस्साहस
877.	The use of many words where only a few are necessary	Circumlocution	(N.)	शब्द-बाहुल्य
878.	Clues available at a scene	Circumstantial	(Adj.)	परिस्थितिक
879.	A fortress typically one on high ground above a city	Citadel	(N.)	किला
880.	Making a loud and confused noise	Clamorous	(Adj.)	कोलाहलपूर्ण
881.	An extreme fear of being in a small confined place	**Claustrophobia**	(N.)	छोटे जगह में होने का अत्यधिक डर
882.	Customers collectively	Clientele	(N.)	ग्राहक गण
883.	Land beside a sea	Coast	(N.)	समुद्र तट
884.	A spider's home	Cobweb	(N.)	मकड़ी का जाला
885.	A small compartment in an aircraft for the pilot	Cockpit	(N.)	वायु-यान में चालक कक्ष
886.	A drink usually made from a mixture of one or more alcoholic drinks	Cocktail	(N.)	मिश्रित शराब

S.N.	Phrases	One Word	PoS	Hindi
887.	An instruction that is added later to a will, usually to change a part of it	Codicil	(N.)	वसीयत नामे के बाद का परिवर्तन पत्र
888.	Use of force or threats to get someone to agree to something	Coercion	(N.)	जोर जबरदस्ती
889.	A strongbox or small chest for holding valuables	Coffer	(N.)	तिजोरी
890.	A collection of slaves	Coffle	(N.)	काफिला
891.	A remarkable concurrence of events or circumstances without apparent causal connection	Coincidence	(N.)	संयोग
892.	A person that one work with at the same place, in a profession or a business	Colleague	(N.)	सहकर्मी
893.	People who work together at the same place	Colleagues	(N.)	सहकर्मी
894.	Mutual discourse	Colloquy	(N.)	वार्तालाप
895.	A gigantic statue	Colossus	(N.)	विशालमूर्ति
896.	To keep a great person or event in people's memory	Commemorate	(V.)	स्मरण करना
897.	Money given to agent on sales	Commission	(N.)	दलाली
898.	People who belong to the same country	Compatriots	(N.)	हमवतन, स्वदेशवासी
899.	Master of ceremonies	Compere	(N.)	कार्यक्रम-उद्घोषक
900.	Satisfied, with no desire to change or improve	Complacent	(Adj.)	आत्मसंतुष्ट
901.	To make perfect or complete	Complement	(N.)	पूरक
902.	One who sets type for books, newspapers, etc.	Compositor	(N.)	अक्षरयोजक
903.	Having too much pride in yourself and what you do	Conceited	(Adj.)	अभिमानी
904.	Capable of being imagined or grasped mentally	Conceivable	(Adj.)	कल्पनीय
905.	Living together of a man and woman without being married to each other	Concubinage	(N.)	बिना विवाह के
906.	An apartment building in which each apartment is owned separately by the people living in it, but also containing shared areas	Condominium	(N.)	फ्लैटी की तरह
907.	Forgive or pardon some wrongdoing or an offence	Condone	(V.)	माफ़ करना
908.	A company or person that makes or sells sweets or chocolate	Confectioner	(N.)	मिठाई बेचने वाला
909.	To officially take something away from somebody	Confiscate	(V.)	जब्त करना
910.	Combustibles - flammable	Conflagrant	(Adj.)	जलता हुआ

S.N.	Phrases	One Word	PoS	Hindi
911.	Place where two or more rivers meet	Confluence	(N.)	संगम
912.	Pertaining to an individual from birth	Congenital	(Adj.)	जन्मजात
913.	A corporation made up of a number of different companies that operate in diversified field	Conglomerate	(N.)	कॉम्पनियों का समूह
914.	An assembly of worshippers / A gathering at a religious place / the group of people who attend a particular church	Congregation	(N.)	धार्मिक सभा
915.	An opinion or conclusion formed on the basis of incomplete information	Conjecture	(N.)	निराधार कल्पना
916.	A man who knows a lot about things like food, music and art	Connoisseur	(N.)	विशेषज्ञ, पारखी
917.	Feeling inside you which tells you what is right and what is wrong	Conscience	(N.)	जमीर, अन्तरात्मा
918.	Guided by one's sense of duty	Conscientious	(Adj.)	कर्तव्यनिष्ठ
919.	A careful preservation and protection of wildlife is the need of the hour.	Conservation		प्राकृतिक संरक्षण
920.	Opposed to great or sudden change.	Conservative	(N.)	रूढ़िवादी, अपरिवर्तनवादी
921.	Comfort someone at a time of grief or disappointment	Console	(V.)	सांत्वना देना
922.	A group of stars that forms a shape in the sky and has a name	Constellation	(N.)	नक्षत्र
923.	State of anxiety or dismay causing mental confusion	Consternation	(N.)	घबराहट
924.	Imposed a restriction on	Constrained	(Adj.)	विवश किया हुआ
925.	Extremely skilled	Consummate	(Adj.)	उत्कृष्ट
926.	Easily spread from one person to another (disease)/ A disease which spreads with contact	Contagious	(Adj.)	संक्रामक
927.	Something made impure by exposure to polluting substances	Contaminated	(Adj.)	दूषित
928.	Belonging to the same time/ A person living in the same age with another	Contemporary	(Adj.)	समकालीन
929.	Someone who is satisfied with life is general	Contented	(Adj.)	संतुष्ट
930.	Touching along the side or boundary	Contiguous	(Adj.)	निकटवर्ती
931.	An event that may / may not happen	Contingency	(N.)	आकस्मिता

S.N.	Phrases	One Word	PoS	Hindi
932.	Prohibited by law or treaty from being imported or exported	Contraband	(N.)	वर्जित माल
933.	A man who is recovering from illness.	Convalescent	(N.)	बीमारी से ठीक होना
934.	A place where nuns live and work	Convent	(N.)	मठ
935.	Ceremony of crowning a king	Coronation	(N.)	राजतिलक करना
936.	To confirm with the help of evidence	Corroborate	(V.)	पुष्टि करना
937.	Science of the constitution of the whole universe	Cosmography	(N.)	सृष्टिवर्णन
938.	A person who can make himself/herself feel at home in any country / One who is a citizen not of a country but of the world	Cosmopolitan	(Adj.)	सर्वदेशीय
979.	A stanza having two lines in verse	Couplet	(N.)	द्वीपदी दोहा
940.	A person who takes care of cattle	Cowherd	(N.)	ग्वाला
941.	That can be believed or trusted	Credible	(Adj.)	विश्वसनीय
942.	A person who readily believes others easily	Credulous	(Adj.)	भोलाभाला
943.	A system of religious belief; a faith	Creed	(N.)	संप्रदाय
944.	A place where a dead person's body is burnt.	Crematorium	(N.)	शवदाहग्रह
945.	Turning point of danger / disease	Crisis	(N.)	संकट
946.	A principle or standard by which anything is or can be judged	Criterion	(N.)	मापदंड
947.	One who finds nothing good in anything	Critic	(N.)	आलोचक
948.	Break or fall apart into small fragments in the process of deterioration	Crumble	(V.)	चूर चूर होना
949.	A dynamic campaign for political, social or religious chang	Crusade	(N.)	जिहाद
950.	A device for deciphering codes and ciphers	Cryptograph	(N.)	कूट-लेखन
951.	Guilty of the crime	Culpable	(Adj.)	अपराधिक
952.	All the arts, beliefs and social institutions etc. characteristic of a race	Culture	(N.)	संस्कृति
953.	A person in charge of a museum	Curator	(N.)	संग्रहालय अध्यक्ष
954.	Signal under martial law for people to remain indoors	Curfew	(N.)	निषेधाज्ञा
955.	A strong desire to know or learn something	Curiosity	(N.)	जिज्ञासा
956.	The system of money used in a particular country	Currency	(N.)	मुद्रा
957.	One who sneers at the aims and beliefs of his fellow men. / A person who believes that only selfishness motivates human actions	Cynic	(N.)	निंदक, मानवदोषी

S.N.	Phrases	One Word	PoS	Hindi
958.	Extreme fear of dogs	Cynophobia	(N.)	कुत्ते से असाधारण भय
959.	Centre of attraction	Cynosure	(N.)	आकर्षण-बिन्दु
960.	A secret or disguised way of writing	Cypher	(N.)	गुप्त लिखावट
961.	Dealing with cells	Cytology	(N.)	कोशिका विज्ञान
962.	A situation when no progress is possible	Deadlock	(N.)	गतिरोध
963.	A period of ten years	Decade	(N.)	दशक
964.	Act of injuring another's reputation by any slanderous communication	Defamation	(N.)	मानहानि
965.	To injure one's reputation	Defame	(V.)	बदनाम करना
966.	Open refusal to obey orders	Defiance	(N.)	अवज्ञा
967.	A shortage of vitamins, minerals, etc. needed for good health	Deficiency	(N.)	पोषक तत्वों की कमी
968.	To give one's authority to another	Delegate	(V.)	प्रतिनिधि
969.	Slow and careful movement or thought	Deliberation	(N.)	सोच समझ कर
970.	A young person tending to commit crime, particularly minor crime.	Delinquent	(Adj.)	अपराधी
971.	Become liquid, typically during decomposition	Deliquesce	(V.)	गलना
972.	A political leader appealing to popular desires and prejudices	Demagogue	(N.)	जनोत्तेजक नेता
973.	A system of government in which all the people of a country can vote to elect their representatives	Democracy	(N.)	जनतंत्र
974.	The study of population	Demography	(N.)	जनसांख्यिकी
975.	Take away or alter the natural qualities of	Denature	(V.)	विकृत करना
976.	Criticize unfairly	Denigrate	(V.)	बदनाम करना
977.	Portray in words	Depict	(V.)	शब्दों में वर्णन करना
978.	Person who gives written testimony for use in a law court	Deponent	(N.)	गवाह
979.	Morally corrupt	Depraved	(Adj.)	भ्रष्ट
980.	To feel and express strong disapproval	Deprecate	(V.)	विरोध करना
981.	To become less valuable over a period of time	Depreciate	(V.)	मूल्य कम करना
982.	Unable to think clearly because of a mental illness	Deranged	(Adj.)	अव्यवस्थित
983.	A person without a home, a job or property	Derelict	(Adj.)	अवारा व्यक्ति
984.	Failing to discharge one's duty	Dereliction	(N.)	कर्त्तव्य का त्याग

S.N.	Phrases	One Word	PoS	Hindi
985.	To laugh at something in a cruel way	Deride	(V.)	उपहास करना
986.	A doctor who studies and treats skin diseases	Dermatologist	(N.)	त्वचा विशेषज्ञ
987.	The scientific study of skin diseases	Dermatology	(N.)	त्वचाविज्ञान
988.	The abandonment of one's country or cause	Desertion	(N.)	परित्याग
989.	A person without money, food and other things necessary for life	Destitute	(Adj.)	बदहाली
990.	One who investigates and solves crimes	Detective	(N.)	जासूस
991.	The action of discouraging an action or event through instilling doubt or fear of the consequences	Deterrence	(N.)	रुकावट डालना
992.	Showing a skilful use of underhand tactics to achieve goals	Devious	(Adj.)	धूर्त
993.	Skilful with your hands	Dexterous	(Adj.)	निपुण
994.	Determine the nature of the disease	Diagnose	(V.)	रोग पहचानना
995.	The process of deciding the nature of a disease by examination	Diagnosis		रोग की पहचान
996.	A particular form of a language which is peculiar to a specific region	Dialect	(N.)	बोली
997.	Bitter and violent attack in words	Diatribe	(N.)	आक्षेप
998.	A ruler with total power over a country, typically one who has obtained control by force	Dictator	(N.)	तानाशाह
999.	Giving orders in a manner that permits no refusal	Dictatorial	(Adj.)	तानाशाही
1000.	A book giving meaning of various words	Dictionary	(N.)	शब्दकोष
1001.	Spread over a wide area or between a large number of people	Diffuse	(Adj.)	फैला हुआ
1002.	a situation in which you have to make a difficult choice between two or more things	Dilemma	(N.)	दुविधा
1003.	A dabbler in the art and literature	Dilettante	(N.)	मस्तमौला
1004.	Showing care and effort in your work / duties	Diligent	(Adj.)	मेहनती
1005.	Irresistible craving for alcoholic drinks	Dipsomania	(N.)	शराब की लत
1006.	A book of names and addresses	Directory	(N.)	नाम और पते की पुस्तक
1007.	A song sung in the past at a funeral or for a dead person	Dirge	(N.)	शोकगीत
1008.	An act that has disastrous consequences	Disaster	(N.)	आपदा
1009.	A heavy round plate of metal thrown by an athlete	Discus	(N.)	चक्का फेंक प्रतियोगिता

S.N.	Phrases	One Word	PoS	Hindi
1010.	The state of being deprived of a right or privilege, especially the right to vote.	Disenfranchise-ment	(N.)	मताधिकार से वंचित करना
1111.	An act that makes feel morally bad or ashamed.	Disgraceful	(Adj.)	शर्मनाक
1112.	Change the appearance to deceive or to hide the identity	Disguise	(V.)	भेष बदलना
1113.	Break up into small parts as the result of impact or decay	Disintegrate	(V.)	विघटित हो जाना
1114.	Causing a mood of gloom and depression	Dismal	(Adj.)	निराशपूर्ण
1115.	To throw an event into confusion or disorder	Disrupt	(V.)	तितर बितर करना
1116.	Country treated as permanent home by an individual	Domicile		मूल निवास
1117.	An area of land that is controlled by a ruler	Dominion	(N.)	अधिराज्य
1118.	Not active or growing	Dormant	(Adj.)	निष्क्रिय
1119.	A large bedroom for a number of people in a school or institution	Dormitory	(N.)	शयनागर, छात्रवास
1120.	Situated on back	Dorsal	(Adj.)	सतहीय
1121.	A heavy fall of rain that often starts suddenly	Downpour	(N.)	मूसलधार बारिश
1122.	A game in which no one wins	Draw	(V.)	अनिर्णित करना
1123.	The nest of a squirrel, typically in the from of a mass of twigs in a tree	Drey	(N.)	गिलहरी का घोषला
1124.	Light rain falling in small drops	Drizzle	(V.)	बूंदा बादी होना
1125.	Mania for travel	Dromomania	(N.)	यात्रा की धुन
1126.	Dry weather with no rainfall	Drought	(N.)	सूखा
1127.	A herd or flock of animals being driven in a body	Drove	(N.)	झुंड
1128.	(a metal) that can be made into a thin wire	Ductile	(Adj.)	तन्य, कोमल
1129.	A contest between two people to settle a point of honour	Duel	(N.)	द्वंद्व युद्ध
1130.	One who can't speak	Dumb	(Adj.)	गूंगा
1131	A person, animal or plant much below the usual height	Dwarf	(N.)	बौना आदमी
1132.	A wall built to prevent the sea or a river from flooding an area	Dyke	(N.)	बांध
1133.	Succession of rulers belonging to one family.	Dynasty	(N.)	राजवंश
1134.	One who listens secretly to private conversation	Eavesdropper	(N.)	छिपकर बातें सुनने वाला

S.N.	Phrases	One Word	PoS	Hindi
1135.	A man with abnormal habits	Eccentric	(Adj.)	विचित्र
1136.	Sound reflected back as in mountains	Echo	(N.)	प्रतिध्वनि
1137.	One who studies and cares about environment	Ecologist	(N.)	पर्यावरण विज्ञानशास्त्री
1138.	Study of the interaction of people with their environment	Ecology	(N.)	पर्यावरण विज्ञान
1139.	Careful in the spending of money, time, etc.	Economical	(Adj.)	किफायती
1140.	A thing fit to be eaten	Edible	(Adj.)	खाद
1141.	Instruct or improve someone morally or intellectually.	Edify	(V.)	उपदेश देना
1142.	To prepare written material for publication by correcting or modifying it	Edit	(V.)	संपादन करना
1143.	Rub or wipe out	Efface	(V.)	मिटाना
1144.	A change which is the result of an act or some cause	Effect	(V.)	प्रभाव
1145.	Man behaving more like a woman than as a man	Effeminate	(Adj.)	नारी जैसा
1146.	Favouring social equality	Egalitarian	(Adj.)	समानधिकारवादी
1147.	One who is preoccupied with his own interests	Egoist	(N.)	आत्महितैषी
1148.	A person who talks too much of himself / A person who speaks always in praise of himself	Egotist	(N.)	अहंवादी
1149.	All the people in a country or area who are entitled to vote in an election	Electorate	(N.)	मतदाता
1150.	A poem that express lament for the dead	Elegy	(N.)	शोकगीत
1151.	A small mischievous fairy	Elf	(N.)	शरारती परी
1152.	The art of effective speaking	Elocution	(N.)	वाककला
1153.	To run away secretly with a romantic partner	Elope	(V.)	भाग जाना
1154.	Fluent or persuasive in speaking or writing	Eloquent	(Adj.)	सुवक्ता
1155.	A paradise with perfect bliss	Elysium	(N.)	स्वर्ग
1156.	The act of setting free from bondage of any kind	Emancipation	(N.)	मुक्ति
1157.	Fix an object firmly and deeply in surrounding mass	Embed	(V.)	अंत:स्थापित करना
1158.	A small piece of burning or glowing coal or wood in a dying fire	Ember	(N.)	अंगार
1159.	Steal or misappropriate money	Embezzle		गबन करना
1160.	An act of misappropriation of money	Embezzlement	(N.)	गबन

S.N.	Phrases	One Word	PoS	Hindi
1161.	Be an expression of or give a tangible or visible form to an idea, quality, or feeling	Embody	(V.)	मूर्त रूप देना
1162.	One who is honourably discharged from service	Emeritus	(Adj.)	अवकाश प्राप्त
1163.	Medicine that causes vomiting	Emetic	(N.)	वमनकारी औषध
1164.	A person who leaves his country to live in another	Emigrant	(N.)	देश त्यागी
1165.	One who goes for a secret official mission	Emissary	(N.)	गुप्तचर
1166.	The ability to understand another person's feelings, experience, etc.	Empathy	(N.)	संवेदना
1167.	One who employs	Employer	(N.)	काम देने वाला
1168.	A reference work (often in several volumes) containing articles on various topics (often arranged in alphabetical order) dealing with the entire range of human knowledge or with some particular specialty	Encyclopedia	(N.)	विश्वकोष
1169.	Regularly found in a particular place or among a particular group of people and difficult to get rid of/ a disease that is prevalent in a particular area	Endemic	(Adj.)	स्थानिक
1170.	To sweep over something so as to surround it completely	Engulf	(V.)	निगल जाना
1171.	A state of mental weariness from lack of occupation	Ennui	(N.)	ग्लानि
1172.	Preserve a right, tradition, or idea in a form that ensures it will be protected and respected	Enshrine	(V.)	प्रतिष्ठापित करना
1173.	A scientist who studies insects	Entomologist	(N.)	कीटविज्ञानी
1174.	The scientific study of insects	Entomology	(N.)	कीट विज्ञान
1175.	Likely to arouse envy	Enviable	(Adj.)	ईर्ष्या के योग्य
1176.	Lasting for a very short time	Ephemeral	(Adj.)	छणिक
1177.	Long poem based on a noble theme	Epic	(N.)	महाकाव्य
1178.	Devoted to pleasure and enjoy yourself	Epicurean	(Adj.)	भोगवादी
1179.	Widespread outbreak of a disease which affects large populations at the same time	Epidemic	(N.)	महामारी
1178.	A disease causing a person to fall unconscious involuntarily	Epilepsy	(N.)	मिर्गी
1179.	A short speech at the end of a play	Epilogue	(N.)	उपसंहार
1180.	A verse letter	Epistle	(N.)	काव्यपत्र
1181.	An inscription on a tombstone in the memory of the person who has died	Epitaph	(N.)	समाधि-लेख
1182.	A person or thing that is a perfect example of a particular quality or type	Epitome	(N.)	साक्षात् उदाहरण

S.N.	Phrases	One Word	PoS	Hindi
1183.	Imaginary line dividing Earth into northern and southern hemispheres	Equator	(N.)	भूमध्य रेखा
1184.	A state of perfect balance	Equilibrium	(N.)	समतुल्यता
1185.	The dates when days and nights are of equal length	Equinox	(N.)	जब दिन और रात समान लंबाई के हो
1186.	Which can be rooted out	Eradicable	(Adj.)	उन्मूलनीय
1187.	Rub out writing	Erase	(V.)	मिटाना
1188.	Excessive desire to work.	Ergomania	(N.)	काम करने की अत्यधिक इच्छा
1189.	A lover of work	Ergophile	(N.)	काम का प्रेमी
1190.	A mistake in a book	Erratum	(N.)	किताब में अशुद्धि
1191.	Profound scholarly knowledge	Erudition	(N.)	पांडित्य
1192.	A person in a vehicle or on horseback escorting another vehicle	Escort	(N.)	मार्गरक्षी
1193.	The condition of being honoured (esteemed or respected or well regarded)	Esteem	(N.)	आदर
1194.	Something which lasts forever	Eternal	(Adj.)	अनंत
1195.	Infinite or unending time	Eternity	(N.)	अनंतकाल
1196.	The philosophical study of moral values and rules	Ethics	(N.)	आचार विचार
1197.	Science of the races of mankind	Ethnology	(N.)	मानव जाति विज्ञान
1198.	Make pale by excluding light	Etiolate	(V.)	पीला करना
1199.	The customary code of polite behaviour in society	Etiquette	(N.)	शिष्टाचार
1200.	The study of the origin and history of words	Etymology	(N.)	शब्दों के उद्गम का शास्त्र
1201.	A science of race, culture and human development	Eugenics	(N.)	मनुष्यों की संतति सुधार का अध्ययन
1201.	Praise highly in speech or writing	Eulogise	(V.)	प्रशंसा करना
1202.	A formal expression of praise for someone who has died.	**Eulogy**	(N.)	प्रशंसा भाषण
1203.	Substitution of a mild for a very blunt expression	Euphemism	(N.)	कठोर बात को कोमल रीति से कहना
1204.	Bringing about gentle and painless death from ncurable disease	Euthanasia	(N.)	इच्छा मृत्यु

S.N.	Phrases	One Word	PoS	Hindi
1205.	Soon passing out or of a short duration	Evanescent	(Adj.)	क्षणिक
1206.	Expel someone from a property, especially with the support of the law	Evict	(V.)	बेदखल करना
1207.	To develop gradually	Evolved	(V.)	विकसित
1208.	Represent something as larger, better or worse than it really is	Exaggerate	(V.)	बढ़ा चढ़ा कर
1209.	A person who is examined	Examinee	(N.)	परीक्षार्थी
1210.	A short piece of writing, music, film, etc. taken from a longer whole	Excerpt	(N.)	अंग
1211.	A short journey for pleasure	Excursion	(N.)	पर्यटन
1212.	Critical explanation or interpretation of a text, especially of scriptu	Exegesis	(N.)	व्याख्या
1213.	An urgent need or demand	Exigency	(N.)	तत्कालिक
1214.	A situation in which many people leave a place at the same time	Exodus	(N.)	कूच
1215.	To free somebody from all blame	Exonerate	(V.)	दोषमुक्त करना
1216.	A large open area of land, water or sky	Expanse	(N.)	विस्तार
1217.	A person who lives outside his native country	Expatriate	(N.)	निर्वासित
1218.	To make atonement for one's sins	Expiate	(V.)	प्रायश्चित करना
1219.	To come to an end	Expire	(V.)	समाप्त होना
1220.	To remove an objectionable part from a book.	Expurgate	(V.)	छाँटना
1221.	A speech or a presentation made without previous preparation.	Extempore	(Adj.)	बिना तैयारी के
1222.	Stop something from burning	Extinguish	(V.)	बुझाना
1223.	To send back a criminal or an unwanted person to the country of his/her origin	Extradite	(V.)	भागे हुए अधिकारी को सौंपना
1224.	A person who wastes his money on luxury	Extravagant	(Adj.)	फ़िज़ूल ख़र्च
1225.	A lively and confident person who enjoys being with other people , one who is outgoing	Extrovert	(N.)	बहिर्मुखी
1226.	The scientific study of the mind and how it influences behaviour	**Psychology**	(N.)	मनोविज्ञान
1227.	Careful in performing duties	Punctilious	(Adj.)	अति शिष्टाचारी
1228.	A person who gambles, places a bet, or makes a risky investment	Punter	(N.)	जुआरी

S.N.	Phrases	One Word	PoS	Hindi
1229.	The scientific study of the mind and how it influences behaviour	**Psychology**	(N.)	मनोविज्ञान
1230.	Careful in performing duties	Punctilious	(Adj.)	अति शिष्टाचारी
1231.	A person who gambles, places a bet, or makes a risky investment	Punter	(N.)	जुआरी
1232.	To run after	Pursue	(V.)	पीछे लगे रहना
1233.	Decay of organic matter producing a fetid smell	Putrefy	(V.)	सड़ना, गलना
1234.	An obsessive desire to set fire to things	Pyromania	(N.)	आग लगने का पागलपन
1235.	Sound made by ducks	Quack	(V.)	बत्तख की आवाज
1236.	A court or open space usually rectangular and enclosed by a building	Quadrangle	(N.)	चतुर्भुजाकार
1237.	Any creature with four feet	Quadruped	(N.)	चौपाया
1238.	A shake or tremble in a person's voice	Quaver	(V.)	थरथराना
1239.	Search for something	Quest	(N.)	खोज
1240.	A feather used as a pen	Quill	(N.)	पंख की कलम
1241.	An event which happens once in five years	Quinquennial	(Adj.)	पंचवार्षिक
1242.	A person preoccupied with an unrealistically optimistic approach to life	Quixotic	(Adj.)	ख्याली
1243.	A person who is good at telling stories in an interesting and amusing way	Raconteur	(N.)	मज़ेदार कहानियां सुनाने वाला
1244.	The act of spreading outward from a central source	Radiation	(N.)	विकिरण
1245.	A person who advocates complete political or social change	Radical	(N.)	उग्र सुधारवादी
1246.	Medical doctors who specialise in diagnosing diseases using X-rays, CT scans and ultrasound	Radiologist	(N.)	विकिरण चिकित्सक
1247.	The science dealing with x-rays and other high-energy radiation, especially for the diagnosis and treatment of disease.	Radiology	(N.)	विकिरण चिकित्सा विज्ञान
1248.	Having a stale smell or taste	Rancid	(Adj.)	बासी
1249.	Characterized by bitterness or resentment	Rancorous	(Adj.)	शत्रुतापूर्ण
1250.	To free prisoner on payment	Ransom	(N.)	फिरौती
1251.	Greedy for money	Rapacious	(Adj.)	अतिलोभी
1252.	Reduction in tax or debt	Rebate	(N.)	छूट

S.N.	Phrases	One Word	PoS	Hindi
1253.	To take back, withdraw or renounce	Recant	(V.)	मुकर जाना
1254.	A hollow object used to contain something.	Receptacle	(N.)	पात्र
1255.	One who receives something	Recipient	(N.)	प्राप्तकर्ता
1256.	Give and receive mutually	Reciprocate	(V.)	विनिमय करना
1257.	A person who withdraws from the world to live in seclusion and often in world to live in seclusion and often in solitude	Recluse	(N.)	वैरागी
1258.	When something moves in a straight line	Rectilineal	(Adj.)	सीधा
1259.	A process involving too much official formality	Red-tapism	(N.)	लाल फीताशाही
1260.	That which is no longer useful	Redundant	(Adj.)	अनावश्यक
1261.	An act when people vote in order to make a decision about a particular subject or policy ratherthan voting for a perso	Referendum	(N.)	जनमत संग्रह
1262.	An involuntary action under a stimulus is described	Reflex	(N.)	अनैच्छिक क्रिया
1263.	The system which is observed to do progress	Reformism	(N.)	संशोधनवाद
1264.	A person who has been forced to leave his country home, because there is a war or for political religious or social reasons	Refugee	(N.)	शरणार्थी
1265.	Dress with medals, ribbons worn at official ceremony.	Regalia	(N.)	पदक, तमगा
1266.	The act of killing a king	Regicide	(N.)	राज-हत्या
1267.	Restore (someone) to health or normal life after imprisonment, addiction, or illness	Rehabilitate	(V.)	पूर्व दशा में लाना
1268.	A deceased holy person's remains or belongings kept for reverence	Relic	(N.)	अवशेष
1269.	Send back a criminal into custody for further investigation	Remand	(V.)	जेल वापसी
1270.	To brought back to mind	Reminded	(V.)	याद दिलाना
1271.	A characteristic of one thing that is suggestive of another	Reminiscence	(N.)	संस्मरण
1272.	Amount paid to a man for his labour	Remuneration	(N.)	पारिश्रमिक
1273.	Artistic, musical or dramatic interpretation	**Rendition**	(N.)	प्रस्तुतिकरण
1274.	One who deserts his principles or party	Renegade	(N.)	पाखंडी
1275.	Restore something to better condition	Renovate	(V.)	नवीनीकरण
1276.	The return of someone to his own country	Repatriation (3)	(N.)	स्वदेश लौटना
1277.	Atonement for one's sins	Repentance	(N.)	पछतावा

S.N.	Phrases	One Word	PoS	Hindi
1278.	An exact or a very close copy (of something)	Replica	(N.)	नकल
1279.	Postponing or remitting punishment	**Reprieve**	(N.)	दंड विराम
1280.	Causing a strong dislike	Repulsive	(Adj.)	घिनौना
1281.	A large natural or artificial lake used as a source of water supply	**Reservoir**	(N.)	जलाशय
1282.	The process by means of which plants and animals breathe.	Respiration	(N.)	श्वसन
1283.	Postponement or delay permitted in the suffering of a penalty or the discharge of an obligation.	Respite	(N.)	मोहलत
1284.	Return the same sort of attack / give tit for tat	Retaliate	(V.)	बदला लेना
1285.	A person very reserved in speech	Reticent	(Adj.)	अल्पभाषी
1286.	Go back over the same route that one has just taken	Retrace	(V.)	दोहराना
1287.	Withdraw from a forward position in battle	**Retreat**	(V.)	पीछे हटना
1288.	Action of reviewing past events in one's life	Retrospection	(N.)	पश्चावलोकन
1289.	A tune that is played to wake soldiers in the morning	**Reveille**	(N.)	जगाने का बिगुल
1290.	Take great pleasure.	**Revel**	(V.)	आनंद लेना
1291.	Criticize in an abusive or angrily insulting manner	Revile	(V.)	गाली देना
1292.	Meaningless language with an exaggerated style intended to impress. / The art of effective or persuasive speaking or writing	Rhetoric	(N.)	शब्दाडंबर
1293.	A specialist in diseases of the nose	**Rhinologist**	(N.)	नाक के रोगों में विशेषज्ञ
1294.	Scale used for measuring the strength of an earthquake	Richter	(N.)	भूकंप की गति मापने का स्केल
1295.	Full of criticism and mockery	Ridicule	(V.)	उपहास
1296.	One who has fixed opinions and beliefs or Hard and difficult to bend	Rigid	(Adj.)	दृढ / कठोर
1297.	Solemn religious acts	Rites	(N.)	संस्कार
1298.	Circular building or hall with a dome	Rotunda	(N.)	गोल-घर
1299.	The broken parts of objects found in an ancient site	Ruins	(N.)	खंडहर
1300.	Move with urgent haste	Rush	(V.)	जल्दबाज़ी करना
1301.	Deliberately destroy something for military advantage	Sabotage	(N.)	तोड़-फोड़
1302.	Violation of something holy or sacred	Sacrilege	(N.)	अपवित्रीकरण

S.N.	Phrases	One Word	PoS	Hindi
1303.	Deriving pleasure from inflicting pain	Sadistic	(Adj.)	परपीड़न-कामुक
1304.	The quality of being particularly noticeable	Salience	(N.)	विशेषता
1305.	The firing of many guns at the same time to mark an occasion	Salvo	(N.)	फौजी सलामी
1306.	One who helps a person in need	Samaritan	(N.)	नेक आदमी
1307.	The clandestine copying and distribution of literature banned by the state	Samizdat	(N.)	प्रतिबंधित साहित्य की नकल और वितरण
1308.	A place of good climate for invalids	Sanatorium	(N.)	आरोग्य निवास
1309.	The state or quality of being holy	Sanctity	(N.)	पवित्रता
1310.	A protected place for birds and animals / A nature reserve for birds or animals	Sanctuary	(N.)	अभयारण्य
1311.	Optimistic in an apparently difficult situation	Sanguine	(Adj.)	आशावादी
1312.	The use of irony to mock or convey contempt	Sarcasm	(N.)	ताना
1313.	Full of criticism and mockery	Satire	(N.)	हास्य व्यंग्य
1314.	Taste good food or drink and enjoy it to the full	Savouring	(V.)	स्वाद लेना
1315.	A sheath for the blade of a sword	Scabbard	(N.)	म्यान
1316.	Tale that brings bad reputation to somebody	Scandal	(N.)	कलंकपूर्ण कृत्य
1317.	Barely sufficient or adequate	Scant	(Adj.)	अपर्याप्त
1318.	A person who is blamed for the wrong doings of others	Scapegoat	(N.)	बलि का बकरा
1319.	The state of being in short supply.	Scarcity	(N.)	अभाव
1320.	A person who is forgetful and unable to concentrate or think clearly	Scatterbrain	(N.)	अस्थिर व्यक्ति
1321.	Search for and collect anything usable from discarded waste	Scavenge	(V.)	कूड़े में उपयोगी चीज ढूंढना
1322.	Someone who habitually doubts accepted beliefs	Sceptic	(N.)	संदेहवादी
1323.	An ornamented staff carried by rulers on ceremonial occasions as a symbol of sovereignty	Sceptre	(N.)	राजाधिकार
1324.	A plan of what is to be done and when	Schedule	(N.)	समय सारणी
1325.	A grant or payment to support a student's education	Scholarship	(N.)	छात्र वृत्ति
1326.	A vivacious and lively experience	Scintillating	(Adj.)	बहुत शानदार

S.N.	Phrases	One Word	PoS	Hindi
1327.	A set of twenty	Score	(N.)	बीस का एक सेट
1328.	A loud, harsh, piercing cry	Screech	(N.)	फटा आवाज़
1329.	Small room where dishes are washed	Scullery	(N.)	बर्तन मांजने की जगह
1330.	Making or spreading scandalous claims about someone with the intention of damaging their reputation	Scurrilous	(Adj.)	अभद्र
1331	Relating to worldly things or to things that are not regarded as religious, spiritual, or sacred	Secular	(N.)	धर्म निरपेक्ष
1332.	A drug or other substance that induces sleep	Sedative	(N.)	शांतिकर औषधि
1333.	Marked by care and persistent effort	Sedulous	(Adj.)	परिश्रमी
1334.	The scientific study of earthquakes	Seismology	(N.)	भूकंप विज्ञान
1335.	That which is arranged by conferring or discussing	Seminar	(N.)	संगोष्ठी
1336.	Aware of and able to understand other people and their feelings	Sensitive	(Adj.)	संवेदनशील
1337.	A person between the ages of 70 and 79	Septuagenarian	(N.)	सत्तर वर्ष की
1338.	The occurrence and development of events by chance in a happy or beneficial wa	Serendipity	(N.)	आकस्मिक लाभ
1339.	Consisting of or arranged in a series, rank, or row. serial order	Serial	(Adj.)	अनुक्रमिक
1340.	Rearing of silk worm	Sericulture	(N.)	रेशम कीट-पालन
1341.	To cut something into two pieces	Sever	(V.)	काटकर अलग करना
1342.	A person between the ages of 60 and 69	Sexagenarian	(N.)	साठ वर्ष का
1343.	A vertical passageway into a mine	Shaft	(N.)	ऊर्ध्वाधार मार्ग
1344.	A close-fitting cover for a sword or knife	Sheath	(N.)	म्यान
1345.	A large number of fish swimming together.	Shoal	(N.)	मछलियों का समुदाय
1346.	Fragments from an exploded artillery shell, mine, or bomb	Shrapnel	(N.)	बम का टुकड़ा
1347.	A short rest or sleep taken after lunch	Siesta	(N.)	दोपहर का आराम
1348.	A figure of speech by which a thing is spoken of as being that which it only resembles	Simile	(N.)	उपमा

S.N.	Phrases	One Word	PoS	Hindi
1349.	Happening or being done at exactly the same time	Simultaneous	(N.)	समक्षणिक
1350.	An office with high salary but no work	Sinecure	(N.)	आराम की नौकरी
1351.	An or internal or external framework of bones	Skeleton	(N.)	कंकाल
1352.	Reduce decrease in speed or intensity	Slacken	(V.)	धीमा पड़ जाना
1353.	Have saliva dripping copiously from the mouth	Slobber	(V.)	लार टपकना
1354.	Kill someone by covering their nose and mouth so that they suffocate	Smother	(V.)	गला घोंटकर मारना
1355.	A person regarded as arrogant and annoying	Snob	(N.)	घमंडी
1356.	The study and classification of human societies	Sociology	(N.)	समाज शास्त्र
1357.	A brief or short stay at a place	Sojourn	(N.)	थोड़े दिन का निवास
1358.	A very delicate flaw or mistake which is not expected from the person making it	Solecism	(N.)	अशिष्टता
1359.	A speech made to oneself	Soliloquy	(N.)	आत्मभाषण
1360.	The state of being alone, especially when you find this pleasant	Solitude	(N.)	एकांत
1361.	Being able to pay one's debt	Solvent	(Adj.)	अपने ऋण चुकाने में समर्थ
1362.	Walking in sleep	Somnambulism	(N.)	नींद में चलना
1363.	Someone who walks about in sleep	Somnambulist	(N.)	नींद में चलने वाला
1364.	One who talks in sleep	Somniloquist	(N.)	नींद में बोलने वाला
1365.	The act or habit of talking in one's sleep	Somniloquy	(N.)	नींद में बोलने की आदत
1366.	A fourteen-line poem	Sonnet	(N.)	चौदह लाइन की कविता
1367.	A drug or other substance that induces sleep	Soporific	(N.)	नींद लाने वाला
1368.	A type of magic in which spirits, especially evil ones, are used to make things happen	Sorcery	(N.)	जादू-टोना
1369.	The murder of one's sister	Sororicide	(N.)	बहन की हत्या
1370.	Something kept as a reminder of an event	Souvenir	(N.)	निशानी
1371.	Sudden involuntary muscular contraction	Spasm	(N.)	ऐंठन
1372.	an example of a particular type of thing, especially intended to be studied by experts or scientists	Specimen	(N.)	नमूना

S.N.	Phrases	One Word	PoS	Hindi
1374.	The forming of a theory or conjecture without firm evidence	Speculation	(N.)	परिकल्पना
1375.	Study of caves	Speleology	(N.)	गुफा विज्ञान
1376.	One who spends money recklessly	Spendthrift	(N.)	खर्चीला
1377.	An old unmarried woman	Spinster	(N.)	अधेड़ अविवाहित
1378.	One who speaks on behalf of others	Spokesman	(N.)	प्रवक्ता
1379.	ccurring at irregular intervals in time	Sporadic	(N.)	छिटपुट
1380.	Not being what it purports to be	Spurious	(Adj.)	जाली
1381.	A sudden rush of a large number of frightened people or animals.	Stampede	(N.)	आकस्मिक भगदड़
1382.	An upright bar, post, or frame forming a support or barrier	Stanchion	(N.)	स्तंभ
1383.	A computer printout sent out by a bank regarding debits and credits in your accoun	Statement	(N.)	विवरण पत्र
1384.	An attractively tall, graceful, and dignified woman	Statuesque	(Adj.)	सुडौल
1385.	Written law of a legislative body	Statute	(N.)	कानून
1386.	Not able to produce children	Sterile	(Adj.)	बांझ
1387.	One who loads and uploads ships	Stevedore	(N.)	जहाजी कुली
1388.	A person who can endure pain or hardship without showing his feelings/complaining	Stoic	(N.)	सहनशील व्यक्ति
1389.	Indifference to pleasure and pain	Stoicism	(N.)	सहनशीलता
1390.	One who hides away on a ship to obtain a free passage	Stowaway	(N.)	छिपकर यात्रा करना
1391.	A government by the military class	Stratocracy	(N.)	सैन्य वर्ग द्वारा सरकार
1392.	Showing a dislike of anything improper.	Strict	(Adj.)	कड़क, सख्त
1393.	Angry or bitter disagreement over fundamental issues	Strife	(N.)	विवाद
1394.	Speaking with a stammer or lisp.	Stuttering	(N.)	हकलाना
1395.	Too willing to obey other people	Subservient	(Adj.)	अनुसेवी
1396.	Bare minimum needed for survival	Subsistence	(N.)	जीवन निर्वाह
1397.	Having juicy or fleshy and thick tissues	Succulent	(Adj.)	रसीला
1398.	The right to vote in political elections	Suffrage	(N.)	मताधिकार
1399.	The action of killing oneself intentionally	Suicide	(N.)	आत्महत्या

S.N.	Phrases	One Word	PoS	Hindi
1400.	A brief account of a subject	Summary	(N.)	सारांश
1401.	Splendid and expensive-looking	Sumptuous	(Adj.)	आलीशान
1402.	Of the highest quality	Superlative	(Adj.)	श्रेष्ठतासूचक
1403.	Speed greater than that of sound	Supersonic	(Adj.)	पराध्वनिक
1404.	The belief that particular events happen in a way that cannot be explained by reason/ science	Superstition	(N.)	अंधविश्वास
1405.	Ask or beg for something earnestly or humbly	Supplicate	(V.)	विनती करना
1406.	Move suddenly and powerfully forward or upward	Surge	(N.)	लहर
1407.	Having something more than required	Surplus	(N.)	अधिकता
1408.	Kept secret, especially because it would not be approved of	Surreptitious	(Adj.)	छल से किया हुआ
1409.	A person's last performance	Swan song	(N.)	अंतिम प्रदर्शन
1410.	A collection of bees	Swarm	(N.)	मधुमक्खियों का झुंड
1411.	An edged, bladed weapon that is longer than a knife	Sword	(N.)	तलवार
1412.	A part of a word that can be pronounced separately	Syllable	(N.)	शब्दांश
1413.	Reasoning method involving two statements from which a conclusion is reached	Syllogism	(N.)	न्यायवाक्य
1414.	Traditionally in sonata form	Symphony	(N.)	स्वर की समता
1415.	A building where the jews meet for religious worship and teaching	Synagogue	(N.)	यहूदियों का
1416.	Words of the same meanings	Synonyms	(N.)	समानर्थक शब्द
1417.	cheap and of poor quality and/or not in good taste	Tacky	(Adj.)	खराब स्वाद
1418.	Of or connected with the sense of touch	Tactile	(Adj.)	स्पर्श योग्य
1419.	A rough, violent, troublesome person	Tartar	(N.)	चिड़चिड़ा मनुष्य
1420.	Indelible mark on the skin made by inserting pigment into the skin	Tattoo	(V.)	गोदान
1421.	A statement in which you say the same thing twice in different words	Tautology	(N.)	अलग-अलग शब्दों में दो बार एक ही बात करना
1422	A person who preserves skin of animals	Taxidermist	(N.)	चर्म प्रसाधक
1423.	The art of cleaning and preserving animal skins	Taxidermy	(N.)	चर्म प्रसाधन

S.N.	Phrases	One Word	PoS	Hindi
1424.	Science regarding principles of classification	Taxonomy	(N.)	वर्गीकरण
1425.	The application of scientific knowledge for practical purposes	Technology	(N.)	तकनीकी
1426.	A person who never takes alcoholic drinks	Teetotaller	(N.)	पूर्णतया मद्यत्यागी
1427.	Power of reading thought of others	Telepathy	(N.)	दूर संवेदन
1428.	A violent windstorm	Tempest	(N.)	तूफ़ान
1429.	Lasting only for a very short while	Temporary	(Adj.)	अस्थायी
1430.	Station at the end of a route	Terminus	(N.)	अंतिम स्टेशन
1431.	A written statement about someone's character, usually provided by an employer	Testimonial	(N.)	प्रशंसा पत्र
1432.	Government of a country by religious leaders	Theocracy	(N.)	धर्मशास्त्र
1433.	One who studies God and religion	Theologian	(N.)	धर्मशास्त्री
1434.	Relating to the study of the nature of god and religious belief	Theological	(Adj.)	आध्यात्मविद्या
1435.	The study of the nature of god and religious beliefs	Theology	(N.)	धर्मशास्त्र
1436.	Relating to the healing of diseases	Therapeutic	(Adj.)	चिकित्सा संबंधी
1437.	An instrument for measuring body temperature	Thermometer	(N)	तापमापी
1438.	Complete with regard to every detail.	Thorough	(Adj.)	संपूर्ण
1439.	A busy, main road for public use	Thoroughfare	(N.)	सार्वजनिक मार्ग
1440.	Showing a lack of courage or confidence	Timid	(Adj.)	कायर
1441.	A long, angry speech of criticism or accusation	Tirade	(N.)	कड़ी निंदा
1442.	Existing only in name	Titular	(Adj.)	नाममात्र का
1443.	A young child just beginning to walk	Toddler	(N.)	नन्हा बच्चा
1444.	A strong and fast moving stream of water	Torrent	(N.)	प्रचंड धारा
1445.	Full of twists and turns	Tortuous	(Adj.)	घुमावदार
1446.	A system of government in which only one political party is allowed to function	Totalitarianism	(N.)	सर्वसत्तावाद
1447.	Something that is poisonous or unhealthy	Toxic	(Adj.)	विषैला
1448.	A person who works against his country	Traitor	(N.)	गद्दार
1449.	Free from disturbance	Tranquil	(Adj.)	शांतचित्त
1450.	Beyond or above the range of normal or physical human experience	Transcendent	(Adj.)	सर्वोत्कृष्ट
1451.	An apparatus for reducing or increasing the voltage of an alternating current.	Transformer	(N.)	परिवर्तक

S.N.	Phrases	One Word	PoS	Hindi
1452.	Someone who violates a law or command	Transgressor	(N.)	उल्लंघन करने वाला
1453.	Lasting for only a short time	Transient	(N.)	क्षणिक
1454.	A portable radio set	Transistor	(N.)	ले जाने योग्य रेडियो
1455.	That which lasts for a short time	Transitory	(Adj.)	क्षणसाथी
1456.	Change in form, nature, or substance	Transmute	(V.)	बदल देना
1457.	Relating to speeds close to that of sound	Transonic	(N.)	लगभग हवा में ध्वनि के बराबर गति
1458.	Allowing you to see through it (glass etc.)	Transparent	(Adj.)	पारदर्शक
1459.	To move back and forth or sideways	Traverse	(V.)	पर्वत पर तिरछे चढ़ना
1460.	Distorted representation of something	Travesty	(N.)	उपहासात्मक रचना
1461.	The crime of betraying one's country	Treason	(N.)	देशद्रोह
1462.	Shaking movement of the ground,	Tremor	(N.)	भूकंप के झटके
1463.	Those who pass through this gate without permission will be prosecuted.	Trespassers	(N.)	अनधिकार प्रवेश
1464.	Stream flowing into another big river	Tributary	(N.)	सहायक नदी
1465.	Happening every three years	Triennial	(Adj.)	त्रैवार्षिक
1466.	A set of three related works by the same author	Trilogy)	(N.)	तीन रचनाओं का सेट
1467.	A stand having three legs	Tripod	(N.)	तिपाई
1468.	A group of three powerful people	Triumvirate	(N.)	तिकड़ी
1469.	Not important or serious, not worth considering, obvious and dull	Trivial	(Adj.)	तुच्छ
1470.	An award for success in war, hunting , something given as a token of victory	Trophy	(N.)	विजय चिन्ह
1471.	A student who idly or without excuse absents himself, hersef from school	Truant	(N.)	गैरहाजिर रहने वाला
1472.	Defiantly aggressive	Truculent	(Adj.)	लड़ाकू
1473.	An obviously true or hackneyed statement	Truism	(N.)	सामान्य सत्य
1474.	The sound made by an elephant	Trumpet	(V.)	हाथी का चिंघाड़ना

S.N.	Phrases	One Word	PoS	Hindi
1475.	An extremely large wave in the sea caused by an earthquake	Tsunami	(N.)	भूकंप तरंग
1476.	One who changes sides	Turncoat	(N.)	दलबदलू
1477.	Protection of or authority over someone	Tutelage	(N.)	संरक्षण
1478.	Two children born together	Twins	(N.)	जुड़वा
1479.	One who is new to a profession	Tyro	(N.)	नौसिखिया
1480.	By everyone in a particular group	Unanimously	(Adj.)	सर्वसम्मति से
1481.	To put two and two together	Understand	(V.)	अर्थ समझना
1482.	That can't be captured	Ungrippable	(Adj.)	जिस पर कब्जा नहीं किया जा सकता
1483.	Not having knowledge or experience of a particular subject or activity	Uninitiated	(Adj.)	अदीक्षित
1484.	Found all over the world	Universal	(Adj.)	सार्वभौमिक
1484a	Not knowable	Unknowable	(Adj.)	अज्ञात
1485.	Something never done or known before	Unprecedented	(Adj.)	अभूतपूर्व
1486.	Having no moral principles	Unscrupulous	(Adj.)	अनैतिक
1487.	Something that cannot be handled easily	Unwieldy	(Adj.)	दुष्कर
1488.	The upward force that a fluid exerts on a body floating in it	Upthrust	(N.)	तरल में तैरते हुए शरीर पर ऊपर की ओर बल
1489.	A large vase that usually has a pedestal or feet	Urn	(N.)	कलश
1490.	A person who shows people their seats	Usher	(N.)	प्रवेश करने वाला
1491.	One who lends money on high rates of interest	Usurer	(N.)	सूदखोर
1492.	The practice of taking exorbitant or excessive interest on the money lent	Usury	(N.)	सूदखोरी
1493.	An imagined society where everything is perfect and everyone is happy/ A place of ideal perfection especially in laws, government, and social conditions	Utopia	(N.)	आदर्श राज्य
1494.	An imaginary ideal society free of poverty and suffering	Utopian	(Adj.)	आदर्शवादी
1495.	One extremely fond of one's wife	Uxorious	(Adj.)	जोरू का गुलाम

S.N.	Phrases	One Word	PoS	Hindi
1496.	A person without a settled home or regular work who wanders from place to place and lives by begging.	Vagrant	(N.)	खानाबदोश
1497.	A person who is unduly anxious about his/her health	Valetudinarian	(N.)	बीमारी की अत्यधिक चिंता करने वाला
1498.	One who damages public property	Vandal	(N.)	उग्रवादी
1499.	Killer of prophet	Vaticide	(N.)	पैगंबर का हत्यारा
1500.	One who eats no animal flesh	Vegetarian	(N.)	शाकाहारी
1501.	Showing strong feeling	Vehement	(Adj.)	उग्र
1502.	The speed of something in a particular direction	Velocity	(N.)	वेग
1503.	Committing murder in revenge	Vendetta	(N.)	प्रतिशोध
1504.	A person who is greatly respected because of wisdom	Venerable	(Adj.)	सम्मानित
1505.	Regard with great respect	Venerate	(V.)	सम्मानित करना
1506.	Seeking to harm someone in return for a perceived injury.	Vengeful	(Adj.)	प्रतिहिंसक
1507.	A slight fault that can be forgiven.	Venial		मामूली गलती
1508.	One who has the art of speaking in such a way that the sound seems to come from another person, place.	Ventriloquist	(N.)	तरह तरह की आवाज़े निकाल सकने वाला
1509.	A new project or business activity involving some risk	Venture	(N.)	उपक्रम
1510.	Conformity to facts	Veracity	(N.)	सच्चाई
1511.	In exactly the same words as were used originally	Verbatim	(Adj.)	शब्द प्रति शब्द
1512.	The use of too many words or of more difficult words than are needed to express an idea	Verbiage	(N.)	शब्दाडंबर
1513.	Using or containing more words than are needed.	Verbosity	(N.)	शब्दाडंबर
1154.	A decision that is made by a jury in a court	Verdict	(N.)	फैसला
1515.	Someone having many skills	Versatile	(Adj.)	सर्वगुण सम्पन्न
1516.	Evening prayer in church	Vespers	(N.)	गिरजाघर में सायंकाल की प्रार्थना
1517.	A person who is long experienced or practiced in an activity	Veteran	(N.)	अनुभवी
1518.	The area near or surrounding a particular place	Vicinity	(N.)	आस-पास

S.N.	Phrases	One Word	PoS	Hindi
1519.	Person who portrays bad character roles in cinema	Villain	(N.)	खलनायक
1520.	To show or state that someone or something is not guilty of something	Vindicate	(V.)	निर्दोष ठहराना
1521.	One who is determined to take full revenge for wrongs done to him.	Vindictive	(Adj.)	प्रतिशोधी
1522.	A person highly skilled in music	Virtuoso	(N.)	कला प्रवीण व्यक्ति
1523.	Of a disease or poison extremely severe or harmful in its effects	Virulent	(Adj.)	विषैला
1524.	One who can think about the future with imagination and wisdom	Visionary	(Adj.)	काल्पनिक
1525.	The cultivation of grapevines.	Viticulture	(N.)	अंगूर की खेती
1526.	Having a lively, attractive personality.	Vivacious		फूर्तीला, जोश पूर्ण
1527.	A substance easily evaporated at normal temperatures.	Volatile	(Adj.)	परिवर्तनशील
1528.	The faculty or power of using one's will.	Volition	(N.)	इच्छा शक्ति
1529.	A group of arrows	Volley	(N.)	तीर की बौछार
1530.	Of one's own free willfor	Voluntary	(Adj.)	स्वयंसेवी
1531.	One who offers his service of his own freewill	Volunteer	(N.)	स्वयं सेवक
1532.	One who is greedy	Voracious	(Adj.)	लालची
1533.	A long sea journey	voyage	(N.)	समुद्री यात्रा
1534.	Exposed to the possibility of being attacked or harmed, either physically or emotionally	Vulnerable	(Adj.)	असुरक्षित
1535.	A jocular person who is full of amusing anecdotes	Wag	(N.)	मसखरा
1536.	A raised passageway in a building	Walkway	(N.)	पैदल रास्ता
1537.	A place where clothes are kept	Wardrobe	(N.)	अलमारी
1538.	A steep descent of water of a stream or river	Waterfall	(N.)	झरना
1539.	A list of passengers and luggage	Waybill	(N.)	यात्री की सूची
1540.	To take someone somewhere suddenly and quickly	Whisk	(V.)	फुरती से ले जाना
1541.	Speak in a very low tone	Whisper	(V.)	फुसफुसाकर बोलना
1542.	Reduce something in size, amount, or extent by a gradual series of steps	Whittle	(V.)	तराशना

S.N.	Phrases	One Word	PoS	Hindi
1543.	Someone who buys and sells goods in large amounts to shops and businesses	Wholesaler	(N.)	थोक व्यापारी
1544.	A woman whose husband is dead especially one who has not remarried	Widow	(N.)	विधवा
1545.	A man whose wife is dead	Widower	(N.)	विधुर
1546.	Done deliberately, although the person doing it knows that it is wrong	Wilfully	(Adv.)	जान-बूझकर
1547.	A plant, leaf, or flower becoming limp	Wilt	(V.)	मुरझाना
1548.	An unexpected piece of good fortune	Windfall	(N.)	अप्रत्याशित लाभ
1549.	To separate husk from the grain	Winnow	(V.)	फटकना
1550.	The practice of magic	Witchery	(V.)	जादू-टोना
1551.	A decorative ring of flowers and leaves	Wreath	(N.)	पुष्पांजलि
1552.	The remains of something that has been badly damaged	Wreckage	(N.)	मलबे
1553.	To move along with quick, short twistings	Wriggle	(N.)	छटपटाना
1554.	Fear of foreigners	Xenophobia	(N.)	विदेशी लोगों का डर
1555.	A feeling of intense longing for something	Yearning	(N.)	ललक
1556.	A wooden object used for connecting animals that are pulling a vehicle	Yoke	(N.)	घोड़ागाड़ी में घोड़ो को जोड़ने वाली लकड़ी
1557.	A person who is fanatical and uncompromising in pursuit of their religious, political, or other ideals	Zealot	(N.)	कट्टरपंथी
1558.	The highest point	Zenith	(N.)	शीर्ष बिंदु
1559.	A solution for all difficulties or diseases	Panacea	(N.)	रामबाण इलाज
1560.	Something no longer in use	Obsolete	(Adj.)	अप्रचलित
1561.	A place where birds are kept	Aviary	(N.)	पक्षीशाल
1562.	An inscription on a tombstone in the memory of the person who has died	Epitaph	(N.)	समाधि-लेख
1563.	One who cannot be corrected / One who is beyond reform	Incorrigible	(Adj.)	असंशोधनीय
1564.	Something that cannot be avoided	Inevitable	(Adj.)	अटल
1565.	An extreme fear of being in a small confined place	Claustrophobia	(N.)	छोटे जगह में होने का अत्यधिक डर
1566.	Handwriting which is difficult or impossible to read	Illegible	(Adj.)	अपठनीय

S.N.	Phrases	One Word	PoS	Hindi
1567.	A person who can endure pain or hardship without showing his feelings/complaining	Stoic	(N.)	सहनशील व्यक्ति
1568.	An imagined society where everything is perfect and everyone is happy/ A place of ideal perfection especially in laws, government, and social conditions	Utopia	(N.)	आदर्श राज्य
1569.	A person who helps another to commit a crime or to do something morally wrong	Accomplice	(N.)	सह-अपराधी
1570.	Someone who makes charitable donations intended to increase human wellbeing	Altruist	(N.)	परोपकारी
1571.	Able to use the left hand and right hand equally well	Ambidextrous	(N.)	उभयहस्त
1572.	Belonging to the same time / A person living in the same age with another	Contemporary	(Adj.)	समकालीन
1573.	Something that cannot be heard	Inaudible	(Adj.)	अश्राव्य
1574.	A person who eats human flesh	Cannibal	(N.)	नरभक्षक
1575.	A person employed to drive a private or hired car	Chauffeur	(N.)	मोटर-चालन
1576.	A person who leaves his country to live in another	Emigrant	(N.)	उत्प्रवासी
1577.	To free somebody from all blame	Exonerate	(V.)	दोषमुक्त करना
1578.	One who is difficult to please	Fastidious	(Adj.)	ढीठ, हठी
1579.	An animal that lives in groups/ Tending to associate with others of one's kind	Gregarious	(Adj.)	झुण्ड में रहने वाला
1580.	(used about a person) believing and trusting people too easily, and therefore easily tricked	Gullible	(Adj.)	आसानी से धोखा खाने वाला
1581.	(used about a person) never making mistakes or being wrong	Infallible)	(Adj.)	अचूक
1562.	A person whose job is to write dictionaries	Lexicographer	(N.)	शब्दकोश के लेखक

UNIT 2

Most Important One-Word Substitutions

Given below are the most important one word substitutions asked in various competitive Examinations.

S.N.	Phrases	One Word	PoS	Hindi
1.	Someone who opposes war or violence as a means of settling disputesy	Pacifist	(N.)	शांतिवादी
2.	A person who gives money or gifts to charities, or helps needy people in other ways	**Philanthropist**	(N.)	जन हितैषी
3.	A person who knows or write more than one languages	Polyglot	(N.)	बहुभाषी
4.	An animal that kills and eats other animals	Predator	(N.)	परजीवी
5.	A fictitious name especially one assumed by an author	Pseudonym	(N.)	उपनाम
6.	A person who withdraws from the world to live in seclusion and often in solitude	Recluse	(N.)	वैरागी
7.	A person very reserved in speech	Reticent	(Adj.)	अल्पभाषी
8.	A protected place for birds and animals/ A nature reserve for birds or animals	Sanctuary	(N.)	अभयारण्य
9.	Government not connected with religious or spiritual matters	**Secular**	(Adj.)	धर्म निरपेक्ष
10.	A close-fitting cover for a sword or knife / Cover for the blade of a weapon or a tool	Sheath	(N.)	म्यान
11.	An office with high salary but no work	**Sinecure**	(N.)	आराम की नौकरी
12.	Found all over the world	**Universal**	(Adj.)	सार्वभौमिक
13.	One who lends money on high rates of interest	Usurer	(N.)	सूदखोर
14..	A person who is long experienced or practiced in an activity	Veteran	(N.)	अनुभवी
15.	A decorative ring of flowers and leaves	Wreath	(N.)	पुष्पांजली
16.	To decide and state officially in court that somebody is not guilty of a crime	Acquit	(V.)	बरी करना
17.	A word formed from the first letters of the words that make up the name of something	Acronym	(N.)	शब्दों के पहले अक्षरों से बना एक शब्द

S.N.	Phrases	One Word	PoS	Hindi
18.	Concerned with beauty or the appreciation of beauty	Aesthetic	(Adj.)	सौन्दर्यबोधी
19.	A person belonging to a foreign country / different from what you are used to	Alien	(N.)	अजनबी
20.	A person who believes that laws and governments are not necessary	Anarchist	(N.)	अराजकतावादी
21.	The study of human race, especially of its origin, development, customs and beliefs	Anthropology	(N.)	मानव विज्ञान
22.	Strong dislike between two persons / A deep-seated feeling of aversion	Antipathy	(N.)	घृणा, चिढ़
23.	The feeling of not being interested in or enthusiastic	Apathy	(N.)	उदासीनता
24.	A person who works for an expert to learn a trade	Apprentice	(N.)	शिक्षार्थी
25.	A person who is chosen to settle a disagreement/ a person appointed by two parties to resolve a dispute	Arbitrator	(N.)	पंच
26.	A person who is trained to travel in space	Astronaut	(N.)	अन्तरिक्ष यात्री
27.	Place that provides refuge // a hospital where people who were mentally ill could be cared for, often for a long time	Asylum	(N.)	शरणस्थल
28.	A large bundle bound for storage or transport	Bale	(N.)	गटा
29.	An instrument used for measuring atmospheric pressure	Barometer	(N.)	वायु-दाब-मापक
30.	Place given to soldiers to live in	Barracks	(N.)	सैनिकों के लिये बने घर
31.	A list of the books referred to in a scholarly work	**Bibliography**	(N.)	ग्रन्थसूची
32.	A person who is intolerant towards those holding different opinions	Bigot		कटर व्यक्ति
33.	The study of plant life	Botany	(N.)	वनस्पति विज्ञान
34.	Harsh or discordant sound / Loud confusing	**Cacophony**	(N.)	कोलाहल
35.	Beautiful handwriting that you do with a special pen / brush.	Calligraphy	(N.)	सुलेख
36.	A small building / room used for christian worship in a school, prison, large private house etc	Chapel	(N.)	छोटा गिरजाघर
37.	A group of singers in a church	Choir	(N.)	गायक-मंडली
38.	The use of many words where only a few are necessary	Circumlocution	(N.)	शब्द-बहुल्य
39.	Use of force or threats to get someone to agree to something	**Coercion**	(N.)	जोर जबरदस्ती

S.N.	Phrases	One Word	PoS	Hindi
40.	A person that one work with at the same place, in a profession or a business	Colleague	(N.)	सहकर्मी
41.	Easily spread from one person to another (disease) / A disease which spreads with contact	Contagious	(Adj.)	संक्रामक
42.	A person who can make himself/herself feel at home in any country / One who is a citizen not of a country but of the world	**Cosmopolitan**	(Adj.)	सर्वदेशीय
43.	A person in charge of a museum	Curator	(N.)	संग्रहालय अध्यक्ष
44.	A period of ten years	Decade	(N.)	दशक
45.	A system of government in which all the people of a country can vote to elect their representatives	Democracy	(N.)	जनतंत्र
46.	A doctor who studies and treats skin diseases	Dermatologist	(N.)	त्वचा विशेषज्ञ
47.	One who listens secretly to private conversation	Eavesdropper	(N.)	छिपकर बातें सुनने वाला
48.	A man with abnormal habits	Eccentric	(Adj.)	विचत्र
49.	Study of the interaction of people with their environment	Ecology	(N.)	पर्यावरण विज्ञान
50.	One who is preoccupied with his own interests	**Egoist**	(N.)	आत्महितैषी
51.	The ability to understand another person's feelings, experience, etc.	Empathy	(N.)	संवेदना
52.	Lasting for a very short time	**Ephemeral**	(Adj.)	छणिक
53.	Widespread outbreak of a disease which affects large populations at the same time	Epidemic	(N.)	महामारी
54.	Something which lasts forever	Eternal	(Adj.)	अनंत
55.	A formal expression of praise for someone who has died.	Eulogy	(N.)	प्रशंसा भाषण
56.	A person who wastes his money on luxury	**Extravagant**	(Adj.)	फिजूल खर्च
57.	A short story with a moral, usually with animals as characters	Fable	(N.)	कल्पित कहानी
58.	A person motivated by irrational enthusiasm	**Fanatic**	(N.)	कटरपंथी
59.	A group of ships sailing together	Fleet	(N.)	जहाजों का बेड़ा
60.	The plants and vegetation of a region	Flora	(N.)	वनस्पति
61.	Something which gets broken easily	Fragile	(Adj.)	भंगुर
62.	An act of murdering one's brother	Fratricide	(N.)	भ्रातृहत्या
63.	One who runs away from justice or the law	Fugitive	(N.)	भगोड़ा
64.	Science of heredity	Genetics	(N.)	आनुवंशिकी

S.N.	Phrases	One Word	PoS	Hindi
65.	A perception without objective reality	Hallucination	(N.)	माया
66.	A building in which aircraft are housed	Hangar	(N.)	विमानशाला
67.	A transport vehicle for conveying the coffin at a funeral	Hearse	(N.)	शवयान
68.	The study of growing garden plants	Horticulture	(N.)	उद्यान-विज्ञान
69.	A box or cage for rabbits or small animals	Hutch	(N.)	छोटे जानवरों के रहने का घर
70.	A person who dishonestly pretends to be somebody else	Imposter	(N.)	बहुरूपिया
71.	Something that is difficult to understand	Incomprehen-sible	(Adj.)	समझ से बाहर
72.	Being unable to pay one's debt	Insolvent	(Adj.)	दिवालिया
73.	Well-known for being bad/ A person of evil reputation	Notorious	(Adj.)	कुख्यात
74.	That through which light cannot pass	Opaque	(Adj.)	अपारदर्शी
75.	To give up one's authority or throne	Abdicate	(V.)	पद त्यागना
76.	The study of human history and prehistory through the excavation of sites	Archaeology	(N.)	पुरातत्त्व
77.	A person who does not believe in God	Atheist	(N.)	नास्तिक
78.	Hard but easily broken // liable to break easily	Brittle	(Adj.)	भंगुर
79.	A person who draws or makes maps	Cartographer	(N.)	मानचित्रकार
80.	An arrangement of events or dates in the order of their occurrenc	Chronology	(N.)	कालक्रम
81.	A group of stars that forms a shape in the sky and has a name	Constellation	(N.)	नक्षत्र
82.	A speech or a presentation made without previous preparation.	Extempore	(Adj.)	बिना तैयारी के
83.	A person who suffers from an imaginary illness / A person who is abnormally anxious about his health	Hypochondriac	(N.)	रोगभ्रमी
84.	A person pretending to be somebody he isn't	Hypocrite	(N.)	पाखंडी
85.	A plan of a journey, including the route and the places that you visit	Itinerary	(N.)	यात्रा कार्यक्रम
86.	A person with strong desire to steal.	Kleptomania	(N.)	चोरी करने की बीमारी
87.	A place where money is coined by authority of the government	Mint	(N.)	टकसाल
88.	A person who dislikes women	Misogynist	(N.)	स्त्री द्वेषी

S.N.	Phrases	One Word	PoS	Hindi
89.	Giving undue favours to one's own kith and kin.	Nepotism	(N.)	भाई-भतीजावाद
90.	A large number of fish swimming together.	Shoal	(N.)	मछलियों का समुदाय
91.	A person who never takes alcoholic drinks	Teetotaller	(N.)	पूर्णतया मद्यत्यागी
92.	Animals that can live on land and water	Amphibians	(N.)	उभयचर जन्तु
93.	A situation in a country, an organization, etc. in which there is no government, order / contro	Anarchy	(N.)	अराजकता
94.	Animals and plants growing or living in, or near water	Aquatic	(Adj.)	जलीय
95.	One who makes an official examination of accounts/financial records	Auditor	(N.)	लेखा परीक्षक
96.	An account of a person's life written by self	Autobiography	(N.)	अत्मकथा
97.	One who is a great lover of books	Bibliophile	(N.)	पुस्तक प्रेमी
98.	Words uttered impiously about God/ The act of speaking irreverently about sacred things.	Blasphemy	(N.)	ईश्वर की निंदा
99.	An arrangement of flowers that is usually given as a present	Bouquet	(N.)	गुलदस्ता
100.	House or shelter of a gipsy / A group of people travelling together, especially in a desert	Caravan	(N.)	काफिला
101.	A complete list of books	Catalogue	(N.)	सूची
102.	One who plans the steps and moves in a dance	Choreographer	(N.)	नृत्य-निर्देशक
103.	A thing fit to be eaten	Edible	(Adj.)	खाद्य
104.	The scientific study of insects	Entomology	(N.)	कीटविज्ञान
105.	A short speech at the end of a play	Epilogue	(N.)	उपसंहार
106.	Causing or ending in death	Fatal	(Adj.)	घातक
107.	A person who sells and arranges cut flowers	Florist	(N.)	फूलवाला
108.	One who eats too much	Glutton	(N.)	खाऊ, पेटू
109.	Holding an office without receiving a pay	Honorary	(Adj.)	मानवीय
110.	Extreme fear of water	Hydrophobia	(N.)	पानी से भय
111.	One who destroys images or attacks popular beliefs	Iconoclast	(N.)	मूर्ती तोड़ने वाला
112.	A person who cannot read or write	Illiterate	(Adj.)	निरक्षर
113.	That which cannot be believed	Incredible	(Adj.)	अविश्वसनीय
114.	That which cannot be satisfied	Insatiable	(Adj.)	लालची
115.	The condition of being unable to sleep over a period of time	Insomnia	(N.)	अनिद्रा

S.N.	Phrases	One Word	PoS	Hindi
116.	One who dies without a will	Intestate	(Adj.)	बिन वसीयत मरा हुआ
117.	That which cannot be called back	Irrevocable	(Adj.)	अटल
118.	Sentimental longing for a period in the past	Nostalgia	(N.)	अतीत की घटनाओं की याद
119.	A person who collects coins	Numismatist	(N.)	मुद्राशास्त्री
120.	Government or rule by a small group of people	Oligarchy	(N.)	अल्पतंत्र
121.	One who knows everything	Omniscient	(Adj.)	सर्वज्ञानी
122.	One who see bright side of things	Optimist	(N.)	आशावादी
123.	A person who loves, supports and defends his country	Patriot	(N.)	देश-भक्त
124.	A person who walks on foot and not travelling in a vehicle	Pedestrian	(N.)	पैदल यात्री
125.	A person who collects or studies stamps	Philatelist	(N.)	डाक के टिकट का संग्रहक
126.	Violation of something holy or sacred	Sacrilege	(N.)	अपवित्रीकरण
127.	Someone who walks about in sleep	Somnambulist	(N.)	नींद मे चलने वाला
128.	To reduce to a shorter form intended to stand for the whole	Abbreviation	(N.)	संक्षेपण
129.	Study of sound	Acoustics	(N.)	ध्वनि-विज्ञान
130.	The period between the beginning of puberty and adulthood	Adolescence	(N.)	किशोरावस्था
131.	A list of items to be discussed at a meeting	Agenda	(N.)	कार्यसूची
132.	One who plays for pleasure rather than as a profession/ A person who is neither well experienced nor professional	Amateur	(N.)	शौकीन व्यक्ति
133.	Capable of being understood in either of two or more possible senses, and therefore not definite.	Ambiguous	(Adj.)	अनेकार्थी
134.	A partial or total loss of memory	Amnesia	(N.)	भूलने की बिमारी
135.	An official pardon // the formal act of liberating someone	Amnesty	(N.)	राज-क्षमा
136.	A person who presents a radio / television programme	Anchor	(N.)	समाचार उद्घोषक
137.	The date on which an event happened in some previous year	Anniversary	(N.)	सालगिरह
138.	A medicine to nullify the effect of poison	Antidote	(N.)	विषहर औषध

S.N.	Phrases	One Word	PoS	Hindi
139.	A glass tank where fish and water plants are kept	Aquarium	(N.)	मछलीघर
140.	A large body of water with many islands	Archipelago	(N.)	द्वीपसमूह
141.	The place where public, government or historical records are kept	Archives	(N.)	अभिलेखागार
142.	A government by the nobles / government by person of highest social order	Aristocracy	(N.)	श्रेष्ठ जनों के द्वारा राज्य शासन
143.	One who denies oneself ordinary bodily pleasures	Ascetic	(N.)	तपस्वी
144.	The scientific study of celestial bodies like sun, moon, stars, planets, etc.	Astronomy	(N.)	खगोल शास्त्र
145.	A person who can speak only two languages	Bilingual	(Adj.)	द्विभाषिक
146.	A government run by officials in a state	Bureaucracy	(N.)	नौकरशाही
147.	Hole excavated by an animal as dwelling	Burrow	(N.)	बिल
148.	A doctor who specializes in the study or treatment of heart diseases	Cardiologist	(N.)	हृदय रोग विशेषज्ञ
149.	Animals that eat meat	Carnivorous	(N.)	मांसभक्षी
150.	The art or process of drawing or making maps	Cartography	(N.)	मानचित्रकारी
151.	An assembly of worshippers / A gathering at a religious place/ A group of people who have come together in a religious building for worship and prayer	Congregation	(N.)	धार्मिक सभा
152.	A man who knows a lot about things like food, music and art	Connoisseur	(N.)	विशेषज्ञ, पारखी
153.	A man who is recovering from illness.	Convalescent	(N.)	बिमारी से ठीक होना
154.	A person who readily believes others easily	Credulous	(Adj.)	भोला-भाला
155.	The scientific study of skin diseases	Dermatology	(N.)	त्वचा विज्ञान
156.	A large bedroom for a number of people in a school or institution	Dormitory	(N.)	शयनागार
157.	A game in which no one wins	Draw	(N.)	अनिर्णित करना
158.	Man behaving more like a woman than as a man	Effeminate	(Adj.)	नारी जैसा
159.	A person who talks too much of himself/ A person who speaks always in praise of himself / A person who is excessively conceited and self-absorbed	Egotist	(N.)	अहंवादी
160.	A poem that express lament for the dead	Elegy	(N.)	शोकगीत
161.	An act of misappropriation of money	Embezzlement	(N.)	गबन

S.N.	Phrases	One Word	PoS	Hindi
162.	Bringing about gentle and painless death from incurable disease	Euthanasia	(N.)	इच्छामृत्यु
163.	The murder of a whole race or a group of people	Genocide	(N.)	जातिसंहार
164.	The line when the land and sky seems to meet	Horizon	(N.)	क्षितिज
165.	Incapable of being approached	Inaccessible	(Adj.)	दुर्गम
166.	Incapable of feeling tired or exhausted	Indefatigable	(Adj.)	न थकनेवाला
177.	That can burn / catches fire easily	Inflammable	(Adj.)	ज्वलनशील
168.	A copy of a book, piece of music, etc. before it has been printed	Manuscript	(N.)	हस्तलिपि
169.	A soldier who will fight for any country / group that offers payment	Mercenary	(N.)	किराये का सैनिक
170.	A person who hates and avoids other people	Misanthrope	(N.)	मानवद्वेषी
171.	A system of government by a king / a queen	Monarchy	(N.)	राज तंत्र
172.	A person or thing that has the same name as another	Namesake	(N.)	हमनाम
173.	A notice of a person's death	Obituary	(N.)	शोक सन्देश
174.	A geometrical figure with eight sides	Octagon	(N.)	अष्टभुज
175.	One who is all powerful	Omnipotent	(Adj.)	सर्वशक्तिमान
176.	A piece of land / garden, in which fruit trees are grown	Orchard	(N.)	फलोद्यान

UNIT 3

Examwise One Word Substitutions

Given below are a number of one word substitutions asked in SSC Exams.

S.N.	Origin	Definition
	SSC CGL 2020	
1	Central character in a story or play	Protagonist
2	Only on the surface of something	Superficial
3	An entertainer who performs difficult physical feats	Acrobat
4	To free from restraint	Emancipate
5	A decision on which one cannot go back	Irrevocable
6	A long wooden seat with a back for people to sit on in a church	Pew
7	One who possesses several talents	Versatile
8	Strong dislike between two persons	Antipathy
9	Study of diseases	Pathology
10	No longer in use	Obsolete
11	A period of thousand years	Millennium
12	A mass of snow, ice and rocks falling rapidly down a mountainside.	Avalanche
13	The original natives of a country	Aborigines
14	Too great to be expressed or described in words	Ineffable
15	A person who is neither well experienced nor professional	Amateur
16	A set of rooms specially in a hotel for the use of one person or his family	Suite
17	Made of artificial substance or material	Synthetic
18	One who accompanies somebody to protect him	Escort
19	Soil deposited by flowing water	Alluvium
20	Something which is considered to be very important	Cardinal
21	Substance used for killing troublesome small animals like insects, mice etc.	Pesticide
22	A cruel and oppressive ruler	Tyrant
23	The sovereign head of a state	Monarch

	Many word (SSC CPO 2020 Tier-2)	
1	Branch of science that studies structure, classification and genetics of plants	botany
2	One who talks in sleep	somniloquist

S.N.	Origin	Definition
3	An entrance hall in a building used by the public, especially a hotel or theatre	foyer
4	One who is beyond reform	incorrigible
5	A person skilled in cutting, dressing, and laying stone in buildings.	mason
6	A doctor who attends to bone problems	orthopaedist
7	One who is violently against established traditions and beliefs	iconoclast
8	A traveller who moves from one region or country to another	migrant
9	A small mischievous fairy	elf
10	An arrangement of flowers that is usually given as a present	bouquet

Many Word (SSC Selection Post 2021 - 10th Level)		
1	The sound made by a hen	Cluck
2	pictures given in a book to explain things	Illustration
3	The young one of a cow	Calf
4	A group of people, especially traders or pilgrims, travelling together across a desert	Caravan
5	A place where government records are kept	Archive
6	a low area of land between hills	valley
7	The sound made by sheep	Bleat
8	to walk unsteadily as if about to fall	stagger
9	A blank book for keeping a collection of photographs, stamps or pictures.	Album
10	The sound made by a camel	Grunt
11	Able to be heard	Audible
12	A doctor who specialises in X-rays and other kind of radiations	Radiologist
13	Vertebrate animals that crawl on the ground	Reptiles
14	A remark that expresses approval or admiration	Compliment
15	Having or showing no emotion	Apathetic
16	An animal that can live in water as well as on land	Amphibian
17	To stay longer than necessary	Linger
18	All the customers of a business	Clientele
19	Full of people	Populous
20	An afternoon performance of a play, film or show	Matinee
21	An image of God used for worship	Idol
22	Officially make a student leave a school for ever	Expel
23	A group of vehicles travelling together, typically one accompanied by armed troops	Convoy

S.N.	Origin	Definition
24	Not allowed to do or be something	Ineligible
25	A person, animal or plant belonging originally to a place	Native
26	To steal and pass off ideas and words of another as one's own	Plagiarize
27	The young one of a sheep	Lamb
28	A place where bread and cakes are made	Bakery
29	The belief that people cannot change or avoid what happens	Fatalism
30	A given space, time or position	Slot
31	A lions' home	Den
32	A person who wanders from place to place without a home or job.	Vagabond
33	A place where pigs are kept	Sty
34	To have a strong feeling of sympathy with a desire to help.	Compassion
35	A room where food, crockery and cutlery are kept	Pantry
36	A person who studies the Earth and the materials of which it is made	Geologist

Many word (SSC Selection Post 2021-12th Level)		
1	One who is easily deceived	Gullible
2	A group of cattle or sheep	Herd
3	Study of the earth and its structure and processes	Geology
4	Something that is no longer in use	Obsolete
5	A group of birds	Flock
6	One who does one's work thoroughly and seriously	Conscientious
7	Safe to drink	Potable
8	To protect from harm or danger	Defend
9	The study of plants	Botany
10	A disease persisting for a long time or recurring again and again	Chronic
11	Scientific study of the human mind and behavior	Psychology
12	Someone who looks at the brighter side of things	Optimist
13	One who doesn't believe in the existence of God	Atheist
14	Fear of water	Hydrophobia
Many word (SSC Selection Post 2021-Grand Level)		
1	The state of being unmarried by choice	Celibacy
2	Capable of bending easily without breaking	Pliable
3	The dark shape and outline of something visible against a bright background	Silhouette
4	Following or occurring after death	Posthumous
5	An original model from which later forms are developed	Prototype

S.N.	Origin	Definition
	Many word (SSC Selection Post 2021-Grand Level)	
1	One who supervises students in an examination hall	Invigilator
2	Walk or move at a slow, relaxed pace	Amble
3	A sound that cannot be heard	Inaudible
4	A glass container to keep fish	Aquarium
5	The study of earthquakes	Seismology
6	To walk aimlessly	Amble
7	A fictional being from another world	Alien
8	Showing great attention to detail and correct behaviour	Punctilious
9	A medical condition in which somebody partly or completely loses their memory	Amnesia
10	The examination or observation of one's own mental and emotion processes	Introspection
11	In exactly the same words as the original	Verbatim
12	Formally put an end to a system, practice, or institution	Abolish
13	Indifferent to pleasure and pain	Stoic
14	Sharpness and accuracy of judgment	Acumen
15	Something that is strong and lasts a long time without breaking becoming weaker.	Durable
16	A tank for fish or water plants	Aquarium
17	An image of a God used for worship,	Idol
18	Drawings or writing scribbled on walls in public places	Graffiti
19	Study of insects	Entomology
20	A seat for a passenger on a bicycle or motorbike	Pillion
21	One who knows everything	Omniscient
22	Unfairly take something belonging to another for one's use	Misappropriate
23	A problem that is so difficult that it cannot be answered	Insoluble
	Many word (SSC CGL 2021-Tier-1)	
24	One who can read and write	Literate
25	Drawings or writing on a wall in a public place	Graffiti
26	A style of cooking food, characteristic of a particular country or region	Cuisine
27	Unable to express feelings clearly	Inarticulate
28	An animal with a spinal cord	Vertebrate
29	Able to be happy, successful, etc. again after something difficult or bad has happened	Resilient
30	A fixed sum paid annually	Annuity
31	A person who travels on foot.	Pedestrian

S.N.	Origin	Definition
32	A spear used for hunting large fish	Harpoon
33	A room or large cupboard for storing food	Larder
34	Place where objects of importance are exhibited	Museum
35	Lacking interest or excitement	Mundane
36	Easily hurt emotionally	Sensitive
37	A group of people	Crowd
38	Policy of racial discrimination	Apartheid
39	A person who works in a shop that sells cut flowers and plants	Florist
40	A four-footed animal	Quadruped
41	A person above a hundred years in age	Centenarian
42	A person who collects or studies stamps	Philatelist
	Many Word (SSC CHSL 2021Tier-1)	
1	Zeal; burning enthusiasm; passion	Ardour
2	someone who was only interested in the amount of money that he could get from a situation	Mercenary
3	the scientific study of sound	Acoustics
4	connoisseur of food	Gourmet
5	knows everything and has unlimited knowledge	Omniscient
6	The action of examining with care or reading carefully	Perusal
7	pretending to be what he is not	Hypocrite
8	A short text written on tombstone	Epitaph
9	a report giving the news of the death and details about the life of the deceased	Obituary
10	A pause between the acts of a play.	Interlude
11	An instrument for detecting an earthquake	Seismograph
12	Fall back or sink again (into a worse state after an improvement)	Relapse
13	Looking or sounding foreign, bizarre, strange, unfamiliar	Outlandish
14	unable to pay his debts	Bankrupt
15	A person who leaves his/her own country to live in another country permanently	Emigrant
16	One thing that can be divided	Divisible
17	Unselfish interest in the welfare of others	Altruism
18	Unable to speak distinctly or express oneself clearly	Inarticulate
19	A small organised dissenting group within a larger one	Faction
20	inexperienced at this job	Novice
21	The study of population and its dynamics	Demography

S.N.	Origin	Definition
22	Speaks many languages	Polyglot
23	One who is well-versed in the knowledge of plants	Botanist
24	Eternal; lasting forever or indefinitely	Perpetual
25	Wastes his money on luxurious objects	Extravagant
26	An outlook that is influenced by people from all over the world	Cosmopolitan
27	naturally able to eat both, plants and flesh	Omnivorous
28	helping other people willingly without expecting any payment for her services	Volunteer
29	The state of being full or complete	Plenitude
30	A remedy to counteract the effects of poison	Antidote
31	One who gives money or help to another person or cause	Benefactor
32	The love of man or mankind	Philanthropy
33	whose names are not known	Anonymous
34	One who loves the company of others	Gregarious
35	One who believes in the existence of a god or gods	Theist
36	someone who draws maps	Cartographer
37	Someone who is shy and spends time alone rather than being with others	Introvert
38	To dispute angrily	Wrangle
39	One who has many skills	Versatile
40	Direct and outspoken	Forthright
41	Allowing or assisting to discover	Heuristic
42	The area where animals are slaughtered for the market	Abattoir
43	To renovate or improve	Revamp
44	Lasting for a very short period of time	Ephemeral
45	A journey undertaken by a group of people with a particular purpose, especially that of exploration or research	Expedition
46	A sudden unsteady movement; a stagger	Lurch
47	Reject as invalid, especially by legal procedure	Quash
48	Merry, convivial, hearty and good humoured	Jovial
49	Something that is pertaining to controversy	Polemical
50	A person as a source of intellectual light or moral inspiration	Luminary
51	living in the same time period	Contemporaries
52	Something that will cure all illnesses	Panacea
53	Situation of no organisation and control due to the lack of an effective government	Anarchy
54	Strong taste or liking for something	Penchant

S.N.	Origin	Definition
55	An omission of duty	Delinquency
56	The art of beautiful handwriting	Calligraphy
57	The work inscribed on the tomb in the memory of the person	Epitaph
58	Take and use the thoughts, inventions, etc. of another person as one's own	Plagiarise
59	One who makes an active effort to promote human welfare	Philanthropist
60	A person who loves and collects books	Bibliophile
61	The activity of writing dictionaries	Lexicography
62	One who is well versed in many languages	Polyglot
63	Easily provoked	Irascible
64	One who makes an active effort to promote human welfare	Philanthropist
65	has come to a different country from his own country for settling	Immigrant
66	One who knows many languages	Polyglot
67	A word that has the same or nearly the same meaning as another word in the same language	Synonym
68	Number of fishes getting caught	Haul

	Story of an individual written by himself	
1	The expression of a wish that misfortune or doom befall a person	Curse
2	A place for ammunition and weapons	Arsenal
3	Property left to someone by a will	Legacy
4	One who is unable to pay his debts	Bankrupt
5	One who does not tire easily	Indefatigable
6	A person who looks at the bright side of things	Optimist
7	Climb or move with difficulty or a lot of effort, typically using one's hands and feet	Clamber
8	A keeper or custodian of a museum	Curator
9	Any award, honour or laudatory notice	Accolade
10	Something happening in three years	Triennial
11	Story of an individual written by himself	Autobiography
12	A person exhibiting excessive worry about one's health	Hypochondriac
13	One who feeds on human flesh	Cannibal
14	A person who believes in or tries to bring about a state of lawlessness	Anarchist
15	One who believes in fate	Fatalist
16	The collection and study of postage stamps	Philately
17	A person who sells flowers	Florist
18	A disturbed state of mind caused by an illness	Delirium

S.N.	Origin	Definition
19	One who collects coins	Numismatist
20	A large bundle bound for storage or transport	Bale
21	Made in imitation so as to be passed off fraudulently as genuine	Counterfeit
22	Killing one self	Suicide
23	An imaginary name assumed by an author	Pseudonym
24	The study of human mind and behaviour	Psychology
25	One who studies insect life	Entomologist
26	Of or relating to the moon	Lunar
27	A system of government by the wealthy class	Plutocracy
28	One who has a long experience of any occupation	Veteran
29	An agreement between enemies or opponents to stop fighting, arguing, etc., for a certain period of time	Truce
30	One who knows all	Omniscient
31	One who runs away from justice or a dangerous situation	Fugitive
32	Having or forming a hard outer layer	Crusted
33	The study of the heart and its action and disease	Cardiology
34	Incapable of making mistakes or being wrong	Infallible
35	Someone working or acting merely for money or other rewards	Mercenary
36	A non-professional who is inept at a particular activity	Amateur
37	Having a common centre, as circles or spheres	Concentric
38	One who can use either hand with ease	Ambidextrous
39	Existing or happening in the same time period	Contemporary
40	A room in a public building where outdoor clothes or luggage may be left	Cloakroom
41	A place for breeding and keeping birds.	Aviary
42	The action of using someone or something as a model	Imitation
43	A game in which no one wins	Draw
44	One who is outspoken and outgoing	Extrovert
45	Someone who is silent or uncommunicative in speech	Reserved
46	A place where bees are kept	Apiary
47	One who does a thing for pleasure and not as a profession	Amateur
48	Incapable of making mistakes or being wrong	Infallible
49	Someone working or acting merely for money or other rewards	Mercenary
50	Government by king or queen	Monarchy
51	Violation or misuse of what is regarded as sacred	Sacrilege
52	Occurring after the death of the said person	Posthumous
53	A place where dead bodies are kept for identification	Morgue

S.N.	Origin	Definition
54	Feelings of great happiness and excitement	Euphoria
55	In exactly the same words as were used originally	Verbatim
56	The life history of a person written by himself	Autobiography
57	An unconventional style of living	Bohemian
58	One who dislikes art and culture	Philistine
59	An abbreviation formed from the initial letters of other words and pronounced as a word	Acronym
60	An unlikely chance or occurrence, especially a piece of good luck	Fluke
61	Make (something bad or unsatisfactory) better	Ameliorate
62	An afternoon performance in a theatre or cinema	Matinee
63	An ability to find ways and directions	Navigate
64	A person who produces beautiful handwriting	Calligrapher
65	A state of perfect balance	Equilibrium
66	A collection of selected writings of various authors	Anthology
67	A short story with a moral	Parable
68	A place for storing grain	Granary
69	A group of fish	School
70	The science or art of political government	Politics
71	A book or paper written by hand	Manuscript
72	One who dies for a noble cause	Martyr
73	A place where government records are kept	Archive
74	A book that contains information on various subjects	Encyclopaedia
75	A thing or substance that is liable to catch fire easily	Inflammable
76	A group of guns or missile launchers operated together at one place	Battery
77	One who hates mankind	Misanthrope
78	Someone who attacks cherished ideas or traditional institutions	Iconoclast
79	One who collects stamps	Philatelist
80	Deliberately and maliciously set something (buildings usually) on fire	Arson
81	A cage for small animals	Hutch
82	One who is not sure about God's existence	Agnostic
83	The study of different skin diseases	Dermatology
84	One who is hostile and violent	Aggressive
85	Not fit to eat	Inedible
86	A large group of people, especially the nomadic	Horde
87	An action of making amends for a wrong or injury	Atonement
88	Animals that live in water	Aquatic

S.N.	Origin	Definition
89	That which can be easily broken	Fragile
90	Weakness and poor health	Frailty
91	To own up to something as true	Confess
92	A person incapable of making mistakes	Infallible
93	A sound that is pleasing to hear	Melodious
94	A person who makes maps	Cartographer
	Many Word (selection post 2022 - 10th Level)	
1	Reminder of the place	Souvenir
2	The inner soft part of a seed, fruit or nut	Kernel
3	An official inspection of a company's, or individual's, accounts	Audit
4	An arrangement of flowers that is usually given as present.	Bouquet
5	Safe to drink	Potable
6	Something that lasts only for a short time	Ephemeral
7	The arrangement of events or dates in the order of their occurrence	Chronology
8	the men living in the same age	Contemporaries
9	make perfectly clear	Elucidate
10	A herd of cattle or animals driven in a body.	Drove
11	Delay in doing something to a later time	Procrastination
12	A large group of people	Horde
13	A funeral procession	Cortege
14	Widespread occurrence of an infectious disease crossing international boundaries	Pandemic
15	A meal that is usually taken late in the morning that combines a late breakfast and an early lunch	Brunch
16	Absence of Government	Anarchy
	Many Word (selection post 2022 - 12th Level)	
1	One who loves wisdom and hence pursues it	Philosopher
2	One who is extravagantly romantic, chivalrous and impractical.	Quixotic
3	The killing of a whole race	Genocide
4	A highly unpleasant, annoying, objectionable sound.	Nasty
	Many Word (selection post 2022 - Grad. Level)	
1	To the utmost or most absolute extent or degree	Quite
2	Easy to understand	Lucid
3	The supervising person during an examination	Invigilator

S.N.	Origin	Definition
4	An arrangement of parts or elements in a particular form or figure	Configuration
5	Short accounts of real and interesting incidents	Anecdotes
6.	Really coming from its stated, advertised or reputed source	Genuine
	Many Word (SSC CGL 2021 Tier-2)	
1	A book or set of books giving information on many subjects or on many aspects of one subject and typically arranged alphabetically.	Encyclopedia
2	A case for keeping a sword	Sheath
3	A doctor who specializes in heart diseases	Cardiologist
4	A large single detached house with single or double story	Bungalow
5	An animal or person that eats a variety of food of both plant and animal origin.	Omnivore
6	One who is all powerful	Omnipotent
7	One who lives on others	Parasite
8	One who speaks for others	Spokesperson
9	One who talks to oneself	Soliloquist
10	A person who moves from one place to another, with intentions of finding work and settling, permanently or temporarily, at a new location	Migrant
11	Symbols of royalty	Regalia

	Many Word (SSC DP Head Constable 2022)	
1	Younger looking skin.	Rejuvenated
2	A disorder that involve difficulty in reading, interpret words	Dyslexia
3	Piece of enclosed land planted with fruit trees.	Orchard
4	One who loves to speak	Loquacious
5	Great sorrow or distress	Woe
6	A paper written by hand	Manuscript
7	The study of secret writing and coded language or words	Cryptography
8	Extremely high.	Exorbitant
9	Not quite coinciding with a central position	Off-Centre
10	Changing frequently	Fickle
11	Public oratory skills	Elocution
12	Using (an idea, term, or name) frequently in casual talk	Bandying
13	A person who is unsure about God's existence	Agnostic
14	Extreme physical or mental sufferings	Agony
15	Something which can be copied	Imitable

S.N.	Origin	Definition
16	Mark with spots or smears of colour	Mottle
17	Causing or affected by anxiety or stress	Fraught
18	In a quick manner.	Hurriedly
19	A room filled with equipment for games and physical exercise.	Gymnasium
20	A group of things that have been hidden in some place	Cache
21	A soldier who fights for the sake of money	Mercenary
22	Fill up again	Replenish
23	Performed or occurring as a result of a sudden impulse	Spontaneous
24	Something that is modern or existing in the prevailing times	Contemporary
25	Ceremony to formally congratulate success.	Felicitating
26	Involvement with or influence in the community.	Outreach
27	Unable to pay his debts.	Insolvent
28	One who has the qualities like shyness and openness at the same time	Ambivert
29	Science of speech sounds	Phonetics
30	Someone who is friendly and good natured	Amicable
31	Study of the various aspects of aging	Gerontology
32	the art or practice of garden cultivation and management	Horticulture
33	Indifferent to the pains and pleasures of life.	Stoic
34	Having or showing the ability to speak fluently and coherently	Articulate
35	Lack of order in a country	Anarchy
36	An unknown author.	Anonymous
37	A community that is smaller than a village.	Hamlet
38	The quality of being new and original	Novelty
39	One who walks in sleep	Somnambulist
40	Extreme form of patriotism	Jingoism
41	Certain to happen	Inevitable
42	The act of killing a king	Regicide
43	Showing a lack of experience, wisdom or judgment	Naïve
44	Concerning or consisting of money.	Pecuniary
45	One who is very curious to know things and asks questions	Inquisitive
46	Feeling or showing deep and solemn respect	Reverent
47	Well known for bad qualities	Notorious
48	Religious madness (wherein the patient think he is the deity)	Theomania
49	One who knows everything and has infinite understanding	Omniscient
50	One who knows everything	Omniscient
51	Sentimental longing	Nostalgia

S.N.	Origin	Definition
52	A range of different things	Diversity
53	A place of burial	Sepulchre
54	Denoting the second or second mentioned of two people or things	Latter
55	Repetition of a sound caused by reflection of sound waves.	Echo
56	Proved to be right in court	Vindicated
57	Small shelter for dog	Kennel
58	One who is capable of using both hands	Ambidextrous
59	Walk or move in a leisurely or aimless way	Wander
60	Study of statistics of population	Demography
61	One who is violently against established beliefs and traditions	Iconoclast
62	No longer in use.	Archaic
63	Government by military class	Stratocracy
64	To take own life.	Suicide

Many Word (SSC DP Head Constable 2022)		
1	Showing astute powers of judgement; clever and judicious	Shrewd
2	One who does a thing for pleasure and not as a profession	Amateur
3	A place for storage of arms and ammunition	Arsenal
4	Evoking a keen sense of sadness or regret	Poignant
5	Profitable, yielding financial gain	Lucrative
6	One who takes a dark view of things	Pessimist
7	Cause to continue; keep up; preserve (a state of affairs, an activity etc)	Maintain
8	A person who introduces the performers or contestants in a variety show	Compere
9	Taking heed or care; being conscious	Mindful
10	The scientific study of worms and insects	Entomology
11	The quality of being honest and having strong moral principles	Integrity
12	The one who makes maps and charts	Cartographer
13	The scientific study of the behaviour, structure, physiology, classification and distribution of animals	Zoology
14	Honour given for some achievement	Laurel
15	Killing of a person by another	Homicide
16	fast moving water	Torrent
17	Treat with a vaccine, usually by injection to promote immunity against a disease	Inoculate
18	One who knows all things	Omniscient
19	A group of worshippers	Congregation

S.N.	Origin	Definition
20	Someone who is reserved and shy	Introvert
21	A happy development or happening of events by chance.	Serendipity
22	To become a strong person in spite of many difficulties.	Resilient
23	A large group of people	Horde
24	Person living at the same time	Contemporary
25	One who believes in his fate	Fatalist
26	Take hold of forcibly or suddenly	Seize
27	Someone who does not believe that God exists	Atheist
28	The arrangement of events or dates in the order of their occurrence	Chronology
29	Rarely; not often	Seldom
30	So delicate or precise as to be difficult to analyse or describe	Subtle
31	A person who regards the whole world as his country	Cosmopolitan
32	Try hard to do or achieve something	Endeavour
33	Rapid or sudden rise	Upsurge
34	person hired to drive our car	Chauffeur
35	One who is bad in spellings	Cacographer
36	Hatred	Malevolence
37	The main character in a story.	Protagonist
38	A letter, poem etc. whose author is unknown.	Anonymous

Some More Important One Word Substitutions		
1	Someone who attacks cherished ideas or traditionalinstitutions	Iconoclast
2	Charging an important public figure with a serious crime	Impeach
3	Urging or requesting (someone) solemnly or earnestly to dosomething	Adjure
4	Extreme physical or mental sufferings	Agony
5	A large gathering of people of a particular type	Bevy
6	First time someone does in public or for the public	Debut
7	Orders that must be followed	Diktat
8	Difficult to understand; having or seeming to have a hidden meaning	Cryptic
9	A family of young animals	Brood
10	Ideas or inventions which are considered to be a particularperson's creation	Brainchild
11	A person who draws or produces maps	Cartographer
12	One who believes in fate	Fatalist

S.N.	Origin	Definition
13	Journals or newspapers, especially the official one ofanorganization or institution	Gazette
14	A storehouse for threshed grain	Granary
15	Journeys especially by a group of people for a specificpurpose	Expedition
16	One hard to please (very selective in his habits)	Fastidious
17	An angry and usually long speech or piece of writing thatstrongly criticizes someone or something	Diatribe
18	The art or practice of garden cultivation and management	Horticulture
19	An action of marrying a person of a superior caste or class	Hypergamy
20	Conclusion or opinions that are formed because of knownfacts or evidence	Inference
21	Freedom from punishment, harm, or loss	Impunity
22	Someone who attacks cherished ideas or traditionalinstitutions	Iconoclast
23	Charging an important public figure with a serious crime	Impeach
24	Killing of one's mother	Matricide
25	A person who dislikes humankind and avoids human society	Misanthrope
26	One who collect coins as hobby	Numismatist
27	Japanese art of folding paper into shapes that look likebirds, animals, etc.	Origami
28	The branch of science concerned with the origin, structure,and composition of rocks	Petrology
29	Measures designed merely to humour or placate someone	Placebo
30	Partial refunds to someone who has paid too much for tax,rent, or a utility	Rebate
31	A large natural or artificial lake used as a source of watersupply	Reservoir
32	An act of destroying or damaging something deliberately sothat it does not work correctly	Sabotage
33	Easily annoyed or angered and likely to argu	Truculent
34	The scientific study of the behaviour, structure, physiology, classification, and distribution of animals	Zoology
35	Seeming to be seen everywhere	Ubiquitous
36	Lack of solidity or substance; thinness	Tenuity
37	A person who is indifferent to the pains and pleasures oflife	Stoic
38	Honor or respect that is felt for or shown to (someone orsomething)	Reverence
39	Used in reference to luxurious accommodations	Ritz
40	Persons who are in charge of or takes care of something	Warden

S.N.	Origin	Definition
41	Having a strong, sharp taste or smell	Pungent
42	Objects that are used to do a particular activity or are of aparticular kind.	Paraphernalia
43	Feeling of being sorry for doing something bad or wrong inthe past	Remorse
44	One who lives in solitude	Recluse
45	Very complicated and difficult to understand	Turgid
46	Feeling a strong desire	Yearn
47	Condition in which someone is not able to think normallybecause of being drunk, drugged, tired, etc.	Stupor
48	Long and complicated series of events	Saga
49	Reasons that you give to hide your real reason for doingsomething	Pretext
50	A news article that reports the recent death of a person	Obituary

UNIT 4 Revision: One-Word Substitutions and Practice Sets

Let us revise and practice.

1. One who knows many languages. **– Linguist**
2. Being unable to pay one' debts. **– Insolvent**
3. Having an evil reputation. **– Notorious**
4. One who leaves his country to settle elsewhere. **– Emigrant**
5. A person who lives at the same time as another. **– Contemporary**
6. A person who can neither read nor write. **– Illiterate**
7. A person who spends his money recklessly. **– Spendthrift**
8. A person who lives by himself. **– Recluse**
9. A woman whose husband is dead. **– Widow**
10. A man whose wife is dead. **– Widower**
11. A child whose parents are dead. **– Orphan**
12. A minister representing a sovereign or state in a foreign country. **– Ambassador**
13. A person sent on a mission (usually official). **– Emissary**
14. A person who is indifferent to pleasure or pain. **– Stoic**
15. One who defends or is zealous for his country's freedom or rights. **– Patriot**
16. One who makes an eloquent public speech. **– Orator**
17. One who undergoes penalty of death for sticking to his faith. **– Martyr**
18. One who abandons his religious faith. **– Apostate**
19. One who is given to questioning the truth of facts and the soundness of inferences. **– Sceptic**
20. Belonging to all parts of the world; a person familiar with many different countries. **– Cosmopolitan**
21. One who resides in a country of which he is not a citizen. **– Alien**
22. One who comes as a settler into a foreign country. **– Immigrant**
23. Being present everywhere. **– Omnipresent**
24. Being all-powerful. **– Omnipotent**
25. One who knows everything. **– Omniscient**
26. Beyond making a mistake. **– Infallible**
27. One who eats human flesh. **– Cannibal**
28. One who looks at the dark side of things. **– Pessimist**
29. One who looks at the bright side of things. **– Optimist**
30. Not being able to be elected or selected under the rules. **– Ineligible**
31. One who loves and works for his fellow men. **– Philanthropist**
32. One who hates mankind. **– Misanthropist**
33. One who lives on vegetables. **– Vegetarian**
34. One who has belief in the existence of God. **– Theist**
35. One who has no belief in the existence of God. **– Atheist**
36. One who believes in fate. **– Fatalist**
37. One who plays a game for pleasure and not professionally. **– Amateur**
38. One who has grown old in or has long experience of (specially military) service or occupation. **– Veteran**

39. One who lends money at exhorbitant rates of interest. **– Usurer**
40. A member of a council. **– Councillor**
41. The practice of having more than one wife at the same time. **– Polygamy**
42. A general pardon of political offenders. **– Amnesty**
43. Fond of entertaining guests. **– Hospitable**
44. One who totally abstains from alcoholic drinks. **– Teetotaller**
45. One who walks on foot. **– Pedestrian**
46. Taking of one's own life. **– Suicide**
47. Murder of a king. **– Regicide**
48. Murder of a new-born infant. **– Infanticide**
49. Murder of one's own father/mother/brother. **– Patricide/Matricide/Fratricide**
50. The killing of human beings. **– Homicide**
51. A child born after the death of his father or a book published after the death of its author. **– Posthumous**
52. Forbidden, prohibited by law. **– Illicit**
53. A man whose manners are more like those of a woman. **– Effeminate**
54. A medicine to counteract the effect of poison. **– Antidote**
55. A speech made without preparation. **– Extempore**
56. A language that is no longer spoken. **– Dead**
57. The word which is no longer in use. **– Obsolete**
58. The motive merely to get money. **– Mercenary**
59. Existing for ever – without any beginning or end. **– Eternal**
60. Subject to death. **– Mortal**
61. Resulting in death. **– Fatal or mortal**
62. Property inherited from one's father or ancestors. **– Patrimony**
63. A paper written by hand. **– Manuscript**
64. The result of the match where neither party wins. **– Draw**
65. Animals which give birth to babies and feed them with their milk. **– Mammals**
66. Method of sending messages without the help of wires. **– Wireless or radio**
67. A place for burial of dead bodies. **– Cemetery**
68. Counterfeiting of document. **– Forgery**
69. Of one's own free will. **– Voluntary**
70. Give tit for tat. **– Retaliate**
71. The cessation of warfare before a treaty is signed. **– Armistice**
72. The science of reasoning. **– Logic**
73. Belonging to all parts of the world. **– Universal**
74. A figure with many angles or sides. **– Polygon**
75. An instrument for measuring temperature. **– Thermometer**
76. Compulsory enlistment for military or other services. **– Conscription**
77. A place where young plants are reared. **– Nursery**
78. The absence of government in a country. **– Anarchy**
79. A state in which the Government is carried on nominally, and also, by the people or their elected representatives without a monarch. **– Republic**
80. Government carried on by an absolute ruler. **– Dictatorship**
81. Government by the representatives of the people. **– Democracy**
82. Government by officials. **– Bureaucracy**
83. An absolute government. **– Autocracy**
84. The life history of a person written by another. **– Biography**

85. The life history of a person written by himself. —**Autobiography**
86. Conferred as an honour, or performed without pay. —**Honorary**
87. The yearly return of a date. —**Anniversary**
88. Of unknown or unadmitted authorship. —**Anonymous**
89. Allowing the passage of rays of light. —**Transparent**
90. Not allowing the passage of light. —**Opaque**
91. A substance that kills insects. —**Insecticide**
92. Occurring at the same time. —**Simultaneous**
93. An assembly of worshippers. —**Congregation**
94. An assembly of listeners. —**Audience**
95. A substance that kills germs. —**Germicide**
96. A cure for all diseases. —**Panacea**
97. All of one mind. —**Unanimous**
98. Contrary to law. —**Illegal**
99. Not definitely or clearly expressed. —**Inexplicit**
100. That which cannot be excused. —**Inexcusable**
101. That which cannot be taken by force of arms. —**Impregnable**
102. That which cannot be admitted or allowed. —**Inadmissible**
103. That which cannot be reached. —**Inaccessible**
104. That which cannot be perceived by sense. —**Imperceptible**
105. That which cannot be destroyed. —**Indestructible**
106. That which cannot be altered or recalled. —**Irrevocable**
107. That which cannot be dispensed with. —**Indispensable**
108. That which cannot be burnt. —**Incombustible**
109. That which cannot be divided. —**Indivisible**
110. That which cannot be reconciled. —**Irreconcilable**
111. That which cannot be recovered. —**Irrevocable**
112. That which cannot be seen. —**Invisible**
113. That which cannot be read. —**Illegible**
114. That which cannot be heard. —**Inaudible**
115. That which cannot be conquered. —**Invincible**
116. That which cannot be wounded. —**Invulnerable**
117. That which cannot be believed. —**Incredible**
118. That which can be easily set on fire. —**Inflammable**
119. That which can not be avoided. —**Unavoidable**
120. That which cannot be expressed in words. —**Inexpressible**
121. The only one of its type. —**Unique**
122. A man who is the head of a monastery or an abbey. —**Abbot**
123. A form of a word, phrase, etc. that is shorter than the full form. —**Abbreviation**
124. A quantity that is more than enough. —**Abundance**
125. A word formed from the first letters of a group of words. —**Acronym**
126. A public notice offering or asking for goods, services, etc. —**Advertisement**
127. Planting areas of land with trees to form a forest. —**Afforestation**
128. A building without a roof containing rows of seats rising in steps round an open space. —**Amphitheatre**
129. The loss of ability to feel pain while still conscious. —**Analgesia**
130. A part of the sea, or of a large lake, enclosed by a wide curve of the shore. —**Bay**

131. A stretch of sand or stones along the edge of the sea or a lake. **—Beach**
132. The driver of a taxi. **—Cabby**
133. Entertainment provided in a restaurant or club while the customers are eating and drinking. **—Cabaret**
134. A person who draws maps and charts. **—Cartographer**
135. A person, an animal or a plant that lives, grows or is often found in a particular place. **—Denizen**
136. The medical study of the skin and its diseases. **—Dermatology**
137. A shopkeeper selling cloth and clothing. **—Draper**
138. A sudden serious event or situation requiring immediate action. **—Emergency**
139. A false or mistaken belief. **—Fallacy**
140. A long pole on which a flag is flown. **—Flagstaff**
141. All the plants of a particular area or period of time. **—Flora**
142. A state of extreme excitement. **—Frenzy**
143. Injury to the nose, fingers or toes, caused by extreme cold. **—Frostbite**
144. A room or building for showing works of art. **—Gallery**
145. To play games of chance, etc. for money. **—Gamble**
146. A drug that causes one to hallucinate. **—Hallucinogen**
147. Existing only in the mind. **—Imaginary**
148. A manager or director of a ballet, a concert, a theatre or an opera company. **—Impresario**
149. A newspaper or magazine that deals with a particular subject or professional activity. **—Journal**
150. A person sent to teach the Christian religion to people who are ignorant of it. **—Missionary**

PRACTICE SET-1

A. Fill up the blanks in the following sentences using an appropriate one-word substitution for each:

1. First inhabitants are called ________.
2. ________ is the science of sound.
3. A statement on oath is ________.
4. One who is able to use left as well as right hand is ________.
5. ________ is the plea that a person charged with a crime was elsewhere when it was committed.
6. ________ means allowance due to a wife from her husband on separation.
7. One who is habitually good to others is an ________.
8. ________ is a kind of substance in the blood tending to neutralise matter that is harmful.
9. ________ is the cultivation and maintenance of beehives.
10. Animals living in water are ________.
11. ________ is the other side of the globe.
12. ________ means total loss of voice.
13. A person guilty of malicious setting on fire of property, etc. is known as ________.
14. Cultivation of trees or shrubs is ________.
15. Study of antiquities especially of prehistoric period is ________.

16. ____________ is the theory that gods and goddesses have human form.
17. ____________ is the mistake of placing something in the wrong period of time.
18. One who is a great lover of books is a ____________.
19. A man with narrow, prejudiced views, especially about politics and religion is a ____________.
20. The act of speaking disrespectfully about sacred things is____________.
21. A man of free and easy habits, socially unconventional is a____________.
22. ____________denotes a fall from the sublime to the ridiculous.
23. ____________is a hospital for mad persons.
24. ____________is the art of beautiful handwriting.
25. A person who is hundred years old is a ____________.
26. A____________ is an empty pretender to knowledge or skill.
27. ____________ is a roundabout way of expression.
28. A hackneyed and trite literary phrase or saying is a ____________.
29. That which spreads through actual contact is ____________.
30. A ____________is a sneering critic of everything.
31. An expert who understands the value of art, antiques, etc. is a ____________.
32. A man who has invested lot of money in the private sector is a ____________.
33. ____________ expresses the inability of a person to do without alcoholic drinks.
34. Account of facts relating to formation and meaning of words is____________.
35. ____________is the science of production of fine offspring.
36. ____________ is a personal peculiarity of temperament, an unusual trait.
37. ____________is a perverted mental condition characterised by indecent exposure of the person.
38. ____________is the philosophy of life that reality as existence can be lived, but cannot become the object of thought.
39. One who is always seeking to escape from the bitter realities of life is an ____________.
40. ____________is a state of mental weariness from lack of occupation or interest.
41. Writing inscribed on a tomb is ____________.
42. Fruit eating animals are called____________.
43. Meat eating animals are called ____________
44. ____________is the study of man as an animal.
45. ____________denotes the animals of a particular region or epoch.
46. One who is genuinely interested in the welfare and emancipation of a woman is____________
47. ____________ denotes the tendency to grow downwards.
48. ____________is the science of the earth's crust.
49. ____________is the scientific study of old age and its diseases.
50. ____________signifies animals which live in groups.
51. Animals living on grass are ___.
52. ____________ is the doctrine that the sensual pleasure is the main aim of life.
53. ____________ is the art of garden cultivation.
54. ____________ is one who expresses ideas not in conformity with conventional religious thinking.
55. A person who is given to turning inwards is an ____________.
56. That which is not recognised by law is ___.
57. ____________ is a personal peculiarity of temperament.

58. One who breaks images is ____________.
59. A person who has the most uncompromising attitude, specially in politics is ____________.
60. A single pillar construction is ____________.
61. ____________ denotes an excessively morbid desire to steal.
62. One who makes/compiles a dictionary is ____________.
63. ____________ is a free thinker on religion.
64. ____________ is the philosophy of practising duplicity in statecraft.
65. One who is a hater of woman is ____________
66. ____________ is a ridiculous confusion and misuse of words.
67. ____________ is the theory of heredity tending to reduce to numerical law the recurrence of inherited characters.
68. A person who hates marriage is ____________
69. ____________ is the study of the forms of animals, plants, or words.
70. A place where dead bodies are kept is ____________.
71. Coining a new word is ____________
72. ____________ denotes undue favour to one's relatives.
73. ____________ is the one who believes in the philosophy that nothing has real existence.
74. ____________ is the science that treats of coins and medals.
75. ____________ is a definite system of names, especially in classification.
76. ____________ is Government by the few.
77. ____________ is the science regarding the study of birds.
78. ____________ is the art of spelling words correctly.
79. ____________ is the science of languages.
80. ____________ is the doctrine that God is everything and everything is God.
81. The science of diseases is ____________.
82. ____________ is the science of dealing with stamp collection.
83. ____________ is the science of vocal natural sounds.
84. ____________ is a statement showing remarkable degree of prediction.
85. ____________ is the study of ancient writings and inscriptions.
86. That which relates to the common people is ____________.
87. One indifferent to art and literature is ____________.
88. Artificial rearing of fish is ____________.
89. Government by the rich is known as ____________.
90. A literary theft is ____________.
91. The practice of a woman having more than one husband is ____________.
92. ____________ is the operation of the body after death.
93. ____________ stands for ancester of a person, animal or plant.
94. One who makes love, now to one, and now to another is a ____________.
95. Original model is ____________.
96. ____________ is a form of work of an art in which objects are glued to a backing to form a picture.
97. ____________ means false arguments intended to deceive.
98. ____________ is an offence against grammar or idiom.
99. ____________ is the doctrine of ascribing sacrificial fractions and supernatural powers to the ordained person.
100. ____________ is a person who helps even a stranger in difficulty.
101. ____________ is a health resort.

102. __________ is the production of raw silk.
103. Talking loudly when alone is __________.
104. One who walks in sleep is a __________.
105. An elderly unmarried woman is a __________
106. Communication between mind and mind is __________.
107. __________ is the science regarding principles of classification.
108. __________ is the art of preparing and mounting skins of animals in life-like manner.
109. That which relates to a barber or his work is __________.
110. __________ is the representation on map of natural and artificial features of a town/ district, etc.
111. A student who runs away from the class or the school without permission is __________.
112. One who easily gives up his party or principles is a __________.
113. Happening once in three years is denoted by __________.
114. A truth which is often repeated is __________
115. __________ is the theory that actions are right because they are useful.
116. An ideal state is called a __________ state.
117. Broadcast report of a public event or news of an invalid's condition is a __________.
118. A rule of law which is applicable to the past is __________.
119. An appointed place of meeting, specially of troops is __________.
120. __________ is fear of being enclosed in a small closed space.

ANSWERS

1. aborigines	2. acoustics	35. Eugenics	36. Eccentricity
3. affidavit	4. ambidextrous	37. Exhibitionism	38. Existentialism
5. Alibi	6. Alimony	39. escapist	40. Ennui
7. Altruist	8. Antibody	41. epitaph	42. frugivorous
9. Epiculture	10. aquatic	43. carnivorous	44. Anthropology
11. Antipodes	12. Aphonia	45. Fauna	46. feminist
13. arsonist	14. arbori-culture	47. Geotropism	48. Geology
15. archaeology	16. Anthropomorphism	49. Gerontology	50. Gregarious
17. Anachronism	18. bibliophile	51. graminivorous	52. Hedonism
19. bigot	20. blasphemy	53. Horticulture	54. Heretic
21. bohemian	22. Bathos	55. introvert	56. illegitimate
23. Asylum	24. Calligraphy	57. Idiosyncracy	58. iconoclast
25. centenarian	26. charlatan	59. intransigent	60. monolithic
27. circumlocution	28. cliche	61. Kleptomania	62. lexicographer
29. contagious	30. cynic	63. Libertine	64. Machiavellism
31. connoisseur	32. capitalist	65. misogynist	66. Malapropism
33. Dipsomania	34. etymology	67. Mendelism	68. misogamist

69.	Morphology	70.	mortuary	95.	prototype	96.	Collage
71.	neologism	72.	Nepotism	97.	Sophism	98.	Solecism
73.	Nihilist	74.	Numismatics	99.	Sacerdotal	100.	Samaritan
75.	Nomenclature	76.	Oligarchy	101.	Sanatorium	102.	Sericulture
77.	Ornithology	78.	Orthography	103.	soliloquy	104.	somnambulist
79.	Philology	80.	Pantheism	105.	spinster	106.	telepathy
81.	pathology	82.	Philately	107.	Taxology	108.	Taxidermy
83.	Phonology	84.	Prophecy	109.	tonsorial	110.	Topography
85.	Palaeography	86.	plebian	111.	truant	112.	turncoat
87.	philistine	88.	pisciculture	113.	triennial	114.	truism
89.	plutocracy	90.	plagiarism	115.	Utilitarianism	116.	utopian
91.	polyandry	92.	Postmortem	117.	bulletin	118.	retrospective
93.	Progenitor	94.	philanderer	119.	rendezvous	120.	Claustrophobia

PRACTICE SET- 2

In questions given below out of four alternatives, choose the one which can be substituted for the given word/sentence.

1. Extreme old age when a man behaves like a fool
   (a) Imbecility (b) Senility
   (c) Dotage (d) Superannuation

Ans. (c).

2. That which cannot be corrected
   (a) Unintelligible (b) Indelible
   (c) Illegible (d) Incorrigible

Ans. (d).

3. The study of ancient societies
   (a) Anthropology (b) Archaeology
   (c) History (d) Ethnology

Ans. (b).

4. A person of good understanding knowledge and reasoning power
   (a) Expert (b) Intellectual
   (c) Snob (d) Literate

Ans. (b).

5. A person who insists on something
   (a) Disciplinarian (b) Stickler
   (c) Instantaneous (d) Boaster

Ans. (b).

6. State in which the few govern the many
   (a) Monarchy (b) Oligarchy
   (c) Plutocracy (d) Autocracy

Ans. (b).

7. A style in which a writer makes a display of his knowledge
   (a) Pedantic (b) Verbose
   (c) Pompous (d) Ornate

Ans. (a).

8. List of the business or subjects to be considered at a meeting
   (a) Schedule (b) Timetable
   (c) Agenda (d) Plan

Ans. (c).

9. Leave or remove from a place considered dangerous
   (a) Evade (b) Evacuate
   (c) Avoid (d) Exterminate

Ans. (b).

10. A prima facie case is such
    (a) As it seems at first sight
    (b) As it is made to seem at first sight
    (c) As it turns out to be at the end
    (d) As it seems to the court after a number of hearings

Ans. (a).

11. A person pretending to be somebody he is not

(a) Magician (b) Rogue

(c) Liar (d) Imposter

Ans. (d).

12. A person who knows many foreign languages

(a) Linguist (b) Grammarian

(c) Polyglot (d) Bilingual

Ans. (a).

13. One who has little faith in human sincerity and goodness

(a) Egoist (b) Fatalist

(c) Stoic (d) Cynic

Ans. (d).

14. One who possesses many talents

(a) Versatile (b) Nubile

(c) Exceptional (d) Gifted

Ans. (a).

15. Words inscribed on tomb

(a) Epitome (b) Epistle

(c) Epilogue (d) Epitaph

Ans. (d).

16. One who eats everything

(a) Omnivorous (b) Omniscient

(c) Irrestible (d) Insolvent

Ans. (a).

17. Malafide case is one

(a) Which is undertaken in a good faith

(b) Which is undertaken in a bad faith

(c) Which is undertaken after a long delay

(d) Which is not undertaken al all

Ans. (b).

18. The custom or practice of having more than one husband at same time

(a) Polygyny (b) Polyphony

(c) Polyandry (d) Polychromy

Ans. (c).

19. Tending to move away from the centre or axis

(a) Centrifugal (b) Centripetal

(c) Axiomatic (d) Awry

Ans. (a).

20. Teetotaller means

(a) One who abstains from theft

(b) One who abstains from meat

(c) One who abstains from taking wine

(d) One who abstains from malice

Ans. (c).

21. A person interested in collecting, studying and selling of old things

(a) Antiquarian (b) Junk-dealer

(c) Crank (d) Archealogist

Ans. (a).

ONE WORD SUBSTITUTIONS ASKED IN 2022

1. Extreme old age when a man behaves like a fool

(a) Imbecility (b) Senility

(c) Dotage (d) Superannuation

2. That which cannot be corrected

(a) Unintelligible (b) Indelible

(c) Illegible (d) Incorrigible

3. The study of ancient societies

(a) Anthropology (b) Archaeology

(c) History (d) Ethnology

4. A person of good understanding knowledge and reasoning power

(a) Expert (b) Intellectual

(c) Snob (d) Literate

5. A person who insists on something

(a) Disciplinarian (b) Stickler

(c) Instantaneous (d)Boaster

6. State in which the few govern the many

(a) Monarchy (b) Oligarchy

(c) Plutocracy (d) Autocracy

7. A style in which a writer makes a display of his knowledge

(a) Pedantic (b) Verbose

(c) Pompous (d) Ornate

8. List of the business or subjects to be considered at a meeting
(a) Schedule (b) Timetable
(c) Agenda (d) Plan
9. Leave or remove from a place considered dangerous
(a) Evade (b) Evacuate
(c) Avoid (d) Exterminate.
10. A prima facie case is such
(a) As it seems as first sight
(b) As it is made to seem at first sight
(c) As it turns out to be at the end
(d) As it seems to the court after a number of hearings
11. A person pretending to be somebody he is not
(a) Magician (b) Rogue
(c) Liar (d) Imposter
12. A person who knows many foreign languages
(a) Linguist (b) Grammarian
(c) Polyglot (d) Bilingual
13. One who has little faith in human sincerity and goodness
(a) Egoist (b) Fatalist
(c) Stoic (d) Cynic
14. One who possesses many talents
(a) Versatile (b) Newbie
(c) Exceptional (d) Gifted
15. Words inscribed on tomb
(a) Epitome (b)Epistle
(c) Epilogue (d) Epitaph
16. One who eats everything
(a) Omnivorous (b) Omniscient
(c) Irrestible (d) Insolvent
17. Malafide case is one
(a) Which is undertaken in a good faith
(b) Which is undertaken in a bad faith
(c) Which is undertaken after a long delay
(d) Which is not undertaken at all
18. The custom or practice of having more than one husband at same time
(a) Polygyny (b) Polyphony
(c) Polyandry (d) Polychromy
19. Tending to move away from the centre or axis
(a) Centrifugal (b) Centripetal
(c) Axiomatic (d) Awry
20. Teetotaller means
(a) One who abstains from theft
(b) One who abstains from meat
(c) One who abstains from taking wine
(d) One who abstains from malice
21. A person interested in collecting, studying and selling of old things
(a) Antiquarian (b) Junk-dealer
(c) Crank (d) Archealogist
22. A drawing on transparent paper
(a) Red print (b) Blue print
(c) Negative (d) Transparency
23. One who is not easily pleased by anything
(a) Maiden (b) Mediaeval
(c) Precarious (d) Fastidious
24. A remedy for all diseases
(a) Stoic (b) Marvel
(c) Panacea (d) Recompense
25. One who is fond of fighting
(a) Bellicose (b) Aggressive
(c) Belligerent (d) Militant

ANSWER KEYS

1. c 2. d 3. b 4. b 5. b 6. b 7. a 8. c 9. b 10. a 11. d 12. a 13. d 14. a 15. d 16. a 17. b 18. c 19. a 20. c 21. a 22. d 23. d 24. c 25. c

UNIT 5

Synonyms and Antonyms with Hindi Meaning

Given below are a number of synonyms and antonyms. Synonyms are words that have the same, or almost the same, meaning as another word. Antonyms are words that have the opposite meaning of another word. Choosing the right synonym refines your writing. Learning common antonyms sharpens your sense of language and expands your vocabulary

S.N.	Words (Hindi Meaning)	Synonyms	Antonyms (Hindi Meaning)
1.	Advance (आगे बढ़ना)	Progress, Move Forward	Retreat (पीछे हटना)
2.	Aggravate (भड़काना)	Irritate, Intensify	Alleviate (शान्त करना)
3.	Allure (आकर्षित करना)	**Tempt, Attract**	Repulse (खदेड़ना)
4.	Ample (प्रचुर)	Sufficient	Scarce, Meagre (अपर्याप्त)
5.	Assault (हमला)	Attack	Defend, Retreat (बचाव, पीछे हटना)
6.	Assist (मदद करना)	Help, Facilitate,	Obstruct (बाधा डालना)
7.	Awkward (बेढंगा)	Clumsy	Convenient, Graceful (सुविधाजनक, गरिमापूर्ण)
8.	Barbarous (असभ्य)	Crude	Civilized (सभ्य)
9.	Bleak (उदास)	Depressing, Grim	Bright (उज्ज्वल)
10.	Brutal (क्रूर)	Savage, Cruel	Humane(दयालू)
11.	Cease (रोकना)	Stop	Initiate, Continue, Start (जारी रखना)
12.	Censure (निंदा)	Criticise	Praise, Applause (प्रशंसा)
13.	Chaste (पवित्र)	Pure	Corrupt (भ्रष्ट)
14.	Complacent (आत्मसंतुष्ट)	Satisfied, Smug	Concerned (चिंतित)
15.	Conceited (अभिमानी)	Proud, Smug, Arrogant	Modest (विनम्र)
16.	Congenial (अनुकूल)	Favourable, Cordial Compatible	Unpleasant(अप्रिय)
17.	Defile (अशुद्ध करना)	Corrupt	Purify, Honour, Elevate (शुद्ध) करना, सम्मान करना)
18.	Deliberate (जानबूझकर)	International, Intended, Planned	Spontaneous (स्वाभाविक)

S.N.	Words (Hindi Meaning)	Synonyms	Antonyms (Hindi Meaning)
19.	Despise (घृणा)	Undervalue, Abhor	Admire (प्रशंसा)
20.	Devout (धार्मिक)	Pious	Treacherous (अधर्मी)
21.	Diffident (संकोची)	Timid	Confident, Aggressive (आत्मविश्वासी, आक्रामक)
22.	Dispute (झगड़ा)	Quarrel	Concede, Agreement (हार मानना, समझौता करना)
23.	Docile (आज्ञाकारी)	Submissive	Opposing, Unwilling (विरोधी, असम्मत)
24.	Eradicate (मिटा देना)	Abolish, Uproot	Preserve (बचाना)
25.	Fatigue (थकान)	Tiredness, Weariness	Strength (ताकत)
26.	Feeble (कमज़ोर)	Weak	Strong, Effective (प्रभावी)
27.	Ferocious (उग्र)	Fierce	Mild, Gentle (विनम्र)
28.	Fickle (अस्थिर)	Unstable	Constant, Stable, Firm (स्थिर)
29.	Enigmatic (रहस्यपूर्ण)	Puzzling,	Plain, Straightforward (सीधा, साधा)
30.	Eternal (निरन्तर)	Perpetual, Forever, Ageless, Everlasting	Temporary (अस्थाई)
31.	Exaggerate (अतिश्योक्ति करना)	Magnify	Understate, Compress (पर्दा डालना, संक्षिप्त करना)
32.	Exceptional (असाधारण)	Extraordinary	Common, Unremarkable, Ordinary (साधारण)
33.	Gloomy (उदास)	Murky, Dull	Bright, Radiant (alfa) (दीप्तिमान)
34.	Harmony (तालमेल)	Consensus, Peace	Strife, Conflict (विवाद)
35.	Insipid (बेस्वाद)	Bland	Tasty (स्वादिष्ट)
36.	Intrepid (निडर)	Fearless, Gallant	Meek, Cowardly (डरपोक)
37.	Invincible (अजय)	Unassailable, Unbeatable	Vulnerable, Powerless (कमजोर शक्तिहीन)
38.	Jubilant (उल्लसित)	Ecstatic, Rejoicing, Happy	Sorrowful, Depressed (3) (उदास)
39.	Lament (विलाप)	Mourn	Celebrate, Rejoice (आनंद)
40.	Latent (छुपा हुआ)	Hidden	Obvious, Evident (स्पष्ट)
41.	Lethal (घातक)	Malignant, Fatal	Harmless (हानिरहित)
42.	Meagre (अल्प)	Inadequate	Plentiful, Sufficient (प्रचुर पर्याप्त)

S.N.	Words (Hindi Meaning)	Synonyms	Antonyms (Hindi Meaning)
43.	Morbid (रोगग्रस्त)	Depressed, Ghastly, Nasty	Cheerful (आनंदित)
44.	Mundane (साधारण)	Ordinary, Everyday, Commonplace	Extraordinary (असाधारण)
45.	Ominous (अशुभ)	Threatening	Auspicious (शुभ)
46.	Opulent (धनी)	Rich, Luxurious, Sumptuous	Poor (गरीब)
47.	Profuse (अत्यधिक)	Aplenty, Abundant	Sparse, Meager, Scant (अल्प)
48.	Quiescent (निष्क्रिय)	Dull	Active, Animated (सक्रिय)
49.	Sordid (घटिया)	Unpleasant, Dirty	Reputable (सम्मानित)
50.	Spurious (अप्रमाणिक)	Fake	Authentic, Genuine (प्रमाणिक)
51.	Thrive (उन्नति करना)	Flourish, Prosper	Fail, Shrink (सिकुड़ना)
52.	Triumph (सफलता)	Victory	Defeat, Sorrow, Failure (हार, दुख)
53.	Abrupt (एकाएक)	Sudden	Gradual, Smooth (धीरे-धीरे)
54.	Absolve (दोषमुक्त करना)	Acquit, Pardon	Blame (दोष लगाना)
55.	Accede (मान लेना)	Consent, Comply	Deny (मना करना)
56.	Adept (निपुण)	Skilled	Inept (अयोग्य)
57.	Admonish (डांटना)	**Chide**	Praise, Applaud (प्रशंसा करना)
58.	Colossal (विशाल)	**Enormous, Gigantic**	Small, Minimal, Tiny, Teeny(छोटा)
59.	Cordial (दोस्ताना)	Friendly, Amicable, Warm	Hostile (शत्रुतापूर्ण)
60.	Futile (व्यर्थ)	Useless	Worthy, Productive, Fruitful, Useful (योग्य, उपयोगी)
61.	Illicit (अवैध)	Illegal, Unlawful	Lawful, Legal (वैध, कानूनी)
62.	Liberty (स्वतंत्रता)	**Freedom**	Dependence, Slavery, Bondage (गुलामी, बंधन)
63.	Mitigate (कम करना)	Lessen, Reduce	Enhance, Intensify, Increase(बढ़ाना, तीव्र करना)
64.	Morose (उदास)	**Gloomy, Sullen**	Cheerful (हंसमुख)
65.	Pernicious (हानिकारक)	Injurious, Dangerous,	Beneficial, Kind (लाभकारी, दयालु)
66.	Rectify (सुधारना)	Spiteful	Falsify(असत्य बनाना)

S.N.	Words (Hindi Meaning)	Synonyms	Antonyms (Hindi Meaning)
67.	Reprimand (फटकार)	Correct, Amend	Reward, Forgiveness, Compliment(क्षमा, प्रसंशा)
68.	Stern (कठोर)	Rebuke, Reproach, **Strict**	Lenient, Light (उदार)
69.	Timid (डरपोक)	Coward, Shy, Humble	Brave, Bold (बहादुर)
70.	Tranquil (शांत)	Peaceful, Calm, Sober	Stormy, Disturbed, Violent (अशांत करना)
71.	Vigilant (सतर्क)	Watchful	Inattentive, Rash, Numb, Careless, (गूंगा)
72.	Abstain (संयम रखना)	Refrain	Indulge, Pursue (लिप्त होना)
73.	Absurd (बेतुका)	**Ridiculous**	Sensible, Reasonable (समझदार)
74.	Adversity (विपत्ति)	Misfortune, Misery	Prosperity (समृद्धि)
75.	Affluence (सम्पन्नता)	Wealth, Richness	Poverty (दद्रिता)
76.	Agile (फुर्तीला)	Active, Quick, Nimble	Lethargic (सुस्त)
77.	Amateur (नौसिखिया)	Beginner	Professional (पेशेवर)
78.	Benevolent (परोपकारी)	Kind, Generous	Malevolent, Merciless, Stingy (द्वेषी, निर्दयी, कंजूस)
79.	Curtail (घटाना)	**Downsize**	Resume, Enlarge, Lengthen\ (फिर से शुरू, बढ़ाना, लंबा करना)
80.	Demolish (ध्वस्त करना)	Dismantle	Build, Establish, Construct (बनानाए निर्माण करना)
81.	Despair (निराशा)	**Misery, Sad**	Hope (आशा)
82.	Eminent (प्रतिष्ठित)	Famous, Promi nent, Renowned	Ordinary, Inconspicous
83.	Candid (निष्कपट, स्पष्ट)	Frank, Honest, Forthright	Devious, Cunning, (कुटिल) Artful, Deceitful, Blunt, Biased (चालाक धोकेबाज)
84.	Barren (बांझ)	Unproductive, Infertile, Desolate	Fertile (उपजाऊ)
85.	Genuine (वास्तविक)	Original, Authentic, Real	Fake, Spurious, Dubious (नकली, झूठा)
86.	Insolent (असभ्य)	Disrespectful, Rude, Bold	Humble, Submissive, Mannerly, Courteous (विनम्र, सभ्य)

S.N.	Words (Hindi Meaning)	Synonyms	Antonyms (Hindi Meaning)
87.	Obscene (अश्लील)	Indecent	Decent, Clear, Distinct (सभ्य)
88.	Prudent (विवेकी)	Cautious, Wise, Frugal	Unwise, Careless, Indiscreet, Wasteful (अविवेकी)
89.	Transparent (पारदर्शक)	Lucid, Clear	Opaque (अपारदर्शी)
90.	Dubious (संदिग्ध)	Doubtful, Fishy	Likely, Certain (निश्चित)
91.	Persuade (राजी करना)	Coax, Convince	Dissuade, Prevent, Halt (रोक लगाना)
92.	Turbulent (अशांत)	**Violent, Agitation**	Placid, Calm, Peaceful (शांत शांतिपूर्ण)
93.	Abandon (छोड़ देना)	Forsake, Desert	Retain, Support (बनाये रखना)
94.	Abundant (प्रचुर)	Plentiful	Meagre, Scarce, Insufficient (अल्प, दुलर्भ)
95.	Affluent (धनी)	Prosperous, Wealthy	Poor (गरीब)
96.	Apparent (स्पष्ट)	Obvious, Manifest	Ambiguous, Hidden (अस्पष्ट)
97.	Coarse (खुरदुरा, अशोधित)	Rough, Crude	Smooth, Gentle, Refined (कोमल)
98.	Commence (आरंभ करना)	Start, Launch, Initiate	Conclude, Close, Terminate (समाप्त करना)
99.	Diligent (परिश्रमी)	Industrious, Hardworking, Assiduous, Untiring	Lazy (आलसी)
100.	Emerge (प्रकट होना)	Appear	Vanish, Disappear (गायब)
101.	Erudite (विद्वान)	**Scholarly, Learned**	Unscholarly, Ignorant (अज्ञानी)
102.	Impeccable (त्रुटिहीन)	Perfect, Flawless, Faultless	Inexact, Imperfect, Flawed (अशुद्ध, त्रुटिपूर्ण, दोषपूर्ण)
		Faultless	(अशुद्ध, त्रुटिपूर्ण, दोषपूर्ण)
103.	Lucid (स्पष्ट अर्थ का)	Clear	Vague, Confusing (अस्पष्ट)
104.	Obstinate (जिद्दी)	**Stubborn**	Flexible, Docile (विनम्र)
105.	Amiable (मैत्रीपूर्ण)	Friendly	Hostile (शत्रुतापूर्ण)
106.	Boisterous (कोलाहल पूर्ण)	Noisy, Clamorous	Calm, Peaceful, Rstrained (शांत, संयमित
107.	Abolish (हटाना)	Eliminate	Continue (जारी रखना)
108.	Accord (सहमति)	Confer	Disagreement (असहमति)
109.	Accustomed (अभ्यस्त)	Habituated	Unusual (असामान्य)

S.N.	Words (Hindi Meaning)	Synonyms	Antonyms (Hindi Meaning)
110.	Adorn (सजाना)	Beautify	Disfigure (बिगाड़ना)
111.	Alert (सतर्क)	Watchful	Careless (लापरवाह)
112.	Anxiety (व्याकुलता)	Worry	Certainty (निश्चय)
113.	Anxious (चिंतित)	Nervous	Calm (शांत)
114.	Apparition (भूत-प्रेत)	Spirit	Realness (वास्तविकता)
115.	Applause (वाहवाही)	Approval	Criticism (आलोचना)
116.	Apprise (सूचित)	Inform	Hide (छिपा देना)
117.	Assert (दृढ़ता)	Emphasize	Abandon (छाड़ना)
118.	Attenuate (कमजोर होना)	Weaken	Strong (शतिशाली)
119.	Avoid (टालना)	Evade	Meet (मिलना)
120.	Bane (श्राप)	Curse	Boon (वरदान)
121.	Barbaric (असभ्य)	Uncivilized	Civilised (सभ्य)
122.	Barrier (अवरोध)	Bound	Opening (खुली जगह)
123.	Beautiful (सुंदर)	Handsome	Ugly (कुरूप)
124.	Beneficial (लाभदायक)	Advantageous	Harmful (हानिकारक)
125.	Benign (अनुकूल)	Favourable	Malignant (घातक)
126.	Bliss (परमानंद)	Happiness	Sorrow (शोक)
127.	Bountiful (प्रचुर)	Generous	Meager (अल्प)
128.	Brittle (नाजुक,भंगुर)	Fragile	Strong (मजबूत)
129.	Callous (संवेदनाहीन)	Insensitive	Caring (परवाह करने वाला)
130.	Camouflage (छुप जाना)	Disguise	Reveal (दिखाना)
131.	Capable (सक्षम)	Competent	Inept (अयोग्य)
132.	Cavalier (घमंडी)	Curt	Humble (सादगी पूर्ण)
133.	Chagrin (शर्मिंदगी)	Embarrassment	Pleasure (खुशी)
134.	Chastise (सजा देना)	Upbraid	Praise (प्रशंसा करना)
135.	Chronic (दीर्घ)	Persistent	Infrequent (कभी-कभी)
136.	Circuitous (घुमावदार)	Roundabout	Direct (सीधा)
137.	Clumsy (अनाड़ी)	Unskilful	Graceful (गरिमापूर्ण)
138.	Compassion (दया)	Pity	Meanness (नीचता)
139.	Compassionate (सहानुभुति)	Sympathetic	Heartless (बेरहम)
140.	Conceal (छिपाना)	Hide	Reveal (प्रकट करना)
141.	Conjecture (अनुमान)	Guess	Certainty (निश्चय)
142.	Contrary (विरोध)	Opposite	Agreeable (सहमत)
143.	Courage (साहस)	Valour	Cowardice (कायरता)

S.N.	Words (Hindi Meaning)	Synonyms	Antonyms (Hindi Meaning)
144.	Crafty (चालाक)	Cunning	Unskilled (अनाड़ी)
145.	Cumbersome (भारी भरकम)	Heavy	Convenient (सुविधाजनक,आसान)
146.	Piquant (चटपटा)	Spicy, Appealing	Bland (बेस्वाद)
147.	Precise (सटीक)	Accurate	Vague (अस्पष्ट)
148.	Predicament (कठिन परिस्थित)	Plight, Dilemma	Solution (समाधान)
149.	Prevent (रोकना)	Avert, Block	Induce (प्रेरित करना)
150.	Procrastinate (विलम्ब करना)	Delay	Expedite, Do (शीघ्र,करना)
151.	Prompt (शीघ्र)	Immediate, Quick	Sluggish (सुस्त)
152.	Prosperity (समृद्धि)	Wealth	Adversity (विपत्ति)
153.	Quash (रद्द करना, अस्वीकार करना)	Reject, Crush	Support (सर्मथन करना)
154.	Querulous (शिकायती)	Grouchy, Complaining	Uncomplaining (शिकायत न करने वाला)
155.	Recede (कम होना)	Wane	Advance, Extend (उन्नति, विस्तार)
156.	Redundant (अनावश्यक)	Unnecessary	Required, Concise (आवश्यक, संछिप्त)
157.	Relinquish (त्यागना)	Discard	Retain, Continue (बनाये रखना)
158.	Reticent (अल्पभाषी)	Silent	Communicative, Talkative (बातुनी)
159.	Retreat (पीछे)	Withdrawl	Advance (आगे बढ़ाना)
160.	Savage (बर्बर)	Brutal	Civilized, Cultured (सभ्य)
161.	Scanty (अल्प)	Limited, Meagre	Profuse (अधिक)
162.	Serene (शांत)	Calm	Ruffled, Stressed (रूखा / अत्यधिक
163.	Slender (पतला)	Slim	Stout (मोटा)
164.	Subsequent (आगामी)	Consecutive	Prior, Preceding (पहले, पूर्ववर्ती)
165.	Subtle (कोमल)	Understated	Harsh (कठोर)
166.	Sufficient (पर्याय)	Enough	Inadequate (अपर्याप्त)
167.	Superficial (सतही)	Shallow	Genuine (सच्चा)
168.	Superfluous (अनावश्यक, अतिरिक्त)	Extra	Necessary (आवश्यक)
169.	Surreptitious (गुप्त)	Secret, Secretive	Open (स्पष्ट)
170.	Unruly (अनियंत्रित)	Lawless, Disobedient	Orderly (व्यवथित)
171.	Vital (महत्वपूर्ण, अत्यावश्यक)	Essential, Crucial	Trivial (मामूली)
172.	Wary (होशियार)	Alert	Rash, Careless (जल्दबाज, लापरवाह)

S.N.	Words (Hindi Meaning)	Synonyms	Antonyms (Hindi Meaning)
173.	Weary (थका मांदा होना)	Exhausted, Tired	Refreshed (तरोताजा)
174.	Weird (अजीब)	Strange	Usual, Normal (सामान्य)
175.	Aberration (असामान्यता, विचलन)	Deviation	Normality (सामान्यता)
176.	Abjure (त्यागना)	Renounce	Acquire (प्राप्त करना)
177.	Haggard (थका, मंदा)	Exhausted	Fresh (ताज़ा)
178.	Handy (आसान)	Convenient	Heavy (भारी)
179.	Harass (परेशान करना)	Bother, Molest	Relieve (दु:ख दूर करना)
180.	Humane (दयालु)	Sympathetic	Cruel, Unkind (निर्दयी)
181.	Immense (विशाल)	Massive	Tiny (बहुत छोटा)
182.	Impoverished (गरीब)	Penniless	Affluent, Rich (धनी)
183.	Inclement (निर्दयी)	Unfavourable,	Mild (विनम्र)
184.	Indolent (आलसी, निष्क्रिय)	Dignified, Lazy	Diligent, Lively (मेहनती,जीवंत)
185.	Indomitable (अदम्य, अजेय)	Unconquerable, Invincible	Cowardly (कायर)
186.	Industrious (मेहनती)	Diligent	Lethargic, Indolent (सुस्त, निष्क्रय)
187.	Infirm (कमजोर)	Weak	Strong (बलवान)
188.	Initiate (आरंभ)	Start	Finish, Conclude (खतम करना)
189.	Instant (तुरंत)	Immediate	Delayed, Gradual (विलंबित)
190.	Jettison (बाहर फेंक देना)	Hurl, Eject	Accept (स्वीकार करना)
191.	Knack (कुशलता)	Dexterity	Dullness, Inability (नीरसता, अक्षमता)
192.	Lackadaisical (आलसी भावुक)	Careless	Enthusiastic (उत्साही)
193.	Lethargic (सुस्त)	Inactive, Lazy	Lively (जीवंत)
194.	Loquacious (बातूनी)	Talkative	Taciturn (अल्पभाषी)
195.	Mammoth (विशाल)	Gigantic, Enormous	Infinitesimal (अति सूक्ष्म)
196.	Meander (दिशाहीन घूमना)	Curve, Wander	Determine (निर्धारित करना)
197.	Mellow (मधुर)	Genial	Hard (कठिन)
198.	Naive (भोला)	Ingenuous	Artful, Experienced (धूर्त, अनुभवी)
199.	Novel (अद्‌भुत, नया)	Unique	Banal, Old (तुच्छ, पुराना)
		Unknown	
201.	Orthodox (परंपरागत)	Traditional	Heretical, Unconventional (विधर्मी, अपरंपरागत)

S.N.	Words (Hindi Meaning)	Synonyms	Antonyms (Hindi Meaning)
202.	Ostracize (निष्काशित)	Expel, Banish	Patronize (संरक्षण देना)
203.	Pacify (शांत करना)	Calm Down, Soothe	Enrage (क्रोधित करना)
204.	Perilous (संकटपूर्ण)	Hazardous, Dangerous	Safe (सुरक्षित)
205.	Philanthropist (परोपकारी)	Benefactor, Humanitarian	Miser (लोभी)
206.	Pinnacle (शिखर)	Summit, Culmination	Base (आधार)
207.	Culmination (समापन)	Climax	Beginning, Commencement (शुरुआत)
208.	Culpable (दोषी)	Guilty	Innocent, Blameless (निर्दोष)
209.	Defy (विरोध करना)	Repel, Disobey	Yield (स्वीकार करना)
210.	Demure (शर्मीला)	Sober	Strong, Bold (दृढ़, साहसिक)
211.	Deny (इनकार करना)	Refuse	Agree, Accept (सहमत होना)
212.	Derogatory (अपमानजनक)	Disparaging, Sarcastic	Complimentary (प्रशंसात्मक)
213.	Deter (रोक लगाना)	Hinder	Incite, Encourage (प्रोत्साहित करना)
214.	Dilate (फैलाना)	Widen	Contract, Compress (संकुचित करना)
215.	Diminish (घटाना)	Reduce	Increase (बढ़ना)
216.	Dishevelled (अस्त व्यस्त)	Untidy	Tidy (साफ)
217.	Eager (उत्सुक)	Keen	Disinterested, Indifferent (उदासीन)
218.	Efficacious (प्रभावी)	Effective	Ineffective, Useless (प्रभावहीन)
219.	Efficient (कुशल)	Capable, Competent	Idle (बेकार)
200.	Elated (उत्तेजित)	Exalted	Disheartened, Depressed (निराश)
211.	Evade (बच निकलना)	Avoid, Bypass	Confront (सामना करना)
222.	Evasive (कपटपूर्ण)	Devious	Categorical, Frank (स्पष्ट करना)
233.	Exorbitant (अत्यधिक)	Excessive, High	Modest (मामूली)
244.	Extinct (विलुप्त)	Abolished	Alive, Living (जीवित)
255.	Fake (नकली)	False	Real, Genuine (असली)

S.N.	Words (Hindi Meaning)	Synonyms	Antonyms (Hindi Meaning)
266.	Felicity (परम सुख)	Bliss	Sorrow (शोक)
277.	Fictitious (काल्पनिक)	False	Real, Factual (असली)
288.	Flourish (समृद्ध होना)	Thrive	Degenerate, Hinder (बिगड़ना, बाधा डालना)
299.	Former (भूतपूर्व)	Previous	After, Latter (बाद)
300.	Forsake (त्यागना)	Abandon, Desert	Revert (लौट आना)
301.	Fortify (मज़बूत करना)	Strengthen, Secure	Undermine (दुर्बल बना देना)
302.	Frail (दुर्बल)	Feeble, Fragile	Robust (सुदृढ़)
303.	Frugal (अल्पव्ययी, किफ़ायती)	Economical	Extravagant (खर्चीला)
304.	Gallant (वीर,शौर्य)	Courageous, Brave	Cowardly (कायरतापूर्ण)
305.	Gather (एकत्र करना)	Congregate	Divide, Disperse (फैल जाना, छितराना)
306.	Genial (मिलनसार)	Cordial	Boorish, Hostile (शत्रुतापूर्ण)
307.	Glee (आनंद)	Happiness	Woe (शोक)
308.	Guile (छल कपट)	Cunning, Deceit	Honesty (ईमानदारी)
309.	Taciturn (अल्पभाषी)	Silent, Reticent	Talkative (बातूनी)
310.	Thwart (विफल करना)	Impede, Curb	Assist (सहायता करना)
311.	Transient (क्षणिक)	Transitory, Fleeting, Temporary	Permanent (स्थायी)
312.	Vacillate (निश्चय न कर पाना)	Waver, Irresolute	Decide (निश्चय करना)
313.	Abeyance (ठहराव)	Inactivity, Suspension	Continuation (जारी रखना)
314.	Absolute (पूर्ण)	Complete	Limited (सीमित)
315.	Accomplish (सफल होना)	Achieve	Fail (असफल होना)
316.	Acute (धारदार)	Sharp	Blunt (भोथरा)
317.	Affinity (लगाव सहानुभूति)	Empathy	Aversion (घृणा)
318.	Altruistic (परोपकारी)	Philanthropic	Selfish (स्वार्थी)
319.	Ameliorate (सुधारना)	Improve	Worsen (बदतर करना)
320.	Amicable (मैत्रीपूर्ण)	Friendly	Hostile (शत्रुतापूर्ण)
321.	Apposite (उपयुक्त)	Appropriate	Inappropriate (अनुपयुक्त)
322.	Arcane (गुप्त)	Mysterious, Hidden	Public (सार्वजनिक)
323.	Articulate (सुस्पष्ट)	Distinct	Unclear (अस्पष्ट)

S.N.	Words (Hindi Meaning)	Synonyms	Antonyms (Hindi Meaning)
324.	Ascend (ऊपर उठना)	Climb	Descend (नीचे उतरना)
325.	Ascertain (सुनिश्चित करना)	Discover	Overlook, Disprove (अनदेखी करना, खडन करना)
326.	Audacious (साहसी)	Bold	Cowardly (कायर)
327.	Audacity (धृष्टता)	Boldness	Cowardice,Timidity (कायरता)
328.	Audacity (विश्वसनीय)	Certain, Genuine	False (असत्य)
329.	Beseech (याचना करना)	Beg	Command (हुक्म देना)
330.	Cajole (फुसलाना)	Flatter, Entice	Repulse (प्रतिरोध करना)
331.	Capricious (मनमौजी)	Whimsical	Firm, Reasonable (दृढ़, तर्कसंगत)
332.	Cherish (पोषण)	Nurture	Abandon (छोड़ देना)
333.	Chivalrous (शौर्यवान)	Heroic	Cowardly, Defiant (कायर)
334.	Clandestine (गुप्त)	Secret	Open, Honest (खुला, निष्कपट)
335.	Comic (हास्य)	Funny	Tragic (दुखद)
336.	Command (आदेश)	Instruct	Opposition, Permission (विपक्ष, अनमति)
337.	Concise (संक्षिप्त)	Brief	Lengthy (लंबा)
338.	Confine (सीमित)	Restrict	Liberate (मुक्त करना)
330.	Consensus (आम सहमति)	Unanimity	Disagreement, Discord (असहमति कलह)
340.	Contaminate (दूषित करना)	Pollute	Cleanse (शुद्धी करना)
341.	Copious (प्रचुर)	Plentiful	Scarce (दुर्लभ)
342.	Courteous (विनम्र)	Polite	Rude (अशिष्ट)
343.	Flimsy (कमजोर)	Weak, Feeble	Sturdy, Strong (तगड़ा)
344.	Fragile (नाजुक, भंगुर)	Brittle	Tough, Strong (मजबूत)
345.	Garrulous (बातूनी)	Talkative, Voluble	Taciturn (अल्पभाषी)
346.	Haste (जल्दी)	Hurry	Delay (देरी)
347.	Incredible (अतुल्य, अविश्वसनीय)	Unbelievable	Possible, Believable (संभव, विश्वसनीय)
348.	Inept (कुख्यात)	Clumsy	Skillful, Talented, (योग्य) Competent
349.	Innocuous (अहानिकर)	Harmless, Inoffensive	Pernicious, Harmful (हानिकारक)
350.	Integration (एकीकरण)	Unity, Unification	Fragmentation (विखंडन)

S.N.	Words (Hindi Meaning)	Synonyms	Antonyms (Hindi Meaning)
351.	Judicious (विवेकीकरण)	Wise, Prudent Catious,	Rash (अविवेकी)
352.	Lavish (प्रचुर)	Expensive, Bountiful	Scarce, Frugal (दुर्लभ, अल्पव्ययी)
353.	Magnificent (शानदार)	Splendid, Grand	Modest (विनम्र)
354.	Malice (दुर्भावना)	Bitterness	Goodwill, Kindness (सद्भावना)
355.	Meticulous (सतर्क)	Careful, Methodical, Perfectionist	Careless (लापरवाह)
356.	Monotonous (नीरस एकसमान)	Dull, Boring	Interesting, Varied (दिलचस्प, विभिन्न)
357.	Nefarious (दुष्कर्मी)	Wicked, Iniquitous	Pleasing (सुखदायी)
358.	Notorious (कुख्यात)	Disreputable	Popular, Reputed, Famous (प्रतिष्ठित, प्रसिद्ध)
359.	Paucity (कमी)	Shortage	Plethora, Surplus (बहुतायत अतिरिक्त)
360.	Peculiar (अड़े रहना)	Strange	Usual, Normal (सामान्य)
361.	Persist (खतरनाक)	Insist, Continue	Cease, Discontinue (बन्द करना)
362.	Precarious (पसंद)	Perilous, Dangerous, Insecure	Safe (सुरक्षित)
363.	Predilection (पसंद)	Preference	Dislike, Aversion, Enmity (नापसंद, घृणा, शत्रुता)
364.	Revive (पुनजीवित करना)	Restore, Recover	Ruin, Damage (बर्बाद करना)
365.	Sacred (धार्मिक)	Holy	Profane (अपवित्र)
366.	Salient (मुख्य)	Prominent, Noticeable	Insignificant, Negligible (तुच्छ, नगण्य)
367.	Stable (स्थिर)	Anchored	Shaky (अस्थिर)
368.	Stringent (सख्त)	Tough, Strict, Rigorous	Lenient (नरम)
369.	Current (वर्तमानकालिक)	Present	Past (अतीत)
370.	Debacle (पराजय)	Downfall	Success (सफलता)
371.	Debonair (आर्कषक)	Elegant	Cheerless (निराश)
372.	Decamp (भाग जाना)	Flee	Remain (ठहरना)
373.	Deliberately (जान-बूझकर)	Intentionally	Unintentionally (अनजाने में)

S.N.	Words (Hindi Meaning)	Synonyms	Antonyms (Hindi Meaning)
374.	Delight (आनंद)	Joy	Sorrow (शोक)
375.	Delusion (भ्रम)	Illusion	Reality (हकीकत)
376.	Demented (पागल)	Idiotic	Sensible (समझदार)
377.	Devoid (खली)	Empty	Full (भरा हुआ)
378.	Dexterity (निपुणता)	Adroitness	Ignorance (अज्ञानता)
379.	Disaster (आपदा)	Misfortune	Success (सफलता)
380.	Discreet (सावधान)	Careful	Tactless (अव्यावहारिक)
381.	Disperse (छितराना)	Eject	Gather (एकत्र करना)
382.	Dissuade (रोकना)	Discourage	Persuade (राजी करना)
383.	Divulgence (पर्दाफाश)	Revelation	Repudiation (इनकार)
384.	Doleful (दुख भरा)	Mournful	Cheerful (आनंदित)
385.	Dwindle (घटना)	Decrease	Increase (बढ़ना)
386.	Elaborate (विस्तृत)	Detailed	Minimal (कम से कम)
387.	Eloquent (सुवक्ता)	Fluent	Inarticulate (व्यक्त करने मे असमर्थ)
388.	Encountered (सामना करना)	Faced	Avoided (टालना)
389.	Endeavour (प्रयत्न करना)	Attempt	Laziness (कामचोरी)
390.	Ensconce (छिपना)	**Conceal**	Unveil (दिखना)
391.	Enthusiasm (उत्साह)	**Zeal**	Lethargy (सुस्ती)
392.	Epidemic (व्यापक रोग)	Widespread	Limited (सीमित)
393.	Epitome (प्रतीक)	Type	Enlargement (विस्तारण)
394.	Erode (नष्ट करना)	Disintegrate	Fix (ठीक कर)
395.	Esoteric (गुप्त)	Abstruse	Familiar (परिचित)
396.	Eventual (अंतिम)	Ultimate	Initial (प्रारंभिक)
397.	Evince (व्यक्त)	Show	Conceal (छिपाना)
398.	Exasperating (तंग करना)	Frustrating	Soothing (प्रसन्न करने वाला)
399.	Exotic (असाधारण)	Strange	Ordinary (साधारण)
400.	Fallacy (भ्रम)	Bias	Truth (सच्चाई)
401.	Fidelity (वफ़ादारी)	Loyalty	Treachery (दगाबाजी)
402.	Fiendish (क्रूर)	Cruel	Friendly (मित्रतापूर्ण)
403.	Fragrance (सुगंध)	Aroma	Stench (दुर्गंध)
404.	Frigid (बहुत)	Freezing	Warm (गरम)
405.	Frivolous (तुच्छ)	Puerile	Wise (विद्वान)

S.N.	Words (Hindi Meaning)	Synonyms	Antonyms (Hindi Meaning)
406.	Genius (प्रतिभावान)	A person with uncommon intellect	Dumb (बेवक़ूफ)
407.	Graceful (गरिमापूर्ण)	Elegant	Awkward (बेढंगा)
408.	Gradual (क्रमशः)	Continuous	Abrupt (एकाएक)
409.	Gruesome (कुरूप)	Hideous	Gracious (सुन्दर)
410.	Gullible (भोला-भाला)	Innocent	Wise (समझदार)
411.	Gumption (बुद्धिमानी)	Acumen	Stupidity (मूर्खता)
412.	Guzzle (बहुत खाना पीना)	Imbibe	Starve (भूखा मरना)
413.	Hasty (जल्दबाज, अविचारी)	Quick	Cautious (सतर्क)
414.	Hesitate (हिचकिचाना)	Pause	Advance (अग्रसर होना)
415.	Honest (ईमानदार)	Upright	Corrupt (भ्रष्ट)
416.	Hospitable (सौहार्दपूर्ण)	Congenial	Rude (अशिष्ट)
417.	Hostility (दुश्मनी)	Enmity	Friendship (मित्रता)
418.	Humble (विनम्र)	Meek	Arrogant (घमडी)
419.	Illuminate (उजाला करना)	Brighten	Darken (अंधेरा करना)
420.	Impetuous (जल्दबाज़ी में)	Hasty	Cautious (सावधानी से)
421.	Incapacitate (असमर्थ बनाना)	Cripple	Facilitate (सुविधा देना)
422.	Incessant (निरंतर)	Persistent	Intermittent (रुक-रुक कर)
423.	Incorrigible (असंशोधनीय)	Unalterable	Reformable (संशोधनीय)
424.	Indelible (स्थायी)	Inerasable	Temporary (अस्थायी)
425.	Indict (अभियोग लगाना)	Charge	Exonerate (दोषमुक्त करना)
426.	Inevitable (अपरिहार्य, अटल)	Unavoidable	Avoidable (परिहार्य)
427.	Invade (आक्रमण)	Ravage	Surrender (आत्मसमर्पण)
428.	Irascible (चिड़चिड़ा)	Irritable	Amiable (सुशील)
429.	Isolation (अलगाव, एकांत)	Separation	Association (संघ)
430.	Just (न्याय संगत)	Fair	Corrupt (भ्रष्ट)
431.	Lassitude (थकान)	Sluggishness	Enthusiasm (उत्साह)
432.	Levity (छिछोरापन)	Funniness	Gravity (गंभीरता)
433.	Logical (तर्कसंगत)	Rational	Contradictory (असंगत)
434.	Maintain (देखभाल करना)	Care	Abandon (छोड़ना)
435.	Malevolent (बुरा चाहने वाला)	Despiteful	Kind (दयालु)
436.	Meek (विनम्र, आज्ञाकारी)	Submissive	Assertive (हठ धर्मी)
437.	Melancholy (उदासी)	Sorrowful	Cheerful (हंसमुख)
438.	Melodious (मधुर)	Tuneful	Tuneless (बेसुरा)
439.	Miniature (लघु)	Diminutive	Large (विशाल)

S.N.	Words (Hindi Meaning)	Synonyms	Antonyms (Hindi Meaning)
440.	Modest (विनम्र)	Humble	Vain (अहंकारी)
441.	Muddle (अव्यवस्था)	Difficulty	Order (क्रम)
442.	Nascent (आरंभ होना)	Budding	Withering (नष्ट होना)
443.	Nebulous (धुंधला)	Vague	Clear (स्पष्ट)
444.	Nugatory (निरर्थक)	Futile	Productive (उत्पादक)
445.	Obedient (आज्ञाकारी)	Devoted	Disobedient (अवज्ञाकारी)
446.	Obsequious (चापलूस)	Servile	Domineering (घमंडी)
447.	Ostentation (आडम्बर)	Pomp	Modesty (विनम्रता)
448.	Outrageous (शर्मनाक)	Shocking	Jolly (विनादपूर्ण)
449.	Pandemonium (कोलाहल)	Chaos	Harmony (सामंजस्य)
450.	Paradox (विरोधाभास)	Puzzle	Evidence (प्रमाण)
451.	Penitence (अफसोस करना)	Repentance	Brazenness (बेशर्मी)
452.	Penury (गरीबी)	Poverty	Wealth (धन)
453.	Peril (संकट)	Danger	Safety (सुरक्षा)
454.	Pious (पवित्र)	Religious	Sinful (पापी)
455.	Pompous (आडंबरपूर्ण)	Boastful	Humble (विनम्र)
456.	Porous (छिद्रयुक्त)	Permeable	Impermeable (अभेद्य)
457.	Praise (प्रशंसा करना)	Compliment	Accuse (आरोप लगाना)
458.	Proficient (कुशल)	Adept	Clumsy (अनाड़ी)
459.	Radiance (चमक)	Sparkle	Dullness (धुंधलापन)
460.	Rampart (किले की दीवार)	Parapet	Ditch (खाई)
461.	Rational (तर्कसंगत)	Logical	Illogical (विसंगत)
462.	Ravish (मोहलेना)	Enthral	Repel (पीछे हटाना)
463.	Receive(प्राप्त करना)	Get	Give (देना)
464.	Regret (अफसोस)	Repent	Contentment (सन्तुष्टता)
465.	Remember (याद रखना)	Recall	Forget (भूलना)
466.	Remorse (अफसोस)	Regret	Indifference (उदासीनता)
467.	Resolute (दृढ़)	Determined	Agreeable (स्वीकार्य)
468.	Retain (बनाये रखना)	Maintain	Release (मुक्त करना)
469.	Revel (आनंद लेना)	Make Merry	Mourn (शोक मनाना)
470.	Robust (मज़बूत)	Healthy	Feeble (कमज़ोर)
471.	Sanguine (आशावादी)	Buoyant	Hopeless (निराशाजनक)
472.	Scarce (दुर्लभ)	Limited	Ample (प्रचुर)
473.	Seize (पकड़ना)	Catch	Loosen (ढीला करना)

S.N.	Words (Hindi Meaning)	Synonyms	Antonyms (Hindi Meaning)
474.	Shrink (कम होना)	Diminish	Expand (फैलाना)
475.	Sneer (उपहास)	Mock	Praise (प्रशंसा)
476.	Solicit (विनती करना)	Request	Prohibit (मना करना)
477.	Stationary (स्थिर)	Fixed	Moving (गतिमान)
478.	Sterile (बाँझ)	Barren	Fertile (उपजाऊ)
479.	Strange (अपरिचित)	Abnormal	Familiar (परिचित)
480.	Stretch (विस्तार)	Extend	Compress (संक्षेप करना)
481.	Sustenance (जीविका)	Aid	Starvation (भुखमरी)
482.	Swift (तेज़)	Quick	Slow (धीरे)
483.	Synthetic (कृत्रिम)	Fake	Natural (प्राकृतिक)
484.	Tedious (ग़ैरदिलचस्प)	Dull	Interesting (दिलचस्प)
485.	Toxic (विषैला)	Poisonous	Healthy (स्वास्थ्यवर्धक)
486.	Traitor (कद्दार)	Deceiver	Patriot (देश-भक्त)
487.	Trepidation (घबराहट)	Nervousness	Calm (शांत)
488.	Trivial (मामूली)	Superficial	Profound (पारंगत)
489.	Truculent (उग्र, लड़ाकू)	Ferocious	Amiable (मिलनसार)
490.	Tumult (हंगामा)	Uproar	Calmness (सन्नाटा)
491.	Urge (तीव्र इच्छा)	Impulse	Deter (रोक रखना)
492.	Vague (अस्पष्ट)	Unclear	Clear (स्पष्ट)
493.	Valiant (बहादुर)	Courageous	Cowardly (कायरतापूर्ण)
494.	Vanquish (पराजित करना)	Defeat	Surrender (हार मानना)
495.	Venial (क्षमा योग्य)	Pardonable	Unpardonable (अक्षम्य)
496.	Vicious (अनैतिक, निर्दयी)	Cruel	Virtuous (नैतिक)
497.	Vintage (प्राचीन)	Classic	Modern (आधुनिक)
498.	Violent (हिंसक, उग्र)	Aggressive	Gentle (सुशील)
499.	Virulent (घातक)	Deadly	Amicable (मैत्रीपूर्ण)
500.	Volition (इच्छा)	Choice	Compulsion (विवशता)
501.	Vulnerable (असुरक्षित)	Exposed	Secure (सुरक्षित)
502.	Wholesome (स्वास्थ्य के लिए अच्छा)	Sound	Impure (असुद्ध)
503.	Yell (चिल्लाना)	Shout	Whisper (धीरे-धीरे बोलना)

UNIT 6

Synonyms with Hindi and English Meaning

Given below are a number of synonyms with their Hindi and English meanings.

S.N.	Word (Hindi Meaning)	Hindi Meaning	Synonyms
1	Abbreviate	संक्षिप्त करना	Shorten, shorten, reduce, cut
2	Abdicate	त्यागना	Abandon, disown, turn down, spurn, reject
3	Abettor	अपराध में सहयोगी	Accomplice
4	Ability	योग्यता	Capacity
5	Ablaze	जलता हुआ, उत्तेजित	Furious
6	Ablution	स्नान	Washing
7	Abnegation	अस्वीकार	Denial
8	Abnormal	असामान्य	Unnatural
9	Abode	घर	Dwelling
10	Abolition	उन्मूलन	Cancellation
11	Abort	बंद कर देना	End
12	Abortive	निष्फल	Unsuccessful
13	Abrogate	रद्द कर देना	Repeal, Abolish
14	Abruptly	एकाएक	Suddenly
15	Absolutely	बिल्कुल	Definitely
16	Absorbing	दिलचस्प	Engrossing
17	Abuse	गाली	Misuse, Exploit
18	Abysmal	बहुत खराब, बेबुनियादी	Aful, deplorable
19	Accessories	सहायक सामग्री	Attachments
20	Acclaim	प्रशंसा करना	Praise
21	Accountable	जवाबदेह	Answerable
22	Accoutrements	उपकरण	Equipment
23	Accrue	इकट्ठा करना	Accumulate, Collect
24	Accurate	शुद्ध	Precise, Correct, Exact
25	Accurately	शुद्धता से	Correctly
26	Accused	अभियुक्त	Indicted, Arraigned

S.N.	Word (Hindi Meaning)	Hindi Meaning	Synonyms
27	Achieve	पाना	Accomplish, Succeed,
28	Acknowledgement	अभिस्वीकृति	Confirmation
29	Acquaint	परिचय कराना	Introduce, Familiarise
30	Acquiescent	बात मानने वाला	Tractable
31	Active	कार्यरत	Busy
32	Actuate	उकसाना	Move
33	Adapt	अनुकूल बनाना	Adjust
34	Adequate	पर्याप्त	Sufficient, Enough
35	Adhere	पालन करना	Comply
36	Adjust	अनुकूल बनाना	Adapt
37	Adjustment	सामंजस्य	Balancing
38	Admonition	चेतावनी	Warning
39	Adulation	चापलूसी	Flattery, Adoration
40	Adulterated	मिलावटी	Contaminated
41	Advantageous	लाभदायक	Favourable
42	Adversary	विरोधी	Rival, Opponent
43	Adverse	विपरीत	Unfavourable
44	Advocate	समर्थक	Support
45	Affectionate	स्नेही	Sympathetic
46	Afflict	सताना	Annoy
47	Aggregate	कुल	Total
48	Agitated	व्यथित, परेशान	Upset
49	Agony	कष्ट	Pain
50	Aim	उद्देश्य	Purpose
51	Aisle	गलियारा	Passage
52	Alarm	खतरे का संकेत	Panic
53	Allay	शांत करना	Relieve
54	Allege	आरोप लगाना	Charge
55	Alleviate	कम करना	Mitigate
56	Allow	अनुमति देना	Permit
57	Alluring	आकर्षक	Attractive
58	Aloof	अलग-थलग	Detached
59	Alter	बदलना	Transform
60	Alteration	फेरबदल	Modification

S.N.	Word (Hindi Meaning)	Hindi Meaning	Synonyms
61	Altruist	परोपकारी	Philanthropist
62	Amalgam	मिश्रण	Mixture
63	Amend	संसोधन	Alter
64	Amorous	कामुक	Erotic
65	Amplify	बढ़ाना	Magnify, Boost
66	Amusing	मनोरंजक	Laughable
67	Ancestor	पूर्वज	Forefather
68	Anger	गुस्सा	Displeasure
69	Angry	गुस्सा	Enraged
70	Anguish	दुख, पीड़ा	Agony, Ache, Sorrow
71	Annihilate	विनाश करना	Destroy
72	Annoy	झुंझला देना	Offend, Irritate
73	Anodyne	पीड़ा नाशक	Benign
74	Anomalous	असंगत, अजीब	Peculiar
75	Antagonist	विरोधी	Opponent
76	Anthology	संग्रह	Collection
77	Anticipate	पूर्वानुमान	Expect
78	Antipathy	घृणा	Dislike
79	Antique	प्राचीन	Ancient
80	Apathetic	उदासीन	Indifferent
81	Apathy	उदासीनता	Indifference
82	Apex	शिखर	Top
83	Appalling	भयावह	Shocking
84	Apparently	स्प्ष्ट रूप से	Seemingly
85	Appeal	आकर्षण	Charm
86	Appear	प्रतीत होना	Seem
87	Appease	शांत करना	Pacify
88	Appraise	आंकना	Judge
89	Apprehend	गिरफ्तार	Arrest
90	Arbitrary	मनमाना	Random
91	Ardent	उत्साही	Passionate
92	Arduous	कठिन	Difficult, Strenuous
93	Aroma	सुगंध	Scent
94	Artful	धूर्त	Cunning, Crafty

S.N.	Word (Hindi Meaning)	Hindi Meaning	Synonyms
95	Ascription	आरोपण	Attribution
96	Assemble	एकत्रित होना	Amass
97	Assertion	दावा	Declaration
98	Assertive	निश्चयात्मक	Domineering
99	Assess	आकलन	Measure
100	Astonish	चकित करना	Surprise
101	Astonishment	आश्चर्य	Wonder
102	Atrocity	अत्याचार	Violence, Barbarity
103	Attain	प्राप्त	Achieve
104	Attract	आकर्षित करना	Fascinate, Entice
105	Attribute	गुण	Characteristic, Quality
106	August	गरिमापूर्ण, भव्य	Majestic, Dignified
107	Aura	प्रभामंडल	Halo
108	Auspicious	शुभ	Favourable
109	Austere	सादा, सख्त	Strict, unadorned
110	Autocratic	निंरकुश	Dictatorial
111	Avarice	लोभ	Greed
112	Avenge	बदला लेना	Punish
113	Aversion	घृणा	Dislike
114	Awe	श्रद्धा	Admiration
115	Awry	विकृत	Crookedly
116	Baffle	चकरा देना	Puzzle, Confuse, Perplex
117	Ban	निषेध	Prohibit
118	Banal	तुच्छ	Commonplace
119	Bang	जोर से मारना	Beat
120	Banish	निर्वासित करना	Expel, Exile
121	Banner	पताका	Poster
122	Bargain	मोलभाव करना	Deal
123	Bashful	संकोची	Shy
124	Batter	पीटना	Beat
125	Beckon	इशारे से बुलाना	Call
126	Beguile	मोहना, ठगना	Deceive
127	Behaviour	व्यवहार	Conduct
128	Behoove	योग्य होना	Necessary

S.N.	Word (Hindi Meaning)	Hindi Meaning	Synonyms
129	Belligerent	लड़ाकू	Hostile, Antagonistic
130	Beneficiaries	लाभार्थी	Recipients
131	Benevolence	भलाई	Kindness
132	Bereft	वंचित	Deprived
133	Bewitched	मोहित	Captivated
134	Bifurcated	दो शाखाओं में बांटना	Divided into Two
135	Bind	बांधना	Unite, Fasten
136	Blabber	गप्पी, बक-बक करना	Nonsense
137	Blister	छाला	Wound, Bubble
138	Blunder	बड़ी भूल	Mistake
139	Board	खानपान	Food
140	Boast	झूठा गर्व	Pride
141	Bogus	जाली	Fake
142	Bolster	सहारा देना	Strengthen
143	Bonanza	अप्रत्याशित लाभ	Bonus
144	Bonhomie	मिलनसारिता	Companionship
145	Brace	तैयार करना	Fortify
146	Brat	बिगड़ैल बच्चा	Spoilt Child
147	Breach	उल्लंघन	Violation
148	Breakthrough	महत्वपूर्ण खोज	Discovery
149	Breezy	हवादार	Airy
150	Brevity	संक्षेप	Crispness
151	Brisk	तेज	Quick
152	Brutalize	निर्दयी व्यवहार	Ill-Treat
153	Bull-Headed	हठीला	Headstrong
154	Bumptious	अहंकारी, घमण्डी	Conceited
155	Bustle	हलचल	Haste
156	Cadence	लय ताल	Rhythm
157	Calculation	हिसाब	Counting
158	Caliber	क्षमता	Capacity
159	Calm	शांत	Peaceful, Relaxed, Quiet
160	Cancel	रद्द करना	Abolish
161	Canny	चालाक	Clever
162	Cantankerous	झगड़ालू	Quarrelsome

S.N.	Word (Hindi Meaning)	Hindi Meaning	Synonyms
163	Capitulate	हथियार डालना	Surrender
164	Caricature	व्यंग्य-चित्र	Grotesque
165	Carnage	मार काट	Slaughter
166	Carouse	खान पान कर आनंद मनाना	Frolic, Quaff
167	Casual	आकस्मिक	Occasional
168	Catastrophe	तबाही, आपदा	Calamity, Tragedy, Disaster
169	Cavort	कूदना	Jump
170	Celebrate	मनाना	Honour
171	Ceremonial	शिष्टाचार-युक्त	Formal
172	Certain	निश्चित	Sure
173	Chafe	झुझलाना, क्रोध करना	Irritate
174	Challenge	आपत्ति उठाना	Objection
175	Change	परिवर्तन	Alter
176	Chaos	अराजकता	Disorder, Mix-Up, Confusion, Turmoil
177	Character	चरित्र	Trait
178	Charisma	प्रतिभा	Charm
179	Chauvinism	कट्टरता	Zealotry
180	Chide	डांटना	Rebuke
181	Choke	जाम होना	Block
182	Choosy	चयनात्मक	Selective, Picky
183	Chorus	सहगान	Signing Group
184	Citadel	गढ़	Fortress
185	Clamour	कोलाहल	Uproar
186	Clasp	पकड़	Catch
187	Clean	साफ	Honest
188	Clement	दयालू	Mild
189	Climax	चरम बिन्दु	Culmination
190	Clinched	पक्का करना	Finalized
191	Cloistered	तनहा	Isolated
192	Cluster	समूह	Assemblage
193	Coddle	लाड़ प्यार करना	Satisfy
194	Coerce	मजबूर करना	Pressurize

S.N.	Word (Hindi Meaning)	Hindi Meaning	Synonyms
195	Cogent	प्रभावशाली, निश्च्यात्मक	Effective, Convincing
196	Coincidence	इत्तफ़ाक	Chance
197	Collate	एकत्र करना	Assemble
198	Colloquial	बोल-चाल का	Familiar
199	Combustible	ज्वलनशील	Inflammable
200	Commemorate	मनाना	Celebrate
201	Commendable	सराहनीय	Praiseworthy
202	Common	सामान्य	Usual
203	Commotion	हल्ला गुल्ला	Disturbance, Fuss
204	Compensate	कमी पूर्ति	Make Up For
205	Competent	सक्षम	Capable
206	Compliant	आज्ञाकारी	Submissive
207	Complicated	जटिल	Complex
208	Comply	पालन करना	Obey
209	Compose	संग्रह करना	Collect
210	Comprehend	समझना	Understand
211	Concealed	गुप्त	Hidden
212	Concession	रियायत	Allowance
213	Concise	संक्षिप्त	Short
214	Conclude	समाप्त होना	End
215	Concocted	मनगढ़ंत	Dubious
216	Concurrence	सहमति	Agreement
217	Condemn	निंदा करना	Criticize, Punish, Denounce
218	Condescending	प्रोत्साहक ढंग से	Patronising
219	Condescension	तुच्छ समझना	Disdain
220	Condone	ध्यान देना	Overlook
221	Confederate	संधि करना	Combined
222	Confess	कबूल करना	Admit
223	Confidential	गोपनीय	Secret
224	Conflagration	आग	Fire
225	Conflict	टकराव	Clash
226	Confusion	अव्यवस्था	Muddle
227	Congregation	मण्डली	Assembly, Meeting

S.N.	Word (Hindi Meaning)	Hindi Meaning	Synonyms
228	Congruent	सर्वांगसम	Identical
229	Congruous	उपयुक्त	Balanced
230	Conjurer	जादूगर	Magician
231	Çonnoisseur	विशेषज्ञ	Discerning Judge
232	Connote	भाव बतलाना	Convey
233	Conscientious	ईमानदार	Honest
234	Consciousness	चेतना	Awareness
235	Conscript	भरती होने वाला	Draftee
236	Consequence	परिणाम	Outcome
237	Consequent	फलस्वरूप	Ensuing
238	Conservation	संरक्षण	Preservation
239	Considerate	विचारशील	Thoughtful
240	Consignee	पाने वाला	Nominee, beneficiary, collector, payee, acceptor, assignee,
241	Consort	सहचारी	Partner
242	Conspicuous	प्रत्यक्ष	Evident
243	Consternation	घबराहट	Dismay
244	Constrain	विवश करना	Restrict
245	Constraint	प्रतिबंध	Control
246	Consult	राय लेना	Discuss
247	Contemplation	चिंतन	Meditation, Design
248	Contempt	घृणा	Hatred
249	Contingent	आकस्मिक	Accidental
250	Contraband	वर्जित	Smuggled
251	Contradict	खंडन	Confront, Refute
252	Contravene	अवहेलना करना	Breach
253	Contrite	पछतावा	Regretful
254	Control	नियंत्रण करना	Regulate
255	Controvert	प्रतिवाद करना	Contradict
256	Convalesce	अच्छा हो जाना	Recover
257	Converse	बातचीत	Talk
258	Convert	परिवर्तित करना	Transform
259	Convict	अपराधी	Criminal, Culprit
260	Corridor	बरामदा	Passage

S.N.	Word (Hindi Meaning)	Hindi Meaning	Synonyms
261	Counterfeit	नकली	Fake
262	Cove	छोटी खाड़ी, खोह	Bay
263	Covenant	प्रतिज्ञापत्र	Contract, Bond
264	Coveted	आकांक्षित	Desired
265	Credible	विश्वसनीय	Believable
266	Credulous	भोला	Gullible
267	Creep	छुपकर सरक जाना	Tiptoe
268	Crescendo	चढ़ाई, उत्कर्ष	Escalation
269	Crucial	अत्यंत महत्वपूर्ण	Vital
270	Cruddy	मैला	Dirty
271	Crude	कच्चा	Unrefined
272	Cruel	क्रूर	Brutal
273	Crumble	अधीन करना	Submissive
274	Crusade	धर्मयुद्ध	Campaign
275	Crust	उपरी तह	Shell
276	Cunning	धूर्त	Shrewd
277	Cupidity	लोभ	Greed
278	Curative	उपचारात्मक	Healing
279	Curious	जिज्ञासु	Inquisitive
280	Cute	आकर्षक	Charming
281	Cynicism	कुटिलता	Bitterness
282	Dame	महिला	Lady
283	Damp	नम	Wet
284	Damsel	अविवाहित युवती	Maiden
285	Dangerous	खतरनाक	Hazardous
286	Daring	साहसी	Courageous
287	Dauntless	निडर	Brave
288	Dearth	अकाल	Scarcity, Shortage
289	Debilitate	दुर्बल करना	Weaken
290	Decay	क्षय	Decompose
291	Deceptive	कपटी	Cheat
292	Decimated	नाश करना	Destroyed
293	Declension	पतन	Decay
294	Decrease	घटना	Decline

S.N.	Word (Hindi Meaning)	Hindi Meaning	Synonyms
295	Decrepit	निर्बल	Feeble
296	Decrepitude	निर्बलता	Feebleness
297	Dedicate	समर्पित करना	Devote
298	Dedicated	समर्पित	Committed
299	Dedication	निष्ठा	Commitment
300	Deepen	गहरा करना	Intensify
301	Defect	दोष	Flaw
302	Defer	टालना	Postpone, Delay
303	Deference	सम्मान	Respect, Obeisance, Compliance
304	Defiance	अवज्ञा, चुनौती	Resistance
305	Defiant	अवज्ञाकारी	Rebellious
306	Deficiency	कमी	Inadequacy, Shortage
307	Deficient	अपूर्ण	Lacking
308	Definite	निश्चित	Complete
309	Dejected	उदास	Depressed
310	Delectable	स्वादिष्ट	Luscious
311	Delegate	नियुक्त करना	Nominate
312	Delicate	कोमल	Frail
313	Delineate	वर्णन करना	Explain
314	Delinquent	अपराधी	Offending
315	Deluge	बाढ़	Flood, Overflow
316	To Demise	मृत्यु	Death
317	Demonstrate	प्रदर्शित करना	Show
318	Denial	इंकार	Dismissal
319	Denouement	उपसंहार	Climax
320	Dense	घना	Thick
321	Depict	वर्णन करना	Characterize
322	Deplete	कम करना	Reduce
323	Deplore	विलाप करना	Regret
324	Deposition	महाभियोग	Impeachment
325	Deride	मज़ाक उड़ाना	Mock
326	Derision	उपहास	Ridicule
327	Derive	प्राप्त	Obtain
328	Desert	परित्याग करना	Abandon

S.N.	Word (Hindi Meaning)	Hindi Meaning	Synonyms
329	Desiccated	शुष्क	Dry
330	Desolate	उजड़ा हुआ	Bleak
331	Desperation	निराश	Hopelessness
332	Despicable	घिनौना	Hateful, Contemptible
333	Despondent	हताश	Dejected, Depressed
334	Destroy	नष्ट करना	Ruin, Demolish
335	Desultory	अनियमित	Frugal
336	Detain	रोकना	Delay
337	Deteriorate	खराब होना	Worsen
338	Determined	निर्धारित	Resolved, Resolute
339	Detractors	आलोचक	Critics
340	Detrimental	हानिकारक	Harmful
341	Deviate	पथभ्रष्ट	Veer
342	Dictator	तानाशाह	Tyrant
343	Diffidence	संकोच	Meekness
344	Dilemma	दुविधा	Predicament
345	Diminutive	छोटा सा	Petite
346	Disastrous	अनर्थकारी	Calamitous
347	Discern	पहचानना	Discriminate, Perceive
348	Discontent	असंतोष	Dissatisfaction
349	Discover	खोजना	Find
350	Discriminate	भेदभाव	Distinguish
351	Disease	रोग	Illness
352	Disgrace	कलंक	Dishonour
353	Disgust	घृणा	Dislike
354	Disheartened	निराश	Depressed
355	Dishevel	बिखेरना	Clutter
356	Disparity	असमानता	Difference
357	Disproportionately	अनुपातहीन	Unreasonably
358	Disrupt	भंग करना	Break, Disturb
359	Disseminate	फैलाना	Disperse
360	Distaste	अरुचि, पूर्ण	Loathing
361	Distasteful	अरुचिकर	Unpleasant
362	Divisive	बांटने वाला	Conflicting

S.N.	Word (Hindi Meaning)	Hindi Meaning	Synonyms
363	Divulge	भेद खोलना	Reveal
364	Dodge	चकमा देना	Avoid
365	Dour	रूखा, बेदर्द	Morose
366	Drag	खींचना	Pull
367	Dreaded	भयानक	Feared
368	Drivel	बकवास	Blather
369	Drizzle	बूंदा बांदी	Sprinkle
370	Drowsy	निद्रालु	Sleepy
371	Duct	नलिका	Canal
372	Dulcet	मीठा	Sweet
373	Duo	जोड़ी	Pair
374	Duplication	प्रतिलिपि	Copying
375	Earn	कमाना	Achieve
376	Ebb	अवनति	Sink
377	Ebullient	जोशीला	Enthusiastic
378	Echelon	उपाधि	Rank
379	Eclectic	चयनशील	Diverse
380	Economical	किफ़ायती	Thrifty
381	Ecstasy	परमानंद	Joy, Happiness
382	Efface	खत्म करना	Abolish
383	Effect	नतीजा	Result
384	Efficiency	दक्षता	Capability
385	Effigy	पुतला	Dummy
386	Elapsed	गुजर चुके	Ceased
387	Elastic	लोचदार	Flexible
388	Elegant	सुंदर	Graceful
389	Eliminate	निकालना	Remove, Exclude
390	Elope	भागना	Abscond
391	Elude	बच निकलना	Escape
392	Elusive	मायावी	Intangible, Baffling
393	Emancipate	स्वतंत्र करना	Liberate
394	Embargo	पाबंदी	Barrier
395	Embed	गाड़ना	Bury
396	Embezzle	गबन करना	Misappropriate

S.N.	Word (Hindi Meaning)	Hindi Meaning	Synonyms
397	Emblem	प्रतीक	Symbol
398	Embrace	स्वीकार करना	Accept
399	Embroil	उलझना	Confuse
400	Emit	उत्सर्जित करना	Discharge
401	Emphasize	ज़ोर देना	Stress, Significance
402	Emphatic	जोरदार	Firm
403	Empirical	प्रयोगात्मक	Practical
404	Emulate	अनुकरण करना	Imitate
405	Encroach	अतिक्रमण	Intrude
406	Encumbrance	रुकावट, बाधा	Obstacle
407	Engage	व्यस्त रखना	Occupy
408	Engross	तल्लीन	Absorb
409	Engulf	निगल जाना	Envelop, Inundate
410	Enhance	बेहतर करना	Improve
411	Enigma	पहेली	Puzzle, Riddle
412	Enjoyable	आनंदमय	Delightful
413	Enliven	सजीव करना	Cheer
414	Ennui	नीरसता	Boredom
415	Enormous	विशाल	Immense, Huge, Massive
416	Enrage	क्रोधित करना	Infuriate
417	Entangle	फंसाना	Implicate
418	Enthrall	मंत्रमुग्ध करना	Mesmerize, Enchant
419	Entice	लुभाना	Lure, Entrap
420	Enunciate	स्पष्ट उच्चारण करना	Articulate
421	Equanimity	समभाव, शांत	Calm
422	Erect	उठाना	Raise
423	Errand	कार्य	Assignment
424	Erroneous	ग़लत	False, Invalid, Wrong, Inaccurate
425	Erstwhile	भूतपूर्व	Former
426	Espionage	जासूसी	Spying
427	Essential	आवश्यक	Vital
428	Esteem	आदर	Regard
429	Estimate	अनुमान	Assess
430	Estranged	अलग-थलग	Separated

S.N.	Word (Hindi Meaning)	Hindi Meaning	Synonyms
431	Ethical	नैतिक	Equitable
432	Eulogy	गुणगान	Praise
433	Eventually	आखिरकार	Finally
434	Everlasting	चिरस्थायी	Eternal
435	Evidence	सबूत	Indication
436	Evident	प्रत्यक्ष	Clear
437	Exalt	प्रशंसा करना	Praise
438	Exasperate	भड़काना	Infuriate
439	Exceed	ज्यादा होना	Surpass
440	Excerpt	अंश	Extract
441	Excogitate	ईजाद करना	Invent
442	Execrate	कोसना	Curse
443	Execute	पालन करना	Implement
444	Exempt	मुक्त, छूट	Immune, Exclude
445	Exhaustible	समाप्त हो जानेवाला	Temporary
446	Exhort	उकसाना	Pressure
447	Expandable	लचीला	Flexible
448	Expensive	मूल्यवान	Dear
449	Explicit	स्पष्ट	Clear, Lucid
450	Expose	बेनकाब	Reveal
451	Extract	निकालना	Withdraw
452	Extricate	मुक्त करना	Free, Remove
453	Extrovert	बहिर्मुखी	Talkative
454	Exuberant	उत्सुक	Eager
455	Exude	रिसना, टपकना	Ooze
456	Exultation	उल्लास	Jubilation
457	Fabulous	शानदार	Marvellous
458	Façade	मुखैटा	Frontage
459	Facility	कौशल	Skill
460	Facsimile	नकल	Replica
461	Fanatic	कट्टर	Enthusiast
462	Fare (V)	प्रगति करना	Progress
463	Fascinate	मंत्र मुग्ध करना	Captivate
464	Fascinating	आकर्षक	Appealing

S.N.	Word (Hindi Meaning)	Hindi Meaning	Synonyms
465	Fascination	आकर्षण	Appeal
466	Fasten	बान्धना	Affix
467	Fatal	जानलेवा	Deadly
468	Fatuous	मूर्ख	Silly, Irrational
469	Favoured	पसंदीदा	Preferred
470	Feign	बहाना करना	Pretend
471	Felicitated	सम्मानित	Congratulated
472	Festivity	उत्सव का समय	Celebration
473	Fetch	लाना	Bring
474	Fiction	कल्पना	Fantasy
475	Fillip	प्रोत्साहन	Boost
476	Filthy	गंदा	Dirty
477	Fissure	दरार	Cleavage
478	Flabbergasted	स्तंभित	Dumbfounded, Astonished
479	Flair	विशिष्ट योग्यता	Talent
480	Flaunt	दिखावा	Exhibit
481	Fledgling	अनुभवहीन मनुष्य	Apprentice
482	Fleeting	अस्थायी, क्षणभंगुर	Momentary, Brief
483	Float	बहना, तैरना	Slide
484	Flung	छितराना, फेकना	Threw
485	Fluorescent	चमक	Glowing
486	Flutter	स्पंदन	Flicker
487	Foliage	वनस्पति	Greenery
488	Foment	भड़काना	Incite
489	Forbid	रोकना	Ban, Preclude, Prohibit
490	Foreboding	पूर्वाभास	Alarm
491	Forego	त्यागना	Leave, Give Up
492	Forgive	माफ करना	Pardon
493	Forsaken	छोड़ा हुआ	Abandoned
494	Forswear	शपथपूर्वक त्यागना	Forsake
495	Forthright	मुँहफट	Outspoken
496	Fossilize	मिलकर पत्थर बन जाना	Amalgamate
497	Foundation	आधार	Base

S.N.	Word (Hindi Meaning)	Hindi Meaning	Synonyms
498	Fowl	पक्षी	Bird
499	Foyer	प्रवेश कक्ष	Lobby
500	Frantic	उत्तेजित	Violent
501	Fraternise	सहयोगी	Associate
502	Fraudulent	कपटपूर्ण	Deceitful
503	Freelance	अत्मनिर्भर, स्वच्छंद	Self-Employed
504	Frontier	सीमा	Boundary
505	Fruitful	फलदायक	Productive
506	Fundamental	आधारभूत	Basic
507	Furbish	चमक लाना	Shine
508	Furtive	गुप्त	Secretive
509	Fury	रोष	Anger
510	Fuse	मिलना, जोड़ना	Combine
511	Fustian	अभिमानी	Arrogant
512	Futility	निरर्थकता	Uselessness
513	Gaff	गुप्त तरीका	Trick
514	Gambol	उछल कूद करना	Frisk
515	Garble	तोड़ना-मोड़ना	Confuse
516	Garnish	सजाना	Adorn
517	Gasp	हांफना	Fight for Breath
518	Gaudy	भड़कीला	Flashy
519	Generic	सामान्य	Universal
520	Genre	शैली, प्रकार	Category
521	Glare	चमक	Dazzle
522	Gleam	प्रकाश की किरण, मंद प्रभा	Sheen, Shine
523	Glib	चालाक	Artful
524	Glorious	शानदार	Splendid
525	Glum	उदास	Dismal
526	Gnome	बौना	Dwarf
527	Gospel	धर्म शिक्षा	Faith
528	Gourmet	पेटू	Gastronome
529	Grab	लपकना	Catch, Seize
530	Grandeur	शानदार	Magnificence

S.N.	Word (Hindi Meaning)	Hindi Meaning	Synonyms
531	Grasp	पकड़ना	Clinch
532	Gratification	संतुष्टि	Satisfaction
533	Gratuitous	अकारण	Spontaneous
534	Grave	गंभीर	Serious
535	Gravity	गंभीरता	Depth
536	Greet	नमस्कार	Welcome
537	Grim	निर्दय	Stern
538	Grisly	भयानक	Gruesome
539	Groan	कराहना	Grumble
540	Grudging	ईर्ष्यालु	Envious
541	Gruff	कर्कश	Rough
542	Grumble	बड़बड़ाना	Complain, Murmur, Groan
543	Gullibility	भोलापन	Simplicity
544	Hackneyed	घिसा-पिटा	Tired
545	Hallucination	मतिभ्रम	Delusion
546	Hamper (V)	बाधा डालना	Hinder, Restrict
547	Hapless	अभाग	Unlucky
548	Happiness	खुशी	Bliss
549	Hard	कठिन	Difficult
550	Hardly	मुश्किल से	Barely
551	Hardship	कष्ट	Misery
552	Hate	नफरत	Detest
553	Haughty	घमंडी	Conceited, Arrogant
554	Hazardous	खतरनाक	Dangerous, Risky
555	Hearsay	अफ़वाह	Buzz
556	Herald	संदेशवाहक, घोषणा	Messenger, Announce
557	Herculean	बलशाली	Strong
558	Heretic	विधर्मी	Cynic
559	Hind	पिछला	Rear
560	Holistic	संपूर्ण रूप से	Comprehensive
561	Honour	सम्मान	Respect
562	Hoodwink	आंख में धूल झोंकना	Deceive, Cheat, Defraud
563	Horrid	भयंकर	Offensive
564	Hound	शिकारी कुत्ता	Beagle

S.N.	Word (Hindi Meaning)	Hindi Meaning	Synonyms
565	Howl	चिल्लाना	Wail
566	Huge	विशाल	Big
567	Humdrum	नीरस	Monotonous, Boring
568	Humiliation	निरादर	Dishonour
569	Humorous	हास्यपूर्ण	Witty
570	Hurdle	बाधा	Obstacle
571	Hybrid	मिश्र प्रजाति	Composite
572	Hyperbole	अतिश्योक्ति	Overstatement
573	Hysteria	पागलपन	Madness
574	Iconic	आदर्श	Exemplary
575	Identical	समान	Same, Similar
576	Ideology	विचारधारा	Belief
577	Idleness	आलस्य	Lethargy
578	Ignominious	शर्मिंदा करने वाला	Disgraceful
579	Ignominy	कलंक	Disgrace
580	Ill-Bred	असभ्य	Uncouth
581	Imaginary	काल्पनिक	Fictitious
582	Imbecile	मूर्ख	Idiot, Foolish
583	Imitate	नकल	Copy, Ape, Mimic
584	Imitation	नकली	Artificial, Fake
585	Immerse	डुबो देना	Submerge
586	Imminent	निकटस्थ	Forthcoming
587	Impair	कमजोर करना	Weakness
588	Impediment	बाधा	Obstruction
589	Imperial	साम्राज्य संबंधी	Sovereign
590	Impervious	अभेद्य	Impenetrable
591	Impetus	प्रेरणा	Encouragement
592	Impious	अधर्मी	Irreverent, Irreligious
593	Implicit	अंतर्निहित	Tacit, Unspoken
594	Implore	विनती करना	Plead
595	Impolite	रूखा	Rude
596	Importune	जिद करना	Appeal
597	Impost	चुंगी	Tax
598	Imprudent	बेपरवाह	Careless

S.N.	Word (Hindi Meaning)	Hindi Meaning	Synonyms
599	Inadvertent	बेपरवाह	Unintentional
600	Inanition	भोजन के कमी की वजह से सुस्ती	Lethargy
601	Inarticulate	अस्पष्ट	Incoherent
602	Incensed	क्रोधित	Exasperated
603	Inception	आरंभ	Beginning
604	Incessantly	निरंतर	Continuously, Steadily
605	Inclination	रुझान	Aptitude
606	Incumbent	आवश्यक	Required
607	Index	सूची	Guide
608	Indictment	अभियोग	Accusation
609	Indignation	रोष	Anger
610	Indiscreet	असावधानीपूर्ण	Careless
611	Indissoluble	स्थायी	Permanent
612	Indistinguishable	समरूप	Equivalent
613	Indulgence	अनुग्रह	Leniency
614	Ineffable	अवर्णनीय	Inexpressible
615	Ineluctable	अनिवार्य	Irremovable
616	Inexpensive	सस्ता	Cheap
617	Infamy	बदनामी	Notoriety
618	Infatuation	मुग्धता	Passion
619	Inference	निष्कर्ष	Conclusion
620	Infructuous	निष्फल	Fruitless
621	Infuriate	क्रोधित करना	Enrage
622	Infuse	उड़ेलना	Fill
623	Ingenuous	निष्कपट	Innocent, Candid
624	Inhibitor	अवरोध करनेवाला	Determent
625	Inimical	विरोधी	Harmful, Hostile
626	Innuendo	इशारा	Implication
627	Insane	पागल	Crazy, Mad
628	Insensitive	असंवेदनशील	Callous
629	Insidious	घातक	Crafty
630	Insignia	प्रतीक चिह्न	Symbol
631	Inspire	प्रेरित करना	Animate

S.N.	Word (Hindi Meaning)	Hindi Meaning	Synonyms
632	Instigate	भड़काना	Kindle
633	Insult	अपमान	Offend
634	Insuperable	अजेय	Insurmountable
635	Integrant	अविभाज्य	Item
636	Integrate	जोड़ना	Unite, Assimilate
637	Intensify	सशक्त करना	Strengthen
638	Interdiction	निषेध आज्ञा	Decree
639	Interference	दखल अंदाजी	Obstruction, Barring
640	Interrogate	पूछताछ	Investigate
641	Interspersed	छितराया हुआ	Scattered
642	Intricate	जटिल	Complex, Complicated
643	Intriguing	लुभावना, साज़िश	Gripping
644	Invariable	स्थिर	Constant
645	Invective	अपशब्द	Abusive
646	Inventory	सामान सूची	Catalogue
647	Investigate	जांच करना	Search, Examine
648	Invidious	अपमानजनक	Hateful
649	Invigorating	स्फूर्तिदायक	Refreshing
650	Invoice	चालान	Statement
651	Iota	कण	Bit
652	Irregular	अनियमित	Uneven
653	Irreproachable	त्रुटिहीन	Faultless
654	Irresolute	अनिश्चित	Undecided
655	Irreverence	अपमान	Disrespect
656	Irrevocable	अटल	Unalterable
657	Isolate	अलग	Detach, Secluded
658	Jabber	गपशप	Chatter
659	Jaded	थका हुआ	Tired
660	Jangle	झगड़ा	Disagree
661	Jealous	ईर्ष्या	Envied, Envious
662	Jeopardy	खतरा	Risk, Peril
663	Jovial	आनन्दित	Joyous
664	Jubilation	आनंदोत्सव	Rejoicing
665	Junk	कचरा	Waste

S.N.	Word (Hindi Meaning)	Hindi Meaning	Synonyms
666	Juvenile	लड़कपन	Childish
667	Keen	उत्सुक	Eager
668	Kinship	रिश्तेदारी	Relationship
669	Kiosk	गुमटी, छोटी दुकान	Store
670	Kit	साज-सामान	Equipment
671	Knave	धूर्त	Scoundrel
672	Knavish	कपटी, बेईमान	Unscrupulous
673	Labyrinth	भूलभुलैया	Meandering, Maze
674	Laconic	संक्षिप्त	Concise, Crisp, Brief
675	Laden	लदा हुआ, भरा हुआ	Full
676	Laud	प्रशंसा	Acknowledge
677	Launching	शुभारंभ	Introducing
678	Lax	लापरवाह	Negligent
679	Layout	नक्शा	Arrangement
680	Lean	दुबला	Thin
681	Leisurely	आराम से	Relaxed
682	Lethargy	सुस्ती	Drowsy
683	Level (Adj)	समान स्तरीय	Flat
684	Leverage	प्रभाव	Influence
685	Liability	देनदारी	Debt
686	Limpid	पारदर्शक	Clear, Lucid
687	Lint	रोआँ	Fur
688	Lithe	लचीला	Flexible
689	Litter	कूड़ा-कर्कट	Trash
690	Little	थोड़ा	Trivial
691	Livid	आगबबूला	Furious
692	Lofty	ऊंचा	Towering
693	Longevity	दीर्घायु	Durability
694	Longing	लालसा	Yearning
695	Lousy	घटिया	Awful, Terrible
696	Loyal	वफादार	Devoted
697	Loyalty	वफादारी	Faithfulness
698	Lucidity	स्पष्टता	Clarity
699	Lucrative	लाभप्रद	Worthwhile

S.N.	Word (Hindi Meaning)	Hindi Meaning	Synonyms
700	Lure	लुभाना	Attract
701	Lurid	सनसनीखेज	Over-Bright, Shocking
702	Lurk	घात में रहना	Sneak, Prowl
703	Luxuriant	विलासी	Abundant, Lush
704	Lyrical	गीतात्मक	Musical
705	Madness	पागलपन	Insanity
706	Maestro	माहिर	Genius
707	Magnanimous	उदार चरित्र	Charitable
708	Magnify	बढ़ा देना	Enlarge
709	Malady	बीमारी	Illness
710	Malignant	घातक	Harmful, Vicious
711	Mandate	आदेशपत्र	Official Order
712	Mandatory	अनिवार्य	Compulsory, Essential, Imperative
713	Mandible	जबड़ा	Jaw
714	Mania	उन्माद	Madness
715	Manual	नियम पुस्तिका	Handbook
716	Marvellous	अद्भुत	Wonderful
717	Masqueraded	स्वाँग रचना	Acted
718	Massive	बड़ा	Huge
719	Mastery	प्रभुत्व	Authority
720	Masticate	चबाना	Chew
721	Mayhem	अफरा तफरी	Chaos
722	Meddle	हस्तक्षेप करना	Interfere
723	Mediation	बीच बचाव	Intervention
724	Mellifluous	मधुर	Dulcet
725	Memoir	संस्मरण, वृत्तान्त	Diary
726	Menace	खतरा	Threat, Nuisance
727	Mentor	गुरु	Guide
728	Mercurial	अस्थिर	Volatile
729	Mercy	दया	Sympathy
730	Merge	मिलना	Blend
731	Mimic	अनुकरण करने वाला	Copy, Imitator
732	Mince	छोटे-छोटे टुकड़े करना	Crumble
733	Mirth	आनन्द	Delight

S.N.	Word (Hindi Meaning)	Hindi Meaning	Synonyms
734	Misfortune	आपदा	Calamity
735	Missive	राजनीतिक संदेश	Letter
736	Mistake	गलती	Error
737	Mock	उपहास करना	Taunt
738	Mollify	शांत करना	Pacify
739	Momentous	सबसे महत्वपूर्ण	Important
740	Monolithic	विशालकाय	Huge
741	Morale	हौसला	Self-Confidence
742	Mordant	व्यंग्य मिश्रित	Bitter, Sarcastic
743	Moribund	मरता हुआ	Dying
744	Mortal	मरणशील	Deadly
745	Motif	रूपरेखा	Design
746	Motive	मकसद	Intention, Reason
747	Multitude	भीड़	Mass
748	Munch	चबाना	Chew
749	Munificent	उदार	Generous
750	Nap	झपकी	Siesta
751	Nauseous	घिनौना	Loathsome
752	Neglected	उपेक्षित	Ignored
753	Negotiation	मोल भाव	Bargaining
754	Niggard	कंजूस	Miser
755	Nincompoop	मूर्ख	Foolish, Fool
756	Noble	प्रतिष्ठित	Dignified
757	Nomadic	घुमंतू	Roving, Wandering
758	Nonplussed	भौचक	Puzzled
759	Novice	नौसिखिया	Beginner
760	Noxious	हानिकारक	Harmful
761	Nudge	कुहनी से हल्के धक्का देना, आकर्षित करना	Poke
762	Numerous	बहुत	Several
763	Nurture	पालन-पोषण करना	Grow
764	Oasis	मरु उद्यान	Spring
765	Obdurate	जिद्दी	Stubborn
766	Obligation	दायित्व	Commitment

S.N.	Word (Hindi Meaning)	Hindi Meaning	Synonyms
767	Obligatory	अनिवार्य	Necessary, Mandatory
768	Obliterate	पूर्ण विनाश	Annihilate
769	Oblivious	अनजान	Ignorant
770	Obnoxious	घृणित	Disgusting
771	Obsession	जुनून	Pre-Occupation
772	Obstacle	बाधा	Barrier
773	Obstreperous	कोलाहलमय	Noisy, Unruly
774	Obstruction	बाधा	Hindrance
775	Obtain	हासिल करना	Achieve
776	Obvious	स्पष्ट	Evident
777	Occult	अलौकिक	Supernatural
778	Occur	घटित होना	Happen
779	Odious	अप्रिय	Hateful
780	Offend	परेशान करना	Annoy
781	Omniscient	अंतर्यामी	All-Knowing
782	Onerous	कठिन	Arduous
783	Onus	दायित्व	Responsibility, Burden
784	Opinion	विचार	View, Idea
785	Opportune	समय पर	Timely
786	Optimist	आशावादी	Idealist
787	Oracular	रहस्यमय	Cryptic
788	Ossify	हड्डी बन जाना	Make or become like a bone
789	Ostentatious	भड़कीला, आडंबरपूर्ण	Flashy
790	Outraged	बेहद नाराज	Angry
791	Ovation	अभिनंदन	Applause
792	Over	समाप्त	Bygone
793	Oversee	निरीक्षण करना	Supervise
794	Overwhelmed	व्याकुल, अभिभूत	Surprised, Awesome
795	Pacific	शांत	Peaceful
796	Pail	बाल्टी	Bucket
797	Pale	फीका	Colourless
798	Palliate	कम करना	Relieve
799	Pallid	पीला पड़ना	Pale
800	Panacea	रामबाण इलाज	Cure-All

S.N.	Word (Hindi Meaning)	Hindi Meaning	Synonyms
801	Panic	उन्माद	Frenzy
802	Panorama	चारों ओर का दृश्य	Scene
803	Paranoid	शंकास्पद	Suspicious
804	Parity	समानता	Closeness
805	Parsimony	कंजूसी	Miserliness, Frugality
806	Passion	जुनून	Desire
807	Pathetic	दयनीय	Pitiful
808	Pathos	करुणा	Sorrow
809	Patrol	पहरा देना	Inspect
810	Patron	प्रायोजक	Sponsor
811	Pawn	गिरवी रखना	Pledge
812	Pedigree	वंशावली	Lineage
813	Pejorative	अपमानजनक	Derogatory
814	Penchant	विशेष रुचि	Liking, Fondness
815	Pensive	चिंताग्रस्त	Reflective
816	Perceive	जानना समझना	Notice, Recognise
817	Perdurable	चिरस्थायी	Long-Lasting
818	Perennial	चिरस्थायी	Lasting
819	Perfidious	बेका	Disloyal
820	Perforate	छिद्र करना	Pierce
821	Periodic	नियमित	Regular
822	Perish	मर जाना	Die, Decease
823	Perky	प्रफुल्लित	Cheerful
824	Perpetuate	स्थायी बनाना	Preserve
825	Perplex	हैरान करना	Bewilder
826	Perquisite	विशेषाधिकार	Privilege
827	Persecution	अत्याचार	Oppression
828	Perseverance	दृढ़ता	Endurance
829	Persevere	दृढ़ रहना	Persist
830	Perspicacious	चतुर	Shrewd
831	Perspicuous	सुगम	Precise
832	Pert	आकर्षक	Lively
833	Peruse	ध्यान से पढ़ना	Examine, Read
834	Perverse	विकृत	Nefarious

S.N.	Word (Hindi Meaning)	Hindi Meaning	Synonyms
835	Pester	परेशान करना	Annoy
836	Petition	याचिका	Appeal
837	Petrify	पत्थर बनाना	Harden
838	Phonetic	ध्वनि-संबंधी	Spoken
839	Pillage	डाका डालना	Desecrate
840	Pioneer	पथप्रदर्शक	Primary
841	Piquancy	चटपटापन	Flavouring
842	Pitfall	खतरा	Hazard
843	Pithy	संक्षिप्त	Brief
844	Pity	दया	Mercy
845	Plaudit	प्रशंसा	Praise
846	Plea	दलील	Appeal
847	Plead	निवेदन	Request
848	Pleasant	सुखदायक	Amusing, Refreshing
849	Pleasure	आनंद	Happiness
850	Plebiscite	जनमत संग्रह	Referendum
851	Pledged	प्रतिज्ञा करना	Promised
852	Plentiful	प्रचुर	Ample
853	Plight	दुर्दशा	Difficulty
854	Plod	थके कदमों से चलना	Drag
855	Plump	मोटा	Fat
856	Poach	अवैध शिकार करना	Hunt
857	Podium	मंच	Dais
858	Poignant	मार्मिक	Emotional, Sad, Touching
859	Pollute	दूषित	Contaminate
860	Pollution	प्रदूषण	Contamination
861	Ponder	विचार करना	Meditate
862	Popular	लोकप्रिय	Favourite
863	Posterior	पीठ-संबंधी	Dorsal
864	Potent	शक्तिशाली	Powerful
865	Practical	व्यावहारिक	Sensible
866	Pragmatic	व्यावहारिक	Realistic
867	Preamble	प्रस्तावना	Introduction
868	Precedence	प्रधानता	Priority

S.N.	Word (Hindi Meaning)	Hindi Meaning	Synonyms
869	Precision	सटीक	Accuracy
870	Preferred	पसंदीदा	Favoured
871	Prejudice	पक्षपात करना	Bias
872	Premonition	पूर्व-सूचना	Forewarning
873	Preponderance	प्रभुत्व	Dominance
874	Presumptuous	अभिमानी	Arrogant
875	Pretend	बहाना करना	Feign
876	Prevalent	प्रचलित	Common
877	Preventive	निवारक	Protective
878	Primitive	प्राचीन	Basic, Ancient
879	Principle	सिद्धांत	Axiom
880	Priority	प्राथमिकता	Precedence, Preference
881	Proactive	अग्रसक्रिय	Enthusiastic
882	Probe	जाँच	Investigate
883	Proclaim	घोषित करना	Declare
884	Procure	प्राप्त करना	Obtain
885	Prodigal	फिजूलखर्ची	Wasteful, Lavish, Extravagant
886	Prodigious	अति विशाल	Immense
887	Prodigy	प्रतिभाशाली	Genius
888	Profane	असभ्य	Coarse
889	Profess	दावा करना	Admit
890	Profligate	अपव्ययी	Wasteful, Immoral
891	Prognosis	पूर्वानुमान	Forecast
892	Prohibition	निषेध	Exclusion
893	Proliferate	पैदा करना	Reproduce
894	Prolific	फलदायक	Productive
895	Promiscuous	अविवेकी	Indiscriminate
896	Promising	आशाजनक	Bright
897	Promotion	तरक्की	Elevation
898	Prophylactic	रोगनिरोधी	Preventive
899	Propinquity	निकटता	Nearness
900	Propitiate	संतुष्ट करना	Appease
901	Propitious	अनुकूल	Hopeful
902	Proposition	प्रस्ताव	Proposal

S.N.	Word (Hindi Meaning)	Hindi Meaning	Synonyms
903	Proscribe	बहिष्कार करना	Ban
904	Protest	विरोध	Oppose, Object
905	Protrude	उभरा होना	Bulge
906	Provoke	उत्तेजित करना	Enrage
907	Proximity	निकटता	Closeness
908	Purge	शुद्ध करना	Evacuate
909	Puzzled	उलझा हुआ	Confused
910	Quack	ठग	Fake
911	Quake	काँपना	Tremble
912	Quarantine	अलग करना	Isolation
913	Quarrelsome	झगड़ालु	Querulous
914	Quarry	शिकार	Victim
915	Quest	तलाश	Search
916	Quicken	शीघ्र करना	Accelerate
917	Quiver	काँपना	Tremble, Shake
918	Rabid	कट्टर, दिवाना	Extreme
919	Radical	पूर्ण, उग्र	Absolute, Profound
920	Ragged	फटा पुराना	Torn
921	Rambling	दूर तक फैला हुआ	Long-Winded
922	Ramification	जटिल, अनपेक्षित परिणाम	Consequence
923	Rampant	अनियंत्रित	Excessive
924	Random	अनियमित	Arbitrary
925	Rapid	तेज	Quick
926	Rapturous	आनन्दित	Delighted
927	Rare	दुर्लभ	Scarce
928	Ravage	बरबाद कर देना	Demolish, Damage
929	Ravine	दर्रा	Abyss
930	Realm	क्षेत्र	Field, Dimension
931	Recapitulation	संक्षिप्त	Recall, Summary
932	Recently	हाल में	Lately
933	Receptacle	पात्र	Container
934	Recipients	प्राप्तकर्ता	Receivers
935	Reckless	लापरवाह	Thoughtless, Rash

S.N.	Word (Hindi Meaning)	Hindi Meaning	Synonyms
936	Recollect	याद करना	Remember
937	Recommend	सिफारिश	Approve
938	Reconcile	समझौता कराना	Resolve
939	Recover	पुनः प्राप्त करना	Regain
940	Redeem	मुक्त करना	Save
941	Redundancy	फालतूपन	Excess
942	Refuge	शरण	Shelter
943	Regard	सम्मान	Respect
944	Regime	शासन	Authority, Rule
945	Regress	पीछे हटना	Backslide
946	Regular	नियमित	Usual
947	Reiterate	दोहराना	Repeat
948	Rejuvenate	फिर से युवा करना	Update, Refresh
949	Release	रिहाई	Acquit
950	Relevant	उपयुक्त	Applicable
951	Reliable	भरोसेमंद	Trusted, Dependable
952	Relief	राहत	Aid
953	Relish	आनंद	Enjoy, Adore
954	Reluctant	अनिच्छुक	Unwilling
955	Rely	निर्भर होना	Depend
956	Remedial	उपचारात्मक	Corrective
957	Remedy	उपचार	Cure
958	Reminisce	याद दिलाना	Remember
959	Renown	प्रसिद्ध	Fame
960	Repartee	हाजिर जवाबी	Response
961	Repeal	रद्द करना	Cancellation
962	Repeated	दोहराया गया	Reiterated
963	Repel	पीछे हटाना	Drive away, Resist
964	Repercussion	प्रतिक्रिया	Reaction
965	Replaced	बदला गया	Substituted
966	Replenish	फिर से भरना	Restore
967	Replete	परिपूर्ण	Full
968	Repose	आराम करना	Rest
969	Reproach	धिक्कारना	Berate

S.N.	Word (Hindi Meaning)	Hindi Meaning	Synonyms
970	Reproof	फटकार लगाना	Rebuke
971	Reprove	निंदा करना	Scold
972	Repudiate	त्याग करना	Renounce
973	Repugnance	घृणा	Aversion
974	Repulsive	घिनौना	Disgusting
975	Request	निवेदन	Ask
976	Requisite	आवश्यक	Obligatory, Precondition
977	Rescind	रद्द कर देना	Revoke
978	Resilient	लचीला	Supple
979	Resistant	अवरोध	Opposing
980	Resolution	संकल्प	Decision
981	Respite	विराम	Hiatus
982	Resplendent	चमकीला	Dazzling
983	Restive	अशांत	Restless
984	Restrain	नियंत्रित करना	Control
985	Restrict	रोकना	Prohibit
986	Result	परिणाम	Outcome
987	Resurgence	नवीनीकरण	Renewal
988	Retaliate	बदला लेना	Avenge
989	Reticence	शांत रहना	Reserve
990	Retort	प्रत्युत्तर	Reply
991	Retrieve	वापस पा लेना	Recover
992	Revamp	मरम्मत करना	Restructure
993	Revelation	रहस्योद्घाटन	Break
994	Revenue	राजस्व	Income
995	Revere	आदर करना	Respect
996	Reverie	विचारों में खोना	Day-Dream
997	Revile	गाली देना	Abuse
998	Revolt	विद्रोह	Riot
999	Rhythm	ताल	Tempo
1000	Riddle	पहेली	Puzzle
1001	Rift	टूटना	Break
1002	Right	सही	Correct
1003	Rind	छिलका	Peel

S.N.	Word (Hindi Meaning)	Hindi Meaning	Synonyms
1004	Rip	फाड़ना	Tear
1005	Rivalled	प्रतिद्वंद्वी होना	Competed
1006	Rivet	स्थिर रखना	Engage
1007	Rotund	गोल-मटोल	Round
1008	Rough	खुरदरा	Coarse
1009	Rout	घोर पराजय	Defeat
1010	Rowdy	फसादी	Boisterous
1011	Royal	राजकीय	Kingly
1012	Ruck	जनसाधारण	Mass
1013	Rumour	अफवाह	Hearsay
1014	Ruse	चाल	Trick
1015	Saga	गाथा	Narrative
1016	Salacious	कामातुर	Lustful
1017	Salvage	बचाना	Save
1018	Sanction	मंजूरी	Approval, Permit
1019	Sane	समझदार	Sensible
1020	Sarcastic	व्यंग्यात्मक	Arrogant
1021	Sauciness	ढिठाई	Impudence
1022	Savour	स्वाद	Taste
1023	Scandalized	स्तंभित करना	Shocked
1024	Scatter	तितर-बितर	Disperse
1025	Scintillating	चमकता हुआ	Glittering
1026	Scion	वंशज	Heir
1027	Scorn	घृणा करना	Condemn, Despise, Mockery
1028	Scour	पिसना	Scrub
1029	Scowl	भौंह चढ़ाना	Frown
1030	Scrap	अस्वीकार करना	Reject
1031	Scrawny	दुबला पतला	Skinny
1032	Scream	चीखना	Cry
1033	Scrumptious	स्वादिष्ट	Tasty, Delicious
1034	Scurrility	अति दुष्ट व्यवहार	Atrocity
1035	Scuttle	जल्दी बाजी में चलना	Scamper
1036	Secure (Verb)	सुरक्षित	Protect

S.N.	Word (Hindi Meaning)	Hindi Meaning	Synonyms
1037	Selection	चयन	Preference, Choice, Selecting, Election, Choosing, Picking, Decision, Option, Nomination
1038	Serious	गंभीर	Earnest, Earnest, Grave, Sedate, Sober, Solemn, Staid
1039	Severity	कठिनाई	Seriousness
1040	Sham	बनावटी	Fake, Pretence, Fake, Act, Fiction, Simulation, Imposture Fraud, Feint, Lie
1041	Sheath	आवरण	Coat, Arrayed, Attired, Clothed, Covered, Dressed, Face, Garbed, Robed
1042	Shimmer	चमकना	Shine, Glint, Glisten, Flicker, Twinkle, Sparkle, Flash, Scintillate, Flare, Glare
1043	Shine	चमक	Glitter
1044	Shove	ठेलना	Poke, Push, Thrust, Propel Impel, Send, Press, Drive, Plunge Stick, Force, Shoot, Ram, Barge Bump, Knock, Strike, Hit, Jolt
1045	Shrewd	धूर्त/चतुर	Judicious
1046	Shriek	चिल्लाकर बोलना	Yell
1047	Shudder	कांपना	Shiver
1048	Shuffle	हेर फेर	Stagger
1049	Silt	अवसाद	Residue
1050	Similar	समरूप	Alike
1051	Sinuous	टेढ़ा मेढ़ा	Serpentine
1052	Slack	ढीला	Feeble, Careless
1053	Slither	सरकते हुए जाना	Slide
1054	Smear	धब्बा	Discolour
1055	Smudge	धब्बा	Stain
1056	Snaky	टेढ़ा मेढ़ा	Sinuous
1057	Snooze	झपकी लेना	Sleep
1058	Sole	एकमात्र	Only
1059	Solemn	गंभीर	Pensive, Serious
1060	Solid	दृढ़	Firm
1061	Solitary	अकेला	Lonely, Singular

S.N.	Word (Hindi Meaning)	Hindi Meaning	Synonyms
1062	Sombre	निराशाजनक	Gloomy
1063	Somnolent	निद्राजनक	Drowsy
1064	Soothe	शांत करना	Mollify
1065	Spectrum	विस्तृत श्रेणी	Range
1066	Speculate	अनुमान लगाना	Guess
1067	Spell Bound	सम्मोहित	Enthralled
1068	Spill	गिरना	Drop
1069	Spine	रीढ़ की हड्डी	Vertebrae
1070	Spirited	साहसी	Ardent, Enthusiastic
1071	Spontaneous	स्वाभाविक	Impulsive
1072	Sporadic	छिट पुट	Scattered, Occasional
1073	Spruce	सजाना	Smart, Natty, Neat, Well groomed, Well turned out, Well dressed, Besuited, Smart, Trim, Dapper, Snazzy, Spiffy, Trig
1074	Spume	झाग	Foams
1075	Spunky	साहसी	Enthusiastic
1076	Spurn	तिरस्कार करना	Despise
1077	Startled	आश्चर्यचकित	Amazed
1078	Steady	नियमित	Abiding, Stable
1079	Stentorian	बुलन्द	Extremely Loud
1080	Stimulation	उत्तेजना	Provocation
1081	Stoical	उदासीन	Apathetic
1082	Stray	भटक जाना, बेघर	Wander, Homeless
1083	Strenuous	कठिन प्रयास	Difficult
1084	Stroll	चहलकदमी	Walk
1085	Stubborn	जिद्दी	Adamant, Obstinate
1086	Stun	चकित होना	Shock
1087	Stupor	अर्धचेतनावस्था	Slumber
1088	Sturdy	हट्टा कट्टा	Tough
1089	Stymie	रोक लगाना	Impede
1090	Subjugate	पराजित करना	Conquer
1091	Submerge	डुबोना	Drown
1092	Submissive	आज्ञाकारी	Obedient

S.N.	Word (Hindi Meaning)	Hindi Meaning	Synonyms
1093	Subside	कम होना	Descend
1094	Substitute	जगह लेना	Replace
1095	Substitution	प्रतिस्थापन	Exchange
1096	Successive	क्रमिक	Consecutive
1097	Succulent	रसीला	Juicy
1098	Suffix	अंत में जोड़ना	Addition
1099	Suitable	उपयुक्त	Appropriate
1100	Sullen	रूठा हुआ	Grim
1101	Sumptuous	आलीशान	Opulent
1102	Superannuated	सेवा-निवृत्त	Retired
1103	Supercilious	घमंडी	Arrogant
1104	Supernatural	अलौकिक	Mystical
1105	Supersede	निकाल फेंकना	Set Aside
1106	Superstitious	अंधविश्वासी	Irrational
1107	Supporting	सहायक	Agreeing
1108	Supreme	सर्वोच्च	Head, Matchless
1109	Surge	तेजी से चढ़ना	Rush
1110	Surly	कर्कश और अमित्रतापूर्ण	Unfriendly
1111	Surmount	काबू पाना	Overcome
1112	Survey	सर्वेक्षण	Examine
1113	Sustain	बनाए रखना	Continue, Support
1114	Swap	अदला बदली	Exchange
1115	Sycophant	चापलूस	Flatterer
1116	Symptomatic	लक्षणात्मक	Characteristic
1117	Systematically	व्यवस्थित ढंग से	Methodically
1118	Taboo	निषेध	Unacceptable
1119	Tackle	निपटना	Deal
1120	Tag (N)	उपनाम	Label
1121	Tame	पालतू	Domesticated
1122	Tangled	उलझा हुआ	Knotted
1123	Tarnish	कलंकित करना	Damage
1124	Temerity	ढिठाई	Audacity, Boldness
1125	Temperate	संतुलित	Moderate

S.N.	Word (Hindi Meaning)	Hindi Meaning	Synonyms
1126	Tempest	तूफान	Storm
1127	Tenacity	दृढता	Firmness
1128	Tend (V)	देखभाल करना	Care For
1129	Tenet	धारणा	Belief
1130	Tensile	तन्य	Stretchable
1131	Tension	तनाव	Strain
1132	Tenuous	सूक्ष्म	Thin
1133	Tepid	गुनगुना	Warm
1134	Termination	समाप्ति	Conclusion
1135	Terse	संक्षिप्त	Brief
1136	Testify	गवाही देना	Announce, Affirm
1137	Threat	खतरा	Risk
1138	Thrifty	किफायती	Economical, Frugal
1139	Tilt	झुकाव	Slant
1140	Tinsel	सजाना	Decoration, Garnish
1108	Supreme	सर्वोच्च	Head, Matchless
1109	Surge	तेजी से चढ़ना	Rush
1110	Surly	कर्कश और अमित्रतापूर्ण	Unfriendly
1111	Surmount	काबू पाना	Overcome
1112	Survey	सर्वेक्षण	Examine
1113	Sustain	बनाए रखना	Continue, Support
1114	Swap	अदला बदली	Exchange
1115	Sycophant	चापलूस	Flatterer
1116	Symptomatic	लक्षणात्मक	Characteristic
1117	Systematically	व्यवस्थित ढंग से	Methodically
1118	Taboo	निषेध	Unacceptable
1119	Tackle	निपटना	Deal
1120	Tag (N)	उपनाम	Label
1121	Tame	पालतू	Domesticated
1122	Tangled	उलझा हुआ	Knotted
1123	Tarnish	कलंकित करना	Damage
1124	Temerity	ढिठाई	Audacity, Boldness
1125	Temperate	संतुलित	Moderate

S.N.	Word (Hindi Meaning)	Hindi Meaning	Synonyms
1126	Tempest	तूफान	Storm
1127	Tenacity	दृढ़ता	Firmness
1128	Tend (V)	देखभाल करना	Care For
1129	Tenet	धारणा	Belief
1130	Tensile	तन्य	Stretchable
1131	Tension	तनाव	Strain
1132	Tenuous	सूक्ष्म	Thin
1133	Tepid	गुनगुना	Warm
1134	Termination	समाप्ति	Conclusion
1135	Terse	संक्षिप्त	Brief
1136	Testify	गवाही देना	Announce, Affirm
1137	Threat	खतरा	Risk
1138	Thrifty	किफायती	Economical, Frugal
1139	Tilt	झुकाव	Slant
1140	Tinsel	सजाना	Decoration, Garnish
1141	Tirade	कड़ी निंदा	Rant
1142	To admonish	फटकार लगाना	To Reprimand
1143	To astound	चकित करना	To Bewilder
1144	To confront	सामना करना	To Accost
1145	To reproach	फटकारना	To Admonish
1146	Toil	कठिन परिश्रम	Work Hard, Sweat
1147	Toilsome	कष्टमय	Tiresome
1148	Tolerance	सहनशक्ति	Endurance
1149	Torpid	निष्क्रिय	Inactive
1150	Tousled	अस्त व्यस्त	Disarranged
1151	Trail	रास्ता	Path
1152	Tramp	घुमक्कड़	Wanderer
1153	Transcend	हावी होना	Eclipse
1154	Transition	परिवर्तन	Change
1155	Transmission	परिवहन	Conveyance
1156	Transmit	प्रसारित करना	Convey
1157	Trauma	मानसिक आघात	Emotional Shock
1158	Travail	पीड़ा	Agony
1159	Treacherous	विश्वासघाती	Unfaithful

S.N.	Word (Hindi Meaning)	Hindi Meaning	Synonyms
1160	Tread	चलना	Walk
1161	Tremendous	अद्भुत	Remarkable, Huge
1162	Tribulation	पीड़ा	Suffering
1163	Trimming	कतरन	Cutting
1164	Trite	साधारण	Commonplace
1165	Trust (N)	भरोसा	Belief
1166	Tryst	भेंट	Meeting
1167	Umpteen	अनेक	Countless
1168	Unanimous	एकमत	Undisputed
1169	Uncanny	विचित्र	Mysterious
1170	Vacant	रिक्त	Bare
1171	Vagabond	आवारा	Tramp
1172	Valedictory	बिदाई का	Terminal
1173	Valuable	मूल्यवान	Precious
1174	Vanish	गायब	Disappear
1175	Velocity	वेग	Speed
1176	Venal	भ्रष्टाचारी	Corrupt
1177	Venerable	माननीय	Esteemed
1178	Venerate	सम्मानित करना	Revere
1179	Venture	जोखिम उठाना	Attempt
1180	Veracious	एकदम सही	Accurate
1181	Veracity	सच्चाई	Truth
1182	Verbatim	शब्द प्रति शब्द	Exactly
1183	Verisimilitude	सत्य का आभास	Authenticity
1184	Versatile	बहुमुखी	Flexible
1185	Viable	करने योग्य	Workable
1186	Vie	स्पर्धा करना	Compete
1187	Vindicate	साबित करना	Justify
1188	Vindictive	प्रतिशोधी	Spiteful, Revengeful
1189	Violation	उल्लंघन	Breach
1190	Virtuoso	गुणी कलाकार	Ace
1191	Visceral	शारीरिक (आंत का)	Bodily
1192	Visible	दृश्य	Apparent
1193	Vituperate	गाली देना	Abuse

S.N.	Word (Hindi Meaning)	Hindi Meaning	Synonyms
1194	Vivacious	जोशपूर्ण	Lively
1195	Vocation	पेशा	Occupation
1196	Voracious	लालची	Greedy
1197	Wander	घूमना	Roam, Deviate
1198	Wane	घटना	Decline
1199	Wastrel	खर्चीला	Spendthrift
1200	Welter	उथल-पुथल	Turmoil
1201	Whine	कराहना	Gripe
1202	Whinny	ऊँचे स्वर में	Loud
1203	Whirl (V)	घूमना	Spin
1204	Wily	धूर्त	Cunning, Artful, Crafty
1205	Winsome	मनोहर	Charming
1206	Wistful	उदास	Sorrowful
1207	Wobble	डगमगाना	Vibrate
1208	Worth	कीमत	Value
1209	Wreak	करना	Cause
1210	Wrench	झटके से खींचना	Wrest
1211	Wry	कुटिल	Crooked
1212	Yardstick	मापदंड	Standard
1213	Yearn	लालसा करना	Strong Desire, To Crave
1214	Yield	राजी होना	Submit
1215	Yield (n)	पैदावार	Harvest
1216	Yoke	घोड़े का साज	Harness
1217	Zest	उत्साह	Enthusiasm
1218	Accurate	शुद्ध	Precise, Correct, Exact
1219	Baffle	चकरा देना	Puzzle, Confuse, Perplex
1220	Laconic	संक्षिप्त	Concise, Crisp, Brief
1221	Catastrophe	तबाही, आपदा	Calamity, Tragedy, Disaster
1222	Chaos	अराजकता	Disorder, Mix-Up, Confusion, Turmoil
1223	Condemn	निंदा करना	Criticize, Punish, Denounce
1224	Defer	टालना	Postpone, Delay
1225	Erroneous	गलत	False, Invalid, Wrong, Inaccurate
1226	Hurdle	बाधा	Obstacle

S.N.	Word (Hindi Meaning)	Hindi Meaning	Synonyms
1227	Mandatory	अनिवार्य	Compulsory, Essential, Imperative
1228	Prodigal	फिजूलखर्ची	Wasteful, Lavish, Extravagant
1229	Solitary	अकेला	Lonely, Singular
1230	Wander	घूमना	Roam, Deviate
1231	Wily	धूर्त	Cunning, Artful, Crafty
1232	Achieve	पाना	Accomplish, Succeed, Accomplish
1233	Anguish	दुख, पीड़ा	Agony, Ache, Sorrow
1234	Calm	शान्त	Peaceful, Relaxed, Quiet
1235	Cantankerous	झगड़ालू	Quarrelsome
1236	Convict	अपराधी	Criminal, Culprit
1237	Dearth	अकाल	Scarcity, Shortage
1238	Deference	सम्मान	Respect, Obeisance, Compliance
1239	Detrimental	हानिकारक	Harmful
1240	Drag	खींचना	Pull
1241	Enormous	विशाल	Immense, Huge, Massive
1242	Exempt	मुक्त, छूट	Immune, Exclude
1243	Feign	बहाना करना	Pretend
1244	Forbid	रोकना	Ban, Preclude, Prohibit
1245	Fury	रोष	Anger
1246	Grumble	बड़बड़ाना	Complain, Murmur, Groan
1247	Haughty	घमंडी	Conceited, Arrogant
1248	Herald	संदेशवाहक, घोषणा	Messenger, Announce
1249	Hoodwink	आंख में धूल झोंकना	Deceive, Cheat, Defraud
1250	Imitate	नकल	Copy, Ape, Mimic
1251	Inimical	विरोधी	Harmful, Hostile
1252	Jeopardy	खतरा	Risk, Peril
1253	Massive	बड़ा	Huge
1254	Mimic	अनुकरण करने वाला	Copy, Imitator
1255	Poignant	मार्मिक	Emotional, Sad, Touching
1256	Priority	प्राथमिकता	Precedence, Preference
1257	Relish	आनंद	Enjoy, Adore
1258	Scorn	घृणा करना	Condemn, Despise, Mocker
1259	Sustain	बनाए रखना	Continue, Support
1260	Vindictive	प्रतिशोधी	Spiteful, Revengeful

S.N.	Word (Hindi Meaning)	Hindi Meaning	Synonyms
1261	Abrogate	रद्द करना	Repeal, Abolish
1262	Abuse	गाली	Scorn, Harm
1263	Accrue	इकट्ठा करना	Accumulate, Collect
1264	Acquaint	परिचय कराना	Introduce, Familiarise
1265	Adapt	अनुकूल बनाना	Adjust
1266	Adequate	पर्याप्त	Sufficient, Enough
1267	Adulation	चापलूसी	Flattery, Adoration
1268	Adversary	विरोधी	Rival, Opponent
1269	Amplify	बढ़ाना	Magnify, Boost
1270	Annihilate	विनाश करना	Destroy
1271	Annoy	झुंझला देना	Offend, Irritate
1272	Anticipate	पूर्वानुमान	Expect
1273	Antipathy	घृणा	Dislike
1274	Arduous	कठिन	Difficult, Strenuous
1275	Aroma	सुगन्ध	Scent
1276	Artful	धूर्त	Cunning, Crafty
1277	Atrocity	अत्याचार	Violence, Barbarity
1278	Attract	आकर्षित करना	Fascinate, Entice
1279	Attribute	गुण	Characteristic, Quality
1280	August	गरिमापूर्ण, भव्य	Majestic, Dignified
1281	Austere	सादा, सख्त	Strict, unadorned
1282	Banish	निर्वासित करना	Expel, Exile
1283	Bashful	संकोची	Shy
1284	Beguile	मोहना, ठगना	Deceive
1285	Belligerent	लड़ाकू	Hostile, Antagonistic
1286	Bind	बांधना	Unite, Fasten
1287	Blister	छाला	Wound, Bubble
1288	Brisk	तेज	Quick
1289	Carouse	खान पान कर आनंद मनाना	Frolic, Quaff
1290	Choosy	चयनात्मक	Selective, Picky
1291	Cogent	प्रभावशाली, निश्चयात्मक	Effective, Convincing
1292	Commotion	हल्ला गुल्ला	Disturbance, Fuss

S.N.	Word (Hindi Meaning)	Hindi Meaning	Synonyms
1293	Competent	सक्षम	Capable
1294	Complicated	जटिल	Complex
1295	Condone	ध्यान न देना	Overlook
1296	Congregation	मण्डली	Assembly, Meeting
1297	Consternation	घबराहट	Dismay
1298	Contemplation	चिंतन	Meditation, Design
1299	Contradict	खंडन	Confront, Refute
1300	Contrite	पछतावा	Regretful
1301	Covenant	प्रतिज्ञापत्र	Contract, Bond
1302	Decimated	नाश करना	Destroyed
1303	Deficiency	कमी	Inadequacy, Shortage
1304	Deluge	बाढ़	Flood, Overflow
1305	Despicable	घिनौना	Hateful, Contemptible
1306	Despondent	हताश	Dejected, Depressed
1307	Destroy	नष्ट करना	Ruin, Demolish
1308	Determined	निर्धारित	Resolved, Resolute
1309	Discern	पहचानना	Discriminate, Perceive
1310	Discover	खोजना	Find
1311	Disrupt	भंग करना	Break, Disturb
1312	Ebullient	जोशीला	Enthusiastic
1313	Ecstasy	परमानंद	Joy, Happiness
1314	Elastic	लोचदार	Flexible
1315	Eliminate	निकालना	Remove, Exclude
1316	Elusive	मायावी	Intangible, Baffling
1317	Emancipate	स्वतंत्र करना	Liberate

UNIT 7

Synonyms asked in various SSC Exams

Given below are the list of synonyms appeared in recent SSC GD cnstable, CPO Tier 1 and CGL Tier-1, SSC CHSL, Steno, MTS and other exams

S.N.	Word-Synonyms	S.N.	Word-Synonyms
1	Affinity - Empathy	28	Suitable - Appropriate
2	Cumbersome - Heavy	29	Apparent - Obvious
3	Stray - Wander	30	Curative - Healing
4	Adulterated - Contaminated	31	Integration - Unification,
5	Abruptly - Suddenly	32	Isolation - Separation
6	Plea - Appeal	33	Stubborn – Obstinate
7	Elapsed - Ceased	34	Relish - Enjoy
8	O Bountiful - Generous	35	Compassion - Pity
9	Riddle - Puzzle	36	Gratification - Satisfaction
10	Implicit - Tacit	37	Imitation - Artificial
11	Breach - Violation	38	Façade - Frontage
12	Flimsy - Feeble	39	Magnificent - Grand
13	Gallant - Courageous	40	Suitable – Appropriate
14	Eradicate - Abolish	41	Everlasting - Eternal
15	Patron - Sponsor	42	Fanatic - Enthusiast
16	Exhaustible - Temporary	43	Gullible - Innocent
17	Delight - Joy	44	Elaborate - Detailed
18	Incredible - Unbelievable	45	Thrive - Prosper
19	Madness - Insanity	46	Morale - Self-confidence
20	Lucid - Clear	47	Gloomy - Dull
21	Passion - Desire	48	Menace - Nuisance
22	Relevant - Applicable	49	Amiable - Friendly
23	Prosperity - Wealth	50	Turbulent - Violent
24	Procure - Obtain	51	Impeccable - Flawless
25	Confine - Restrict	52	Slender - Slim
26	Contrary - Opposite	53	Agile - Active

S.N.	Word-Synonyms	S.N.	Word-Synonyms
27	Condemn - Criticize	54	Melodious - Tuneful
55	Obscure - Unknown	89	Forsake - Abandon
56	Vague - Unclear	90	Favoured - Preferred
57	Precise - Accurate	91	Glee - Happiness
58	Annoy - Irritate	92	Identical - Same
59	Handy - Convenient	93	Baffle Confuse
60	Nomadic - Roving	94	Impair - Weakness
61	Incorrigible - Unalterable	95	Gallant - Courageous
62	Dishevelled - Untidy	96	Lithe - Flexible
63	Mitigate - Lessen	97	Accessories - Attachments
64	Industrious - Diligent	98	Aisle - Passage
65	Ability - Capacity	99	Lavish - Expensive
66	Character - Trait	100	Mandatory - Compulsory
67	Extrovert - Talkative	101	Futile - Useless
68	Commendable - Praiseworthy	102	Vagabond - Tramp
69	Ecstasy - Happiness	103	Fillip - Boost
70	Affluent - Wealthy	104	Drag - Pull
71	Feign - Pretend	105	Tread - Walk
72	Dame - Lady	106	Profess - Admit
73	Amplify - Magnify	107	Damsel - Maiden
74	Replete - Full	108	Infuse - Fill
75	Forego - Give up	109	Persuade - Convince
76	Massive - Huge	110	Hardship - Misery
77	Harass - Bother	111	Indistinguishable - Equivalent
78	Nincompoop - Foolish	112	Discern - Discriminate
79	Avoid – Evade	113	Compliant - Submissive
80	Execute - Implement	114	Launching – Introducing
81	Remedy - Cure	115	Stimulation - Provocation
82	Velocity - Speed	116	Replaced - Substituted
83	Accurate - Precise	117	Contaminating - Polluting
84	Immerse - Submerge	118	Beneficiaries - Recipients
85	Awkward - Clumsy	119	Neglected - Ignored
86	Radical - Absolute	120	Disproportionately - Unreasonably
87	Fake - False	121	Pledged - Promised

S.N.	Word-Synonyms	S.N.	Word-Synonyms
88	Extricate - Remove	122	Preventive - Protective
123	Substitute - Replace	156	Enigmatic Mysterious
124	Gratuitous - Grateful	157	Exasperating - Frustrating
125	Lyrical - Musical	158	Imminent - Forthcoming
126	Contravene - Breech	159	Clinched - Finalized
127	Memoir - Diary	160	Elusive - Intangible
128	Detractors - Critics	161	Requisite - Obligatory
129	Chronic Persistent	162	Exalt - Praise
130	Coerce-Pressurize	163	Concise - Brief
131	Garrulous - Talkative	164	Assist - Help
132	Tilt - Slant	165	Intricate - Complex
133	Inept - Clumsy	166	Initiate - Start
134	Inarticulate - Incoherent	167	Adept - Skilled
135	Indelible - Inerasable	168	Endeavour - Attempt
136	Triumph - Victory	169	Obstacle- Barrier
137	Entice - Entrap.	170	Hostility - Enmity
138	Dubious - Fishy	171	Insult - Offend
139	Drag - Pull	172	Attribute - Quality
140	Engulf - Envelop	173	Fuse - Combine
141	Lethal - Fatal	174	Renown - Fame
142	Prevalent - Common	175	Devout - Pious
143	Rampant - Excessive	176	Converse - Talk
144	Exempt - Exclude	177	Austere - Strict
145	Fury - Anger	178	Expose - Reveal
146	Sterile - Barren	179	Adversary - Rival
147	Precarious - Dangerous	180	Hind - Rear
148	Vindictive - Revengeful	181	Innuendo - Implication
149	Pensive - Reflective	182	Current - Present
150	Repudiate - Renounce	183	Adhere - Comply
151	Lament - Mourn	184	Combustible - Inflammable
152	Defer - Delay	185	Embed - Bury
153	Perplex - Bewilder	186	Enthrall - Mesmerize
154	Mammoth - Gigantic	187	Fortify - Secure
155	Taciturn - Reticent	188	Erode - Disintegrate

S.N.	Word-Synonyms	S.N.	Word-Synonyms
189	Entangle - Implicate	223	Miniature - Diminutive
190	Thwart - Impede	224	Camouflage - Disguise
191	Handy - Convenient	225	Climax - Culmination
192	Avenge - Punish	226	Manual - Handbook
193	Scrap - Reject	227	Sordid – Dirty
194	Sane - Sensible	228	Efficient - Competent
195	Opportune - Timely	229	Fleeting - Brief
196	Pathetic - Pitiful	230	Spontaneous - Impulsive
197	Thrifty - Frugal	231	Distasteful - Unpleasant
198	Stern - Strict	232	Resolution - Decision
199	Temperate - Moderate	233	Candid - Forthright
200	Defiance - Resistance	234	Howled - Wailed
201	Reprimand - Reproach	235	Pernicious - Spiteful
202	Pitfall - Hazard	236	Abundant - Plentiful
203	Vital - Essential	237	Deceptive - Cheat
204	Discover - Find	238	Vanquish - Defeat
205	Ignominious - Disgraceful	239	Emphasize - Stress
206	Orthodox - Traditional	240	Massive - Huge
207	Quest – Search	241	Scrumptious - Delicious
208	Ideology - Belief	242	Cherish - Nurture
209	Meddle - Interfere	243	Luxuriant - Lush
210	Anomalous - Peculiar	244	Conceited - Smug
211	Fleeting - Momentary	245	Despise - Abhor
212	Identical - Similar	246	Cordial - Amicable
213	Ostentatious - Flashy	247	Revamp - Restructure
214	Radiance - Sparkle	248	Mediation - Intervention
215	Recapitulation - Summary	249	Herculean - Strong
216	Wary - Alert	250	Competent - Capable
217	Recede - Wane	251	Erstwhile - Former
218	Accurate - Precise	252	Vindictive - Revengeful
219	Dedication - Commitment	253	Expandable - Flexible
220	Leisurely - Relaxed	254	Tangled - Knotted
221	Eminent - Prominent	255	Proclaim - Declare
222	Commence - Start	289	Exceptional - Extraordinary

S.N.	Word-Synonyms	S.N.	Word-Synonyms
257	Assert - Emphasize	290	Brisk - Quick
258	Prohibition - Exclusion	291	Enhance - Improve
259	Complicated - Complex	292	Hate - Detest
260	Alteration - Modification	293	Awkward - Clumsy
261	Overwhelming - Awesome	294	Dedicate - Devote
262	Distaste – Loathing	295	Aroma - Scent
263	Deepen - Intensify	296	Remember - Recall
264	Courage - Valour	297	Slender - Slim
265	**Misfortune - Calamity**	298	Apparent - Obvious
266	**Capable - Competent**	299	Fundamental - Basic
267	Demolish - Dismantle	300	Detain - Delay
268	Chide - Rebuke	301	Calm - Peaceful
269	Immense - Massive	302	Relevant.- Applicable
270	Former - Previous	303	Swift - Quick
271	Lavish - Bountiful	304	Massive - Huge
272	Accountable - Answerable	305	Revive - Recover
273	Courteous - Polite	306	Engage - Occupy
274	Infuriate - Enrage	307	Integration - Unification
275	Obvious - Evident	308	Acclaim - Praise
276	Optimist - Idealist	309	Vigilant - Watchful
277	Benevolent - Generous	310	Lucid - Clear
278	Harass-Molest	311	Affluence - Wealth
279	Profuse - Aplenty	312	Zest - Enthusiasm
280	Rectify - Amend	313	Intricate - Complicated
281	Forgive - Pardon	314	Ferocious - Fierce
282	Agile - Quick	315	Beneficial - Advantageous
283	Eager - Keen	316	Dubious - Doubtful
284	Strange - Abnormal	317	Abandoned - Deserted
285	Advantageous - Favourable	318	Stoical - Apathetic
286	Anthology - Collection	319	Magnify - Enlarge
287	Absolved - Pardoned	320	Applause - Approval
288	Distroy - Ruin	321	Magnify - Enlarge
322	Popular - Favourite	354	Agitated - Upset

S.N.	Word-Synonyms	S.N.	Word-Synonyms
323	Humdrum - Monotonous	355	Eliminate - Remove
324	Obtain - Achieve	356	Mandatory - Compulsory
325	Encumbrance - Obstacle	357	Robust - Healthy
326	Recently - Lately	358	Proximity - Closeness
327	Artful - Crafty	359	Corridor - Passage
328	Morbid - Nasty	360	Missive Letter
329	Persuade - Coax	361	Insipid - Bland
330	Inclination - Aptitude	362	Contaminate - Pollute
331	Impious - Irreligious	363	Subsequent - Consecutive
332	Prodigy - Genius	364	Adequate - Sufficient
333	Judicious-Prudent	365	Tranquil - Calm
334	Chaste - Pure	366	Fascinating - Appealing
335	Mock - Taunt	367	Engulf - Inundate
336	Contempt - Hatred	368	Offend - Annoy
337	Anxious - Nervous	369	Parsimony - Frugality
338	Control - Regulate	370	Apparent - Obvious
339	Drowsy - Sleepy	371	Fatigue - Weariness
340	Enormous - Huge	372	Redundant - Unnecessary
341	Cogent - Convincing	373	Trivial - Superficial
342	Diminutive - Petite	374	Scanty - Meagre
343	Evidence Indication	375	Complacent - Smug
344	Impoverished - Penniless	376	Flourish - Thrive
345	Mercurial - Volatile	377	Fatigue - Weariness
346	Onerous - Arduous	378	Sanction - Approval
347	Persist - Continue	379	Jeopardy - Peril
348	Philanthropist - Humanitarian	380	Ignominy - Disgrace
349	Perpetuate - Preserve	381	Opinion - View
350	Discern - Perceive	382	Loyal - Devoted
351	Inimical - Hostile	383	Incredible - Unbelievable
352	Applause - Approval	384	Aloof - Detached
353	Solid - Firm	385	Intensify - Strengthen

S.N.	Word-Synonyms	S.N.	Word-Synonyms
385	Deficiency - Inadequacy	399	Penitence - Repentance
386	Exasperate - Infuriate	401	Implore - Plead
387	Feign - Pretend	402	Glorious - Splendid
388	Efficacious - Voracious	403	Revere - Respect
389	Beguile - Deceive	404	Prevent - Avert
390	Deference - Obeisance	405	Acknowledgement - Confirmation
391	Disastrous - Calamitous	406	Prodigal - Extravagant
392	Fatigue - Tiredness	407	Fury - Anger
393	Surreptitious - Secretive	408	Solitary - Singular
394	Reprimand – Rebuke	409	Expensive - Dear
395	Malady – Illness	410	Retain - Maintain
396	Obligatory - Mandatory	411	Erudite - Learned
397	Scintillating - Glittering	412	Violent - Aggressive
398	Pathetic - Pitiful		

UNIT 8

Antonyms with Hindi Meaning

Antonyms are words that have the opposite meaning of another word. Learning common antonyms sharpens your sense of language and expands your vocabulary

S.N.	Words	Antonyms
1	Abbreviate (संक्षिप्त करना)	Expand (विस्तार करना)
2	Abolish (समांप्त करना)	Build up, Create (निर्माण करना)
3	Abominable (घटिया	**Delightful** (आनंदप्रद)
4	Aboriginal (मूल निवासी)	Immigrant (अप्रवासी)
5	Above (ऊपर)	Below नीचे
6	Abridge (संक्षेप करना)	Stretch विस्तार
7	Abscond (फ़रार होना)	Remain (टिकना)
8	Absorb (सोख लेना)	Eject, Emit (निकालना)
9	Abstract (निराकार, अमूर्त)	Concrete (ठोस)
10	Abundance (प्रचुरता)	Scarcity (कमी)
11	Abusive (अपमानजनक)	Laudatory (प्रशंसात्मक)
12	Abutting (सटा हुआ)	Far (दूर)
13	Accelerate (गति बढ़ाना)	**Delay** (देरी करना)
14	Accentuate (जोर देना)	Disparage (उपेक्षा करना)
15	Accept (स्वीकार)	Reject (अस्वीकार)
16	Accessible (पहुंने योग्य)	**Restricted** (वर्जित)
17	Accolade (सम्मान)	**Blame** (दोष लगाना)
18	Accumulate (जमा करना)	Disperse, Squandered (बिखेरना, गंवाना)
19	Accusation (आरोप लगाना)	Exculpation, Defenders (सफ़ाई देना, बचाना)
20	Acerbican (कड़वा सच)	Bland (बेस्वाद, अरोचक)
21	Acknowledge (स्वीकार करना)	Deny, Decline (मना करना)
22	Acquit (दोषमुक्त करना)	Condemn, Convict, Blame (दोष लगाना)
23	Adamant (अटल)	Yielding, Gullible, Flexible (नर्म, लचीला)
24	Add (जोड़ना)	Remove (हटाना)
25	Adjacent (सटा हुआ)	Distant (अलग)
26	Admiration, (प्रशंसा)	Contempt (निंदा)

S.N.	Words	Antonyms
27	Admire (प्रशंसा)	Dislike (नापसंद)
28	Adulteration (मिलावट)	Purification (शुद्धिकरण)
29	Adultery (व्यभिचार)	Purity (पवित्रता)
30	Advanced (उन्नत)	Retarded (मंद)
31	Advocacy (समर्थन)	Discouragement (हतोत्साह)
32	Affable (मिलनसार)	Surly (बदमिजाज़)
33	Affiliation (संबंध)	Detachment (वियोग)
34	Affirm (स्वीकार करना)	Refuse, Disagree, Denial (मना करना, असहमत होना)
35	Affliction (यातना)	Pleasure (आनंद)
36	Aggrandize (शक्ति बढ़ाना)	Belittle (महत्व घटाना)
37	Aggressive (आक्रमक)	Peaceful, (शांतिपूर्ण)
38	Agitate (उत्तेजित करना)	Pacify, Calm (शांत करना)
39	Agony (कष्ट)	Pleasure, Ecstasy, Delight, Comfort (आनंद, उत्साह, आराम)
40	Agree (सहमत)	Oppose (विरोध)
41	Agreement (समझौता)	Discord (अनबन)
42	Airy (हवादार)	Stuffy (घुटन-भरा)
43	Alacrity (तत्परता)	Indifference (उदासीनता)
44	Alien (विदेशी)	Native (देशी)
45	Alight (उतरना)	**Embark** (चढ़ना)
46	Alike (एक जैसा)	Different (अलग-अलग)
47	Alive (जिंदा)	Dead (मृत)
48	Allergic (एलर्जी संबंधी)	**Immune** (प्रतिरक्षा)
49	Alliance (संधि)	Separation (पृथकरण)
50	Alluring (मोहक)	**Repulsive** (अरुचिकर)
51	Ally (मित्र)	Enemy (दुश्मन)
52	Altercation (तकरार)	Compromise (समझौता)
53	Altruism (परोपकारिता)	Spite (द्वेष करना)
54	Always (हमेशा)	Never (कभी नहीं)
55	Amass (एकत्र करना)	**Distribute** (वितरित करना)
56	Ambiguous (अस्पष्ट)	Precise, Clear (स्पष्ट)
57	Amorphous (अनाकार)	Definite (निश्चित)
58	Ample (प्रचुर)	Meagre (अल्प)

S.N.	Words	Antonyms
59	Amuse (मन बहलाना)	**Bore** (उबा देना)
60	Analogous (अनुरूप)	Disagreeing (भिन्न होना)
61	Anarchic (अराजक)	Normal (साधारण)
62	Angst (आक्रोश)	Casualness (लापरवाही)
63	Anile (बुढ़िया जैसा)	Young (युवा)
64	Animosity (बैर)	**Benevolence, Love** (परोपकार, मोब्बत)
65	Antique (प्राचीन)	Recent, Modern (हाल का, आधुनिक)
66	Antithesis (विपरीत)	**Harmony** (समानता)
67	Apex (शिखर)	Base (तल)
68	Apocryphal (मणगढ़ंत)	Authentic (विश्वसनीय)
69	Appalling (डरावना)	Consoling, Appealing (सांत्वना, अपील)
70	Applaud (सराहना)	Denounce, Criticize, Censure (निंदा)
71	Appoint (नियुक्त करना)	Dismiss (खारिज)
72	Appreciation (प्रशंसा)	Antipathy (घृणा)
73	Approach (पास आना)	Avoid (टाल जाना)
74	Approached (संपर्क किया)	Retreated (पीछे हटा)
75	Appropriate (उपयुक्त)	Unsuitable (अनुपयुक्त)
76	Approve (मंजूर)	**Reject** (अस्वीकार)
77	Argue (तर्क करना)	Agree (सहमत होना)
78	Arid (बंजर)	**Wet, Fertile** (गीला, उपजाऊ)
79	Arouse (उत्तेजित करना)	**Cease** (बंद करना)
80	Arraign (दोष लगाना)	Free (मुक्त होना)
81	Arrogance (अहंकार)	Humility (विनम्रता)
82	Arrogant (अभिमानी)	Modest, Humble (विनम्र)
83	Artifice (धोखा)	Truthfulness (सच्चाई)
84	Ascent (चढ़ाव)	Descent (गिराव)
85	Assemble (इकट्ठा करना)	**Disperse, Scatter** (बिखेरना)
86	Assent (समर्थन)	Dissent (मतभेद)
87	Assiduous (परिश्रमी)	Neglectful (बेपरवाह)
88	Assuage (शांत करना)	**Provoke** (उकसाना)
89	Astonished (चकित करना)	Calm (शांत)
90	Atheist (नास्तिक)	Believer (आस्तिक)
91	Attachments (बंधन)	Opposition विरोध
92	Attack (आक्रमण)	Defence (रक्षा)

S.N.	Words	Antonyms
93	Attract (आकर्षित)	Repel (पीछे हटाना)
94	Augment (बढ़ाना)	Degrade, Decrease, Diminish (घटाना)
95	Auspicious (सौभाग्यशाली)	Unlucky (बदकिस्मत)
96	Authenticated (प्रमाणीकृत)	Disprove (झूठा ठहराना)
97	Autonomy (स्वराज्य)	Dependence (निर्भरता)
98	Awake (जागना)	Asleep, Hypnotized (सोना, सम्मोहित)
99	Aware (अवगत)	Ignorant (अनभिज्ञ)
100	Awkward (अटपटा)	Graceful (सुशोभित)
101	Babel (कोलाहल)	Quiet (शांत)
102	Baffling (रहस्यमय)	Comprehensible (समझने लायक)
103	Balmy (सुखदायी)	Hard (कठिन)
104	Baneful (विनाशकारी)	Lucky (सौभाग्यशाली)
105	Banter (मज़ाक)	Praise (प्रशंसा)
106	Bare (नंगा)	Covered (ढका हुआ)
107	Baroque (विचित्र)	Plain (सामान्य)
108	Befuddle (मदहोश होना)	Explicate (समझाना)
109	Belittle (छोटा महसूस कराना)	Extol (प्रशंसा करना)
110	Beneath (नीचे)	Above (ऊपर)
111	Benediction (आशीर्वाद)	Criticism (आलोचना)
112	Benign (दयालु)	Hostile (शत्रुतापूर्ण)
113	Benison (शुभकामना)	Execration (फटकार)
114	Bequest (वसीयत, दान)	Withdraw (निकालना)
115	Betrayal (विश्वासघात)	Loyalty, Stand By (स्वाभाविक)
116	Better (बेहतर)	Worsen (बदतर)
117	Betterment (सुधार होना)	Deterioration (बिगड़ना)
118	Bewildered (उलझन में डालना)	Enlighten (स्पष्ट करना)
119	Bias (पक्षपात)	Fairness (निष्पक्षता)
120	Bifurcate (द्विशाखित)	Combine (जोड़ना)
121	Bigot (कट्टर)	Liberal (उदार)
122	Bizarre (विचित्र)	Usual, Ordinary (साधारण)
123	Blame (आरोप)	Praise (प्रशंसा)
124	Bland (अरोचक)	Exciting (रोमांचक)
125	Blasphemous (अपवित्रकारी)	Pious (पवित्र)
126	Blemish (दोष)	Perfection (निपुणता)

S.N.	Words	Antonyms
127	Bless (आशीर्वाद)	Curse (अभिशाप)
128	Bloated (फूला हुआ)	Deflated (पिचका हुआ)
129	Block (रोक लगाना)	Clear (पास करना)
130	Blunt (भौंथरा)	Sharp (नुकीला)
131	Bold (साहसिक)	Timid (डरपोक)
132	Bondage (बंधन)	Liberty (स्वतंत्रता)
133	Boring (अरुचिकर)	Exciting (रोमांचक)
134	Bossy (धौंस देने वाला)	Polite (सभ्य)
135	Bravery (वीरता)	Cowardice (कायरता)
136	Brazen (बेशर्म)	Modest (विनम्र)
137	Breadth (चौड़ाई)	Narrowness (रिहाई)
138	Bridle (लगाम)	Release (बेरंग)
139	Brief (संक्षिप्त)	Elaborate (संकीर्णता)
140	Bright (चमकदार)	Bleak (विस्तृत)
141	Brindled (चितकबरा)	Unflecked (बेदाग)
142	Broad (चौंड़ा)	Narrow (संकीर्ण)
143	Brutality (निर्दयता)	Humanity (मानवता)
144	Bucolic (ग्रामीण)	Urban (नगरीय)
145	Buoyant (तैरता हुआ)	Weighted (भारी)
146	Buoyant (प्रसन्नचित)	Gloomy (उदासीपूर्वक)
147	Burgeon (फलना फूलना)	Shrivel (सूखना)
148	Cacophony (कोलाहल)	Harmony (सामंजस्य)
149	Calamity (आपदा)	Happiness (खुशी)
150	Calculative (षड्यंत्रकारी)	Naive (भोला-भाला)
151	Callous (कठोर)	Sensitive, Sympathetic, Concerned (संवेदनशील, सहानुभूति, चिंतित)
152	Callow (अनुभवहीन)	Sophisticated (जटिलता)
153	Calm (शान्त)	Excited (उत्तेजित)
154	Canonicality (धर्मवैधानिक)	Unorthodoxen (अपरंपरागत)
155	Capacious (विशाल)	Cramped (तंग)
156	Captivate (मंत्रमुग्ध होना)	Distract, Disillusion (विचलित, मोह-भंग)
157	Captivity (क़ैद)	Liberty, Freedom (स्वतंत्रता)
158	Capture (कब्जा)	Release (रिहाई)
159	Carnal (शारीरिक)	Spiritual (आध्यात्मिक)

S.N.	Words	Antonyms
160	Casual (आकस्मिक)	Planned (आयोजित)
161	Caustic (कटु)	Kind (दयालु)
162	Cautious (सतर्क)	Negligent, Reckless (लापरवाह)
163	Celestial (स्वर्गीय)	Hellish (नारकीय)
164	Certainty (निश्चित)	Doubt (संदेह)
165	Certify (प्रमाणित)	Disapproves (अस्वीकार करना)
166	Cessation (समाप्ति)	Commencement (प्रारंभ)
167	Chaotic (अस्तव्यस्त)	Organised (संगठित)
168	Charity (दान पुण्य)	Stealing (चोरी)
169	Charming (आकर्षक)	Repulsive (अरुचिकर)
170	Chicken Hearted (डरपोक)	Courageous (निडर)
171	Churlish (अभद्र)	Courteous (विनम्र)
172	Cite (उल्लेख करना)	Forget (भूलना)
173	Clammy (चिपचिपा)	Dry (सूखा)
174	Clamorous (कोलाहलमय)	Suppression (अवरोध, रूकावट)
175	Clash (टकराव)	Harmony (सामंजस्य)
176	Classic (उत्कृष्ट)	Atypical (असामान्य)
177	Clear (स्पष्ट)	Nebulous, Opaque, Murky, Dim (अस्पष्ट, अपारदर्शी, धुंधला)
178	Cloudy (धुंधला)	Transparent (पारदर्शक)
179	Coax (फुसलाना)	Dissuade (मना करना)
180	Coherent (सुसंगत)	Disorganized, Illogical (अव्यवस्थित, अतार्किक)
181	Collect (इकट्ठा करना)	Disperse (बिखेरना)
182	Combative (लड़ाकू)	Peaceful (शांतिपूर्ण)
183	Comedy (हास्य)	Tragedy (शोकपूर्ण घटना)
184	Comfort (सांत्वना)	Discontentment (असंतोष)
185	Commiserate (हमदर्दी)	Indifferential (उदासीन)
186	Committed (प्रतिबद्ध)	Uncertain (अनिश्चित)
187	Compatriot (हमवतन)	Outsider (परदेशी)
188	Compel (बल से कराना)	Dissuade (न करने के लिए समझाना)
189	Compendium (सारांश)	Expansion (विस्तार)
190	Complete (पूर्ण)	Partial (आंशिक)
191	Complex (जटिल)	Simple (सरल)

S.N.	Words	Antonyms
192	Comply (आज्ञापालन करना)	Oppose, Challenge (आपत्ति करना)
193	Comprehensive (विस्तृत)	Restricted (सीमित)
194	Compromise (समझौता)	Dissent (मतभेद)
195	Compulsory (अनिवार्य)	Optional (ऐच्छिक)
196	Comrade (साथी)	Enemy (दुश्मन)
197	Concealed (गुप्त)	Revealed (खुलासा)
198	Conceive (विचार करना)	Misunderstand (गलत समझना)
199	Concentrated (घड़ा)	Diluted (पतला)
200	Conciliation (समझौता)	Confrontation (मुकाबला)
201	Conclusive (निर्णयात्मक)	Ambiguous (अस्पष्ट)
202	Concur (सहमत होना)	Disagree (असहमत)
203	Condense (संघनित करना)	Expand (फैलाना)
204	Confident (आत्म विश्वासी)	Diffident (संकोची)
205	Confirm (निश्चित करना)	Reject (अस्वीकार करना)
206	Conform (अनुरूप)	Differ, Deviation (अलग, विचलन)
207	Confront (सामना करना)	Avoid (टालना)
208	Congested (भरा हुआ)	Cleared (टालना)
209	Connect (जुड़ना)	Detach (अलग होना)
210	Consanguinity (रक्तसंबंध)	Disunion (विच्छेद)
211	Consent (सहमति)	Dissent (मतभेद)
212	Conserve (सुरक्षित रखना)	Destroy (नष्ट)
213	Conspicuous (सुस्पष्ट)	Obscure (अस्पष्ट)
214	Constant (स्थिर)	Varying, Fluctuating (परिवर्तनीय)
215	Construe (समझाना)	Obscure (अस्पष्ट)
216	Consume (उपभोग करना)	Save (बचत करना)
217	Contemplate (विचार करना)	Ignore (अनसुनी करना)
218	Contemplative (विचारशील)	Unreflective (असावधान)
219	Contented (संतुष्ट)	Dissatisfied (असुंष्ट)
220	Contentious (विवादास्पद)	Agreeable (सहमत)
221	Contest (संघर्ष)	Stillness (स्थिरता)
222	Contextual (संबंधित)	Unrelated (असंबंधित)
223	Contiguous (मिला हुआ)	Separated (अलग-थलग)
224	Contradiction (परस्पर विरोध)	Agreement (समझौता)
225	Contribute (योगदान करना)	Take (लेना)

S.N.	Words	Antonyms
226	Controlled (नियंत्रित)	Excited (उत्तेजित)
227	Controversial (विवादास्पद)	Undisputed, Indisputable, Agreement (निर्विवाद)
228	Convene (आयोजित करना)	Disperse (भंग करना)
229	Convenience (सहूलियत)	Hindrance (अड़चन)
230	Convex (उत्तल)	Concave (अवतल)
231	Convicted (दोषी ठहराया)	Acquitted (बरी कर दिया)
232	Convincing (यकीनी)	Doubtable (संदेहास्पद)
233	Convulsion (ऐंठन)	Restful (शांत)
234	Corroborate (समर्थन)	Contradict, Oppose (खंडन करना)
235	Corrupt (भ्रष्ट)	Honest (ईमानदार)
236	Courtesy (शिष्टाचार)	Rudeness (अशिष्टता)
237	Courtly(सभ्य)	Rough (असभ्य)
238	Covert (गुप्त)	Public (सार्वजनिक)
239	Covetous (लालची)	Benevolent (भलाई करने वाला)
240	Cozen (धोखा देना)	Honest (ईमानदार)
241	Create (सृजन करना)	Destroy (नष्ट करना)
242	Credit (जमा धन)	Debit (निकाला गया धन)
243	Crestfallen (हताश, उदास)	Triumphant (विजयी)
244	Crisp (करारा)	Tender (मुलायम)
245	Critical (आलोचनात्मक)	Complimentary (प्रशंसात्मक)
246	Criticise (आलोचना करना)	Commend, Approve (सराहना करना)
247	Crook (अपराधी)	Law (कानून)
248	Crooked (मुड़ा हुआ)	Straight (सीधा)
249	Crucial (महत्वपूर्ण)	Trivial (तुच्छ)
250	Cruel (निर्दयी)	Kind (मेहरबान)
251	Curb (नियंत्रण)	Allow, Freedom (अनुमति, आजादी)
252	Curse (अभिशाप)	Boon (वरदान)
253	Cursory (अधूरा)	Thorough (संपूर्ण)
254	Curt (रूखा)	Polite (विनम्र)
255	Dainty (सजीला)	Clumsy (बेढंगा)
256	Damage (टूट-फूट)	Mend (मरम्मत)
257	Dank (नम)	Dry (सूखा)
258	Darken (अंधेरा छाना)	Illuminated (प्रकाशित होना)

S.N.	Words	Antonyms
259	Dashed (धराशायी)	Encouraged (प्रोत्साहित)
260	Daunt (भयभीत करना)	Encourage (प्रोत्साहित करना)
261	Deathly (प्राणघातक)	Blooming (फलता फूलता)
262	Debauched (ऐयाश, पथभ्रष्ट)	Honourable (माननीय)
263	Decay (क्षय)	Growth (वृद्धि)
264	Deceit (छल)	Honesty, Plain (ईमानदारी,निष्कपट)
265	Deceive (धोखा देना)	Support (सहायता करना)
266	Decimate (बरबाद करना)	Preserve (रक्षा करना)
267	Decry (दोष देना)	Praise (प्रशंसा करना)
268	Deep (गहरा)	Shallow (उथला)
269	Defence (रक्षा)	Offence (अपराध)
270	Defend (बचाव)	Surrender (आत्मसमर्पण)
271	Defend (रक्षा करना)	Abandon (छोड़ देना)
272	Deferential (आदरसूचक)	Arrogant (अभिमानी)
273	Deficiency (कमी)	**Excess** (अति)
274	Deficit (अभाव)	**Abundance, Surplus** (प्रचुरता)
275	Defuse (शांत करना)	Agitate (उत्तेजित करना)
276	Dejected (उदास)	Cheerful (आनन्दित)
277	Delectation (आनंद)	Sorrow (शोक)
278	Delicate (नाजुक)	Firm (दृढ़)
279	Delicious (स्वादिष्ट)	Insipid, Distasteful (फीका, बेस्वाद)
280	Demand (मांग)	Supply (आपूर्ति)
281	Demean (नीचा दिखाना)	Admire (प्रशंसा करना)
282	Denounce (आरोप लगाना)	Praise, Compliment (प्रशंसा करना)
283	Dense (सघन)	Sparse (विरल)
284	Depict (शब्दों में वर्णन करना)	Hide (छिपा देना)
285	Deplete (कम करना)	Expand (विस्तार करना)
286	Deport (निकला देना)	Permit (अनुमति देना)
287	Deposit (जमा)	Withdraw (निकालना)
288	Depredation (विध्वंस)	Construction (निर्माण)
289	Depth (गहराई)	Shallow (उथला)
290	Derisive (व्यंग्यात्मक)	Respectful (सम्मान पूर्ण)
291	Descent (उतार)	Ascent (चढ़ाव)
292	Desecrate (अपवित्र करना)	Sanctify (पवित्र करना)

S.N.	Words	Antonyms
293	Desecration (अपवित्रीकरण)	Consecration, Veneration (पवित्र करण, मन्नत)
294	Deserter (भगोड़ा)	Loyalist (वफादार)
295	Desist (रोकना)	Continued (जारी रहना)
296	Desperate (बेताब)	Content (संतुष्ट)
297	Destination (मंजिल)	Origin (प्रारंभ)
298	Destroy (नष्ट करना)	Preserve (रक्षा करना)
299	Destructive (विनाशकारी)	Constructive (रचनात्मक)
300	Detest (घृणा करना)	like, Adore (पसंद करना)
301	Detest (नफरत करना)	Adore (प्यार करना)
302	Developed (विकसित)	Backward (पिछड़ा)
303	Deviate (भटकना)	Concentrate (ध्यान केन्द्रित करना)
304	Devious (चालाक)	Straight (सीधा)
305	Diabolical (शैतानी)	Moral (नैतिक)
306	Differ (मतभेद होना)	Concurrent (सहमत होना)
307	Difference (अंतर)	Similarity (समानता)
308	Different (विभिन्न)	Similar (समान)
309	Diffidence (संकोच)	Self-Assurance (अत्मविस्वास)
310	Dignified (प्रतिष्ठित)	Ordinary (मामूली)
311	Digress (पीछे हटना)	Stay (टिकना)
312	Disable (अयोग्य बनाना / बंद करना)	Permit (मंजूरी देना)
313	Disapprove (निंदा करना)	Commend (सराहना करना)
314	Disarming (शांत करने वाला)	Detestable (घिनौना)
315	Disavowal (इनकार)	Approval (स्वीकृति)
316	Discard (छोड़ना)	Adopt, Acceptan (अपनाना)
317	Disclose (जाहिर करना)	Conceal (गुप्त रखना)
318	Disconsolate (निराश)	Joyous (आनंदित)
319	Discord (कलह)	Harmony (सामंसजस्य)
320	Discordant (असहमत)	Agreeable (सहमत)
321	Discreet (सावधान)	Heedless (असावधान)
322	Discrimination (भेदभाव)	Equality (समानता)
323	Disdain (तिरस्कार)	Admiration, Favour (प्रशंसा, एहसान)
324	Disgrace (अपमान)	Honour (सम्मान)
325	Dishearten (हतोत्साह करना)	Encourage (उत्साहित करना)

S.N.	Words	Antonyms
326	Disheveled (विखरा हुआ)	Ordered (सुव्यवस्थित)
327	Disillusioned (निराशाग्रस्त)	Enthusiastic (उत्साह पूर्ण)
328	Disjointed (संबंध तोड़ा हुआ)	Connected (जुड़ा हुआ)
329	Dismay (निराश करना)	Gladden (प्रसन्न करना)
330	Disorderly (उल्टा पुल्टा)	Arranged (व्यवस्थित)
331	Disparate (भिन्न)	Similar (समान)
332	Dissension (कलह)	Harmony (सामंजस्य)
333	Dissent (मतभेद)	Agreement (समझौता)
334	Dissident (मतभेद करने वाला)	Orthodox (परम्परावादी)
335	Distant (दूर)	Close, Near (पास)
336	Distinctive (विशेष)	Close (अभिन्न)
337	Distract (विचलित करना)	Clarify (स्पटीकरण करना)
338	Distraught (व्याकुल)	Serene (शांत)
339	Distress (दु:ख)	Pleasure (आनंद)
340	Diurnal (दैनिक)	Nocturnal (रात्रिकालीन)
341	Diverge (अलग अलग होना)	Collect (एकत्रित होना)
342	Diverge (छितरना)	Converge (एकाग्र)
343	Diverse (भिन्न)	Identical (समान)
344	Divest (वंचित करना)	Give (अदा करना)
345	Divide (विभाजित करना)	Unite (जोड़ना)
346	Dividing (विभाजक)	Connecting (संयोग)
347	Divine (दिव्य)	Lowly (नीच)
348	Divulge (भेद खोलना)	Conceal, Hide (छिपना)
349	Dogmatic (कट्टर)	Flexible (लचीला)
350	Dominant (प्रभावशाली)	Submissive (विनम्र)
351	Dominate (हावी)	Surrender (अत्मसमर्पण)
352	Dormant (निष्क्रिय)	Active (सक्रिय)
353	Downcast (निराश)	Cheerful (हंसमुख)
354	Drab (फीका)	Bright (चमकदार)
355	Drawn (तैयार)	Relaxed (आराम)
356	Dull (सुस्त)	Keen, Exciting (उत्सुक, रोमांचक)
357	Dummy (दिखावटी)	Original (असली)
358	Duplicate (नक़ल)	Original (मुल प्रति)
359	Dwe (बस जाना)	Move (आगे बढ़ना)

S.N.	Words	Antonyms
360	Dye (रंग रंजक)	Bleach (सफद विरंजक)
361	Dynamic (गतिशील)	Static (स्थिर)
362	Earthly (पृथ्वी संबंधी)	Celestial (अकाशीय)
363	Eccentric (सनकी)	Normal (साधारण)
364	Eccentricity (सनक)	Normalcy (सामान्य स्थिति)
365	Effeminacy (कायरता)	Manliness (बहादुरपन)
366	Effeminate (नारी जैसा)	Manly (मर्दाना)
367	Effervescen (उत्तेजित)	Stale (पुराना)
368	Egoist (अहंवादी)	Selfless (स्वार्थरहित)
369	Egregious (अत्यंत)	Mild (सौम्य)
370	Elasticity (लोच)	Rigidity (कठोरता)
371	Elegance (शिष्टता)	Vulgarity, Gracelessness (असभ्यता, बेहयायी)
372	Elegant (शिष्ट)	Crude (अशिष्ट)
373	Elementary (सामान्य)	Complex (जटिल)
374	Elevation (ऊंचाई)	Depression (गिराव)
375	Emaciated (निर्बल)	Fat, Healthy (स्वस्थ)
376	Emancipation (मुक्ति)	Bondage (गुलामी)
377	Emerge (उभरना)	Disappear (गायब होना)
378	Empathy (सहानुभूति)	Apathy (उदासीनता)
379	Encouraged (प्रोत्साहित)	Discouraged, Opposed (हतोत्साहित, विरोध)
380	Encroach (अतिक्रमण करना)	Keep Away (दूर रहना)
381	End (समाप्त)	Start (शुरू)
382	Endangered (संकटग्रस्त)	Protected (संरक्षित)
383	Endorse (समर्थन)	Disapprove, Renounce (अस्वीकार करना)
384	Endow (प्रदान करना)	Deprive (वंचित)
385	Enduring (स्थायी)	Transient (क्षणिक)
386	Enigma (पहेली)	Clarity (स्पष्टता)
387	Enlarge (विस्तार करना)	Condense (संक्षेप करना)
388	Enlighten (प्रकाशित करना)	Befog (अंधेरा करना)
389	Enliven (सजीव करना)	Dishearten (उदास करना)
390	Enmity (शत्रुता)	Amicability (मित्रतापूर्णता)
391	Ennui (ग्लानि)	Excitement (उत्तेजना)
392	Enraged (ख़फ़ा)	Pleased (प्रसन्न)

S.N.	Words	Antonyms
393	Enrich (बढ़ाना)	Reduce (काम करना)
394	Ensue (पीछे होना)	Precede (आगे होना)
395	Enthusiasm (उत्साह)	Apathy (उदासीनता)
396	Entire (संपूर्ण)	Partial (अंशिक)
397	Entrance (प्रवेश)	Exit (निकास)
398	Ephemeral (अल्पकालिक)	Eternal (अनन्त)
399	Equilibrium (संतुलन)	Imbalance (असंतुलन)
400	Equivalent (समतुल्य)	Dissimilar (भिन्न)
401	Erase (मिटाना)	Create (बनाना)
402	Escalate (बढ़ाना)	Reduce (घटाना)
403	Establish (स्थापित करना)	Destroy (नष्ट करना)
404	Esteem (आदर)	Disregard (उपेक्षा)
405	Estimate (आकलन)	Actual (वास्तविक)
406	Eternity (अनंत काल)	Bounds (सीमा)
407	Eulogistic (प्रशंसात्मक)	Critical (आलाचनात्मक)
408	Euphoria (उत्साह)	Lethargy (सुस्ती)
409	Evanescent (क्षणभंगुर)	Permanent (स्थायी)
410	Evident (प्रत्यक्ष)	Obscure, Doubtful (अस्पष्ट,संदिग्ध)
411	Evoke (आह्वान करना)	Stop (रोकना)
412	Exasperation (रोष)	Enjoyment (आनन्द)
413	Excitable (उत्तेजनीय)	Placid (शांत)
414	Excited (उत्तेजित)	Bored (ऊबा हुआ)
415	Exclusive (छोड़ कर)	Inclusive (मिला कर)
416	Exemptions (छूट)	Inclusions (सम्मिलन)
417	Exhale (सांस छोड़ना)	Inhale (सांस लेना)
418	Exhaustive (संपूर्ण)	Incomplete (अधूरा)
419	Exhausts (थका देना)	Invigorates (शक्ति देना)
420	Exhume (खोदकर निकलना)	Hide (छिपाना)
421	Exigent (अत्यावश्यक)	Usual (सामान्य)
422	Exodus (निर्गमन, प्रस्थान)	Arrival, Influx (भीतर जाना)
423	Exonerate (निर्दोषी ठहराना)	Convict, Sentence (अपराधी घोषित करना, सज़ा देना)
424	Expand (विस्तार)	Contract, Shrink (सिकुड़ना)

S.N.	Words	Antonyms
425	Expansion (विस्तार)	Contraction, Compression (संकुचन, संचीड़न)
426	Expel (निकाल देना)	Absorb (सोख लेना)
427	Explicit (सुस्पष्ट)	Ambiguous (अस्पष्ट)
428	Expunge (निकालना)	Insert, Add (डालना)
429	Expurgate (बेकार चीज हटाना)	Permit (अनुमति देना)
430	Exquisite (अति सुंदर)	Rough (असभ्य)
431	Extant (मौजूदा प्रचलित)	Extinct, Destroyed (विलुप्त, नष्ट)
432	Extensive (विस्तृत)	Intensive (गहन)
433	Extenuate (शांत करना)	Strengthen (शक्तिशाली बनना)
434	Extol (प्रशंसा करना)	Censure (निंदा करना)
435	Extraneous (असंगत)	Relevant (संगत)
436	Extravagant (फ़िजूल खर्च)	Economical, Thrifty (किफयती)
437	Extreme (चरम)	Mild (सौमय)
438	Exultant (उल्लसित)	Depressed (उदास)
439	Fabricate (निर्माण)	Brenk (टुटना)
440	Facilitate (सुविधा प्रदान करना)	Hinder (बाधा पहुचाना)
441	Fair (निष्पक्ष)	Unjust (अन्यायपूर्ण)
442	Fallible (पतनशील)	Unerring (अचूक)
443	Familiar (परिचित)	Strange (अपरिचित)
444	Famous (प्रसिद्ध)	Obscure, Unknown (अज्ञात)
445	Far-Fetched (अवास्तविक)	Realistic (वास्तविक)
446	Farsighted (दूरदर्शी)	Unwise (अज्ञानी)
447	Fastidious (तुनुक मिजाज)	Easy going, Adjustable (समझनेवाला)
448	Fati (मोटा)	Lean (दुबला)
449	Fatigued (थका हुआ)	Energised (जोश में)
450	Feasible (संभव)	Implausible, Impractical (असंभव)
451	Fecund (उपजाऊ)	Barren, Sterile, Sparse (बाँझ,विरल)
452	Fertile (उपजाऊ)	Barren (बंजर)
453	Fervent (उत्सुक)	Dispassionate (उदासीन)
454	Festal (उत्सव-संबंधी)	Solemn (गंभीर)
455	Fetter (बेड़ी डालना)	Liberate (स्वतंत्र करना)
456	Finite (सीमित)	Endless (अनंत)

S.N.	Words	Antonyms
457	Flagitious (घोर अपराधी)	Virtuous (धार्मिक)
458	Flamboyant (चमकीला)	Understand, Modest (मामूली)
459	Flaunt (दिखावा)	Cover (छिपाना)
460	Flaw (खोट)	Perfection (निपुणता)
461	Flawless (निर्दोष)	Defective (दोषपूर्ण)
462	Flee (भाग जाना)	Submit (समर्पण करना)
463	Flexible (लचीला)	Rigid, Stiff (कठोर)
464	Flicker (झिलमिलाहट)	Burn Steadily (नित्य, जलने वाला)
465	Flippant (गंभीर न होना)	Serious, Earnest (गंभीर, ईमानदार)
466	Flood (बाढ़)	Drought (सूखा)
467	Florid (गहरे रंग का)	Plain, Pale (सादा,फीका)
468	Fluctuate (उतार चढ़ाव)	Stabilize (स्थिर)
469	Fluent (धाराप्रवाह)	Halting (लड़खड़ाता)
470	Focus (केंद्रित प्रभाव)	Disperse (बिखेरना)
471	Foment (भड़काना)	Quell (शांत करना)
472	Foreign (विदेश)	Native (देशी)
473	Foremost (सबसे महत्वपूर्ण)	Unimportant (महत्वहीन)
474	Foresight (दूरदर्शिता)	Indiscretion (मूर्खता)
475	Forgo (त्यागना)	Conquer (जीतना)
476	Forlorn (निराश)	Joyful, Elated (आनंदपूर्ण)
477	Formal (औपचारिक)	Informal (अनौपचारिक)
478	Formidable (डरावना)	Trivial (तुच्छ)
479	Foul (बेईमानी)	Fair (ईमानदारी)
480	Frailty (निर्बलता)	Strength (मज़बूती)
481	Freed (मुक्त किया गया)	Imprisoned (कैद किया हुआ)
482	Freedom (आजादी)	Captivity (कारावास)
483	Friend (मित्र)	Foe (शत्रु)
484	Friendly (मित्रतापूर्ण)	Hostile (शत्रुतापूर्ण)
485	Friendship (मित्रता)	Enmity (शत्रुता)
486	Fritter (व्यर्थ नष्ट करना)	Save, Hoard (बचाना, इकट्ठा करना)
487	Frugality (कमखर्ची)	Prodigality, Generosity (उदारता, दानशीलता)
488	Fruitless (निरर्थक)	Successful (सफल)

S.N.	Words	Antonyms
489	Fugitive (भगोड़ा)	Captive (बंदी)
490	Furtive (गुपचुप)	Straight (स्पष्ट)
491	Gaunt (दुबला-पतला)	Plump (मोटा)
492	Generous (उदार)	Stingy (कंजूस) Inconsiderate (अविवेकी)
493	Genteel (सज्जन)	Uncivilized (असभ्य)
494	Gentleman (सज्जन)	Boor (गंवार)
495	Gigantic (विशाल)	Tiny (बहुत छोटा)
496	Glittering (शानदार)	Dull (फीका)
497	Glossy (चमकदार)	Dull (फीका)
498	Goodwill (ख्याति)	Hostility (शत्रुता)
499	Gorgeous (मनमोहक)	Ordinary (साधारण)
500	Graceful (गरिमापूर्ण)	Awkward (बेढ़गा)
501	Gracious (दयालू)	Miserable (दयनीय, दुखी)
502	Gradual (धीरे-धीरे)	Rapid (तीव्र)
503	Gradually (क्रमशः)	Abruptly (एकाएक)
504	Grandiose (वैभवशाली)	Moderate (मध्यम)
505	Gratify (प्रसन्न करना)	Disappoint, Annoy (निराश, झुझला देना)
506	Grating (कर्कश)	Musical (मधुर)
507	Gregarious (सुसामाजिक)	Unsociable, Introvert (एकांतप्रिय,. अंतर्मुखी)
508	Grieve (शोक)	Rejoice (आनंद)
509	Grim (भयंकर)	Pleasant (सुहावना)
510	Grotesque (विकृत, कुरूप)	Attractive, Natural, Plain (आकर्षक सादा)
511	Group (समूह)	Individual (अकेला)
512	Grudge (असन्तोष)	Goodwill (सद्भाव)
513	Grumpy (तुनुकमिज़ाज)	Pleasant (हँसमुख)
514	Guilty (अपराधी)	Innocent (मासूम)
515	Hail (ओला पड़ना)	Dribble (झींसी पड़नेवाली वर्षा)
516	Halcyon (शांतिपूर्ण)	Agitated (उत्तेजित)
517	Harmonious (सुसंगत)	Discordant (असंगत)
518	Harmony (सामंजस्य)	Hatred, Discord (नफरत, अनबन)
519	Harrowing (शोकजनक)	Pleasant (खुशनुमा)
520	Harsh (कठोर)	Gentle, Lenient (कोमल, नरम)
521	Hassled (परेशान)	Relaxed (तनाव मुक्त)

S.N.	Words	Antonyms
522	Haste (जल्दी)	Delay (विलंब)
523	Hazard (खतरा)	Safety (सुरक्षा)
524	Hazardous (संकटपूर्ण)	Secure (संरक्षित)
525	Hazy (धुंधला)	Clear (स्पष्ट)
526	Hearty (मिलनसार)	Aloof (अलग)
527	Heed (सावधान रहना)	Neglect (असावधानी)
528	Heedless (असावधान)	Observant (तेज़ नज़र)
529	Hefty (तगड़ा)	Slight (हलका)
530	Hegemony (नेतृत्व)	Subordination (अधीनता)
531	Heighten (बढ़ाना)	Decrease (कमी)
532	Heinous (घृणित)	Agreeable (सुखद)
533	Hereditary (अनुवांशिक)	Acquired (अर्जित)
534	Hidden (छिपा हुआ)	Apparent (स्पष्ट)
535	Hideous (घिनौना)	Beautiful, Charming (सुंदर, आकर्षक)
536	Highlight (V.) (विशिष्टता दर्शाना)	Downplay (काम करके बताना)
537	Hilarious (उल्लसित)	Sad (दुखी)
538	Hinder (बाधा पहुंचाना)	Aid, Help (सहायता)
539	Hindrance (बाधा)	Advantage (सुविधा)
540	Hoarse (कर्कश)	Smooth (कोमल)
541	Hollow (खोखला)	Solid (ठोस)
542	Hope (आशा)	Doubt, Despair (संदेह, निराशा)
543	Hopeful (आशाजनक)	Pessimistic (निराशावादी)
544	Horizontal (क्षैतिज)	Vertical (खड़ा)
545	Horrendous (भयानक)	Pleasant (सुखदायक)
546	Hostile (शत्रुतापूर्ण)	Amiable, Friendly, Sympathetic, Gentle (दोस्ताना, सहानुभुती, कोमल)
547	Huddle (ढेर लगाना)	Sort (छांटना)
548	Humble (विनम्र)	Naughty (नटखट)
549	Humility (विनम्रता)	Pride, Arrogance, Vanity (अभिमान, अंहकार)
550	Hummock (टीला)	Ditch (खाई)
551	Identical (समान)	Different (भिन्न)
552	Idiosyncrasy (अनोखापन)	Generality (सामान्य)

S.N.	Words	Antonyms
553	Ignite (आग लगाना)	Extinguish (बुझाना)
554	Ignoble (नीचे)	Dignified (सम्मानित)
555	Ignorance (अज्ञान)	Knowledge (ज्ञान)
556	Ignorant (अज्ञानी)	Learned (ज्ञानी)
557	Illusive (भ्रामक)	Factual, Reality (वास्तविक)
558	Illustrious (शानदार)	Obscure (अस्पट)
559	Imbroglio (उलझन)	Composure (मानसिक संतुलन)
560	Immaculate (बेदाग)	Filthy, Messy, Foul (गंदा, बेईमानी से)
561	Immortal (अमर)	Temporary (अस्थाई)
562	Immune (प्रतिरक्षित)	Vulnerable, Sensitive (असुरक्षित, नाजुक)
563	Impartial (निष्पक्ष)	Biased (पक्षपाती)
564	Impede (बाधा डालना)	Expedite, Advance, Facilitate (प्रगति करना)
565	Impel (उत्तेजित करना)	Repress (दबाना)
566	Impertinent (विसंगत)	Respectful (सम्मान पूर्ण)
567	Impromptu (बिना पहले सोचे हुए)	Premeditated, Prepared, Planned (पूर्व निर्धारित, तैयार)
568	Impudent (बेशर्म)	Polite, Modest (सभ्य)
569	Impugnable (विवादस्पद)	Indubious (स्पष्ट)
570	Impute (आरोप लगाना)	Defend (रक्षा करना)
571	In Toto (पूर्णतया)	Partially (आंशिक रूप से)
572	Inadvertently (अनजाने में)	Deliberately (जान - बूझकर)
573	Incarcerate (क़ैद कर देना)	Release (रिहाई)
574	Incentive (प्रोत्साहन)	Hindrance (बाधा)
575	Incite (उत्तेजित करना)	Prohibit, Discourage, Restrain (हतोत्साहित करना)
576	Include (शामिल)	Eliminate, Reject (हटाना, अस्वीकार करना)
577	Incoherent (असंगत)	Intelligible (सुगम)
578	Incongruous (असंगत)	Harmonious (सामंजस्यपूर्ण)
579	Incorporate (शामिल करना)	Exclude (निकालना)
580	Increase (बढ़ना)	Diminish (घटना)
581	Indicted (दोषी ठहराया)	Released (मुक्त करना)
582	Indifferent (उदासीन)	Attentive (सचेत)

S.N.	Words	Antonyms
583	Indignant (क्रोधित)	Pleased (प्रसन्न)
584	Induce (प्रेरित करना)	Prevent (रोकना)
585	Inert (निष्क्रिय)	Active (सक्रिय)
586	Inertia (जड़ता)	Vigour, Energy (शक्ति, ऊर्जा)
587	Inexpensive (सस्ता)	Dear (मंहगा)
588	Infallible (अचूक)	Imperfect, Faulty (त्रुटिपूर्ण)
589	Inferior (घटिया)	Superior (बेहतर)
590	Infinite (अनंत)	Limited (सीमित)
591	Infirmity (दुर्बलता)	Strength (मज़बूती)
592	Ingenious (प्रतिभावना)	Pedestrian (मामूली)
593	Ingratiating (खुशामद भरा)	Proud (अभिमानी)
594	Inhale (सांस लेना)	Exhale (सांस छोड़ना)
595	Inhibit (रोकना)	Allow, Approve (स्वीकृति देना)
596	Iniquity (अधर्मी)	Good (भलाई)
597	Initiated (आरंभ करना)	Concluded (समापन करना)
598	Innate (जन्मजात)	Acquired (अर्जित)
599	Innocent (मासूम)	Cunning (चालाक)
600	Inoffensive (अहानिकारक)	Rude (अशिष्ट, असभ्य)
601	Inordinate (अनियमित)	Reasonable (उचित)
602	Inquisitive (जिज्ञासु)	Indifferent, Unconcerned, Ignore (उदासीन, बेपरवाह)
603	Insatiable (लालची)	Content (संतुष्ट)
604	Insert (डालना)	Extract (निकालना)
605	Insidious (घातक)	Sincere (निष्कपट)
606	Instinctive (स्वाभाविक)	Rational (तर्कसंगत)
607	Insular (द्वीपीय, सीमित)	Cosmopolitan (सर्वदेशीय)
608	Intangible (न छूने योग्य)	Concrete (ठोस)
609	Intelligible (बोध गम्य)	Confused (परेशान)
610	Intentional (जान-बूझकर)	Accidental (आकस्मिक)
611	Interim (अल्पकालीन)	Permanent (स्थायी)
612	Interrogate (प्रश्न करना)	Reply (जवाब देना)
613	Inundate (बाढ़ लाना)	Underwhelm (उत्साहहीन करना)
614	Inundation (सैलाब)	Drought (सूखा)

S.N.	Words	Antonyms
615	Invaluable (अमूल्य)	Worthless (मूल्यहीन)
616	Invert (पलटना)	Straighten (सीधा करना)
617	Irk (गुस्सा दिलाना)	Please (आनंदित करना)
618	Irrelevant (बेमतलब)	Consequential (फल स्वरूप)
619	Irreversible (अपरिवर्तनीय)	Repairable (मरम्मत योग्य)
620	Irritate (चिढ़ना)	Delight (आनंद)
621	Jade (थका डालना)	Cheer (उत्साहित करना)
622	Jeopardize (खतरे में डालना)	Protect (रक्षा करना)
623	Jest (मज़ाक)	Gravity (गंभीरता)
624	Jinx (बदकिस्मती)	Spell (जादू - टोना)
625	Jolly (प्रसन्न)	Serious (गंभीर)
626	Jovial (उल्लासपूर्ण)	Gloomy Sorrowful (उदास)
627	Juicy (रसीला)	Dry (सूखा)
628	Keen (इच्छुक)	Blunt, Dull (मंदबुद्धि)
629	Kind (दयालु)	Cruel, Meanness (निर्दयी, दरिद्रता)
630	Knowledge (ज्ञान)	Ignorance (अज्ञान)
631	Lack-Lustre (बिना चमक का)	Radiant (चमकीला)
632	Laid-Back (शांतिचित)	Ambitious (महत्वाकांक्षी)
633	Lambency (उज्ज्वलता)	Dullness (मंदता)
634	Languid (कमजोर)	Energetic (शक्तिशाली)
635	Launch (प्रारंभ करना)	Withdraw (वापस लेना)
636	Lavish (खर्चीला)	Moderate (मध्य श्रेणी का)
637	Lead (नेतृत्व करना)	Follow (अनुसरण करना)
638	Learned (सीखा हुआ)	Instinctive (स्वाभाविक)
639	Lechery (कामुकता)	Benevolence (परोपकार)
640	Lenient (उदार)	Strict (कठोर)
641	Lessen (घटाना)	Increase (बढ़ाना)
642	Liberal (उदार)	Intolerant, Stingy (असहिष्णु)
643	Liberation (आज़ादी)	Bondage (गुलामी)
644	Linger (देर तक ठहरना)	Quicken (शीघ्र करना)
645	Lively (जीवंत)	Sluggish (सुस्त)
646	Loathe (घृणा करना)	Like, Love, Admire (पसंद, प्यार)
647	Lofty (ऊंचा)	Below (नीचे)

S.N.	Words	Antonyms
648	Loiter (टाल-मटोल करना)	Hasten, Punctual (समयानुकूल)
649	Loosen (ढीला करना)	Fasten (जकड़ना)
650	Loyalty (वफादारी)	Treason (विश्वासघात)
651	Lugubrious (उदास)	Optimistic (आशावादी)
652	Lunacy (पागलपन)	Sanity (अक्लमंदी)
653	Lustre (चमक)	Matte (चमकरहित)
654	Luxury (विलासिता)	Poverty (दरिद्रता)
655	Madder (क्रोधित होना)	Calm (शांत)
656	Maestro (माहिर)	Amateur (शौकीन व्यक्ति)
657	Make (बनाना)	Break (तोड़ना)
658	Malaise (अस्वस्थता)	Healthy (स्वस्थ)
659	Malicious (दुर्भावनापूर्ण)	Benign, Decent (सौम्य)
660	Malignant (घातक)	Benign (अनुकूल)
661	Malleable (लचीला)	Intractable (हठीला)
662	Manage (सफल होना)	Fail (असफल होना)
663	Manifest (स्पष्ट)	Disguise (भेष बदलना)
664	Marginal (किनारे का)	Core (भीतरी भाग)
665	Maverick (अपरंपरागत)	Conventional (परम्परागत)
666	Meandering (घुमावदार)	Straight (सीधा)
667	Meddle (दख़ल देना)	Ignore (अनदेखा करना)
668	Mediocre (औसत दर्जे का)	Exceptional (असाधारण)
669	Melody (राग)	Cacophony (कोलाहल)
670	Menace (हानिकारक)	Comfort (आराम)
671	Menacing (धमकाने वाला)	Helping (मदद करनेवाला)
672	Mental (मानसिक)	Physical (शारीरिक)
673	Meretricious (दिखावे का)	Natural (प्राकृतिक)
674	Metropolitan (महानगर संबंधी)	Provincial (प्रान्तीय)
675	Mettle (उत्साह)	Cowardice (कायरता)
676	Migrate (स्थानांतरण करना)	Return (वापसी)
677	Minuscule (बहुत छोटा)	Massive, Gigantic (विशाल)
678	Misanthropist (मानवद्वेषी)	Philanthropist (जन-हितैषी)
679	Miserable (दुखी)	Happy, Cheerful, Joyful (खुश, खुशहाल)
680	Misery (कष्ट)	Bliss (परमानंद)

S.N.	Words	Antonyms
681	Moderate (मध्यम)	Extreme (अत्यधिक)
682	Modern (आधुनिक)	Ancient (प्राचीन)
683	Monumental (अति महान)	Insignificant (तुच्छ)
684	Moot (विवादास्पद)	Definite (निश्चित)
685	Mortality (मरण)	Birth (जन्म)
686	Mould (सांचे में ढालना)	Genuine (अकृत्रिम)
687	Mournfur (शोकाकुल)	Joyous (आनंदित)
688	Movement (गतिविधि)	Static (स्थिर)
689	Multifaceted (बहुमुखी)	Simple (सरल)
690	Muster (इकट्ठा करना)	Disperse (छितराना)
691	Mutilate (विकृत करना)	Mend (मरम्मत करना)
692	Myopic (दूरदर्शी)	Farsighted (दूरदृष्टिता)
693	Myth (कल्पित)	Fact (तथ्य)
694	Nab (पकड़लेना)	Free (मुक्त करना)
695	Nadir (पतन)	Zenith (सर्वोत्तम अवस्था)
696	Naive (सीधा-सादा)	Experienced, Sophisticated (अनुभवी, जटिल)
697	Narrow (संकीर्ण)	Wide (चौड़ा)
698	Nasty (बुरा)	Pleasant (सुखद)
699	Native (मूल निवासी)	Alien, Foreign (विदेशी)
700	Neat (स्वच्छ)	Sloppy, Messy (मैला, अव्यस्थित)
701	Nebulous (अस्पष्ट)	Definite (निश्चित)
702	Neglect (लापरवाही)	Care (देखभाल)
703	Negligent (लापरवाह)	Careful (सावधान)
704	Negotiate (मोलतोल)	Remain (टिकना)
705	Nervous (घबराने वाला)	Composed (शांतचित्त)
706	Never (कभी नहीं)	Always (हमेशा)
707	Niggardly (कंजूसी से)	Lavishly, Generous (भव्य, उदार)
708	Noble (महान)	Servile (चापलूस)
709	Noisily (ऊंचे स्वर से)	Quietly (चुपचाप)
710	Nominate (मनोनीत)	Rejected (अस्वीकृत)
711	Nonconformist (संप्रदायवादी)	Conventional (परम्परागत)
712	Nondescript (गुमनाम)	Distinguished (प्रसिद्ध)

S.N.	Words	Antonyms
713	Normal (साधारण)	Strange (अजीब)
714	Notion (ख्याल)	Need (जरूरत)
715	Nourish (लालन-पालन)	Starve (भूखा)
716	Nuisance (परेशानी)	Pleasure (आनंद)
717	Numerous (प्रचुर)	Scarce (दुर्लभ)
718	Obese (मोटा)	Thin, Slim, Skinny (पतला दुबला)
719	Obfuscate (उलझाना)	Clarify (स्पष्ट करना)
720	Objective (निष्पक्ष)	Prejudiced (पक्षपातपूर्ण)
721	Obligate (बाध्य करना)	Let Off (मुक्त करना)
722	Obliging (उपकारी)	Unfriendly (अमित्रतापूर्ण)
723	Oblivious (बेख़बर)	Conscious (स्पष्ट)
724	Obscure (अस्पष्ट)	Clear (सचेत)
725	Obsolescence (प्रचलन)	Modernity (आधुनिकता)
726	Obsolete (अप्रचलित)	Recent (हाल का)
727	Obstruct (रोक लगाना)	Clear (पास करना)
728	Obtuse (मंद बुद्धि)	Sharp Witted (समझदार)
729	Offbeat (असामान्य)	Conventional (परंपरागत)
730	Officious (परेशान करने वाला)	Timid (डरपोक)
731	Offset (बराबर कर देना)	Disproportion (असमानता)
732	Omit (छोड़ देना)	Include (शामिल)
733	Opaque (अपारदार्शक)	Transparent, Clear (पारदर्शक, स्पष्ट)
734	Opponent (प्रतिद्वंदी)	Supporter (समर्थक)
735	Oppose (विरोध)	Favour (समर्थन)
736	Opprobrium (अपमान)	Adulation (अतिप्रशंसा)
737	Optimistic (आशावादी)	Pessimistic (आशावादी)
738	Optional (ऐच्छिक)	Compulsory (अनिवार्य)
739	Opulence (अधिकता)	Poverty (दरिद्रता)
740	Oral (मौखिक)	Written (लिखा हुआ)
741	Orderly (व्यवस्थित)	Chaotic (अराजक)
742	Originate (प्रारंभ करना)	Terminate (अंत करना)
743	Ostracise (बहिष्कृत करना)	Welcome, Embrace (स्वागत)
744	Outlandish (विचित्र, बाहरी)	Ordinary (सामान्य)

S.N.	Words	Antonyms
745	Outspoken (मुंहफट)	Secretive (रहस्यात्मक)
746	Outstanding (शानदार)	Ordinary (सामान्य)
747	Overlook (अनदेखी करना)	Notice (ध्यान देना)
748	Overt (प्रत्यक्ष)	Hidden, Concealed (छिपा हुआ)
749	Overweening (ज्यादा ही आत्मविश्वास)	Modest (आडंबरहीन)
750	Pacifist (शांतिवादी)	Warmonger (युद्धोत्तेजक)
751	Palatial (आलीशान)	Poor (गरीब)
752	Pale (फीका)	Bright (तीव्र)
753	Paltry (तुच्छ)	Substantial (पर्याप्त)
754	Panegyric (प्रशंसात्मक)	Criticism (आलोचना)
755	Panicky (घबराया हुआ)	Calm (शांत)
756	Pardon (क्षमा)	Punish (सज़ा)
757	Parochial (संकीर्ण)	Global (वैश्विक)
758	Parsimonious (किफायती)	Extravagant, Lavish (अतिशयोक्तिपूर्ण, भव्य)
759	Particularly (विशेष रूप से)	Generally (आम तौर पर)
760	Partner (साथी)	Opponent (प्रतिद्वंदी)
761	Passive (निष्क्रिय)	Agitated (उत्तेजित)
762	Passivity (निष्क्रियता)	Interest (दिलचस्पी)
763	Peculiar (अनोखा)	Familiar (जाना-पहचाना)
764	Peer (कुलीन)	Inferior (नीचा)
765	Pellucid (पारदर्शक)	Murky (धुंधला)
766	Penurious (दरिद्र)	Opulent (धनी)
767	Penury (दरिद्रता)	Wealth (दौलत)
768	Perish (मरजाना)	Grow (उत्पन्न होना)
769	Permanent (स्थायी)	Temporary (अस्थायी)
770	Permit (अनुमति)	Forbid (रोकना)
771	Perpetrate (पाप करना)	Prevent (प्रतिबंध करना)
772	Perpetual (लगातार)	Intermittent, Transitory (रुक-रुक कर, अस्थायी)
773	Perseverance (दृढ़ता)	Instability (क्षणभंगुरता)
774	Perspicuity (स्पष्टता)	Vagueness (अस्पष्टता)
775	Perturb (व्याकुलता)	Soothe (शांत करना)
776	Pessimist (निराशावादी)	Optimist (आशावादी)

S.N.	Words	Antonyms
777	Petty (छोटा)	Big (बड़ा)
778	Philanthropic (परोपकारी)	Self Centred (स्वकेंद्रित)
779	Phlegmatic (सुस्त)	Ardent (उत्साही)
780	Pilferer (चोर)	Police (पुलिस)
781	Placate (शांत करना)	Enrage (क्रोधित करना)
782	Placid (शांत)	Stormy (तूफ़ानी)
783	Plausible (संभाव्य)	Implausible, Unlikely (अविश्वसनीय, असंभव)
784	Pliable (लचीला)	Rigid (कठोर)
785	Plunge (कूदना)	Rise (ऊपर उठना)
786	Pompous (गर्वित)	Humble (विनीत)
787	Possess (दखल करना)	Release (छोड़ देना)
788	Potent (प्रबल)	Weak (कमज़ोर)
789	Potential (क्षमता)	Lacking (अभाव)
790	Precious (कीमती)	Worthless, Cheap (बेकार सस्ता)
791	Preclude (बंद करना)	Include (शामिल)
792	Predecessor (पूर्वज)	Successor (वारिस)
793	Premium (मूल्यवान)	Inferior (घटिया)
794	Preposterous (ऊटपटांग)	Reasonable (वाजिब)
795	Prestige (प्रतिष्ठा)	Disregard (अनादर)
796	Prevail (जीत लेना)	Surrender (हार मानना)
797	Prim (नियमानुकूल)	Informal, Dishevelled (अनौपचारिक)
798	Primed (दुरुस्त)	Unready (कच्चा)
799	Prior (पूर्व)	Subsequent (आगामी)
800	Probationer (परखाधीन)	Master (उस्ताद)
801	Probity (ईमानदार)	Deceit (छल)
802	Proceed (आगे जाना)	Recede (दूर जाना)
803	Proceeding (कार्यवाही)	Passiveness (निष्क्रियता)
804	Produce (निर्माण करना)	Destroy (नष्ट करना)
805	Professional (पेशेवर)	Amateur (शौक़ीन व्यक्ति)
806	Profound (गहन)	Superficial, Ignorant (सतही, अज्ञानी)
807	Profusion (प्रचुरता)	Scarcity (कमी)
808	Progress (प्रगति)	Decline, Retreat (पीछे हटना)

S.N.	Words	Antonyms
809	Progressive (प्रगतिशील)	Conservative (अपरिवर्तनवादी)
810	Prolific (फलदायक)	Unproductive (अनुत्पादक)
811	Prolong (लंबा करना)	Shorten (छोटा करना)
812	Prominent (प्रसिद्ध)	Obscure, Unknown, Inconspicuous (अस्पष्ट, अज्ञात, तुच्छ)
813	Protean (बहुरूपिया)	Unchanging (अपरिवर्तनीय)
814	Protect (रक्षा करना)	Harm (हानि पहुंचाना)
815	Protract (विलंब करना)	Advance (अग्रसर होना)
816	Provide (प्रदान करना)	Deny (मना करना)
817	Provident (दूरदर्शी)	Wasteful (अपव्ययी)
818	Provincial (प्रांतीय)	Metropolitan (महानगर)
819	Provisional (अस्थायी)	Permanent, Definite (स्थायी, निश्चित)
820	Provoke (भड़कना)	Soothe, Appease (शांत करना)
821	Public (सार्वजनिक)	Private (निजी)
822	Publicise (प्रचारित करना)	Withhold (रोक)
823	Puissant (ओजस्वी)	Lazy (आलसी)
824	Punctilious (बारीकियों पर ध्यान देने वाला)	Easy Going (आरामपसंद)
825	Pungent (तीखा)	Mild (सौम्य)
826	Purloin (चुराना)	Compensate (कमी पूर्ति)
827	Putrefy (गलना, सड़ना)	Combine (जोड़ना)
828	Quaint (विचित्र)	Common (सामान्य)
829	Quarrel (झगड़ा)	Harmony (सामंजस्य)
830	Quell (शांत करना)	Agitate (उत्तेजित करना)
831	Quiet (शांत)	Noisy (शोर)
832	Rambling (घुमावदार)	Coherent, Direct (संगत सीधा)
833	Ramify (श्रेणी विभाजन होना)	Unite (सम्मिल हो जाना)
834	Rampage (हंगामा करना)	Harmony (सामंजस्य)
835	Rancid (बासी)	Fresh (ताजा)
836	Random (क्रमरहित)	Specific (विशिष्ट)
837	Rapid (तीव्र)	Slow (धीरे)
838	Rapture (उत्साह)	Calmness (शांति)
839	Rash (जल्दबाजी)	Careful (सावधान)
840	Ratification (पुष्टीकरण)	Disapproval (अस्वीकार)

S.N.	Words	Antonyms
841	Raucous (कर्कश)	Subdued, Dulcet (सुरीला)
842	Rear (पिछला भाग)	Front (सामने का)
843	Reason (विचार करना)	Charge (धावा बोलना)
844	Reasonable (उचित)	Outrageous (बेहिसाब)
845	Reassure (आश्वस्त)	Discourage (हतोत्साह करना)
846	Rebate (छूट)	Increase (बढ़ना)
847	Rebellion (विद्रोह)	Submission (आधीनता)
848	Rebuff (दुतकारना)	Praise (प्रशंसा)
849	Rebuke (फटकारना)	Flattery (चापलूसी)
850	Recalled (स्मरण)	Forgotten (भुला दिया)
851	Reckless (लापरवाह)	Cautious (सतर्क)
852	Recluse (एकांतवासी)	Extrovert (बर्हिमुखी व्यक्ति)
853	Recondite (जटिल)	Straightforward (सरल)
854	Recovered (बरामद)	Lost (खोया)
855	Rectitude (इंसाफ)	Infamy (बदनामी)
856	Refined (शुद्ध किया हुआ)	Crude (कच्चा)
857	Refulgent (उज्ज्वल)	Dark (अंधेरा)
858	Reign (हुकुमत करना)	Yield (समर्पण करना)
859	Relationship (संबंध)	Opposition (विरोध)
860	Relaxed (तनावमुक्त)	Tense (तनाव में)
861	Release (रिहाई)	Confine (बंद करना)
862	Relentless (निष्ठुर)	Yielding (बात मान लेनेवाला)
863	Reluctant (अनिच्छुक)	Eager, Willing (तैयार इच्छुक)
864	Remarkable (असाधारण)	Normal (साधारण)
865	Remnant (अवशेष)	Whole (पूरा का पूरा)
866	Remote (दूरस्थ)	Close (पास)
867	Renaissance (नवजागरण)	Decadence (पतन)
868	Renowned (प्रसिद्ध)	Unknown, Obscure (अनजान, अप्रसिद्ध)
869	Repel (पीछे हटाना)	Attract (आकर्षित करना)
870	Reprimanded (फटकारना)	Praised (सराहना की)
871	Repugnant (प्रतिकूल)	Pleasant (प्रतिकूल)
872	Repulsion (घृणा)	Attraction (आकर्षण)
873	Repulsive (प्रतिकारक, अप्रिय)	Attractive, Pleasing (आकर्षक, मनभावक)

S.N.	Words	Antonyms
874	Reserved (संकोची)	Communicative, Friendly (मिलनसार)
875	Resign (त्यागपत्र देना)	Join (नियुक्त होना)
876	Resist (विरोध करना)	Yield, Allow (स्वीकार करना)
877	Resolve (संकल्प)	Indecision, Refuse (असमंजस)
878	Resource (साधन)	Lack (अभाव)
879	Responsible (ज़िम्मेदार)	Irresponsible (गैर ज़िम्मेदार)
880	Restricted (सीमित)	Unbounded (अपार)
881	Restrictive (प्रतिबंधक)	Liberal (उदारवादी)
882	Resume (फिर आरंभ करना)	Finish (समाप्त)
883	Retaliation (प्रतिशोध)	Reconciliation (सुलह)
884	Retard (धीमा करना)	Hurry (जल्दी करना)
885	Retrench (छटनी करना)	Recruit (नियुक्त करना)
886	Retrieve (सुधारना)	Damage (क्षति पहुंचाना)
887	Reveal (प्रकट करना)	Hide, Conceal (छिपाना)
888	Revered (आदरणीय)	Despised (तिरस्कृत)
889	Reverence (सम्मान)	Contempt (अपमान)
890	Revoke (वापस लेना)	Implement, Proclaim (लागू करना)
891	Reward (इनाम)	Punish (सज़ा देना)
892	Ribald (अशिष्ट)	Clean (स्वच्छ)
893	Ridiculous (बेतुका)	Reasonable (उचित)
894	Rigid (कठोर)	Flexible (लचीला)
895	Rotund (गोल मटोल)	Slim (पतला)
896	Rough (खुरदुरा)	Smooth (कोमल)
897	Routine (सामान्य)	Different (विभिन्न)
898	Rueful (उदास)	Joyful (प्रफुल्लित)
899	Ruefully (उदास)	Cheerful, Defiant (प्रसन्नतापूर्वक, अवज्ञापूर्ण)
900	Rugged (खुरदरा)	Smooth (कोमल)
901	Ruined (तबाह)	Mended (मरम्मत किया हुआ)
902	Rustic (देहाती)	Urban (शहरी)
903	Ruthless (क्रूर)	Kind, Compassionate (मेहरबान)
904	Sabotage (तोड़फोड़)	Create (निर्माण करना)
905	Sacrifice (त्याग)	Acquire (प्राप्त)
906	Safe (सुरक्षित)	Insecure (असुरक्षित)

S.N.	Words	Antonyms
907	Sagacious (चतुर)	Ignorant (अनभिज्ञ)
908	Salve (खुशामदी करना)	Blockage (रुकावट)
909	Sarcasm (ताना)	Flattery (खुशामद)
910	Savant (विद्वान)	Amateur (शौक़ीन)
911	Scarcity (कमी)	Plenty (खूब)
912	Scholarly (विद्वतापूर्ण)	Ignorant (अंजाम)
913	Scoff (हंसी उड़ाना)	Praise (प्रंशसा करना)
914	Scorn (तिरस्कार)	Praise (प्रशंसा)
915	Scrimp (बचत करना)	Squander (गंवाना)
916	Scrutable (परीक्षा करने योग्य)	Occult (रहस्यमय)
917	Scurrilous (अपमानजनक)	Complimentary (प्रशंसात्मक)
918	Seamy (अनैतिक)	Pure (पवित्र)
919	Secede (किसी मंडली से हटना)	Unite (सम्मिलित होना)
920	Secure (सुरक्षित)	Endangered (संकटग्रस्त)
921	Sedate (शांत)	Exciting (उत्तेजित)
922	Segregate (प्रथक करना)	Integrate (एकीकृत करना)
923	Seize (ज़ब्त करना)	Release (मुक्त करना)
924	Semblance (अनुरूपता)	Difference (अंतर)
925	Sentience (चेतना)	Disregard (उदासीनता)
926	Servant (नौकर)	Master (स्वामी)
927	Servile (चापलूस)	Defiant (विद्रोही)
928	Sever (अलग करना)	Unite (सम्मिलित करना)
929	Severe (कठोर)	Mild (सौम्य)
930	Shabby (जर्जर)	Nice (सुहावना)
931	Shallow (उथला)	Deep (गहरा)
932	Shimmering (झिलमिलाती)	Gloomy (उदास)
933	Shrewd (चालाक)	Naive (भोला)
934	Shun (दूर रहना / बचना)	Cherish (अच्छा लगना)
935	Skeptic (संदेहवादी)	Believer (विश्वास करनेवाला)
936	Slacken (कम करना)	Increase, Intensify (बढ़ना)
937	Slander (बदनामी)	Admire (प्रशंसा करना)
938	Slave (दास)	Master (स्वामी)
939	Slavish (दास संबंधी)	Assertive (अड़ियल)

S.N.	Words	Antonyms
940	Sleek (आकर्षक)	Dull (फीका)
941	Slothful (आलसी)	Lively (जीवन्त)
942	Sluggish (सुस्त)	Active, Alert (चौकन्ना)
943	Slur (बदनामी)	Compliment (प्रशंसा)
944	Sly (धूर्त)	Honest (ईमानदार)
945	Smoulder (सुलगना)	Froze (जम जाना)
946	Smug (दंभी)	Modst (आडंबरहीन)
947	Sober (शांत)	Agitated (उत्तेजित)
948	Sobriety (संयम)	Drunkenness (मादकता)
949	Society (समाज)	Hate (नफ़रत)
950	Soggy (गीला)	Dry (सूखा)
951	Solace (आश्वासन)	Disharmony (असामंजस्य)
952	Somber (निराशाजनक)	Cheerful (हंसमुख)
953	Span (फैलाव)	Concentrate (इकट्ठा)
954	Spare (अतिरिक्त)	Necessary (आवश्यक)
955	Sparse (विरल)	Abundant, Dense (सघन)
956	Specific (विशिष्ट)	General (आम)
957	Speculate (विचार करना)	Dismiss (खारिज करना)
958	Spellbound (मंत्रमुग्ध)	Disenchanted (मोहभंग)
959	Spiritual (आध्यात्मिक)	Physical, Material (भौतिक)
960	Split (विभाजन)	Join (जुड़ना)
961	Sprightly (उत्साहयुक्त)	Lethargic (आलसी)
962	Squalid (मैला)	Clean (साफ़)
963	Squall (चिल्लाहट)	Peace (शांति)
964	Squander (फिजूलखर्ची, धन लुटाना)	Skimp, Hoard, Saving (कंजूसी, जमा करना, बचत)
965	Stability (स्थिरता)	Inconsistency (असंगति)
966	Stale (बासी)	Fresh (ताज़ा)
967	Stalwart (साहसी)	Cowardly (कायर)
968	Startle (चौंकना)	Soothe (शांत करना)
969	Stationary (स्थिर)	Moving, Shifting, Unsteady (गतिशील, सरकाना, अस्थिर)
970	Steep (ढालवांपन)	Flat (समतल)

S.N.	Words	Antonyms
971	Stiff (कठोर)	Tender (नरम)
972	Still (स्थिर)	Active (सक्रिय)
973	Stingy (कंजूस)	Generous, Extravagant (उदार, फ़िज़ूल खर्च)
974	Stout (मोटा)	Thin (पतला)
975	Stratagem (कपट)	Frankness (सरलता)
976	Strife (कलह)	Peace (शांति)
977	Stunning (तेजस्वी)	Unattractive (बदसूरत)
978	Stupendous (अति विशाल)	Awful (भद्दा)
979	Suave (सौम्य)	Rude (अशिष्ट)
980	Suavity (मधुरता)	Misbehavior (दुराचार)
981	Subdued (नियंत्रित)	Excited (उत्साहित)
982	Sublime (उत्कृष्ट)	Ludicrous, Inferior (ऊटपटांग, हीन)
983	Submissive (विनम्र)	Stubborn (ज़िद्दी)
984	Substantial (पर्याप्त)	Doubtful, Flimsy (अनिश्चित, छिछला)
985	Succeed (सफल होना)	Lose (हार जाना)
986	Successor (वारिस)	Predecessor (पूर्वज)
987	Succinct (संक्षिप्त)	Lengthy (लंबा)
988	Sullen (हठी)	Agreeable (सहमत)
989	Sultry (कामोत्तेजक)	Frigid (उदासीन)
990	Summit (शिखर)	Bottom (तल)
991	Summon (बुलवाना)	Dismiss (खारिज)
992	Sunder (अलग करना)	Combine (जोड़ना)
993	Supplant (कपट से हटाना)	Surrender (आत्मसमर्पण)
994	Supple (लचीला)	Brittle (भुंगुर)
995	Suppress (दबाना)	Incite Reveal (उकसाना, प्रकट करना)
996	Supreme (उच्चतम)	Inferior (नीचा)
997	Surveillance (निगरानी)	Neglect (लापरवाही)
998	Survival (उत्तरजीवित)	Extinction (विलुप्त होने)
999	Susceptible (ग्रहणशील)	Immune (प्रतिरक्षित)
1000	Suspend (निलंबित करना)	Continue, Persist (दृढ़ रहना)
1001	Suspicion (संदेह)	Trust (भरोसा)
1002	Suspicious (संदेहजनक)	Trustworthy (भरोसेमंद)
1003	Sweltering (तपना)	Freezing (जमना)

S.N.	Words	Antonyms
1004	Swerve (मुड़ना)	Straighten (सीधा-होना)
1005	Swindle (धोखा देना)	Honesty (इमानदारी)
1006	Sympathy (सहानुभूति)	Cruelty (क्रूरता)
1007	Synopsis (सार-संग्रह)	Amplification (विस्तारण)
1008	Tacit (अल्पभाषी)	Explicit (सुस्पष्टवादी)
1009	Tactful (शिष्ट)	Careless (लापरवाह)
1010	Taint (कलंक)	Purify (शुद्ध)
1011	Takes Off (उड़ना)	Lands (भूमि पर उतरना)
1012	Tame (शांत)	Upset (परेशान)
1013	Tardy (मंदा)	Prompt, Quick, Early (शीघ्र)
1014	Tasty (स्वादिष्ट)	Insipid (फीका)
1015	Tempestuous (तूफ़ानी)	Calm (शांत)
1016	Temporal (सांसारिक)	Spiritual (आध्यात्मिक)
1017	Temporary (अस्थायी)	Lasting (स्थायी)
1018	Tender (कोमल)	Rough (रूखा)
1019	Tense (तना हुआ)	Relaxed (ढीला)
1020	Tentative (संभावित)	Definite (निश्चित)
1021	Terminate (बर्खास्त)	Begin, Commence (आरंभ करना)
1022	Terrible (भयानक)	Nice (सुहावना)
1023	Testimony (गवाही)	Disproof (खंडन)
1024	Theoretical (सैद्धांतिक)	Practical (व्यवहारिक)
1025	Thorough (संपूर्ण)	Cursory (सतही)
1026	Thoroughly (पूर्णता)	Superficially (अल्पज्ञाता से)
1027	Threaten (धमकाना)	Commend (सराहना करना)
1028	Timorous (डरपोक)	Bold (साहसिक)
1029	Tiresome (थकानेवाला)	Energising (स्फूर्तिदायक)
1030	To avert (टालना)	To aid (मदद करना)
1031	To filch (चुराना)	To philanthropy (परोपकार के लिए)
1032	To indict (अभियोग लगाना)	To exonerate (दोषमुक्त करना)
1033	To maneuver (पैंतरेबाज़ी करना)	To cease (समाप्त होना)
1034	Tolerate (धैर्य धारण करना)	Disapprove (अस्वीकार करना)
1035	Traditional (परंपरागत)	Unusual, Modern (असामान्य, आधुनिक)
1036	Tragedy (शोकपूर्ण घटना)	Fortune (सौभाग्य)

S.N.	Words	Antonyms
1037	Tranquility (शांति)	Disturbance (अशांति)
1038	Transience (क्षणिक होना)	Eternity (अनंत काल)
1039	Treacherous (नमक हराम)	Faithful (वफादार)
1040	Treachery (धोखा)	Loyalty (इमानदारी)
1041	Tremulous (डरपोक)	Steady, Stable (स्थिर)
1042	Trigger (शुरू करना)	Halt (रोक लगाना)
1043	Tropical (उष्ण)	Cold (सर्द)
1044	Turbid (मटमैला)	Clear (साफ़)
1045	Turgid (आडंबरी)	Humble (सादगीपूर्ण)
1046	Tyranny (अत्याचार)	Autonomy (स्वराज्य)
1047	Tyrant (तानाशाह)	Benefactor (दान देनेवाला)
1048	Tyro (नौसिखिए)	Professional (पेशेवर)
1049	Ulterior (गुप्त)	Overt (प्रत्यक्ष)
1050	Unanimity (सर्व-सम्मति)	Disagreement (मतभेद)
1051	Unapproachable (पहुंच से बाहर का)	Accessible (पहुंचने योग्य)
1052	Uncanny (अलौकिक)	Ordinary (साधारण)
1053	Uncouth (अशिष्ट)	Refined (संस्कारयुक्त)
1054	Unfair (अनुचित)	Just (न्याय संगत)
1055	Unfeeling (निर्मम)	Affectionate (स्नेही)
1056	Unforeseen (आकस्मिक)	Expected (अपेक्षित होना)
1057	Unitary (एकात्मक)	Multiple, Incomplete (एकाधिक, अपूर्ण)
1058	United (संयुक्त)	Separated (विभाजित)
1059	Unprecedented (अभूतपूर्व)	Known (जानने वाला)
1060	Unpredictable (अप्रत्याशित)	Dependable, Reliable (भरोसमंद, विश्वसनीय)
1061	Unscrupulous (अनैतिक)	Conscientious (ईमानदार)
1062	Unusual (असामान्य)	Commonplace (सामान्य)
1063	Unworthy (अयोग्य)	Deserving (योग्य)
1064	Uphold (समर्थन)	Oppose (विरोध)
1065	Urban (शहरी)	Rural (ग्रामीण)
1066	Urbane (शिष्ट)	Crude (अशिष्ट)
1067	Usurp (हड़पना)	Restore, Surrender, Release (पुर्नस्थापित, आत्मसमर्पण, त्यागना)
1068	Vacate (खाली करना)	Occupy (दख़ल करना)

S.N.	Words	Antonyms
1069	Vacillation (चंचलता)	Steadfastness (दृढ़ता)
1070	Vagrant (आवारा)	Settled (स्थायी)
1071	Vaguely (अस्पष्ट रूप से)	Distinctly (साफ़ तौर पर)
1072	Vanguard (अग्र-दल)	Follower (अनुसरणकर्ता)
1073	Vanity (घमंड)	Modesty, Humility (शील, नम्रता)
1074	Vast (व्यापक)	Small (छोटा)
1075	Veneration (आदर)	Disrespect, Contempt (अनादर, अवमानना)
1076	Verbose (शब्द बहुल)	Brief (संक्षिप्त)
1077	Verdant (हरा भरा)	Dying (मरता हुआ)
1078	Verity (सचाई)	Falsehood (झूठ)
1079	Versatile (अस्थाई)	Inflexible (अटल)
1080	Veteran (अनुभवी)	Novice (नौसिखिए)
1081	Vexatious (तंग करने वाला)	Soothing (संतुष्ट करनेवाला)
1082	Vibrant (फुरतीला)	Listless (उदासीन)
1083	Vice (बुराई)	Virtue (गुण)
1084	Victor (विजेता)	Laser (परास्त)
1085	Vigilance (जागरूकता)	Indifference (उदासीनता)
1086	Vigorous (जोरदार)	Spiritless (बेजान)
1087	Vile (नीच)	Decent (सभ्य)
1088	Virtual (आभासी)	Authentic (विश्वसनीय)
1089	Virtue (गुण)	Vice (बुराई)
1090	Virtuous (धार्मिक)	Vicious, Sinful (पापी)
1091	Visionary (काल्पनिक)	Pragmatist, Realist, Pragmatic (व्यवहारिक, यथार्थवाद
1092	Vista (दृश्य)	Blindness (अंधापन)
1093	Vitiate (नुकसान पहुंचाना)	Affirm (समर्थन करना)
1094	Vocal (स्वर)	Silent (मूक)
1095	Volatile (परिवर्तनशील)	Certain (निश्चित)
1096	Voluble (बातूनी)	Reserved (संकोची)
1097	Voluntary (स्वयंसेवी)	Mandatory (अनिवार्य)
1098	Vulnerable (असुरक्षित)	Secure (सुरक्षित)
1099	Waggish (मज़ाकिया)	Solemn (गंभीर)
1100	Wane (कम होना)	Increase (बढ़ना)

S.N.	Words	Antonyms
1101	Warm (गरम)	Cool (ठंडा)
1102	Waver (डगमगाना)	Steady (स्थिर)
1103	Wavering (अस्थिर)	Unchanging (स्थिर)
1104	Weakness (कमजोरी)	Strength (मज़बूती)
1105	Wicked (दुष्ट)	Good, Righteous (अच्छा, धर्मी)
1106	Widespread (बड़े पैमाने पर)	Limited (सीमित)
1107	Widespread (व्यापक)	Limited (सीमित)
1108	Wisdom (बुद्धिमान)	Stupidity (मूर्खता)
1109	Wither (मुरझाना)	Bloom, Grow (फूल खिलना, उगाना)
1110	Worsen (बदतर)	Improve (बेहतर)
1111	Wreck (विनाश)	Build (निर्माण)
1112	Yield (मान लेना)	Resist (विरोध करना)
1113	Zany (नासमझ)	Sober, Serious (शांत, गंभीर)
1114	Zeal (उत्साह)	Apathy (उदासीनता)
1115	Zealous (उत्साही)	Indifferent (उदासीन)
1116	Zenith (शीर्ष बिंदु)	Nadir (सबसे निम्न बिंदु)

Most Repeated Antonyms asked in SSC Exams

1	Hostile (शत्रुतापूर्ण)	Amiable, Friendly, Sympathetic, Gentle (दोस्ताना, सहानुभूति, कोमल)
2	Arrogant (अभिमानी)	Modest, Humble, Humility (foeuz) (विनम्र)
3	Shallow (उथला)	Deep (गहरा)
4	Acquit (दोषमुक्त करना)	Condemn, Convict, Blame (दोष लगाना)
5	Adamant (अटल)	Yielding, Gullible, Flexible (नर्म, लचीला)
6	Agony (कष्ट)	Pleasure, Ecstasy, Delight, Comfort (आनंद, उत्साह और आराम)
7	Flexible (लचीला)	Rigid, Stiff (कठोर)
8	Stingy (कंजूस)	Generous, Extravagant (उदार, फिजूल ख़र्च)
9	Vanity (घमंड)	Modesty, Humility (नम्रता)
10	Affirm (स्वीकार करना)	Refuse, Disagree, Denial (मना करना, असहमत होना)
11	Ambiguous (अस्पष्ट)	Precise, Clear (स्पष्ट)
12	Arid (बंजर)	Wet, Fertile (गीला, उपजाऊ)

S.N.	Words	Antonyms
13	Autonomy (स्वराज्य)	Dependence (निर्भरता)
14	Callous (कठोर)	Sensitive, Sympathetic, Concerned (संवेदनशील, सहानुभूति, चिंतित)
15	Distant (दूर)	Close, Near (पास)
16	Dormant (निष्क्रिय)	Active (सक्रिय)
17	Harsh (कठोर)	Gentle, Lenient (कोमल, नरम)
18	Impede (बाधा डालना)	Expedite, Advance, Facilitate (प्रगति करना)
19	Inquisitive (जिज्ञासु)	Indifferent, Unconcerned, Ignore (उदासीन, बेपरवाह)
20	Miserable (दुखी)	Happy, Cheerful, Joyful (खुश, खुशहाल)
21	Opaque (अपारदर्शक)	Transparent, Clear (पारदर्शक, स्पष्ट)
22	Profound (गहन)	Superficial, Ignorant (सतही, अज्ञानी)
23	Rapid (तीव्र)	Slow (धीरे)
24	Reluctant (अनिच्छुक)	Eager, Willing (तैयार, इच्छुक)
25	Repulsive (प्रतिकारक, अप्रिय)	Attractive, Pleasing (आकर्षक, मनभावन)
26	Severe (कठोर)	Mild (सौम्य)
27	Sparse (विरल)	Abundant, Dense (सघन)
28	Stationary (स्थिर)	Moving, Shifting, Unsteady (गतिशील, सरकाना, अस्थिर)
29	Traditional (परंपरागत)	Unusual, Modern (असामान्य, आधुनिक)
30	Virtue (गुण)	Vice (बुराई)
31	Abundance (प्रचुरता)	Scarcity (कमी)
32	Ample (प्रचुर)	Meagre (अल्प)
33	Applaud (सराहना)	Denounce, Criticize, Censure (निंदा)
34	Appoint (नियुक्त करना)	Dismiss (खारिज)
35	Attract (आकर्षित)	Repel (पीछे हटाना)
36	Augment (बढ़ाना)	Degrade, Decrease, Diminish (घटाना)
37	Bold (साहसिक)	Timid (डरपोक)

UNIT 9 Synonyms and Antonyms (Miscellaneous)

9.1 One Word has Many Synonyms

A synonym is a word which conveys a meaning similar to the given word. While giving a synonym, a student should always remember that a synonym should be in the same part of speech in which the given word is. For examples.

The correct synonym of envy is jealousy and not jealous because envy and jealousy are nouns while jealous is an adjective.

1.	Adaptation	conformation, harmonization, synchronization.
2.	Apt	applicable, germane, appropriate, pertinent.
3.	Adjust	fit, suit, adapt, accommodate, conform, synchronize, attune.
4.	Accelerate	intensify, redouble, step up, stimulate, energize,
5.	Add	sum, total.
6.	All	aggregate, total, whole, gross, sum.
7.	Accumulation	agglomeration, conglomeration, aggregation, concentration,
8.	Accuse	calumniate, slander, malign, denigrate, blacken, tarnish, sully.
9.	Abnormal	unnatural, aberrant, freakish, eccentric, anomalous.
10.	Apathetic	unenthusiastic. unambitious, unstirred, unimpassioned, uninspired, unmoved.
11.	Authoritarian	masterful, domineering, lordly, bossy, autocratic, dictatorial.
12.	Association	league, alliance, axis, federation.
13.	Abandon	desertion, defection, secession, withdrawal.
14.	Abash	embarrass, modest, timid, be ashamed.
15.	Abhor	loathe, abominate, detest, hate.
16.	Abode	dwelling, residence, home.
17.	Adieu	farewell, good-bye, valediction.
18.	Bate	diminish, decrease, lessen, deduct.
19.	Bond	chain, tie, band, yoke, nexus, link, liaison.
20.	Bedevil	confuse, confound, complicate, perplex, involve, entangle, embroil.
21.	Bewitch	charm, enchant, fascinate.
22.	Bizarre	strange, curious, odd, queer, funny, peculiar, grotesque.
23.	Barbaric	wild, savage, brutish, uncivilized, uncultured, primitive.
24.	Behaviour	demeanour, conduct, deportment.
25.	Breeze	zephyr, gale, wind.
26.	Beseech	appeal, implore, crave, beg.

27.	Beauty	elegance, grace, charm, attractiveness.
28.	Babble	nonsense, bombast, jargon.
29.	Bandit	robber, plagiarist.
30.	Bashful	reserve, shy, coy, demure.
31.	Bemoan	lament, mourn, grieve, weep over.
32.	Booty	spoil, plunder, prey.
33.	Burnished	polished, sleek, glossy.
34.	Circumstance	factor, situation, condition.
35.	Copy	reproduction, replica, fascimile, tracing, transcription, impression.
36.	Compensatory	compensating, countervailing, balancing.
37.	Connect	attach, annex, tag, clip, contact.
38.	Continuity	cohesion, connectedness, tenaciousness.
39.	Comprehensive	omnibus, encyclopaedic, all-embracing, full-length.
40.	Constitute	compose, form, make, construct, organise, build.
41.	Complex	intricate, complicated, mazy, winding.
42.	Curial	judicial, inquisitional.
43.	Caress	love, fondle, dandle, pat, hug.
44.	Contend	combat, strive, struggle, fight, campaign, tussle, wrestle, grapple.
45.	Co-operation	reciprocity, sympathy, co-existence, league, amity, compatibility.
46.	Cajole	flatter, wheedle, inveigle.
47.	Celibacy	bachelorhood, chastity.
48.	Cling	stick, adhere, hug.
49.	Calamity	disaster, affliction, distress.
50.	Cheerless	dejected, gloomy, mournful, sad.
51.	Competent	capable, learned, efficient, clever.
52.	Degree	proportion, ratio, scale.
53.	Disjoin	disunite, dissociate, divorce, part, sever, disconnect, unplug.
54.	Disorder	incoordination, muddle, chaos, anarchy.
55.	Disclose	reveal, expose, unveil, unfold.
56.	Devil	fiend, imp, satan.
57.	Divine	holy, sanctified, sacred, celestial, sublime, numinous, superhuman.
58.	Distant	remote, far-away, asunder.
59.	Disinterested	dispassionate, impersonal, uninvolved, detached, impartial, indifferent.
60.	Dislike	repugnance, detestation, loathing, abhorrence, disfavour, disaffection.
61.	Degrading	lowering, demeaning, ignominious, derogatory.
62.	Dangerous	dreadful, fearsome, awesome.

63.	Defiant	proud, provocative, bellicose, militant, disobedient
64.	Disfigure	deform, cripple, maim, deface.
65.	Damn	curse, swear, scold, denounce.
66.	Dandy	coxcomb, puppy, man about town.
67.	Deceit	fraud, bluff, guile, knavery.
68.	Deity	omnipotence, providence, God.
69.	Demise	death, decease, eternal rest, expiry.
70.	Devoid	release, exempt from, immune from, empty.
71.	Existence	life, being, absoluteness.
72.	Ethnic	racial, tribal, phyletic, clannish.
73.	Equilibrium	equipoise, balance, steadiness, poise.
74.	Extensive	far-ranging, far-flying, far-reaching, far-stretching, vast.
75.	Enormous	immense, vast, colossal, monumental.
76.	Ending	final, terminal, last, ultimate, extreme, polar, conclusive, crowning.
77.	Ecclesiastical	ecclesiastic, churchly, theocratic, heavenly.
78.	Endorse	legislate, pass, enact, ordain, en-force, agree.
79.	Enrage	upset, discompose, ruffle, irritate, annoy, vex, anger.
80.	Erotic	aphrodisiac, erotogenic, amatory.
81.	Excellent	overwhelming, awesome, awe-inspiring, breath-taking.
82.	Enchant	fascinate, bewitch, captivate, enrapture.
83.	Earnest	serious, solemn, impressive.
84.	Elevation	eminence, loftiness, sublimity, height, zenith, culmination.
85.	Eccentricity	informality, anomaly, peculiarity, exception.
86.	Effulgence	arrogance, haughtiness, shamelessness.
87.	Extempore	at once, on the spur of the moment.
88.	Fragmentary	broken, brashy, crumbly, in bits, in pieces.
89.	Foreigner	alien, stranger, outlandish, expatriate.
90.	First	initial, maiden, starting, natal, original.
91.	Forgiving	placable, condoning, unresentful, forbearing.
92.	Flatterer	sycophant, sponger, hanger-on.
93.	Feelingly	unctuously, earnestly, devoutly, sincerely.
94.	Fervent	fervid, passionate, intense, earnest, impassioned.
95.	Fatigue	overtax, extort, suck, squeeze, grind, tiredness, exhaust
96.	Fat	stout, plump, obese, chubby.
97.	Frigid	cold, chilly, biting, nipping, shivering.
98.	Fructify	generate, impregnate, multiply.

99.	Fame	reputation, glory, renown.
100.	Feeble	frail, languid, faint, weak.
101.	Fickle	changeable, wavering, irresolute, unsteady, amenable.
102.	Fraud	imposture, impostor, deception. duplicity.
103.	Greatness	largeness, bigness, vastness, gigantism, enormousness.
104.	Group	constellation, galaxy, cluster, bevy, flock, team.
105.	Generalise	broaden, widen, universalise.
106.	Gluttony	greediness, rapacity, insatiability, voracity, gulosity.
107.	Grave	serious, sober, solemn, sedate, staid, demure, stern.
108.	Given	bestowed, gifted, gratuitous, gratis.
109.	Gab	jabber, chatter, prattle, twaddle.
110.	Gesticulate	wink, nod, beck, nudge, gesture,
111.	Grasp	hold, seize, snatch, grip, grab.
112.	Generous	liberal, bountiful, magnanimous.
113.	Gratitude	thankfulness, gratefulness, indebtedness.
114.	Hymn	song, religious lyric, psalm, anthem, paean.
115.	Heathen	amoralist, materialist, worldling, rude, barbarous.
116.	Hypocritical	traitorous, treasonous, disloyal.
117.	Hard	harsh, rigorous, intolerant, severe, cruel, difficult.
118.	Humbled	unimportant, withered, tarnished.
119.	Hire	rent, lease, charter.
120.	Hindrance	impediment, obstruction, restriction, hampering, barrier.
121.	Hallucination	delusion, illusion, dream.
122.	Hoodwink	mystify, puzzle, deceive, lead astray.
123.	Handsome	beautiful, graceful, elegant, exquisite.
124.	Henpecked	enslaved, under one's thumb, tied to one's apron string.
125.	Heap	pile, gather, collect, board, store.
126.	Harass	trouble, afflict, inflict.
127.	Imitate	ape, parrot, flatter, echo, mirror, reflect.
128.	Inaptitude	unfitness, incapacity, incompetence.
129.	Innocent	blameless, sinless, guiltless.
130.	Intact	untouched, unaffected, unbroken, unimpaired, unabridged.
131.	Illegal	illegitimate, illicit, contraband, impermissible.
132.	Indict	impeach, arraign, complain, charge, convict.
133.	Insolence	hubris, arrogance, naughtiness, loftiness.
134.	Inimical	unfriendly, loveless, unsympathetic, disenchanted.

135.	Intolerable	insufferable, impossible, unendurable, unbearable, extreme.
136.	Join	conjoin, yoke, hyphenate, assemble, unite.
137.	Jolly	merry, jubilant, lively, festive, gay. jovial, mirthful, hilarious, joyous.
138.	Justice	impartiality, equity, fairness, right, integrity, justness.
139.	Kinship	relationship, alliance, ties of blood.
140.	Keen	sharp, acute, penetrating, eager.
141.	Kill	murder, assassinate, destroy, slay, massacre, butcher, slaughter.
142.	Knowledge	scholarship, erudition, learning, attainments, education, acquirements.
143.	Lifelike	realistic, photographic, exact, verisimilitude, natural.
144.	Large	substantial, considerable, sizeable, bulky, massy, massive.
145.	Lenient	gentle, tender, squeamish, placable, unhardened, tolerant, mild.
146.	Lax	loose, slack, disorganized.
147.	Mismatch	mismate, misadapt, misfit, miscast.
148.	Middle class	bourgeois, black-coat worker, white-collar worker.
149.	Mixture	mingling, blending, harmonization, interpolation.
150.	Modesty	lowliness, unpretentiousness, meekness, resignation, self-depreciation, self-effacement, humble.
151.	Miscarry	abort, misfire, fizzle out, crash.
152.	Native	indigenous, original, inbred, real primitive, intrinsic.
153.	Natural	normal, usual, consistent, regular, inevitable.
154.	Necessary	needful, indispensable, expedient, requisite, essential, unavoidable, inevitable.
155.	Neighbouring	adjacent, near to, contiguous, bordering, close to, proximate.
156.	Nervous	timorous, shaky, timid, hesitant.
157.	Noble	stately, dignified, magnanimous, elevated, exalted, lordly
158.	Overstep	exceed, pass, surpass, overtrump, outshine, eclipse, overshadow.
159.	Orderless	disordered, disorganised, jumbled, in disarray.
160.	Occultist	mystic, transcendentalist, esoteric, theosophist, spiritualist, alchemist.
161.	Offender	villain, scoundrel, crook, imposter.
162.	Ornamental	decorative, fancy, glamorous, picturesque, quaint.
163.	Oppress	tyrannize, overawe, intimidate, terrorize.
164.	Obstruct	shield, hinder, armour, fortify.
165.	Opposition	disharmony, dissonance, jar, recrimination, bickering, friction, hostility.
166.	Opponent	opposer, adversary, antagonist.
167.	Plenitude	fullness, maximum, saturation, abundance.
168.	Precursor	predecessor, ancestor, forbear.
169.	Profane	unholy, unsanctified, sacrilegious, God-forsaken, infidel, pagan, gentile.

170.	Pietistic	fervent, seraphic, inspired, austere.
171.	Plebeian	common, simple, untitled, ignoble.
172.	Promote	help, raise, exhort, advocate, elevate.
173.	Patience	forbearance, endurance, tolerance, sufferance.
174.	Prodigal	spender, waster, spendthrift, squanderer.
175.	Quantify	allot, rate, ration.
176.	Quake	shake, tremble, quiver, shiver, shudder, stutter.
177.	Queer	eccentric, abnormal, strange, whimsical, wayward, odd, quaint, peculiar.
178.	Relation	reference, respect, regard, rapport.
179.	Referral	allusion, mention, citation, quotation.
180.	Remainder	residue, residuals, result, left over.
181.	Ritualistic	ceremonious, formalistic, sabbatarian, liturgical.
182.	Repentant	contrite, remorseful, regretful, apologetic, sorry.
183.	Ridiculous	sardonic, derisive, sarcastic, ironical, quizzical.
184.	Relinquish	retire, disclaim, surrender.
185.	Retaliatory	retaliative, retributive, revengeful.
186.	Repulsive	ugly, repelling, odious, revolting, offensive, loathsome.
187.	Renounce	abandon, discard, leave, abdicate.
188.	Rumour	hearsay, scandal.
189.	Similarity	resemblance, likeness, similitude, semblance.
190.	Superiority	sublimity, transcendence, loftiness.
191.	Shortening	severance, detraction, amputation, excision, curtailing.
192.	Suitable	appropriate, eligible, relevant, befitting, convenient.
193.	Scission	section, cleavage, division, dichotomy.
194.	Sequent	following, succeeding, incoming ensuing, next.
195.	Sort	type, variety, kind.
196.	Sorcery	witchery, spellbinding, magic, wizardry.
197.	Sensual	earthly, gross, unspiritual.
198.	Selfish	ego-centric, egoistic, self-absorbed, narcissistic.
199.	Secluded	private, sequestered, retired, hidden, buried.
200.	Stimulate	provoke, urge, instigate, incite.
201.	Spontaneous	instinctive, unrestricted, natural, unchecked.
202.	Suppress	check, impede, restrain, bridle.
203.	Temperament	temper, humour, disposition, mood, spirit.
204.	Turmoil	turbulence, tumult, frenzy, storm, upheavel, convulsion.
205.	Terminate	conclude, close, determinate, finish, consummate.

206.	Trustworthy	reliable, dependable, trusty, faithful, loyal.
207.	Thankless	rewardless, bootless, unacknowledged.
208.	Tasteful	gracious, dignified, choice, exquisite.
209.	Tragedy	calamity, disaster, catastrophe, affliction.
210.	Tyrant	oppressor, bully, despot, persecutor, autocrat.
211.	True	exact, accurate, faithful, authentic, veracious.
212.	Tremble	shiver, quake, quiver, shudder, vibrate, oscillate.
213.	Travel	journey, voyage, tour, roam, wander, ramble.
214.	Tough	tenacious, strong, firm, stiff, fibrous, rigid, durable.
215.	Theory	doctrine, hypothesis, supposition, belief, speculation, presumption, postulate, assumption.
216.	Unborn	uncreated, unmade, unconceived, undiscovered, uninvented, unimagined.
217.	Unimitated	inimitable, transcendent, unique, uplagiarized.
218.	Unravel	untangle, comb out, unweave, uncoil, untwist, untwine.
219.	Unfortunate	ill-fated, unlucky, ill-starred, starcrossed, unblest, luckless, doomed.
220.	Unbeaten	unsubdued, unvanquished, unbeatable, invincible, undefeated.
221.	Understand	peceive, apprehend, grasp, discern, realise.
222.	Unfair	unjust, wrongful, dishonest, partial, dishonourable.
223.	Urge	spur, incite, prompt, impel, goad, stimulate, drive, force.
224.	Use	exercise, employ, utilise, practise.
225.	Unconcerned	apathetic, indifferent, cool, disinterested.
226.	Vice	fault, demerit, infirmity, frailty, foible.
227.	Virtuous	law-abiding, honest, scrupulous, principled, soul-searching, incorruptible, stainless.
228.	Violent	atrocious, brutal, fierce, savage.
229.	Vain	shameless, unblushing, unabashed, brazen, conceited.
230.	Variegated	inlaid, enamelled, embroidered.
231.	Vindicator	patron, paladin, loyalist, guard, sentinel, escort.
232.	Veracity	reality, honesty, truthfulness, frankness.
233.	Vulgar	indecent, unrefined.
234.	Vivid	clear, apparent, bright.
235.	Volunteer	proffer, tender, propose, offer, undertake, tend.
236.	Vibrate	quiver, oscillate, swing, sway, shiver, shake.
237.	Value	appreciate, prize, esteem, treasure.
238.	Vacant	empty, unoccupied, void, unfulfilled, exhausted.
239.	Weighty	ample, voluminous, capacious.
240.	Whole	total, universal, holistic, integral.

241.	Worship	honour, revere, venerate, adore.
242.	Wicked	bad, unvirtuous, immoral.
243.	Wooing	courting, spooning, flirting.
244.	Wonderful	wondrous, marvellous, miraculous, phenomenal, stupendous.
245.	Warlike	militaristic, bellicose, aggressive, combative, unpacific, chaotic.
246.	Wealth	riches, abundance, fortune, plenty.
247.	Warmth	fervour, ardour, affection.
248.	Yield	forego, surrender, concede.
249.	Zenith	summit, acme, pinnacle, culmination, height, top, apex, climax.
250.	Zero	nought, nil, nothing, cipher.

9.2 Synonyms-Objective Multiple Choice Type

Directions : Choose the word from among the four options (a), (b), (c) and (d) which is nearest in meaning to the given word.

1. Abrupt
   (a) uneven (b) sudden
   (c) unlawful (d) irritating
2. Abeyance
   (a) obedience (b) suspension
   (c) servile humility (d) lassitude
3. Abysmal
   (a) despairing (b) long discourse
   (c) total sum (d) bottomless
4. Abstinence
   (a) self-denial
   (b) lack of control
   (c) failure to be present
   (d) indifference
5. **Aberrate**
   (a) to wander or deviate from
   (b) wandering of the intellect
   (c) mental lapse
   (d) queer
6. Abject
   (a) cast away (b) mean
   (c) worthless (d) grovelling
7. Absolve
   (a) to set free (b) to pardon
   (c) to acquit (d) to accomplish
8. Absonant
   (a) discordant (b) absurd
   (c) unnatural (d) contrary to reason
9. Abstract
   (a) to draw away (b) to separate
   (c) to remove quietly (d) a thing existing only in India
10. Acclimatize
   (a) announce (b) accustom
   (c) approve (d) make tall claims
11. Accrue
   (a) to keep hold of (b) to overcome
   (c) to obtain secretly (d) to accumulate
12. Acme
   (a) the top (b) highest point
   (c) the culmination (d) zenith
13. Acquiesce
   (a) to rest satisfied
   (b) not making any opposition to a situation
   (c) to assent
   (d) quiet submission
14. Accumulate
   (a) overcome (b) spread
   (c) collect (d) disperse
15. Accurate
   (a) apprehend (b) guess
   (c) improve (d) exact
16. Addiction
   (a) remainder (b) long discourse
   (c) total (d) slavish habit
17. Admonish
   (a) to warn (b) to reproof
   (c) to counsel (d) to advise
18. Adumbrate
   (a) to give a faint shadow of
   (b) to shadow forth
   (c) to fore-shadow
   (d) to over shadow
19. Adulation
   (a) fawning (b) praise
   (c) embarrassment (d) veneration
20. Adversary
   (a) companion (b) accomplice
   (c) opponent (d) partner

21. Agrarian
    (a) relating to land
    (b) conserving the management of land
    (c) land distribution
    (d) cultivation of land

22. Alight
    (a) to dismount (b) to descend
    (c) to perch (d) to settle

23. Alleviate
    (a) to dilute (b) to lessen
    (c) to humiliate (d) to make excuses

24. Ameliorate
    (a) to appease (b) to make endurable
    (c) to humiliate (d) to release

25. Ambient
    (a) going round
    (b) surrounding
    (c) that which encompasses
    (d) the air or sky

26. Ample
    (a) unlimited (b) extravagant
    (c) abundant (d) scanty

27. Amnesty
    (a) approval (b) acquittal
    (c) eloquence (d) general pardon.

28. Annulment
    (a) ignorance (b) boredom
    (c) abolition (d) numbness

29. Annihilate
    (a) to reduce
    (b) to put out of existence
    (c) to crush by word
    (d) to wither by look

30. Anomaly
    (a) irregularity
    (b) deviation from the rule
    (c) incongruous
    (d) an oddity

31. Appease
    (a) to anger (b) to assist
    (c) to pacify (d) to surrender

32. Archaic
    (a) awkward
    (b) damaged
    (c) lame
    (d) belonging to an earlier period

33. Arrant
    (a) downright (b) mitigated
    (c) out and out (d) notorious

34. Assiduously
    (a) persistently (b) bitterly
    (c) hopefully (d) enthusiastically

35. Askance
    (a) awry
    (b) obliquely
    (c) to look with disdain
    (d) disapprobation

36. Assuage
    (a) to soften (b) to reduce
    (c) to allay (d) to abate or subside

37. Austere
    (a) proud (b) rigorous
    (c) revered (d) very poor

38. Aura
    (a) fame (b) crown
    (c) subtle emanation (d) holiness

39. Averruncate
    (a) to ward off (b) to uproot
    (c) to avert (d) to weed out

40. Axiom
    (a) a self-evident truth
    (b) universal principle
    (c) a postulate assumption
    (d) true worth

41. Banal
    (a) hostile (b) commonplace
    (c) forbidden (d) genial

42. Baffle
(a) annoy (b) irritate
(c) puzzle (d) destroy

43. Balm
(a) consolation (b) painful
(c) soft (d) cool

44. Barbarous
(a) quarrelsome (b) savage
(c) rough (d) civilized

45. Beguile
(a) benefit (b) betray
(c) deceive (d) beware

46. Beleaguer
(a) blacken (b) besiege
(c) bereft (d) surrender

47. Benign
(a) radiant (b) religious
(c) kindly (d) hopeful

48. Benevolence
(a) active kindness (b) troublesome
(c) honesty (d) respectful

49. Beseech
(a) deceive (b) entreat
(c) advise (d) betray

50. Berserk
(a) clever (b) happy
(c) noisy (d) uncontrollably wild

51. Bestial
(a) shallow (b) brutish
(c) wild (d) ugly

52. Boisterous
(a) happy
(b) tolerance
(c) noisy and cheerful
(d) excited

53. Bonhomie
(a) unity
(b) tolerance
(c) happiness
(d) hearty pleasantness of manner

54. Bravura
(a) spirited
(b) dashing in execution
(c) an impression of supreme ease
(d) florid air

55. Brunt
(a) load (b) impact
(c) weight (d) consequence

56. Burlesque
(a) ludicrous
(b) a piece of literature or acting that mocks its original by grotesque exaggeration
(c) jocular
(d) jocund

57. Cacophony
(a) a disagreeable sound
(b) discord of sounds
(c) harsh sounding
(d) jarring sound

58. Callous
(a) careless (b) forgetful
(c) deceptive (d) unfeeling

59. Calamity
(a) fortune (b) peaceful
(c) smooth (d) disaster

60. Camaraderie
(a) suspicion (b) hostility
(c) frank (d) friendliness

61. Candid
(a) frank (b) excited
(c) overjoyed (d) enthusiastic

62. Capitulate
(a) emphasize (b) to rush
(c) overturn (d) to surrender

63. Capricious
(a) greedy (b) unreliable
(c) conceited (d) stingy

64. Carnal
(a) natural (b) primitive
(c) sensual (d) spiritual

65. Catastrophe
(a) great destruction (b) development
(c) dependence (d) danger

66. Cavil
(a) to make fun of (b) to find fault
(c) to insult (d) to whine

67. Cantankerous
(a) cross-grained (b) perverse in temper
(c) irritable (d) short-tempered

68. Censorious
(a) rude (b) sarcastic
(c) severely critical (d) annoying

69. Chauvinish
(a) blind patriotism (b) political trickery
(c) buffoonery (d) defeatism

70. Chide
(a) to make fun of (b) to rebuke
(c) to cheat (d) deprive

71. Chastisement
(a) punishment (b) opposition
(c) harassment (d) rudeness

72. Circumlocution
(a) using more words than
(b) evasive talk
(c) long speech
(d) irrelevant details

73. Circumspect
(a) curious (b) wary
(c) cautious (d) prudent

74. Clandestine
(a) concealed (b) hidden
(c) private (d) on the sly

75. Concede
(a) demand (b) approve
(c) benefit (d) admit

76. Congenial
(a) kindred spirit
(b) cold
(c) existing at or from birth
(d) weak in character

77. Concomitant
(a) the which accompanies or attends
(b) agreeable friend
(c) contestant
(d) collaborator

78. Contour
(a) rout (b) appearance
(c) outline (d) frame

79. Cogitate
(a) to turn a thing over in one's mind
(b) to meditate
(c) to ponder
(d) to think deeply

80. Cognition
(a) knowledge
(b) apprehension
(c) knowing in the widest sense
(d) to be conscious of

81. Commodious
(a) suitable (b) convenient
(c) roomy (d) spacious

82. Complaisant
(a) desirous of pleasing
(b) obliging
(c) facile
(d) ready to condone

83. Compunction
(a) guilt
(b) pricking of conscience
(c) remorse
(d) regret tinged with pity

84. Concur
(a) to run together (b) to meet on one point
(c) to coincide (d) to act together

85. Confound
(a) to overthrow
(b) to confuse
(c) to throw into disorder
(d) to defeat in argument

86. Consecrate
    (a) to render holy (b) venerable
    (c) hallowed (d) devoted
87. Contingent
    (a) dependent on something else
    (b) liable
    (c) not certain to happen
    (d) accidental
88. Contraband
    (a) excluded by law (b) prohibited
    (c) illegal traffic (d) smuggled goods
89. Corollary
    (a) an easy inference (b) a consequence
    (c) result (d) a supplement
90. Corroborate
    (a) to confirm (b) to make certain
    (c) to ascertain (d) to ensure
91. Craven
    (a) cowardly
    (b) a spiritless fellow
    (c) to surrender
    (d) one who gives in without a fight
92. Daunt
    (a) discourage (b) disable
    (c) terrify (d) tackle
93. Dank
    (a) damp (b) dark
    (c) gloomy (d) ill
94. Dastard
    (a) a coward
    (b) one who does a brutal act without giving his victim a chance
    (c) shrinking from danger
    (d) lack of courage
95. Dearth
    (a) abundance (b) scarcity
    (c) vogue (d) end
96. Debacle
    (a) unable (b) depart
    (c) downfall (d) obstruct
97. Debility
    (a) carelessness (b) weakness
    (c) tenseness (d) awkwardness
98. Decrepit
    (a) destroyed (b) made weak
    (c) awful (d) dependent
99. Despicable
    (a) lengthy (b) difficult
    (c) contemptible (d) determined
100. Deport
    (a) to leave (b) to imprison
    (c) to banish (d) to make known
101. Deplete
    (a) to flatten (b) to conquer
    (c) to finish (d) to exhaust
102. Debonair
    (a) superficial (b) pleasing and gracious
    (c) in high style (d) flighty
103. Declaim
    (a) to make a set or rhetorical speech
    (b) to harangue
    (c) to recite
    (d) to utter
104. Decree
    (a) an order by one in authority
    (b) an edict or law
    (c) a judicial decision
    (d) a predetermined purpose
105. Deflect
    (a) to turn aside
    (b) to swerve
    (c) to deviate from the proper course
    (d) bending
106. Defray
    (a) to pay (b) to satisfy
    (c) to appease (d) to meet the expenses
107. Degage
    (a) unembarrassed (b) unconstraimed
    (c) easy (d) unconcerned

108. Deja'vu
(a) unoriginal material
(b) old stuff
(c) an illusion of having experienced something before actually doing so
(d) first time

109. Delectable
(a) delightful (b) pleasing
(c) gives pleasure (d) makes happy

110. Delineate
(a) to mark out with lines
(b) to represent by a sketch or picture
(c) to draw
(d) to leave

111. Denouement
(a) unravelling of a plot or story
(b) the issue
(c) event
(d) outcome

112. Desiderate
(a) long for (b) earnestly desire
(c) want (d) miss

113. Deprecate
(a) to try to ward off by prayer
(b) to desire earnestly the prevention of
(c) to invoke or beseech
(d) to regret deeply

114. Derelict
(a) forsaken (b) dejected
(c) falling in ruins (d) neglectful of duty

115. Devious
(a) out of the way (b) roundabout
(c) winding (d) erring

116. Diatribe
(a) variety
(b) bitter and violent attack in words
(c) confusing
(d) rubbish

117. Dirge
(a) prophecy (b) music of mourning
(c) curfew (d) scarcity

118. Disparate
(a) radically different (b) discouraged
(c) reckless (d) stingy

119. Discourse
(a) conversation (b) reasoning faculty
(c) a treatise (d) a process of combat

120. Dissimulate
(a) to pretend (b) to conceal
(c) to disguise (d) to dissemble

121. Dogmatic
(a) angry
(b) powerful
(c) vicious
(d) excessively opinionated

122. Doughty
(a) strong and able (b) coarse
(c) foolish (d) impudent

123. Dubious
(a) treacherous (b) doubtful
(c) demanding (d) delighted

124. Duress
(a) stress (b) pressure
(c) threat (d) risk

125. Drivel
(a) to slaver like a child
(b) to be foolish
(c) to speak like an idiot
(d) to talk nonsense

126. Ecstasy
(a) a state of temporary mental alienation
(b) altered or diminished consciousness
(c) excessive joy
(d) exalted feeling

127. Edifice
(a) pride (b) imposing building
(c) strength (d) beauty

128. Edacious
(a) given to eating (b) gluttonous
(c) fond of eating (d) greedy for food

129. Effeminate
(a) womanish (b) unmanly
(c) weak (d) voluptuous

130. Effete
(a) exhausted (b) degenerate
(c) decadent (d) become barren

131. Effrontery
(a) shameless insolence
(b) imprudence
(c) insolence
(d) defiance

132. Egress
(a) admittance (b) exit
(c) crossing (d) trespass

133. Eke
(a) to dilute (b) to supplement
(c) to coax (d) to irritate

134. Embellish
(a) employ (b) arrange
(c) decorate (d) design

135. Embezzle
(a) attract (b) dazzle
(c) decorate (d) misuse

136. Empiric
(a) one who experiments
(b) one whose knowledge is got from experience only
(c) a quack
(d) not actually conversant with the subject

137. Emulate
(a) strive to equal or excel
(b) to rival successfully
(c) to imitate
(d) eager to rival

138. Encomium
(a) very economic (b) very high praise
(c) enlighten (d) devotion

139. Enthral
(a) to captivate (b) to imprison
(c) to banish (d) to make known

140. Entail
(a) to win
(b) to impose or result in
(c) to weaken
(d) to lag behind

141. Envisage
(a) to face
(b) to seek
(c) to foresee in imagination
(d) to understand

142. Enunciate
(a) to censure publicly
(b) to state formally
(c) to emphasize
(d) to promote

143. Ennui
(a) a feeling of weariness
(b) langour
(c) boredom
(d) tired

144. Equipoise
(a) equally balanced (b) equilibrium
(c) equidistant (d) midpoint

145. Equivocal
(a) open to doubt (b) critical
(c) enquiring (d) silent

146. Erudite
(a) recalcitrant (b) reserved
(c) scholarly (d) curious

147. Eschew
(a) imply (b) avoid
(c) control (d) prevent

148. Evince
(a) to show plainly (b) to see clearly
(c) to be interested (d) to perform

149. Exacerbate
(a) harass (b) malign
(c) enhanced (d) irritate

150. Excruciating
(a) chronic (b) aggravated
(c) enraged (d) acute

151. Exigency
(a) crisis (b) emergency
(c) swiftness (d) tenacity

152. Explicit
(a) sure (b) determined
(c) definite (d) deplorable

153. Extricate
(a) avoid (b) devoid
(c) disentangle (d) distance

154. Expunge
(a) to block out (b) to borrow from
(c) to squeeze dry (d) to forgive

155. Exotic
(a) foreign (b) temperamental
(c) vain (d) clear

156. Expedite
(a) to free from impediments
(b) to hasten
(c) to weaken the force of
(d) to palliate

157. Extenuate
(a) to lessen
(b) to underrate
(c) to weaken the force of
(d) to palliate

158. Fabricate
(a) oppose (b) make up
(c) pretend (d) deceive

159. Fascinate
(a) charm (b) encourage
(c) employ (d) exchange

160. Fatality
(a) final (b) falsehood
(b) misfortune (d) neglect

161. Flagrant
(a) widely scattered (b) poisonous
(c) scandalous (d) absurd

162. Faux pas
(a) fox-like (b) passage
(c) furious (d) folly

163. Facient
(a) facial (b) smooth
(c) agent (d) humorous

164. Fecund
(a) fertile (b) powerful
(c) strange (d) pure

165. Ferocious
(a) frightening (b) fierce
(c) threatening (d) horrible

166. Feline
(a) delicate (b) cat-like
(c) very feminine (d) sleek

167. Fealty
(a) feeling (b) truth
(c) faculty (d) loyalty

168. Fixation
(a) single-mindedness
(b) obsession
(c) inspiration (d) expression

169. Frugal
(a) quiet (b) economical
(c) shy (d) generous

170. Filum
(a) cinema (b) silent film
(c) thread (d) fulfil

171. Fissure
(a) scar (b) leg bone
(c) act of melting (d) crack

172. Fictitious
(a) unreal (b) imaginary
(c) obvious (d) factual

173. Frisk
(a) fry (b) fly
(c) gamble (d) gambol

174. Garish
(a) beautifully decorated
(b) hasty
(c) bold
(d) unpleasantly gaudy

175. Genre
(a) giant (b) birth
(c) style (d) gear

176. Glabrous
(a) gloomy (b) gaseous
(c) bald (d) gall

177. Gladiator
(a) blissful (b) gradual
(c) trained fighter (d) flier

178. Gird
(a) to honour
(b) to prod
(c) to prepare for action
(d) to shackle

179. Gourmand
(a) excessive eater (b) strength
(c) clumsy person (d) special dish

180. Grand
(a) optimistic (b) impressive
(c) generous (d) handsome

181. Grubby
(a) dirty (b) rinse
(c) grasping (d) grit

182. Grandeur
(a) high flown (b) decoration
(c) magnificence (d) impression

183. Grandiose
(a) high (b) imposing
(c) inspiring (d) attractive

184. Habitat
(a) habits (b) home
(c) area (d) locality

185. Handicap
(a) hindrance (b) annoyance
(c) disability (d) deformity

186. Havoc
(a) heighten (b) hinder
(c) destruction (d) terrify

187. Hazard
(a) jarring noise (b) blockade
(c) hindrance (d) risk

188. Hackneyed
(a) chopped (b) cheerful
(c) chortle (d) banal

189. Halidom
(a) sanctity (b) holiday
(c) present (d) hell

190. Histrionic
(a) theatrical (b) historically
(c) talented (d) deceive

191. Hovel
(a) cry (b) heave
(c) outhouse (d) aircraft

192. Hum-drum
(a) noisy (b) chaotic
(c) dull (d) harassing

193. Ideograph
(a) symbol (b) data
(c) opinion (d) imagination

194. Impetuous
(a) hasty (b) stimulating
(c) erratic (d) disrespectful

195. Impetus
(a) courage (b) impatience
(c) arrogance (d) driving energy

196. Impeach
(a) accuse
(b) to remove from office
(c) to slander
(d) to put in jail

197. Impasse
(a) unpassable (b) insurmountable
(c) hurdle (d) deadlock

198. Incense
    (a) to worship (b) to enrage
    (c) to stimulate (d) to inhale

199. Infringe
    (a) to encroach (b) to surround
    (c) to decorate (d) to limit

200. Ingenuous
    (a) skillful (b) intelligent
    (c) artless (d) genius

201. Inexorable
    (a) angry (b) liable
    (c) exit (d) relentless

202. Inquisition
    (a) punishment
    (b) long speech
    (c) thorough investigation
    (d) curiosity

203. Invidious
    (a) deceptive (b) malicious
    (c) hypercritical (d) stealthy

204. Insinuate
    (a) pierce (b) sinful
    (c) suggest (d) low

205. Incubus
    (a) interior (b) nightmare
    (c) apparatus (d) imposing

206. Inordinate
    (a) unruly (b) disorderly
    (c) excessive (d) elusive

207. Inscrutable
    (a) mysterious (b) insurmountable
    (c) dull (d) impenetrable

208. Instigate
    (a) involve (b) interpret
    (c) unhinge (d) incite

209. Intimidate
    (a) mislead (b) misplace
    (c) frighten (d) demoralize

210. Jubilant
    (a) joyful (b) excited
    (c) triumphant (d) enticing

211. Jocose
    (a) merry (b) fat
    (c) clumsy (d) foolish

212. Knit
    (a) weave (b) mix
    (c) knot (d) rugged

213. Knoll
    (a) nil (b) negative
    (c) merit (d) mound

214. Labyrinth
    (a) bewildering maze (b) tunnel
    (c) temple (d) tomb

215. Levitate
    (a) float (b) impose
    (c) levity (d) invite

216. Lave
    (a) wash (b) impose
    (c) jest (d) stream

217. Lectern
    (a) latticed (b) tasselled
    (c) singing desk (d) plait

218. Lenitive
    (a) lying (b) pulse-live
    (c) nitwit (d) soothing

219. Leonine
    (a) lotion (b) lying
    (c) lion like (d) submissive

220. Lecherous
    (a) salacious (b) salty
    (c) smooth (d) polite

221. Literatus
    (a) emblem (b) highly educated
    (c) novel (d) award

222. Luscious
    (a) lasting (b) shining
    (c) attractive (d) trivial

223. Lucid
(a) sensational (b) lucky
(c) melodious (d) detailed

224. Lucrative
(a) attractive (b) profitable
(c) thoughtful (d) ordeal

225. Machinations
(a) mechanical (b) mobilising
(c) scheming (d) moralising

226. Macabre
(a) memorable (b) mysterious
(c) gruesome (d) hateful

227. Magnanimous
(a) magnified (b) mobilize
(c) essential (d) generous

228. Malevolent
(a) spiteful (b) horrible
(c) treacherous (d) tricky

229. Manoeuvre
(a) mobilize (b) planned movement
(c) mystify (d) miniature

230. Mete
(a) Meet (b) give
(c) receive (d) measure

231. Meagre
(a) abundant (b) scanty
(c) heapful (d) copious

232. Model
(a) parade (b) procession
(c) paradigm (d) idle

233. Nadir
(a) height (b) lowest point
(c) nullify (d) hopeless

234. Nag
(a) praise highly
(b) find fault with continuously
(c) deceive
(d) frustration

235. Narcotic
(a) that which produces total insensibility
(b) that which frustrates
(c) annoying
(d) fulfilling

236. Nescience
(a) knowledgeable
(b) absence of knowledge
(c) noncommittal
(d) numbness

237. Nefarious
(a) wicked (b) outrageous
(c) untiring (d) abiding

238. Nemesis
(a) outcome (b) deserved fate
(c) devoid (d) reward

239. Nonplussed
(a) beyond control (b) unlawful
(c) harmful (d) completely puzzled.

240. Nostalgia
(a) nauseous (b) repulsive
(c) home-sickness (d) hopelessness

241. Nurture
(a) dependence (b) training
(c) temperament (d) rumination

242. Obdurate
(a) stubborn (b) unconvinced
(c) harmful (d) inconvenient

243. Obese
(a) jolly (b) very bright
(c) very fat (d) rigorous

244. Obfuscate
(a) abandon (b) annoy
(c) defy (d) bewilder

245. Obviate
(a) get rid of (b) frustrate
(c) impede (d) assure

246. Odious
(a) enhanced (b) hateful
(c) attentive (d) foul smelling

247. Officious
(a) dealing with office work
(b) office routine
(c) too eager to help or advise
(d) to hinder smooth working

248. Ominous
(a) pleasant (b) threatening
(c) promising (d) luring

249. Onerous
(a) honourable (b) inquiring
(c) burdensome (d) benign

250. Opprobrious
(a) abusive (b) opportunist
(c) autocratic (d) insensitive

251. Perpetuate
(a) to cause to last indefinitely
(b) to enter into
(c) to pass through
(d) to perform

252. Pontificate
(a) to speak authoritatively
(b) to raise to higher office
(c) to act clumsily
(d) to constitute

253. Prolific
(a) skilful (b) swift
(c) fertile (d) wearisomely verbose

254. Profess
(a) to become expert at
(b) to proclaim
(c) to foretell
(d) to enlarge

255. Prodigious
(a) enormous (b) extravagant
(c) persistent (d) powerful

256. Propitiate
(a) to yield (b) to encourage
(c) to fawn upon (d) to appease

257. Quay
(a) take (b) wharf
(c) bay (d) mouth of a river

258. Quagmire
(a) rugged cliff (b) bay
(c) fog (d) whirlpool

259. Quench
(a) to extinguish (b) to kindle
(c) to make silent (d) to saturate

260. Quintessence
(a) over-fussiness (b) good taste
(c) purest part (d) vanity

261. Quash
(a) to suppress (b) to slacken
(c) to press into pulp (d) to splinter

262. Replenish
(a) to spread around
(b) to fulfill
(c) to indulge
(d) to provide a new supply for

263. Recapitulate
(a) to recover properly
(b) to sum up
(c) to repeat oneself tiresomely
(d) to surrender again

264. Reckless
(a) irresponsible (b) without fault
(c) hopeless (d) wicked

265. Rhetorical
(a) convincing
(b) pleading
(c) satirical
(d) designed for showy oratorial effect

266. Reticence
(a) modesty (b) caution
(c) tendency (d) garrulous

267. Riddle
(a) to entangle (b) to question
(c) to explain (d) to fill with holes

268. Sagacious
(a) excessively grasping
(b) truthful
(c) lustful
(d) discerning

269. Siesta
(a) farm
(b) carnival
(c) East Indian Market
(d) afternoon nap

270. Solicit
(a) to command
(b) to worry
(c) to sympathize with
(d) to ask for

271. Spurious
(a) pertaining to heraldry
(b) stubborn
(c) angry
(d) not genuine

272. Splay
(a) to slash (b) to spread out
(c) to split in two (d) to unsex

273. Supercilious
(a) foolish (b) shallow-minded
(c) scornfully superior
(d) aggressive

274. Stringent
(a) shrinking (b) long drawn out
(c) sarcastic (d) severe

275. Tactile
(a) considerate
(b) sharp
(c) pertaining to the organs of touch
(d) strong

276. Tantalize
(a) to delay (b) to tease
(c) to flatter (d) to puzzle

277. Temporal
(a) mild (b) holy
(c) worldly (d) angry

278. Thwart
(a) to strike vigorously
(b) to enrage
(c) to injure
(d) to frustrate

279. Topography
(a) art of painting
(b) physical features of a region
(c) soil chemistry
(d) signalling by light

280. Tour-de-force
(a) long journey (b) feat of skill
(c) spectacle (d) show of force

281. Triumph
(a) defeat (b) joy
(c) victory (d) happiness

282. Truculent
(a) tenacity (b) aggressive
(c) inhuman (d) without pity

283. Tumultuous
(a) trembling (b) tricky
(c) disorderly (d) travelling

284. Turbid
(a) confused (b) tight
(c) daunting (d) puzzling

285. Turmoil
(a) upheaval (b) agitation
(c) terrible (d) noisy

286. Turpitude
(a) audacity (b) opaqueness
(c) wickedness (d) defiance

287. Tutelage
(a) guardianship (b) following
(c) teachings (d) worship

288. Twaddle
(a) turn around (b) foolish talk
(c) to face squarely (d) to evade an issue

289. Tyrannize
(a) rule cruelly and unjustly
(b) behave selfishly
(c) shout at somebody
(d) preside

290. Unanimous
(a) showing complete agreement
(b) lack of interest

(c) undecided
(d) unconquered

291. Uncanny
(a) unable to (b) mysterious
(c) untiring (d) wild

292. Unbecoming
(a) unable to achieve
(b) unlikely to be understood
(c) not suitable
(d) tiresome

293. Usurp
(a) acquire
(b) achieve
(c) acquire wrongfully
(d) capture

294. Vacillate
(a) waver (b) to shake violently
(c) to feel elated (d) to loose control

295. Vanquish
(a) threaten (b) terrify
(c) defeat (d) deceive

296. Venerate
(a) regard suspiciously
(b) regard humorously
(c) regard with deep respect
(d) worship

297. Waft
(a) to dream (b) to move gracefully
(c) to pass by (d) to convey by floating

298. Wrought
(a) made or fashioned
(b) broken
(c) complicated
(d) strengthened

299. Wreak
(a) to twist
(b) to emit an unpleasant odour
(c) to inflict
(d) to sweat

300. Wrest
(a) take violently away
(b) impose
(c) to warn
(d) to jerk violently

301. Whit
(a) grain (b) least
(c) adorn (d) amour

302. Wrath
(a) happiness (b) anger
(c) doom (d) apply

303. Yearning
(a) pleasing (b) strong desire
(c) least possible (d) modified

304. Yield
(a) give in (b) obstruct
(c) prevent (d) prolong

305. Yokel
(a) horn (b) plough
(c) rustic (d) devoid

306. Yonder
(a) past (b) over there
(c) beyond (d) after

307. Zap
(a) guild (b) mourn
(c) mystify (d) defeat

308. Zeal
(a) enthusiasm (b) lukewarm
(c) unwilling (d) pleasure

309. Zenith
(a) low (b) depth
(c) highest point (d) defeat

310. Zest
(a) energy (b) weakness
(c) gain (d) gusto

ANSWERS

1. (b) 2. (b) 3. (d) 4. (a) 5. (a) 6. (c) 7. (a) 8. (b) 9. (a) 10. (b)
11. (d) 12. (d) 13. (d) 14. (c) 15. (d) 16. (d) 17. (a) 18. (b) 19. (a) 20. (c)
21. (a) 22. (b) 23. (b) 24. (b) 25. (b) 26. (c) 27. (d) 28. (c) 29. (b) 30. (a)
31. (c) 32. (d) 33. (a) 34. (a) 35. (b) 36. (d) 37. (b) 38. (c) 39. (a) 40. (a)
41. (b) 42. (c) 43. (a) 44. (b) 45. (c) 46. (b) 47. (c) 48. (a) 49. (b) 50. (d)
51. (b) 52. (c) 53. (d) 54. (c) 55. (b) 56. (b) 57. (d) 58. (d) 59. (d) 60. (d)
61. (a) 62. (d) 63. (b) 64. (c) 65. (a) 66. (b) 67. (d) 68. (c) 69. (a) 70. (b)
71. (a) 72. (b) 73. (b) 74. (c) 75. (d) 76. (a) 77. (a) 78. (c) 79. (b) 80. (c)
81. (a) 82. (a) 83. (b) 84. (c) 85. (a) 86. (a) 87. (d) 88. (d) 89. (b) 90. (a)
91. (a) 92. (a) 93. (a) 94. (a) 95. (b) 96. (c) 97. (b) 98. (b) 99. (c) 100. (c)
101. (d) 102. (b) 103. (a) 104. (a) 105. (a) 106. (d) 107. (a) 108. (c) 109. (a) 110. (b)
111. (a) 112. (a) 113. (b) 114. (a) 115. (b) 116. (b) 117. (b) 118. (a) 119. (a) 120. (d)
121. (d) 122. (a) 123. (b) 124. (c) 125. (d) 126. (d) 127. (b) 128. (b) 129. (a) 130. (a)
131. (a) 132. (b) 133. (b) 134. (c) 135. (d) 136. (a) 137. (a) 138. (b) 139. (c) 140. (b)
141. (c) 142. (b) 143. (a) 144. (b) 145. (a) 146. (c) 147. (b) 148. (a) 149. (b) 150. (d)
151. (b) 152. (c) 153. (a) 154. (a) 155. (a) 156. (b) 157. (a) 158. (b) 159. (a) 160. (c)
161. (c) 162. (d) 163. (c) 164. (a) 165. (b) 166. (b) 167. (d) 168. (b) 169. (b) 170. (c)
171. (d) 172. (a) 173. (d) 174. (d) 175. (c) 176. (c) 177. (c) 178. (c) 179. (a) 180. (b)
181. (a) 182. (a) 183. (b) 184. (b) 185. (c) 186. (c) 187. (d) 188. (d) 189. (a) 190. (a)
191. (c) 192. (c) 193. (a) 194. (a) 195. (d) 196. (a) 197. (d) 198. (b) 199. (a) 200. (c)
201. (d) 202. (c) 203. (b) 204. (c) 205. (b) 206. (c) 207. (a) 208. (d) 209. (c) 210. (a)
211. (a) 212. (a) 213. (d) 214. (a) 215. (a) 216. (a) 217. (c) 218. (d) 219. (c) 220. (a)
221. (b) 222. (c) 223. (a) 224. (b) 225. (c) 226. (c) 227. (d) 228. (a) 229. (b) 230. (d)
231. (b) 232. (c) 233. (b) 234. (b) 235. (a) 236. (b) 237. (a) 238. (b) 239. (d) 240. (c)
241. (b) 242. (a) 243. (c) 244. (d) 245. (a) 246. (b) 247. (c) 248. (b) 249. (c) 250. (a)
251. (d) 252. (d) 253. (c) 254. (b) 255. (a) 256. (d) 257. (d) 258. (c) 259. (a) 260. (c)
261. (a) 262. (d) 263. (b) 264. (a) 265. (d) 266. (c) 267. (d) 268. (d) 269. (d) 270. (d)
271. (d) 272. (b) 273. (c) 274. (d) 275. (c) 276. (b) 277. (c) 278. (d) 279. (b) 280. (b)
281. (c) 282. (b) 283. (c) 284. (a) 285. (b) 286. (c) 287. (a) 288. (b) 289. (a) 290. (a)
291. (b) 292. (c) 293. (c) 294. (a) 295. (c) 296. (c) 297. (d) 298. (a) 299. (c) 300. (a)
301. (b) 302. (b) 303. (b) 304. (a) 305. (c) 306. (b) 307. (d) 308. (a) 309. (c) 310. (d)

9.3 Synonyms in Context

Many words in English have more than one meaning or have different shades of meaning. The meaning differs according to the use of the word in different contexts. The sentences are followed by four options. Out of those, you are required to tick mark the one which comes nearest in meaning to the bold word in the particular context. By way of illustration, one question has been done for you.

* One should try to overlook the **weakness** of fellow beings.
(a) feebleness (b) frailty
(c) shortcomings (d) strength

The answer is (c). Although the word weakness by itself means feebleness, in this particular context, it refers to short-comings or faults.

1. The sad news caused depression in the family.
(a) debasement (b) hollowness
(c) prostration (d) dejection
2. The manager's lascivious ways antagonised all of them.
(a) ambitious (b) lustful
(c) erotic (d) treacherous
3. The servant promised that he would be back in a trice and left for the market.
(a) a trifle (b) a triangle
(c) an instant (d) three minutes
4. Nobody paid much attention to the trite remarks he kept passing.
(a) hackneyed (b) sharp
(c) illogical (d) cutting
5. The motives behind the burglary could not be ascertained.
(a) about (b) before
(c) for (d) after
6. The newspaper is an inexhaustible source of news.
(a) impartial (b) unending
(c) authentic (d) continuous
7. There can be different ways of solving the same problem.
(a) routes (b) manners
(c) methods (d) path
8. For all your efforts at sounding, convincing, no one is going to buy your story.
(a) purchase (b) acknowledge
(c) believe (d) demand
9. Habitual consumption of hot food played havoc with his health.
(a) warm (b) cold
(c) spicy (d) sweet
10. The subordinate had to mind the business in the absence of his superiors.
(a) take offence (b) look after
(c) think up (d) neglect
11. It had never been foreseen that the audience would pass unsavoury comments on your recitation.
(a) delicious (b) tasteless
(c) nasty (d) pleasant
12. Repeated attacks on his works has rendered the author immune to criticism.
(a) exempt (b) hostile
(c) disturbing (d) insensitive
13. The man was so tall that his presence seemed to dwarf the rest of the people in the room.
(a) elongate
(b) decrease
(c) dwindle the height
(d) render tall
14. A successful leader remains cool in the face of any adverse comments or situations.
(a) hot (b) calm
(c) unaffected (d) quiet
15. The scene in the play presents a replica of the one in the novel by the same author.

(a) copy (b) facsimile
(c) replacement (d) double

16. The clergy was instrumental in the downfall of the government.
(a) cause (b) responsible
(c) indifferent (d) ambivalent

17. The changes in contemporary lifestyle are being described as outrageous by the older generation.
(a) shameful (b) dreadful
(c) horrible (d) enraging

18. Your involvement with undesirable elements is bound to blemish your reputation as an upright man.
(a) disfigure (b) tarnish
(c) mystify (d) brighten

19. The student's perseverance ultimately brought him success after so many futile attempts.
(a) steadfastness (b) endurance
(c) persistence (d) patience

20. The lost child was restored to its parents amidst smiles.
(a) united (b) shown
(c) returned (d) reinstated

21. The ruin of his health was caused by excessive drinking.
(a) destruction (b) perdition
(c) debacle (d) desolation

22. The bomb blast mutilated the bodies of the victims.
(a) annihilated (b) demolished
(c) mangled (d) dismantled

23. It is good if all traces of the tragedy are obliterated from the victim's mind.
(a) overturned (b) perished
(c) effaced (d) liquidated

24. Ultimately, one of the parties to the dispute relinquished his claim to the ownership of the property.
(a) yielded (b) ceded
(c) resigned (d) gave up

25. Air, water and wind are all signs of the bounty of nature.
(a) donation (b) contribution
(c) award (d) largesse

26. It is difficult to obtain a licence for owning gunfire.
(a) take (b) receive
(c) procure (d) gain

27. The foreign settlers have refused to adopt the lifestyle of the host country.
(a) borrow (b) assume
(c) appropriate (d) simulate

28. One cannot possess a human being the way one can do a car or a house.
(a) seize (b) contain
(c) annex (d) own

29. The appearance of the culprit intensified the mood of expectation in the people.
(a) heightened (b) abated
(c) amplified (d) magnified

30. Steps were being taken to mitigate the sufferings of the victims of earthquake.
(a) assuage (b) lessen
(c) palliate (d) subdue

31. The child's parents always cushioned her against the harsh realities of life.
(a) rested (b) protected
(c) relaxed (d) eased

32. The warring factions have decided upon an immediate cessation of hostilities.
(a) resistance (b) discontinuance
(c) recess (d) stoppage

33. Elegance of language outweighs all other qualities in an individual.
(a) smartness (b) distinction
(c) refinement (d) affectation

34. A balanced piece of writing should never digress from the subject-matter.
(a) deviate (b) expatiate
(c) perorate (d) develop

35. Obedience of the court rulings is mandatory for all according to the law of the land.
(a) proper (b) binding
(c) perceptive (d) demanding

36. After being caught committing forgery, the man was incarcerated.
(a) arrested (b) imprisoned
(c) restrained (d) pursued

37. In the course of his freedom struggle, the leader had to countenance many hardships.
(a) suffer (b) sanction
(c) indulge (d) permit

38. All the parties have joined hands to conspire and overthrow the government.
(a) collaborate (b) collude
(c) concur (d) concert

39. The hall reverberated with applause from the audience when the performance ended.
(a) reflected (b) rebounded
(c) resounded (d) replied

40. The food being dished out was insipid to say the least.
(a) tasteless (b) weak
(c) unappealing (d) unpromising

41. The price of all commodities in the market is exorbitant.
(a) exaggerated (b) preposterous
(c) sumptuous (d) excessive

42. With the entry of the new brands, the value of the product is bound to depreciate.
(a) improve (b) slash
(c) devalue (d) thrift

43. No one is allowed to transgress beyond the line of control.
(a) exceed (b) trespass
(c) wander (d) confine

44. Respect for individual dignity is held sacrosanct by all religions.
(a) inviolable (b) pure
(c) holy (d) biased

45. Lack of education has retarded the nation's progress.
(a) impeded (b) slackened
(c) eased (d) accelerated

46. Many people emulated Gandhiji by embracing the principles of non-violence.
(a) hugging (b) enfolding
(c) adopting (d) clasping

47. The manager of the hotel was asked to see if he could accommodate two more guests.
(a) equip (b) provide
(c) lodge (d) store

48. In defence services, one is required to accommodate in all sorts of circumstances.
(a) enjoy (b) tolerate
(c) adjust (d) equip

49. The government's policies have alienated a large section of the people.
(a) estranged (b) infuriated
(c) roused (d) degraded

50. The mountain air coming from the north has proved salubrious for the people settled here.
(a) wholesome (b) toxic
(c) virulant (d) pleasant

ANSWERS

1. (d)	2. (b)	3. (c)	4. (a)	5. (c)	6. (b)	7. (c)	8. (c)	9. (c)	10. (b)
11. (c)	12. (d)	13. (c)	14. (b)	15. (b)	16. (b)	17. (a)	18. (b)	19. (a)	20. (c)
21. (a)	22. (c)	23. (c)	24. (d)	25. (d)	26. (c)	27. (d)	28. (d)	29. (a)	30. (b)
31. (b)	32. (d)	33. (d)	34. (a)	35. (b)	36. (b)	37. (a)	38. (b)	39. (c)	40. (a)
41. (d)	42. (c)	43. (b)	44. (a)	45. (b)	46. (c)	47. (b)	48. (c)	49. (a)	50. (a)

9.4 One Word has many Antonyms

An antonym is often defined as a word that is contrary in meaning to another; Hot is the antonym of cold. Remember that an antonym must be in the same port of speech in which the given word is.

Also the answer should be in the same tense form in which the key-word is. The correct answer is that which is similar in voice to the key-word.

Examples

The correct antonym of Fidelity is disloyalty and not disloyal because fidelity and disloyalty are in the same part of speech the noun while disloyal is the adjective.

1.	Abandon	continue, pursue, remain, carry on.
2.	Above	below, down, under.
3.	Abolish	confirm, uphold, promote, encourage.
4.	Ability	incompetence, disability, incapacity.
5.	Abridge	enlarge, prolong, expand, magnify.
6.	Absolve	punish, chastise, castigate, penalise.
7.	Absurd	wise, rational, sensible, reasonable.
8.	Abundance	lack, dearth, shortage, want.
9.	Accumulate	distribute, dissipate, scatter, spread.
10.	Acquit	charge, blame, accuse, involve.
11.	Adapt	differ, misfit, disagree, irregularise.
12.	Admiration	hate, condemnation.
13.	Ample	meagre, scanty, insufficient, limited.
14.	Amuse	annoy, tire, bore.
15.	Atrocious	noble, excellent, worthy, laudable.
16.	Attract	reject, repulse, repel, rebuff.
17.	Awareness	ignorance, innocence, foolishness.
18.	Awake	dormant, asleep, latent, slumbering.
19.	Backward	forward, advance, onward, prompt.
20.	Beautiful	loathsome, horrible, ugly.
21.	Before	after, subsequently, succeeding.
22.	Beg	challenge, claim, demand, contend.
23.	Belief	disbelief, suspicion, misgiving, distrust.
24.	Benevolence	malice, venom, enmity, hatred.
25.	Beseech	challenge, insist, demand, contend.
26.	Bewilder	illuminate, edify, enlighten.
27.	Bitter	mellow, genial, sugary, sweet.
28.	Blame	extol, praise, applaud, compliment.

29.	Bliss	sorrow, affliction, woe, distress.
30.	Bold	fearful, diffident, timid, afraid.
31.	Breed	annihilate, murder, destroy, kill.
32.	Brutal	humane, tender, compassionate, merciful.
33.	Bright	opaque, cloudy, dull, tarnished.
34.	Brief	diffuse, verbose, long, detailed.
35.	Busy	inactive, indolent, lazy, idle.
36.	Calamity	fortune, peace, happiness, joy.
37.	Calm	excite, perturb, agitate, disturb.
38.	Cancel	confirm, establish, endorse, ratify.
39.	Careless	cautious, thoughtful, vigilant, attentive.
40.	Certain	ambiguous, dubious, obscure, uncertain.
41.	Charm	repulse, repel, deter, rebuff.
42.	Cheap	expensive, costly, dear, worthy.
43.	Cheerful	torpid, lifeless, inert, sluggish.
44.	Claim	renounce, forego, waive, drop.
45.	Coarse	elegant, polite, cultured, refined.
46.	Cold	fiery, tepid, warm, scalding.
47.	Cooperative	rebellious, individual.
48.	Competent	incompetent, inefficient, weak.
49.	Company	individual, isolated, alone, single.
50.	Compliment	criticism, censure, disapprobation.
51.	Confide	suspect, doubt, apprehend, distrust.
52.	Dainty	coarse, vulgar, crude, rough.
53.	Decide	hesitate, vacillate, waver, falter.
54.	Defeat	triumph, vanquish, prevail, win.
55.	Delicacy	roughness, robustness, crudeness, heaviness.
56.	Delight	grief, anguish, displeasure, sorrow.
57.	Deny	verify, confirm, comply, endorse.
58.	Desire	detest, hate, despite, loathe.
59.	Deviate	abide, persist, converge, perpetuate.
60.	Diligent	idle, slack, slothful, lazy.
61.	Disclose	conceal, veil, cloak, suppress.
62.	Disgust	please, delight, charm, gratify.
63.	Dishonest	reliable, just, fair, trustworthy.

64.	Dispute	consent, comply, agree, accede.
65.	Dutiful	defiant, seditious, rebellious.
66.	Enchanted	disgusted, repulsed, nauseated.
67.	Encourage	discourage, depress, dishearten.
68.	Endanger	protect, defend, shield, safeguard.
69.	Entice	rebuff, repel, defer, repulse.
70.	Error	accuracy, verify, exactitude.
71.	Establish	destroy, demolish.
72.	Evasion	defence, reply, rejoinder, response.
73.	Everlasting	transitory, passing, transient, temporal
74.	Expand	contract, condense, curtail, reduce.
75.	Extra-ordinary	normal, ordinary, common, usual.
76.	False	veritable, accurate, authentic, reliable.
77.	Famous	obscure, notorious, unknown, anonymous.
78.	Feeble	robust, strong, vigorous, brawny.
79.	Fertile	infertile, sterile, arid, barren.
80.	Flexible	rigid, stiff, austere, unbending.
81.	Foe	ally, comrade, colleague, associate.
82.	Foolish	sane, wise, discreet, rational.
83.	Generous	mean, stingy, miserly, parsimonious.
84.	Gloomy	merry, jolly, bright, jocund.
85.	Graceful	awkward, ungainly, uncouth.
86.	Great	obscure, humble, unknown, trivial.
87.	Happiness	sorrow, sadness, grief, distress.
88.	Hard	soft, flexible, pliable.
89.	Hasten	impede, retard, hinder, delay.
90.	Hatred	liking, love, adoration, affection.
91.	Hesitate	decide, resolve, settle, determine.
92.	Horrible	agreeable, pleasant, delightful, charming.
93.	Humble	vain, proud, brazen, immodest.
94.	Ignorant	cultured, educated, literate, knowledgeable.
95.	Impartial	partial, biased, unjust, unfair.
96.	Impede	expedite, hasten, quicken, urge.
97.	Impulsive	cautious, heedful, thoughtful, wary.
98.	Innocent	wicked, guilty, criminal, culpable.

99.	Irritate	calm, appease, soothe, pacify.
100.	Jolly	gloomy, dismal, unhappy, sad.
101.	Just	unfair, partial, biased, prejudiced.
102.	Kind	cruel, hard, callous, harsh.
103.	Kill	create, produce, originate.
104.	Lasting	transient, transitory, evanescent.
105.	Lead	mislead, misguide, misdirect, deceive.
106.	Liberty	service, bondage, submission, slavery.
107.	Loyalty	disloyalty, perfidy, treachery.
108.	Majestic	insignificant, paltry, abject.
109.	Malice	charity, benevolence, humanity.
110.	Mild	savage, wild, fierce, ferocious.
111.	Miserable	joyous, happy, cheerful, blissful.
112.	Modern	old, ancient, obsolete, primitive.
113.	Modest	arrogant, haughty, proud, disdainful.
114.	Muscular	feeble, weak, frail, infirm.
115.	Narrow	wide, spacious, broad, extensive.
116.	Neat	untidy, disorderly, slovenly, unkempt.
117.	Nervous	bold, fearless, valiant, undaunted.
118.	Noisy	peaceful, quiet, placid.
119.	Notorious	reputable, famous, noted.
120.	Obedient	obstinate, disobedient, stubborn, recalcitrant.
121.	Obstinate	docile, compliant, yielding, amenable.
122.	Odd	ordinary, normal, commonplace.
123.	Oppose	aid, assist, encourage, support.
124.	Organise	disrupt, disintegrate, disarrange.
125.	Ordinary	unusual, rare, uncommon, queer.
126.	Order	disorder, confusion, chaos, anarchy.
127.	Own	deny, renounce, disclaim.
128.	Pacify	irritate, exasperate, provoke, annoy.
129.	Painful	soothing, pleasant, agreeable.
130.	Passionate	cold, impassive, torpid, phlegmatic.
131.	Pathetic	funny, comic, ludicrous, farcical.
132.	Peculiar	natural, ordinary, usual, normal.
133.	Peevish	cordial, jovial, genial, hearty.

134.	Permanent	temporary, transient, fleeting.
135.	Persuade	deter, discourage, dissuade, restrain.
136.	Pleasant	offensive, obnoxious, horrible.
137.	Please	offend, outrage, affront, injure.
138.	Plenty	scanty, deficiency, dearth, lack.
139.	Polite	rude, uncivil, churlish, insolent.
140.	Praise	blame, censure, condemn, reprove.
141.	Precious	cheap, useless.
142.	Preserve	destroy, demolish, eradicate, desolate.
143.	Pretty	ugly, loathsome, uncomely.
144.	Prevent	help, assist, aid, abet.
145.	Pride	modesty, humility, humbleness.
146.	Profuse	scanty, insufficient, meagre, limited.
147.	Sad	cheerful, happy, joyous, mirthful.
148.	Scanty	profuse, ample, sufficient, abundant.
149.	Scatter	hoard, amass, store, accumulate.
150.	Scold	compliment, praise, commend, applaud.
151.	Scorn	revere, respect, esteem, venerate.
152.	Selfish	generous, liberal, lavish, charitable.
153.	Serious	gay, cheerful, jovial, merry.
154.	Shocking	pleasant, charming, delightful.
155.	Shy	bold, confident, audacious, assuming.
156.	Silence	uproar, disorder, turmoil, noise.
157.	Similar	different, dissimilar, diverse, differing.
158.	Simple	complex, intricate, complicated.
159.	Sin	virtue, integrity, purity, morality.
160.	Skilful	clumsy, incompetent, awkward, unskilful.
161.	Slander	praise, laud, extol, applaud.
162.	Slender	plump, fat, buxom, stout.
163.	Slow	active, alert, prompt, swift.
164.	Smooth	uneven, rough.
165.	Soft	hard, inflexible, rigid, firm.
166.	Soothe	irritate, exasperate, provoke, agitate.
167.	Spiteful	benign, benevolent, benignant, beneficent.
168.	Steady	irregular, inconsistent, unstable, fickle.

169.	Stiff	flexible, supple, lissom, elastic.
170.	Stimulate	discourage, deter, dissuade, hinder.
171.	Stupid	wise, sagacious, rational, sensible.
172.	Sublime	ridiculous, comic, absurd, ludicrous.
173.	Successful	unlucky, unfortunate, disastrous.
174.	Sudden	anticipated, gradual, progressive.
175.	Suppress	excite, provoke, incite, agitate.
176.	Suspicious	trustful, honest, straightforward.
177.	Systematic	irregular, casual, occasional.
178.	Talkative	taciturn, reserved, silent, mute.
179.	Tame	wild, savage, ferocious, untamed.
180.	Tasteless	savoury, delicious, appetising.
181.	Tear	repair, mend, rectify, restore.
182.	Thin	fat, corpulent, stout, obese.
183.	Thoughtful	carefree, remiss, reckless.
184.	Tie	unfasten, loosen, disconnect, unbind.
185.	Timid	bold, courageous, unafraid.
186.	Torture	allay, relief, ease, comfort.
187.	Tough	soft, tender, fragile, delicate, feeble.
188.	Tragic	comic, farcical, propitious, amusing.
189.	Trained	unskilled, inefficient, clumsy, inexpert.
190.	Treacherous	faithful, loyal, reliable, devoted.
191.	True	false, untrue, wrong, incorrect.
192.	Trust	doubt, distrust, suspicion, misgiving.
193.	Tune	disharmony, discord, dissonance.
194.	Try	quit, leave, relinquish, drop.
195.	Typical	unusual, singular, peculiar, abnormal.
196.	Trouble	relief, joy, luck, prosperity.
197.	Trembling	steady, firm, stable, still.
198.	Teacher	student, pupil, disciple, learner.
199.	Tire	revive, invigorate, refresh, relax.
200.	Ugly	lovely, beautiful, comely, gracious.
201.	Universal	sectional, factional, sectarian.
202.	Uncertain	certain, definite, undoubted, indisputable.
203.	Unfair	just, fair, honest.

204.	Untidy	neat, tidy, immaculate, smart.
205.	Unusual	usual, common, everyday, hackneyed.
206.	Utility	worthless, useless.
207.	Urgent	petty, trivial, insignificant.
208.	Usual	unusual, uncommon, rare, singular.
209.	Vain	modest, unassuming, unpretentious.
210.	Valuable	worthless, cheap, base.
211.	Versatile	steady, constant, permanent, invariable.
212.	Violent	quiet, placid, peaceful, calm.
213.	Wakeful	lethargic, asleep, inactive.
214.	Yield	withhold, restrain, resist, withstand, oppose.
215.	Zenith	base, basis, nadir, bottom.

9.5 Antonyms- Objective Multiple Choice Type

Directions : Below are given some words followed by four answers. Tick the answer which you believe gives the opposite meaning of the word.

1. Lewd
   (a) lazy (b) amusing
   (c) decent (d) beautiful

2. Gallantry
   (a) brave (b) cowardice
   (c) sharp (d) hard

3. Knave
   (a) jester (b) knight
   (c) bachelor (d) gentleman

4. Zest
   (a) morose (b) bright
   (c) intelligence (d) irritation

5. Impious
   (a) holy (b) mischievous
   (c) shrewd (d) diplomatic

6. Scurry
   (a) to hurry or hasten (b) to tremble
   (c) to be ashamed (d) to languid

7. Enigmatic
   (a) displeased (b) simple
   (c) short-sighted (d) learned

8. Sporadic
   (a) epidemic (b) stagnant
   (c) spontaneous (d) regular

9. Ascetic
   (a) germ-free (b) artistic
   (c) gloomy (d) worldly

10. Repugnant
    (a) plain (b) brutal
    (c) agreeable (d) pungent

11. Stigma
    (a) obstinacy (b) honour
    (c) disgrace (d) vision

12. Recoup
    (a) to worsen (b) to strengthen
    (c) to trap (d) to recover

13. Slacken
    (a) to activate (b) to quench
    (c) to delight (d) to muse

14. Irrevocable
    (a) solid (b) fast
    (c) transitional (d) interruption

15. Rotundity
    (a) erect (b) deviate
    (c) angular (d) arch

16. Scepticism
    (a) doubt (b) assent
    (c) confess (d) gullibility

17. Salient
    (a) chief (b) insignificant
    (c) lend (d) supernatural

18. Redundance
    (a) paucity (b) bare
    (c) rejection (d) crucial

19. Valorous
    (a) discretion (b) parasite
    (c) fascinating (d) timid

20. Indiscretion
    (a) circumspection (b) magnitude
    (c) inclination (d) ambition

21. Dexterous
    (a) courageous (b) dumb
    (c) clumsy (d) empty

22. Guile
    (a) forsake (b) innocence
    (c) paradox (d) hard

23. Facilitate
    (a) to hinder (b) to recommend
    (c) to serve (d) to correct

24. Opponent
    (a) freedom (b) liberation
    (c) restraint (d) auxiliary

25. Boisterous
    (a) frenzied (b) sobriety
    (c) casual (d) harmful

26. Complacency
    (a) worse (b) corrode
    (c) destroy (d) dissatisfaction

27. Aggravate
    (a) humorous (b) soothing
    (c) fragrance (d) painful

28. Exhilaration
    (a) modern (b) worthy
    (c) despondency (d) elation

29. Pensive
    (a) penetrate (b) subject
    (c) glum (d) jubilant

30. Adornment
    (a) blemish (b) perfect
    (c) sincere (d) approve

31. Refinement
    (a) spotless (b) courage
    (c) vulgarity (d) poverty

32. Optimism
    (a) dread (b) despair
    (c) abandon (d) straightforward

33. Laud
    (a) to censure (b) to respect
    (c) to connive (d) to descend

34. Reverence
    (a) rejection (b) disdain
    (c) dislike (d) honour

35. Sycophant
    (a) psychic (b) elegant
    (c) slanderer (d) arrangement

36. Ignominious
    (a) selfish (b) villain
    (c) honorable (d) victorious

37. Magnanimous
    (a) dishonest (b) covetous
    (c) gracious (d) faithful

38. Penitence
    (a) penniless (b) cowardice
    (c) naughty (d) remorseless

39. Asceticism
    (a) gambler (b) austere
    (c) sinister (d) debauchery

40. Famish
    (a) famous (b) pure
    (c) devouring (d) mistake

41. Chastity
(a) injustice (b) grossness
(c) discourage (d) enlighten

42. Purgatory
(a) reward (b) flawless
(c) celestial (d) proximity

43. Veneration
(a) sacrilege (b) static
(c) downfall (d) religious

44. Allegiance
(a) accuse (b) confer
(c) violation (d) puny

45. Zenith
(a) colossal (b) weak
(c) nadir (d) break

46. Aromatic
(a) reeking (b) unscrupulous
(c) assist (d) mean

47. Augment
(a) atone (b) decrease
(c) irregular (d) ugly

48. Ensconce
(a) evade (b) recover
(c) active (d) to be ill at ease

49. Inimical
(a) celebrity (b) friendly
(c) speedy (d) radiant

50. Inopportune
(a) right (b) truthful
(c) harsh (d) timely or suitable

51. Toxic
(a) harmless (b) swollen
(c) insulting (d) tonic

52. Titanic
(a) early (b) puny
(c) silence (d) balance

53. Prolix
(a) common (b) attractive
(c) short and crisp (d) bulging out

54. Penurious
(a) painless (b) expert
(c) great (d) rich

55. Pliable
(a) tortuous (b) inflexible
(c) childish (d) suffocating

56. Lucrative
(a) happy (b) illegal
(c) unprofitable (d) unkempt

57. Soft
(a) blunt (b) thin
(c) delicate (d) stubborn

58. Copious
(a) dearth (b) stout
(c) nervous (d) false

59. Restive
(a) restless (b) relaxed
(c) deceitful (d) grasping

60. Puerility
(a) strength (b) manliness
(c) maturity (d) calmness

61. Harmony
(a) dissonance (b) shyness
(c) harmless (d) falsehood

62. Divulge
(a) soiled (b) clever
(c) conceal (d) deplore

63. Impair
(a) strengthen (b) injure
(c) repair (d) spread

64. Vacillation
(a) withdrawal (b) reasonable
(c) determination (d) confusion

65. Infuse
(a) enforce (b) extract
(c) enrich (d) ignore

66. Gawky
(a) simple (b) decorated
(c) distorted (d) graceful

67. Innocuous
(a) innocent (b) harmful
(c) definite (d) homeless

68. Vainglorious
(a) glorified (b) modest
(c) vain (d) empty

69. Fortitude
(a) forgetfulness (b) generosity
(c) cowardice (d) simplicity

70. Lassitude
(a) shallowness (b) weariness
(c) peace of mind (d) alertness

71. Jaded
(a) rejected (b) zestful
(c) wicked (d) frank

72. Transparent
(a) covered (b) opaque
(c) clear (d) misty

73. Coagulate
(a) thicken (b) dissipate
(c) descend (d) none of the above

74. Poignant
(a) sharp (b) sweet
(c) dull (d) bland

75. Epochal
(a) crucial (b) suspicious
(c) insignificant (d) stupendous

76. Phrenetic
(a) intense (b) composed
(c) deteriorative (d) eccentric

77. Inchoate
(a) terse (b) implicit
(c) chaotic (d) developed

78. Fragmented
(a) undivided or whole
(b) temporary
(c) crumbled
(d) partial

79. Nascent
(a) budding (b) mature
(c) elderly (d) initial

80. Yearn
(a) struggle (b) stubborn
(c) loathe (d) none of the above

81. Harmony
(a) discord (b) similar
(c) peace (d) differ

82. Morbid
(a) diseased (b) languid
(c) rigid (d) healthy

83. Pathetic
(a) sympathetic (b) hale and hearty
(c) healthy (d) farcical

84. Endear
(a) cheap (b) attach
(c) alienate (d) help

85. Voluminous
(a) bulky (b) slight
(c) compulsory (d) voluntary

86. Mellifluous
(a) mutual (b) common
(c) hoarse (d) contented

87. Pastime
(a) entertain (b) leisure
(c) future (d) work

88. Cupidity
(a) wine-worshipping
(b) atrocity
(c) clarity
(d) generosity

89. Brunette
(a) brown (b) bland
(c) blonde (d) thorny

90. Callow
(a) hollow (b) sallow
(c) experienced (d) fertile

91. Esoteric
(a) concentric (b) exoteric
(c) meteoric (d) categoric

92. Debilitate
(a) strengthen (b) rehabilitate
(c) torture (d) soothe

93. Sparse
(a) assault (b) dense
(c) point (d) deficient

94. Juvenile
(a) senile (b) trope
(c) delinquent (d) kneel

95. Insipid
(a) separate (b) inhale
(c) interesting (d) initial

96. Abridge
(a) summarise (b) dilate
(c) over-bridge (d) curb

97. Predilection
(a) proposal (b) previous
(c) aversion (d) boisterous

98. Nebulous
(a) stars (b) curved
(c) homesickness (d) crystal clear

99. Reminisce
(a) remind (b) retrace
(c) forget (d) curtail

100. Erudite
(a) eradicate (b) ignorant
(c) pendant (d) pauper

101. Alienate
(a) enliven (b) endear
(c) leaning (d) uprising

102. Accomplice
(a) opponent (b) escort
(c) accessory (d) desertion

103. Apocalyptic
(a) high-sounding (b) appealing
(c) concealed (d) poetic

104. Ardent
(a) eager (b) casual
(c) fierce (d) none of the above

105. Avant-garde
(a) up-to-date (b) old fashioned
(c) rise-up (d) boasting

106. Absolve
(a) free (b) blame
(c) absorb (d) total

107. Brusque
(a) sweep (b) sudden
(c) obsequious (d) immediate

108. Benefactor
(a) beneficent (b) benediction
(c) beneficiary (d) none of the above

109. Brag
(a) show off (b) proud
(c) laud (d) humble

110. Benign
(a) novice (b) sympathetic
(c) malignant (d) beginning

111. Credulous
(a) innocent (b) creditable
(c) unbelieving (d) worth

112. Curb
(a) help (b) incite
(c) restrain (d) aggravate

113. Calumny
(a) pillar (b) slander
(c) praise (d) lump

114. Churlish
(a) quarrelsome (b) curly
(c) suave (d) curvy

115. Conservative
(a) reactionary (b) orthodox
(c) iconoclast (d) saving

116. Complaint
(a) obliging (b) inhabitant
(c) misfit (d) recalcitrant

117. Cryptic
(a) wail (b) manifest
(c) underground (d) rude

118. Contemptible
(a) foolish (b) unworthy
(c) dull (d) likeable

119. Distinguished
(a) ordinary (b) marked
(c) confused (d) straightened

120. Disparage
(a) eject (b) appreciate
(c) compare (d) jump

121. Droll
(a) roller (b) shout
(c) customary (d) whimsical

122. Dissipate
(a) upgrade (b) lavish
(c) spit (d) economise

123. Debonair
(a) unelegant (b) safe
(c) fashionable (d) fresh

124. Dainty
(a) delicate (b) polished
(c) coarse (d) plain

125. Delicious
(a) pleasant (b) odious
(c) sweet (d) none of the above

126. Deviate
(a) stray (b) conform
(c) abide (d) change

127. Diligent
(a) careful (b) lazy
(c) intelligent (d) harmless

128. Emerge
(a) disappear (b) outcome
(c) appear (d) none of the above

129. Effeminate
(a) virile (b) feminine
(c) philogynist (d) misogynist

130. Epilogue
(a) epigraph (b) prologue
(c) prelude (d) vogue

131. Extolled
(a) condemned (b) sang
(c) criticized (d) praised

132. Ennui
(a) introduce (b) excitement
(c) powerless (d) tiredness

133. Esoteric
(a) concentric (b) categoric
(c) rhetoric (d) none of the above

134. Endemic
(a) epidemic (b) hateful
(c) assaulting (d) lethargic

135. Ephemeral
(a) temporal (b) everlasting
(c) polite (d) temporary

136. Fickle
(a) steadfast (b) independent
(c) permanent (d) silly

137. Fatuous
(a) predestined (b) impatient
(c) purposeful (d) silly

138. Firmament
(a) earth (b) hell
(c) sky (d) heaven

139. Fetish
(a) object of love (b) object to hate
(c) object to harm (d) object of dispute

140. Fructify
(a) enrich (b) fruitful
(c) upgrade (d) sterilize

141. Feeble
(a) weak (b) robust
(c) meek (d) emaciated

142. Fundamental
(a) essential (b) subordinate
(c) cardinal (d) none of the above

143. Ghastly
(a) healthy (b) frightful
(c) spectral (d) horrible

144. Garrulous
(a) pabulum (b) prolific
(c) phlegmatic (d) parliamentary

145. Graceful
(a) awkward (b) ugly
(c) slim (d) kind

146. Grip
(a) release (b) fight
(c) hold (d) stretch

147. Gumption
(a) rigidity (b) guess
(c) stupidity (d) sticking

148. Gratify
(a) unpleasant (b) frustration
(c) displease (d) ingratitude

149. Gullible
(a) fish (b) credulous
(c) shrewd (d) traveller

150. Gauche
(a) mistake (b) abusive
(c) attractive (d) gaunt

151. Honorary
(a) professional (b) unpaid
(c) insulting (d) permanent

152. Holiness
(a) evil (b) profanity
(c) devotion (d) none of the above

153. Hunch
(a) slavery (b) kingly
(c) empirical (d) hindrance

154. Hedonism
(a) socialism (b) asceticism
(c) revivalism (d) intoxication

155. Heretic
(a) heresy (b) hermit
(c) devoted (d) pious

156. Humorous
(a) ludicrous (b) serious
(c) dull (d) funny

157. Inborn
(a) acquired (b) congenial
(c) outborn (d) snatched

158. Idiosyncrasy
(a) insanity (b) sanity
(c) normal (d) singularity

159. Insipid
(a) separate (b) inhale
(c) interesting (d) initial

160. Intransigent
(a) surrendering (b) corrigible
(c) urgent (d) porous

161. Impede
(a) hinder (b) expedite
(c) insect (d) stop

162. Imply
(a) declare (b) denote
(c) hint (d) none of the above

163. Impulsive
(a) impetuous (b) slow
(c) heedful (d) wayward

164. Infringement
(a) contravention (b) compliance
(c) encroachment (d) dislocation

165. Kernel
(a) husk (b) core
(c) centre (d) heart

166. Keen
(a) dull (b) edge
(c) sharp (d) weak

167. Legendary
(a) historical (b) mythical
(c) practical (d) none of the above

168. Lament
(a) rejoice (b) deplore
(c) cry (d) complain

169. Loyalty
(a) constancy (b) perfidy
(c) allegiance (d) dishonesty

170. Misgiving
(a) assurance (b) presence
(c) doubt (d) understanding

171. Momentous
(a) heavy (b) snort-lived
(c) frivolous (d) timely

172. Mollify
(a) twist (b) continue
(c) terminate (d) harden

173. Mope
(a) duty (b) sweep
(c) sulk (d) gay

174. Marine
(a) naval (b) land
(c) bird (d) none of the above

175. Modesty
(a) coyness (b) ostentation
(c) relegation (d) peering

176. Noxious
(a) nasal (b) sneezing
(c) notary (d) sanitary

177. Nervous
(a) agitated (b) fearless
(c) shaky (d) timorous

178. Overt
(a) secret (b) open
(c) coy (d) divert

179. Obese
(a) fat (b) thin
(c) explode (d) obedient

180. Oversight
(a) omission (b) observation
(c) inattention (d) none of the above

181. Pedestrian
(a) equestrian (b) driver
(c) hawker (d) none of the above

182. Protract
(a) retrace (b) distract
(c) curtail (d) expose

183. Particularise
(a) impartial (b) dislike
(c) generalise (d) union

184. Perennial
(a) occasional (b) permanent
(c) frequent (d) rare

185. Pacify
(a) calm (b) irritate
(c) quarrel (d) none of the above

186. Peevish
(a) timid (b) cordial
(c) cruel (d) hard

187. Protege
(a) carnage (b) patron
(c) prototype (d) producing

188. Cordiality
(a) proposal (b) boisterous
(c) friendship (d) antagonism

189. Parsimonious
(a) generous (b) selfish
(c) religious (d) hereditary

190. Philistine
(a) brighten (b) cultured
(c) spaning (d) primitive

191. Peremptory
(a) final (b) debatable
(c) ending (d) introductory

192. Pariah
(a) outcast (b) idol
(c) prologue (d) father

193. Prototype
(a) favour (b) canvass
(c) repeat (d) duplicate

194. Piquant
(a) sharp (b) insipid
(c) witty (d) poignant

195. Relegate
(a) repulse (b) welcome
(c) substitute (d) regale

196. Renegade
(a) negate (b) novice
(c) loyal (d) renewal

197. Rancour
(a) farm (b) affection
(c) heal (d) loud

198. Refrain
(a) react (b) avoid
(c) indulgence (d) sunder

199. Rotund
(a) remaining (b) girth
(c) angular (d) crammed

200. Rebuke
(a) applaud (b) criticise
(c) accuse (d) blame

201. Robust
(a) automatic (b) weak.
(c) restored (d) none of the above

202. Rigid
(a) feasible (b) flexible
(c) easy (d) helpful

203. Rejoice
(a) lament (b) make merry
(c) dance (d) hate

204. Remarkable
(a) average (b) noteworthy
(c) commendable (d) none of the above

205. Repeal
(a) annual (b) revoke
(c) cancel (d) apply

206. Spasmodic
(a) together (b) frequent
(c) nature (d) passive

207. Supine
(a) superior (b) lupine
(c) prostrate (d) painful

208. Sententious
(a) strident (b) stem
(c) prolix (d) laxity

209. Solicitude
(a) solitary (b) nonchalant
(c) seriousness (d) company

210. Succinctness
(a) seriousness (b) terseness
(c) inner (d) redundancy

211. Surfeit
(a) superior (b) fined
(c) underfed (d) tall

212. Simulated
(a) feign (b) genuine
(c) imitate (d) separate

213. Stubborn
(a) obstinate (b) ductile
(c) stub (d) life

214. Sublime
(a) ordinary (b) ridiculous
(c) superb (d) bright

215. Suppress
(a) restrain (b) provoke
(c) show (d) punish

216. Traverse
(a) assist (b) cross
(c) negotiate (d) hinder

217. Truant
(a) delinquent (b) talkative
(c) sedulous (d) none of the above

218. Tractable
(a) inexorable (b) countable
(c) plateau (d) hilly

219. Terrestrial
(a) earthly (b) worldly
(c) celestial (d) celebrity

220. Taciturnity
(a) bluntness (b) rudeness
(c) eloquence (d) adulation

221. Transverse
(a) straight (b) opaque
(c) parallel (d) horizontal

222. Foggy
(a) covered (b) opaque
(c) clear (d) misty

223. Transmutation
(a) immortality (b) perpetuation
(c) morality (d) change

224. Tortuous
(a) fulsome (b) noisy
(c) hypocritical (d) straight

225. Undulating
(a) smooth (b) uneven
(c) adulation (d) respect

226. Ugliness
(a) banal (b) smooth
(c) grotesque (d) pulchritude

227. Unruly
(a) dirty (b) orderly
(c) noisy (d) none of the above

228. Urge
(a) incite (b) deter
(c) desire (d) power

229. Unanimous
(a) concordant (b) discordant
(c) unity (d) none of the above

230. Warp
(a) swim (b) woof
(c) cautious (d) equip

231. Venial
(a) corrupt (b) clean
(c) nervous (d) serious

232. Vain
(a) majestic (b) useless
(c) modest (d) boasting

233. Vapid
(a) pungent (b) tame
(c) rapid (d) slow

234. Vindicate
(a) censure (b) favour
(c) indicate (d) eradicate

235. Versatile
(a) volatile (b) variable
(c) constant (d) moody

236. Violent
(a) impetuous (b) placid
(c) ruthless (d) none of the above

237. Vivid
(a) clear (b) dim
(c) glare (d) sharp

238. Vital
(a) trivial (b) essential
(c) significant (d) none of the above

239. Vociferate
(a) bore (b) plough
(c) whisper (d) level

240. Verbose
(a) oral (b) final
(c) epigrammatic (d) grammatical

241. Whimsical
(a) freakish (b) staid
(c) laughter (d) normal

242. Wizened
(a) shrewd (b) foolish
(c) smooth (d) zooming

243. Wellbred
(a) coarse (b) polite
(c) ugly (d) none of the above

244. Wizard
(a) crook (b) magician
(c) ordinary (d) villain

245. Wilt
(a) weaken (b) die
(c) revive (d) to limp

246. Worthy
(a) despicable (b) laudable
(c) bad (d) foolish

247. Yearn
   (a) struggle (b) stubborn
   (c) loathe (d) none of the above

248. Yield
   (a) withhold (b) abandon
   (c) denounce (d) distribute

249. Vibrant
   (a) dull (b) lively
   (c) bright (d) none of the above

250. Vulgar
   (a) cheap (b) expensive
   (c) refined (d) impure

ANSWERS

1. (c)	2. (b)	3. (d)	4. (a)	5. (a)	6. (d)	7. (b)	8. (d)	9. (d)	10. (c)
11. (b)	12. (a)	13. (a)	14. (c)	15. (a)	16. (d)	17. (b)	18. (a)	19. (a)	20. (a)
21. (c)	22. (b)	23. (a)	24. (d)	25. (b)	26. (d)	27. (b)	28. (c)	29. (d)	30. (a)
31. (c)	32. (b)	33. (a)	34. (b)	35. (c)	36. (c)	37. (b)	38. (d)	39. (d)	40. (c)
41. (b)	42. (c)	43. (a)	44. (c)	45. (c)	46. (a)	47. (b)	48. (d)	49. (b)	50. (d)
51. (a)	52. (b)	53. (c)	54. (d)	55. (b)	56. (c)	57. (d)	58. (a)	59. (b)	60. (c)
61. (a)	62. (c)	63. (a)	64. (c)	65. (b)	66. (d)	67. (b)	68. (b)	69. (c)	70. (d)
71. (b)	72. (b)	73. (b)	74. (c)	75. (c)	76. (b)	77. (d)	78. (a)	79. (b)	80. (c)
81. (a)	82. (d)	83. (d)	84. (c)	85. (b)	86. (c)	87. (d)	88. (d)	89. (c)	90. (c)
91. (a)	92. (a)	93. (b)	94. (b)	95. (c)	96. (b)	97. (c)	98. (d)	99. (c)	100. (b)
101. (b)	102. (c)	103. (c)	104. (b)	105. (b)	106. (b)	107. (c)	108. (c)	109. (d)	110. (c)
111. (c)	112. (d)	113. (c)	114. (c)	115. (c)	116. (d)	117. (b)	118. (d)	119. (a)	120. (b)
121. (c)	122. (d)	123. (a)	124. (c)	125. (b)	126. (c)	127. (b)	128. (a)	129. (a)	130. (b)
131. (a)	132. (b)	133. (d)	134. (a)	135. (b)	136. (a)	137. (c)	138. (a)	139. (b)	140. (d)
141. (b)	142. (b)	143. (a)	144. (c)	145. (a)	146. (a)	147. (c)	148. (c)	149. (c)	150. (c)
151. (a)	152. (b)	153. (c)	154. (b)	155. (d)	156. (b)	157. (a)	158. (c)	159. (c)	160. (a)
161. (b)	162. (a)	163. (c)	164. (b)	165. (a)	166. (a)	167. (a)	168. (a)	169. (b)	170. (a)
171. (c)	172. (d)	173. (d)	174. (b)	175. (b)	176. (d)	177. (b)	178. (a)	179. (b)	180. (b)
181. (a)	182. (c)	183. (c)	184. (a)	185. (b)	186. (b)	187. (b)	188. (d)	189. (a)	190. (b)
191. (b)	192. (b)	193. (d)	194. (b)	195. (b)	196. (c)	197. (b)	198. (c)	199. (c)	200. (a)
201. (b)	202. (b)	203. (a)	204. (a)	205. (d)	206. (b)	207. (c)	208. (c)	209. (b)	210. (d)
211. (c)	212. (b)	213. (b)	214. (a)	215. (b)	216. (d)	217. (c)	218. (a)	219. (c)	220. (c)
221. (c)	222. (c)	223. (b)	224. (d)	225. (a)	226. (d)	227. (b)	228. (b)	229. (b)	230. (c)
231. (d)	232. (c)	233. (a)	234. (a)	235. (c)	236. (b)	237. (b)	238. (a)	239. (c)	240. (c)
241. (d)	242. (c)	243. (a)	244. (c)	245. (c)	246. (a)	247. (c)	248. (a)	249. (a)	250. (c)

9.6 Antonyms in Context

In this section, you are required to spot antonyms. As you know, many words in English have more than one meaning or have different shades of meaning. The meaning differs according to the use of the word in different contexts. Here, the words for which you are required to find antonyms have been used in sentences and are given in bold. The sentences are followed by four options. Out of these, you are required to tick mark the one which conveys the opposite of the meaning that the bold word has in this particular context. By way of illustration, one question has been solved for you.

* An over-indulgent mother is always **blind** to her child's faults.
(a) unable to see (b) sensitive
(c) ignorant (d) aware

The answer is (b). Though the word blind in itself means inability to see, in this context, it means insensitive. It is not as if the indulgent mother cannot see her child's faults. She sees them, but is not sensible to their being faults at all.

1. The news produced a sour expression on her face.
(a) sweet (b) pleasant
(c) attractive (d) amused

2. The temperature touched 40 degree centigrade yesterday.
(a) affected (b) contacted
(c) did not reach (d) disconnected

3. The situation took an ugly turn in yesterday's meeting.
(a) beautiful (b) dry
(c) lovely (d) pleasant

4. The teacher always spoke to her students in a sharp tone.
(a) soft (b) blunt
(c) fine (d) sweet

5. She forgets herself when she is among friends.
(a) behaves properly (b) remembers
(c) recalls (d) improves

6. The child was singing in a sweet voice.
(a) bitter (b) ugly
(c) hoarse (d) sour

7. One should not always be hard on one's subordinates.
(a) severe (b) kind
(c) dull (d) soft

8. They returned from the beautiful picnic spot with a heavy heart.
(a) weightless (b) happy
(c) sombre (d) jovial

9. The issue of tax evasion generated a hot debate.
(a) mild (b) cold
(c) soft (d) perverse

10. The boy laughed in order to cover his nervousness.
(a) reveal (b) uncover
(c) erode (d) expose to view

11. My friend has an agreeable disposition.
(a) amicable (b) haughty
(c) disagreeable (d) charming

12. With deep sorrow, the principal announced the exstudent's death.
(a) profound (b) mild
(c) shallow (d) pronounced

13. The man ordered his servant, in a rough voice, to leave.
(a) hoarse (b) gentle
(c) smooth (d) shrill

14. The well was so deep that it was difficult to draw water from it.
(a) pronounced (b) mild
(c) shallow (d) steep

15. His book took the first prize at the Book Fair Contest.
(a) won (b) gave
(c) lost (d) captured

16. In that country, people are used to wearing

strange clothes.

(a) unusual (b) familiar
(c) rare (d) common

17. This canal was constructed during the first Five Year Plan.
(a) destroyed (b) made
(c) erected (d) fabricated

18. The lady spoke to her friend in a cold voice after their quarrel.
(a) warm (b) hot
(c) friendly (d) expressionless

19. The student gave a neat answer to the puzzling question that was put to him.
(a) clever (b) clumsy
(c) confused (d) dirty

20. Clear thinking can be done by a sound mind.
(a) calm (b) unreasonable
(c) noisy (d) confused

21. His father was in a sombre mood.
(a) light (b) gay
(c) sedate (d) cheerful

22. The teacher gave some valuable advice to the students.
(a) expensive (b) cheap
(c) useless (d) priceless

23. The actor gave a brilliant performance at the function.
(a) dull (b) uninteresting
(c) joyful (d) unexciting

24. Adult franchise has been hailed as a progressive step.
(a) impeding (b) regressive
(c) obstructive (d) retrograde

25. The solution put forward by you is impracticable.
(a) feasible (b) possible
(c) plausible (d) defunct

26. All the residents had gathered in the field to hoist the flag.
(a) elevate (b) lower
(c) exist (d) examine

27. All the cosmetic aids made the model look ghastly.
(a) horrible (b) attractive
(c) disgusting (d) foul

28. The ability to see is nature's best gift to mankind.
(a) display (b) aptitude
(c) deprivation (d) excitement

29. The latest issue of the magazine carries very dull pictures.
(a) sleek (b) ventilating
(c) obscene (d) glossy

30. The latest measures of the government may cause the economy to decay.
(a) grow (b) descend
(c) stagger (d) expand

31. A cheap display of wealth was being done through gaudy dresses.
(a) extravagant (b) cheap
(c) sober (d) ornate

32. The party showed no disposition towards breaking up.
(a) unwillingness (b) temperament
(c) inclination (d) sparking

33. A dull speaker is never able to distinguish between an attentive and an absorbed audience.
(a) applauding (b) distrait
(c) clever (d) absent-minded

34. The construction will not complete on time if the work is done by a bunch of drowsy labourers.
(a) sleepy (b) lazy
(c) active (d) alert

35. Due to keen interest in studies, he came out with a brilliant performance in the examination.
(a) cheerless (b) dismal
(c) gay (d) happy

36. Your recitation of the poem was looked at with disdain by the rest of the class.
(a) haughtiness (b) admiration

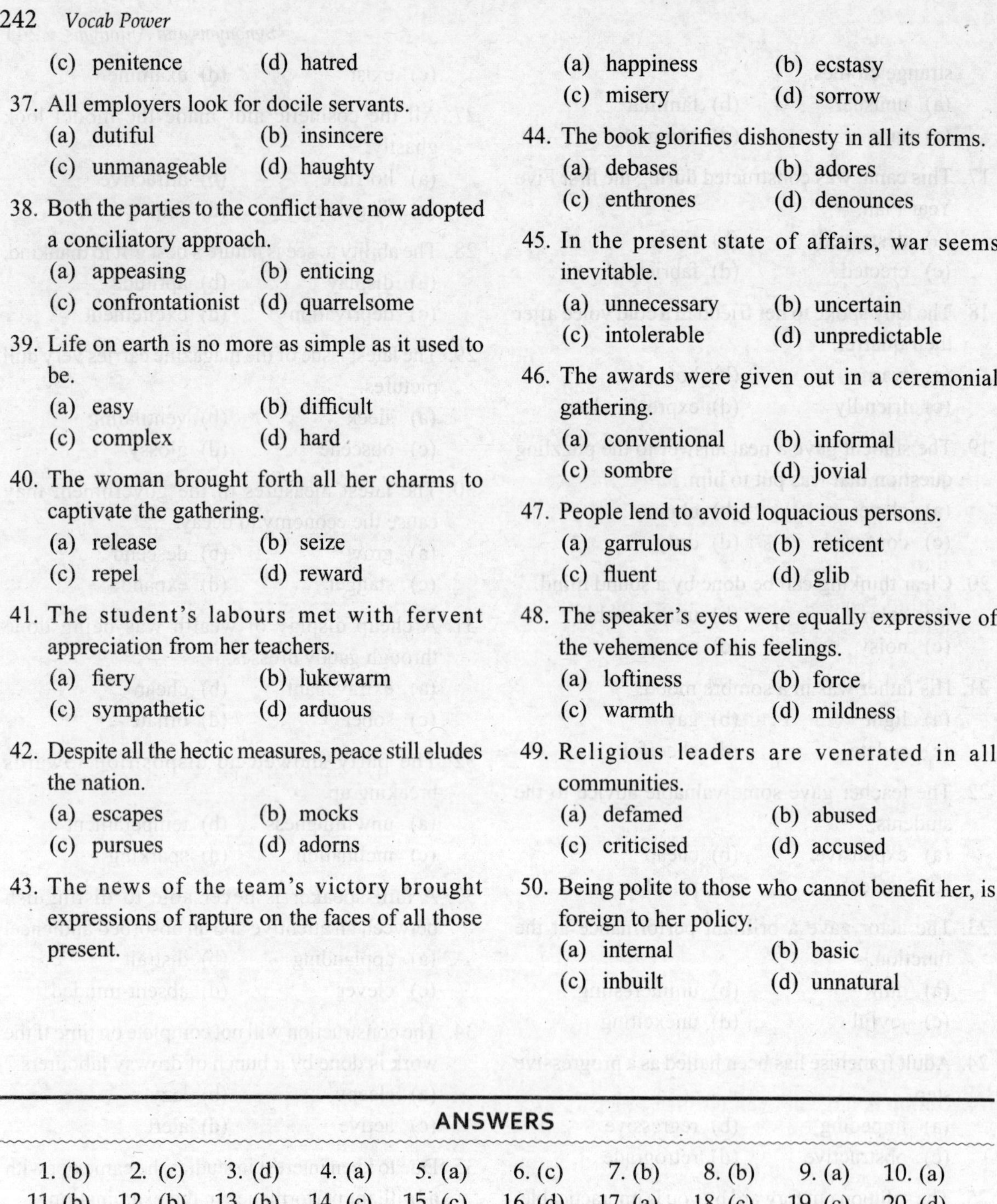

(c) penitence (d) hatred

37. All employers look for docile servants.
(a) dutiful (b) insincere
(c) unmanageable (d) haughty

38. Both the parties to the conflict have now adopted a conciliatory approach.
(a) appeasing (b) enticing
(c) confrontationist (d) quarrelsome

39. Life on earth is no more as simple as it used to be.
(a) easy (b) difficult
(c) complex (d) hard

40. The woman brought forth all her charms to captivate the gathering.
(a) release (b) seize
(c) repel (d) reward

41. The student's labours met with fervent appreciation from her teachers.
(a) fiery (b) lukewarm
(c) sympathetic (d) arduous

42. Despite all the hectic measures, peace still eludes the nation.
(a) escapes (b) mocks
(c) pursues (d) adorns

43. The news of the team's victory brought expressions of rapture on the faces of all those present.
(a) happiness (b) ecstasy
(c) misery (d) sorrow

44. The book glorifies dishonesty in all its forms.
(a) debases (b) adores
(c) enthrones (d) denounces

45. In the present state of affairs, war seems inevitable.
(a) unnecessary (b) uncertain
(c) intolerable (d) unpredictable

46. The awards were given out in a ceremonial gathering.
(a) conventional (b) informal
(c) sombre (d) jovial

47. People lend to avoid loquacious persons.
(a) garrulous (b) reticent
(c) fluent (d) glib

48. The speaker's eyes were equally expressive of the vehemence of his feelings.
(a) loftiness (b) force
(c) warmth (d) mildness

49. Religious leaders are venerated in all communities.
(a) defamed (b) abused
(c) criticised (d) accused

50. Being polite to those who cannot benefit her, is foreign to her policy.
(a) internal (b) basic
(c) inbuilt (d) unnatural

ANSWERS

1. (b)	2. (c)	3. (d)	4. (a)	5. (a)	6. (c)	7. (b)	8. (b)	9. (a)	10. (a)
11. (b)	12. (b)	13. (b)	14. (c)	15. (c)	16. (d)	17. (a)	18. (c)	19. (c)	20. (d)
21. (d)	22. (c)	23. (b)	24. (b)	25. (a)	26. (b)	27. (b)	28. (c)	29. (d)	30. (a)
31. (c)	32. (a)	33. (b)	34. (c)	35. (b)	36. (b)	37. (c)	38. (d)	39. (c)	40. (c)
41. (b)	42. (a)	43. (c)	44. (d)	45. (b)	46. (b)	47. (b)	48. (d)	49. (a)	50. (b)

Contronyms

Contronym is a word which has two meanings, both contradictory to each other. Contronyms are a combination of homonyms (words with similar spelling or pronunciation) and antonyms (words with opposite meaning).

1. **Apology** A statement of contrition for an action, or a defense of one
2. **Aught** All, or nothing
3. **Bill** A payment, or an invoice for payment
4. **Bolt** To secure, or to flee
5. **Bound** Heading to a destination, or restrained from movement
6. **Buckle** To connect, or to break or collapse
7. **Cleave** To adhere, or to separate
8. **Clip** To fasten, or detach
9. **Consult** To offer advice, or to obtain it
10. **Continue** To keep doing an action, or to suspend an action
11. **Custom** A common practice, or a special treatment
12. **Dike** A wall to prevent flooding, or a ditch
13. **Discursive** Moving in an orderly fashion among topics, or proceeding aimlessly in a discussion
14. **Dollop** A large amount (British English), or a small amount
15. **Dust** To add fine particles, or to remove them
16. **Enjoin** To impose, or to prohibit
17. **Fast** Quick, or stuck or made stable
18. **Fine** Excellent, or acceptable or good enough
19. **Finished** Completed, or ended or destroyed
20. **First degree** Most severe in the case of a murder charge, or least severe in reference to a burn
21. **Fix** To repair, or to castrate
22. **Flog** To promote persistently, or to criticize or beat
23. **Garnish** To furnish, as with food preparation, or to take away, as with wages
24. **Give out** To provide, or to stop because of a lack of supply
25. **Go** To proceed or succeed, or to weaken or fail
26. **Grade** A degree of slope, or a horizontal line or position
27. **Handicap** An advantage provided to ensure equality, or a disadvantage that prevents equal achievement
28. **Help** To assist, or to prevent or (in negative constructions) restrain
29. **Hold up** To support, or to impede
30. **Lease** To offer property for rent, or to hold such property
31. **Left** Remained, or departed
32. **Let** Allowed, or hindered
33. **Liege** A feudal lord, or a vassal
34. **Literally** Actually, or virtually
35. **Mean** Average or stingy, or excellent
36. **Model** An exemplar, or a copy

37. **Off** Deactivated, or activated, as an alarm
38. **Out** Visible, as with stars showing in the sky, or invisible, in reference to lights
39. **Out of** Outside, or inside, as in working out of a specific office
40. **Overlook** To supervise, or to neglect
41. **Oversight** Monitoring, or failing to oversee
42. **Peer** A person of the nobility, or an equal
43. **Presently** Now, or soon
44. **Put out** Extinguish, or generate
45. **Puzzle** A problem, or to solve one
46. **Quantum** Significantly large, or a minuscule part
47. **Quiddity** Essence, or a trifling point of contention
48. **Quite** Rather (as a qualifying modifier), or completely
49. **Ravel** To entangle, or to disentangle
50. **Refrain** To desist from doing something, or to repeat
51. **Rent** To purchase use of something, or to sell use
52. **Rock** An immobile mass of stone or figuratively similar phenomenon, or a shaking or unsettling movement or action
53. **Sanction** To approve, or to boycott
54. **Sanguine** Confidently cheerful, or bloodthirsty
55. **Scan** To peruse, or to glance
56. **Screen** To present, or to conceal
57. **Seed** To sow seeds, or to shed or remove them
58. **Shop** To patronize a business in order to purchase something, or to sell something
59. **Skin** To cover, or to remove
60. **Skinned** Covered with skin, or with the skin removed
61. **Splice** To join, or to separate
62. **Stakeholder** One who has a stake in an enterprise, or a bystander who holds the stake for those placing a bet
63. **Strike** To hit, or to miss in an attempt to hit
64. **Table** To propose (in British English), or to set aside
65. **Temper** To soften, or to strengthen
66. **Throw out** To dispose of, or to present for consideration
67. **Transparent** Invisible, or obvious
68. **Trim** To decorate, or to remove excess from
69. **Trip** A journey, or a stumble
70. **Unbending** Rigid, or relaxing
71. **Variety** A particular type, or many types
72. **Wear** To endure, or to deteriorate
73. **Weather** To withstand, or to wear away
74. **Wind up** To end, or to start up
75. **With** Alongside, or against

UNIT 11 Hetronyms

Heteronyms mostly come in pairs. Heteronyms are words that have the same spellings but have different pronunciations. They have different meanings according to pronunciation. Two words never are homophones but can be homographs. For example "**Row**" when a row is pronounced as "**ROUW**" its meaning is "a fight" and when we pronounced it as "**ROH**" its meaning is "a line".

Affect *ehFEKT-* to change; *AFFekt-* a person's feelings or emotion

Alternate *ALternit-* the next choice; *ALternait-* switch back and forth

Are *AHR-* plural present tense of "to be"; *AIR-* 100 square meters (1/100th of a hectare) [although may also be pronounced *AHR*]

Ares *AIRS-* 100 square meter units [plural]; *AIReez-* Greek god of war [capitalized]

Attribute *ahTRIByoot-* to consider resulting from; *AHtribyoot-* a characteristic of someone (12)

August *AUgust-* month [capitalized]; *auGUST-* important, eminent

Axes *AKsiz-* more than one ax or axe; *AKseez-* the plural of axis

Bass *BASE-* a string instrument; *(rhymes with mass)-* a fish

Bow *BAU-* to lower one's head or the front of a ship; *BOH-* used to shoot arrows

Bowed *BAU-d-* to bend over; *BOH-d-* bent

Buffet *BUFFet-* to pound or bump; *booFAY-* place where you serve yourself

Close *CLOZE-* to shut; *CLOS-* near

Combine *komBYNE-* put together; *KOMbyne-* a threshing machine

Conduct *KONduckt-* behavior; *kunDUCKT-* to lead (see this heteronym below)

Conflict *kunFLIKT-* to act against; *KAHNflict-* a fight or disagreement

Console *KAHNsole-* an upright case; *kunSOLE-* to comfort

Content *KAHNtent-* meaning; *kunTENT-* satisfied

Contest *kunTEST-* to argue; *KAHNtest-* a match of skill

Contract *CONtract-* an agreement; *conTRACT-* to shrink or to agree on a project

Convert *conVERT-* to change one's belief; *CONvert-* one whose belief was changed

Converse *KAHNvers-* the opposite; *kunVERS-* to talk

Convict *kunVIKT-* to find guilty; *KAHNvikt-* a prisoner

Crooked *KROOKt-* to bend your neck; *KROOK-ed-* having a curve

Deliberate *diLIBerit-* carefully considered; *diLIBerATE-* to consider

Desert *dihZURT-* to leave ; *DEZert-* arid region

Digest *DYEjest-* collection of published material; *dieJEST-* absorb nutrients

Do *DOO-* to accomplish; *DOE-* a musical note

Does *DUZ-* performs; *DOZE-* more than one female deer

Dove *DUV-* a bird; *DOEV-* jumped off

Drawer *DROR-* the compartment you pull out from the dresser; *DRAWer-* one who draws

Excuse *EKskyooz-* to let someone off; *EKskyoos-* a reason or explanation

House *HAUS-* a building that serves as living quarters; *HOWZ-* to provide with living quarters

Incense *INsens-* burnt aromatic; *inSENS-* to make angry

Intern *INtern-* a physician in training; *inTERN-* confine to prescribed area

Invalid *inVALLid*- not valid; *INvallid*- an ill person

Laminate *LAMinate*- to construct by adding layers; *LAMinit* [although both pronunciations are listed]- the cover itself

Lather *(rhymes with rather)*- foam or suds; *(rhymes with bath fur)*- a worker who installs lath (lattice work)

Lead *LEED*- to guide; *LED*- a metallic element

Minute *MINNit*- 60 seconds; *myNOOT*- tiny

Moderate *MODerit*- keeping within reason; *MODerATE*- to preside over

Mow *MOH*- to cut grass; *MAU*- a pile of hay

Multiply *MULLtihPLIE*- multiply two numbers; *MULLtihplee*- in a multiple manner

Number *NUMber*- one, two, three …; *NUMMER*- more numb [many dictionaries do not list this use, which suggests that "more numb" is preferred.

Nun *NUN*- women in religious order; *NOON*- 14th letter in Hebrew alphabet

Object *ubJEKT*- to complain; *AHBjekt*- a thing

Pasty *PAstee*- like glue; *PASStee*- a meat pie

Pate *PAIT*- a bald head; *paTAY*- a minced food; *PAHT*- a porcelain paste [diacritics in pâté and pâte don't count!]

Perfect *PERfekt*- exactly correct; *perFEKT*- to make correct

Periodic *PEERreeODDik*- occasional; *PUREeyeODDik*- an iodine compound

Permit *perMIT*- to allow some event to occur; *PERmit* [although both pronunciations are listed]- a document giving permission

Polish *POElish*- from Poland; *PAHLish*- shine [capitalization doesn't count!]

Present *PREZent*- a gift; *preeSENT*- to give a talk

Primer *PRIHMer*- an elementary book; *PRYmer*- the preparatory coat of paint

Produce *PROdoos*- vegetables; *proDOOS*- bring forth

Project *proJEKT*- to show a movie; *PRAHjekt*- a task

Pussy *PUHSee*- having pus; *POOHSee*; a kitten

Raven *RAYven*- black bird; *RAVen*- hungry

Rebel *REBBell*- a resister; *rihBELL*- to resist

Record *RECKord*- a list; *reKORD*- to write down

Recreation *rek-ree-Ashun*- pastime; *REEcreeAshun*- remake (also, **recreate**)

Refuse *reFUSE*- to deny; *REFFyoos*- garbage

Relay *reeLAY*- to put it down again, such as a carpet; *REElay*- a race by teams; *rihLAY*- to pass along, such as information .

Rerun *reRUN*- to race again or to repeat a show on television; RErun- a repeated TV show

Reside reZIDE- to stay put; RE-SYD- [Slang] to change places (change teams) [usu. hyphenated as re-side] (

Resign *reZYN*- to quit; *reSYN*- to sign again (e.g., a contract) [usu. hyphenated as re-sign]

Resume *reeZOOM*- to restart; *REHZoomay*- a document of experience [also résumé; diacritics don't count!]

Row *ROH*- a line; *ROUW*- a fight

Sake *SAHkey*- alcoholic drink; *SAYK*- a purpose

Secrete *seeKREET*- to discharge; *sehKRET*- an armored skullcap [secrète, diacritics don't count!]

Secreted *seeKREETed*- having put out; *SEEkrehted*- placed out of sight

Separate *SEPerATE*- to divide into groups; *SEPret*- not joined together

Sewer *SOwer*- one who sews; *SOOwer*- place for human waste

Slough *SLUFF*- the outer layer of skin of a snake; [*rhymes with OW!*]- a hole of deep mud or mire; *SLOO*- a marshy pond

Sow *SOUW*- a pig; *SO*- to plant seed

Subject *SUBjekt*- the theme; subJEKT- to force upon someone

Tear *TARE*- to rip; *TEER*- fluid in eye

Wind *WHINEd*- to coil up; *WINd*- the blowing air

Wound *WOOND*- to injure; *WOWND*- coiled up

UNIT 12

Palindrome

If a word is a palindrome, that means it's spelled the same both backward and forwards. That means, you can write any one of these words on a mirror and not have to worry about it being reversed!

For example, B-i-B. A fun clue for this palindrome word could be "it's something that a baby wears when they eat!"

A list of Palindromes

1. Abba
2. Aibohphobia
3. Bib
4. Bob
5. Civic
6. Deified
7. Detartrated
8. Dewed
9. Eve
10. Hannah
11. Kayak
12. Level
13. Madam
14. Malayalam
15. Minim
16. Mom
17. Murdrum
18. Noon
19. Nun
20. Otto
21. Peep
22. Pop
23. Racecar
24. Radar
25. Redder
26. Refer
27. Repaper
28. Rotator
29. Rotavator
30. Sagas
31. Sis
32. Solos
33. Stats
34. Tattarrattat
35. Tenet
36. Yay
37. Wow

Palindrome sentences and Phrases

Not only can a palindrome show up as a single word, but if you're careful, you can create a full sentence or a phrase that is a palindrome. Here are some examples:

1. Taco cat
2. Never odd or even
3. Madam, I'm Adam

4. Mr. Owl ate my metal worm.
5. Was it a car or a cat I saw?
6. Murder for a jar of red rum.
7. Go hang a salami, I'm a lasagna hog.
8. Do geese see God?
9. Evil olive
10. Amore, Roma
11. A man, a plan, a canal: Panama
12. My gym
13. No lemon, no melon
14. Top spot
15. Sit on a potato pan, Otis!
16. Ah. Satan sees Natasha.
17. Cigar? Toss it in a can. It is so tragic.
18. Did Hannah See bees? Hanna did.
19. You, banana boy!
20. Borrow, or rob?
21. Eva, can I see bees in a cave?
22. Poor Dan is in a droop.
23. Oozy rat in a sanitary zoo.
24. Step on no pets.
25. Able was I ere I saw Elba.
26. Sir, I demand, I am a maid named Iris.
27. We panic in a pew.
28. Won't lovers revolt now?
29. Don't nod.

UNIT 13

Pangram

A pangram is a sentence that includes every single letter of the alphabet, from A to Z, at least once. The most challenging pangrams are the ones with the fewest letters. For instance, a perfect pangram includes just 26 letters. They're the most difficult to come up with. Here are 14 phrases that epitomize pangrams.".

1. Waltz, bad nymph, for quick jigs vex. (28 letters)
2. Quick zephyrs blow, vexing daft Jim. (29 letters)
3. Sphinx of black quartz, judge my vow. (29 letters)
4. Two driven jocks help fax my big quiz. (30 letters)
5. Five quacking zephyrs jolt my wax bed. (31 letters)
6. The five boxing wizards jump quickly. (31 letters)
7. Pack my box with five dozen liquor jugs. (32 letters)
8. The quick brown fox jumps over the lazy dog. (35 letters)
9. Jinxed wizards pluck ivy from the big quilt. (36 letters)
10. Crazy Fredrick bought many very exquisite opal jewels. (46 letters)
11. We promptly judged antique ivory buckles for the next prize. (50 letters)
12. A mad boxer shot a quick, gloved jab to the jaw of his dizzy opponent. (54 letters)
13. Jaded zombies acted quaintly but kept driving their oxen forward. (55 letters)
14. The job requires extra pluck and zeal from every young wage earner. (55 letters)
15. Go, lazy fat vixen; be shrewd, jump quick.
16. When zombies arrive, quickly fax Judge Pat.
17. Amazingly few discotheques provide jukeboxes.
18. Puzzled women bequeath jerks very exotic gifts.
19. The quick onyx goblin jumps over the lazy dwarf.
20. Brawny gods just flocked up to quiz and vex him.
21. Watch "Jeopardy!", Alex Trebek's fun TV quiz game.
22. Six big devils from Japan quickly forgot how to waltz.
23. Five or six big jet planes zoomed quickly by the tower.
24. Jack amazed a few girls by dropping the antique onyx vase.
25. A quick movement of the enemy will jeopardize six gunboats.
26. No kidding—Lorenzo called off his trip to Mexico City just because they told him the conquistadors were extinct.

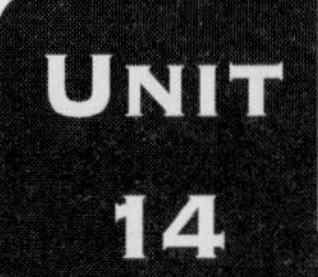

Superfluous Expressions

Those words which are unnecessary and are just redundant in an expression are known as Superfluous words. For example – for a long period of time. Here we can remove 'of time' or period. The correct expression will be – for a long period or for a long time.

So we can say that superfluous words means 'more than required'.

They are redundant words in the expression.

What are SLANG?

Those words or phrases which are used by a particular group but they are not used in standard English (by everyone) are called SLANG.

For example- 'Fake news' is a slang. This phrase was made popular by President Donald Trump. This word is supposed to describe inaccurate and fabricated news but now a days this phrase is used to describe the news which is against one's views.

Another Example of Slang- my family member – its right phrase will be – a member of my family

Some features of Slang:-

- Slang is an informal language.
- A slang is used and spoken in particular context.
- We sometimes misinterpret using slang as being cool.
- For example sometimes we use 'sis' for sister.

Superfluous Antonym :

1. required
2. relevant
3. useful
4. necessary
5. needed
6. reasonable

These are the antonyms of Superfluous.

Superfluous Synonym

1. excessive
2. redundant
3. useless
4. needless
5. unnecessary
6. profuse
7. surplus

Superfluous Etymology

Superfluous is a combination of two Latin words – 'Super' and 'Fluere'. 'Super' means over and 'Fluere' means to flow.

Redundant Meaning

1. Repetition of same sense in different words
2. More than is needed, desired, or required

Superfluous Grammar

Superfluous is an important topic of Grammar if we want to avoid common errors in English speaking and writing. Sometimes we write and speak words which are unnecessary. So we should know all these words if we want to improve our English language. Now we are going to start the word list.

Superfluous Expression and SLANG word list

There are some words which start with 're'. After some of them we don't have to add back or again. There words are as follow:

1. return, reimburse, retreat, recede, recall, recapitulate, repeat, recast, rewrite – never use back after them.

   reborn, rebuild, reiterate, recast, recall, recede- never use again after them.

2. After these words never use over.

   over-ride, overturn, overshadow, overshoot, overtop

3. There are some words after which we do not have to use not. Otherwise it will make the expression superfluous expression.

   until, unless, forbid, prevent, dissuade, deny, refuse, lest.

Superfluous Words – Incorrect and Correct Uses

	Incorrect		Correct
1.	equally as good as (Wrong)	1.	as good as
2.	mutual agreement (Wrong)	2.	agreement
3.	mutual friend (Wrong)	3.	common friend
4.	mutual dislike of each other (Wrong)	4.	mutual dislike
5.	freeship (Wrong)	5.	freestudentship
6.	lecturership (Wrong)	6.	lectureship
7.	cousin brother (Wrong)	7.	cousin
8.	cousin sister (Wrong)	8.	cousin
9.	consensus opinion (Wrong)	9.	consensus
10.	consort husband (Wrong)	10.	consort
11.	consort wife (Wrong)	11.	consort
12.	final conclusion (Wrong)	12.	conclusion
13.	kindly requested (Wrong)	13.	requested
14.	funeral service (Wrong)	14.	funeral
15.	supposing if (Wrong)	15.	supposing
16.	suppose if (Wrong)	16.	either use suppose or if
17.	during the period of war (Wrong)	17.	during the war
18.	during the war period (Wrong)	18.	during the war
19.	with bag and baggage (Wrong)	19.	bag and baggage
20.	my family member (Wrong)	20.	a member of my family
21.	an English teacher (Wrong)	21.	a teacher of English
22.	passing marks (Wrong)	22.	pass marks
23.	linking road (Wrong)	23.	link road
24.	suddenly come across (Wrong)	24.	come across
25.	come across with (Wrong)	25.	come across
26.	coward man (Wrong)	26.	coward
27.	flee away (Wrong)	27.	flee
28.	and who (Wrong)	28.	who
29.	and which (Wrong)	29.	which
30.	and that (Wrong)	30.	that
31.	reason because (Wrong)	31.	reason that / reason why
32.	two twins (Wrong)	32.	twins
33.	divide into four quarters (Wrong)	33.	divide into four
34.	await for (Wrong)	34.	await (= wait for)
35.	comprise of (Wrong)	35.	comprise (= consist of)
36.	investigate into (Wrong)	36.	investigate (= inquire into)

Legal Words

A list of common legal terms that every entrepreneur, business owners and common man must know. Knowing the meaning of the following legal terms can help you easily understand a conversation with a Lawyer and comprehend legal matters.

1.	Contract	a binding agreement that is enforceable by law
2.	Consideration	the process of giving careful thought to something
3.	Negligence	failure to act with the prudence of a reasonable person
4.	Precedent	an example that is used to justify similar occurrences
5.	Infringement	an act that disregards an agreement or a right
6.	Perjury	criminal offense of making false statements under oath
7.	Statute	an act passed by a legislative body
8.	Sue	institute legal proceedings against; file a suit against
9.	Challenge	a call to engage in a contest or fight
10.	Void	an empty area or space
11.	Lewd	suggestive of or tending to moral looseness
12.	Detention	a state of being confined (usually for a short time)
13.	Parole	a conditional release from imprisonment
14.	Misdemeanor	a crime less serious than a felony
15.	Injunction	a judicial remedy to prohibit a party from doing something
16.	Summons	a request to be present
17.	Writ	a legal document issued by a court or judicial officer
18.	Frustration	an act of hindering someone's plans or efforts
19.	Bar	a rigid piece of metal or wood
20.	Bench	a long seat for more than one person
21.	Trespass	enter unlawfully on someone's property
22.	Interrogation	an instance of questioning
23.	Apprehend	anticipate with dread or anxiety
24.	Magistrate	a lay judge or civil authority who administers the law
25.	Marshal	a military officer of highest rank
26.	Embezzlement	the fraudulent appropriation of funds or property
27.	Malpractice	professional wrongdoing that results in injury or damage
28.	Fugitive	someone who is sought by law officers
29.	Torture	infliction of suffering to punish or obtain information

30.	Acquitted	declared not guilty of a specific offense or crime
31.	Affidavit	written declaration made under oath
32.	Barrister	a British lawyer who speaks in the higher courts of law
33.	Solicitor	a British lawyer who gives legal advice
34.	Chancellor	the person who is head of state (in several countries)
35.	Equity	thc quality of bcing fair, rcasonablc, or impartial
36.	Piracy	the act of plagiarizing
37.	Grill	a framework of metal bars used as a partition or a grate
38.	Class Action	a lawsuit brought by a representative member of a large group of people on behalf of all members of the group
39.	Common-Law Marriage	a marriage relationship created by agreement and cohabitation rather than by ceremony
40.	Canon Law	the body of official rules governing the affairs of a church
41.	Boarding	the act of passengers and crew getting aboard a ship or aircraft
42.	Jurisprudence	the branch of philosophy concerned with the law
43.	Libel	a false and malicious publication
44.	Curfew	an order that after a certain time activities are prohibited
45.	Espionage	the systematic use of spies to obtain secrets
46.	Treason	a crime that undermines the offender's government
47.	Abduction	the criminal act of carrying someone away by force
48.	Autopsy	an examination and dissection of a dead body
49.	Impeachment	the act of charging an official with an offense committed while in office
50.	Collective Bargaining	negotiation between an employer and a trade union
51.	Verdict	findings of a jury on issues submitted to it for decision
52.	Legislation	the act of making or enacting laws
53.	Repudiate	refuse to acknowledge, ratify, or recognize as valid
54.	Perpetrator	someone who commits wrongdoing
55.	Offender	a person who transgresses moral or civil law
56.	Culprit	someone or something responsible for harm or wrongdoing
57.	Estoppel	a rule of evidence whereby a person is barred from denying the truth of a fact that has already been settled
58.	Tenancy	the act or state of being an occupant
59.	Deed	a legal document to effect a transfer of property
60.	Surety	something clearly established

61.	Clause	a separate section of a legal document
62.	Performance	the act of doing something successfully
63.	Implied Trust	a trust inferred by operation of law
64.	Foreclosure	proceedings initiated to repossess the collateral for a loan
65.	Bankruptcy	a legal process for a corporation declared to be insolvent
66.	Roundup	the activity of gathering livestock together so that they can be counted or branded or sold
67.	Security Interest	any interest in a property that secures the payment of an obligation
68.	Juvenile Delinquency	an antisocial misdeed in violation of the law by a minor
69.	Expiration	a coming to an end of a contract period
70.	Convict	find or declare guilty
71.	Ordinance	an authoritative rule
72.	Suspended	supported or kept from sinking or falling by buoyancy
73.	Sentence	a string of words satisfying grammatical rules of a language
74.	Discovery	the act of finding something
75.	Felony	a serious crime, such as murder or arson
76.	Adjudicate	hear a case and sit as the judge at the trial of
77.	Arraign	accuse of a wrong or an inadequacy
78.	Bail	money forfeited if the accused fails to appear in court
79.	Assault	attack someone physically or emotionally
80.	Dissent	a difference of opinion
81.	Non Compos Mentis	not of sound mind, memory, or understanding
82.	Fiat	a legally binding command or decision
83.	Evict	expel or eject without recourse to legal process
84.	Aggravated	made more severe or intense especially in law
85.	Refutation	the act of determining that something is false
86.	Force Majeure	a natural and unavoidable catastrophe
87.	Complaint	an expression of grievance or resentment

UNIT 16 Collocations

Collocations are words that are frequently placed together. So, a collocation in English is a group of two or more words that are often found together either in English speech or English writing.

Collocations with HAVE & DO & MAKE

Have	Do	Make
a conversation	a job	a decision
a look	business	a mistake
a meal	damage	a change
a nap	research	an effort
a party	sports	a difference
a bath	homework	a cake
fun	something	a fortune
a good time	justice	a living
a sense of	harm	a point
an impact	well	a difference

Collocations with PAY & SAVE & KEEP

Pay	Save	Keep
attention	money	a secret
a bill	time	a distance
a compliment	energy	a promise
a fine	a life	a balance
a visit	a seat	a record
a visit	the peace	a job
a price	a fortune	a low profile
a salary	the environment	a lookout
respect	a distance	a secret
a debt	water	a memory

Collocations with TAKE and BREAK & CATCH

Take	Break	Catch
a bath	a break	a cold
a nap	a rest	a flight
a walk	a vacation	a glimpse
a trip	a chance	a meal
a photo	a dance	a thief
a shower	a breath	a ride
a test	a lunch	a fish
a risk	a nap	a ball
a sip	a leave	a game
a stand	a pause	a fever

Collocations with COME and GO & GET

Come	Go	Get
along	ahead	along
back	away	around
down	back	at
in	by	away
out	down	back
over	for	behind
through	in	up
up	off	down
with	on	over
without	out	rid

Collocations with Time

spend time	waste time
make time for	save time
free time	have a hard time
have time	take your time
on time	just in time
take time off	run out of time
leisure time	spare time
stall for time	pass the time
take your time	this/the same time tomorrow
to tell time	to keep time
precious time	set time
kill time	have a great time

Collocations with Catch

Catch a ball	Catch a cold
Catch a glimpse	Catch a thief
Catch (on) fire	Catch a whiff
Catch a bus/ a train	Catch sight of
Catch a chill	Catch someone's eye
Catch you later!	Catch the flu
Catch someone's attention	Catch your breath
Catch someone Red-Handed	Catch Someone In The Act

Collocations with Come

Come close	Come clean about
Come complete with	Come on time
Come last	Come up with
Come to an agreement	Come right back
Come to a stand still (idiom)	Come to a compromise
Come to an end	Come to a conclusion
Come late	Come to a decision
Come first	Come to a realization
Come prepared	Come to a stop
Come early	Come to life
Come into view	Come to sb's rescue
Come under attack	Come to terms with

Collocations with Give

Give thought (to)	Give a call (a ring, a buzz)
Give evidence	Give a choice
Give notice	Give a lecture or speech or performance
Give sb a chance	Give a chance
Give sb a lift	Give a ride
Give sth a go	Give a damn
Give an answer	Give a hug or kiss
Give an example	Give a hand
Give an idea	Give a headache
Give an opinion	Give advice
Give birth	Give permission
Give credit	Give rise to
Give priority	Give sb a call
Give the impression	Give the impression
Give up	Give up
Give up hope	Give up hope
Give way	Give way
Give someone a lift	Give an idea
Give sth a go	Give an opinion
Give an answer	Give birth
Give an example	Give credit
Give priority	

Collocations with Go

Go astray	Go smoothly
Go bad	Go to the beach/to the movie
Go bald	Go to war

Go bankrupt	Go abroad
Go deaf	Go crazy
Go insane (idiom)	Go blind
Go mad/angry	Go missing
Go on a date	Go out of business
Go on a picnic	Go overseas
Go on foot	Go quiet
Go online	Go smoothly
Go finishing	Go abroad
Go sailing	Go to war
Out of fashion	

Collocations with Have

Have a baby	Have a jog
Have a backache	Have a lecture
Have a bad fall	Have a Jacuzzi
Have a birthday	Have depression/etc.
Have a break	Have a discussion
Have a bath	Have a stroke
Have a bad temper	Have a swim
Have a competition	Have a talk
Have a chat	Have a taste
Have a bite	Have a temperature
Have a dream	Have a touch
Have a drink	Have a try
Have a feeling	Have a walk
Have a fight	Have sympathy
Have a fit	Have the chance (to)
Have a game	Have time
Have a haircut	Have trouble
Have a hard time	Have work
Have a headache	Have a snack
Have a holiday	Have a business trip
Have a goal	Have a busy day
Have a good time	Have a career/goal
Have a good/nice/etc day!	Have a chance
Have a great weekend	Have a cold
Have a laugh	Have a laugh
Have a drill	Have a drill
Have a glass of wine	Have a glass of wine
Have a go	Have a go
Have a lesson	Have a lesson
Have a lie-down	Have a lie-down
Have a limp	Have a limp
Have a lisp	Have a lisp
Have a listen	Have a listen
Have a look	Have a look
Have a massage	Have a massage
Have a meal	Have a meal
Have a dispute	Have a dispute

Collocation With Make

Make a bed	Make a remark
Make a break with somebody	Make a reservation
Make a cake	Make a rude gesture
Make a confession/an admission	Make a salad
Make a fool of yourself	Make a move
Make a fortune	Make a note (of)
Make a bundle (idiom)	Make a pass at
Make a fuss	Make a phone call
Make a joke	Make an objection
Make a dress	Make an observation
Make a habit	Make arrangements
Make a difference	Make believe
Make a living	Make breakfast/lunch/dinner
Make a cup of tea	Make coffee
Make a decision	Make contact
Make a list	Make a statement
Make a deal	Make a mess
Make a promise	Make an offer
Make a recovery	Make sense

Have a confrontation	Make an exception
Have a conversation/ chat	Make an excuse
Have a cup of tea/ coffee	Make an impression
Have a dance	Make ends meet
Have a day off	Have a confrontation
Have a meeting	Have a conversation/ chat
Have a moment	Have a cup of tea/ coffee
Have a nap	Have a dance
Have a nightmare	Have a day off
Have a party/concert	Have a meeting
Have a passion for	Have a moment
Have a plan	Have a nap
Have a problem	Have a nightmare
Have a quarrel	Have a party/concert
Have a relationship	Have a passion for
Make an exception	Have a plan
Make an excuse	Have a problem
Make an impression	Have a quarrel
Make ends meet	Have a relationship
Make someone angry/ mad/happy/sad	Have a rest
Make sth easy	Have a ride
Make sure	Have a right
Make the bed	Have a run
Make time	Have a safe journey
Make tracks	Have a salad
Make trouble	Have a sandwich
Make up	Have a scrub
Make up your mind	Have a shave
Make war	Have a shower
Make your bed	Have a smell
Make changes	Have a snooze
Make a call	Have a stretch

Make a choice	Have a wash
Make a comment	Have a wish
Make a complaint	Have a word
Make a contract	Have a workout
Make a discovery	Have a doubt
Make a fire	Have a think
Make a mistake	Have access (to)
Make a point	Have an accident
Make a prediction	Have an appointment with
Make a presentation	Have an argument
Make a profit	Have an effect (on)
Make a sales call	Have an energy bar
Make a sandwich	Have an event
Make a snack	Have an exam
Make a sound	Have an excuse
Make a speech	Have an experience
Make a suggestion	Have an ice-cream
Make a takeover bid	Have an idea
Make a tea	Have an interview
Make a threat	Have an opportunity
Make amends	Have breakfast/lunch/ dinner
Make an agreement	Have difficulty
Make an allusion	Have faith
Make an appearance	Have food
Make an appointment	Have fun/a good time
Make an arrangement	Have no education
Make an attempt	Have no fear
Make an effort	Have patience
Make an effort	Have rest
Make an enquiry	Have room
Make food	Have something to eat
Make friends	Have soul
Make fun of someone	Have success
Make progress	Make room

UNIT 17 Paronyms and Homonyms

1.	Access (approach)	It is very difficult to have access to the President of a Nation.
2.	Accession (coming to throne)	The accession of the prince to the throne was welcomed by the people.
3.	Excess (more than desired)	Excess of everything is bad.
4.	Accept (to take)	The teachers accepted the invitation of the students on the Teacher's Day.
5.	Except (leaving out)	Everybody except Sameera was invited to the party.
6.	Expect (hope)	I never expected that my Known ones would desert me in the lurch.
7.	Alter (change)	Ayesha is so obstinate that no one can alter hes views.
8.	Altar (place of worship)	When I visited the temple, I saw him kneeling at the altar.
9.	Assent (agree)	I got assent of my father to study in a boarding school.
10.	Ascent (climbing up)	The ascent to Kargil hills is very arduous.
11.	Adopt (take up)	One should not adopt the bad habits of others.
12.	Adapt (adjust)	One must learn to adapt oneself to the circumstances of life.
13.	Adept (expert)	Shruti is adept in the art of painting .
14.	Amicable (friendly)	Finally the two brothers came to an amicable settlement.
15.	Amiable (lovable, obliging)	Being an amiable house wife she is liked by her kith and kin.
16.	Accede (accept)	The director was kind enough to accede to the request of the labourers.
17.	Exceed (surpass)	Your essay should not exceed three hundred words.
18.	Concede (agree)	The prisoner did not concede to the argument of the jailor.
19.	Alteration (change)	There is no alteration In the programme yet.
20.	Altercation (wordy quarrel)	There was altercation between the shop keeper and my brother.
21.	Apposite (suitable)	Her remarks about the character of her friends are quite apposite.
22.	Opposite (contrary)	Sita's behavior is opposite to that of her brother.
23.	Affect (to influence, to pretend)	Continuous attack of asthma has affected his health.
24.	Effect (influence)	Excessive hard work in life had adverse effect on her health.
25.	Allusion (reference)	The poem is explained properly by the help of many allusions.
26.	Illusion (unreal)	According to the Vedantists life is an illusion.
27.	Ail (suffer)	Rohit is getting weaker day by day, we don't know what ails him.

28.	Ale (intoxicating drink)	He visits ale house daily even against the advice of doctors.
29.	Apprehend (fear, perceive, arrest)	The soothsayer apprehended the day of Shruti's death.
30.	Comprehend (understand)	She could not comprehend the meaning of the passage.
31.	Admission (to get admitted, acceptance)	These days in order to get admission to convent schools you must give a lot of money.
32.	Admittance (entry)	No admittance without permission.
33.	Antique (of ancient times)	There are many antique pieces in the museum.
34.	Antic (odd, tricks)	Antics of the juggler regaled the children.
35.	Alternate (by turns)	We have a moral science class on every alternate day.
36.	Alternative (one of the two choices)	There is no alternative to honesty in dealing with the people.
37.	Artful (clever)	She was able to change the behavior of her in-laws towards her by artful means.
38.	Artistic (pertaining to art)	Everybody admires her for artistic temperament.
39.	Artist (one who practices fine art)	He is a frivolous artist.
40.	Artiste (performing)	There was no security for the artiste, who had come to perform for the charity show.
41.	Artisan (one who does handicraft)	The artisans of Moradabad are very skilful.
42.	Affection (love, kindly feeling)	My mother is held in high affection and respect by all the members of the family.
43.	Affectation (unnatural behavior, pretence)	I always feel vexed at her affectation.
44.	Abstain (keep form things (eating, drinking, voting)	We would abstain from drinking.
45.	Refrain (keep from bad habits)	You should refrain from telling a lie.
46.	Avenge (just punishment)	Hamlet delayed avenging the murder of his father.
47.	Revenge (to punish out of personal grudge)	He revenged himself on his enemy by abducting his minor child.
48.	Adulteration (making impure)	The owners of the milk dairy were charged with adulteration of milk.
49.	Adultery (having extra marital relations)	Her husband accused her of adultery and deserted her.
50.	Aspersion (slander)	We should not cast aspersions on our friends.
51.	Aspiration (ambition, desire)	You can attain your aspiration only by hard work.
52.	Avert (to check)	A little common sense averted a major mishap.
53.	Advert (refer to)	He adverted to the problem of Indian security in his speech.

54.	Birth (to be born)	The exact date of the birth of a person is known from his birth certificate.
55.	Berth (a seat in a train)	I have got two berths booked in the Rajdhani Express.
56.	Bridle (reins)	It is very difficult to control a horse without a bridle.
57.	Bridal (of bride)	The bridal dress must have cost a lot.
58.	Barbaric (savage, simple)	She was selected to play the part of village damsel because of her barbaric beauty.
59.	Barbarous (inhuman)	The Mughal invaders were barbarous in their wars.
60.	Barbarity (cruelty)	Hitler's barbarity is too terrible to be related.
61.	Barbarism (uncivilized conditions)	Barbarism still prevails in most of the tribal regions of the world.
62.	Beneficial (useful)	Nutritious food is beneficial for health.
63.	Beneficent (kind)	Everybody paid rich tribute to the king as he was beneficent to all and sundry.
64.	Beside (by the side of)	He sat beside her father.
65.	Besides (in addition to)	Besides English she is also learning French.
66.	Bear (tolerate, carry, give birth)	Mohan cannot bear being insulted by his boss.
67.	Bare (naked)	He was bitten by a snake as he was bare foot.
68.	Borne (carried)	The dead body was borne by his friends.
69.	Born (take birth)	Pearl was born in Ashwini Hospital at Mumbai.
70.	Bail (security)	His application for release on bail was rejected.
71.	Bale (bundle of cloth)	He was carrying a bale of cotton on his head.
72.	Beatific (feeling joy & peace)	The saints are always in a beatific state of mind.
73.	Beatitude (state of bliss, blessedness)	He experienced beatitude before he died.
74.	Caste (class of society)	In ancient times people were divided into different castes according to the work they did.
75.	Cast (throw)	We cast away old clothes and buy new ones.
76.	Cost (price)	The cost of living has risen a lot.
77.	Childlike (simple, innocent as a child)	Her childlike face has won over many hearts.
78.	Childish (silly)	No body likes him for his childish habits.
79.	Canvass (propagate)	Because of approaching elections people are canvassing for their candidates.
80.	Canvas (rough cloth)	While jogging he always wears canvas shoes.
81.	Cite (to quote)	The advocate cited many examples to prove his case.

82.	Site (place)	It is a very spacious site for constructing a nursing home.
83.	Sight (scenery, vision)	The mutilated body of a child was a ghastly sight.
84.	Continuous (without break)	He has been sleeping for an hour continuously.
85.	Continual (continuity with break)	It has been drizzling continually since last night.
86.	Cemetery (burial place)	The dead body was taken to the cemetery for burial.
87.	Symmetry (quality of harmony or balance in size and design)	The building looks exquisite only because of its remarkable symmetry.
88.	Career (vocation, profession)	If we want to make a good career we must work.
89.	Carrier (that one carries)	The goods were taken to the destination on public carrier.
90.	Confident (certain, sure)	I am very confident of my friend's success in the interview.
91.	Confidant (one who shares a secret)	Once his confidant, now Dinesh is the arch enemy of his mentor.
92.	compliment (regards)	I complimented my friend on her success.
93.	Complement (that completes)	Both husband and wife are complement to each other.
94.	Cannon (big gun)	Hundreds of cannons were shot in the battlefield.
95.	Canon (principle, a law)	Canons of any religion are not easy to follow.
96.	Creditable (praiseworthy)	It is really creditable for a village boy to have topped the university.
97.	Credible (believable)	Your excuse is not credible.
98.	Credulous (simple, artless)	Children are credulous by nature.
99.	Coma (state of unconsciousness)	After the accident my friend had been in state of coma for several hours.
100.	Comma (a mark of punctuation)	Comma is a very important part of learning punctuation.
101.	Corporal (physical)	In our school the children are not given corporal punishment.
102.	Corporeal (having body, material)	Ghosts are not corporeal beings.
103.	Comprehensive (exhaustive, extensive)	Comprehensive steps have been taken to meet with unforeseen emergency.
104.	Contagious (that spreads by contact)	Small pox is a contagious disease.
105.	Contiguous (adjacent)	New Delhi and Noida are contiguous.
106.	Censure (blame, criticize)	Censure motion tabled by the opposition fell through.
107.	Censor (examination of films and plays)	The film "The Bandit Queen" has not been approved of by the censor board.
108.	Collision (striking against (face to face)	Due to heavy fog the car met with a collision.
109.	Collusion (nexus)	There was a collusion between the smugglers and the political leaders.

110.	Contemptible (deserving contempt)	The conduct of the taxi driver was highly mean and contemptible.
111.	Contemptuous (expressing contemptuous)	She dismissed the servant with contemptuous gesture.
112.	Considerable (large, to great extent)	The industrialist spent considerable amount of money to uplift the living conditions of his workers.
113.	Considerate (thoughtful of others)	He is beneficent and considerate to his subordinates.
114.	Ceremonious (formal)	One should not be very ceremonious in the marriage of daughters.
115.	Ceremonial (of ceremony)	I could not attend the ceremonial function of his marriage.
116.	Complaisant (pleasing, obliging)	He is popular with his friends on account of his complaisant nature.
117.	Complacent (self satisfied)	Most of the students of my class are complacent in their outlook and will not revolt against the principal.
118.	Conscious (aware)	We should always be conscious of what is going on around the world.
119.	Conscience (inner voice)	I always act according to my conscience.
120.	Consensus (general agreement)	Government should be run by consensus.
121.	Conscientious (honest, scrupulous)	Being a conscientious worker he never shirks work.
122.	Coherent (intelligible)	She was so nervous that her words were not coherent.
123.	Inherent (inborn quality)	Sincerity is inherent in her character.
124.	Collaborate (work together)	Indian industries are compelled to collaborate with multinational companies for survival.
125.	Corroborate (confirm)	The principal corroborated the teacher's statement made to the police.
126.	Casual (occasional)	He is on casual leave today.
127.	Causal (relating to cause)	There is definite causal relationship between population and poverty.
128.	Council (an assembly)	The legislative council has passed the Bill.
129.	Counsel (advice)	His counsel proved very beneficial in the end.
130.	Councillor (member of council)	He is a Councillor of the Legislative Council.
131.	Counselor (adviser)	I have engaged a noted counselor to defend my case.
132.	Corpse (dead body)	A mutilated corpse was found in a locked house.
133.	Corps (body of troops)	He is serving in the Army Ordnance Corps.
134.	Carcass (dead body of animal)	A carcass of a dog was lying in the road.
135.	Coarse (rough)	Though he is quite rich, he wears coarse clothes.

136.	Course (line of action)	He has given up an immoral course of life.
137.	Century (one hundred)	Twentieth century will be known as the age of science.
138.	Centenary (100th anniversary)	Centenary of Indian National Movement was celebrated in 1985 AD.
139.	Conservation (preservation)	Conservation of forests is very important for our survival.
140.	Conservatism (orthodox ideas)	I am quite liberal and do not believe in conservatism.
141.	Conform (adhere to)	You must conform to the rules laid down by your company.
142.	Confirm (ratify)	I shall confirm my programme tomorrow.
143.	Capacity (ability to contain)	The hall has a seating capacity for five hundred students.
144.	Capability (power of, doing things)	My friend has capability to do any difficult task.
145.	Commonplace (ordinary, usual)	We are fed up with the commonplace speeches of our leaders.
146.	Common place (place for all)	The street is a common place for everyone.
147.	Commandeer (seize for military purpose)	When martial Law was imposed in Bhutan huge area of vacant land was commandeered for building air strip.
148.	Commander (one who commands)	The commander of the army ordered the soldiers to capture the fort.
149.	Disease (illness)	My friend is suffering from an incurable disease.
150.	Decease (death)	On account of the decease of his father, the burden of the family fell on his shoulders.
151.	Deny {refers to past (action, knowledge)}	She denied that she had gone to the movie last night.
152.	Refuse {refers to future (request, order)}	Meeta refused that she would not return the money.
153.	Duel (fight between two persons)	In ancient times, many duels were fought in order to settle disputes.
154.	Dual (double)	She follows dual policy and misguides her husband.
155.	Deference (regards)	All children should have deference for their elders.
156.	Difference (distinction)	There is no difference among the basic concepts of all the religions.
157.	Deferment (postponement)	His application for deferment of hearing was turned down.
158.	Decent (right and suitable)	She always wears decent clothes.
159.	Descent (coming down)	The descent of the hill is very dangerous.
160.	Dissent (disagreement)	Only a few members expressed dissent to my suggestion.
161.	Desert (noun) (sandy land)	The government has greatly solved the problem of pure drinking water in the desert.
162.	Desert (verb) (leave)	She was deserted by her husband.

163.	Dessert (sweet dish)	Dessert was served after dinner.
164.	Dominant (dominating)	Sohan is very dominant in our class.
165.	Domineer (to dominate)	Mothers in law try to domineer over their daughters in law.
166.	Drought (lack of rain)	Last year most of the areas of Uttar Pradesh suffered from a severe drought.
167.	Draught (Current of wind, quantity of liquid)	A draught of cool wind was very refreshing.
168.	Defective (having defect)	As he met with a severe accident last year, one of his legs is defective.
169.	Deficient (lacking)	Though young he is deficient in common sense.
170.	Divers (different)	The two children of one family may have diverse temperaments.
171.	Deduce (several)	(i) He has consulted diverse doctors about his disease. (ii) Those who dive into the river/sea, are divers. (infer) It is difficult to deduce any conclusion from your ambiguous remarks.
172.	Deduct (subtract)	Two days' wages will be deducted from your monthly salary.
173.	Deliverance (freedom, emancipation)	Lord Buddha preached an eightfold path to attain deliverance from sorrows of life.
174.	Delivery (giving letters etc.)	The delivery of the letter was just in time.
175.	Decry (criticize)	The foreign policy of the Congress party has always been decried.
176.	Descry (dimly seen)	We could descry only a traveler in the bleak evening.
177.	Defy (violate)	How dare you defy my orders?
178.	Deify (to worship)	Swami Vivekananda is deified by every Indian.
179.	Doze (sleep)	The teacher caught him dozing in the class.
180.	Dose (of medicine)	You should not take heavy doses of medicine.
181.	Dam (barrier built to reserve water)	A dam has been built on the river.
182.	Damn (condemn)	The book was damned by the critics.
183.	Diversion (change in direction)	There is a diversion on the road ahead.
184.	Diversity (variety)	Diversity is the chief feature of our civilization.
185.	Enviable (causing envy)	All the people are jealous because of his enviable position in the society.
186.	Envious (feeling of envy)	Her friends were envious of her success in the medical entrance examination.
187.	Exception (objection)	There are always exceptions to rules in every language.
188.	Exceptional (rare, to a large extent)	In his own class, Rohit is a boy with exceptional abilities.

189.	Exceptionable (objectionable)	I objected to her exceptional remarks against my parents.
190.	Eminent (famous)	Shakespeare was an eminent playwright.
191.	Imminent (impending)	Third world war is imminent.
192.	Immanent (present everywhere)	Divine force is immanent in the universe.
193.	Eligible (fit to be chosen)	Untrustworthy people are not eligible for responsible posts.
194.	Illegible (that cannot be read)	I Can't read this letter as her handwriting is illegible.
195.	to a great extent (good sense)]	One of my cousins is an exceedingly rich person.
196.	Exceedingly [to a great extent (bad sense)]	They spent money on the feast lavishly and excessively.
197.	Exhausting (tiring)	Teaching nursery classes is a very exhausting job.
198.	Exhaustive (detailed, comprehensive)	The teacher gave to the students exhaustive notes on English Grammar.
199.	Exhausted (tired)	He was exhausted and went to bed immediately.
200.	Economical (frugal)	A housewife should always be economical if she wants to run her house smoothly.
201.	Economic (pertaining to economy)	India is yet to cross many hurdles to Overcome the economic crisis.
202.	Economics (a subject)	Economics is an interesting subject.
203.	Elude (escape)	Sohan was so clever that he eluded the police and escaped from the prison.
204.	Allude (refer, cite)	The speaker alluded to many examples from the Gita.
205.	Excite (stir up feelings)	The people got very excited when the police refused to take any action against the culprits.
206.	Incite (rousing to action)	The communai speech of the leader incited the mob to violence.
207.	Insight (ability to see the truth)	India needs leaders of great insight.
208.	Envelop (cover, wrap)	As the dark clouds covered the sky, the whole town was enveloped in darkness.
209.	Expeditious (a letter Over)	Please put the letter in the envelope.
210.	Expedient (quick, prompt)	Dattu is very expeditious in answering letters.
211.	Expedition (practical, contrary to principles)	Selfish persons are always expedient in their approach to life.
212.	Esteem (a journey to unknown place)	They will go on an expedition to Everest.
213.	Estimate (respect)	As Mahesh is very sociable, he is held in high esteem by his friends.
214.	Estimation (calculate)	Can you give me the estimate of the cost of the house?
215.	Estimation (opinion, judgment)	In my estimation he is the fool of the first water.

216.	Exposure (reveal, exposed to heat or cold)	She will not attend office today as she is suffering from exposure.
217.	Exposition (explanation)	Tilak's exposition of the Gita is remarkable.
218.	Egotist (one who talks a lot of oneself)	It is difficult to stand the company of an egotist.
219.	Egoist (one who believes in self interest, proud)	An egoist is moved only by self-interest while helping others.
220.	Emerge (Come out)	It is hoped that he will emerge successful out of these Trying conditions.
221.	Immerse (plunge into absorb in)	Being a man of contemplative nature, he is always immersed in a pensive mood.
222.	Eruption (hursting)	The eruption of the volcano caused heavy destruction on the island.
223.	Irruption (Sudden attack)	The Irruption of the Afghanistan Army was successfully repulsed.
224.	Elemental (of nature, elements)	In Spite of elemental hardships Columbus discovered America.
225.	Elementary (beginning, introductory)	You must have elementary knowledge of science.
226.	Excursion (picnic)	The students will go on an excursion tomorrow.
227.	Incursion (sudden attack)	Incursions by Pakistan and China into our borders speak of our weakness.
228.	Entrance (opening, gate)	The entrance to the fair by this route has been blocked up.
229.	Entry (coming into)	The entry of student leaders into college premises is banned.
230.	Expensive (costing much money)	She bought a less expensive dress.
231.	Valuable (useful)	The book provides valuable data for further study.
232.	Fatal (causing death)	On his way to school, he met with an accident and received a fatal wound in the leg.
233.	Fateful (very significant)	The formation of I.N.A. was a fateful event.
234.	Fatalist (believer in fate)	Indians are fatalists by nature.
235.	Forceful (strong and powerful)	Netaji had a forceful personality.
236.	Forcible (by force, compulsion)	He was evicted from the house forcibly.
237.	Feign (pretend)	In order to save himself the accused feigned madness in the court.
238.	Fain (gladly)	She would fain do anything for her friends.
239.	Forgo (give up)	Parents forgo their own comforts for the sake of their children.
240.	Forego (go before)	This point has been dealt with in detail in the foregoing passage.
241.	Facility (convenience, dexterity)	The hotel provides all kinds of facilities to its customers.

242.	Felicity (apt expression, joy)	May God bless you with felicity !
243.	Facilitate (make easy)	The new agreement will facilitate the development of the trade.
244.	Felicitate (to congratulate)	I Felicitated him on his success.
245.	Fair (a show, just, color)	Let us go to the Nauchandi fair.
246.	Fare (passage money, meal)	There is a steep rise in railway fare.
247.	Formality (show ceremony)	True friends never observe formality with each other.
248.	Formalism (observance of rites)	Swami Dayanand taught the Hindus to shun formalism in religion.
249.	Fiscal (of public revenue)	Government is trying to bring down the Fiscal deficit in the next budget.
250.	Financial (monetary)	He suffered huge financial loss in the business.
251.	Gentle (not harsh)	We should be gentle and polite to our elders.
252.	Genteel (well mannered, of the upper class)	People belonging to middle class try to maintain the style of the genteel class of society.
253.	Gamble (to play for stake)	On the occasion of Diwali people gamble for money.
254.	Gambol (to frisk)	It is a beautiful sight to see a deer gamboling in a forest.
255.	Graceful (beautiful)	She has a graceful gait.
256.	Gracious (kind, merciful)	God is gracious.
257.	Gate (door)	The dacoits entered the house through the main gate.
258.	Gait (manner of walking)	Her gait is graceful.
259.	Gravitation (pulling towards, attracting)	Theory of gravitation was invented by Newton.
260.	Gravity (quality of being serious)	One must observe gravity on solemn occasions.
261.	Hoard (amass, to store)	As he is a smuggler, he has a hoard of gold and silver in his house.
262.	Horde (a gang)	A horde of militants intruded into Indian territory.
263.	Historic (likely to be famous in history)	Kapil Dev scored historic victory by winning the World Cup in 1983.
264.	Histrionic (art of acting)	Rekha is known for her histrionic talents.
265.	Historical (of history)	I visited many historical buildings in Delhi while I was in school.
266.	Humility (politeness)	Humility in victory is a rare virtue.
267.	Humiliation (insult, disgrace0)	All respectable persons prefer death to humiliation.
268.	Honorary (unpaid)	My sister taught in a college as an honorary tutor.
269.	Honourable (deserving honour)	He is regarded honourable member of the club.

270.	Human (race of man)	On account of ecological disturbances, the existence of human beings is endangered.
271.	Humane (kind)	Doctors are supposed to be considerate and humane.
272.	Hail (belong to, welcome, frozen rain)	Those hailing from Bangladesh are living illegally in this country.
273.	Hale (healthy)	he is hale and hearty and enjoys life to his fill.
274.	Healthy (having health)	Inspite of his old age he is quite healthy.
275.	Healthful (promoting health)	The climate of hill stations is healthful.
276.	Hypocritical (guilty of hypocrisy)	I do not like his hypocritical attitude towards his friends.
277.	Hypercritical (too critical)	It does not pay in life to be hyporcritical of trivial matters.
278.	Humanity (mankind, quality of being kind)	One must act in the larger interest of humanity.
279.	Humanism (devotion to human interest)	Act of humanism is always apopreciated.
280.	Hollow (not solid, with hole, false)	The stick is hollow; nothing is inside the year.
281.	Hallow (ed) (sacred)	The hallowed shrine is visited by the devotees throughout the year.
282.	Halo (circle of light around the head)	Holy men are painted with halo around their heads.
283.	Industrial (pertaining to industry)	Industrial progress in India has not been rapid.
284.	Industrious (hard working)	My friendis a n industrious man and he achieved success in life.
285.	Impossible (that is not possible)	If we make up our mind and work hard nothing is impossible in this world.
286.	Impassable (that cannot be passed through)	Many passes in the Himalayas are impassable during winter.
287.	Ingenious (skilful, clever)	She devised an ingenious scheme to hoodwink the police.
288.	Ingenuous (frank, innocent)	Children are liked for their ingenuous nature.
289.	Imaginary (fanciful, unreal)	Don't be daunted by imaginary troubles.
290.	Imaginative (contemplative)	poets and artists are imaginative by temperament.
291.	Intelligible (understandable)	Your remarks are not intelligible to me.
292.	Intelligent (wise and sensible)	Only intelligent students are found to succeed in this world of stiff competition.
293.	Immoral (not according to morality)	An immoral person suffers in the long run.
294.	Unmoral (non-moral, amoral)	Unmoral persons are not concerned with morality or the immorality of an action.

295.	Incomparable (without equal)	She was a damsel of incomparable beauty.
296.	Uncomparable (having no similarity)	The security problems of India and Pakistan are uncomparable.
297.	Invert (to put upside down)	Put this statement in inverted commas.
298.	Inert (passive)	Invert gases are without active chemical properties.
299.	Inept (incompetent)	Inept handling of situation resulted in riots.
300.	Inapt (unsuitable)	The title of the story is inapt.
301.	Incidental (happening as natural or a part of)	The risk of loss is always incidental to any business.
302.	Accidental (by chance)	It was just an accidental meeting between the two school mates.
303.	Jealous (full of jealousy)	All his friends are jealous of him.
304.	Zealous (enthusiastic)	My brother is very zealous about his new appointment.
305.	Judicious (wise, thoughtful)	We must be judicious in the choice of our career.
306.	Judicial (pertaining to judiciary)	He was sent to judicial lock up by the Magistrate.
307.	Kindly (acts, feelings)	I shall never forget your kindly act.
308.	Kind (tender, pitiful)	He is a kind man who helps every body.
309.	Lighting (flash of light)	Lighting struck his house and set the whole house on fire.
310.	Lightening (make light)	He is always interested in lightening the financial burden of his father.
311.	Luxurious (pertaining to luxury)	As she is the daughter of a rich industrialist, she lives a very luxurious life.
312.	Luxuriant (rich in growth)	the hills of Uttarakhand are teeming with luxuriant forests.
313.	Loathe (detest)	The rich should not loathe the poor.
314.	Loth (loath) (unwilling)	She was loth to go with him alone.
315.	Limit (extent)	You must spend within your limits.
316.	Limitation (shortcomings)	There are many limitations in Parliamentary form of government in backward countries.
317.	Loud (loud sound)	Everyone was alarmed when there was a loud blast in the locality.
318.	Loudly (in a loud manner)	The teacher forbade them to speak loudly.
319.	Aloud (audible)	The students requested the teacher to speak aloud.
320.	Learned (erudite, educated)	He is not only rich but also learned and wise/
321.	Learnt (past of learn)	He learnt his lesson very well.
322.	Literal (expressed in words)	Most of the words are used in literal and figurative sense.
323.	Literary (of literature)	He is a literary man and reads a lot of books.
324.	Maze (winding paths)	The walled city is full of mazes.

325.	Maize (a kind of corn)	Maize grows in abundance in Africa.
326.	Memorable (worthy of remembering)	In the plays of Shakespeare we find a lot of memorable quotation.
327.	Memorial (statue or anything in the memory of)	We collected money to erect memorial in the memory of war heroes.
328.	Immemorial (longer than people can remember)	The religious rites of the Hindus are immemorial tradition.
329.	Momentary (short lived)	One should not run after the wordly pleasures as they are momentary.
330.	Momentous (very important)	Operation 'Shakti' at Pokhran was the momentous event in the history of independent india.
331.	Morale (the state of spirit, confidence)	The morale of the army should always be high.
332.	Moral (sense of right and wrong, lesson)	We are advised to pursue a moral course of life.
333.	maritime (relating to sea, or ships)	Once Britain was great maritime power.
334.	Marine (found in the sea/trade by sea)	India should develop marine trade to earn foreign exchange.
335.	Manifest (obvious, evident)	It should be manifest to all by now that China and Pakistan are inciting trouble on our borders.
336.	Manifestation (act or desire that makes obvious)	Indiscipline among the youth is just a manifestation of serious national level.
337.	Negligible (unimportant)	The dacoits attacked his house yesterday night but his loss is negligible.
338.	Negligent (careless in duty)	We should not be negligent in our duty.
339.	Neglectful (careless)	He is so neglectful that he doesn't care for his family's interest.
340.	Notable (creditable)	India has made a notable progress in the field of agriculture.
341.	Noticeable (easy to notice)	There is noticeable improvement in the patient.
342.	Notorious (famous (unfavourable)	Our political leaders are notorious for their apthy to public interest.
343.	Noted (famous)	The leader is noted for his honesty.
344.	Observance (compliance)	In order to remain healthy observance of certain simple rules is required.
345.	Observation (notice)	Children have very keen observation power.
346.	Ordinance (a government order)	The government has issued an ordinance against the people who do not pay the taxes on time.
347.	Ordnance (a gun)	There is an ordnance factory at Kanpur.

348.	Official (pertaining to office)	You are bound to maintain official secrecy.
349.	Officious (ready to offer services, flatterer)	Beware of officious fellows.
350.	Organisation (institution)	He is working in a non-government organization.
351.	Organism (living beings with parts working together)	Human organism is a complex system.
352.	Organic (of an organ)	Organic diseases destroy the organs.
353.	Petrol (fuel)	Petrol is very costly these days.
354.	Patrol (go round)	The patrol van is regularly moving on the highway day and night for our protection.
355.	Providential (divine)	My friend's providential escape at the critical moment saved his life.
356.	Provident (frugal, thrifty)	She is quite provident and economical in household expenses.
357.	Providence (divine force)	Trust in Providence for good days.
358.	Practical (not theoretical)	The scientist gave a practical demonstration of his experiment.
359.	Practicable (Capable of being practiced)	Only practicable schemes are adopted by our Managing Director.
360.	Proscribe (ban, prohibit)	Indecent books are generally proscribed by the government.
361.	Prescribe (recommend, advise)	Doctor has prescribed a very efficacious medicine for the treatment of the disease.
362.	Popular (admirable)	As Mrs. Neena is a very kind teacher, she is very popular with her students.
363.	Populous (thickly populated)	China is the most populous country in the world.
364.	Pale (bloodless, yellowish)	Due to his prolonged sickness he looks very pale now.
365.	Pail (container)	A pail full of milk was lying in the kitchen.
366.	Pair (double of a thing)	I gave a pair of new shoes to my brother on his birthday.
367.	Pare (trim)	Please pare your finger nails regularly.
368.	Pane (window glass)	Our window pane was broken by the children who were playing Cricket outside our house.
369.	Pain (suffering of mind or body)	She was feeling pain in her neck.
370.	Peel (to remove the skin)	Please wash the mangoes before you peel them.
371.	Peal (a loud sound)	On hearing his jokes all of us went into a peal of laughter.
372.	Personal (private)	We were asked to express our personal views on this subject in the debate.
373.	Personnel (persons employed)	the personnel department has issued termination notice to Sachin.
374.	Punctual (at fixed time)	Punctual students alone deserve a splendid success.

375.	Punctilious (very careful in duty)	We are taught to be very punctilious in our work in the school.
376.	Prudent (wise, careful, foresight)	It is prudent on her part to break with selfish friends.
377.	Prudential (of prudent actions, policy)	The prudential actions of my father saved the family from financial crisis.
378.	Precedent (previous examples)	The lawyer cited many precedents in support of his case.
379.	President (Head of Institution)	Indian President is only de jure head of the government.
380.	Physique (physical health)	He is a smart youngman with a good physique.
381.	Physic (medicine)	No physic has het been discovered to cure cancer.
382.	Physics (a subject)	Physics is my favourite subject.
383.	Prey (hunt and kill)	As a national bird the Peacock is not a bird of prey.
384.	Pray (offer prayer)	He prays to God daily.
385.	Proceed (to move forward)	Inspite of difficulties he proceeded with his enterprise.
386.	Politic (prudent, wise)	It is not politic to flog the dead horse.
387.	Political (of politics)	The political parties in India have no concern for the poor.
388.	Prosecute (File a suit in the court)	You are likely to be prosecuted in the court for violation of rules.
389.	Persecute (oppress)	She was mercilessly persecuted for not bringing a care in downy.
390.	Pitiable (deserving pity)	The condition of the family is pitiable on account of poverty.
391.	Pitiful (making one feel pity)	It was pitiful sight to see a beggar woman suffering from cancer.
392.	Polity (form of government)	Indian polity is not in a healthy state these days.
393.	Policy (plan of action)	Honesty is the best policy.
394.	Proscription (prohibition)	The proscription of the newspaper was resented by the people.
395.	Prescription (recommendation)	The prescription of medicine by the doctor proved very useful.
396.	Putrefy (to rot)	Many unclaimed dead bodies lay putrefying in the field.
397.	Petrify (turn into stone, stun)	We were petrified with terror to see the ghastly sight of the carnage.
398.	Righteous (just, truthful)	The Principal's anger was righteous for he could not tolerate the indiscipline in the college.
399.	Rightful (having right)	He is the rightful owner of the property.
400.	Raise (increase)	The traders have raised the prices of food grains.
401.	Raze (wipe out)	All the huts of the poor were razed to the ground as they needed land to build a five star hotel.
402.	Reign (rule)	The reign of Gupta dynasty, is known as golden period in the history of India.
403.	Rein (bridle of horse)	He reined the horse and escaped a fall.
404.	Rite (ceremony)	The marriage was performed according to Hindu rites.
405.	Wright (give a shape)	He is a great playwright.

406.	Write (Compose)	Please write in the note-book.
407.	Rout (put to defeat)	The enemy was routed by Indian forces.
408.	Route (path)	you should not go by long route.
409.	Respective (belonging to each)	After the match we left for our respective homes.
410.	Respectable (enjoying respect)	His father is a respectable man of the city.
411.	Respectful (showing respect)	You must be respectful to your elders.
412.	Rapt (fully attentive)	They listened to the speech of the Prime Minister with rapt attention.
413.	Wrapt (lost in, absorbed)	She did not notice my arrival as she was wrapt in her thoughts.
414.	Recourse (means of action)	I do not advise you to have recourse to legal action in this matter.
415.	Resource (means, raw material)	India is a land teeming with natural resources.
416.	Symbol (sign, to represent something)	Vinoba Bhave was a symbol of simplicity and honesty.
417.	Cymbal (a musical instrument)	The melodious sound of the cymbals impressed every body.
418.	Stationery (writing material)	His father deals in office stationery.
419.	stationary (static, fixed)	The sun is stationary.
420.	Soar (rise, fly)	Birds are soaring in the sky.
421.	Sore (wound, painful)	People are sore because the prices are soaring.
422.	Sour (bitter)	the grapes are sour.
423.	Suspect (to think to be true)	The whole class suspects Rohan to have stolen Rita's money.
424.	Doubt (to think to be untrue)	I doubt if she will get through the examination.
425.	Sociable (fond of mixing with people)	Because of her sociable behavior she is liked by all the members of her family.
426.	Social (pertaining to society)	Man is a social animal.
427.	Sensual (voluptuous, exciting sense)	We should not indulge in sensual pleasures or we will repent later on.
428.	Sensuous (that affects the senses)	John Keats poetry is sensuous.
429.	Spacious (having large space)	My house contains many spacious rooms.
430.	Specious (outwardly attractive)	No body was impressed with his specious arguments.
431.	Spiritual (opposed to material, of spirit)	Indians should not give up their spiritual heritage.
432.	Spirituous (containing intoxicating drink)	Excessive consumption of spirituous drinks is injurious to health.
433.	Stimulant (that which stimulates)	Tea is a stimulant for a worker after a day's hard work.
434.	Stimulus (incentive)	Man hardly acts if there is no stimulus before him.

435.	Special (specific)	He came here on a special mission to bring about reconciliation between the two parties.
436.	Especial (to a great degree)	It is especially hot these days.
437.	Storey (upper part of a building)	He lives in the second storey of the house.
438.	Story (tale)	It is a very interesting story.
439.	Suit (a set of clothes, a lawsuit)	He presented me with a woolen suit.
440.	Suite (a set of rooms)	He has booked a suite in the hotel.
441.	Sham (pretend to be, pretence)	What he says is all sham.
442.	Shame (feeling of humiliation)	He felt shame at having told a lie.
443.	Severe (violent, rigorous)	She is suffering from severe headache.
444.	Sever (separate)	You can never sever relations with your family.
445.	Statue (figure of animal/man in stone or wood)	The statue of Dr. Ambedkar was unveiled by the President.
446.	Statute (law passed by law making bodies)	The statute was passed by the Parliament unanimously.
447.	Temperance (Moderation in habits)	We should observe temperance in eating and drinking habits because it leads to healthy way of life.
448.	Tolerable (bearable)	The food that was served in his daughter's marriage was tolerable.
449.	Tolerant (liberal in ideas)	Every religion teaches us to be tolerant of the religious views held by others.
450.	Temporal (worldly, physical)	We should not hanker after temporal glory.
451.	Temporary (lasting for short time)	He was given the job on the temporary basis only.
452.	Tamper (meddle with)	Please do not tamper with my papers.
453.	Temper (emotional state of mind, soften)	One must not lose one's temper.
454.	Teem (full of)	India is a country teeming with natural resources.
455.	Team (group of players)	(His name has not been included in college cricket team.
456.	Uninterested (having no interest)	Gaurav is uninterested in the study of science.
457.	Disinterested (free from personal motive)	A disinterested leader of the party always commands respect from his followers.
458.	Variation (change)	Variation in his blood pressure worried the doctors.
459.	Variance (Opposite)	My views are always at variance with my father's.
460.	Vocation (profession)	Singing is both his vocation and avocation.
461.	Avocation* (hobby)	Gardening is a very favourite avocation of my father.
462.	Virtuous (having virtues)	She is a virtuous and devoted house wife.

463.	Virtual (real)	Her mother is the virtual head of the family.
464.	Voracity (greed)	He is detested on account of his voracity for wealth.
465.	Veracity (truthfulness)	It is very difficult to verify the veracity of her statement since she is very clever.
466.	Vane (weather cock)	The wind vane points to the direction of the wind.
467.	Vain (proud, useless)	She is vain of her wealth.
468.	Wane ((decline)	His popularity as a political leader is on the wane.
469.	Vein (a blood vein)	All the veins carry blood to heart.
470.	Vassal (a slave)	In ancient times prisoners of war were made vassals.
471.	Vessel (a small ship, utensil)	Empty vessels make much noise.
472.	Venal (corruptible)	The venal leaders are bane of Indian polity.
473.	Venial (to be forgiven)	The fault is so slight that it is thought to be venial.
474.	Wreak (take revenge)	At last he wreaked vengeance by killing his enemy.
475.	Wreck (destroy)	the fury of the storm wrecked many houses.
476.	Wither (fade)	The plants kept in the shade will wither for want of Sun and light.
477.	Whither (where)	Modern man is so much confused that he does not know whither he is heading for.
478.	Willing ((ready)	We should always be willing to help the needy.
479.	Wilful (deliberate)	His marriage was a total failure on account of his willful nature.
480.	Wave (sea or river wave)	The waves rose sky high when the storm blew up.
481.	Waive (remove, forgo)	Government has at last agreed to waive excise duty on cloth.
482.	Wrest (snatch by force)	The enemy wrested his gun and killed him.
483.	Rest (peace)	Please go and take rest now.
484.	Womanly (of woman (good sense)	My mother has womanly virtues.
485.	Womanish (of woman (bad sense)	His voice is womanish as it is quite shrill.
486.	Whet (increase interest)	Lemon will whet your appetite for more food.
487.	Vet (screening)	The candidates were vetted for security reasons.
488.	Wet (covered with water/liquid)	He got wet in the rain and is not well.

UNIT 18

Acronyms

An acronym is a pronounceable word formed from the first letter (or first few letters) of each word in a phrase or title. It is the shortened form of a phrase or word. It is created to make communication faster and easier. Students should learn and be familiar with the most commonly used acronyms in order to improve their communication skills.

1.	AIDS	Acquired Immunodeficiency Syndrome
2.	ASAP	As Soon As Possible
3.	AWOL	Absent Without Official Leave (or Absent Without Leave)
4.	IMAX	Image Maximum
5.	LASER	Light Amplification by the Stimulated Emission of Radiation
6.	PIN	Personal Identification Number
7.	RADAR	Radio Detection and Ranging
8.	SCUBA	Self-Contained Underwater Breathing Apparatus
9.	SMART	Specific, Measurable, Achievable, Relevant, Timely
10.	TASER	Thomas A. Swift's Electric Rifle
11.	WASP	White Anglo-Saxon Protestant
12.	POTUS	President of the United States
13.	DND	Do Not Disturb
14.	FBI	Federal Bureau of Investigation
15.	UN	United Nations
16.	MOTOS	Member of the Opposite Sex
17.	IDK	I Don't Know
18.	CPT	Captain
19.	AIDS	Acquired Immune Deficiency Syndrome
20.	TBA	To Be Announced
21.	MD	Medical Doctor
22.	OTC	Over The Counter
23.	DIY	Do It Yourself
24.	ABS	Anti-lock Braking System
25.	NFL	National Football League
26.	IRL	In Real Life
27.	ADHD	Attention Deficit Hyperactivity Disorder
28.	CST	Central Standard Time
29.	PAWS	Progressive Animal Welfare Society

30.	EG	Evil Grin
31.	AFK	Away From Keyboard
32.	MADD	Mothers Against Drunk Driving
33.	POS	Point Of Service
34.	EST	Eastern Standard Time
35.	PANS	Pretty Awesome New Stuff
36.	SWF	Single White Female
37.	SMH	Shaking My Head
38.	TS	Transsexual
39.	MLA	Modern Language Association
40.	FAQ	Frequently Asked Questions
41.	GIF	Graphics Interchange Format
42.	NHL	National Hockey League
43.	BBL	Be Back Later
44.	BBIAB	Be Back In A Bit
45.	MBA	Masters of Business Administration
46.	OT	Overtime
47.	PST	Pacific Standard Time
48.	AA	Alcoholics Anonymous
49.	SGT	Sergeant
50.	SCOTUS	Supreme Court of the United States
51.	TBD	To Be Determined
52.	OMG	Oh My God
53.	TED	Tell me, Explain to me, Describe to me
54.	UFO	Unidentified Flying Object
55.	CC	Copy To
56.	BBS	Be Back Soon
57.	LOL	Laughing Out Loud
58.	ASAP	As Soon As Possible
59.	CPS	Child Protective Services
60.	GF	Girlfriend
61.	GIB	GI Bill
62.	IR	Interracial
63.	AARP	American Association of Retired Persons
64.	PPV	Pay Per View
65.	AMA	American Medical Association
66.	DAFB	Dover Air Force Base

67.	POS	Parents Over Shoulder
68.	ESL	English As A Second Language
69.	SONAR	Sound Navigation And Ranging
70.	DZ	Drop Zone
71.	Navy SEALs	Navy Sea Air Land forces
72.	AMA	Against Medical Advice
73.	PHAT	Pretty, Hot, And Tempting
74.	POW	Prisoner Of War
75.	RADAR	Radio Detection And Ranging
76.	MAJ	Major
77.	HR	Human Resources
78.	ADD	Attention Deficit Disorder
79.	ROFL	Rolling On the Floor Laughing
80.	AWOL	Absent Without Leave
81.	DMV	Division of Motor Vehicles
82.	SUV	Sports Utility Vehicle
83.	DOD	Department of Defense
84.	F2F	Face to Face
85.	SWM	Single White Male
86.	CPL	Corporal
87.	CDC	Centers for Disease Control and Prevention
88.	WWE	World Wrestling Entertainment
89.	DAEMON	Disk And Execution Monitor
90.	LMK	Let Me Know
91.	RNC	Republican National Committee
92.	DBA	Doing Business As
93.	IQ	Intelligence Quotient
94.	CIA	Central Intelligence Agency
95.	KISS	Keep It Simple, Stupid
96.	BTW	By The Way
97.	PR	Public Relations
98.	CSI	Crime Scene Investigation
99.	DNC	Democratic National Committee
100.	TTYL	Talk To You Later
101.	NAFTA	North American Free Trade Agreement
102.	BF	Boyfriend
103.	VBD	Very Bad Date

104.	ADA	American Dental Association
105.	PS	PostScript
106.	MIA	Missing In Action
107.	BBW	Big Beautiful Woman
108.	AKA	Also Known As
109.	AFL	American Football League
110.	FYI	For Your Information
111.	BEG	Big Evil Grin
112.	APA	American Psychological Association
113.	PGA	Professional Golfer's Association
114.	YOLO	You Only Live Once
115.	IMO	In My Opinion
116.	DON	Department of the Navy
117.	LDR	Long Distance Relationship
118.	SO	Significant Other
119.	OFC	Of Course
120.	DOB	Date Of Birth
121.	NBA	National Basketball Association
122.	NYOB	None of Your Business
123.	EDS	Electronic Data Systems
124.	DOA	Dead On Arrival
125.	BRB	Be Right Back
126.	ID	Identification
127.	MOTSS	Member Of The Same Sex
128.	WTH	What The Heck
129.	SWAT	Special Weapons And Tactics
130.	ZIP code	Zone Improvement Plan code
131.	REAP	Reserve Education Assistance Program
132.	USAF	United States Air Force
133.	ETA	Estimated Time of Arrival
134.	ADP	Automated Data Processing
135.	HIV	Human Immunodeficiency Virus
136.	EOD	End of Day
137.	DARE	Drug Abuse Resistance Education
138.	MST	Mountain Standard Time

UNIT 19

Defining Words with their Meanings

19.1 General Defining Words with their Meanings

S.N.	Words	Definitions
1	Aborticide	destruction of a fetus in the uterus; feticide. a drug or other agent that causes abortion.
2	Acaricide	a pesticide that kills mites and ticks.
3	Algicide	killer of algae
4	Amicicide	murder of a friend
5	Aphicide	killer of aphids (very small insects)
6	Avicide	killing of birds
7	Bacillicide	killer of bacteria
8	Bactericide	**killer of bacteria**
9	Biocide	killing living material
10	Bovicide	slaughter of cattle; one who kills cattle
11	Ceticide	**killing of whales and other cetaceans**
12	Cimicide	substance used to kill bed-bugs
13	Deicide	**destruction or killing of a god**
14	Ecocide	destruction of the environment
15	Episcopicide	killing of bishops
16	Famicide	one who destroys another's reputation; slanderer
17	Felicide	killing of a cat
18	Femicide	**killing of a woman**
19	Feticide	killing of a fetus
20	Filicide	killing of one's own child
21	Floricide	killing or killer of flowers
22	Foeticide	**killing a fetus**
23	Formicide	substance that kills ants
24	Fratricide	killing of one's brother
25	Fungicide	killing of fungus
26	Genocide	killing of a race or ethnic group
27	Germicide	**substance that kills germs**

S.N.	Words	Definitions
28	Giganticide	killing of a giant, a person who kills giants.
29	Gynaecide	**killing of women**
30	Herbicide	killing of plants
31	Hereticide	killing of heretics
32	Homicide	killing of a human being
33	Infanticide	killing of an infant
34	Insecticide	killing of insects
35	Larvicide	killing of larvae
36	Liberticide	destruction of liberty
37	Lupicide	killing of a wolf
38	Mariticide	killing or killer of one's husband
39	Matricide	**killing of one's mother**
40	Menticide	reduction of mind by psychological pressure
41	Microbicide	**killing or killer of microbes**
42	Miticide	**agent which kills mites**
43	Molluscicide	killing of mollusks
44	Muscicide	substance for killing flies
45	Neonaticide	killing or killer of a newborn infant
46	Ovicide	killing insect eggs
47	Ovicide	sheep-killing
48	Parasiticide	**killing of parasites**
49	Parasuicide	apparent attempted suicide without the actual intention of killing oneself
50	Parenticide	killing or killer of one's parents
51	Parricide	**killing of parents or a parent-like close relative**
52	Patricide	killing of one's father
53	Perdricide	killer of partridges
54	Pesticide	killing of pests
55	Prolicide	killing of offspring; killing of the human race
56	Pulicide	flea-killer
57	Raticide	substance or person who kills rats
58	Regicide	killing of a monarch
59	Rodenticide	killing of rodents
60	Senicide	killing of old men
61	Serpenticide	killing or killer of a snake

S.N.	Words	Definitions
62	Siblicide	killing or killer of a sibling
63	Silvicide	substance that kills trees
64	Sororicide	killing of one's own sister
65	Speciocide	destruction of an entire species
66	Spermicide	killing of sperm
67	Sporicide	killing of spores
68	Suicide	killing of oneself
69	Taeniacide	killing of tapeworms
70	Tauricide	killing or killer of a bull
71	Trypanocide	killing of trypanosomes
72	Tyrannicide	killing or killer of a tyrant
73	Urbicide	destruction of a city
74	Ursicide	killing or killer of a bear
75	Utricide	one who stabs an inflated skin vessel instead of killing someone
76	Uxoricide	killing of one's own wife
77	Vaticide	killing or killer of a prophet
78	Verbicide	destroying the meaning of a word
79	Vermicide	killing of worms
80	Vespacide	substance or person who kills wasps
81	Viricide	killing of viruses; killing of men or of husbands
82	Virucide	killing of viruses
83	Vulpicide	killing of a fox
84	Weedicide	something that kills weeds
85	Denarian	a person between 10 and 19 years old
86	Vicenarian	a person between 20 and 29 years old
87	Tricenarian	a person between 30 and 39 years old
88	Quadragenarian	a person between 40 and 49 years old
89	Quinquagenarian	a person between 50 and 59 years old
90	Sexagenarian	a person between 60 and 69 years old
91	Septuagenarian	a person between 70 and 79 years old
92	Octogenarian	a person between 80 and 89 years old
93	Nonagenarian	a person between 90 and 99 years old
94	Centenarian	a person between 100 and 109 years old
95	Supercentenarian	a person 110 years old or older
96	Methuselah	a person who is very old

S.N.	Words	Definitions
97	Dyssomnia	a difficulty in falling asleep, or in remaining sleeping
98	Hypersomnia	excessive sleepiness.
99	Hyposomnia	inadequate sleep
100	Insomnia	the condition of being unable to sleep
101	Parasomnia	any of several sleep disorders
102	Semisomnia	a chronic state of low-grade exhaustion caused by too little or fitful sleep.
103	Sexsomnia	a form of non-rapid eye movement parasomnia that causes people to engage in various sexual acts while they are asleep.
104	Somnambulism	walking in sleep
105	Somnambulist	someone who walks about in sleep
106	Somnial	of or pertaining to sleep or dreams.
107	Somniloquism	talking in sleep
108	Somniloquist	someone who talks while asleep
109	Somnolence	the state of being almost asleep
110	Abattoir	a place where animals are slaughtered for the market
111	Apiary	a place where bees are kept
112	Aquarium	a tank for fishes
113	Archives	a place where government records are kept
114	Arena	a place for wrestling
115	Arsenal	a place for ammunition and weapons
116	Asylum	a place for lunatics, and political refugees
117	Aviary	a place where birds are kept
118	Burrow	the dwelling place of an animal underground
119	Cache	a place where ammunition is hidden
120	Cage	a place for birds
121	Caravan	the house or shelter of a gipsy
122	Casino	a place with gambling tables etc.
123	Cemetery	a graveyard where the dead are buried
124	Chalet	the house or shelter of a swiss peasant
125	Cloakroom	a place for luggage at a railway station
126	Convent	a residence for nuns
127	Crèche	a nursery where children of working parent are cared for while their parents are at work
128	Crematorium	a cremation ground where the last funeral rites are performed
129	Decanter	an ornamental glass bottle for holding wine or other alcoholic drinks

S.N.	Words	Definitions
130	Den	the home of a lion
131	Dispensary	a place where medicines are compounded
132	Dormitory	the sleeping rooms in a college or public institution
133	Dovecot	a house or box in which live pigeons or doves
134	Dowar	the house or shelter of an Arab
135	Drey	a squirrel's home
136	Elysium	a paradise with perfect bliss
137	Eyrie, Aerie	a nest of a bird of prey
138	Granary	a place for storing grain
139	Gymnasium	a place where athletic exercises are performed
140	Hangar	a place for housing aeroplanes
141	Hive	a place for bees
142	Hutch	a wooden box with a front of wire for rabbits
143	Igloo	the house or shelter of an eskimo
144	Infirmary	a home for old persons
145	Insectarium	a place for keeping or breeding insects
146	Kabitka	the house or shelter of a kirghis
147	Kennel	a house of shelter for a dog
148	Lair / Den	the resting place of a wild animal
149	Menagerie	a place for wild animals and birds
150	Mint	a place where money is coined
151	Monastery	a residence for monks or priests
152	Morgue	a place where dead bodies are kept for identification
153	Mortuary	a place where dead bodies are kept for post mortem
154	Orchard	a place where fruit trees are grown
155	Orphanage	a place where orphans are housed
156	Pen, Byre	a house or shelter for a cow
157	Portfolio	a portable case for holding papers, drawing etc.
158	Reservoir	a place where water is collected and stored
159	Resort	a place frequented for reasons of pleasure or health
160	Sanatorium	a place for the sick to recover health
161	Scullery	a place where plates, dishes, pots and other cooking utensils are washed up
162	Sheath, Scabbard	a case in which the blade of sword is kept
163	Stable	a house of shelter for a horse
164	Sty	a place where pigs are kept

S.N.	Words	Definitions
165	Tannery	a place where leather is tanned
166	Wardrobe	a place for clothes
167	Wigwam, Tepee	the house or shelter of an American Indian

19.2 Defining Words Related to 'Logy'

S.N.	Words	Definitions
1	Acarology	study of mites, the scientific study of ticks and mites is known as acarology, and scientists, like Selina, who study these tiny animals are called acarologists
2	Accidence	a part of grammar that deals with inflections, grammar book, science of inflections in grammar
3	Aceology	therapeutics, the science of remedies, or of therapeutics ; iamatology
4	Acology	study of medical remedies
5	Acoustics	science of sound
6	Adenology	study of glands
7	Aedoeology	science of generative organs
8	Aerobiology	study of airborne organisms
9	Aerodonetics	science or study of gliding
10	Aerodynamics	dynamics of gases; science of movement in a flow of air or gas or gas
11	Aerolithology	study of aerolites; meteorites
12	Aerology	study of the atmosphere
13	Aeronautics	study of navigation through air or space
14	Aerophilately	collecting of air-mail stamps
15	Aerostatics	science of air pressure; art of ballooning
16	Agonistics	art and theory of prize-fighting
17	Agriology	the comparative study of primitive peoples
18	Agrobiology	study of plant nutrition; soil yields
19	Agrology	study of agricultural soils
20	Agronomics	study of productivity of land
21	Agrostology	science or study of grasses
22	Alethiology	study of truth
23	Algedonics	science of pleasure and pain
24	Algology	study of algae
25	Anaesthesiology	study of anaesthetics
26	Anaglyptics	art of carving in bas-relief
27	Anagraphy	art of constructing catalogues

S.N.	Words	Definitions
28	Anatomy	study of the structure of the body
29	Andragogy	science of teaching adults
30	Anemology	study of winds
31	Angelology	study of angels
32	Angiology	study of blood flow and lymphatic system
33	Anthropobiology	study of human biology
34	Anthropology	study of human cultures
35	Aphnology	science of wealth
36	Apiology	study of bees
37	Arachnology	study of spiders
38	Archaeology	study of human material remains
39	Archelogy	the study of first principles
40	Archology	science of the origins of government
41	Arctophily	study of teddy bears
42	Areology	study of Mars
43	Aretaics	the science of virtue
44	Aristology	the science or art of dining
45	Arthrology	study of joints
46	Astacology	the science of crayfish
47	Astheniology	study of diseases of weakening and aging
48	Astrogeology	study of extraterrestrial geology
49	Astrology	study of influence of stars on people
50	Astrometeorology	study of effect of stars on climate
51	Astronomy	study of celestial bodies
52	Astrophysics	study of behaviour of interstellar matter
53	Astroseismology	study of star oscillations
54	Atmology	the science of aqueous vapour
55	Audiology	study of hearing
56	Autecology	study of ecology of one species
57	Autology	scientific study of oneself
58	Auxology	science of growth
59	Avionics	the science of electronic devices for aircraft
60	Axiology	the science of the ultimate nature of values
61	Bacteriology	study of bacteria
62	Balneology	the science of the therapeutic use of baths
63	Barodynamics	science of the support and mechanics of bridges

S.N.	Words	Definitions
64	Barology	study of gravitation
65	Batology	the study of brambles
66	Bibliology	study of books
67	Bibliotics	study of documents to determine authenticity
68	Bioecology	study of interaction of life in the environment
69	Biology	study of life
70	Biometrics	study of biological measurement
71	Bionomics	study of organisms interacting in their environments
72	Botany	study of plants
73	Bromatology	study of food
74	Brontology	scientific study of thunder
75	Bryology	the study of mosses and liverworts
76	Cacogenics	study of racial degeneration
77	Caliology	study of bird's nests
78	Calorifics	study of heat
79	Cambistry	science of international exchange
80	Campanology	the art of bell ringing
81	Carcinology	study of crabs and other crustaceans
82	Cardiology	study of the heart
83	Caricology	study of sedges
84	Carpology	study of fruit
85	Cartography	the science of making maps and globes
86	Cartophily	the hobby of collecting cigarette cards
87	Castrametation	the art of designing a camp
88	Catacoustics	science of echoes or reflected sounds
89	Catalactics	science of commercial exchange
90	Catechectics	the art of teaching by question and answer
91	Cetology	study of whales and dolphins
92	Chalcography	the art of engraving on copper or brass
93	Chalcotriptics	art of taking rubbings from ornamental brasses
94	Chaology	the study of chaos or chaos theory
95	Characterology	study of development of character
96	Chemistry	study of properties of substances
97	Chirocosmetics	beautifying the hands; art of manicure
98	Chirography	study of handwriting or penmanship
99	Chirology	study of the hands

S.N.	Words	Definitions
100	Chiropody	medical science of feet
101	Chorology	science of the geographic description of anything
102	Chrematistics	the study of wealth; political economy
103	Chronobiology	study of biological rhythms
104	Chrysology	study of precious metals
105	Ciselure	the art of chasing metal
106	Climatology	study of climate
107	Clinology	study of aging or individual decline after maturity
108	Codicology	study of manuscripts
109	Coleopterology	study of beetles and weevils
110	Cometology	study of comets
111	Conchology	study of shells
112	Coprology	study of pornography
113	Cosmetology	study of cosmetics
114	Cosmology	study of the universe
115	Craniology	study of the skull
116	Criminology	study of crime; criminals
117	Cryobiology	study of life under cold conditions
118	Cryptology	study of codes
119	Cryptozoology	study of animals for whose existence there is no conclusive proof
120	Ctetology	study of the inheritance of acquired characteristics
121	Cynology	scientific study of dogs
122	Cytology	study of living cells
123	Dactyliology	study of rings
124	Dactylography	the study of fingerprints
125	Dactylology	study of sign language
126	Deltiology	the collection and study of picture postcards
127	Demology	study of human behaviour
128	Demonology	study of demons
129	Dendrochronology	study of tree rings
130	Dendrology	study of trees
131	Deontology	the theory or study of moral obligation
132	Dermatoglyphics	the study of skin patterns and fingerprints
133	Dermatology	study of skin
134	Desmology	study of ligaments

S.N.	Words	Definitions
135	Diabology	study of devils
136	Diagraphics	art of making diagrams or drawings
137	Dialectology	study of dialects
138	Dioptrics	study of light refraction
139	Diplomatics	science of deciphering ancient writings and texts
140	Diplomatology	study of diplomats
141	Docimology	the art of assaying
142	Dosiology	the study of doses
143	Dramaturgy	art of producing and staging dramatic works
144	Dysgenics	the study of racial degeneration
145	Dysteleology	study of purposeless organs
146	Ecclesiology	study of church affairs
147	Eccrinology	study of excretion
148	Ecology	study of environment
149	Economics	study of material wealth
150	Edaphology	study of soils
151	Egyptology	study of ancient Egypt
152	Ekistics	study of human settlement
153	Electrochemistry	study of relations between electricity and chemicals
154	Electrology	study of electricity
155	Electrostatics	study of static electricity
156	Embryology	study of embryos
157	Emetology	study of vomiting
158	Emmenology	the study of menstruation
159	Endemiology	study of local diseases
160	Endocrinology	study of glands
161	Enigmatology	study of enigmas
162	Entomology	study of insects
163	Entozoology	study of parasites that live inside larger organisms
164	Enzymology	study of enzymes
165	Ephebiatrics	branch of medicine dealing with adolescence
166	Epidemiology	study of diseases; epidemics
167	Epileptology	study of epilepsy
168	Epistemology	study of grounds of knowledge
169	Eremology	study of deserts
170	Ergology	study of effects of work on humans

S.N.	Words	Definitions
171	Ergonomics	study of people at work
172	Escapology	study of freeing oneself from constraints
173	Eschatology	study of death; final matters
174	Ethnogeny	study of origins of races or ethnic groups
175	Ethnology	study of cultures
176	Ethnomethodology	study of everyday communication
177	Ethnomusicology	study of comparative musical systems
178	Ethology	study of natural or biological character
179	Ethonomics	study of economic and ethical principles of a society
180	Etiology	the science of causes; especially of disease
181	Etymology	study of origins of words
182	Euthenics	science concerned with improving living conditions
183	Exobiology	study of extraterrestrial life
184	Floristry	the art of cultivating and selling flowers
185	Fluviology	study of watercourses
186	Folkloristics	study of folklore and fables
187	Futurology	study of future
188	Garbology	study of garbage
189	Gastroenterology	study of stomach; intestines
190	Gastronomy	study of fine dining
191	Gemmology	study of gems and jewels
192	Genealogy	study of descent of families
193	Genesiology	study of reproduction and heredity
194	Genethlialogy	the art of casting horoscopes
195	Geochemistry	study of chemistry of the earth's crust
196	Geochronology	study of measuring geological time
197	Geogeny	science of the formation of the earth's crust
198	Geogony	study of formation of the earth
199	Geography	study of surface of the earth and its inhabitants
200	Geology	study of earth's crust
201	Geomorphogeny	study of the origins of land forms
202	Geoponics	study of agriculture
203	Geotechnics	study of increasing habitability of the earth
204	Geratology	study of decadence and decay
205	Gerocomy	study of old age
206	Gerontology	study of the elderly; aging

S.N.	Words	Definitions
207	Gigantology	study of giants
208	Glaciology	study of ice ages and glaciation
209	Glossology	study of language; study of the tongue
210	Glyptography	the art of engraving on gems
211	Glyptology	study of gem engravings
212	Gnomonics	the art of measuring time using sundials
213	Gnosiology	study of knowledge; philosophy of knowledge
214	Ghotobiology	study of life in germ-free conditions
215	Graminology	study of grasses
216	Grammatology	study of systems of writing
217	Graphemics	study of systems of representing speech in writing
218	Graphology	study of handwriting
219	Gromatics	science of surveying
220	Gynaecology	study of women's physiology
221	Gyrostatics	the study of rotating bodies
222	Haemataulics	study of movement of blood through blood vessels
223	Hagiology	study of saints
224	Halieutics	study of fishing
225	Hamartiology	study of sin
226	Harmonics	study of musical acoustics
227	Hedonics	part of ethics or psychology dealing with pleasure
228	Helcology	study of ulcers
229	Heliology	science of the sun
230	Helioseismology	study of sun's interior by observing its surface oscillations
231	Helminthology	study of worms
232	Hematology	study of blood
233	Heortology	study of religious feasts
234	Hepatology	study of liver
235	Heraldry	study of coats of arms
236	Heresiology	study of heresies
237	Herpetology	study of reptiles and amphibians
238	Hierology	science of sacred matters
239	Hippiatrics	study of diseases of horses
240	Hippology	the study of horses
241	Histology	study of the tissues of organisms
242	Histopathology	study of changes in tissue due to disease

S.N.	Words	Definitions
243	Historiography	study of writing history
244	Historiology	study of history
245	Homiletics	the art of preaching
246	Hoplology	the study of weapons
247	Horography	art of constructing sundials or clocks
248	Horology	science of time measurement
249	Horticulture	study of gardening
250	Hydrobiology	study of aquatic organisms
251	Hydrodynamics	study of movement in liquids
252	Hydrogeology	study of ground water
253	Hydrography	study of investigating bodies of water
254	Hydrokinetics	study of motion of fluids
255	Hydrology	study of water resources
256	Hydrometeorology	study of atmospheric moisture
257	Hydropathy	study of treating diseases with water
258	Hyetology	science of rainfall
259	Hygiastics	science of health and hygiene
260	Hygienics	study of sanitation; health
261	Hygiology	hygienics; study of cleanliness
262	Hygrology	study of humidity
263	Hygrometry	science of humidity
264	Hymnography	study of writing hymns
265	Hymnology	study of hymns
266	Hypnology	study of sleep; study of hypnosis
267	Hypsography	science of measuring heights
268	Tamatology	study of remedies
269	Iatrology	treatise or text on medical topics; study of medicine
270	Iatromathematics	archaic practice of medicine in conjunction with astrology
271	Ichnography	art of drawing ground plans; a ground plan
272	Ichnology	science of fossilized footprints
273	Ichthyology	study of fish
274	Iconography	study of drawing symbols
275	Iconology	study of icons; symbols
276	Ideogeny	study of origins of ideas
277	Ideology	science of ideas; system of ideas used to justify behaviour
278	Idiomology	study of idiom, jargon or dialect

S.N.	Words	Definitions
279	Idiopsychology	psychology of one's own mind
280	Immunogenetics	study of genetic characteristics of immunity
281	Immunology	study of immunity
282	Immunopathology	study of immunity to disease
283	Insectology	study of insects
284	Irenology	the study of peace
285	Iridology	study of the iris; diagnosis of disease based on the iris of the eye
286	Kalology	study of beauty
287	Karyology	study of cell nuclei
288	Kidology	study of kidding
289	Kinematics	study of motion
290	Kinesics	study of gestural communication
291	Kinesiology	study of human movement and posture
292	Kinetics	study of forces producing or changing motion
293	Koniology	study of atmospheric pollutants and dust
294	Ktenology	science of putting people to death
295	Kymatology	study of wave motion
296	Labeorphily	collection and study of beer bottle labels
297	Larithmics	study of population statistics
298	Laryngology	study of larynx
299	Lepidopterology	study of butterflies and moths
300	Leprology	study of leprosy
301	Lexicology	study of words and their meanings
302	Lexigraphy	art of definition of words
303	Lichenology	study of lichens
304	Limacology	study of slugs
305	Limnobiology	study of freshwater ecosystems
306	Limnology	study of bodies of fresh water
307	Linguistics	study of language
308	Lithology	study of rocks
309	Liturgiology	study of liturgical forms and church rituals
310	Loimology	study of plagues and epidemics
311	Loxodromy	study of sailing along rhumb-lines
312	Magirics	art of cookery
313	Magnanerie	art of raising silkworms
314	Magnetics	study of magnetism

S.N.	Words	Definitions
315	Malacology	study of molluscs
316	Malariology	study of malaria
317	Mammalogy	study of mammals
318	Manège	the art of horsemanship
319	Mariology	study of the Virgin Mary
320	Martyrology	study of martyrs
321	Mastology	study of mammals
322	Mathematics	study of magnitude, number, and forms
323	Mazology	mammalogy; study of mammals
324	Mechanics	study of action of force on bodies
325	Meconology	study of or treatise concerning opium
326	Melittology	study of bees
327	Mereology	study of part-whole relationships
328	Mesology	ecology
329	Metallogeny	study of the origin and distribution of metal deposits
330	Metallography	study of the structure and constitution of metals
331	Metallurgy	study of alloying and treating metals
332	Metaphysics	study of principles of nature and thought
333	Metapolitics	study of politics in theory or abstract
334	Metapsychology	study of nature of the mind
335	Meteoritics	the study of meteors
336	Meteorology	study of weather
337	Metrics	study of versification
338	Metrology	science of weights and measures
339	Microanatomy	study of microscopic tissues
340	Microbiology	study of microscopic organisms
341	Microclimatology	study of local climates
342	Micrology	study or discussion of trivialities
343	Micropalaeontology	study of microscopic fossils
344	Microphytology	study of very small plant life
345	Microscopy	study of minute objects
346	Mineralogy	study of minerals
347	Molinology	study of mills and milling
348	Momilogy	study of mummies
349	Morphology	study of forms and the development of structures
350	Muscology	the study of mosses

S.N.	Words	Definitions
351	Museology	the study of museums
352	Musicology	study of music
353	Mycology	0study of funguses
354	Myology	study of muscles
355	Myrmecology	study of ants
356	Mythology	study of myths; fables; tales
357	Naology	study of church or temple architecture
358	Nasology	study of the nose
359	Nautics	art of navigation
360	Nematology	the study of nematodes
361	Neonatology	study of newborn babies
362	Neossology	study of nestling birds
363	Nephology	study of clouds
364	Nephrology	study of the kidneys
365	Neurobiology	study of anatomy of the nervous system
366	Neurology	study of nervous system
367	Neuropsychology	study of relation between brain and behaviour
368	Neurypnology	study of hypnotism
369	Neutrosophy	study of the origin and nature of philosophical neutralities
370	Nidology	study of nests
371	Nomology	the science of the laws; especially of the mind
372	Noology	science of the intellect
373	Nosology	study of diseases
374	Nostology	study of senility
375	Notaphily	collecting of bank-notes and cheques
376	Numerology	study of numbers
377	Numismatics	study of coins
378	Nymphology	study of nymphs
379	Obstetrics	study of midwifery
380	Oceanography	study of oceans
381	Oceanology	study of oceans
382	Odology	science of the hypothetical mystical force of od
383	Odontology	study of teeth
384	Oenology	study of wines
385	Oikology	science of housekeeping
386	Olfactology	study of the sense of smell

S.N.	Words	Definitions
387	Ombrology	study of rain
388	Oncology	study of tumours
389	Oneirology	study of dreams
390	Onomasiology	study of nomenclature
391	Onomastics	study of proper names
392	Ontology	science of pure being; the nature of things
393	Oology	study of eggs
394	Ophiology	study of snakes
395	Ophthalmology	study of eye diseases
396	Optics	study of light
397	Optology	study of sight
398	Optometry	science of examining the eyes
399	Orchidology	study of orchids
400	Ornithology	study of birds
401	Orology	study of mountains
402	Orthoepy	study of correct pronunciation
403	Orthography	study of spelling
404	Orthopterology	study of cockroaches
405	Oryctology	mineralogy or paleontology
406	Osmics	scientific study of smells
407	Osmology	study of smells and olfactory processes
408	Osphresiology	study of the sense of smell
409	Osteology	study of bones
410	Otology	study of the ear
411	Otorhinolaryngology	study of ear, nose and throat
412	Paedology	study of children
413	Paedotrophy	art of rearing children
414	Paidonosology	study of children's diseases; pediatrics
415	Palaeoanthropology	study of early humans
416	Palaeobiology	study of fossil plants and animals
417	Palaeoclimatology	study of ancient climates
418	Palaeolimnology	study of ancient fish
419	Palaeolimnology	study of ancient lakes
420	Palaeontology	study of fossils
421	Palaeopedology	study of early soils
422	Paleobotany	study of ancient plants

S.N.	Words	Definitions
423	Paleo-Osteology	study of ancient bones
424	Palynology	study of pollen
425	Papyrology	study of paper
426	Parapsychology	study of unexplained mental phenomena
427	Parasitology	study of parasites
428	Paroemiology	study of proverbs
429	Parthenology	study of virgins
430	Pataphysics	the science of imaginary solutions
431	Pathology	study of disease
432	Patrology	study of early Christianity
433	Pedagogics	study of teaching
434	Pedology	study of soils
435	Pelology	study of mud
436	Penology	study of crime and punishment
437	Periodontics	study of gums
438	Peristerophily	pigeon-collecting
439	Pestology	science of pests
440	Petrology	study of rocks
441	Pharmacognosy	study of drugs of animal and plant origin
442	Pharmacology	study of drugs
443	Pharology	study of lighthouses
444	Pharyngology	study of the throat
445	Phenology	study of organisms as affected by climate
446	Phenomenology	study of phenomena
447	Philately	study of postage stamps
448	Philematology	the act or study of kissing
449	Phillumeny	collecting of matchbox labels
450	Philology	study of ancient texts; historical linguistics
451	Philosophy	science of knowledge or wisdom
452	Phoniatrics	study and correction of speech defects
453	Phonology	study of speech sounds
454	Photobiology	study of effects of light on organisms
455	Phraseology	study of phrases
456	Phrenology	study of bumps on the head
457	Phycology	study of algae and seaweeds
458	Physics	study of properties of matter and energy

S.N.	Words	Definitions
459	Physiology	study of processes of life
460	Phytology	study of plants; botany
461	Piscatology	study of fishes
462	Pisteology	science or study of faith
463	Planetology	study of planets
464	Plutology	political economy; study of wealth
465	Pneumatics	study of mechanics of gases
466	Podiatry	study and treatment of disorders of the foot; chiropody
467	Podology	study of the feet
468	Polemology	study of war
469	Pomology	study of fruit-growing
470	Posology	science of quantity or dosage
471	Potamology	study of rivers
472	Praxeology	study of practical or efficient activity
473	Primatology	study of primates
474	Proctology	study of rectum
475	Prosody	study of versification
476	Protistology	study of protists
477	Proxemics	study of man's need for personal space
478	Psalligraphy	the art of paper-cutting to make pictures
479	Psephology	study of election results and voting trends
480	Pseudology	art or science of lying
481	Pseudoptics	study of optical illusions
482	Psychobiology	study of biology of the mind
483	Psychogenetics	study of internal or mental states
484	Psychognosy	study of mentality, personality or character
485	Psychology	study of mind
486	Psychopathology	study of mental illness
487	Psychophysics	study of link between mental and physical processes
488	Pteridology	study of ferns
489	Pterylology	study of distribution of feathers on birds
490	Pyretology	study of fevers
491	Pyrgology	study of towers
492	Pyroballogy	study of artillery
493	Pyrography	study of woodburning
494	Quinology	study of quinine

S.N.	Words	Definitions
495	Raciology	study of racial differences.
496	Radiology	study of X-rays and their medical applications
497	Reflexology	study of reflexes
498	Rhabdology	knowledge or learning concerning divining rods
499	Rhabdology	art of calculating using numbering rods
500	Rheology	science of the deformation or flow of matter
501	Rheumatology	study of rheumatism
502	Rhinology	study of the nose
503	Rhochrematics	science of inventory management and the movement of products
504	Runology	study of runes
505	Sarcology	study of fleshy parts of the body
506	Satanology	study of the devil
507	Scatology	study of excrement or obscene literature
508	Schematonics	art of using gesture to express tones
509	Sciagraphy	art of shading
510	Scripophily	collection of bond and share certificates
511	Sedimentology	study of sediment
512	Seismology	study of earthquakes
513	Selenodesy	study of the shape and features of the moon
514	Selenology	study of the moon
515	Semantics	study of meaning
516	Semantology	science of meanings of words
517	Semasiology	study of meaning; semantics
518	Semiology	study of signs and signals
519	Semiotics	study of signs and symbols
520	Serology	study of serums
521	Sexology	study of sexual behaviour
522	Siderography	art of engraving on steel
523	Sigillography	study of seals
524	Significs	science of meaning
525	Silvics	study of tree's life
526	Sindonology	study of the shroud of Turin
527	Sinology	study of China
528	Sitology	dietetics

S.N.	Words	Definitions
529	Sociobiology	study of biological basis of human behaviour
530	Sociology	study of society
531	Somatology	science of the properties of matter
532	Sophiology	science of ideas
533	Soteriology	study of theological salvation
534	Spectrology	study of ghosts
535	Spectroscopy	study of spectra
536	Speleology	study and exploration of caves
537	Spermology	study of seeds
538	Sphagnology	study of peat moss
539	Sphragistics	study of seals and signets
540	Sphygmology	study of the pulse
541	Splanchnology	study of the entrails or viscera
542	Spongology	study of sponges
543	Stasiology	study of political parties
544	Statics	study of bodies and forces in equilibrium
545	Stemmatology	study of relationships between texts
546	Stoichiology	science of elements of animal tissues
547	Stomatology	study of the mouth
548	Storiology	study of folk tales
549	Stratigraphy	study of geological layers or strata
550	Stratography	art of leading an army
551	Stylometry	studying literature by means of statistical analysis
552	Suicidology	study of suicide
553	Symbology	study of symbols
554	Symptomatology	study of symptoms of illness
555	Synecology	study of ecological communities
556	Synectics	study of processes of invention
557	Syntax	study of sentence structure
558	Syphilology	study of syphilis
559	Systematology	study of systems
560	Taxidermy	art of curing and stuffing animals
561	Tectonics	science of structure of objects, buildings and landforms
562	Tegestology	study and collecting of beer mats
563	Teleology	study of final causes; analysis in terms of purpose
564	Telmatology	study of swamps

S.N.	Words	Definitions
565	Teratology	study of monsters, freaks or malformations etc
566	Teuthology	study of cephalopods
567	Textology	study of the production of texts
568	Thalassography	science of the sea
569	Thanatology	study of death and its customs
570	Thaumatology	study of miracles
571	Theology	study of religion; religious doctrine
572	Theriatrics	veterinary medicine
573	Theriogenology	study of animals' reproductive systems
574	Thermodynamics	study of relation of heat to motion
575	Thermokinematics	study of motion of heat
576	Thermology	study of heat
577	Therology	study of wild mammals
578	Thremmatology	science of breeding domestic animals and plants
579	Threpsology	science of nutrition
580	Tidology	study of tides
581	Timbrology	study of postage stamps
582	Tocology	obstetrics; midwifery
583	Tonetics	study of pronunciation
584	Topology	study of places and their natural features
585	Toponymics	study of place-names
586	Toreutics	study of artistic work in metal
587	Toxicology	study of poisons
588	Toxophily	love of archery; archery; study of archery
589	Traumatology	study of wounds and their effects
590	Tribology	study of friction and wear between surfaces
591	Trichology	study of hair and its disorders
592	Trophology	study of nutrition
593	Tsiganology	study of gypsies
594	Turnery	art of turning in a lathe
595	Typhlology	study of blindness and the blind
596	Typography	art of printing or using type
597	Typology	study of types of things
598	Ufology	study of alien spacecraft
599	Uranography	descriptive astronomy and mapping
600	Uranology	study of the heavens; astronomy

S.N.	Words	Definitions
601	Urbanology	study of cities
602	Urenology	study of rust molds
603	Urology	study of urine; urinary tract
604	Venereology	study of venereal disease
605	Vermeology	study of worms
606	Vexillology	study of flags
607	Victimology	study of victims
608	Vinology	scientific study of vines and winemaking
609	Virology	study of viruses
610	Vitrics	glassy materials; glassware; study of glassware
611	Volcanology	study of volcanoes
612	Vulcanology	study of volcanoes
613	Xylography	art of engraving on wood
614	Xylology	study of wood
615	Zenography	study of the planet Jupiter
616	Zoiatrics	veterinary surgery
617	Zooarchaeology	study of animal remains of archaeological sites
618	Zoochemistry	chemistry of animals.
619	Zoogeography	study of geographic distribution of animals
620	Zoogeology	study of fossil animal remains
621	Zoology	study of animals
622	Zoonomy	animal physiology
623	Zoonosology	study of animal diseases
624	Zoopathology	study of animal diseases
625	Zoophysics	physics of animal bodies
626	Zoophysiology	study of physiology of animals
627	Zoophytology	study of plant-like animals
628	Zoosemiotics	study of animal communication
629	Zootaxy	science of classifying animals
630	Zootechnics	science of breeding animals
631	Zygology	science of joining and fastening
632	Zymology	science of fermentation
633	Zymurgy	branch of chemistry dealing with brewing and distilling
19.3 Defining Words related to 'Phy'		
1	Acoustography	an imaging process that employs a sensor to convert ultrasound into an image in near real-time, analogous to an X-ray

S.N.	Words	Definitions
2	Acrography	a method of relief etching on wood, metal, or stone by means of a coating of compressed chalk
3	Angiography	roentgenographic examination of blood vessels after injection of a radiopaque contrast medium; produces an angiogram
4	Arteriography	roentgenographic examination of arteries
5	Autobiography	a biography of yourself
6	Autography	ariting done with one's own hand.
7	Autoradiography	producing a radiograph by means of the radiation emitted from the specimen being photographed
8	Bibliography	a list of writings with time and place of publication (such as the writings of a single author or the works referred to in preparing a document etc.)
9	Biogeography	dealing with the geographical distribution of animals and plants
10	Biography	an account of the series of events making up a person's life
11	Cacography	poor handwriting
12	Calligraphy	beautiful handwriting
13	Cardiography	diagnostic procedure consisting of recording the activity of the heart electronically with a cardiograph (and producing a cardiogram)
14	Cartography	the making of maps and charts
15	Chirography	beautiful handwriting
16	Cholangiography	roentgenographic examination of the bile ducts after a contrast medium has been injected
17	Choreography	a notation used by choreographers
18	Chorography	the systematic description and mapping of particular regions
19	Chromatography	a process used for separating mixtures by virtue of differences in absorbency
20	Cinematography	the act of making a film
21	Cosmography	a representation of the earth or the heavens
22	Cryptography	act of writing in code or cipher
23	Crystallography	the branch of science that studies the formation and structure of crystals
24	Demography	the branch of sociology that studies the characteristics of human populations
25	Encephalography	roentgenography of the brain after spinal fluid has been replaced by a gas (usually oxygen); produces an encephalogram

S.N.	Words	Definitions
26	Epigraphy	the study of ancient inscriptions
27	Ethnography	the branch of anthropology that provides scientific description of individual human societies
28	Geography	study of the earth's surface; includes people's responses to topography and climate and soil and vegetation
29	Hagiography	a biography that idealizes or idolizes the person (especially a person who is a saint)
30	Historiography	the writing of history
31	Holography	the branch of optics that deals with the use of coherent light from a laser in order to make a hologram that can then be used to create a three dimensional image
32	Hydrography	the science of the measurement and description and mapping of the surface waters of the earth with special reference to navigation
33	Iconography	the images and symbolic representations that are traditionally associated with a person or a subject
34	Ideography	the use of ideograms in writing
35	Lexicography	the act of writing dictionaries
36	Lithography	the act of making a lithographic print
37	Lymphography	roentgenographic examination of lymph nodes and lymph vessels after injection of a radiopaque contrast medium; produces a lymphangiogram
38	Mammography	a diagnostic procedure to detect breast tumors by the use of X rays
39	Oceanography	the branch of science dealing with physical and biological aspects of the oceans
40	Orography	the science of mountains
41	Orthography	a method of representing the sounds of a language by written or printed symbols
42	Paleogeography	the study of the geography of ancient times or ancient epochs
43	Paleography	the study of ancient forms of writing (and the deciphering of them)
44	Photography	the occupation of taking and printing photographs or making movies
45	Physiography	the study of physical features of the earth's surface
46	Planography	the process of printing from a surface on which the printing areas are not raised but are ink receptive (as opposed to ink repellent)
47	Polarography	an electrochemical method of chemical analysis

S.N.	Words	Definitions
48	Pornography	creative activity (writing or pictures or films etc.) of no literary or artistic value other than to stimulate sexual desire
49	Radiography	photography that uses other kinds of radiation than visible light
50	Radiotelegraphy	the use of radio to send telegraphic messages (usually by Morse code)
51	Roentgenography	radiography that uses X rays to produce a roentgenogram the measurement of tremors and shocks and undulatory movements of earthquakes
52	Seismography	the act of making a print by the silkscreen method
53	Serigraphy	using the reflections of high frequency sound waves to construct an image of a body organ (a sonogram); commonly used to observe fetal growth or study bodily organs
54	Sonography	the act or art of writing in shorthand
55	Stenography	the branch of geology that studies the arrangement and succession of strata
56	Stratigraphy	communicating at a distance by electric transmission over wire
57	Telegraphy	photography using a telephoto lens
58	Telephotography	diagnostic technique using a thermograph to record the heat produced by different parts of the body; used to study blood flow and to detect tumors
59	Thermography	(medicine) obtaining pictures of the interior of the body
60	Tomography	the configuration of a surface and the relations among its man made and natural features
61	Topography	the craft of composing type and printing from it
62	Typography	using the reflections of high frequency sound waves to
63	Ultrasonography	construct an image of a body organ (a sonogram); commonly used to observe fetal growth or study bodily organs
64	Venography	roentgenographic examination of veins
65	Xerography	forming an image by the action of light on a specially coated charged plate; the latent image is developed with powders that adhere only to electrically charged areas
66	Xeroradiography	radiography using X rays and xerographic (rather than roentgenographic) techniques
19.4 Words related to Form of Government		
1	Acracy	government by none; anarchy
2	Adhocracy	government in an unstructured fashion; an unstructured organization

S.N.	Words	Definitions
3	Albocracy	government by white people
4	Anarchy	government by none
5	Androcracy	government by men
6	Anemocracy	government by the wind
7	Angelocracy	government by angels
8	Antarchy	opposition to government; anarchy
9	Argentocracy	government by money
11	Aristocracy	government by the nobility
12	Arithmocracy	government by simple majority
13	Autarchy	government by an absolute ruler
14	Autocracy	government by one individual
15	Barbarocracy	government by barbarians
16	Beerocracy	government by brewers or brewing interests
17	Bestiocracy	rule by beasts
18	Biarchy	government by two people; diarchy
19	Binarchy	government by two people; diarchy
20	Bureaucracy	government by civil servants
21	Cannonarchy	government by superior firepower or by cannons
22	Capelocracy	government by shopkeepers
23	Chiliarchy	government by one thousand people
24	Chirocracy	government by physical force
25	Chromatocracy	government by rulers of a particular skin colour
26	Chrysoaristocracy	government by the wealthy; plutocracy
27	Chrysocracy	government by the wealthy; plutocracy
28	Corpocracy	government by corporate bureaucrats
29	Cosmarchy	rulership over the entire world, esp. by the devil
30	Cottonocracy	government by those involved in the cotton trade
31	Cryptarchy	secret rulership
32	Decadarchy	government by ten individuals; decarchy
33	Decarchy	government by ten individuals
34	Demarchy	government by the people; popular government
35	Democracy	government by the people
36	Demonarchy	government by a demon
37	Demonocracy	government by demons or evil forces
38	Despotocracy	government by despots or tyrants
39	Diabolocracy	government by the Devil

S.N.	Words	Definitions
40	Diarchy	government by two people
41	Dinarchy	government by two people; diarchy
42	Dodecarchy	government by twelve people
43	Doulocracy	government by slaves
44	Duarchy	government by two people; diarchy
45	Dulocracy	government by slaves; doulocracy
46	Dyarchy	government by two people; diarchy
47	Ecclesiarchy	government by clerics or ecclesiastical authorities
48	Endarchy	centralised government
49	Ergatocracy	government by the workers or the working class
50	Ethnarchy	government over an ethnic group
51	Ethnocracy	government by an ethnic group or race
52	Exarchy	government by bishops
53	Foolocracy	government by fools
54	Gerontocracy	government by the aged
55	Gunarchy	government by women; gynarchy
56	Gymnasiarchy	government over a school or academy
57	Gynaecocracy	government by women; gynarchy
58	Gynarchy	government by women
59	Gynocracy	government by women; gynarchy
60	Hagiarchy	government by saints or holy persons
61	Hagiocracy	government by holy men
62	Hamarchy	government by a cooperative body of parts
63	Hecatarchy	government by one hundred people; hecatontarchy
64	Hecatontarchy	government by one hundred people
65	Hendecarchy	government by eleven people
66	Heptarchy	government by seven people
67	Heroarchy	government by heroes
68	Hetaerocracy	government by paramours
69	Heterarchy	government by a foreign ruler
70	Hierarchy	government by a ranked body; government by priests
71	Hierocracy	government by priests or religious ministers
72	Hipparchy	rule or control of horses
73	Hoplarchy	government by the military
74	Hyperanarchy	condition of extreme anarchy
75	Hyperarchy	excessive government

S.N.	Words	Definitions
76	Iatrarchy	government by physicians
77	Idiocracy	personal rule; self-rule
78	Infantocracy	government by an infant
79	Isocracy	equal political power
80	Jesuitocracy	government by Jesuits
81	Juntocracy	government by a junta
82	Kakistocracy	government by the worst
83	Kleptocracy	government by thieves
84	Kritarchy	government by judges
85	Landocracy	government by the propertied class; timocracy
86	Logocracy	government of words
87	Matriarchy	government by women or mothers
88	Meritocracy	government by the meritorious
89	Merocracy	government by a part of the citizenry
90	Mesocracy	government by the middle classes
91	Metrocracy	government by mothers or women; matriarchy
92	Millionocracy	government by millionaires
93	Millocracy	government by mill owners
94	Mobocracy	government by mobs or crowds
95	Monarchy	government by one individual
96	Moneyocracy	government by the monied classes
97	Monocracy	government by one individual
98	Myriarchy	government by ten thousand individuals
99	Narcokleptocracy	government by those who profit from trade in illegal drugs
100	Navarchy	rulership over the seas
101	Neocracy	government by new or inexperienced rulers
102	Nomocracy	government based on legal system; rule of law
103	Ochlocracy	government by mobs
104	Octarchy	government by eight people
105	Oligarchy	government by the few
106	Paedarchy	government by children
107	Paedocracy	government by children; paedarchy
108	Panarchy	universal rule or dominion
109	Pantarchy	government by all the people; world government
110	Pantisocracy	government by all equally
111	Paparchy	government by the pope

S.N.	Words	Definitions
112	Papyrocracy	government by newspapers or literature
113	Parsonarchy	government by parsons
114	Partocracy	government by a single unopposed political party
115	Patriarchy	government by men or fathers
116	Pedantocracy	government by pedants or strict rule-bound scholars
117	Pentarchy	government by five individuals
118	Phallocracy	government by men
119	Philosophocracy	government by philosophers
120	Phylarchy	government by a specific class or tribe
121	Physiocracy	government according to natural laws or principles
122	Pigmentocracy	government by those of one skin colour
123	Plantocracy	government by plantation owners
124	Plousiocracy	government by the wealthy; plutocracy
125	Plutarchy	government by the wealthy; plutocracy
126	Plutocracy	government by the wealthy
127	Polarchy	government by many people; polyarchy
128	Policeocracy	government by police
129	Pollarchy	government by the multitude or a mob; ochlocracy
130	Polyarchy	government by many people
131	Polycracy	government by many rulers; polyarchy
132	Popocracy	government by populists
133	Pornocracy	government by harlots
134	Prophetocracy	government by a prophet
135	Psephocracy	government resulting from election by ballot
136	Prochocracy	government by beggars or paupers; wholesale pauperization
137	Punditocracy	government by political pundits
138	Quangocracy	rule of quasi-autonomous non-governmental organizations
139	Rotocracy	government by those who control rotten boroughs
140	Septarchy	government by seven rulers; heptarchy
141	Shopocracy	government by shopkeepers
142	Slavocracy	government by slave-owners
143	Snobocracy	government by snobs
144	Sociocracy	government by society as a whole
145	Squarsonocracy	government by landholding clergymen
146	Squatterarchy	government by squatters; squattocracy
147	Squattocracy	government by squatters

S.N.	Words	Definitions
148	Squirearchy	government by squires
149	Squirocracy	government by squires; squirearchy
150	Statocracy	government by the state alone, without ecclesiastical influence
151	Stratarchy	rulership over an army
152	Stratocracy	military rule or despotism
153	Strumpetocracy	government by strumpets
154	Synarchy	joint sovereignty
155	Technocracy	government by technical experts
156	Tetradarchy	government by four people; tetrarchy
157	Tetrarchy	government by four people
158	Thalassiarchy	sovereignty of the seas; thalassocracy
159	Thalassocracy	sovereignty of the seas
160	Thearchy	rule by a god or gods; body of divine rulers
161	Theatrocracy	goverment by gathered assemblies of citizens
162	Theocracy	government by priests or by religious law
163	Timarchy	government by the propertied class; timocracy
164	Timocracy	government by the propertied class
165	Triarchy	government by three people
166	Tritheocracy	government by three gods
167	Whiggarchy	government by Whigs
168	Xenocracy	government by a body of foreigners

19.5 Defining Words related to Worship

S.N.	Words	Definitions
1	Aischrolatry	worship of filth, dirt, or smut
2	Allotheism	belief in or worship of strange gods
3	Angelolatry	worship of or belief in angels
4	Anthropolatry	worship of human beings
5	Arborolatry	worship of trees
6	Archaeolatry	worship of archaic things or old customs
7	Astrolatry	worship of stars
8	Autolatry	self-worship
9	Bardolatry	excessive devotion to or worship of Shakespeare
10	Bibliolatry	worship of the Bible or other books
11	Christolatry	worship of Christ
12	Cosmolatry	worship of the world
13	Cynolatry	worship of dogs
14	Demonolatry	worship of or devotion to demons

S.N.	Words	Definitions
15	Dendrolatry	worship of trees
16	Ecclesiolatry	excessive devotion to church tradition and form
17	Epeolatry	worship of words
18	Episcopolatry	worship of bishops
19	Gamidolatry	worship of marriage
20	Gastrolatry	gluttony; excessive love of food
21	Geolatry	earth-worship
22	Grammatolatry	worship of letters and words
23	Gyniolatry	deep respect or devotion for women
24	Hagiolatry	worship or reverence for saints
25	Heliolatry	sun worship
26	Hierolatry	worship of saints or sacred things
27	Hygeiolatry	excessive devotion to health
28	Ichthyolatry	the worship of fish
29	Iconolatry	image-worship
30	Ideolatry	worship of ideas
31	Idiolatry	self-worship; egotism
32	Idolatry	worship of idols
33	Ignicolist	fire-worshipper
34	Litholatry	stone-worship
35	Lordolatry	worship of nobility
36	Mariolatry	worship of the virgin mother
37	Martyrolatry	excessive devotion to martyrs
38	Mechanolatry	worship of machines
39	Monolatry	worship of one god without excluding belief in others
40	Necrolatry	worship of the dead
41	Neolatry	worship of novelty
42	Onolatry	worship of asses or donkeys
43	Ophiolatry	worship of snakes
44	Ophism	snake-worship
45	Pandemonism	worship of spirits dwelling in all forms of nature
46	Parthenolatry	worship of the Virgin Mary
47	Patriolatry	excessive devotion or worship of one's native country
48	Physiolatry	nature-worship
49	Planetolatry	worship of the planets
50	Plutolatry	worship of wealth

S.N.	Words	Definitions
51	Poetolatry	worship of poets
52	Pseudolatry	false worship
53	Pyrolatry	fire-worship
54	Selenolatry	worship of the moon
55	Statolatry	worship of the state
56	Staurolatry	worship of the cross or crucifix
57	Symbolatry	undue worship of symbols
58	Thaumatolatry	worship of miracles or wonders
59	Theriolatry	animal-worship
60	Zoolatry	excessive devotion to animals or pets

19.6 Defining Words related to Scientist Instrument

S.N.	Words	Definitions
1	Absorptiometer	instrument for measuring solubility of gases in liquids
2	Accelerometer	instrument for measuring acceleration or vibrations
3	Acetimeter	instrument for measuring strength of vinegar
4	Acidimeter	instrument for measuring concentration of acids
5	Actinograph	instrument used to calculate time of photographic exposure
6	Actinometer	instrument for measuring incident radiation
7	Aerometer	instrument for measuring weight or density of gas
8	Aethrioscope	instrument for measuring temperature variations due to sky conditions
9	Alcoholometer	instrument for measuring proportion of alcohol in solutions
10	Alcovinometer	instrument to measure strength of wine
11	Algometer	instrument for measuring sensitivity to pain
12	Alkalimeter	instrument for measuring strength of alkalines
13	Altimeter	instrument for measuring altitude
14	Ammeter	instrument for measuring electrical current
15	Anemograph	instrument for measuring pressure and velocity of wind
16	Anemometer	instrument for measuring wind velocity
17	Areometer	instrument used for measuring specific gravity
18	Arthroscope	instrument for examining interior of a joint
19	Atmometer	instrument for measuring evaporating capacity of air
20	Audiometer	instrument for measuring acuity of hearing
21	Auriscope	instrument for examining the ear
22	Auxanometer	instrument for measuring growth of plants
23	Auxometer	instrument for measuring magnifying power
24	Ballistocardiograph	instrument for detecting body movements caused by heartbeat

S.N.	Words	Definitions
25	Barograph	instrument for recording air pressure
26	Barometer	instrument for measuring air pressure
27	Baroscope	weather-glass
28	Bathymeter	instrument for recording contours of deep oceans
29	Bathythermograph	instrument for recording water temperature as compared to depth
30	Bolometer	instrument for measuring radiant energy or infrared light
31	Bronchoscope	instrument for examining the windpipe
32	Calorimeter	instrument for measuring absorbed or evolved heat
33	Cardiograph	instrument for recording movements of the heart
34	Cathetometer	instrument for measuring short vertical distances
35	Ceilometer	instrument for measuring height of cloud ceiling above earth
36	Ceraunograph	instrument for recording thunder and lightning
37	Chlorometer	instrument for measuring amount of chlorine in a solution
38	Chromatograph	instrument for performing chromatographic separations
39	Chromatoptometer	instrument measuring eyes' sensitivity to colour
40	Chronograph	instrument for recording the moment of an event
41	Chronometer	instrument for measuring time
42	Chronoscope	instrument for measuring very short time intervals
43	Clinometer	instrument used to measure slopes and elevations
44	Coercimeter	instrument for measuring coercive force
45	Colonoscope	instrument for viewing the colon
46	Colorimeter	instrument for measuring and determining colour
47	Colposcope	instrument for viewing the neck of the uterus
48	Coronagraph	instrument for viewing the corona of the sun
49	Coulombmeter	instrument for measuring electric charge
50	Coulometer	instrument measuring amount of substance released in electrolysis
51	Craniometer	instrument for measuring the skull
52	Cratometer	instrument for measuring power of magnification
53	Crescograph	instrument for measuring the growth of plants
54	Cryometer	instrument for measuring low temperatures
55	Cryoscope	instrument for determining freezing points of substances
56	Cyanometer	instrument for measuring blueness of the sky or ocean
57	Cyclograph	instrument for describing arcs of circles without compasses
58	Cyclometer	instrument for measuring revolutions of a wheel

S.N.	Words	Definitions
59	Cymograph	instrument for tracing the outline of mouldings
60	Cymometer	instrument for measuring frequency of electrical waves
61	Cystoscope	instrument for examining the bladder
62	Cytometer	instrument for counting cells
63	Decelerometer	instrument for measuring deceleration
64	Declinometer	instrument for measuring magnetic declination
65	Dendrometer	instrument for measuring trees
66	Densimeter	instrument for measuring closeness of grain of a substance
67	Densitometer	instrument for measuring optical or photographic density
68	Diagometer	instrument for measuring electrical conductivity
69	Diagraph	instrument for enlarging or projecting drawings
70	Diaphanometer	instrument for measuring the transparency of air
71	Dichroscope	instrument for examining crystals for dichroism
72	Diffractometer	instrument for determining structure of crystal through light diffraction
73	Dilatometer	instrument for measuring expansion
74	Dioptometer	instrument for measuring focus or refraction of the eyes
75	Dipleidoscope	instrument for measuring moment when an object passes a meridian
76	Diplograph	instrument for writing two lines of text at once
77	Dosimeter	instrument for measuring dose of radiation
78	Dromometer	instrument for measuring speed
79	Drosometer	instrument for measuring dew
80	Durometer	instrument for measuring hardness of substances
81	Dynamograph	instrument for recording mechanical forces
82	Dynamometer	instrument for measuring mechanical force
83	Ebullioscope	instrument for measuring boiling point of liquids
84	Effusiometer	instrument for comparing molecular weights of gases
85	Eidograph	instrument for copying drawings
86	Elatrometer	instrument for measuring gaseous pressure
87	Electrocardiograph	instrument for recording unusual electrical fluctuations of the heart
88	Electrodynamometer	instrument for measuring electrical current
89	Electroencephalograph	instrument for measuring the brain's electrical impulses
90	Electrograph	instrument for recording electrical potential
91	Electrometer	instrument for measuring electrical potential

S.N.	Words	Definitions
92	Electromyograph	instrument for diagnosing neuromuscular disorders
93	Electroretinograph	instrument for measuring electrical activity in the retina
94	Electroscope	instrument for detecting electrical charges in the body
95	Ellipsograph	instrument for describing ellipses
96	Encephalograph	instrument for recording brain images
97	Endoscope	instrument for visualizing interior of a hollow organ
98	Endosmometer	instrument for measuring osmosis into a solution
99	Epidiascope	instrument for projecting images of objects
100	Episcope	instrument for projecting images of opaque objects
101	Ergograph	instrument for measuring and recording muscular work
102	Ergometer	instrument for measuring work performed
103	Eriometer	instrument for measuring very small diameters
104	Eudiometer	instrument for measuring air purity
105	Evaporimeter	instrument for measuring rate of evaporation
106	Extensometer	instrument for measuring deformation in object due to forces applied
107	Fathometer	instrument for measuring underwater depth using sound
108	Fiberscope	instrument using fibre-optics to examine inaccessible areas
109	Floriscope	instrument for inspecting flowers
110	Flowmeter	instrument for measuring properties of flowing liquids
111	Fluorimeter	instrument for measuring fluorescence
112	Fluoroscope	instrument using x-rays to examine internal structure of opaque object
113	Focimeter	instrument for measuring focal length of a lens
114	Galactometer	instrument for measuring specific gravity of milk
115	Galvanometer	instrument for measuring electrical current
116	Galvanoscope	instrument for detecting presence and direction of electric current
117	Gasometer	instrument for holding and measuring gases
118	Gastroscope	instrument for examining interior of the stomach
119	Geothermometer	instrument for measuring subterranean temperatures
120	Goniometer	instrument for measuring angles between faces
121	Gradiometer	instrument for measuring gradient of a physical quantity
122	Gravimeter	instrument for measuring variations in gravitational fields.
123	Gyrograph	instrument for counting a wheel's revolutions
124	Haptometer	instrument measuring sensitivity to touch

S.N.	Words	Definitions
125	Harmonograph	instrument drawing curves representing vibrations
126	Harmonometer	instrument measuring harmonic relations of sounds.
127	Helicograph	instrument for drawing spirals on a plane
128	Heliograph	instrument for measuring intensity of sunlight
129	Heliometer	instrument for measuring apparent diameter of the sun
130	Helioscope	instrument for observing sun without injury to the eyes
131	Hemacytometer	instrument for counting blood cells
132	Hippometer	instrument to measure height of horses
133	Hodoscope	instrument for tracing paths of ionizing particles
134	Hydrometer	instrument for measuring specific gravity of liquids
135	Hydroscope	instrument for viewing under water
136	Hydrotimeter	instrument for measuring water hardness
137	Hyetograph	instrument for recording rainfall
138	Hyetometer	instrument for measuring rainfall
139	Hyetometrograph	instrument for recording rainfall
140	Hygrograph	instrument for recording variations in atmospheric humidity
141	Hygrometer	instrument for measuring air moisture
142	Hygroscope	instrument for displaying changes in air humidity
143	Hypsometer	instrument for measuring height of trees through triangulation
144	Iconometer	instrument for finding size of object by measuring its image
145	Idiometer	instrument for measuring motion of observer in relation to transit of the heavens
146	Inclinometer	instrument for measuring inclination to the horizontal of an axis
147	Interferometer	instrument for analysing spectra of light
148	Iriscope	instrument for exhibiting the prismatic colours
149	Katathermometer	instrument for measuring the cooling power of air
150	Katharometer	instrument measuring changes in composition of gases
151	Keratometer	instrument for measuring curvature of the cornea
152	Keraunograph	instrument for recording distant thunderstorms
153	Kinetoscope	instrument for producing curves by combination of circular movements
154	Konimeter	instrument measuring amount of dust in air
155	Koniscope	instrument for measuring dust in air
156	Kymograph	instrument for recording fluid pressure
157	Labidometer	instrument for measuring size of the head of a fetus

S.N.	Words	Definitions
158	Lactometer	instrument for testing relative density of milk
159	Lactoscope	instrument for measuring purity or richness of milk
160	Lanameter	instrument for measuring quality of wool
161	Laparoscope	instrument for viewing interior of peritoneal cavity
162	Laryngoscope	instrument for examining interior of the larynx
163	Leptometer	instrument for measuring oil viscosity
164	Loxodograph	device used to record ship's travels
165	Lucimeter	instrument for measuring light intensity
166	Luxmeter	instrument for measuring illumination
167	Lysimeter	instrument for measuring percolation of water through soil
168	Magnetograph	instrument for recording measurements of magnetic fields
169	Magnetometer	instrument for measuring intensity of magnetic fields
170	Manometer	instrument for measuring pressure of a liquid or gas
171	Marigraph	instrument for recording tide levels
172	Mecometer	instrument for measuring length
173	Megameter	instrument for determining longitude by observing stars
174	Megascope	instrument for projecting an enlarged image
175	Mekometer	range-finder
176	Meldometer	instrument for measuring melting points of substances
177	Meteorograph	instrument recording a variety of meteorological observations
178	Methanometer	instrument for detecting presence of methane
179	Microbarograph	instrument for recording minute changes in atmospheric pressure
180	Microcalorimeter	instrument for measuring tiny quantities of heat
181	Micrograph	instrument used to write on a very small scale
182	Micrometer	instrument for measuring very small distances
183	Micronometer	instrument for measuring short periods of time
184	Microscope	instrument for magnifying small objects
185	Microseismograph	instrument for recording small or distant earthquakes
186	Microseismometer	instrument for measuring small or distant earthquakes
187	Mileometer	instrument for recording distance travelled in miles
188	Milliammeter	instrument for recording very small electrical currents
189	Myograph	instrument for recording muscular contractions
190	Myringoscope	instrument for viewing the eardrum
191	Nephelometer	instrument for measuring cloudiness
192	Nephograph	instrument for photographing clouds

S.N.	Words	Definitions
193	Nephoscope	instrument for observing direction and velocity of clouds
194	Nitrometer	instrument for measuring nitrogen and its compounds
195	Odograph	odometer; instrument for measuring distance travelled
196	Odometer	instrument for measuring distance travelled
197	Odontograph	instrument for obtaining curves for gear-teeth
198	Oenometer	instrument for measuring alcoholic strength of wine
199	Ohmmeter	instrument for measuring electrical resistance
200	O Oleometer	instrument for measuring amount of oil in a substance
201	Olfactometer	instrument measuring intensity of odour of a substance
202	Ombrometer	rain-gauge
203	Oncometer	instrument measuring change in size of internal organs
204	Oncosimeter	instrument measuring variations in density of molten metal
205	Ondograph	instrument measuring change in wave formations of electricity
206	Oometer	instrument for measuring eggs
207	Opacimeter	instrument for measuring opacity
208	Opeidoscope	instrument for illustrating sound by means of light
209	Ophthalmometer	instrument for measuring the eye
210	Ophthalmoscope	instrument for viewing the interior of the eye
211	Opisometer	instrument for measuring curved lines
212	Opsiometer	instrument for testing vision
213	Optometer	instrument for testing vision
214	Orchidometer	instrument for measuring the size of the testicles
215	Oscillograph	instrument for recording alternating current wave forms
216	Oscillometer	instrument for measuring ship's rollings
217	Oscilloscope	instrument for detecting electrical fluctuations
218	Osmometer	instrument for measuring osmotic pressure
219	Otoscope	instrument for examining the ear
220	Pachymeter	instrument for measuring small thicknesses
221	Pallograph	instrument measuring ship's vibration
222	Pantochronometer	combined sundial and compass
223	Pantograph	instrument for copying drawing to a different scale
224	Passimeter	instrument for issuing automatic tickets
225	Pedometer	instrument for measuring distance travelled on foot
226	Peirameter	instrument measuring resistance of road surfaces to wheel movement

S.N.	Words	Definitions
227	Pelvimeter	instrument for measuring the pelvis
228	Penetrometer	instrument for measuring firmness or consistency of substances
229	Permeameter	instrument for measuring permeability
230	Phacometer	instrument for measuring lenses
231	Phaometer	old instrument for measuring light intensity
232	Pharmacometer	instrument for measuring drugs
233	Pharyngoscope	instrument for inspecting the pharynx
234	Phonautograph	instrument for recording sound vibrations
235	Phonendoscope	device which amplifies small sounds
236	Phonometer	instrument for measuring sound levels
237	Phorometer	instrument used to correct abnormalities in eye muscles
238	Photometer	instrument for measuring light intensity
239	Photopolarimeter	instrument for measuring intensity and polarization of reflected light
240	Phototachometer	instrument for measuring the speed of light
241	Phototelegraph	instrument for transmitting drawings telegraphically
242	Phthongometer	instrument measuring intensity of vowel sounds
243	Piezometer	instrument for measuring pressure or compressibility
244	Pitchometer	instrument for measuring angles of ship's propeller blades
245	Planigraph	instrument for copying drawings at a different scale
246	Planimeter	instrument for measuring area of plane figures
247	Platometer	instrument for measuring area; planimeter
248	Plegometer	instrument for measuring the strength of a blow
249	Plemyrameter	instrument for measuring variations in water level
250	Plethysmograph	instrument for measuring change in body part size due to blood flow
251	Pluviograph	self-registering rain gauge
252	Pluviometer	rain-meter
253	Pneometer	instrument that measures respiration
254	Pneumatometer	instrument for measuring quantity of air breathed
255	Pneumograph	instrument for measuring and recording respiration
256	Polarimeter	instrument for measuring polarised light
257	Polariscope	instrument for detecting polarized light
258	Polygraph	instrument for measuring small changes in pulse and respiration

S.N.	Words	Definitions
259	Porometer	instrument for measuring degree of porosity
260	Poroscope	instrument for investigating porosity
261	Potentiometer	instrument for measuring electromotive forces
262	Potometer	instrument measuring rate at which plants absorb water
263	Prisoptometer	instrument for measuring degree of astigmatism
264	Proctoscope	instrument for examining the rectum
265	Psophometer	instrument measuring audible interference of electrical current
266	Psychograph	instrument that supposedly records spirit messages
267	Psychrometer	instrument that supposedly records spirit messages instrument for measuring air moisture or temperature
268	Psychrometer	instrument for measuring dryness of the atmosphere instrument for measuring the pulse
269	Pulsimeter	instrument for measuring specific gravity or density
270	Pycnometer	instrument measuring solar radiation from the sky's whole hemisphere
271	Pyknometer	instrument for measuring radiation from earth
272	Pyranometer	instrument for measuring heating effect of sun instrument for measuring very high temperatures
273	Pyrgeometer	instrument for measuring intensity of radiant heat apparatus for measuring penetrating power of X-ray beams
274	Pyrheliometer	apparatus for measuring quantity of X-rays
275	Pyrometer	instrument for measuring proportions of elements in
276	Pyroscope	metallic samples
277	Qualimeter	instrument for measuring the spine
278	Quantimeter	instrument for detecting radar signals
279	Quantometer	instrument for finding direction through radio signals
280	Rachiometer	instrument for measuring atmospheric conditions at high altitude
281	Radarscope	instrument measuring radiation energy
282	Radiogoniometer	instrument for viewing objects using X-rays
283	Radiometeorograph	instrument for measuring counting rate of electronic
284	Radiometer	counters
285	Radioscope	old instrument with two arms used for measuring angles
286	Ratemeter	instrument for measuring reflectance of radiant energy
287	Recipiangle	instrument measuring refraction of light
288	Reflectometer	instrument for measuring reflectance of radiant energy
289	Refractometer	instrument measuring refraction of light

S.N.	Words	Definitions
290	Respirometer	instrument for measuring and studying respiration
291	Retinoscope	instrument for measuring and viewing the retina
292	Rheometer	instrument that measures current
293	Rhinoscope	instrument for examining the nose
294	Rhythmometer	instrument for measuring speed of rhythms
295	Riometer	instrument for measuring absorbed cosmic radio waves
296	Rotameter	old instrument for measuring length of curved lines
297	Rotameter	instrument consisting of glass tube with free float for measuring liquid flow
298	Saccharimeter	instrument for measuring amount of sugar in a solution
299	Salinometer	instrument for measuring amount of salt in a solution
300	Scintillometer	instrument measuring scintillation of star
301	Scintilloscope	instrument for measuring gamma rays emitted by a radioactive body
302	Sclerometer	instrument measuring hardness
303	Scoliometer	instrument measuring curvature
304	Scotograph	instrument for writing without seeing
305	Scotoscope	instrument for detecting objects in darkness
306	Seismograph	instrument for recording earthquakes
307	Seismometer	instrument for measuring earthquake intensity
308	Seismoscope	instrument for detecting earthquakes
309	Selenoscope	instrument for viewing the moon
310	Sensitometer	instrument for measuring sensitivity of photographic material
311	Sepometer	instrument for measuring septic matter in the air
312	Serimeter	instrument for testing quality of silk
313	Shuftiscope	instrument used to explore interior of dysentery case
314	Siccimeter	instrument for measuring liquid evaporation
315	Sideroscope	instrument using magnets to detect presence of iron
316	Sigmoidoscope	instrument for examining the interior of the rectum and sigmoid colon
317	Sillometer	instrument measuring speed of ship
318	Skiascope	instrument for measuring eye's refraction from movement of shadows
319	Snooperscope	instrument for viewing infrared radiation
320	Solarimeter	instrument for measuring solar radiation
321	Sonograph	instrument for recording and analysing sound
322	Spectrofluorimeter	instrument for measuring and recording fluorescence spectra

S.N.	Words	Definitions
323	Spectrograph	instrument for viewing a spectrum
324	Spectroheliograph	instrument for taking pictures of the sun
325	Spectroheliokinematograph	camera for taking pictures of the sun
326	Spectrohelioscope	instrument for viewing solar disc in light of a single wavelength
327	Spectrometer	instrument measuring wavelengths of light of a spectrum
328	Spectrophotometer	instrument for measuring speed of different parts of light spectrum
329	Spectroscope	instrument for forming spectra by dispersing rays of light
330	Speedometer	instrument for measuring velocity.
331	Spherometer	instrument measuring curvature
332	Sphygmograph	instrument for recording pulse
333	Sphygmomanometer	instrument for measuring arterial blood pressure
334	Sphygmometer	instrument for measuring arterial blood pressure
335	Sphygmoscope	instrument for making arterial pulsations visible
336	Spinthariscope	instrument for visually detecting alpha particles
337	Spirograph	instrument recording movements of breathing
338	Spirometer	instrument measuring lung capacity
339	Stactometer	pipette with hollow bulb for counting drops
340	Stadiometer	instrument for measuring the length of a curved line
341	Stagmometer	instrument for measuring number of drops in volume of liquid
342	Stalagmometer	instrument for measuring surface tension by drops
343	Statoscope	instrument for measuring small changes in atmospheric pressure
344	Stauroscope	instrument for studying structure of crystals with polarised light
345	Stenometer	instrument for measuring distances
346	Stereometer	instrument for measuring specific gravity
347	Stereoscope	instrument for viewing special three-dimensional photographs
348	Stethometer	instrument measuring chest expansion during breathing
349	Stethoscope	instrument for detecting sounds produced by the body
350	Strabismometer	instrument measuring degree of squinting
351	Strabometer	instrument for measuring strabismus in the eyes
352	Stroboscope	instrument for studying motion using flashes of light
353	Stylometer	instrument for measuring columns
354	Swingometer	instrument for measuring swing in votes during an election
355	Symplesometer	instrument for measuring pressure of a current

S.N.	Words	Definitions
356	Synchroscope	instrument for detecting whether two moving parts are synchronized
357	Tacheometer	instrument for rapidly measuring survey points on a map
358	Tachistoscope	instrument for rapidly showing images on a screen to test perception
359	Tachograph	instrument for recording speed of rotation
360	Tachometer	instrument for measuring speed of rotation
361	Tascometer	instrument for measuring stress in a structure
362	Tasimeter	instrument for measuring changes in pressure
363	Taximeter	instrument for measuring fee for hired vehicle
364	Telemeter	instrument for measuring strain or distance from observer
365	Telescope	instrument for viewing objects at great distances
366	Telespectroscope	instrument for analysing radiation omitted by distant bodies
367	Telestereoscope	instrument for viewing distant objects stereoscopically
368	Tellurometer	instrument using microwaves to measure distance
369	Tenderometer	instrument for measuring tenderness of fruits and vegetables
370	Tensimeter	instrument for measuring vapour pressure
371	Tensiometer	instrument for measuring tension
372	Thalassometer	instrument for measuring tides
373	Thermograph	instrument for recording changes in temperature
374	Thermometer	instrument for measuring temperature
375	Thermometrograph	instrument for recording changes in temperature
376	Thermoscope	instrument indicating change in temperature
377	Thoracoscope	instrument for viewing the thorax and chest wall
378	Tiltmeter	instrument for measuring tilting of earth's surface
379	Tocodynamometer	instrument for measuring uterine contractions during childbirth
380	Tomograph	instrument for viewing section of an object using X-rays
381	Tonometer	instrument measuring pitch of musical tones
382	Topophone	instrument to determine direction and distance of a fog- horn
383	Torsiograph	instrument for recording torsional vibrations on an object
384	Transmissometer	instrument for measuring transmission of light through a fluid
385	Trechometer	instrument for determining distance travelled; odometer
386	Tremograph	instrument for recording involuntary muscular motion
387	Tribometer	instrument measuring friction
388	Trigonometer	instrument for solving triangles

S.N.	Words	Definitions
389	Trocheameter	instrument counting wheel's revolutions
390	Tromometer	instrument for measuring slight earthquake shocks
391	Tropometer	instrument measuring rotation
392	Turbidimeter	instrument for measuring turbidity of liquids
393	Turgometer	instrument for measuring turgidity
394	Typhlograph	instrument to help the blind write clearly
395	Udometer	instrument for measuring rainfall
396	Ultramicroscope	instrument for viewing extremely small objects
397	Urethroscope	instrument for viewing the interior of the urethra
398	Urinometer	instrument for measuring specific gravity of urine
399	Vaporimeter	instrument for measuring vapour pressure
400	Variometer	instrument for measuring magnetic declination
401	Velocimeter	instrument for measuring velocity
402	Velometer	instrument for measuring speed of air
403	Viameter	instrument for measuring revolutions of a wheel
404	Vibrograph	instrument for recording vibrations
405	Vibrometer	instrument for measuring vibrations
406	Viscometer	instrument for measuring viscosity
407	Visometer	instrument for measuring focal length of the eye
408	Voltameter	instrument for measuring electrical current indirectly
409	Voltmeter	instrument for measuring electrical potential
410	Volumenometer	instrument for measuring volume of a solid
411	Volumeter	instrument for measuring volume of a liquid or gas
412	Wattmeter	instrument for measuring electrical power
413	Wavemeter	instrument for measuring wavelengths
414	Weatherometer	instrument for measuring weather-resisting properties of paint
415	Xanthometer	instrument for measuring colour of sea or lake water
416	Xylometer	instrument measuring specific gravity of wood
417	Zymometer	instrument for measuring fermentation
418	Zymosimeter	instrument for measuring fermentation

UNIT 20

Figures of Speech

A figure of speech or rhetorical figure is a word or phrase that intentionally deviates from ordinary language use in order to produce a rhetorical effect. Figures of speech are traditionally classified into schemes, which vary the ordinary sequence of words, and tropes, where words carry a meaning other than what they ordinarily signify.

Figures of speech come in many varieties. The aim is to use the language inventively to accentuate the effect of what is being said. A few examples follow:

1. "Round and round the rugged rocks the ragged rascal ran" is an example of alliteration, where the consonant *r* is used repeatedly. "Sister Suzy's sewing socks for soldiers" is a particular form of alliteration called sibilance, repeating an s sound. Both are commonly used in poetry.
2. "She would run up the stairs and then a new set of curtains" is a variety of zeugma called a syllepsis. Run up can refer either to a quick ascent or to manufacture. The effect is enhanced by the momentary suggestion, through a pun, that she might be climbing the curtains. The ellipsis or omission of the second use of the verb makes the reader think harder about what is being said.
3. "Painful pride" is an oxymoron, where two contradictory ideas are placed in the same sentence.
3. "An Einstein" is an example of synecdoche, as it uses a particular name to represent a class of people: geniuses.
4. "I had butterflies in my stomach" is a metaphor, referring to a nervous feeling as if there were flying insects in one's stomach.
5. To say "it was like having some butterflies in my stomach" would be a simile, because it uses the word like which is missing in the metaphor.
6. To say "It was like having a butterfly farm in my stomach", "It felt like a butterfly farm in my stomach", or "I was so nervous that I had a butterfly farm in my stomach" could be a hyperbole, because it is exaggerated.
7. "That filthy place was really dirty" is an example of tautology, as there are the two words ('filthy' and 'dirty') having almost the same meaning and are repeated so as to make the text more emphatic.

S.N.	Words	Definition
1	Ballad	A ballad is a form of verse, often a narrative set to music. Ballads derive from the medieval French chanson balladée or ballade, which were originally "dance songs".

S.N.	Words	Definition
2	Concrete	Concrete poems are objects composed of words, letters, colors, and typefaces, in which graphic space plays a central role in both design and meaning. Concrete poets experimented boldly with language, incorporating visual, verbal, kinetic, and sonic elements.
3	Couplet	Two lines of poetry that rhyme
4	Elegy	This is a particular type of lyric that is written to mourn the passing of something or someone.
5	Epic	This is a very, very long poem that tells a story. Epic poems are narrative poems that are long enough to be in a book of their own, rather than an anthology
6	Epigram	These are very short, witty poems that make a pithy pronouncement about something. Usually they are written as a couplet.
7	Epitaphs	Epitaphs are poems about the dead that are written to be on a tombstone; this means they are usually very short.
8	Euphony	Sounds that are very pleasant to the ear. The opposite of cacophony
9	Idyll	A short poem which depicts the rustic life of people
10	Metaphor	A direct comparison between two dissimilar items. She is a monster is a metaphor comparing a girl to a monster.
11	Metonymy	This is a type of metaphor in which a reference point is substituted for the thing to which reference is actually made. The pen is mightier than the sword
12	Novel	A fictitious prose narrative of book length, typically representing character and action with some degree of realism
13	Octave	Eight lines of poetry that have a rhyme scheme
14	Ode	This is a very serious form of the lyric; it is written about a serious topic and is very dignified, if not stately, in tone and style
15	Oxymoron	An oxymoron is a pair of single word opposites placed side by side for dramatic effect. A contradiction in terms. For example, "cold fire" or "sick health" or "jumbo shrimp".
16	Paradox	A large oxymoron. An apparently contradictory statement that, despite the contradiction, has an element of truth in it. Wordsworth's "the child is the father of the man" is a paradoxical statement.

S.N.	Words	Definition
17	Parody	A parody is a mockery of another piece of literature; it copies the style and voice, and sometimes language of the original for comedic effect
18	Pastoral	A pastoral is a poem that is set in the countryside. It often presents an unrealistic, idealistic notion of country living: happy shepherds, lovely shepherdesses, contented flocks of sheep, sunny meadows, and gentle weather
19	Personification	A comparison between a non-human item and a human so that the non-human item is given human characteristics.
20	Quatrain	Four lines of poetry that have a rhyme scheme
21	Satire	A style of writing that has the goal of mocking or scorning an individual, an institution, or society as a whole.
22	Sestet	Six lines of poetry that have a rhyme scheme
23	Simile	A comparison between two dissimilar items using "like" or "as" to make the comparison. The stars are like diamonds in the sky is a simile, comparing stars to diamonds.
24	Sonnet	A fourteen-line lyric written in iambic pentameter

UNIT 21 Words often Confused and Misused

There are certain words and phrases the usage of which generally confuses us. Two words in English language may have the same meaning while their implied meanings may be different. Good writing and speaking depend largely on one's ability to select the right word in the given context. The students are very often confused when they find two or more words for the same meaning. But these words differ in usage. For example, in the English language we have two words for the same meaning, e.g. **Crime** and **Sin**. The word **crime** means 'an offence, for which there is severe punishment by law'. Hence we say : 'The business of the law court is to punish **crime**'. While **sin** means 'an offence against the principle of morality'. So we say " 'Man is liable to **sin**'.

The users of English should be competent to find the correct word or expression that best suits in a particular context. This part of the book will enable the students to learn this efficiency. The following is a list of some commonly confused words. Their meaning and correct usage will be of great help to all the students.

21.1 Confusing Words and Phrases

1. Ago, Before

Ago is used with *time* that is *gone-by*. It is also used with an *action that had happened in the past.*

Examples :

(i) It was seven years ago that my uncle died. (An action taken place in the past)

(ii) I finished my studies long ago. (A time gone by)

Note :

(a) Ago can be used only with simple past tense. It should not be used with past perfect.

Don't Say : I *had* finished my studies long *ago*.

Say : I finished my studies long *ago*.

(b) Ago cannot be used in a sentence that has present or future tense.

Don't Say : He *shall finish* his work three months *ago*.

Say : He *finished* his work three months *ago*.

(c) Ago is used as an adverb of time. It is never used as a conjunction of time or a preposition of time.

Before is used in the following three ways :

(i) Adverb of Time : As an adverb of time, it means, at an earlier rime or in the past or already.

Examples :

(i) You should have told me so before. (At an earlier time)

(ii) That had happened long before. (Already)

(iii) It had been fine the day before. (In the past)

(ii) Conjunction of Time : As a conjunction of time, it means, earlier than the time when.

Examples :

(i) It will be a long time before we finish this work. (Earlier than the time when)

(ii) I shall not do his work before I have taken money.

(iii) Apologise before it is too late.

(iii) As a Preposition of Time : As a preposition of time, it means, earlier than.

Examples :

(i) He will start for Nagpur before Monday next.

(ii) He finished the paper before time.

Before is also used in the place of :

(i) In front of, e.g.,

The devotee knelt *before* the idol and said his prayers.

(ii) Ahead of, e.g.,

Your name comes *before* mine on the list.

(iii) In the presence of, e.g.,

I am prepared to make a statement *before* the judge.

(iv) To be considered, e.g.,

The proposal went *before* the Board.

(v) Rather than, e.g.,

I will kill myself *before* I apologise to him.

2. Already, Yet, All Ready

Already is used especially with the perfect tense of a verb. It suggests the meaning *before now or before a stated or suggested time in the past.*

Examples :

(i) Mr. Mehta had already left when I phoned.

(ii) I have already seen that movie.

Yet is used in the negative and interrogative sentences. It is generally used with past perfect tense. It means, *by this or that time, or until now/then.*

Examples :

(i) I have not paid the house tax yet.

(ii) Has not the postman come yet ?

All ready are two different words. Jointly, they give the sense of *preparedness.*

3. Artist, Artisan, Artiste

Artist means one who is *skilled in a fine art.*

Examples :

(i) A painter is an artist.

(ii) He is a graphic artist.

Artisan means a *craftsman.*

Examples :

(i) A carpenter is an artisan.

(ii) Local artisans displayed handwoven textiles.

Artiste means a *professional entertainer,* e.g., *a singer, a dancer or an actor.*

Examples :

(i) She is a very clever artiste.

(ii) He is a very popular artiste.

4. Avocation, Vocation

Avocation means *subordinate occupation* usually pursued for pleasure.

Examples :

(i) My avocation is gardening.

(ii) What is your avocation ?

Vocation means *calling; regular and habitual pursuit.*

Examples :

(i) His vocation is banking.

(ii) She has found her true vocation.

5. Battle, War, Fight

Battle refers to *combat* especially *between large organised forces at a limited place and time.*

Examples :

(i) A pitched battle was fought between the two armies.

(ii) The first battle of Panipat took place in 1526 A.D.

War refers to hostilities between nations conducted by their armed forces for unlimited period of time and spread over different places.

Examples :

(i) The First World War took place in 1914.

(ii) The Border incident led to war between India and Pakistan.

Fight refers to *combat between two or more persons or parties* and it is *a still shorter result of a quarrel.*

Examples :

(i) There was a regular fight between the merchants, and the labourers.

(ii) There was a fight between Ram and Madan.

6. Deny, Refuse

Deny means *declare untrue* or *non-existent.*

Examples :

(i) He denied the charge.

(ii) He denied the existence of God.

Refuse means *not to accept.*

Examples :

(i) He refused my offer.

(ii) I refused to carry out her orders.

7. Disinterested, Uninterested

Disinterested means *free from bias or prejudice.*

Examples :

(i) A judge must be disinterested in a case.

(ii) A parent should love his children in a disinterested manner.

Uninterested means *lacking in interest.*

Examples :

(i) A judge should not be uninterested in a case.

(ii) I am completely uninterested in politics.

8. Other, Another

Other can be used for persons as well as things. Remember the following points about the use of *other*.

(a) Other means additional to that or those previously mentioned or implied.

Examples :

(i) Mr. Bhatia and three other persons were present at the meeting.

(ii) Other people may look down upon you, but I have all respects for you.

(b) Other is generally followed by a plural of a noun and is used in the affirmative statements.

Example :

Mohan was sitting quietly, though *other* students were making noise.

(c) Other may be followed by a singular noun if it is preceded by some or any.

Examples :

(i) Bring me some other book.

(ii) I have not read any other book on this subject.

(d) Other followed by than means, except.

Examples :

(i) The boy was no other than my friend's son.

(ii) You will not have time to visit places other than those mentioned in the list.

(e) When *other* is preceded by *the*, it means, *the second of the two*.

Example :

Two boys were driving the machine, one was dumb and *the other* was deaf.

Note : The *other day, morning, week,* etc. refer to *recent past.*They cannot be used for the remote past.

Examples :

(i) I saw him in the market the other day.

(ii) The other week was a terrible week for us.

Another can also be used for *persons* and *things*. Please remember the following points about *another*.

(a) Another means, an additional person or thing.

(b) Another is followed by a singular countable noun.

Examples :

(i) Would you like another cup of tea ?

(ii) She will soon have another baby.

Note : *Another* can also be used in the sense of a *different person or thing*.

Example : I don't like this pair, let us choose *another*.

9. Wait, Await

Wait is used as an intransitive verb. It is generally followed by the preposition, *for* or *to*.

Examples :

(i) We are waiting for the rain to stop.

(ii) The principal is waiting to begin.

Await is used as a transitive verb. It means *to wait for some-one* or *something*.

It is not followed by any preposition.

Examples :

(i) A warm welcome awaits the Polish Prime Minister in India.

(ii) I am awaiting your reply.

10. Had better

Had better is used to convey the sense of *ought to do something*. Remember the following facts about *had better* :

(a) Had better is an independent use.

(b) It is never followed by the third form of the verb.

(c) It is always followed by the first form of the verb.

(d) The presence of better in this expression does not mean that it can be used for expressing some comparison.

(e) *Have better* cannot be written in place of *had better*.

Examples :

(i) You had better go home now.

(ii) You had better not wake me in the night.

11. Seem, Appear

Seem means, *have or give the impression or appearance of being or doing something*. Please keep in mind the following facts about *seem*.

(a) Seem cannot be used in progressive tenses.

(b) Seems can be followed by the word like.

Examples :

(i) She seems to be right. (She may or may not be right, but seems right to the speaker)

(ii) Do whatever seems best. (I should do whatever appears to me best)

Note :

(a) It is not possible to use as in place of like with seem.

Don't Say : It *seemed* as a disaster at the time.

Say : It *seemed like* a disaster at the time.

(b) Seemed means, to appear to oneself.

Appear means, *come into view or become visible. Appear is never followed by like.*

Examples :

(i) A comet suddenly appeared in the sky.

(ii) A light appeared at the end of the tunnel.

(iii) The streets appeared deserted.

12. Play, Game

Play refers to the *activity of conducting a game.*

Examples :

The students were *playing* football.

Game refers to the *form of play or sport.*

Example :

Football is an interesting *game.*

13. No more, No longer

No more is used to express *quantity* or *degree.*

Example :

There is *no more* sugar in the store.

No longer is used to express, *time.*

Examples :

(i) He no longer attends late night parties.

(ii) He no longer takes drugs.

14. Famous, Notorious

Famous means, *known to many persons.* It is always used in a *positive sense.*

Examples :

(i) Delhi is famous for its historical monuments.

(ii) Nadini is famous as a poet.

Notorious means, *well-known for some bad quality.*

Examples :

(i) He was notorious as a gambler and rake.

(ii) He is a notorious rogue.

15. Attain, Acquire :

Attain refers to *an achievement by labour or exertion.*

Example :

He *attained* the heights of success by dint of hard work.

Acquire refers to *having something and holding it permanently.*

Example :

He has *acquired* a thorough knowledge of Botany.

16. Vacant, Empty

Vacant means *not filled or occupied.*

Examples :

(i) My house is still vacant.

(ii) I have applied for a vacant post.

Empty means *containing nothing.*

Examples :

(i) I found an empty box in the room.

(ii) This is an empty lorry.

21.2 A List of Some Words Often Confused

1. **Ability** (physical or mental power or skill which can be acquired and developed) : He has an **ability** to be a good carpenter.

   Capacity (power which is usually inborn) : He has a wonderful **capacity** for mathematics.

2. **Allow** (not to refuse) : The principal **allowed** the children to use the calculators in the exams.

   Permit (to agree to some action) : He was **permitted** to join the Computer classes.

3. **Abstain** (from a thing) : He **abstains** from beer and wine.

   Refrain (from an action) : One should **refrain** oneself from abusing.

4. **Answer** (a question is answered): The examiner posed some very difficult questions which the average students could not **answer**.

   Reply (a letter or a charge is replied to) : I immediately **replied** to his urgent letter.

5. **Ancient** (opposite of modern) : There are several good books on the history of **ancient** India in our library.

   Old (opposite of new) : **Old** is gold.

6. **Admit** (give assent to); He **admitted** that smoking is a bad habit.

   Confess (not only to admit something wrong but also to acknowledge guilt) : He **confessed** that he had stolen money.

7. **Astonish** (extreme surprise) : I was **astonished** to see my friend after a long gap of 5 years.

   Surprise (feeling caused by something new or unexpected) : His failure was not a great **surprise**.

   Wonder (Surprise combined with admiration) : The tourists are filled with **wonder** when they look at the Taj Mahal.

8. **Anxious** (feeling anxiety) : I am **anxious** about my son's safety at his non-arrival.

   Eager (strongly desirous): He is **eager** for his success.

9. **Bravery** (ready to face danger, pain and suffering) : He is as **brave** as a lion.

   Courage (lies in the mind and is a lofty sentiment) : He has the **courage** to do what he feels right.

   Daring (pushing forward without hesitation; adventurous): The **daring** of the mountaineers deserves praise.

   Valour (bravery esp. in war) : The Indian warriors were known for their deeds of **valour**.

   Boldness (usually transient) : He showed **boldness** in rescuing a drowning child.

   Audacity (Foolish boldness or imprudence in daring) : His **audacity** provoked me much.

10. **Battle** (fight esp. between organized and armed forces) : The **battle** of Philipi resulted in the death of many valiant Romans.

    War (a series of contests between two armies) : **War** between Troy and Greece was fought for the beautiful Helen.

    Fight (a combat between small number of persons) : Indians **fought** for their freedom.

11. **Beautiful** (used for the beauty of women) : She is known as the most **beautiful** woman of her city.

    Handsome (fine appearance of men) : He is a **handsome** fellow.

12. **Behaviour** (treatment shown towards others) : Tom is liked by all his classmates for his good **behaviour**.

    Conduct (behaviour esp. moral) : A good **conduct** prize was given to a child at school.

    Deportment (manners) : Young ladies used to have lessons in **deportment**.

13. **Blemish** (a stain that spoils the beauty or perfection; some moral defect) : He bears a good character without any **blemish**.

    Defect (fault or imperfection) : There are many **defects** in our system of education.

    Flaw (a defect which is continued such as a crack) : Shakespearean tragic heroes often suffer from some tragic **flaw**.

14. **Begin** (used on all occasions) : The meeting will **begin** at 8 o'clock.

    Start (beginning of a journey, activity etc.) : He decided to **start** a newspaper.

    Commence (used only in formed and official language) : The winter-session of Parliament will **commence** on 2nd December.

15. **Custom** (generally accepted behaviour among members of a social group) : We should not be slave to **customs**.

    Habit (some settled practice esp. that cannot be easily given up) : We should not fall into bad **habits**.

16. **Cite** (mention as an example esp. by quoting from a book to support an arguement etc.) : He **cited** the authority of Abraham Lincoln who stands for his perseverance and hard-working.

Quote (repeat words used by another) : He **quoted** a verse from the Bible.

17. **Contenment** (a state of mind where one does not want more) : **Contenment** is the theme of Pope's famous peom 'Ode On Solitude'

Satisfaction (fulfilment of one's expectations) : Children's success is a great **satisfaction** to their parents.

18. **Ceiling** (under surface or overhead lining of a room) : He has beautified the **ceiling** of his room.

Roof (top covering of a building, tent, bus or car) : The children are playing on the **roof** of their house.

19. **Careful** (paying attention to what one does or says) : One should be **careful** to what one does.

Meticulous (showing great attention to detail) : He is very **meticulous** in his choice of words.

Scrupulous (adherence to what one knows to be true, correct or exact etc.) : The newly appointed Chief Justice is quite **scrupulous** in dispensing justice.

20. **Certain** (something beyond question or doubt) : It is **certain** that two and two make four.

Inevitable (that cannot be avoided) : Death is an **inevitable** end of all the mortals.

Necessary (which has to be done) : Sleep is **necessary** to healt.

21. **Curious** (eager to know) : He is very **curious** about his future.

Inquisitive (inquiring into other people's affairs) : He is **inquisitive** about his neighbour's income.

22. **Charitable** (helping the poor) : The **charitable** institutions help the poor and helpless persons.

Benevolent (kind and helpful) : He is **benevolent** towards all the needy people.

Philanthropic (lover of mankind who gives money on large scale) : His **philanthropic** attitude motivates him to donate large amounts of money for the orphans, widows, disabled and the poor.

Altruistic (unselfish) : He is **altruistic** in serving mankind.

23. **Common** (belong to, used or done by all or nearly all members of a group or society) : In multi-lingual countries, English is a **common** language.

Ordinary (usual or customary) : She went to the party in **ordinary** dress.

Vulgar (ordinary but coarse) : He delivered a speech in the **vulgar** tongue.

Familiar (acquainted) : I am not very **familiar** with the modern mathematics.

24. **Communicate** (pass on news, information, feeling etc.) : Often the children are not able to **communicate** with their parents.

Impart (pass on a secret or news) : I have nothing to **impart** to you today.

25. **Contagious** (disease spreading by contact) : Small-pox is a **contagious** disease.

Infectious (disease spreading through bacteria carried in the atmosphere or in water) : Typhoid is an **infectious** disease.

26. **Correct** (freedom from error) : We learnt the **correct** pronunciation.

Accurate (careful and exact) : His knowledge of phonology is **accurate** to certain extent.

Right (something, just and true) : We should know the difference between **right** and wrong.

27. **Deny** (disown or refuse to acknowledge) : I **denied** the charge of having any hand in the M.P.'s murder.

Refuse (say 'no' to a request or offer) : Her **refused** to help me.

28. **Explore** (inquire into or examine a country etc. by going through it) : The navigators **explored** the ocean's depth for a good knowledge of it.

Discover (find our something that existed before) : Columbus **discovered** America.

Invent (create or design something not existing before) : Graham Bell **invented** ine telephone.

29. **Declare** (make known clearly or formally) : The President of the athletic association **declared** the athletic meet open.

Announce (make known for the time) : His engagement with Sony is ultimately **announced**.

Advertise (make known to people by printing notices in newspapers) : The manufactures **advertise** their goods in the leading newspapers in order to grip the market.

Proclaim (make known publicly by some formal declaration) : He **proclaimed** his nephew his legal heir.

Promulgate (announce officially a decree or a law) : A nee law is **promulgated** by the new government.

30. **Doubt** (incline to disbelieve): Please, don't **doubt** my word.

Suspect (have an idea or feeling [concerning the possibility or likelihood]) : I **suspect** that he is a liar.

31. **Difficulty** (quality of being difficult) : Do you have any **difficulty** in understanding the lectures in History ?

Hardship (severe suffering) : The soldiers bear **hardship** during a war without complaining.

32. **Disaster** (great or sudden misfortune) : His over-confidence had led him to **disaster**.

Catastrophe (final and unhappy event that brings a change) : His failure in the examination was a **catastrophe.**

33. **Desire** (long for; want something earnestly) : I **desire** to possess immense wealth.

Want (wish for something lacking or absent): I don't **want** such friends who meddle in my affairs.

Need (need something that is lacking and necessary) : We **need** nutritive food for good health.

Wish (have a desire that cannot be fulfilled) : I **wish** I were a bird.

34. **Distress** (subjected to strain, anxiety or unhappiness): Brutus was much **distressed** to hear the news of his wife's death.

Suffering (subjected to pain, loss, grief, punishment, wrong etc.) I have been **suffering** from fever for the last two days.

Agonize (subjected to unbearable physical or mental anguish) : She was greatly **agonized** at her child's sufferings.

35. **Envy** (feeling of ill-will at another's better fortune) : Her friend was filled with **envy** at her success. **Jealousy** (feeling of ill-will because of possible or actual loss of rights or love) : Othello's **jealousy** made him to strangle his beloved wife.

36. **Error** (deviation from correct or accurate result) : Brutus suffered on account of this **error** of judgement.

Mistake (wrong idea or act) : We all make **mistakes** occasionally.

Blunder (stupid or careless mistake) : The student was punished for committing **blunders**.

Lapse (slight error in speech or behaviour) : He is criticized for his **lapse** from virtue.

37. **Expect** (think or believe that something will come or happen) : I **expect** that she will come today.

Hope (expectation of something desired) : I live in **hopes** of better times.

38. **Event** (happening usually something important or memorable) : The last two years in India have been full of **events**.

Incident (event but of less importance) : The **incidents** of theft have now become common in the metropolitan cities.

Accident (happening unfortunate and undesirable) : Many passengers died in a recent terrible railway **accident.**

39. **False** (untrue or incorrect): He is **false** to his word.

Wrong (not morally right) : Two **wrongs** don't make a right.

40. **Forbid** (not allow something to be used or done): God **forbade** Adam to eat the apple of the tree of knowledge.

Prohibit (forbid an action by rules or regulations): In schools and colleges, smoking is strictly **prohibited**.

Ban (order with authority that something must not be done) : The censor-board has **banned** the latest multi-starred film.

41. **Freedom** (without restraint) : Children should be granted the **freedom** of speech.

Liberty (free from slavery, imprisonment or despotic control) : Brutus killed Caesar in order to grant **liberty** to the Romans.

42. **Famous** (used in good sense) : Michael Jackson has become **famous** as a pop-singer.

Notorious (used in bad sense) : A **notorious** dacoit was killed by the police in a fake encounter.

Renowned (heaving dignified kind of reputation) : Shakespeare is a **renowned** English dramatist.

43. **House** (building for human habitation) : The government provides loans for building a new **house**.

Home (native land of oneself or one's ancestors) : Cement and bricks cannot make houses the **homes**.

44. **Humble** (having a modest opinion of oneself) : He is aware of his **humble** birth.

Meek (mild and patient or somewhat weak) : She is as **meek** as a lamp.

Modest (not showing too high opinion of one's abilities) : He is **modest** about his achievements and possession.

45. **Idle** (doing no work due to certain circumstances) : Owing to the strike, the machines in the factory are **idle**.

    Lazy (doing no work due to habit) : He is a **lazy** fellow.

46. **Infer** (conclude, reach to an opinion) : I **inferred** from your remarks that he was a fool.

    Imply (give or make a suggestion) : His words **implied** that he was not telling the truth.

47. **Limit** (confine within limits; restrict) : We must **limit** our needs in proportion to our means.

    Circumscribe (marking the limit which intensifies the suggestion of restraint) : He is asked to **circumscribe** his interests.

    Confine (emphasize the limits which cannot be passed) : He is **confined** to bed by illness.

48. **Offend** (do wrong) : Loud noise **offends** the ears.

    Outrage (offended beyond endurance) : He was **outraged** at his misbehaviour.

    Affront (insult) : The son **affronted** the father.

49. **Pleasure** (sensuous enjoyment): Do me the **pleasure** of dining with me.

    Delight (great pleasure) : The romantic poets find **delight** in the lap of nature.
    Bliss (perfect joy; a state of being in heaven) : Serving mankind is a **bliss** to the virtuous souls.

50. **Place** (to put) : Please **place** the lamp on the table.

    Keep (maintain in order) : **Keep** the books properly in the shelf.

51. **Perform** (do a piece of work one is ordered to do) : One should **perform** one's duties properly.

    Execute (carry plan, command, law etc.) The proper **execution** of the law is more important than its formation.

    Accomplish (complete a task or anything) : He **accomplished** his aims successfully.

52. **Power** (faculty of body or mind) : He is a man of great intellectual **power**.

    Force (power of body or mind which accelerates the action) : Christianity has been a **force** for good in the lives of many people.

    Energy (capacity to do things and get things done) : He has so much of **energy** that he can do the work of three men.

    Strength (quality of being strong) : God is our real **strength**. **Might** (physical strength) : **Might** is right.

53. **Possible** (that can exist or happen) : Frost may be **possible** even in the month of May.

    Probable (That may be expected to happen or prove true) : Frost may be possible though not **probable** in the month of May.

54. **Praise** (commend the merit of) : He is **praised** for his courage.

    Admire (regard with pleased surprise) : The beautiful girl is **admired** by all.

55. **Rob** (take property from a place unlawfully and often by force) : She was **robbed** of her ring.

    Steal (take property secretly without right) : My watch had been **stolen**.

56. **Remark** (give casual expression) : He **remarked** that he had become very naughty.

    Comment (give some opinion) : I am not going to **comment** on this book.

57. **Recollect** (call back to the mind) : She **recollects** her childhood days.

Remember (remember something after a lapse) : I could not **remember** his name.

58. **Rescue** (set free) : He **rescued** a child from drowning.

Redeem (deliver from sin or set free by payment) : The terrorists at last **redeemed** the prisoners on certain conditions.

Reclaim (reform a person) : He **reclaimed** him from vice.

59. **Sober** (sane or tranquil) : He is a **sober** man.

Solemn (serious and awe inspiring) : There was a **solemn** silence in the graveyard.

Serious (not given to pleasure seeking) : One should be **serious** to one's work.

60. **Spectator** (on looker esp. of a show or game) : The **spectators** took a lot of interest in the football match.

Beholder (who takes notice of something unusual) : The **beholder** was enchanted by her beauty.

Observer (one who watches carefully) : He was sent there as an **observer**.

61. **Substitute** (acting for or serving for another) : Tea can be a good **substitute** for coffee.

Replace (put back in its place; take the place of) : Nothing can **replace** a mother's love and care.

62. **Say** (utter) : He **said** that the name of his sister was Jane.

Speak (hold conversation) : I request you to **speak** slowly.

Talk (converse) : They were **talking** about their business.

Tell (give detailed account of) : He **told** me about his future plans.

63. **Sight** (anything seen) : It is a beautiful **sight** for the pets.

Scenery (the view of a landscape) : The beautiful **scenery** of Kashmir fascinates the visitors.

Scene (description of an incident) : The historian has truly described the **scene** of a great battle.

64. **Seem** (appear to be) : What **seems** easy is often very difficult. **Appear** (become visible) : The stars **appear** in the cloudless sky.

65. **Shade** (comparative darkness caused by cutting off the direct rays of light) : The trees give a pleasant **shade** to the weary travellers.

Shadow (area or shade; dark shade thrown on the ground, a wall, floor etc.) The earth's **shadow** when falls on the moon causes lunar eclipse.

66. **See** (use the power of sight without effort) : A blind-man cannot **see** anything.

Look (try to see) : I **looked** at the picture but could not find anything beautiful in it.

Watch (see closely) : The boy was **watching** the television.

67. **Teach** (give instruction to, cause to know or be able to do) : He **taught** me French.

Educate (give intellectual and moral training) : To Wordsworth, Nature can **educate** man.

Train (give teaching and practice to someone in order to bring to a desired standard of behaviour) : The children should be **trained** to be good citizens.

68. **Trifle** (thing, event esp. of little value or importance) : It is silly to quarrel over **trifles**.

Trivial (something trifling and lacking seriousness) : Their objectives for future plans were quite **trivial**.

69. **Understand** (know the meaning of) : He didn't **understand** French.

Comprehend (understand fully; grasping with the mind) : He **comprehends** the Aristotelian theory of imitation.

Appreciate (understand and enjoy) : We can't **appreciate** Wordsworth's poems unless we understand his love of nature. **70. Unite** (join) : **United** we stand, divided we fall.

Combine (join together) : We can't always **combine** work with pleasure.

Co-operate (work or act together in order to bring about a result) : A country connot progress unless its people **co-operate** with the government.

71. **Use** (employ for a purpose) : A knife is **used** to cut bread. Employ (give work to, usually for payment) : He is **employed** in a school.

Utilize (use a thing for some profit) : Life can be a bed of roses if we learn to **utilize** the opportunities we get in our life.

72. **Vigorous** (strong, energetic) : He delivered a **vigorous** speech.

Strenuous (using or needing great effort) : He remains busy from dawn to dusk and leads a very **strenuous** life.

73. **Vacant** (not occupied by anyone) : I have applied for a **vacant** post in the Royal Hotel.

Empty (having nothing inside) : The famous big house on the Mall Road is now **empty**.

74. **Wise** (ability of sound judgement) : Only **wise** man can see the things in advance.

Sage (having the wisdom of experience [often ironic]) He behaves just like a **sage**.

Prudent (acting only after careful planning) : A **prudent** man takes up a project after careful forethoughts.

75. **Witty** (things that are brilliantly or sparkingly amusing) : A **witty** comment always appeals to the mind.

Humorous (having a sense of humour) : Mark Twain is a famous **humorous** writer.

Ludicrous (ridiculous; exciting or deserving derision) : His comments are generally **ludicrous**.

Farcical (extremely ludicrous of futile) : His behaviour was **farcical**.

76. **Womanly** (befitting a woman) : She possesses all **womanly** qualities.

Womanish (weak; like women) : The boys of **womanish** qualities cannot stand firm before dangers.

UNIT 22 Foreign Words with their Meanings

Given below are a number of foreign words with their meanings.

S.N.	Words	*Origin*	Definitions
1	ab initio	*Latin*	from the beginning (the agreement should be declared void ab initio)
2	ad hoc	*Latin*	made or done suddenly for a particular purpose
3	ad infinitum	*Latin*	for ever; again and again
4	ad interim	*Latin*	for the meantime
5	ad nauseam	*Latin*	to a tiresomely excessive degree
6	a fortiori	*Latin*	more conclusively
7	annus mirabilis	*Latin*	a remarkable or auspicious year
8	a posteriori	*Latin*	based on reasoning from known facts or past events rather than on assumptions or predictions
9	a priori	*Latin*	based on deduction rather than experience
10	bona fide	*Latin*	genuine; real
11	carpe diem	*Latin*	make the most of the present time
12	caveat emptor	*Latin*	the buyer is responsible for checking the quality of goods before purchasing them
13	compos mentis	*Latin*	sane; in full control of one's mind
14	cui bono?	*Latin*	who stands to gain?
15	de facto	*Latin*	in fact, whether by right or not
16	dei gratia	*Latin*	by the grace of God
17	de jure	*Latin*	rightful; by right
18	deo gratias	*Latin*	thanks be to God
19	deo volente	*Latin*	God willing
20	de profundis	*Latin*	expressing one's deepest feelings
21	deus ex machina	*Latin*	an unexpected event that saves an apparently hopeless situation
22	dramatis personae	*Latin*	the characters in a play
23	ex gratia	*Latin*	(with reference to payment) done from a sense of moral obligation rather than because of any legal requirement

S.N.	Words	Origin	Definitions
24	ex officio	*Latin*	by virtue of one's position or status
25	in absentia	*Latin*	while not present
26	in camera	*Latin*	in private
27	in extremis	*Latin*	in an extremely difficult situation; at the point of death
28	in loco parentis	*Latin*	in the place of a parent
29	in medias res	*Latin*	in or into the middle of things
30	in propria persona	*Latin*	in his or her own person
31	in situ	*Latin*	in the original or appropriate position
32	inter alia	*Latin*	among other things
33	in toto	*Latin*	as a whole
34	ipso facto	*Latin*	by that very fact or act
35	locum tenens	*Latin*	a temporary deputy or stand-in
36	locus classicus	*latin*	the best known or most authoritative passage on a subject
37	magnum opus	*latin*	the most important work of an artist, writer, etc.
38	mea culpa	*latin*	an acknowledgement that something is one's fault
39	memento mori	*latin*	something kept as a reminder that death is inevitable
40	modus operandi	*latin*	a way of doing something
41	modus vivendi	*latin*	an arrangement that allows conflicting parties to coexist peacefully
42	ne plus ultra	*latin*	the best example of something
43	nil desperandum	*latin*	do not despair
44	nolens volens	*latin*	whether one wants or likes something or not
45	non sequitur	*latin*	a conclusion or statement that does not logically follow from the previous statement
46	per annum	*latin*	for each year
47	per capita	*latin*	for each person
48	per se	*latin*	by or in itself or themselves
49	persona non grata	*latin*	a person who is not welcome somewhere
50	prima facie	*latin*	accepted as so until proved otherwise
51	primus inter pares	*latin*	the senior or representative member of a group
52	pro rata	*latin*	proportional; proportionally
53	proxime accessit	*latin*	the person who comes second in an examination or is runner-up for an award
54	quid pro quo	*latin*	a favour or advantage given in return for something

S.N.	Words	*Origin*	Definitions
55	reductio ad absurdum	*latin*	a method of disproving a premise by showing that its logical conclusion is absurd
56	sine die	*latin*	no appointed date for resumption
57	sine qua non	*latin*	a thing that is absolutely essential
58	sub judice	*latin*	being considered by a court of law and therefore not to be publicly discussed elsewhere
59	sub rosa	*latin*	happening or done in secret
60	sui generis	*latin*	constituting a class alone : unique, peculiar.
61	terra firma	*latin*	dry land; the ground
62	terra incognita	*latin*	unknown territory
63	via media	*latin*	a compromise
64	victor ludorum	*latin*	the overall champion in a sports competition
65	vox populi	*latin*	public opinion
66	à cappella	*latin*	sung without instrumental accompaniment
67	al dente	*latin*	(of food, typically pasta) cooked so as to be still firm when bitten
68	alfresco	*latin*	in the open air
69	cognoscenti	*latin*	people who are well informed about something
70	cosa nostra	*latin*	a US criminal organization related to the Mafia
71	dolce far niente	*latin*	pleasant idleness
72	dolce vita	*Italain*	a life of pleasure and luxury
73	papabile	*Italain*	worthy or eligible to be elected pope
74	pococurante	*Italain*	careless or nonchalant
75	sotto voce	*Italain*	in a quiet voice
76	blitzkrieg	*German*	an intense, violent military campaign intended to bring about a swift victory
77	doppelgänger	*German*	an apparition or double of a living person
78	katzenjammer	*German*	a hangover or a severe headache accompanying a hangover
79	unheimlich	*German*	uncanny or weird
80	verboten	*German*	forbidden
81	zeitgeist	*German*	the characteristic spirit or mood of a particular historical period

S.N.	Words	Origin	Definitions
82	à deux	*French*	for or involving two people
83	agent provocateur	*French*	a person who tempts a suspected criminal to commit a crime so that they can be caught and convicted
84	à huis clos	*French*	in private
85	amour propre	*French*	self-respect
86	au courant	*French*	well informed; up to date
87	au fait	*French*	having a good or detailed knowledge
88	au fond	*French*	basically; in essence
89	au naturel	*French*	in the most simple or natural way
90	beau geste	*French*	a noble and generous act
91	beau idéal	*French*	the highest standard of excellence
92	beau monde	*French*	fashionable society
93	beaux arts	*French*	the fine arts
94	bête noire	*French*	a person or thing one particularly dislikes
95	belles-lettres	*French*	literary works written and read for their elegant style
96	billet-doux	*French*	a love letter
97	bon mot	*French*	a clever or witty remark
98	bon vivant	*French*	a person with a sociable and luxurious lifestyle
99	brasserie	*French*	an informal or inexpensive restaurant
100	carte blanche	*French*	complete freedom to act as one wishes
101	cause célèbre	*French*	a controversial issue attracting much public attention
102	c'est la guerre	*French*	used as an expression of resigned acceptance
103	chacun à son gout	*French*	everyone to their own taste
104	chef-d'œuvre	*French*	a masterpiece
105	cherchez la femme	*French*	there is certain to be a woman at the bottom of a problem or mystery
106	comme il faut	*French*	correct in behaviour or etiquette
107	cordon sanitaire	*French*	a guarded l0ine placed around an area infected by disease to prevent anyone from leaving
108	coup de foudre	*French*	love at first sight
109	coup de grâce	*French*	a blow by which a mortally wounded person or thing is mercifully killed
110	coup de main	*French*	a sudden surprise attack

S.N.	Words	*Origin*	Definitions
111	coup d'état	*French*	a sudden violent seizure of power
112	cri de cœur	*French*	a passionate appeal or protest
113	déjà vu	*French*	the sense of having experienced the present situation before
114	de nos jours	*French*	contemporary
115	de rigueur	*French*	obligatory; required by etiquette or current fashion
116	dernier cri	*French*	the very latest fashion
117	de trop	*French*	not wanted; superfluous
118	double entendre	*French*	a word or phrase with two possible interpretations
119	embarras de richesse	*French*	more options or resources than one knows what to do with
120	éminence grise	*French*	a person who has power or influence without holding an official position
121	en famille	*French*	with one's family; in an informal way
122	enfant terrible	*French*	a person whose behaviour is unconventional or controversial
123	en masse	*French*	all together
124	en passant	*French*	by the way
125	entente cordiale	*French*	a friendly understanding between states
126	entre nous	*French*	between ourselves
127	esprit de corps	*French*	a feeling of pride and loyalty uniting the members of a group
128	fait accompli	*French*	a thing that has been done or decided and cannot now be altered
129	faute de mieux	*French*	for want of a better alternative
130	faux pas	*French*	an embarrassing blunder or indiscretion
131	femme fatale	*French*	a seductive woman
132	fête champêtre	*French*	an outdoor entertainment; a garden party
133	fin de siècle	*French*	relating to the end of a century
134	force majeure	*French*	superior strength
135	folie de grandeur	*French*	delusions of grandeur
136	gîte	*French*	a small furnished holiday house in France
137	grande dame	*French*	a woman who is influential within a particular sphere

S.N.	Words	*Origin*	Definitions
138	haute couture	*French*	the designing and making of clothes by leading fashion houses
139	haute cuisine	*French*	high-quality cooking
140	haut monde	*French*	fashionable society
141	hors de combat	*French*	out of action due to injury or damage
142	idee fixe	*French*	an obsession
143	je ne sais quoi	*French*	a quality that is hard to describe
144	jeu d'esprit	*French*	a light-hearted display of wit
145	jeunesse dorée	*French*	wealthy, fashionable young people
146	joie de vivre	*French*	exuberant enjoyment of life
147	laissez-faire	*French*	a non-interventionist policy
148	manqué	*French*	having failed to become what one might have been
149	ménage à trois	*French*	an arrangement in which a married couple and the lover of one of them live together
150	mot juste	*French*	the exactly right word or phrasing
151	noblesse oblige	*French*	privilege entails responsibility
152	nouveau riche	*French*	people who have recently become rich and who display their wealth ostentatiously
153	objet d'art	*French*	a small decorative or artistic object
154	on dit	*French*	a piece of gossip
155	par excellence	*French*	better or more than all others of the same kind
156	parti pris	*French*	a preconceived view; a bias
157	pièce de résistance	*French*	the most important or impressive item
158	pied-à-terre	*French*	a small flat or house kept for occasional use
159	pis aller	*French*	a last resort
160	plat du jour	*French*	a special dish prepared by a restaurant on a particular day
161	plus ça change	*French*	used to express resigned acknowledgement of the fact that certain things never change
162	raison d'être	*French*	the most important reason for someone or something's existence
163	roman-à-clef	*French*	a novel in which real people or events appear with invented names

S.N.	Words	*Origin*	Definitions
164	sangfroid	*French*	the ability to stay calm in difficult circumstances
165	savoir faire	*French*	the ability to act appropriately in social situations
166	soi-disant	*French*	self-styled; so-called
167	table d'hôte	*French*	a restaurant meal offered at a fixed price, with few if any choices
168	tant mieux	*French*	so much the better
169	tant pis	*French*	so much the worse; too bad
170	tête-à-tête	*French*	a private conversation
171	tour de force	*French*	a thing accomplished with great skill
172	tout de suite	*French*	right now, immediately, or straightaway
173	vis-à-vis	*French*	in relation to someone or something (He spoke to the Sports Minister vis-à-vis the arrangement for the World Cup.)

The Hindu Vocabulary (1000 Words)

1000 words from The Hindu Newspapers given with meanings, synonyms and their usages .

1. **Ambivalent (Adjective)**

   Meaning: having mixed feelings or contradictory ideas about something or someone.

   Synonyms: equivocal, uncertain, unsure, doubtful, indecisive, inconclusive, irresolute

   Usage: Some loved her, some hated her, few were ambivalent about her.

2. **Forsake (Verb)**

   Meaning: abandon or leave.

   Synonyms: abandon, desert, leave, quit, depart from, leave behind

   Usage: She forsook her child, giving him up for adoption.

3. **Impudent (Adjective)**

   Meaning: not showing due respect for another person; impertinent.

   Synonyms: impertinent, insolent, cheeky, audacious, brazen

   Usage: He could have strangled this impudent upstart.

4. **Inept (Adjective)**

   Meaning: having or showing no skill; clumsy.

   Synonyms: incompetent, unskillful, unskilled, inexpert, amateurish

   Usage: My attempts at baking were inept but I fumbled on.

5. **Novice (Verb)**

   Meaning: a person new to and inexperienced in a job or situation.

   Synonyms: beginner, learner, inexperienced person

   Usage: He was a complete novice in foreign affairs.

6. **Salient (Adjective)**

   Meaning: most noticeable or important.

   Synonyms: important, main, principal, major, chief, primary, notable

   Usage: The salient points stuck out clearly in her mind.

7. **Umbrage (Noun)**

   Meaning: offence or annoyance.

   Synonyms: take offence, be offended, take exception, bridle, take something personally

   Usage: She took umbrage at his remarks.

8. **Serendipity (Noun)**

   Meaning: the occurrence and development of events by chance in a happy or beneficial way.

   Synonyms: chance, happy chance, accident, happy accident, fluke

   Usage: Technical innovation may be the result of pure serendipity.

9. **Quaint (Adjective)**

   Meaning: attractively unusual or old-fashioned.

   Synonyms: picturesque, charming, sweet, attractive, pleasantly old-fashioned

   Usage: Narrow streets lead to a quaint bridge over the river.

10. **Truculent (Adjective)**

    Meaning: eager or quick to argue or fight;

aggressively defiant.

Synonyms: defiant, aggressive, antagonistic, belligerent, pugnacious, bellicose

Usage: The truculent attitude of farmers to cheaper imports.

11. Intractable (adjective)

Meaning: hard to control or deal with.

Synonyms: unmanageable, uncontrollable, ungovernable, out of control.

Usage: Their problems have become more acute and intractable.

12. Delineate (Verb)

Meaning: describe or portray (something) precisely.

Synonyms: describe, set forth, set out, present, outline, depict, portray.

Usage: The law should delineate and prohibit behaviour which is socially abhorrent.

13. Ascetic (adjective)

Meaning: characterized by severe self-discipline and abstention from all forms of indulgence, typically for religious reasons.

Synonyms: austere, self-denying, abstinent, abstemious.

Usage: An ascetic life of prayer, fasting, and manual labour.

14. Daunt (verb)

Meaning: make (someone) feel intimidated or apprehensive.

Synonyms: intimidate, abash, take aback, shake, ruffle, throw.

Usage: Some people are daunted by technology.

15. Idyllic (adjective)

Meaning: like an idyll; extremely happy, peaceful, or picturesque.

Synonyms: perfect, ideal, idealized, wonderful, blissful.

Usage: An attractive hotel in an idyllic setting.

16. Burgeon (verb)

Meaning: begin to grow or increase rapidly; flourish.

Synonyms: grow rapidly, increase rapidly/exponentially, expand.

Usage: Tourism has burgeoned over the last ten years.

17. Anomalous (adjective)

Meaning: deviating from what is standard, normal, or expected.

Synonyms: abnormal, atypical, non-typical, irregular.

Usage: Nuclear weapons testing may have been responsible for the anomalous weather conditions.

18. Friable (adjective)

Meaning: easily crumbled.

Synonyms: crumbly, easily crumbled, powdery, dusty.

Usage: The soil was friable between her fingers.

19. Protean (adjective)

Meaning: tending or able to change frequently or easily.

Synonyms: ever-changing, variable, changeable, mutable, kaleidoscopic.

Usage: The diverse and protean nature of mental disorders.

20. Recondite (adjective)

Meaning: (of a subject or knowledge) little known; abstruse.

Synonyms: obscure, abstruse, arcane, esoteric, little known.

Usage: The book is full of recondite information.

21. Boisterous (adjective)

Meaning: noisy, energetic, and cheerful

Synonyms: lively, active, animated, exuberant, spirited, bouncy, frisky

Usage: A group of boisterous lads.

22. Inveigle (verb)

Meaning: persuade (someone) to do something by means of deception or flattery

Synonyms: cajole, wheedle, coax, persuade, convince, talk

Usage: He was attempting to inveigle them into doing his will.

23. Sodden (adjective)

Meaning: saturated with liquid, especially water; soaked through.

Synonyms: soaking, soaking wet, soaked, soaked through, wet through

Usage: His clothes were sodden.

24. Perfidious (adjective)

Meaning: deceitful and untrustworthy

Synonyms: treacherous, duplicitous, deceitful, disloyal, faithless

Usage: It is highly risk to hire a perfidious labour.

25. Conundrum (noun)

Meaning: a confusing and difficult problem or question.

Synonyms: problem, difficult question, vexed question, difficulty

Usage: One of the most difficult conundrums for the experts.

26. Denouement (noun)

Meaning: The final part of a play, film, or narrative in which the strands of the plot are drawn together and matters are explained or resolved

Synonyms: final scene, final act, last act

Usage: The film's denouement was unsatisfying and ambiguous.

27. Stolid (adjective)

Meaning: calm, dependable, and showing little emotion or animation

Synonyms: impassive, phlegmatic, unemotional, calm

Usage: A stolid, slow-speaking man.

28. Dissemble (verb)

Meaning: conceal or disguise one's true feelings or beliefs

Synonyms: dissimulate, pretend, deceive, feign, act

Usage: An honest, sincere person with no need to dissemble.

29. Dilatory (adjective)

Meaning: slow to act

Synonyms: slow, unhurried, tardy, unpunctual, lax, slack

Usage: They were dilatory in providing the researchers with information.

30. Garner (Verb)

Meaning: gather or collect (something, especially information or approval)

Synonyms: accumulate, amass, assemble; store

Usage: The police struggled to garner sufficient evidence.

31. Contentious (adjective)

Meaning: causing or likely to cause an argument; controversial.

Synonyms: controversial, disputable, debatable, and disputed

Usage: The contentious issue of abortion.

32. Antipathy (noun)

Meaning: a deep-seated feeling of aversion.

Synonyms: hostility, antagonism, animosity, aversion, animus

Usage: His fundamental antipathy to capitalism.

33. Countenance (noun)

Meaning: a person's face or facial expression

Synonyms: face, features, physiognomy,

profile; facial expression

Usage: His impenetrable eyes and inscrutable countenance give little away.

34. Dogmatic (adjective)

Meaning: inclined to lay down principles as undeniably true

Synonyms: opinionated, peremptory, assertive, imperative, insistent

Usage: She was not tempted to be dogmatic about what she believed.

35. Apropos (adjective)

Meaning: very appropriate to a particular situation

Synonyms: appropriate, pertinent, relevant, apposite, apt

Usage: The song feels apropos to a midnight jaunt.

36. Raffish (adjective)

Meaning: unconventional and slightly disreputable, especially in an attractive way

Synonyms: rakish, jaunty, dapper, dashing, sporty, flashy; unconventional

Usage: His cosmopolitan, raffish air.

37. Vituperate (verb)

Meaning: blame or insult (someone) in strong or violent language

Synonyms: revile, rail against, inveigh against, fulminate against

Usage: He vituperated against all presidents with equal gusto.

38. Diffidence (noun)

Meaning: modesty or shyness resulting from a lack of self-confidence

Synonyms: shyness, bashfulness, unassertiveness, modesty, modestness

Usage: He regretted his diffidence and awkwardness in large groups.

39. Fulminate (verb)

Meaning: express vehement protest

Synonyms: protest, rail, rage, rant, thunder, storm, declaim, inveigh

Usage: Ministers and preachers fulminated against the new curriculum.

40. Assay (noun)

Meaning: the testing of a metal or ore to determine its ingredients and quality

Synonyms: evaluation, assessment, analysis, examination, test

Usage: New plate was taxed when it was brought for assay.

41. Turbid (adjective)

Meaning: (of a liquid) cloudy, opaque, or thick with suspended matter

Synonyms: murky, muddy, thick; opaque, cloudy

Usage: The turbid waters of the river.

42. Erudite (adjective)

Meaning: having or showing great knowledge or learning.

Synonyms: learned, scholarly, well educated, knowledgeable

Usage: He was so erudite that only men who were his equals in scholarship could understand him.

43. Saturnine (adjective)

Meaning: (of a person or their manner) gloomy.

Synonyms: sombre, melancholy, melancholic, moody, miserable

Usage: He was a rather saturnine individual who never spoke an unnecessary word.

44. Abeyance (noun)

Meaning: a state of temporary disuse or suspension.

Synonyms: suspension, a state of suspension,

a state of dormancy, a state of latency, a state of uncertainty

Usage: The project was left in abeyance for the time being.

45. Diaphanous (adjective)

Meaning: (especially of fabric) light, delicate, and translucent.

Synonyms: sheer, fine, ultra-fine, delicate, light, lightweight, thin

Usage: She wore a diaphanous dress of pale gold.

46. Epitome (noun)

Meaning: a person or thing that is a perfect example of a particular quality or type.

Synonyms: personification, embodiment, incarnation, paragon; essence

Usage: She looked the epitome of elegance and good taste.

47. Castigate (verb)

Meaning: reprimand (someone) severely.

Synonyms: reprimand, rebuke, admonish, chastise, chide, upbraid, reprove

Usage: He was castigated for not setting a good example.

48. Apprehension (noun)

Meaning: anxiety or fear that something bad or unpleasant will happen.

Synonyms: alarm, worry, uneasiness, unease, nervousness, **Usage:** He had been filled with apprehension at having to report his failure.

49. Approbation (noun)

Meaning: approval or praise.

Synonyms: acceptance, assent, endorsement, encouragement

Usage: He yearned for popular approbation.

50. Refractory (adjective)

Meaning: stubborn or unmanageable.

Synonyms: obstinate, mulish, bull-headed, intractable

Usage: The refractory students spend a great deal of time in the detention room.

51. Pique (noun)

Meaning: A feeling of irritation or resentment resulting from a slight, especially to one's pride.

Synonyms: irritation, annoyance, resentment, anger, displeasure

Usage: He left in a fit of pique.

52. Turgid (adjective)

Meaning: Swollen and distended or congested.

Synonyms: swollen, congested; in spate, in flood

Usage: A turgid and fast-moving river.

53. Multifarious (adjective)

Meaning: Having many varied parts or aspects.

Synonyms: diverse, many, numerous, various, varied

Usage: The multifarious local and ethnic traditions that are found in the USA.

54. Torpor (noun)

Meaning: A state of physical or mental inactivity; lethargy.

Synonyms: lethargy, torpidity, sluggishness, inertia, inertness, inactivity

Usage: He spent most of the journey in a state of torpor.

55. Audacious (adjective)

Meaning: Showing a willingness to take surprisingly bold risks.

Synonyms: bold, daring, fearless, intrepid, brave, unafraid

Usage: The audience were left gasping at his audacious exploits.

56. Tenacity (noun)

Meaning: The quality or fact of being able to grip something firmly; grip.

Synonyms: persistence, pertinacity, determination, perseverance, doggedness

Usage: The tenacity with which he stuck to his story.

57. Apostate (noun)

Meaning: A person who renounces a religious or political belief or principle.

Synonyms: dissenter, heretic, nonconformist; defector, deserter

Usage: After

50 years as an apostate, he returned to the faith.

58. Discomfit (verb)

Meaning: Make (someone) feel uneasy or embarrassed.

Synonyms: embarrass, make uncomfortable, make uneasy, abash

Usage: He was not noticeably discomfited by her tone.

59. Laconic (adjective)

Meaning: (of a person, speech, or style of writing) using very few words.

Synonyms: brief, concise, terse, succinct, short, economical, elliptical

Usage: His laconic reply suggested a lack of interest in the topic.

60. Ossify (verb)

Meaning: Turn into bone or bony tissue.

Synonyms: turn into bone, become bony, harden, solidify, stiffen

Usage: These cartilages may ossify.

61. Accretion (noun)

Meaning: growth or increase by the gradual accumulation of additional layers or matter.

Synonyms: Accumulation, collecting, gathering, amassing, cumulation.

Usage: The accretion of sediments in coastal mangroves.

62. Acumen (noun)

Meaning: the ability to make good judgements and take quick decisions.

Synonyms: Astuteness, awareness, acuity, sharpness.

Usage: A gullible young man with little or no business acumen.

63. Ephemeral (adjective)

Meaning: lasting for a very short time.

Synonyms: Transitory, transient, fleeting, passing.

Usage: Fashions are ephemeral: new ones regularly drive out the old.

64. Garrulous (adjective)

Meaning: excessively talkative, especially on trivial matters.

Synonyms: Talkative, voluble, chatty.

Usage: A garrulous old man who chattered like a magpie.

65. Fetter (noun)

Meaning: a chain or manacle used to restrain a prisoner, typically placed around the ankles.

Synonyms: shackles, manacles, handcuffs, irons, leg irons, chains.

Usage: He lay bound with fetters of iron.

66. Inure (verb)

Meaning: accustom (someone) to something, especially something unpleasant.

Synonyms: Harden, toughen, season, temper.

Usage: These children have been inured to violence.

67. Pejorative (Adjective)

Meaning: expressing contempt or disapproval.

Synonyms: Disparaging, derogatory, denigratory.

Usage: Permissiveness is used almost universally as a pejorative term.

68. **Tirade (noun)**

Meaning: a long, angry speech of criticism or accusation.

Synonyms: Diatribe, invective, polemic, attack.

Usage: She rounded on Nathan with a devastating tirade.

69. **Yoke (noun)**

Meaning: a wooden crosspiece that is fastened over the necks of two animals and attached to the plough or cart that they are to pull.

Synonyms: Harness, collar, tackle, tack.

Usage: The horses were loosened from the yoke.

70. **Umbrage (noun)**

Meaning: offence or annoyance.

Synonyms: take offence, be offended, take exception, bridle.

Usage: She took umbrage at his remarks.

71. **Abysmal (adjective)**

Meaning: extremely bad; appalling

Synonyms: very bad, dreadful, awful, terrible, frightful

Usage: some of the teaching was abysmal.

72. **Tawdry (adjective)**

Meaning: showy but cheap and of poor quality

Synonyms: gaudy, flashy, showy, garish, loud; tasteless

Usage: she had cheap, tawdry rings on her fingers.

73. **Dross (noun)**

Meaning: something regarded as worthless; rubbish.

Synonyms: rubbish, junk, debris, chaff, draff, detritus

Usage: sometimes it's possible to find a little gem amongst the mass-produced dross.

74. **Ardour (noun)**

Meaning: great enthusiasm or passion.

Synonyms: passion, avidity, fervour, zeal, wholeheartedness, eagerness

Usage: she was unaccustomed to being kissed with such ardour.

75. **Insouciant (adjective)**

Meaning: showing a casual lack of concern

Synonyms: nonchalant, untroubled, unworried, unruffled, unconcerned

Usage: he had an insouciant attitude to their money problems.

76. **Dulcet (adjective)**

Meaning: (especially of sound) sweet and soothing (often used ironically).

Synonyms: sweet, sweet-sounding, mellifluous, euphonious, soothing, mellow

Usage: record the dulcet tones of your family and friends.

77. **Desiccate (Verb)**

Meaning: remove the moisture from (something), typically in order to preserve it.

Synonyms: dried, dried up, dry, dehydrated, powdered

Usage: We can use the desiccated coconut for cooking.

78. **Pellucid (adjective)**

Meaning: translucently clear.

Synonyms: translucent, transparent, clear, crystal clear, crystalline

Usage: mountains reflected in the pellucid waters.

79. Pariah (noun)

Meaning: an outcast.

Synonyms: outcast, persona non grata, leper, reject, untouchable

Usage: they were treated as social pariahs.

80. Taciturn (adjective)

Meaning: (of a person) reserved or uncommunicative in speech; saying little.

Synonyms: untalkative, uncommunicative, reticent, unforthcoming, quiet

Usage: after such gatherings she would be taciturn and morose.

81. Perfunctory (adjective)

Meaning: (of an action) carried out without real interest, feeling, or effort.

Synonyms: cursory, desultory; quick, brief, hasty, hurried, rapid

Usage: The guards gave a perfunctory look up and down the carriage.

82. Transient (adjective)

Meaning: lasting only for a short time; impermanent.

Synonyms: transitory, temporary, short-lived, shortterm, ephemeral

Usage: A transient post-war baby boom.

83. Reprobate (noun)

Meaning: an unprincipled person.

Synonyms: rogue, rascal, scoundrel, good-for-nothing, villain, wretch

Usage: He had to present himself as more of a lovable reprobate than a spirit of Corruption.

84. Libertine (noun)

Meaning: a person, especially a man, who freely indulges in sensual pleasures without regard to moral principles.

Synonyms: philanderer, ladies' man, playboy, rake

Usage: His image as an unbridled libertine is a total myth.

85. Tractable (adjective)

Meaning: (of a person) easy to control or influence.

Synonyms: controllable, manageable, malleable, governable, yielding, **Usage:** She has always been tractable and obedient, even as a child.

86. Sedulous (adjective)

Meaning: (of a person or action) showing dedication and diligence.

Synonyms: diligent, careful, meticulous, thorough, assiduous

Usage: He watched himself with the most sedulous care.

87. Intrepid (adjective)

Meaning: fearless; adventurous (often used for rhetorical or humorous effect).

Synonyms: fearless, unafraid, undaunted, dauntless, undismayed

Usage: The intrepid band braved a precipitous mountain track.

88. Morose (adjective)

Meaning: sullen and ill-tempered.

Synonyms: sullen, sulky, gloomy, bad-tempered, illtempered

Usage: She was morose and silent when she got home.

89. Demur (verb)

Meaning: raise objections or show reluctance.

Synonyms: raise objections, object, take exception, take issue

Usage: Normally she would have accepted the challenge, but she demurred.

90. Equipoise (noun)

Meaning: balance of forces or interests.

Synonyms: equilibrium, balance, evenness, symmetry, parity

Usage: This wine represents a marvellous equipoise of power and elegance.

91. Garrulity (Noun)

Meaning: excessive talkativeness, especially on trivial matters.

Synonyms: talkativeness, garrulousness, loquacity, loquaciousness, volubility, verbosity,

Usage: They were irritated by his ungovernable garrulity.

92. Arrant (Adjective)

Meaning: complete, utter

Synonyms: downright, thoroughgoing, absolute, complete, thorough

Usage: What he is talking is arrant nonsense!

93. Consequential (Adjective)

Meaning: following as a result or effect.

Synonyms: resulting, resultant, ensuing, consequent; following

Usage: A loss of confidence and a consequential withdrawal of funds.

94. Attenuate (Verb)

Meaning: reduce the force, effect, or value of.

Synonyms: weakened, reduced, lessened, decreased, diminished, impaired

Usage: Her intolerance was attenuated by an unexpected liberalism.

95. Precarious (Adjective)

Meaning: dependent on chance; uncertain

Synonyms: uncertain, insecure, unreliable, unsure, unpredictable

Usage: He made a precarious living as a painter.

96. Enervate (Verb)

Meaning: make (someone) feel drained of energy or vitality.

Synonyms: exhaust, tire, fatigue, weary, wear out, devitalize

Usage: The scorching sun enervated her.

97. Equivocate (Verb)

Meaning: use ambiguous language so as to conceal the truth or avoid committing oneself.

Synonyms: prevaricate, be evasive, be non-committal, be vague, be ambiguous

Usage: The government have equivocated too often in the past.

98. Assiduous (Adjective)

Meaning: showing great care and perseverance.

Synonyms: diligent, careful, meticulous, thorough, sedulous, attentive

Usage: She was assiduous in pointing out every feature.

99. Lassitude (Noun)

Meaning: a state of physical or mental weariness; lack of energy

Synonyms: lethargy, listlessness, weariness, languor, sluggishness, enervation

Usage: She was overcome by lassitude and retired to bed.

100. Sycophant (Noun)

Meaning: a person who acts obsequiously towards someone important in order to gain advantage.

Synonyms: toady, creep, crawler, fawner, flatterer, flunkey, truckler

Usage: He was surrounded by flatterers and sycophants.

101. Infant (Noun)

Meaning: a very young child or baby.

Synonyms: Baby, newborn, young child, little child

Usage: Their first year at infant school.

102. Mortality (Noun)

Meaning: the state of being subject to death.

Synonyms: Impermanence, temporality, transience, perishability

Usage: the work is increasingly haunted by thoughts of mortality.

103. Hapless (Adjective)

Meaning: unfortunate

Synonyms: unlucky, luckless, out of luck, cursed, doomed

Usage: The hapless victims of the disaster.

104. Persuade (Verb)

Meaning: induce (someone) to do something through reasoning or argument.

Synonyms: talk someone into, coax, convince, make, get, induce, coerce, prompt

Usage: it wasn't easy, but I persuaded him to do the right thing.

105. Deserters (Noun)

Meaning: a member of the armed forces who deserts.

Synonyms: Runaway, renegade, fugitive, escapee

Usage: deserters from the army.

106. Tenure (Noun)

Meaning: the holding of an office.

Synonyms: incumbency, term of office, term, period of office, time

Usage: his tenure of the premiership would be threatened.

107. Bureaucracy (Noun)

Meaning: excessively complicated administrative procedure.

Synonyms: red tape, rules and regulations, protocol, officialdom

Usage: the unnecessary bureaucracy in local government.

108. Entangle (Verb)

Meaning: cause to become twisted together with or caught in.

Synonyms: Intertwine, entwine, tangle, intertwist, twist, ravel.

Usage: Fish attempt to swim through the mesh and become entangled.

109. Legitimate (Adjective)

Meaning: able to be defended with logic or justification; valid.

Synonyms: valid, sound, admissible, acceptable, well founded

Usage: these are legitimate grounds for unease.

110. Echelons (Noun)

Meaning: a level or rank in an organization, a profession, or society.

Synonyms: Level, rank, grade, step, rung, tier, plane, order, division

Usage: the upper echelons of the business world.

111. Ambivalent (Adjective)

Meaning: having mixed feelings or contradictory ideas about something or someone.

Synonyms: equivocal, uncertain, unsure, doubtful, indecisive, inconclusive, irresolute

Usage: Some loved her, some hated her, few were ambivalent about her.

112. Forsake (Verb)

Meaning: abandon or leave.

Synonyms: abandon, desert, leave, quit, depart from, leave behind

Usage: She forsook her child, giving him up for adoption.

113. Impudent (Adjective)

Meaning: not showing due respect for another person; impertinent.

Synonyms: impertinent, insolent, cheeky, audacious, brazen

Usage: He could have strangled this impudent upstart.

114. Inept (Adjective)

Meaning: having or showing no skill; clumsy.

Synonyms: incompetent, unskilful, unskilled, inexpert, amateurish

Usage: My attempts at baking were inept but I fumbled on.

115. Novice (Verb)

Meaning: a person new to and inexperienced in a job or situation.

Synonyms: beginner, learner, inexperienced person

Usage: He was a complete novice in foreign affairs.

116. Salient (Adjective)

Meaning: most noticeable or important.

Synonyms: important, main, principal, major, chief, primary, notable

Usage: The salient points stuck out clearly in her mind.

117. Umbrage (Noun)

Meaning: offence or annoyance.

Synonyms: take offence, be offended, take exception, bridle, take something personally

Usage: She took umbrage at his remarks.

118. Serendipity (Noun)

Meaning: the occurrence and development of events by chance in a happy or beneficial way.

Synonyms: chance, happy chance, accident, happy accident, fluke

Usage: Technical innovation may be the result of pure serendipity.

119. Quaint (Adjective)

Meaning: attractively unusual or old-fashioned.

Synonyms: picturesque, charming, sweet, attractive, pleasantly old-fashioned

Usage: Narrow streets lead to a quaint bridge over the river.

120. Truculent (Adjective)

Meaning: eager or quick to argue or fight; aggressively defiant.

Synonyms: defiant, aggressive, antagonistic, belligerent, pugnacious, bellicose

Usage: The truculent attitude of farmers to cheaper imports.

121. Persuade (verb)

Definition: induce (someone) to do something through reasoning or argument.

Meaning: prevail on, talk someone into, coax, convince, make, get, press someone into

Usage: He tried to persuade her to come with him.

122. Traverse (Verb)

Definition: travel across or through

Meaning: travel over/across, cross, journey over/across, make one's way across

Usage: He traversed the deserts of Persia and Baluchistan.

123. Indulge (Verb)

Definition: allow oneself to enjoy the pleasure of.

Meaning: wallow in, give oneself up to, give way to, yield to, abandon oneself to

Usage: We indulged in a cream tea.

124. Sway (verb)

Definition: move or cause to move slowly or rhythmically backwards and forwards or from side to side.

Meaning: swing, shake, oscillate, rock, undulate, move from side to side

Usage: The curtains were swaying in the breeze.

125. Deteriorated (Verb)

Definition: become progressively worse.

Meaning: worsen, get worse, decline, be in decline, degenerate, decay

Usage: His condition has deteriorated in the intensive care unit.

126. Ramification (Noun)

Definition: a complex or unwelcome consequence of an action or event.

Meaning: consequence, result, aftermath, outcome, effect, upshot, issue

Usage: Any change is bound to have legal ramifications.

127. Heap (verb)

Definition: put (objects or a loose substance) in a heap.

Meaning: Pile up, pile, stack up, stack, make a pile of, make a stack of

Usage: She heaped logs on the fire.

128. Rebel (noun)

Definition: a person who rises in opposition or armed resistance against an established government or leader.

Meaning: revolutionary, insurgent, mutineer agitator

Usage: The rebels took control of the capital.

129. Substantial (adjective)

Definition: of considerable importance, size, or worth.

Meaning: considerable, real, material, weighty, soild, sizeable

Usage: Substantial progress had been made.

130. Utterly (adverb)

Definition: completely and without qualification; absolutely.

Meaning: completely, totally, absolutely, entirely, fully

Usage: He looked utterly ridiculous.

131. Congenial

Meaning: (of a person) pleasing or liked on account of having qualities or interests that are similar to one's own.

Synonyms: like-minded, compatible, kindred, well suited, easy to get along with

Usage: I was working with a bunch of very congenial people.

132. Strident

Meaning: (of a sound) loud and harsh; grating.

Synonyms: harsh, raucous, rough, grating, rasping, jarring, loud

Usage: A strident voice interrupted the consultation.

133. Confluence

Meaning: the junction of two rivers, especially rivers of approximately equal width.

Synonyms: convergence, meeting, junction, joining, conflux, watersmeet

Usage: The confluence of the Rivers Ouse and Foss.

134. Lavish

Meaning: sumptuously rich, elaborate, or luxurious.

Synonyms: sumptuous, luxurious, luxuriant, lush, gorgeous, costly

Usage: He held lavish dinner parties at his home.

135. Insolent

Meaning: showing a rude and arrogant lack of respect.

Synonyms: impertinent, impudent, cheeky, illmannered

Usage: She hated the insolent tone of his voice.

136. Vagrant

Meaning: a person without a settled home or regular work who wanders from place to place and lives by begging.

Synonyms: tramp, drifter, down-and-out, derelict, beggar, itinerant, wanderer

Usage: The old car was a welcome shelter for the occasional vagrant.

137. Gregarious

Meaning: (of a person) fond of company; sociable.

Synonyms: sociable, social, company-loving, companionable, convivial

Usage: He was a popular and gregarious man.

138. Enigma

Meaning: a person or thing that is mysterious or difficult to understand.

Synonyms: mystery, puzzle, riddle, conundrum, paradox, problem, **Usage:** How it works is a complete enigma to me.

139. Assuage

Meaning: make (an unpleasant feeling) less intense.

Synonyms: Relieve, ease, alleviate, soothe, mitigate, dampen

Usage: The letter assuaged the fears of most members.

140. Sanguine

Meaning: optimistic or positive, especially in an apparently bad or difficult situation.

Synonyms: optimistic, bullish, hopeful, buoyant, positive

Usage: He is sanguine about prospects for the global economy.

141. Apocryphal

Meaning: (of a story or statement) of doubtful authenticity, although widely circulated as being true.

Synonyms: fictitious, made-up, untrue, fabricated, false, **Usage:** An apocryphal story about a former president

142. Adage

Meaning: a proverb or short statement expressing a general truth.

Synonyms: saying, maxim, axiom, proverb, slogan

Usage: It is vital for every pilot to remember the old adage 'safety first

143. Ersatz

Meaning: (of a product) made or used as a substitute, typically an inferior one, for something else.

Synonyms: artificial, substitute, imitation, fake, false

Usage: Ersatz emotion

144. Espionage

Meaning: the practice of spying or of using spies, typically by governments to obtain political and military information.

Synonyms: spying, undercover work, cloak-anddagger activities, surveillance, reconnaissance

Usage: The camouflage and secrecy of espionage

145. Restive

Meaning: (of a person) unable to remain still, silent, or submissive, especially because of boredom or dissatisfaction.

Synonyms: restless, fidgety, edgy, on edge, tense, uneasy

Usage: The crowd had been waiting for hours and many were becoming restive.

146. Accolade

Meaning: an award or privilege granted as a special honour or as an acknowledgement of merit.

Synonyms: honour, recognition, privilege, award, gift, title

Usage: The hotel has won numerous accolades

147. Harbinger

Meaning: a person or thing that announces or signals the approach of another.

Synonyms: sign, indicator, signal, **Usage:** Witch hazels are the harbingers of spring.

148. Restraint

Meaning: unemotional, dispassionate, or moderate behaviour; self-control.

Synonyms: self-control, self-restraint, self-discipline, control

Usage: The customary restraint of the British police

149. Trepidation

Meaning: a feeling of fear or anxiety about something that may happen

Synonyms: fear, apprehension, dread, fearfulness, **Usage:** He sat in the waiting room, full of trepidation

150. Imperturbable

Meaning: unable to be upset or excited; calm.

Synonyms: self-possessed, composed, collected, calm, cool, calm

Usage: My father was a solid, imperturbable man

151. Inevitable

Definition: certain to happen; unavoidable.

Meaning: unavoidable, inescapable, bound to happen, sure to happen, unpreventable, **Usage:** His resignation was inevitable.

152. Unassailable

Definition: unable to be attacked, questioned, or defeated.

Meaning: impregnable, invulnerable, impenetrable, inviolable

Usage: The world's most unassailable fortress.

153. Queer

Definition: strange; odd.

Meaning: odd, strange, unusual, funny, peculiar, curious, bizarre

Usage: It seemed queer to see the windows all dark.

154. Preponderance

Definition: the quality or fact of being greater in number, quantity, or importance.

Meaning: prevalence, predominance, dominance

Usage: The preponderance of women among older people.

155. Redundant

Definition: not or no longer needed or useful; superfluous.

Meaning: unnecessary, not required, inessential, unessential

Usage: An appropriate use for a redundant church.

156. Consensus

Definition: a general agreement.

Meaning: agreement, harmony, concord, likemindedness, concurrence, consent

Usage: There is a growing consensus that the current regime has failed.

157. Debacle

Definition: a sudden and ignominious failure; a fiasco.

Meaning: failure, catastrophe, disaster, disintegration, mess, wreck, ruin; downfall,

Usage: The only man to reach double figures in the second-innings debacle.

158. Beleaguer

Definition: lay siege to.

Meaning: besieged, under siege, blockaded,

surrounded, encircled, hemmed in, under attack

Usage: He led a relief force to the aid of the beleaguered city.

159. Lacklustre

Definition: lacking in vitality, force, or conviction; uninspired or uninspiring

Meaning: uninspired, uninspiring, unimaginative, dull, humdrum, colourless,

Usage: No excuses were made for the team's lacklustre performance.

160. Menace

Definition: a person or thing that is likely to cause harm; a threat or danger.

Meaning: danger, peril, risk, hazard, threat; jeopardy

Usage: A new initiative aimed at beating the menace of drugs.

161. Dampen

Meaning: Humidify, moisten, wet

Definition: Make slightly wet.

Usage: The fine rain dampened her face.

162. Vest

Meaning: invest in, grant to, give to

Definition: confer or bestow (power, authority, property, etc.) on someone.

Usage: Executive power is vested in the President

163. Illicit

Meaning: illegal, unlawful, banned

Definition: forbidden by law, rules, or custom.

Usage: Police were searching for the illicit drugs in the room.

164. glimpse

Meaning: brief look, glance

Definition: a momentary or partial view.

Usage: She caught a glimpse of the ocean

165. Delineation

Meaning: Presentation, description

Definition: the action of describing or portraying something precisely.

Usage: The artist's exquisite delineation of costume and jewellery

166. Intermittent

Meaning: broken, irregular, discontinuous

Definition: occurring at irregular intervals; not continuous or steady.

Usage: They heard intermittent bursts of gunfire

167. Transgression

Meaning: offence, crime, sin, wrong

Definition: an act that goes against a law, rule, or code of conduct; an offence.

Usage: They were granted full amnesty for their transgressions.

168. Sovereignty

Meaning: Power, dominion, supermacy

Definition: Supreme power or authority.

Usage: Full West German sovereignty was achieved in 1955.

169. Blatant

Meaning: flagrant, glaring, obvious

Definition: (of bad behaviour) done openly and unashamedly.

Usage: She forced herself to resist his blatant charm

170. Periphery

Meaning: edge, margin, boundary

Definition: the outer limits or edge of an area or object.

Usage: New buildings on the periphery of the hospital site.

171. Derelict

Meaning: Unsafe, dangerous, hazardous, perilous, insecure

Definition: in a very poor condition as a result of disuse and neglect

Usage: A derelict Georgian mansion

172. Fascinating

Meaning: Engrossing, captivating, absorbing, interesting, enchanting, beguiling, enthralling, riveting

Definition: extremely interesting

Usage: A fascinating book

173. Invoked

Meaning: Pray to, call on, appeal to, plead with, Supplicate, solicit

Definition: call on (a deity or spirit) in prayer, as a witness, or for inspiration

Usage: the antiquated defence of insanity is rarely invoked in England

174. Gadfly

Meaning: as a horsefly, botfly, or warble fly

Definition: a person who annoys others especially with constant criticism

Usage: loud sports commentator who was a tactless gadfly during post-game interviews with the losing team

175. Dissent

Meaning: Disagreement, lack of agreement, difference of opinion, argument, dispute

Definition: the holding or expression of opinions at variance with those commonly or officially held.

Usage: there was no dissent from this view

176. Relevance

Meaning: applicability, application, appositeness, bearing, concernment, germaneness, materiality, pertinence, pertinency, relevancy

Definition: the quality or state of being closely connected or appropriate.

Usage: This film has contemporary relevance

177. Critique

Meaning: Analysis, evaluation, assessment, appraisal, review

Definition: a detailed analysis and assessment of something, especially a literary, philosophical, or political theory

Usage: A critique of Marxist historicism

178. Gestures

Meaning: Signal, signaling, sign, signing, motion, wave, ondication

Definition: a movement of part of the body, especially a hand or the head, to express an idea or meaning.

Usage: he threw out both hands in a gesture of surrender

179. Audacity

Meaning: Boldness, daring, bravery, courage, pluck, insolence

Definition: a willingness to take bold risks.

Usage: he whistled at the sheer audacity of the plan

180. Exemplify

Meaning: typify, epitomize, symbolize, be a typical example of

Definition: illustrate or clarify by giving an example.

Usage: he exemplified his point with an anecdote

181. Assent

Meaning: Agree to, accept, approve, consent to

Definition: express approval or agreement

Usage: the Prime Minister assented to the change

182. Accord

Meaning: Give, grant, tender, present, award, hand, yield

Definition: give or grant someone (power, status, or recognition).

Usage: the powers accorded to the head of state

183. Porch

Meaning: vestibule, foyer, hall, entry, lobby, portal

Definition: a covered shelter projecting in front of the entrance of a building

Usage: the north porch of Hereford Cathedral

184. Fiesta

Meaning: Festival, carnival, holiday, party

Definition: an event marked by festivities or celebration

Usage: the Bristol International Balloon Fiesta

185. Fusion

Meaning: Blend, combination, amalgamation, joining, bonding

Definition: the process or result of joining two or more things together to form a single entity.

Usage: the election results produced pressure for fusion of the parties

186. Traverse

Meaning: cross, negotiate, travel over/across

Definition: travel across or through.

Usage: he traversed the forest

187. Genesis

Meaning: origin, source, root, beginning, start, outset

Definition: the origin or mode of formation of something

Usage: this tale had its genesis in fireside stories

188. Civic

Meaning: Municipal, city, town, urban, metropolitan

Definition: relating to a city or town, especially its administration; municipal.

Usage: a meeting of civic and business leaders

189. Cooper

Meaning: Make, repair, barrel

Definition: a maker or repairer of casks and barrels.

Usage: my father coopered casks and barrels for the ships

190. Rover

Meaning: wanderer, traveler, drifter, brid of passage

Definition: a person who spends their time wandering.

Usage: they became rovers who departed further and further from civilization

191. Regiment

Meaning: Unit, outfit, force

Definition: a permanent unit of an army typically commanded by a lieutenant colonel and divided into several companies, squadrons, or batteries and often into two battalions

Usage: the Royal Highland Regiment

192. Infiltrate

Meaning: penetrate, invade, intrude on, permeate, enter

Definition: enter or gain access to (an organization, place, etc.) surreptitiously and gradually, especially in order to acquire secret information..

Usage: the organization has been infiltrated by informers

193. Interrogation

Meaning: questioning, vross-questioning, carechism, quizzing

Definition: the action of interrogating or the process of being interrogated.

Usage: would he keep his mouth shut under interrogation ?

194. Adjunct

Meaning: Supplement, addition, complement, extra

Definition: a thing added to something else as a supplementary rather than an essential part.

Usage: computer technology is an adjunct to learning

195. Armada

Meaning: fleet, flotilla, navy, squadron

Definition: a fleet of warships.

Usage: an armada of forty-five warships

196. Canon

Meaning: principle, rule, law, tenet, formula

Definition: a general law, rule, principle, or criterion by which something is judged.

Usage: the appointment violated the canons of fair play and equal opportunity

197. Vulnerable

Meaning: at risk, in peril, in danger, unsafe, unprotected

Definition: exposed to the possibility of being attacked or harmed, either physically or emotionally

Usage: we were in a vulnerable position

198. Thrall

Meaning: power, control, grip, grasp, yoke

Definition: the state of being in someone's power, or of having great power over someone.

Usage: she was in thrall to her abusive husband

199. Trammel

Meaning: restraint, curb, check, impediment, barrier

Definition: restrictions or impediments to freedom of action.

Usage: we will forge our own future, free from the trammels of materialism

200. Revere

Meaning: respect, admire, prize, treasure, value

Definition: feel deep respect or admiration for (something) .

Usage: Cezanne's still lifes were revered by his contemporaries

201. Robust

Meaning: durable, resilient, tough, hard-wearing, longlasting, well made,

Definition: (of an object) sturdy in construction

Usage: a robust metal cabinet

202. Perhaps

Meaning: maybe, possibly, conceivably, feasibly

Definition: used to express uncertainty or possibility.

Usage: perhaps I should have been frank with him

203. Towering

Meaning: high, tall, lofty, sky-high, steep

Definition: extremely tall, especially in comparison with the surroundings.

Usage: Hari looked up at the towering buildings

204. Progenitor

Meaning: ancestor, forefather, forebear, parant

Definition: a person who originates a cultural or intellectual movement.

Usage: his children were the progenitors of many of Scotland's noble families

205. Dynamism

Meaning: activity , progress

Definition: the quality of being characterized by vigorous activity and progress.

Usage: the dynamism and strength of the economy

206. Asymmetric

Meaning: lopsided, unsymmetrical, crooked

Definition: having parts which fail to correspond to one another in shape, size, or arrangement; lacking symmetry.

Usage: the church has an asymmetrical plan with an aisle only on one side

207. Prop

Meaning: buttress, support, brace, underpin, reinforce

Definition: support or keep in position

Usage: she propped her chin in the palm of her right hand

208. Assiduous

Meaning: diligent, careful, meticulous, thorough, sedulous, attentive

Definition: showing great care and perseverance.

Usage: She was assiduous in pointing out every feature

209. Episodic

Meaning: intermittent, irregular, sporadic, periodic, fitful

Definition: occurring occasionally and at irregular intervals.

Usage: volcanic activity is highly episodic in nature

210. Impervious

Meaning: impermeable, impenetrable, waterproof

Definition: not allowing fluid to pass through.

Usage: an impervious layer of basaltic clay

211. Capricious

Meaning: fickle, inconstant, changeable, variable, unstable, mercurial, erratic

Definition: given to sudden and unaccountable changes of mood or behaviour..

Usage: A capricious and often brutal administration

212. Empirical

Meaning: seen, factual, actual, real, verifable, firsthand

Definition: based on, concerned with, or verifiable by observation or experience rather than theory or pure logic.

Usage: They provided considerable empirical evidence to support their argument

213. Esoteric

Meaning: abstruse, obscure, arcane, cryptic, difficult, puzzling

Definition: intended for or likely to be understood by only a small number of people with a specialized knowledge or interest.

Usage: Esoteric philosophical debates

214. Inevitable

Meaning: unavoidable, certain, sure, fated, inexorable

Definition: certain to happen; unavoidable.

Usage: war was inevitable

215. Ostentatious

Meaning: showy, loud, fancy, ornate, affected, actorly, kitsch

Definition: characterized by pretentious or showy display; designed to impress.

Usage: A simple design that is glamorous without being ostentatious

216. Poignant

Meaning: moving, sad, touching, tearful, pitiful, tragic

Definition: evoking a keen sense of sadness or regret.

Usage: A poignant reminder of the passing of time

217. Sarcastic

Meaning: Sardonic, ironic, satirical

Definition: marked by or given to using irony in order to mock or convey contempt

Usage: Making sarcastic comments

218. Vain

Meaning: conceited, egoistic, egocentric, self-loving

Definition: having or showing an excessively high opinion of one's appearance, abilities, or worth.

Usage: Their flattery made him vain

219. Trauma

Meaning: Injury, damage, hurt, wound, sore, cut, lesion

Definition: physical injury.

Usage: Rupture of the diaphragm caused by blunt trauma

220. Aloof

Meaning: distant, detached, unresponsive, remote, stuffy

Definition: not friendly or forthcoming; cool and distant.

Usage: They were courteous but faintly aloof

221. Indefatigable

Meaning: tireless, untiring, unwearied, unflagging

Definition: (of a person or their efforts) persisting tirelessly.

Usage: An indefatigable defender of human rights

222. Dilatory

Meaning: slow, unhurried, tardy, lax, slack, idle, lazy

Definition: slow to act.

Usage: He had been dilatory in appointing a solicitor

223. Martinet

Meaning: disciplinarian, taskmaster, tyrant, drill sergeant

Definition: a person who demands complete obedience; a strict disciplinarian.

Usage: The woman in charge was a martinet who treated all those beneath her like children

224. Unlawful

Meaning: illegal, illicit, illegitimate, against the law

Definition: not conforming to, permitted by, or recognized by law or rules.

Usage: The use of unlawful violence

225. Bequest

Meaning: legacy, inheritance, endowment, estate, heritage, bestowal, donation

Definition: the action of bequeathing something.

Usage: A painting acquired by bequest

226. Gullible

Meaning: credulous, trustful, naïve, innocent, ignorant, simple, unguared

Definition: easily persuaded to believe something; credulous

Usage: an attempt to persuade a gullible public to spend their money

227. Deceptive

Meaning: misleading, illusory, illusive, ambiguous, delusive,

Definition: giving an appearance or impression different from the true one; misleading

Usage: He put the question with deceptive casualness

228. Elusive

Meaning: difficult to catch/find, difficult to track down

Definition: difficult to find, catch, or achieve.

Usage: Success will become ever more elusive

229. Tyranny

Meaning: despotism, absolutism, autocracy, dictatorship

Definition: cruel and oppressive government or rule.

Usage: Refugees fleeing tyranny and oppression

230. Rebate

Meaning: refund, repayment, partial refund

Definition: a partial refund to someone who has paid too much for tax, rent, or a utility.

Usage: The scheme eases the move to the council tax by giving rebates in the first year

231. Adhesion

Meaning: sticking, adherence, gluing, fixing, union, festening

Definition: the action or process of adhering to a surface or object.

Usage: The adhesion of the gum strip to the paper

232. Virtuoso

Meaning: genius, expert, master, artist, doyen

Definition: a person highly skilled in music or another artistic pursuit

Usage: A celebrated clarinet virtuoso

233. Waif

Meaning: ragamuffin, guttersnipe

Definition: a homeless, neglected, or abandoned person, especially a child.

Usage: she is foster-mother to various waifs and strays

234. Ulterior

Meaning: Secondary, underlying, undisclosed, unexpressed, unapparent, hidden, covert

Definition: existing beyond what is obvious or admitted; intentionally hidden.

Usage: could there be an ulterior motive behind his request?

235. Telltale

Meaning: revealing, revelatory, meaningful, significant, meaning

Definition: revealing, indicating, or betraying something.

Usage: The telltale bulge of a concealed weapon

236. Stupor

Meaning: daze, state of senselessness

Definition: a state of near-unconsciousness or insensibility

Usage: A drunken stupor

237. Rescind

Meaning: revoke, repeal, cancel, overtrun, annul, withdraw

Definition: revoke, cancel, or repeal (a law, order, or agreement).

Usage: the government eventually rescinded the directive

238. Acrimony

Meaning: rancor, ill feeling, bad blood, animosity, bitterness

Definition: bitterness or ill feeling.

Usage: the AGM dissolved into acrimony

239. Diminish

Meaning: decrease, decline, reduce, lessen

Definition: make or become less.

Usage: The new law is expected to diminish the government's chances

240. Mirth

Meaning: merriment, high spirits, cheer, gaiety, fun, jollity, joy

Definition: amusement, especially as expressed in laughter.

Usage: his six-foot frame shook with mirth

241. Corporeal

Meaning: bodily, fleshly, carnal, human, mortal, earthly

Definition: relating to a person's body, especially as opposed to their spirit.

Usage: He was frank about his corporeal appetites

242. Epigram

Meaning: quip, witticism, gem, jest, pun, sally

Definition: a pithy saying or remark expressing an idea in a clever and amusing way

Usage: a Wildean epigram

243. Laudable

Meaning: admirable, worthy, deserving, noteworthy, reputable, sterling

Definition: (of an action, idea, or aim) deserving praise and commendation.

Usage: laudable though the aim might be, the results have been criticized

244. Reluctant

Meaning: unwilling, disinclined, unenthusiastic, grudging, resisting

Definition: unwilling and hesitant; disinclined.

Usage: She seemed reluctant to answer

245. Plebiscite

Meaning: Vote, ballot, referendum,

Definition: the direct vote of all the members of an electorate on an important public question such as a change in the constitution.

Usage: the administration will hold a plebiscite for the approval of constitutional reforms

246. Amateur

Meaning: non-professional, layman, layperson

Definition: a person who engages in a pursuit, especially a sport, on an unpaid basis.

Usage: it takes five years for a top amateur to become a real Tour de France rider

247. Exorcise

Meaning: drive out, cast out, expel

Definition: rid (a person or place) of a supposed evil spirit.

Usage: infants were exorcised prior to baptism

248. Antagonist

Meaning: adversary, opponent, enemy, foe, rival, competitor

Definition: a person who actively opposes or is hostile to someone or something; an adversary.

Usage: the woman was forcing her antagonist's face into the mud

249. Aberration

Meaning: anomaly, deviation, abnormality, variation, quirk

Definition: a departure from what is normal, usual, or expected, typically an unwelcome one.

Usage: they described the outbreak of violence in the area as an aberration

250. Brusque

Meaning: curt, abrupt, blunt, short, terse, brisk, crisp

Definition: abrupt or offhand in speech or manner

Usage: She could be brusque and impatient

251. Quirky

Meaning: eccentric, odd, outlandish, offbeat, zany, weird

Definition: having or characterized by peculiar or unexpected traits or aspects.

Usage: Her sense of humour was decidedly quirky

252. Reconnaissance

Meaning: survey, exploration, observation, probe, scan

Definition: military observation of a region to locate an enemy or ascertain strategic features

Usage: An excellent aircraft for low-level reconnaissance

253. Humdrum

Meaning: Dull, boring, tedious, monotomous, banal, ordinary, everyday

Definition: lacking excitement or variety; boringly monotonous.

Usage: humdrum routine work

254. Revamp

Meaning: renovate, redecorate, refurbish, recondition, rehabilitate, rebuild, overhaul

Definition: give new and improved form, structure, or appearance to.

Usage: An attempt to revamp the museum's image

255. Covet

Meaning: desire, crave, have one's heart set on

Definition: yearn to possess (something, especially something belonging to another).

Usage: I covet one of their smart bags

256. Inadvertently

Meaning: Accidentally, by accident, unwittingly

Definition: without intention; accidentally.

Usage: His name had been inadvertently omitted from the list

257. Misconstrue

Meaning: misunderstand, misinterpret, misconceive, miss, confuse, confound

Definition: interpret (a person's words or actions) wrongly.

Usage: my advice was deliberately misconstrued

258. Nonchalant

Meaning: Feeling, relaxed, calm

Definition: (of a person or manner) feeling or appearing casually calm and relaxed; not displaying anxiety, interest, or enthusiasm.

Usage: She gave a nonchalant shrug

259. Nexus

Meaning: Connection, focal point

Definition: a connection or series of connections linking two or more things.

Usage: The nexus between industry and political power

260. Arson

Meaning: incendiarism, pyromania, fire-raising, firebombing

Definition: the criminal act of deliberately setting fire to property

Usage: Police are treating the fire as arson

261. Bankrupt

Meaning: Insolvent, without, denuded of, vacant of

Definition: completely lacking in a particular good quality.

Usage: His father went bankrupt and the family had to sell their home

262. Abundant

Meaning: Plentiful, copious, ample, profuse, rich, lavish, liberal, bountiful, bumber

Definition: existing or available in large quantities; plentiful

Usage: there was abundant evidence to support the theory

263. Acquittal

Meaning: Absolution, clearing, exoneration, exculpation,

Definition: a judgement or verdict that a person is not guilty of the crime with which they have been charged.

Usage: the trial resulted in an acquittal

264. Rudimentary

Meaning: Basic, elementary, introductory, early, primary, initial, first

Definition: involving or limited to basic principles.

Usage: He received a rudimentary education

265. Scruple

Meaning: hesitation, compunction, reservation,thoughtd

Definition: a feeling of doubt or hesitation with regard to the morality or propriety of a course of action.

Usage: I had no scruples about eavesdropping

266. Specious

Meaning: misleading, deceptive, false, unsound

Definition: superficially plausible, but actually wrong.

Usage: A specious argument

267. Tenacious

Meaning: firm, tight, fast, clinging, good

Definition: tending to keep a firm hold of something; clinging or adhering closely.

Usage: A tenacious grip

268. Unutterable

Meaning: indescribable, beyond words, unthinkable, inconceivable

Definition: too great or awful to describe.

Usage: Moments of unutterable grief

269. Dissentient

Meaning: dissenting, differing, discordant, negative

Definition: in opposition to a majority or official opinion.

Usage: dissentient voices were castigated as 'hopeless bureaucrats

270. Cynicism

Meaning: scepticism, doubt, mistrust, distrust

Definition: an inclination to believe that people are motivated purely by self-interest; scepticism

Usage: public cynicism about politics

271. Abhorrent

Meaning: detestable, hateful, loathsome, execrable

Definition: inspiring disgust and loathing; repugnant.

Usage: Racism was abhorrent to us all

272. Renounce

Meaning: reject, repudiate, abandon, resign

Definition: formally declare one's abandonment of (a claim, right, or possession)

Usage: Isabella offered to renounce her son's claim to the French Crown

273. Bizarre

Meaning: Strange, peculiar, odd, funny, curious, offbeat, outlandish, queer

Definition: very strange or unusual.

Usage: a bizarre situation

274. Scurrilous

Meaning: abusive, vituperative, derogatory, pejorative, libelous

Definition: making or spreading scandalous claims about someone with the intention of damaging their reputation.

Usage: A scurrilous attack on his integrity

275. Calumny

Meaning: slander, libel, character assassination, calumniation

Definition: the making of false and defamatory statements about someone in order to damage their reputation; slander.

Usage: A bitter struggle marked by calumny and litigation

276. Abundant

Meaning: plentiful, copious, ample, profuse, rich, liberal, opulent

Definition: existing or available in large quantities; plentiful.

Usage: There was abundant evidence to support the theory

277. Applaud

Meaning: clap, cheer, whistle, praise, commend, salute

Definition: show approval or praise by clapping.

Usage: The crowd whistled and applauded

278. Exonerate

Meaning: absolve, clear, acquit, discharge , release, relive, free

Definition: (of an official body) absolve (someone) from blame for a fault or wrongdoing.

Usage: an inquiry exonerated those involved

279. Meritorious

Meaning: praiseworthy, admirable, estimable, creditable, excellent

Definition: deserving reward or praise.

Usage: A medal for meritorious conduct

280. Reproach

Meaning: rebuke, reproof, reproval, admonition, scolding

Definition: the expression of disapproval or disappointment

Usage: He gave her a look of reproach

281. Reticence

Meaning: reserve, restraint, inhibition, shyness, modesty

Definition: the quality of being reticent; reserve.

Usage: The traditional emotional reticence of the British

282. Ruse

Meaning: Ploy, stratagem, tactic, move, device, scheme, trick

Definition: an action intended to deceive someone; a trick

Usage: Emma tried to think of a ruse to get Paul out of the house

283. Preempt

Meaning: Foretall, prevent, secure

Definition: take action in order to prevent (an anticipated event) happening; forestall

Usage: The government pre-empted a coup attempt

284. Rancour

Meaning: bitterness, spite, hate, ill will, vitriol

Definition: bitterness or resentfulness, especially when long standing.

Usage: He spoke without rancour

285. Recluse

Meaning: hermit, ascetic

Definition: a person who lives a solitary life and tends to avoid other people.

Usage: She has turned into a virtual recluse

286. Remorse

Meaning: contrition, repentance, guilt, sorrow, compunction

Definition: deep regret or guilt for a wrong committed.

Usage: They were filled with remorse and shame

287. Sensual

Meaning: physical, carnal, bodily, animal

Definition: of or arousing gratification of the senses and physical, especially sexual, pleasure.

Usage: The production of the ballet is sensual and passionate

288. Undulate

Meaning: rise and fall, surge, wave, billow, roll, swell, ripple

Definition: move with a smooth wave-like motion.

Usage: Her body undulated to the thumping rhythm of the music

289. Wary

Meaning: cautious, careful, chary, alert, prudent

Definition: feeling or showing caution about possible dangers or problems.

Usage: Dogs which have been mistreated often remain very wary of strangers

290. Trite

Meaning: hackneyed, banal, vapid, ordinary, predictabe

Definition: (of a remark or idea) lacking originality or freshness; dull on account of overuse

Usage: This point may now seem obvious and trite

291. Dilatory

Meaning: Slow, unhurried, tardy, lax, sluggish, idle, indolent

Definition: slow to act.

Usage: He had been dilatory in appointing a solicitor

292. Cardinal

Meaning: Fundamental, basic, main, chief, primary, prime, first

Definition: of the greatest importance; fundamental..

Usage: Two cardinal points must be borne in mind

293. Braggart

Meaning: Brag, show-off, trumpeter, poser, egotist

Definition: a person who boasts about their achievements or possessions

Usage: braggart men

294. Assuage

Meaning: Relieve, ease, alleviate, smother, lessen, lower

Definition: make (an unpleasant feeling) less intense

Usage: The letter assuaged the fears of most members

295. Penury

Meaning: extreme/dire poverty, pennilessness, impecuniousness, impoverishment, indigence

Definition: the state of being very poor; extreme poverty.

Usage: He couldn't face another year of penury

296. Tenuous

Meaning: Slight, flimsy, weak, fragile, shaky

Definition: very weak or slight

Usage: The tenuous link between interest rates and investment

297. Turbid

Meaning: murky, muddy, thick,

Definition: (of a liquid) cloudy, opaque, or thick with suspended matter.

Usage: The turbid estuary

298. Verbose

Meaning: wordy, garrulous, talkative, voluble, effusive

Definition: (using or expressed in more words than are needed.

Usage: Much academic language is obscure and verbose

299. Venerate

Meaning: revere, respect, worship, hallow, deify

Definition: regard with great respect; revere

Usage: Philip of Beverley was venerated as a saint

300. Viscous

Meaning: Sticky, gummy, tacky, syrupy

Definition: having a thick, sticky consistency between solid and liquid; having a high viscosity

Usage: Viscous lava

301. Abeyance

Meaning: Suspension, remission, reserve, suspense

Definition: a state of temporary disuse or suspension.

Usage: Matters were held in abeyance pending further enquiries

302. Vacillate

Meaning: dither, teeter, temporize, hesitate, fluctuate

Definition: waver between different opinions or actions; be indecisive.

Usage: I vacillated between teaching and journalism

303. Tantamount

Meaning: equivalent to, equal to, amounting to, as good as, more or less, synonymous with, virtually the same as, much the same as

Definition: equivalent in seriousness to; virtually the same as

Usage: The resignations were tantamount to an admission of guilt

304. Proximity

Meaning: Closeness, nearness, presence, propinquity

Definition: a nearness in space, time, or relationship

Usage: Do not operate microphones in close proximity to television sets

305. Fulsome

Meaning: ample, profuse, generous, liberal, lavish

Definition: complimentary or flattering to an excessive degree

Usage: The press are embarrassingly fulsome in their appreciation

306. Extol

Meaning: praise enthusiastically, go into raptures about/over, wax lyrical about, sing the praises of, praise to the skies, heap praise on,

Definition: praise enthusiastically

Usage: He extolled the virtues of the Russian peoples

307. Insipid

Meaning: tasteless, unflavoured, bland, weak, thin

Definition: lacking flavour; weak or tasteless

Usage: Mugs of insipid coffee

308. Incisive

Meaning: Penetrating, acute, sharp, keen, canny, clever, smart, quick

Definition: (of a person or mental process) intelligently analytical and clear-thinking.

Usage: She was an incisive critic

309. Idolatry

Meaning: idolization, idolizing, fetishization, worship, worshipping, adulation, adoration, adoring, reverence, glorification

Definition: extreme admiration, love, or reverence for something or someone..

Usage: We must not allow our idolatry of art to obscure issues of political significance

310. Disdain

Meaning: scorn, deride, slight, undervalue,

Definition: consider to be unworthy of one's consideration..

Usage: He disdained his patients as an inferior rabble

311. Accolade

Meaning: Honour, recognition, privilege, award, gift, title

Definition: an award or privilege granted as a special honour or as an acknowledgement of merit.

Usage: The hotel has won numerous accolades

312. Acrid

Meaning: pungent, bitter, sharp, sour, tart, harsh, acid, acidic

Definition: unpleasantly bitter or pungent.

Usage: Acrid smoke

313. Adjunct

Meaning: Supplement, addition, accompaniment, complement, additive, accessory

Definition: a thing added to something else as a supplementary rather than an essential part.

Usage: Computer technology is an adjunct to learning

314. Bolster

Meaning: pillow, cushion, support, pad, rest

Definition: a long, thick pillow that is placed under other pillows for support

Usage: the fall in interest rates is starting to bolster confidence

315. Orator

Meaning: Speaker, lecturer, declaimer

Definition: a public speaker, especially one who is eloquent or skilled.

Usage: A theatrically effective orator

316. Pacifist

Meaning: Objector, pacifier, concientious

Definition: a person who believes that war and violence are unjustifiable

Usage: she was a committed pacifist all her life

317. Savour

Meaning: Suggest, smack of, have a suggestion of

Definition: have a suggestion or trace of (a quality or attribute, typically one considered bad).

Usage: Their genuflections savoured of superstition and popery

318. Surfeit

Meaning: Excess, surplus, abundance, oversupply, avalanche, deluge

Definition: an excessive amount of something.

Usage: A surfeit of food and drink

319. Taciturn

Meaning: untalkative, reticent, quiet, mute, dumb, inarticulate

Definition: (of a person) reserved or uncommunicative in speech; saying little.

Usage: After such gatherings she would be taciturn and morose

320. Witticism

Meaning: Joke, quip, witty remark, flash of wit, jest, pun, pleasantry

Definition: a witty remark.

Usage: Maurice roared with laughter at his own witticisms

321. Abdicate

Meaning: resign, retire, quit, stand down

Definition: (of a monarch) renounce one's throne.

Usage: in 1918 Kaiser Wilhelm abdicated as German emperor

322. Atrophy

Meaning: waste, become emaciate, wither, shrivel, wilt

Definition: (of body tissue or an organ) waste away, especially as a result of the degeneration of cells, or become vestigial during evolution

Usage: The calf muscles will atrophy

323. Axiom

Meaning: Accepted truth, general truth, dictum, truism, principle

Definition: a statement or proposition which is regarded as being established, accepted, or selfevidently true.

Usage: The axiom that sport builds character

324. Burnish

Meaning: Shine, brighten, smooth,glaze

Definition: polish (something, especially metal) by rubbing..

Usage: Highly burnished armour

325. Cataclysm

Meaning: disaster, calamity, tragedy, art of God, crisis

Definition: a sudden violent political or social upheaval.

Usage: The cataclysm of the First World War

326. Converge

Meaning: Meet, intersect, cross, connect, link up, coincide

Definition: (of lines) tend to meet at a point..

Usage: a pair of lines of longitude are parallel at the equator but converge toward the poles

327. Delineate

Meaning: describe, set forth, set out, present, outline, depict, portray, represent

Definition: describe or portray (something) precisely..

Usage: The law should delineate and prohibit behaviour which is socially abhorrent

328. Devious

Meaning: underhand, deceitful, dishonest, dubious, dirty

Definition: Showing a skilful use of underhand tactics to achieve goals.

Usage: he's as devious as a politician needs to be

329. Enervate

Meaning: exhaust, tire, weary, devitalize, drain, sap, weaken, enfeeble

Definition: make (someone) feel drained of energy or vitality.

Usage: Enervating heat

330. Esoteric

Meaning: abstruse, obscure, arcane, cryptic, Delphic

Definition: intended for or likely to be understood by only a small number of people with a specialized knowledge or interest

Usage: Esoteric philosophical debates

331. Innate

Meaning: inborn, natural, inbred, inherent, intrinsic, intuitive, untaught

Definition: inborn; natural.

Usage: Her innate capacity for organization

332. Austere

Meaning: Severe, harsh, stiff, reserved, remote, serious

Definition: severe or strict in manner or attitude

Usage: he was an austere man, with a rigidly puritanical outlook

333. Onerous

Meaning: burdensome, heavy, awkward, oppressive

Definition: (of a task or responsibility) involving a great deal of effort, trouble, or difficulty.

Usage: He found his duties increasingly onerous

334. Wanton

Meaning: deliberate, willful, malicious,

spiteful, vicious, evil

Definition: (of a cruel or violent action) deliberate and unprovoked.

Usage: Sheer wanton vandalism

335. Loquacious

Meaning: Talkative, voluble, wordy, rambling

Definition: tending to talk a great deal; talkative.

Usage: Never loquacious, Sarah was now totally lost for words

336. Mortify

Meaning: embarrass, shame, abash, appal, crush

Definition: cause (someone) to feel very embarrassed or ashamed.

Usage: She was mortified to see her wrinkles in the mirror

337. Perdition

Meaning: damnation, eternal punishment

Definition: (in Christian theology) a state of eternal punishment and damnation into which a sinful and unrepentant person passes after death.

Usage: She used her last banknote to buy herself a square meal before perdition

338. Penance

Meaning: atonement, expiation, self-mortification, penalty

Definition: punishment inflicted on oneself as an outward expression of repentance for wrongdoing.

Usage: He had done public penance for those hasty words

339. Vicissitude

Meaning: Change, alteration, transformation, shift, switch, turn

Definition: a change of circumstances or fortune, typically one that is unwelcome or unpleasant.

Usage: Her husband's sharp vicissitudes of fortune

340. Punctilious

Meaning: meticulous, careful, diligent, attentive, studious, rigorous

Definition: showing great attention to detail or correct behaviour..

Usage: He was punctilious in providing every amenity for his guests

341. Terrestrial

Meaning: Earthy, worldly, mundane, earthbound

Definition: on or relating to the earth..

Usage: Increased ultraviolet radiation may disrupt terrestrial ecosystems

342. Laggard

Meaning: layabout, lagger, slug, snail, idler, lounger

Definition: a person who makes slow progress and falls behind others

Usage: Staff were under enormous pressure and there was no time for laggards

343. Aghast

Meaning: horrified, appalled, in shock, wide-eyed, shell-shocked, dismayed

Definition: filled with horror or shock.

Usage: She winced, aghast at his cruelty

344. Pristine

Meaning: immaculate, fresh, new, clean, virgin, pure

Definition: in its original condition; unspoilt.

Usage: Pristine copies of an early magazine

345. Altercation

Meaning: Argument, quarrel, fight, dissension, quarrel

Definition: a noisy argument or disagreement, especially in public.

Usage: I had an altercation with the ticket collector

346. Opulent

Meaning: Luxurious, sumptuous, palatial, grand, magnificent, rich, lush

Definition: ostentatiously costly and luxurious.

Usage: The opulent comfort of a limousine

347. Eulogize

Meaning: praise enthusiastically, go into raptures about/over, wax lyrical about, acclaim, extol

Definition: praise highly in speech or writing.

Usage: He was eulogized as a rock star

348. Astute

Meaning: shrewd, sharp, bright, brilliant, smart, canny, wise, incisive

Definition: having or showing an ability to accurately assess situations or people and turn this to one's advantage.

Usage: An astute businessman

349. Sombre

Meaning: dark, dark-coloured, dull, drab,shady

Definition: dark or dull in colour or tone.

Usage: The night skies were sombre and starless.

350. Errant

Meaning: guilty, culpable, aberrant, deviant, lawless

Definition: erring or straying from the accepted course or standards.

Usage: An errant husband coming back from a night on the tiles

351. Perturb

Meaning: worry, upset, disturb, trouble

Definition: make (someone) anxious or unsettled.

Usage: They were perturbed by her capricious behaviour

352. Imbibe

Meaning: drink, consume, sup, sip, quaff, swallow, down, guzzle, swill, lap

Definition: drink (alcohol).

Usage: They were imbibing far too many pitchers of beer

353. Perjury

Meaning: lying under oath, violation of an oath, giving false evidence/testimony, bearing false witness/testimony

Definition: the offence of wilfully telling an untruth or making a misrepresentation under oath.

Usage: He claimed two witnesses at his trial had committed perjury

354. Vanquish

Meaning: conquer, trounce, annihiliate, worst, overcome, overwhelm,

Definition: defeat thoroughly.

Usage: he successfully vanquished his rival

355. Sombre

Meaning: dark, dark-coloured, dull, drab, dingy, shady

Definition: dark or dull in colour or tone.

Usage: The night skies were sombre and starless

356. Sojourn

Meaning: Stay, visit, stop, stopover, residence

Definition: a temporary stay.

Usage: Her sojourn in Rome

357. Insouciant

Meaning: nonchalant, untroubled, unworried, unruffled, calm, breezy

Definition: showing a casual lack of concern.

Usage: An insouciant shrug

358. Labyrinth

Meaning: Maze, warren, network, web, coil, entanglement

Definition: a complicated irregular network of passages or paths in which it is difficult to find one's way; a maze.

Usage: You lose yourself in a labyrinth of little streets

359. Modicum

Meaning: little bit, small amount, praticle, degree, speck, fragment, scrap, crumb

Definition: a small quantity of a particular thing, especially something desirable or valuable.

Usage: His statement had a modicum of truth.

360. Sonorous

Meaning: resonant, rich, full, booming, vibrant, deep, clear

Definition: (of a person's voice or other sound) imposingly deep and full.

Usage: He read aloud with a sonorous and musical voice

361. Monotonous

Meaning: tedious, dull, unexciting, tiresome, unvaried, prosaic, dreary, colourless

Definition: dull, tedious, and repetitious; lacking in variety and interest..

Usage: The statistics that he quotes with monotonous regularity

362. Annihilate

Meaning: destroy, obliterate, liquidate, eradicate, extinguish, exttinguish

Definition: destroy utterly; obliterate..

Usage: A simple bomb of this type could annihilate them all

363. Expurgate

Meaning: censor, bowdlerize, blue-pencil, redact, cut, edit

Definition: remove matter thought to be objectionable or unsuitable from (a text or account).

Usage: An expurgated English translation

364. Insanity

Meaning: mental illness, lunacy, instability, madness, loss of reason

Definition: the state of being seriously mentally ill; madness..

Usage: He suffered from bouts of insanity

365. Indignation

Meaning: resentment, affront, anger, distress, unhappiness, hurt, pain, upset, pique, spleen

Definition: anger or annoyance provoked by what is perceived as unfair treatment.

Usage: The letter filled Lucy with indignation

366. Passionate

Meaning: intense, ardent, fervent, zealous, fiery, heated, eager, animated, spirited

Definition: having, showing, or caused by strong feelings or beliefs.

Usage: Passionate pleas for help

367. Infuriate

Meaning: enrage, incense, anger, inflame, send into a rage

Definition: make (someone) extremely angry and impatient.

Usage: I was infuriated by your article

368. Brood

Meaning: offspring, young, progeny, spawn

Definition: a family of birds or other young animals produced at one hatching or birth

Usage: A brood of chicks

369. Panacea

Meaning: universal cure, cure-all, wonder drug, magic formula, magic bullet

Definition: a solution or remedy for all difficulties or diseases.

Usage: The panacea for all corporate ills.

370. Reproachful

Meaning: disapproving, reproving, critical, censorious, admonitory

Definition: expressing disapproval or disappointment.

Usage: She gave him a reproachful look

371. Jubilant

Meaning: Overjoyed, exultant, joyful, rejoicing, gleeful, euphoric, ecstatic, transported

Definition: feeling or expressing great happiness and triumph.

Usage: a large number of jubilant fans ran on to the pitch

372. Comprehend

Meaning: understand, grasp, take in, see, apprehend, follow, make sense of, fathom, make out

Definition: grasp mentally; understand.

Usage: he couldn't comprehend her reasons for marrying Lovat

373. Moratorium

Meaning: embargo, ban, prohibition, suspension, stay, stoppage, halt

Definition: a temporary prohibition of an activity

Usage: a moratorium on the use of drift nets

374. Feud

Meaning: quarrel, fight, argue, bicker, squabble, dispute, clash

Definition: be engaged in a prolonged and bitter quarrel or dispute.

Usage: Hoover feuded with the CIA for decades

375. Deafen

Meaning: Make deaf, make temporarily deaf,

Definition: cause (someone) to lose the power of hearing permanently or temporarily.

Usage: We were deafened by the explosion

376. Fortune

Meaning: chance, accident, coincidence, destiny, foruity

Definition: chance or luck as an arbitrary force affecting human affairs.

Usage: some malicious act of fortune keeps them separate

377. Envy

Meaning: Jealousy, desire, enciousness

Definition: a feeling of discontented or resentful longing aroused by someone else's possessions, qualities, or luck.

Usage: She felt a twinge of envy for the people on board

378. Flaunt

Meaning: parade, exhibit, show off, draw attention to

Definition: display (something) ostentatiously, especially in order to provoke envy or admiration or to show defiance

Usage: newly rich consumers eager to flaunt their prosperity

379. Jibe

Meaning: taunt, sneer, jeer, insult, barb

Definition: an insulting or mocking remark; a taunt.

Usage: a jibe at his old rivals.

380. Grisly

Meaning: gruesome, horrid, fearful, hideous,

macabre, dire, awful

Definition: causing horror or disgust.

Usage: The town was shaken by a series of grisly crimes

381. Persuade

Meaning: Coax, sway, prompt, inveigle, enticc, tempt, make, get

Definition: induce (someone) to do something through reasoning or argument.

Usage: It wasn't easy, but I persuaded him to do the right thing

382. Fluff

Meaning: Fuzz, lint, dust

Definition: soft fibres from fabrics such as wool or cotton which accumulate in small light clumps.

Usage: he brushed his sleeve to remove the fluff

383. Hail

Meaning: Sleet, precipitation, beat, rain, fall, drop

Definition: pellets of frozen rain which fall in showers from cumulonimbus clouds

Usage: rain and hail bounced on the tiled roof

384. Allude

Meaning: refer to, suggest, hint at, imply, mention, touch on, cite

Definition: suggest or call attention to indirectly; hint at.

Usage: She had a way of alluding to Jean but never saying her name

385. Defy

Meaning: disobey, refuse to obey, flout, disregard, ignore

Definition: openly resist or refuse to obey.

Usage: a woman who defies convention

386. Elude

Meaning: evade, avoid, get away from, dodge, flee, escape(from)

Definition: escape from or avoid (a danger, enemy, or pursuer), typically in a skilful or cunning way.

Usage: he tried to elude the security men by sneaking through a back door

387. Ambivalent

Meaning: Equivocal, uncertain, unsure, doubtful, indecisive, irresolute, unresolved, mixed

Definition: having mixed feelings or contradictory ideas about something or someone.

Usage: some loved her, some hated her, few were ambivalent about her

388. Anecdote

Meaning: Story, tale, narrative, sketch

Definition: a short amusing or interesting story about a real incident or person

Usage: He told anecdotes about his job

389. Demur

Meaning: object, protest, take issue, take exception,cavil

Definition: raise objections or show reluctance.

Usage: normally she would have accepted the challenge, but she demurred.

390. Discreet

Meaning: careful, circumspect, cautious, wary, chary, guarded, close-mouthed

Definition: careful and prudent in one's speech or actions, especially in order to keep something confidential or to avoid embarrassment.

Usage: We made some discreet inquiries

391. Revive

Meaning: resuscitate, bring back from the edge of death

Definition: restore to life or consciousness.

Usage: both men collapsed, but were revived

392. Eerie

Meaning: uncanny, sinister, ghostly, unnatural, strange, odd, queer, unreal

Definition: strange and frightening.

Usage: An eerie green glow in the sky

393. Confront

Meaning: trouble, bother, burden, distress, vex, irritate, worry, face

Definition: (of a problem or difficulty) present itself to (someone) so that action must be taken.

Usage: The new government was confronted with many profound difficulties.

394. Subside

Meaning: calm, lull, fade, wane, ebb, still, cease, terminate

Definition: become less intense, violent, or severe.

Usage: I'll wait a few minutes until the storm subsides

395. Defendant

Meaning: accused, prisoner at the bar

Definition: an individual, company, or institution sued or accused in a court of law..

Usage: The defendant tried to claim that it was selfdefence

396. Encumbered

Meaning: hamper, hinder, obstruct, impede, check, cramp, limit, slow

Definition: restrict or impede (someone or something) in such a way that free action or movement is difficult.

Usage: She was encumbered by her heavy skirts

397. Calamitous

Meaning: disastrous, woeful, dire, tragic, fatal, direful

Definition: involving calamity; catastrophic or disastrous

Usage: Such calamitous events as fires, hurricanes, and floods

398. Slothful

Meaning: Lazy, idle, indolent, work-shy, inactive, inert, sluggish, dull, heavy

Definition: lazy.

Usage: Fatigue made him slothful

399. Catharsis

Meaning: purgation, relief, exorcism, release, purging

Definition: the process of releasing, and thereby providing relief from, strong or repressed emotions.

Usage: Music is a means of catharsis for them.

400. Revile

Meaning: criticize, censure, attack, lambaste, brand, denounce

Definition: criticize in an abusive or angrily insulting manner.

Usage: He was now reviled by the party that he had helped to lead.

401. Contours

Meaning: outline , shape, form

Definition: an outline representing or bounding the shape or form of something.

Usage: She traced the contours of his face with her finger

402. Anarchy

Meaning: rebellion, disorder, misrule, chaos, tumult, nihilism, mobocracy

Definition: a state of disorder due to absence or nonrecognition of authority or other controlling systems

Usage: He must ensure public order in a country threatened with anarchy

403. Convalesce

Meaning: recuperate, get better, recover, get well

Definition: recover one's health and strength over a period of time after an illness or medical treatment.

Usage: He spent eight months convalescing after the stroke.

404. Fragile

Meaning: breakable, brittle, frangible, flimsy, fine

Definition: (of an object) easily broken or damaged.

Usage: Fragile items such as glass and china

405. Dissuade

Meaning: discourage, deter, prevent, divert, sidetrack

Definition: persuade (someone) not to take a particular course of action.

Usage: His friends tried to dissuade him from flying

406. Lurking

Meaning: skulk, loiter, hide, take cover

Definition: be or remain hidden so as to wait in ambush for someone or something

Usage: A ruthless killer still lurked in the darkness

407. Besmirch

Meaning: sully, tarnish, blacken, stain, taint, smear, spoil, ruin

Definition: damage (someone's reputation).

Usage: He had besmirched the good name of his family

408. Neophyte

Meaning: beginner, learner, novice, newcomer, tyro, fledgling

Definition: a person who is new to a subject or activity

Usage: Four-day cooking classes are offered to neophytes and experts

409. Austere

Meaning: severe, stern, strict, formal, stiff, dour, grim, cold

Definition: severe or strict in manner or attitude.

Usage: He was an austere man, with a rigidly puritanical outlook.

410. Onus

Meaning: burden, responsibility, liability, obligation, duty, weight, load, charge, mantal

Definition: something that is one's duty or responsibility.

Usage: The onus is on you to show that you have suffered loss

411. Intrigue

Meaning: Interest, be of interest to, fascinate, attract, draw, lure, tempt

Definition: arouse the curiosity or interest of; fascinate.

Usage: I was intrigued by your question

412. Nuance

Meaning: shade, gradation, degree, variation

Definition: a subtle difference in or shade of meaning, expression, or sound

Usage: He was familiar with the nuances of the local dialect

413. Accord

Meaning: give, grant, tender, award, hand, yield

Definition: give or grant someone (power, status, or recognition)

Usage: The powers accorded to the head of state.

414. Titter

Meaning: giggle, snigger, tee-hee

Definition: give a short, half-suppressed laugh; giggle

Usage: Her stutter caused the children to titter

415. Cabal

Meaning: clique, faction, group, set, band, camp

Definition: a secret political clique or faction.

Usage: A cabal of dissidents

416. Pious

Meaning: devout, dedicated, reverent, holy, godly, faithful, dutiful, righteous

Definition: devoutly religious

Usage: A deeply pious woman

417. Grotesque

Meaning: Malformed, deformed, distorted, twisted

Definition: comically or repulsively ugly or distorted..

Usage: A figure wearing a grotesque mask

418. Entrench

Meaning: establish, settle, ensconce, lodge, set, root, install

Definition: establish (an attitude, habit, or belief) so firmly that change is very difficult or unlikely

Usage: Ageism is entrenched in our society

419. Obscure

Meaning: unclear, unknown, hidden, doubtful, indeterminate

Definition: not discovered or known about; uncertain.

Usage: His origins and parentage are obscure.

420. Harangue

Meaning: tirade, lecture, homily, rant, fulmination, broadside

Definition: a lengthy and aggressive speech.

Usage: They were subjected to a ten-minute harangue by two border guards

421. Perennial

Meaning: everlasting, perpetual, eternal, unending, never-ending, abiding, lasting,

Definition: lasting or existing for a long or apparently infinite time; enduring or continually recurring.

Usage: His perennial distrust of the media

422. Abnegation

Meaning: rejection, refusal, abandonment, abdication, surrender, disavowal

Definition: the action of renouncing or rejecting something..

Usage: Abnegation of political power

423. Mortal

Meaning: deadly, physical, bodily, fleshly, corporal, earthly, fatal, killing

Definition: (of a living human being, often in contrast to a divine being) subject to death.

Usage: All men are mortal.

424. Somnolent

Meaning: sleepy, drowsy, tired, heavy –eyed, groggy

Definition: sleepy; drowsy

Usage: a somnolent summer day

425. Amicable

Meaning: friendly, cordial, civil, easy, easy-going

Definition: characterized by friendliness and absence of discord.

Usage: An amicable settlement of the dispute

426. Befuddled

Meaning: confused, muddled, addled, dizzy, foggy, fuzzy

Definition: cause to become unable to think clearly

Usage: even in my befuddled state I could see that they meant trouble

427. Callow

Meaning: immature, naïve, green, untried

Definition: (of a young person) inexperienced and immature.

Usage: Earnest and callow undergraduates

428. Foment

Meaning: instigate, incite, provoke, excite, prompt, start, kindle

Definition: instigate or stir up (an undesirable or violent sentiment or course of action)

Usage: They accused him of fomenting political unrest

429. Sneer

Meaning: smirk, snicker, snigger

Definition: a contemptuous or mocking smile, remark, or tone

Usage: He acknowledged their presence with a condescending sneer.

430. Pariah

Meaning: outcast, leper, reject, untouchable, undesirable

Definition: an outcast.

Usage: They were treated as social pariahs.

431. Desist

Meaning: abstain, refrain, forbear, hold back, keep

Definition: stop doing something; cease or abstain.

Usage: Each pledged to desist from acts of sabotage

432. Inscribe

Meaning: crave, write, etch, cut, score, incise

Definition: write or carve (words or symbols) on something, especially as a formal or permanent record.

Usage: His name was inscribed on the new silver trophy

433. Succumb

Meaning: yield, give in, give way, submit, surrender, capitulate, cave in

Definition: fail to resist pressure, temptation, or some other negative force.

Usage: We cannot merely give up and succumb to despair.

434. Mendacious

Meaning: lying, untruthful, dishonest, false, doubledealing, two-faced, perfidious

Definition: not telling the truth; lying

Usage: mendacious propaganda

435. Querulous

Meaning: petulant, testy, touchy, waspish, prickly, crusty, cross, crabby

Definition: complaining in a rather petulant or whining manner..

Usage: She became querulous and demanding

436. Chaos

Meaning: disorder, disarray, confusion, bedlam, furore, babel

Definition: complete disorder and confusion

Usage: Snow caused chaos in the region

437. Alienated

Meaning: estrange, turn away, isolate, detach, distance

Definition: make (someone) feel isolated or estranged.

Usage: An urban environment which would alienate its inhabitants

438. Convalesce

Meaning: recuperate, get better, recover, get well

Definition: recover one's health and strength over a period of time after an illness or medical treatment.

Usage: He spent eight months convalescing after the stroke

439. Besmirch

Meaning: sully, tarnish, blacken, stain, taint, smear, spoil, ruin

Definition: damage (someone's reputation).

Usage: He had besmirched the good name of his family.

440. Disgust

Meaning: revulsion, repugnance, aversion, distaste, loathing

Definition: a feeling of revulsion or strong disapproval aroused by something unpleasant or offensive.

Usage: The sight filled her with disgust.

441. Discrimination

Meaning: prejudice, bias, bigotry, intolerance, partisanship,

Definition: the unjust or prejudicial treatment of different categories of people, especially on the grounds of race, age, or sex.

Usage: Victims of racial discrimination.

442. Consciousness

Meaning: awareness, alertness, sentience, responsiveness, wwakefulness

Definition: the state of being aware of and responsive to one's surroundings.

Usage: She failed to regain consciousness and died two days later

443. Exaggerate

Meaning: overstate, overstress, overvalue, overestimate, magnify

Definition: represent (something) as being larger, better, or worse than it really is.

Usage: She was apt to exaggerate any aches and pains.

444. Debilitate

Meaning: weakening, enervative, tiring, exhausting, devitalizing, draining

Definition: make (someone) very weak and infirm

Usage: He was severely debilitated by a stomach upset

445. Decree

Meaning: order, edict, command, mandate, precept

Definition: an official order that has the force of law.

Usage: The decree guaranteed freedom of assembly

446. Introspection

Meaning: brooding, heart-searching, self-absorption

Definition: the examination or observation of one's own mental and emotional processes.

Usage: Quiet introspection can be extremely valuable

447. Peculiar

Meaning: strange, unusual, odd, funny, curious, weird

Definition: different to what is normal or expected; strange.

Usage: He gave her some very peculiar looks

448. Denial

Meaning: contradiction, rebuttal, repudiation

Definition: the action of denying something.

Usage: She shook her head in denial

449. Probed

Meaning: examine, feel, prod, poke, check

Definition: explore or examine (something), especially with the hands or an instrument.

Usage: Hands probed his body from top to bottom.

450. Engulf

Meaning: flood, deluge, immerse, swamp, inundate

Definition: (of a natural force) sweep over (something) so as to surround or cover it completely.

Usage: The cafe was engulfed in flames

451. Gallant

Meaning: brave, courageous, valiant, bold, plucky, daring, fearless

Definition: (of a person or their behaviour) brave; heroic.

Usage: She had made gallant efforts to pull herself together

452. Hoax

Meaning: practical, joke, joke, jest, prank, trick, jape

Definition: a humorous or malicious deception.

Usage: The evidence had been planted as part of an elaborate hoax

453. Haggle

Meaning: barter, bargain, negotiate, quibble, wrangle

Definition: dispute or bargain persistently, especially over the cost of something.

Usage: The two sides are haggling over television rights.

454. Glut

Meaning: appoint, induct, install, invest, anoint, consecrate

Definition: An excessively abundant supply of something

Usage: there is a glut of cars on the market

455. Firmament

Meaning: the sky, heaven, the blue,

Definition: the heavens or sky.

Usage: Thunder shakes the firmament

456. Intrusive

Meaning: intruding, invasive, obtrusive, interrupting, trespassing, unwanted

Definition: causing disruption or annoyance through being unwelcome or uninvited

Usage: That was an intrusive question

457. Temporize

Meaning: equivocate, stall, delay, prevaricate, hesitate

Definition: avoid making a decision or committing oneself in order to gain time.

Usage: The opportunity was missed because the queen still temporized

458. Lampoon

Meaning: saririze, mock, ridicule, rag, tease

Definition: publicly criticize (someone or something) by using ridicule, irony, or sarcasm.

Usage: The actor was lampooned by the press

459. Grapple

Meaning: wrestle, struggle, tussle

Definition: engage in a close fight or struggle without weapons; wrestle.

Usage: passers-by grappled with the man after the knife attack.

460. Dawdle

Meaning: linger, dally, idle, waste time

Definition: waste time; be slow.

Usage: she mustn't dawdle—she had to make the call now.

461. Rampage

Meaning: riot, tear, run amok, storm, charge

Definition: (especially of a large group of people) move through a place in a violent and uncontrollable manner.

Usage: Several thousand demonstrators rampaged through the city

462. Hostility

Meaning: antagonism, bitterness, malevolence, malice, rancor, venom, anger, hatred

Definition: hostile behaviour; unfriendliness or opposition.

Usage: Their hostility to all outsiders

463. Vacillate

Meaning: dither, teeter, temporize, hesitate, fluctuate,

Definition: waver between different opinions or actions; be indecisive.

Usage: I vacillated between teaching and journalism.

464. Ordained

Meaning: appoint, induct, install, invest, anoint, consecrate

Definition: make (someone) a priest or minister; confer holy orders on

Usage: He was ordained a minister before entering Parliament

465. Provision

Meaning: supply, delivery, furnishing, allocation, distribution, presentation

Definition: The action of providing or supplying something for use.

Usage: New contracts for the provision of services

466. Stipulation

Meaning: condition, precondition, provision, prerequisite, specification

Definition: a condition or requirement that is specified or demanded as part of an agreement

Usage: They donated their collection of prints with the stipulation that they never be publicly exhibited

467. Mausoleum

Meaning: tomb, sepulcher, crypt, vault, catacomb

Definition: a stately or impressive building housing a tomb or group of tombs

Usage: The cathedral was built in 1517 as a royal mausoleum

468. Entrench

Meaning: establish, settle, lodge, set, root, install, plant, embed, anchor, seat

Definition: establish (an attitude, habit, or belief) so firmly that change is very difficult or unlikely.

Usage: Ageism is entrenched in our society

469. Deception

Meaning: deceit, duplicity, fraud, guile, pretence, artifice

Definition: the action of deceiving someone.

Usage: Obtaining property by deception.

470. Astounding

Meaning: amazing, astonishing, shocking, surprising, stunning

Definition: surprisingly impressive or notable

Usage: The summit offers astounding views.

471. Trepidation

Meaning: fear, apprehension, dread, agitation, dismay , alarm

Definition: a feeling of fear or anxiety about something that may happen.

Usage: The men set off in fear and trepidation

472. Certainty

Meaning: Confidence, certitude, fact, truth, validity

Definition: firm conviction that something is the case.

Usage: She knew with absolute certainty that they were dead

473. Scandalising

Meaning: shock, appal, outrage, revolt, repel, sicken

Definition: shock or horrify (someone) by a real or imagined violation of propriety or morality.

Usage: Their lack of manners scandalized their hosts.

474. Stringent

Meaning: Strict, firm, rigid, severe, harsh, tight, exacting, demanding, stiff

Definition: (of regulations, requirements, or conditions) strict, precise, and exacting

Usage: stringent guidelines on air pollution

475. Strained

Meaning: austere, abstinent, Spartan, monastic, simple

Definition: characterized by severe self-discipline and abstention from all forms of indulgence, typically for religious reasons

Usage: an ascetic life of prayer, fasting, and manual labour

476. Entrench

Meaning: establish, settle, ensconce, lodge, set, root, install, plant

Definition: establish (an attitude, habit, or belief) so firmly that change is very difficult or unlikely

Usage: Ageism is entrenched in our society

477. Impair

Meaning: damage, harm, diminish, reduce, weaken, lessen, blunt, impede, disable

Definition: weaken or damage (something, especially a faculty or function)

Usage: a noisy job could permanently impair their hearing

478. Astounding

Meaning: amazing, astonishing, shocking, surprising, striking

Definition: surprisingly impressive or notable.

Usage: The summit offers astounding views

479. Contemplate

Meaning: look at, view, regard, examine, inspect, observe, survey, study

Definition: look thoughtfully for a long time at.

Usage: He contemplated his image in the mirrors.

480. Stupefy

Meaning: stun, daze, knock out, benumb, numb

Definition: make (someone) unable to think or feel properly

Usage: The offence of administering drugs to a woman with intent to stupefy her.

481. Erratic

Meaning: unpredictable, variable, inconstant, uncertain, unstable,

Definition: not even or regular in pattern or movement; unpredictable.

Usage: Her breathing was erratic

482. Prominent

Meaning: important, well known, leading, eminent, pre-eminent, noted, public, foremost, famed, big, top, great, chief, main

Definition: important; famous.

Usage: She was a prominent member of the city council

483. Instincts

Meaning: inclination, drive, compulsion, need

Definition: a natural or intuitive way of acting or thinking.

Usage: They retain their old authoritarian instincts.

484. Prerequisites

Meaning: precondition, condition, essential, requirement, imperative, basic

Definition: a thing that is required as a prior condition for something else to happen or exist

Usage: sponsorship is not a prerequisite for any of our courses

485. Strained

Meaning: drawn, careworn, worn, pinched, tried, weary

Definition: truthful and straightforward; frank

Usage: Jean's pale, strained face

486. Spout

Meaning: nozzle, lip, rose

Definition: a tube or lip projecting from a container, through which liquid can be poured.

Usage: A teapot with a chipped spout

487. Disown

Meaning: reject, cast off, cast aside, abandon, repudiate, renounce, deny

Definition: refuse to acknowledge or maintain any connection with.

Usage: Lovell's rich family had disowned him because of his marriage

488. Speculation

Meaning: conjecture, supposition, guesswork

Definition: the forming of a theory or conjecture without firm evidence.

Usage: There has been widespread speculation that he plans to quit

489. Fragile

Meaning: breakable, brittle, frangible, flimsy, delicate, fine

Definition: (of an object) easily broken or damaged.

Usage: Fragile items such as glass and china.

490. Articulate

Meaning: fluent, eloquent, effective, persuasive, lucid, vocal

Definition: having or showing the ability to speak fluently and coherently

Usage: She was not very articulate.

491. Legitimate

Meaning: legal, lawful, authorized, permitted, permissible, allowable

Definition: conforming to the law or to rules.

Usage: His claims to legitimate authority

492. Snazzy

Meaning: stylish, smart, attractive, lovely, gorgeous, stunning

Definition: stylish and attractive.

Usage: snazzy little silk dresses

493. Sophisticated

Meaning: Underneath, below, further down, lower down

Definition: having, revealing, or involving a great deal of worldly experience and knowledge of fashion and culture.

Usage: a chic, sophisticated woman.

494. Arbitrations

Meaning: adjudication, meditation, negotiation, intervention, interposition

Definition: The use of an arbitrator to settle a dispute

Usage: Tayside Regional Council called for arbitration to settle the dispute

495. Candid

Meaning: frank, outspoken, forthright, open, honest, truthful, direct, bluff

Definition: truthful and straightforward; frank

Usage: His responses were remarkably candid

496. Bicker

Meaning: Squabble, argue

Definition: argue about petty and trivial matters.

Usage: couples who bicker over who gets what from the divorce

497. Fluctuate

Meaning: vary, differ, shift, change, alter, waver, swing, alternate

Definition: rise and fall irregularly in number or amount.

Usage: Trade with other countries tends to fluctuate from year to year

498. Cogent

Meaning: convincing, compelling, strong, forceful, powerful, potent, weighty

Definition: (of an argument or case) clear, logical, and convincing.

Usage: They put forward cogent arguments for British membership

499. Narrative

Meaning: account, story, tale, history, description, record, portrayal, report, rehearsal, recital

Definition: a spoken or written account of connected events; a story.

Usage: A gripping narrative.

500. Plagues

Meaning: afflict, bedevil, torture, torment, trouble, beset, dog

Definition: cause continual trouble or distress to

Usage: He has been plagued by ill health.

501. Proclaim

Meaning: Indicate, show, signify, reveal, manifest, betray, demonstrate

Definition: his high, intelligent forehead proclaimed a strength of mind that was almost tangible.

Usage: indicate clearly

502. Debtor

Meaning: borrower, mortgagor,

Definition: a person, country, or organization that owes money.

Usage: Generally, debtors must negotiate with each creditor separately

503. Hypocrisy

Meaning: cant, humbug, pretence, posturing, empty talk, pietism

Definition: the practice of claiming to have higher standards or more noble beliefs than is the case.

Usage: his target was the hypocrisy of suburban life.

504. Influx

Meaning: inundation, inrush, rush, stream, flood, ingress

Definition: an arrival or entry of large numbers of people or things

Usage: A massive influx of tourists

505. Imperative

Meaning: vital, crucial, critical, essential, exigent, pressing, urgent

Definition: of vital importance; crucial

Usage: immediate action was imperative.

506. Compensate

Meaning: Recompense, repay, pay back, recoup, requite

Definition: give (someone) something, typically money, in recognition of loss, suffering, or injury incurred; recompense.

Usage: Payments were made to farmers to compensate them for cuts in subsidies

507. Diligence

Meaning: assiduity, rigour, heedfulness, carefulness, studiousness

Definition: careful and persistent work or effort.

Usage: Few party members challenge his diligence as an MP

508. Obsolete

Meaning: Out of date, outdated, outmoded, oldfashioned

Definition: no longer produced or used; out of date

Usage: The disposal of old and obsolete machinery

509. Integrate

Meaning: combine, amalgamate, mix, intermix, join, fuse, blend

Definition: combine (one thing) with another to form a whole

Usage: Transport planning should be integrated with energy policy.

510. Alleviate

Meaning: Reduce, ease, relive, dull, lessen, quiet, blunt, moderate

Definition: make (suffering, deficiency, or a problem) less severe.

Usage: He couldn't prevent her pain, only alleviate it.

511. Affirm

Meaning: Declare, state, aver, proclaim, pronounce, attest, swear, avow, vow, guarantee, promise, certify

Definition: state emphatically or publicly.

Usage: He affirmed the country's commitment to peace

512. Travesty

Meaning: misrepresentation, distortion, corruption, poor imitation, parody

Definition: a false, absurd, or distorted representation of something.

Usage: The absurdly lenient sentence is a travesty of justice

513. Reparation

Meaning: amends, restitution, redress, compensation, repayment, atonement.

Definition: the action of making amends for a wrong one has done, by providing payment or other assistance to those who have been wronged.

Usage: The courts required a convicted offender to make financial reparation to his victim.

514. Dissent

Meaning: disagreement, argument, dispute, demur

Definition: the holding or expression of opinions at variance with those commonly or officially held.

Usage: There was no dissent from this view

515. Oppress

Meaning: persecute, abuse, maltreat, ill-treat, suppress, repress, subject

Definition: keep (someone) in subjection and hardship, especially by the unjust exercise of authority

Usage: A system which oppressed working people.

516. Cacophonous

Meaning: loud, noisy, ear-splitting, blaring, booming, deafening,

Definition: involving or producing a harsh, discordant mixture of sounds.

Usage: The cacophonous sound of slot machines

517. Glimpse

Meaning: brief look, quick look

Definition: a momentary or partial view

Usage: She caught a glimpse of the ocean

518. Integrity

Meaning: honest, probity, rectitude, honour, ethics, sincerity, truthfulness, virtue, decency

Definition: the quality of being honest and having strong moral principles.

Usage: A gentleman of complete integrity.

519. Intolerance

Meaning: bigotry, dogmatism, illiberality, parochialism, insularity

Definition: unwillingness to accept views, beliefs, or behaviour that differ from one's own

Usage: A struggle against religious intolerance.

520. Elusive

Meaning: Difficult to catch/find, difficult to track down

Definition: difficult to find, catch, or achieve.

Usage: Success will become ever more elusive.

521. Deem

Meaning: regard as, consider, judge, adjudge, rate, fin, count, esteem, reckon, account

Definition: regard or consider in a specified way.

Usage: The event was deemed a great success

522. Taboo

Meaning: Prohibition, proscription, veto, ban, restriction

Definition: a social or religious custom prohibiting or restricting a particular practice or forbidding association with a particular person, place, or thing

Usage: many taboos have developed around physical exposure

523. Harmonize

Meaning: Coordinate, match, blend, mix, balance

Definition: produce a pleasing visual combination.

Usage: Steeply pitched roofs which harmonize with the form of the main roof.

524. Prolong

Meaning: Lengthen, make longer, extend, elongate

Definition: extend the duration of

Usage: An idea which prolonged the life of the engine by many years

525. Hatch

Meaning: devise, conceive, concoct, brew, invent, plan, design, formulate

Definition: conspire to devise (a plot or plan)

Usage: The little plot that you and Sylvia hatched up last night

526. Pioneer

Meaning: Settler, colonist, explorer, trailblazer

Definition: a person who is among the first to explore or settle a new country or area.

Usage: The pioneers of the Wild West

527. Prone

Meaning: Susceptible, vulnerable, liable, given, disposed

Definition: likely or liable to suffer from, do, or experience something unpleasant or regrettable.

Usage: Farmed fish are prone to disease

528. Implications

Meaning: Suggestions, inference, innuendo, hint, intimation

Definition: the conclusion that can be drawn from something although it is not explicitly stated

Usage: The implication is that no one person at the bank is responsible

529. Utopian

Meaning: unworldly, non-material, immaterial

Definition: modelled on or aiming for a state in which everything is perfect; idealistic.

Usage: It is based on a utopian ideology.

530. Spur

Meaning: stimulus, incentive, encouragement, stimulant, inducement, prompt

Definition: a thing that prompts or encourages someone; an incentive

Usage: Wars act as a spur to practical invention.

531. Legitimate

Meaning: legal, lawful, licit, authorized, valid, upright, allowable

Definition: conforming to the law or to rules.

Usage: His claims to legitimate authority

532. Fiction

Meaning: Novels, stories, narration, story telling

Definition: literature in the form of prose, especially novels, that describes imaginary events and people.

Usage: they were supposed to be keeping up the fiction that they were happily married

533. Abide

Meaning: obey, observe, follow, keep to, conform to, accept, accede to

Definition: accept or act in accordance with (a rule, decision, or recommendation).

Usage: I said I would abide by their decision.

534. Espionage

Meaning: Spying, undercover work, intelligence, cyber-espionage, counter-espionage

Definition: the practice of spying or of using spies, typically by governments to obtain political and military information

Usage: The camouflage and secrecy of espionage

535. Manslaughter

Meaning: Killing, murder, slaying

Definition: the crime of killing a human being without malice aforethought, or in circumstances not amounting to murder

Usage: The defendant was convicted of manslaughter

536. Bankrupt

Meaning: insolvent, without, bare of, denuded of

Definition: (of a person or organization) declared in law as unable to pay their debts.

Usage: His father went bankrupt and the family had to sell their home

537. Prevalent

Meaning: widespread, frequent, usual, common, general, universal

Definition: widespread in a particular area or at a particular time.

Usage: The social ills prevalent in society today

538. Eradicating

Meaning: eliminate, do away with, remove, suppress

Definition: destroy completely; put an end to

Usage: This disease has been eradicated from the world

539. Stern

Meaning: serious, unsmiling, stony, flinty, steely, disapproving, sober

Definition: (of a person or their manner) serious and unrelenting, especially in the assertion of authority and exercise of discipline.

Usage: A smile transformed his stern face.

540. Guts

Meaning: instinctive, intuitive, impulsive,

natural, basic, emotinal

Definition: used in reference to a feeling or reaction based on an instinctive emotional response rather than considered thought

Usage: I had a gut feeling that something was wrong.

541. Blatant

Meaning: Flagrant, glaring, obvious, undisguised, overt, open, manifest

Definition: (of bad behaviour) done openly and unashamedly.

Usage: Blatant lies.

542. Exorbitant

Meaning: extortionate, excessive, sky-high, inordinate, huge, enormous

Definition: (of a price or amount charged) unreasonably high..

Usage: Some hotels charge exorbitant rates for phone calls

543. Frivolous

Meaning: flippant, glib, waggish, joking, jokey, nonserious.

Definition: not having any serious purpose or value.

Usage: Frivolous ribbons and lacy frills.

544. Unprecedented

Meaning: unparalleled, unequalled, unmatched, unrivalled, without equal

Definition: never done or known before

Usage: The government took the unprecedented step of releasing confidential correspondence

545. Dread

Meaning: fear, be afraid of, worry about

Definition: anticipate with great apprehension or fear

Usage: Jane was dreading the party.

546. Disparate

Meaning: contrasting, different, differing, unlike, dissimilar,

Definition: essentially different in kind; not able to be compared.

Usage: They inhabit disparate worlds of thought

547. Accentuate

Meaning: point up, heighten, stress, spotlight, foreground, frature

Definition: make more noticeable or prominent..

Usage: His jacket unfortunately accentuated his paunch

548. Exacerbate

Meaning: aggravate, make worse, worsen, inflame

Definition: make (a problem, bad situation, or negative feeling) worse.

Usage: Rising inflation was exacerbated by the collapse of oil prices.

549. Credence

Meaning: acceptance, belief, faith, trust, confidence, reliance, traction

Definition: belief in or acceptance of something as true

Usage: Psychoanalysis finds little credence among laymen.

550. Suffice

Meaning: be enough, be sufficient, do, serve,

Definition: be enough or adequate.

Usage: A quick look should suffice.

551. Intrusive

Meaning: obtrusive, unwanted, interrupting, unwelcome

Definition: causing disruption or annoyance through being unwelcome or uninvited.

Usage: That was an intrusive question

552. Hesitation

Meaning: pausing, delay, waiting

Definition: the action of pausing before saying or doing something.

Usage: She answered without hesitation.

553. Consequence

Meaning: result, upshot, outcome

Definition: a result or effect, typically one that is unwelcome or unpleasant.

Usage: Inflation is a consequence of a rapid growth in the money supply.

554. Envisage

Meaning: predict, forecast, foretell, expect

Definition: contemplate or conceive of as a possibility or a desirable future event.

Usage: The Rome Treaty envisaged free movement across frontiers.

555. Conventional

Meaning: normal, standard, regular, ordinary

Definition: based on or in accordance with what is generally done or believed.

Usage: A conventional morality had dictated behaviour.

556. Rupture

Meaning: break, fracture, crack

Definition: (especially of a pipe or container, or bodily part such as an organ or membrane) break or burst suddenly.

Usage: If the main artery ruptures he could die.

557. Bumpy

Meaning: uneven, rough, irregular

Definition: (of a surface) uneven, with many patches raised above the rest.

Usage: The car jolted on the bumpy road.

558. Emanate

Meaning: emerge, flow, pour

Definition: (of a feeling, quality, or sensation) issue or spread out from (a source).

Usage: Policy statements which emanate from government departments.

559. Consent

Meaning: agreement, assent, accord

Definition: permission for something to happen or agreement to do something.

Usage: No change may be made without the consent of all the partners.

560. Ostensible

Meaning: apparent, seeming, outward, surface

Definition: stated or appearing to be true, but not necessarily so.

Usage: The real dispute which lay behind the ostensible complaint.

561. Bolster

Meaning: Pillow, cushion, pad, support

Definition: a long, thick pillow that is placed under other pillows for support.

Usage: Most of them were sitting on the floor which was strewn with cushions, bolsters, and rugs.

562. Hover

Meaning: be suspended, be poised, hang, float

Definition: remain in one place in the air.

Usage: Army helicopters hovered overhead.

563. Embark

Meaning: board ship, go on board,

Definition: go on board a ship or aircraft.

Usage: He embarked for India in 1817.

564. Recession

Meaning: economic decline, downturn, depression

Definition: a period of temporary economic decline during which trade and industrial activity are reduced, generally identified by a fall in GDP in two successive quarters.

Usage: the country is in the depths of a recession.

565. Metaphor

Meaning: figure of speech, image, trope, figurative expression

Definition: a figure of speech in which a word or phrase is applied to an object or action to which it is not literally applicable.

Usage: When we speak of gene maps and gene mapping, we use a cartographic metaphor.

566. Pacifism

Meaning: peacemaking, conscientious objection(s), passive resistance, love of peace

Definition: the belief that war and violence are unjustifiable and that all disputes should be settled by peaceful means.

Usage: there remains a powerful undercurrent of pacifism.

567. Nuance

Meaning: fine distinction, shade, shading, gradation, variation

Definition: a subtle difference in or shade of meaning, expression, or sound.

Usage: He was familiar with the nuances of the local dialect.

568. Unrelenting

Meaning: implacable, inflexible, uncompromising, unyielding

Definition: not yielding in strength, severity, or determination.

Usage: He was an unrelenting opponent of the Jacobite cause.

569. Camouflage

Meaning: disguise, hide, conceal, mask, screen

Definition: hide or disguise the presence of (a person, animal, or object) by means of camouflage.

Usage: The caravan was camouflaged with netting and branches from trees.

570. Surmise

Meaning: guess, conjecture, suspect, deduce, infer

Definition: suppose that something is true without having evidence to confirm it.

Usage: He surmised that something must be wrong.

571. Troupe

Meaning: group, company, band, ensemble, set, cast

Definition: a group of dancers, actors, or other entertainers who tour to different venues.

Usage: A dance troupe.

572. Avaricious

Meaning: grasping, acquisitive, covetous, greedy, rapacious, mercenary

Definition: having or showing an extreme greed for wealth or material gain.

Usage: An avaricious, manipulative woman

573. Disconcert

Meaning: unsettle, nonplus, discomfit, confuse, perplex, ruffle, shake, worry.

Definition: disturb the composure of; unsettle.

Usage: The abrupt change of subject disconcerted her.

574. Harangue

Meaning: tirade, lecture, diatribe, homily, polemic, rant, fulmination, broadside, invective

Definition: a lengthy and aggressive speech

Usage: They were subjected to a ten-minute harangue by two border guards

575. Unsceupulous

Meaning: unprincipled, immoral, amoral,

dishonest, cunning, furtive, sly, bad, evil, wicked

Definition: having or showing no moral principles; not honest or fair.

Usage: Unscrupulous landlords might be tempted to harass existing tenants.

576. Preachy

Meaning: moralistic, didactic, dogmatic

Definition: having or showing a tendency to give moral advice in a tedious or self-righteous way.

Usage: His patriotic pictures had a preachy tone

577. Unabashed

Meaning: unashamed, shameless, brazen, confident, immodest, unshrinking, fearless

Definition: not embarrassed, disconcerted, or ashamed

Usage: He was unabashed by the furore his words provoked

578. Melodramatic

Meaning: histrionic, extravagant, overdone, overripe, overemotional, sentimental

Definition: characteristic of melodrama, especially in being exaggerated or overemotional.

Usage: He flung the door open with a melodramatic flourish.

579. Mimic

Meaning: imitate, copy, mock, parody, lampoon, caricature

Definition: imitate (someone or their actions or words), especially in order to entertain or ridicule

Usage: He mimicked Super Star Rajini voice.

580. Protagonist

Meaning: supporter, adherent, backer, proponent, advocate, promoter, exponent, prime mover

Definition: an advocate or champion of a particular cause or idea.

Usage: He's a strenuous protagonist of the new agricultural policy.

581. Jargon

Meaning: Slang, cant, idiom, argot, patter

Definition: special words or expressions used by a profession or group that are difficult for others to understand.

Usage: legal jargon

582. Evocative

Meaning: Reminiscent, suggestive, redolent

Definition: bringing strong images, memories, or feelings to mind

Usage: Powerfully evocative lyrics

583. Beneath

Meaning: Underneath, below, further down, lower down

Definition: extending or directly underneath something.

Usage: A house built on stilts to allow air to circulate beneath.

584. Sheer

Meaning: utter, complete, absolute, total, pure, perfect, patent

Definition: nothing other than; unmitigated (used for emphasis)

Usage: she giggled with sheer delight

585. Plague

Meaning: afflict, bedevil, torment, trouble, beset, dog, curse

Definition: cause continual trouble or distress to

Usage: He has been plagued by ill health

586. Archive

Meaning: file, log, catalogue, pigeonhole

Definition: place or store (something) in an archive.

Usage: The entire directory will be archived

587. Liberate

Meaning: set free, free, release, let out, let go, discharge, deliver

Definition: set (someone) free from imprisonment, slavery, or oppression.

Usage: The serfs had been liberated

588. Retreat

Meaning: withdraw, retire, draw back, pull back, pull out, fall back, give way

Definition: (of an army) withdraw from enemy forces as a result of their superior power or after a defeat

Usage: The French retreated in disarray

589. Combat

Meaning: battle, fighting, action, conflict, war, warfare

Definition: fighting between armed forces.

Usage: Five Hurricanes were shot down in combat.

590. Retract

Meaning: Pull in, draw in, pull back, sheathe, put away

Definition: draw or be drawn back or back in

Usage: She retracted her hand as if she'd been burn.

591. Endurance

Meaning: tolerance, bearing, sufferance

Definition: the ability to endure an unpleasant or difficult process or situation without giving way.

Usage: She was close to the limit of her endurance.

592. Anxiety

Meaning: worry, concern, apprehension

Definition: a feeling of worry, nervousness, or unease about something with an uncertain outcome.

Usage: His anxiety grew as his messages were all left unanswered

593. Secretive

Meaning: uncommunicative, secret, silent

Definition: (of a person or an organization) inclined to conceal feelings and intentions or not to disclose information.

Usage: She was very secretive about her past.

594. Intrusive

Meaning: invasive, obtrusive, unwanted

Definition: causing disruption or annoyance through being unwelcome or uninvited.

Usage: That was an intrusive question.

595. Impresario

Meaning: organizer, manager, producer

Definition: a person who organizes and often finances concerts, plays, or operas.

Usage: A theatrical impresario.

596. Blantant

Meaning: flagrant, glaring, obvious, undisguised

Definition: (of bad behaviour) done openly and unashamedly.

Usage: A blatant lie.

597. Sacrosanct

Meaning: sacred, respected, inviolate

Definition: (especially of a principle, place, or routine) regarded as too important or valuable to be interfered with.

Usage: The individual's right to work has been upheld as sacrosanct.

598. Percolate

Meaning: filter, drain, drip

Definition: (of a liquid or gas) filter gradually

through a porous surface or substance.

Usage: The water percolating through the soil may leach out minerals.

599. Environ

Meaning: surround, encircle, enclose, ring, envelop;

Definition: surround; enclose.

Usage: The stone circle was environed by an expanse of peat soil

600. Usher

Meaning: escort, accompany, help, assist

Definition: show or guide (someone) somewhere.

Usage: He ushered him to a window seat.

601. Pledge

Meaning: Mortgage, guarantee, pawn

Definition: give as security on a loan.

Usage: The creditor to whom the land is pledged

602. Tumultuous

Meaning: loud, deafening, thunderous, thundering, earsplitting, noisy, vociferous

Definition: making an uproar or loud, confused noise.

Usage: Tumultuous applause

603. Coalition

Meaning: alliance, union, partnership, affiliation, bloc, caucus.

Definition: a temporary alliance for combined action, especially of political parties forming a government.

Usage: A coalition between Liberals and Conservatives.

604. Inhibit

Meaning: impede, hinder, hamper, discourage, obstruct, slow, retard

Definition: hinder, restrain, or prevent (an action or process)

Usage: Cold inhibits plant growth

605. Squirm

Meaning: wriggle, wiggle, writhe, twist, slide, slither, turn, shift, fidget

Definition: wriggle or twist the body from side to side, especially as a result of nervousness or discomfort

Usage: He looked uncomfortable and squirmed in his chair.

606. Allegedly

Meaning: reportedly, supposedly, reputedly, ostensibly, apparently, presumedly

Definition: used to convey that something is claimed to be the case or have taken place, although there is no proof

Usage: He was allegedly a leading participant in the coup attempt

607. Creep

Meaning: crawl, squirm, wriggle, writhe, worm, inch, edge

Definition: move slowly and carefully in order to avoid being heard or noticed

Usage: He crept downstairs, hardly making any noise

608. Gimmick

Meaning: stunt, contrivance, scheme, trick, dodge, ploy, stratagem

Definition: a trick or device intended to attract attention, publicity, or trade.

Usage: It is not so much a programme to improve services as a gimmick to gain votes.

609. Provocative

Meaning: annoying, irritating, infuriating, provoking, maddening, goading

Definition: causing anger or another strong

reaction, especially deliberately

Usage: A provocative article.

610. Orthodoxy

Meaning: doctrine, belief, creed, dogma, credo, theory, view, idea, practice

Definition: authorized or generally accepted theory, doctrine, or practice.

Usage: Monetarist orthodoxy.

611. Tendentious

Meaning: partisan, expressing, intending

Definition: expressing or intending to promote a particular cause or point of view, especially a controversial one.

Usage: A tendentious reading of history

612. Credence

Meaning: acceptance, belief, faith, trust, confidence, reliance, traction

Definition: belief in or acceptance of something as true.

Usage: Psychoanalysis finds little credence among laymen

613. Reluctant

Meaning: unwilling, disinclined, grudging, resistant, opposed, antipathetic.

Definition: unwilling and hesitant; disinclined..

Usage: She seemed reluctant to answer.

614. Disingenuous

Meaning: dishonest, deceitful, underhand, underhanded, duplicitous, lying, false

Definition: not candid or sincere, typically by pretending that one knows less about something than one really does.

Usage: This journalist was being somewhat disingenuous as well as cynical

615. Ascribing

Meaning: attribute, assign, put down, set down, accredit, credit

Definition: regard something as being due to (a cause).

Usage: He ascribed Jane's short temper to her upset stomach.

616. Maverick

Meaning: individualist, nonconformist, free spirit, eccentric, outerside

Definition: an unorthodox or independent-minded person.

Usage: He's the maverick of the senate

617. Verdict

Meaning: judgement, adjudication, decision, finding, ruling, resolution, decree, order

Definition: a decision on an issue of fact in a civil or criminal case or an inquest

Usage: The jury returned a verdict of not guilty

618. Embroil

Meaning: Involve, entangle, ensnare, enmesh, catch up, mix up, bog down, mire

Definition: involve (someone) deeply in an argument, conflict, or difficult situation.

Usage: The organization is currently embroiled in running battles with pressure groups.

619. Reckless

Meaning: rash, careless, thoughtless, incautions, heedless, unheeding, inattentive, precipitate

Definition: heedless of danger or the consequences of one's actions; rash or impetuous

Usage: You mustn't be so reckless".

620. Legislative

Meaning: law-making, judicial, juridical, administrative

Definition: having the power to make laws..

Usage: The country's supreme legislative body.

621. Scepticism

Meaning: Doubt, doubtfulness, Dubiousness, lack of conviction

Definition: a sceptical attitude; doubt as to the truth of something.

Usage: These claims were treated with scepticism.

622. Contingent

Meaning: Chance, accidental, fortuitous, possible, unforeseen, unpredictable

Definition: subject to chance.

Usage: The contingent nature of the job.

623. Culmination

Meaning: Climax, pinnacle, peak, high point, Height, crest, zenith

Definition: the highest or climactic point of something, especially as attained after a long time.

Usage: The deal marked the culmination of years of negotiation.

624. Surrogate

Meaning: substitute, proxy, replacement

Definition: a substitute, especially a person deputizing for another in a specific role or office.

Usage: Wives of MPs are looked on as surrogates for their husbands while the latter are at Westminster.

625. Enumerate

Meaning: List, itemize, catalogue, set out, set forth, give

Definition: mention (a number of things) one by one.

Usage: There is not space to enumerate all his works.

626. Altruistic

Meaning: Unselfish, selfless, self-denying

Definition: showing a disinterested and selfless concern for the well-being of others; unselfish.

Usage: It was an entirely altruistic act.

627. Maverick

Meaning: Individualist, nonconformist, free spirit, eccentric, outsider, trendsetter

Definition: an unorthodox or independent-minded person.

Usage: he's the maverick of the senate.

628. Promulgate

Meaning: make public, publicize, announce, proclaim, circulate

Definition: promote or make widely known (an idea or cause).

Usage: These objectives have to be promulgated within the organization .

629. pecuniary

Meaning: financial, money, monetary, fiscal, capital, ccommercial

Definition: relating to or consisting of money.

Usage: He admitted obtaining a pecuniary advantage by deception.

630. Ponderous

Meaning: clumsy, slow, heavy, awkward, graceless

Definition: slow and clumsy because of great weight.

Usage: A swarthy, ponderous giant of a man.

631. Expedite

Meaning: Speed up, accelerate, hurry, hasten, step up, quicken

Definition: make (an action or process) happen sooner or be accomplished more quickly.

Usage: He promised to expedite economic reforms.

632. Conscience

Meaning: moral sense, sense of right, still small voice

Definition: a person's moral sense of right and wrong, viewed as acting as a guide to one's behaviour.

Usage: He had a guilty conscience about his desires

633. Contravene

Meaning: Break, breach, violate.

Definition: offend against the prohibition or order of (a law, treaty, or code of conduct).

Usage: He contravened the Official Secrets Act.

634. Sanctum

Meaning: Holy place, shrine, altar, refuge, foxhole, hiding place

Definition: a sacred place, especially a shrine within a temple or church

Usage: An icon installed within the sanctum of the temple

635. Whopping

Meaning: Huge, massive, enormous, gigantic, very big, very large

Definition: very large

Usage: A whopping $74 million loss.

636. Assassination

Meaning: Murder, killing, political execution, slaughter, butchery, extermination, termination

Definition: the action of assassinating someone

Usage: The assassination of President Kennedy

637. Foil

Meaning: thwart, oppose, baulk, disappoint, impede, obstruct

Definition: prevent (something considered wrong or undesirable) from succeeding.

Usage: A brave policewoman foiled the armed robbery

638. Motley

Meaning: Mixed, diverse, assorted, sundry, varied, disparate

Definition: incongruously varied in appearance or character; disparate.

Usage: A motley crew of discontents and zealots.

639. Facetious

Meaning: Flippant, flip, glib, joking, jocular, playful, impish

Definition: treating serious issues with deliberately inappropriate humour; flippant

Usage: A facetious remark.

640. Murky

Meaning: dark, gloomy, grey, leaden, dull, dim, cloudy

Definition: dark and gloomy, especially due to thick mist.

Usage: The sky was murky and a thin drizzle was falling.

641. Lynch

Synonyms: hang, hang by the neck

Meaning: (of a group of people) kill (someone) for an alleged offence without a legal trial, especially by hanging.

Usage: Her father had been lynched by whites.

642. Arid

Synonyms: dry, dried up, waterless, as dry as a bone, thirsty, Dull

Meaning: lacking in interest, excitement, or meaning..

Usage: His arid years in suburbia

643. Impresario

Synonyms: Organizer, manager, producer, stage manager

Meaning: a person who organizes and often finances concerts, plays, or operas

Usage: Amit Shah plays impresario to this knee-jerk nationalism.

644. Gravitas

Synonyms: dignity, seriousness, solemnity, gravity, loftiness, grandeur

Meaning: dignity, seriousness, or solemnity of manner..

Usage: A post for which he has the expertise and the gravitas

645. Manace

Synonyms: Danger, peril, risk, hazard, threat

Meaning: a person or thing that is likely to cause harm; a threat or danger.

Usage: A new initiative aimed at beating the menace of drugs

646. Fetish

Synonyms: fixation, obsession, compulsion, mania

Meaning: a form of sexual desire in which gratification is linked to an abnormal degree to a particular object, item of clothing, part of the body, etc..

Usage: A man with a fetish for surgical masks

647. Blatant

Synonyms: flagrant, manifest, unmistakable, open, obvious

Meaning: (of bad behaviour) done openly and unashamedly

Usage: Blatant lies

648. Sacrosanct

Synonyms: sacred, hallowed, inviolable, inviolate, untouchable

Meaning: (especially of a principle, place, or routine) regarded as too important or valuable to be interfered with

Usage: The individual's right to work has been upheld as sacrosanct

649. Martyr

Synonyms: suffer from, be a constant sufferer from, have chronic

Meaning: a person who displays or exaggerates their discomfort or distress in order to obtain sympathy

Usage: She wanted to play the martyr

650. Swoop

Synonyms: dive, descend, drop, plunge, pitch

Meaning: (especially of a bird) move rapidly downwards through the air.

Usage: The barn owl can swoop down on a mouse in total darkness

651. Flare

Meaning: Blaze, flash, flame, burn up

Definition: burn or shine with a sudden intensity.

Usage: The bonfire crackled and flared up

652. Trigger

Meaning: Activate, set off, set going, trip

Definition: cause (a device) to function.

Usage: Burglars fled empty-handed after triggering the alarm

653. Evacuate

Meaning: remove, clear, move out, shift, take away, expel, evict.

Definition: remove (someone) from a place of danger to a safer place.

Usage: Several families were evacuated from their homes.

654. Advocacy

Meaning: support for, argument for, arguing for, calling for, pushing for

Definition: public support for or recommendation of a particular cause or policy

Usage: His outspoken advocacy of the agreement has won no friends

655. Allegation

Meaning: claim, assertion, declaration, witness, evidence, hint, intimation

Definition: a claim or assertion that someone has done something illegal or wrong, typically one made without proof.

Usage: He made allegations of corruption against the administration

656. Agitation

Meaning: anxiety, perturbation, distress, concern, alarm, worry

Definition: a state of anxiety or nervous excitement.

Usage: She was wringing her hands in agitation

657. Eradicate

Meaning: get rid of, eliminate, do away with , remove, suppress

Definition: destroy completely; put an end to

Usage: This disease has been eradicated from the world

658. Turmoil

Meaning: confusion, tumult, disorder, commotion, unrest, trouble, upset

Definition: a state of great disturbance, confusion, or uncertainty.

Usage: The country was in turmoil.

659. Assent

Meaning: agree to, approve, bless

Definition: express approval or agreement

Usage: The Prime Minister assented to the change.

670. Assist

Meaning: help, aid, abet, give assistance

Definition: help (someone), typically by doing a share of the work.

Usage: A senior academic would assist him in his work.

671. Flared

Meaning: Blaze, flash, flame

Definition: burn or shine with a sudden intensity.

Usage: A match flared as he lit a cigarette.

672. Triggered

Meaning: activate, set off, set going, trip

Definition: cause (a device) to function.

Usage: Burglars fled empty-handed after triggering the alarm.

673. Advocacy

Meaning: support for, argument for, arguing for, calling for

Definition: public support for or recommendation of a particular cause or policy.

Usage: His outspoken advocacy of the agreement has won no friends.

674. Allegation

Meaning: claim, assertion, declaration, statement

Definition: a claim or assertion that someone has done something illegal or wrong, typically one made without proof.

Usage: He made allegations of corruption against the administration.

675. Agitation

Meaning: anxiety, perturbation, distress, concern

Definition: a state of anxiety or nervous excitement.

Usage: She was wringing her hands in agitation.

676. Eradicate

Meaning: get rid of, eliminate, do away with, remove

Definition: destroy completely; put an end to.

Usage: This disease has been eradicated from the world.

677. Turmoil

Meaning: confusion, disorder, disturbance

Definition: a state of great disturbance, confusion, or uncertainty.

Usage: A time of great political turmoil.

678. Fumigate

Meaning: disinfect, purify, sterilize

Definition: disinfect or purify (an area) with the fumes of certain chemicals.

Usage: We got sulphur candles to fumigate the house.

679. Veer

Meaning: career, swing, wheel, twist

Definition: change direction suddenly.

Usage: An oil tanker that had veered off course.

680. Valiant

Meaning: brave, courageous, fearless

Definition: possessing or showing courage or determination.

Usage: She made a valiant effort to hold her anger in check.

681. Posterity

Meaning: future generations, succeeding generations

Definition: all future generations of people.

Usage: the names of those who died are recorded for posterity on a framed scroll.

682. Relinquish

Meaning: renounce, give up, part with turn over

Definition: voluntarily cease to keep or claim; give up.

Usage: he relinquished his managerial role to become chief executive.

683. Persuade

Meaning: convince, talk someone into, induce

Definition: induce (someone) to do something through reasoning or argument.

Usage: it wasn't easy, but I persuaded him to do the right thing.

684. Ancestry

Meaning: forebears, forefathers, parentage

Definition: one's family or ethnic descent.

Usage: he was proud of his Irish ancestry.

685. Propulsion

Meaning: thrust, motive force, impluse

Definition: the action of driving or pushing forwards.

Usage: they dive and use their wings for propulsion under water.

686. Ephemeral

Meaning: transient, fleeting, passing

Definition: lasting for a very short time.

Usage: fashions are ephemeral: new ones regularly drive out the old.

687. Dissuade

Meaning: discourage, deter, prevent, disincline

Definition: persuade (someone) not to take a particular course of action.

Usage: his friends tried to dissuade him from flying.

688. Persist

Meaning: persevere, continue, carry on

Definition: continue in an opinion or course of action in spite of difficulty or opposition.

Usage: the minority of drivers who persist in drinking.

689. Scarce

Meaning: short, in short supply, scant

Definition: (especially of food, money, or some other resource) insufficient for the demand.

Usage: as raw materials became scarce, synthetics were developed.

690. Perpetual

Meaning: everlasting, never-ending, eternal,

permanent

Definition: never ending or changing.

Usage: the population lived in a perpetual state of fear.

691. Shrewd

Meaning: astute, sharp, acute, intelligent

Definition: having or showing sharp powers of judgement; astute.

Usage: She was shrewd enough to guess the motive behind his gesture.

692. Subvert

Meaning: destabilize, unsettle, overthrow, overtum

Definition: undermine the power and authority of (an established system or institution).

Usage: An attempt to subvert democratic government

693. Emergence

Meaning: disclosure, exposure, publication

Definition: the process of becoming visible after being concealed.

Usage: I misjudged the timing of my emergence.

694. Muster

Meaning: assemble, bring together, mobilize

Definition: assemble (troops), especially for inspection or in preparation for battle.

Usage: They had mustered 50,000 troops.

695. Ordeal

Meaning: trail, tribulation, test.

Definition: a very unpleasant and prolonged experience.

Usage: The ordeal of having to give evidence.

696. Infallible

Meaning: error free, flawless, perfect

Definition: incapable of making mistakes or being wrong.

Usage: She had an infallible sense of timing.

697. Assiduous

Meaning: careful, diligent, attentive

Definition: showing great care and perseverance.

Usage: She was assiduous in pointing out every feature.

698. Shoddy

Meaning: Poor Quality, inferior, rubbishy

Definition: badly made or done.

Usage: We're not paying good money for shoddy goods.

699. Inducement

Meaning: incentive, attraction, encouragement, temptation

Definition: a thing that persuades or leads someone to do something.

Usage: Companies were prepared to build only in return for massive inducements

700. Contemptuous

Meaning: scornful, disdainful, disrespectful, insulting, insolent

Definition: showing contempt; scornful.

Usage: She was intolerant and contemptuous of the majority of the human race.

701. Provincial

Meaning: small-town, non-metropolitan, non-urban, back woods, backwater

Definition: of or concerning a province of a country or empire of or concerning a province of a country or empire.

Usage: Provincial elections.

702. Rebuke

Meaning: reprimand, reproach, scold, admonish, chide, upbraid, criticize

Definition: express sharp disapproval or

criticism of (someone) because of their behaviour or actions express sharp disapproval or criticism of (someone) because of their behaviour or actions.

Usage: she had rebuked him for drinking too much.

703. Lambasted

Meaning: criticize, castigate, chastise, censure, condemn

Definition: criticize (someone or something) harshly.

Usage: They lambasted the report as a gross distortion of the truth.

704. Blare

Meaning: Blast, sound loudly, toot, honk, shriek, screech

Definition: make or cause to make a loud, harsh sound.

Usage: The ambulance arrived outside, siren blaring.

705. Tinkle

Meaning: ring, jingle, jangle, chime, peal, ding, ping

Definition: make or cause to make a light, clear ringing sound.

Usage: Cool water tinkled in the stone fountains.

706. trumpet

Meaning: proclaim, announce, declare, broadcast, blazon

Definition: proclaim widely or loudly.

Usage: The press trumpeted another defeat for the government.

707. Percussion

Meaning: crash, bang, smash, clash, bump, thump

Definition: the striking of one solid object with or against another with some degree of force.

Usage: the clattering percussion of objects striking the walls and the shutters.

708. Wade

Meaning: paddle, wallow, dabble, slop, plod

Definition: walk with effort through water or another liquid or viscous substance.

Usage: He waded out to the boat.

709. Impeccable

Meaning: flawless, faultless, unblemished, spotless, perfect, exemplary

Definition: in accordance with the highest standards; faultless.

Usage: He had impeccable manners.

710. Perplex

Meaning: puzzle, baffle, mystify, worry, befuddle, addle, fog, throw

Definition: make (someone) feel completely baffled

Usage: She was perplexed by her husband's moodiness.

711. Inadvertent

Meaning: unintentional, unintended, accidental, unpremeditated

Definition: not resulting from or achieved through deliberate planning.

Usage: An inadvertent administrative error occurred that resulted in an over payment.

712. Exonerate

Meaning: absolve, clear, acquit,

Definition: (of an official body) absolve (someone) from blame for a fault or wrongdoing.

Usage: The inquiry exonerated Lewis and his company.

713. Hostile

Meaning: antagonistic, aggressive, confrontational, belligerent

Definition: showing or feeling opposition or

dislike; unfriendly.

Usage: He wrote a ferociously hostile attack.

714. Stimulus

Meaning: Spur, encouragement, boost, prompt

Definition: a thing that arouses activity or energy in someone or something; a spur or incentive.

Usage: If the tax were abolished, it would act as a stimulus to exports.

715. Constrain

Meaning: compel, force, drive, oblige

Definition: compel or force (someone) to follow a particular course of action.

Usage: Children are constrained to work in the way the book dictates.

716. Receptive

Meaning: Open-mined, responsive, flexible

Definition: willing to consider or accept new suggestions and ideas.

Usage: A receptive audience.

717. Lethargy

Meaning: sluggishness, inertia, inactivity, inaction,

Definition: a lack of energy and enthusiasm.

Usage: There was an air of lethargy about him.

718. Debilitate

Meaning: weakening, enfeebling, enervating, enervative

Definition: make (someone) very weak and infirm.

Usage: He was severely debilitated by a stomach upset .

719. Aggregate

Meaning:

Definition: a material or structure formed from a mass of fragments or particles loosely compacted together.

Usage: The specimen is an aggregate of rock and mineral fragments.

720. Tumultuous

Meaning: loud, thunderous, ear-shattering

Definition: making an uproar or loud, confused noise.

Usage: He left the stage to tumultuous applause.

721. Rehabilitate

Synonyms: reintegrate, readapt, retrain

Meaning: restore (someone) to health or normal life by training and therapy after imprisonment, addiction, or illness. Usage : helping to rehabilitate former criminals

722. Asylums

Synonyms: mental hospital, mental institution, psychiatric hospital

Meaning: an institution for the care of people who are mentally ill. Usage : he'd been committed to an asylum

723. Prevarication

Synonyms: dishonesty, distortion, lie, equivocation

Meaning: a person dishonest to his organization Usage : My hesitation and prevarication had apparently not inspired my interlocutor with confidence in me.

724. Exacerbating

Synonyms: aggravate, make worse, worsen, inflame, compound

Meaning: make (a problem, bad situation, or negative feeling) worse. Usage : Rising inflation was exacerbated by the collapse of oil prices

725. Indecorously

Synonyms: improper, unseemly, unbecoming, undignified, immodest, indecent, immoral

Meaning: not in keeping with good taste and

propriety; improper Usage : a pub crawl with sundry indecorous adventures

726. Assertion

Synonyms: declaration, contention, statement, claim, submission, swearing

Meaning: a confident and forceful statement of fact or belief Usage : His assertion that his father had deserted the family

727. Incongruity

Synonyms: inappropriateness, dissonance, difference, inconsistency, lack of harmony

Meaning: the state of being incongruous; incompatibility Usage : the incongruity of his fleshy face and skinny body disturbed her the incongruity of his fleshy face and skinny body disturbed her

728. Adjudication

Synonyms: arbitration, refereeing, umpiring

Meaning: The action or process of adjudicating Usage : The matter may have to go to court for adjudication

729. Pervasive

Synonyms: prevalent, penetrating, extensive, general, common, universal, rife

Meaning: (especially of an unwelcome influence or physical effect) spreading widely throughout an area or a group of people. Usage : ageism is pervasive and entrenched in our society

730. Vacillate

Synonyms: dither, teeter, waver, hesitate, oscillate, fluctuate

Meaning: waver between different opinions or actions; be indecisive. Usage : I vacillated between teaching and journalism

731. Pivotal

Synonyms: central, crucial, vital

Meaning: of crucial importance in relation to the development or success of something else.

Usage: Japan's pivotal role in the world economy

732. Afloat

Synonyms: floating, drifting, non-submerged

Meaning: floating in water; not sinking.

Usage: A swimmer fighting to stay afloat

733. Sabotage

Synonyms: wreck, damage

Meaning: deliberately destroy, damage, or obstruct (something), especially for political or military advantage.

Usage: Power lines from South Africa were sabotaged by rebel forces .

734. Contingent

Synonyms: chance, accidental, possible

Meaning: subject to chance.

Usage: The contingent nature of the job

735. Nullify

Synonyms: annul, void, invalidate

Meaning: make legally null and void; invalidate.

Usage: Judges were unwilling to nullify government decisions

736. Verdict

Synonyms: judgment, adjudication, decision, finding

Meaning: a decision on an issue of fact in a civil or criminal case or an inquest.

Usage: The coroner recorded a verdict of death by misadventure

737. Erstwhile

Synonyms: old, past, one-time

Meaning: former

Usage: Written in memory of the composer's erstwhile teacher

738. Conspiracy

Synonyms: plot, scheme, plan

Meaning: a secret plan by a group to do something unlawful or harmful.

Usage: The company was involved in a conspiracy with bookmakers to manipulate starting prices

739. Coterie

Synonyms: set, circle, crowd

Meaning: a small group of people with shared interests or tastes, especially one that is exclusive of other people.

Usage: All prime ministers develop a small coterie of kindred spirits

740. Pervasive

Synonyms: prevalent, penetrating, extensive

Meaning: (especially of an unwelcome influence or physical effect) spreading widely throughout an area or a group of people.

Usage: Ageism is pervasive and entrenched in our society.

741. Commemorative

Meaning: Memorial, remembrance, celebratory, celebrative

Definition: acting as a memorial of an event or person.

Usage: Minister of State ManojSinha today released a commemorative postage stamp on Tourism in India on the occasion of 70th Independence day

742. Disaster

Meaning: catastrophe, tragedy, act of god, calamity

Definition: a sudden accident or a natural catastrophe that causes great damage or loss of life.

Usage: US President Barack Obama issued a disaster declaration for flood-devastated Louisiana

743. Ravage

Meaning: ruin, destroy, raze, damage, lay waste, wipe out.

Definition: cause severe and extensive damage to.

Usage: The hurricane ravaged southern Florida.

744. Swell

Meaning: Expand, bulge, distend, inflate, balloon, bloat, grow, increase, rise

Definition: become or make greater in intensity, number, amount, or volume

Usage: The flooding submerged large parts of the region on Sunday, three days after water-swelled streams and rivers began rising

745. Interim

Meaning: meantime, meanwhile, interval, interlude

Definition: the intervening time

Usage: In the interim I'll just keep my fingers crossed.

746. Curtain

Meaning: hanging, screen, blind, window hanging

Definition: a screen of heavy cloth or other material that can be raised or lowered at the front of a stage

Usage: She drew the curtains and lit the fire

747. Boast

Meaning: Brag, crow, swagger, swank, own, enjoy, have

Definition: talk with excessive pride and selfsatisfaction about one's achievements, possessions, or abilities

Usage: She boasted about her many conquests

748. Intercept

Meaning: Stop, head off, cut off

Definition: obstruct (someone or something) so as to prevent them from continuing to a destination.

Usage: Intelligence agencies intercepted a series of telephone calls.

749. Pave

Meaning: Cover, surface, floor, top, finish

Definition: cover (a piece of ground) with flat stones or bricks; lay paving over

Usage: China Satellite will pave the way to a hackproof communication system.

750. Feasibility

Meaning: Practicability, practicality, workability, viability

Definition: the state or degree of being easily or conveniently done.

Usage: The feasibility of screening athletes for cardiac disease.

751. Quixotic

Meaning: idealistic, unbusinesslike, romatic, extravagant, visionary, unworldly

Definition: extremely idealistic; unrealistic and impractical

Usage: A vast and perhaps quixotic project.

752. Brazen

Meaning: bold, shameless, forward, unashamed, unabashed, unblushing

Definition: bold and without shame.

Usage: He went about his illegal business with a brazen assurance

753. Ingenious

Meaning: inventive, creative, imaginative, original, innovative, resourceful, inspired

Definition: (of a person) clever, original, and inventive.

Usage: He was ingenious enough to overcome the limited budget

754. Naive

Meaning: innocent, artless, guileless, trustful, unaffacted, fond, wide-eyed, simple

Definition: (of a person) natural and unaffected; innocent

Usage: Andy had a sweet, naive look when he smiled

755. Suave

Meaning: charming, sophisticated, debonair, urbane, polished, dignified, gentlemanly, gallant

Definition: (especially of a man) charming, confident, and elegant.

Usage: All the waiters were suave and deferential

756. Epicure

Meaning: gourmet, gourmand, connoisseur,gastronome

Definition: a person who takes particular pleasure in fine food and drink

Usage: They see themselves as epicures—delighting in food that is properly prepared

757. Magnanimous

Meaning: generous, charitable, benevolent, openhanded, bountiful, liberal, princely, kind, kindly

Definition: generous or forgiving, especially towards a rival or less powerful person

Usage: She should be magnanimous in victory

758. Paragon

Meaning: Model, good example, apotheosis, exemplar, paradigm, acme, shining example

Definition: a person or thing viewed as a model of excellence

Usage: Your cook is a paragon.

759. Aesthetic

Meaning: Connoisseur, genteel

Definition: concerned with beauty or the appreciation of beauty

Usage: The pictures give great aesthetic

pleasure.

760. Gregarious

Meaning: sociable, social, companionable, clubbable, convivial

Definition: (of a person) fond of company; sociable

Usage: He was a popular and gregarious man.

761. Abandon

Meaning: Desert, Leave, cast aside,

Definition: cease to support or look after (someone); desert.

Usage: Her natural mother had abandoned her at an early age.

762. Patronage

Meaning: Sponsorship, backing, funding, promotion, support, guaranty, protection

Definition: the support given by a patron.

Usage: The arts could no longer depend on private patronage

763. Traverse

Meaning: cross, negotiate, cross, pass over.

Definition: travel across or through.

Usage: He traversed the forest

764. Recuperate

Meaning: get better, recover, convalesce, get back to normal

Definition: recover from illness or exertion

Usage: She has been recuperating from a knee injury.

765. Alms

Meaning: charity, bounty, subsidy, largesse, endowment

Definition: (in historical contexts) money or food given to poor people

Usage: The riders stopped to distribute alms.

766. Attenuate

Meaning: diminished, impaired, reduced, decreased

Definition: reduce the force, effect, or value of

Usage: Her intolerance was attenuated by an unexpected liberalism

767. Vindictive

Meaning: Vengeful, out for revenge, revengeful, avenging, unforgiving, implacable, bitter

Definition: having or showing a strong or unreasoning desire for revenge

Usage: The criticism was both vindictive and personalized

768. Discomfit

Meaning: embarrass, discomfort, unsettle, unnerve, upset, disturb, perturb, distress

Definition: make (someone) feel uneasy or embarrassed.

Usage: He was not noticeably discomfited by her tone.

769. Accusation

Meaning: allegation, charge, claim, asseveration, blame, criticism, complaint

Definition: a charge or claim that someone has done something illegal or wrong

Usage: accusations of bribery.

770. Indict

Meaning: Charge with, arraign for, take to court for, put on trial for

Definition: formally accuse of or charge with a crime.

Usage: His former manager was indicted for fraud.

771. cacophony

Meaning: din, racket, noise, discord, dissonance, jarring, grating, rasping

Definition: A harsh discordant mixture of sounds

Usage: A cacophony of deafening alarm bells.

772. Brink

Meaning: edge, verge, margin, rim, lip

Definition: the extreme edge of land before a steep slope or a body or water.

Usage: The brink of the cliffs

773. Conscious

Meaning: aware, awake, compos mentis, alert, responsive, reactive, feeling, sentient

Definition: aware of and responding to one's surroundings.

Usage: Although I was in pain, I was conscious

774. Induct

Meaning: admit to, allow into, introduce to, install in,

Definition: admit (someone) formally to a post or organization

Usage: Arrangements for inducting new members to an organization

775. Perceive

Meaning: discern, recognize, tell, grasp, understand, deduce, conclude, sence, divine, intuit

Definition: become aware or conscious of (something); come to realize or understand

Usage: His mouth fell open as he perceived the truth

776. Emphasis

Meaning: Prominence, importance, significance

Definition: special importance, value, or prominence given to something

Usage: They placed great emphasis on the individual's freedom

777. Evident

Meaning: Obvious, apparent, noticeable, conspicuous, perceptible.

Definition: clearly seen or understood; obvious

Usage: She ate the biscuits with evident enjoyment

778. Impatient

Meaning: Irritate, annoyed, angry, testy, tetchy, snappy, cross, crabby, moody

Definition: having or showing a tendency to be quickly irritated or provoked

Usage: An impatient motorist blaring his horn.

779. Sonnet

Meaning: ballad, lyric

Definition: a poem of fourteen lines using any of a number of formal rhyme schemes, in English typically having ten syllables per line

Usage: compose sonnets.

780. Mediocre

Meaning: ordinary, common, commonplace, average

Definition: of only average quality; not very good

Usage: He is an enthusiastic if mediocre painter.

781. Despicable

Meaning: Contemptible, loathsome, hateful, detestable, reprehensible, awful, heinous

Definition: deserving hatred and contempt.

Usage: A despicable crime.

782. Traumatize

Meaning: distrub, shock, bother, hurt, mortify, pain, upset

Definition: subject to lasting shock as a result of a disturbing experience or physical injury.

Usage: The children were traumatized by separation from their families

783. Atrocity

Meaning: iniquity, violation, crime, wrong, offence, affront, scandal, injustice.

Definition: an extremely wicked or cruel act, typically one involving physical violence or injury.

Usage: A textbook which detailed war atrocities

784. incalculable

Meaning: inestimable, untold, immeasurable, uncountable, indeterminable, incomputable

Definition: too great to be calculated or estimated

Usage: An archive of incalculable value.

785. Myopic

Meaning: unimaginative, uncreative, narrow-minded, short-term, small-mind

Definition: lacking foresight or intellectual insight

Usage: The government still has a myopic attitude to public spending.

786. Pertinent

Meaning: Relevant, apposite, appropriate, suitable, fitting, fit, apt, apropos

Definition: relevant or applicable to a particular matter; apposite

Usage: She asked me a lot of very pertinent questions

787. Unsavoury

Meaning: unpalatable, unappetizing, unpleasant, disagreeable, uninviting, unattractive

Definition: disagreeable to taste, smell, or look at

Usage: They looked at the scanty, unsavoury portions of food doled out to them

788. Perspective

Meaning: Outlook, view, viewpoint, point of view, standpoint, position, stand, attitude

Definition: a particular attitude towards or way of regarding something; a point of view.

Usage: Most guidebook history is written from the editor's perspective.

789. Rapture

Meaning: ecstasy, bliss, euphoria, exaltation, joy, transport, rhapsody, delight, pleasure

Definition: a feeling of intense pleasure or joy

Usage: Leonora listened with rapture.

790. Curse

Meaning: Execrate, imprecate, hoodoo

Definition: invoke or use a curse against.

Usage: It often seemed as if the family had been cursed.

791. Hinge

Meaning: depend, hang, rest, turn, pivot, centre, be conditional

Definition: attach or join with or as if with a hinge

Usage: The ironing board was set into the wall and hinged at the bottom.

792. Ballot

Meaning: Vote, poll, election, straw poll, plebiscite

Definition: a system of voting secretly and in writing on a particular issue.

Usage: A strike ballot

793. Disenchant

Meaning: disillusioned, disappointed, let down, fed up, discontented

Definition: cause (someone) to be disappointed

Usage: He may have been disenchanted by the loss of his huge following

794. Cohort

Meaning: unit, outfit, force

Definition: an ancient Roman military unit, comprising six centuries, equal to one tenth of a legion.

Usage: A cohort of civil servants patiently drafting legislation

795. Presumption

Meaning: brazenness, audacity, boldness, temerity, front, pertness, forwardness

Definition: behaviour perceived as arrogant, disrespectful, and transgressing the limits of what is permitted or appropriate

Usage: He lifted her off the ground, and she was enraged at his presumption.

796. Bigoted

Meaning: prejudiced, biased, partial, one-sided, dectarian, discriminatory

Definition: obstinately or unreasonably attached to a belief, opinion, or faction, and intolerant towards other people's beliefs and practices.

Usage: A bigoted group of reactionaries

797. persuade

Meaning: prevail on, induce, win someone over, coax, convince, make get

Definition: induce (someone) to do something through reasoning or argument.

Usage: It wasn't easy, but I persuaded him to do the right thing.

798. Persona

Meaning: image, face, public face, character, personality, identity, self

Definition: the aspect of someone's character that is presented to or perceived by others

Usage: Her public persona.

799. Astonish

Meaning: surprise, stagger, startle, stun, confound, dumbfound

Definition: surprise or impress (someone) greatly.

Usage: You never fail to astonish me.

800. Vicious

Meaning: brutal, savage, violent, dangerous, ruthless, heartless, callous, cruel

Definition: deliberately cruel or violent

Usage: A vicious assault.

801. Adherent

Meaning: follower, supporter, defender, advocate, disciple, votary, member, friend

Definition: someone who supports a particular party, person, or set of ideas

Usage: He was a strong adherent of monetarism.

802. Bystander

Meaning: onlooker, watcher, looker-on, passer-by, eyewitness

Definition: a person who is present at an event or incident but does not take part.

Usage: Water cannons were turned on marchers and innocent bystanders alike

803. Diligence

Meaning: assiduity, rigour, carefulness, conscientiousness, intentness

Definition: careful and persistent work or effort.

Usage: Few party members challenge his diligence as an MP

804. Eulogy

Meaning: accolade, panegyric, paean, encomium, tribute, testimonial

Definition: a speech or piece of writing that praises someone or something highly, especially a tribute to someone who has just died.

Usage: A eulogy to the Queen Mother.

805. Flaccid

Meaning: soft, loose, flabby, yielding, slack, lax, toneless.

Definition: soft and hanging loosely or limply, especially so as to look or feel unpleasant.

Usage: She took his flaccid hand in hers.

806. Demise

Meaning: dying, death, passing, expiry, expiration, end

Definition: a person's death

Usage: Mr Grisenthwaite's tragic demise.

807. Delusion

Meaning: misapprehension, misconception, misleading, mistake, deception, misbelief

Definition: the action of deluding or the state of being deluded.

Usage: What a capacity television has for delusion.

808. Arbitrary

Meaning: capricious, whimsical, random, chance, erratic, unpredictable, wild, casual

Definition: based on random choice or personal whim rather than any reason or system.

Usage: An arbitrary decision.

809. Cynical

Meaning: misanthropic, pessimistic

Definition: believing that people are motivated purely by self-interest; distrustful of human sincerity or integrity.

Usage: He was brutally cynical and hardened to every sob story under the sun

810. Concise

Meaning: Succinct, short, brief, pithy, incisive, crisp.

Definition: giving a lot of information clearly and in a few words; brief but comprehensive.

Usage: A concise account of the country's history.

811. Spawned

Meaning: releases, deposit egg,

Definition: (of a fish, frog, mollusc, crustacean, etc.) release or deposit eggs

Usage: The fish spawn among fine-leaved plants.

812. Casuistry

Meaning: sophistry, sophism, chicanery, quibbling,

Definition: the use of clever but unsound reasoning, especially in relation to moral questions; sophistry.

Usage: The minister is engaging in nothing more or less than casuistry

813. Callous

Meaning: Heartless, unfeeling, uncaring, cold, hard, cruel, harsh

Definition: showing or having an insensitive and cruel disregard for others.

Usage: His callous comments about the murder made me shiver

814. Slovenly

Meaning: scruffy, untidy, messy, unkempt, slatternly, dishavelled, blowsy, down at heel

Definition: (especially of a person or their appearance) untidy and dirty

Usage: A fat, slovenly ex-rock star

815. Verbose

Meaning: wordy, loquacious, garrulous, talkative, voluble, orotund, expansive, babbling, prating

Definition: using or expressed in more words than are needed

Usage: Much academic language is obscure and verbose.

816. Mandate

Meaning: instruction, directive, direction, decree, command, order, injunction, edict, charge

Definition: an official order or commission to do something.

Usage: A mandate to seek the release of political prisoners

817. Smacks

Meaning: slap, blow, spank, cuff, clout, thump, punch, rap, swat, crack

Definition: a sharp slap or blow, typically one given with the palm of the hand.

Usage: She gave Mark a smack across the face.

818. Relentless

Meaning: persistent, continuing, contant, continual, non-stop, lasting, never-ending, steady

Definition: unceasingly intense

Usage: The relentless heat of the desert.

819. Crucify

Meaning: condemn, attack, tear apart, arraign, denounce, pillory, malign, revile, vilify

Definition: criticize (someone) severely and unrelentingly.

Usage: Our fans would crucify us if we lost.

820. Stringent

Meaning: strict, firm, rigid, rigorous, severe, harsh, tight, exacting, stiff

Definition: (of regulations, requirements, or conditions) strict, precise, and exacting

Usage: Stringent guidelines on air pollution.

821. Harness

Meaning: hitch up, put something, saddle, yoke, couple,

Definition: put a harness on (a horse or other draught animal)

Usage: How to groom a horse and harness it.

822. Burgeoning

Meaning: Expand, spring up, shoot up, mushroom, boom, multiply, snowball

Definition: begin to grow or increase rapidly; flourish.

Usage: Manufacturers are keen to cash in on the burgeoning demand

823. Quest

Meaning: Search, hunt, pursuit

Definition: a long or arduous search for something.

Usage: The quest for a reliable vaccine has intensified

824. Evolve

Meaning: develop, progress, make progress, spread, extend

Definition: develop gradually

Usage: The company has evolved into a major chemical manufacturer

825. Obsolete

Meaning: Out of date, outdated, outmoded

Definition: no longer produced or used; out of date

Usage: The disposal of old and obsolete machinery.

826. Affluent

Meaning: wealthy, rich, prosperous, opulent, well off, moneyed, comfortable

Definition: (especially of a group or area) having a great deal of money; wealthy.

Usage: The affluent societies of the western world

827. Relevant

Meaning: pertinent, applicable, apposite, material, apropos, to the point

Definition: closely connected or appropriate to the matter in hand.

Usage: What small companies need is relevant advice.

828. Woe

Meaning: misery, sorrow, distress, sadness, unhappiness, heartache

Definition: great sorrow or distress (often used hyperbolically)

Usage: The Everton tale of woe continued.

829. Multitude

Meaning: army, sea, abundance, profusion, host, horde, mass

Definition: a large number of people or things.

Usage: A multitude of medical conditions are due to being overweight.

830. Herald

Meaning: single, indicate, announce, point to, spell, presage, augur, portent, promis

Definition: be a sign that (something) is about to happen

Usage: The speech heralded a change in policy.

831. Brevity

Meaning: Conciseness, concision, pith, briefness, shortness, compression, crispness

Definition: concise and exact use of words in writing or speech

Usage: The staff will edit manuscripts with a view to brevity and clarity.

832. Feeble

Meaning: Weak, weakly, puny, infirm, delicate, sickly, ailing, failing, helpless, powerless

Definition: lacking physical strength, especially as a result of age or illness.

Usage: By now, he was too feeble to leave his room

833. Miserable

Meaning: Unhappy, sad, dejected, depressed, downcast, downhearted, glum, gloomy, blue, forlorn

Definition: (of a person) wretchedly unhappy or uncomfortable

Usage: Their happiness made Anne feel even more miserable

834. Scanty

Meaning: meagre, scant, minimal, limited, modest, restricted, sparse

Definition: small or insufficient in quantity or amount.

Usage: They paid whatever they could out of their scanty wages to their families

835. Brutal

Meaning: savage, cruel, bloodthirsty, vicious, barbaric, wicked, harsh

Definition: savagely violent

Usage: A brutal murder.

836. Filthy

Meaning: dirty, mucky, grimy, muddy, murky, slimy, unclean

Definition: disgustingly dirty.

Usage: A filthy hospital with no sanitation

837. Combat

Meaning: battle, fighting, action, conflict, armed conflict, war, warfare

Definition: fighting between armed forces.

Usage: Five Hurricanes were shot down in combat.

838. Obstinate

Meaning: Stubborn, headstrong, wilful, unyielding, inflexible, dogged, inexorable

Definition: stubbornly refusing to change one's opinion or chosen course of action, despite attempts to persuade one to do so

Usage: Her obstinate determination to pursue a career in radio.

839. Eloquent

Meaning: persuasive, expressive, articulate, fluent

Definition: fluent or persuasive in speaking or writing.

Usage: An eloquent speech.

840. Impetuous

Meaning: impulsive, rash, hasty, reckless, heedless, foolhardy, injudicious, unthinking

Definition: acting or done quickly and without thought or care

Usage: She might live to rue this impetuous decision.

841. Ballast

Meaning: Heavy material, sand, iron

Definition: heavy material, such as gravel, sand, or iron, placed in the bilge of a ship to ensure its stability

Usage: The hull had insufficient ballast.

842. Deceit

Meaning: deception, duplicity, fraud, craft, chicanery, guile, simulation, lying, bluff

Definition: the use of clever but unsound reasoning, especially in relation to moral questions; sophistry.

Usage: The minister is engaging in nothing more or less than casuistry

843. Synthetic

Meaning: artificial, fake, false, faux, imitation, mock, simulated, ersatz

Definition: (of a substance) made by chemical synthesis, especially to imitate a natural product.

Usage: Synthetic rubber

844. Cohesive

Meaning: adhesive, united

Definition: characterized by or causing cohesion

Usage: Each parish was formerly a cohesive unit

845. Wane

Meaning: disappear, decrease, diminish, dwindle

Definition: (of the moon) have a progressively smaller part of its visible surface illuminated, so that it appears to decrease in size

Usage: The moon is waning.

846. Foster

Meaning: Encourage, promote, further, stimulate, forward, cultivate

Definition: encourage the development of (something, especially something desirable)..

Usage: The teacher's task is to foster learning

847. Swift

Meaning: prompt, rapid, sudden, immediate, instant, without delay

Definition: happening quickly or promptly

Usage: A remarkably swift recovery.

848. Formidable

Meaning: intimidation, forbidding, redoubtable, daunting, alarming, frightening, brooding, awesome, fearsome

Definition: inspiring fear or respect through being impressively large, powerful, intense, or capable

Usage: A formidable opponent

849. Emphatic

Meaning: vehement, firm, forceful, forcible, energetic, vigorous, ardent

Definition: expressing something forcibly and clearly.

Usage: The children were emphatic that they would like to repeat the experience.

850. Drastic

Meaning: extreme, serious, forceful, dire, radical, substantial

Definition: likely to have a strong or far-reaching effect; radical and extreme

Usage: A drastic reduction of staffing levels.

851. Abstain

Meaning: Not vote, decline/refuse to vote

Definition: formally decline to vote either for or against a proposal or motion

Usage: Forty-one voted with the Opposition, and some sixty more abstained.

852. Adulterate

Meaning: Make impure, degrade, debase, spoil, taint, defile, foul, sully

Definition: render (something) poorer in quality by adding another substance.

Usage: The brewer is said to adulterate his beer

853. Laconic

Meaning: brief, terse, succinct, shot, economical, elliptical, crisp, pithy

Definition: (of a substance) made by chemical synthesis, especially to imitate a natural product.

Usage: Synthetic rubber

854. Capricious

Meaning: fickle, inconstant, changeable, variable, unstable, mercurial, volatile

Definition: given to sudden and unaccountable changes of mood or behaviour

Usage: A capricious and often brutal administration

855. Laudable

Meaning: estimable, of note, worthy, admirable, commendable, deserving, reputable

Definition: (of an action, idea, or aim) deserving praise and commendation

Usage: Laudable though the aim might be, the results have been criticized

856. Corroborate

Meaning: confirm, verify, endorse, ratify, validate, certify

Definition: confirm or give support to (a statement, theory, or finding).

Usage: The witness had corroborated the boy's account of the attack

857. Desiccate

Meaning: dried, dried up, dry, powered

Definition: remove the moisture from (something), typically in order to preserve it

Usage: Desiccated coconut.

858. Pedant

Meaning: purist, formalist, doctrinaire, dogmatist

Definition: a person who is excessively concerned with minor details and rules or with displaying academic learning

Usage: The royal palace (some pedants would say the ex-royal palace)

859. Engender

Meaning: Cause, create, generate, rouse, incite, provoke, kindle, trigger, effect

Definition: cause or give rise to (a feeling, situation, or condition).

Usage: The issue engendered continuing controversy.

860. Gullible

Meaning: credulous, trustful, naïve, innocent, unwary, simple

Definition: easily persuaded to believe something; credulous

Usage: An attempt to persuade a gullible public to spend their money.

861. Vacillate

Meaning: Dither, be indecisive, hesitate, oscillate, waver, teeter, temporize

Definition: waver between different opinions or actions; be indecisive

Usage: I vacillated between teaching and journalism.

862. Mitigate

Meaning: reduce, diminish, lessen, weaken, lighten, damp, dull, appease, soothe, still, quell, quiet,

Definition: make (something bad) less severe, serious, or painful.

Usage: Drainage schemes have helped to mitigate this problem

863. Propriety

Meaning: decorum, modesty, civility, courtesy, politeness

Definition: conformity to conventionally accepted standards of behavior or morals.

Usage: He always behaved with the utmost propriety

864. Volatile

Meaning: tense, strained, fraught, uneasy, charged, explosive, turbulent

Definition: liable to change rapidly and unpredictably, especially for the worse

Usage: The political situation was becoming more volatile

865. Malleable

Meaning: pliable, ductile, soft, workable

Definition: (of a metal or other material) able to be hammered or pressed into shape without breaking or cracking.

Usage: A malleable metal can be beaten into a sheet

866. Ostentation

Meaning: showiness, show, showing off,

Definition: the pretentious or showy display of wealth and luxury, designed to impress

Usage: The office was spacious, but without any trace of ostentation

867. Philanthropist

Meaning: benefactor, donor, backer, helper, patron

Definition: a person who seeks to promote the welfare of others, especially by the generous donation of money to good causes

Usage: The trust was founded by an American philanthropist.

868. Enervate

Meaning: exhaust, tire, weary, drain, sap, weaken, enfeeble, indisposed

Definition: make (someone) feel drained of energy or vitality

Usage: Enervating heat.

869. Eulogy

Meaning: Accolade, panegyric, paean, tribute

Definition: a speech or piece of writing that praises someone or something highly, especially a tribute to someone who has just died

Usage: A eulogy to the Queen Mother.

870. Garrulous

Meaning: talkative, voluble, long-winded, chatty, expansive

Definition: excessively talkative, especially on trivial matters

Usage: A garrulous cab driver.

871. Extirpate

Meaning: Weed out, eradicate, stamp out, root out, eliminate, suppress

Definition: eradicate or destroy completely

Usage: Timber wolves were extirpated from New England more than a century ago.

872. Mirth

Meaning: merriment, high spirits, levity, revelry, fun, enjoyment, jollity

Definition: amusement, especially as expressed in laughter.

Usage: His six-foot frame shook with mirth

873. Sagacious

Meaning: wise, clever, intelligent, knoledegeable, sensible

Definition: having or showing keen mental discernment and good judgement; wise or shrewd

Usage: They were sagacious enough to avoid any outright confrontation

874. Sabbatical

Meaning: furlough, leave of absence, recess, ime off, break, holiday, liberty, vacation

Definition: a period of paid leave granted to a university teacher for study or travel, traditionally one year for every seven years worked

Usage: She's away on sabbatical

875. Seemly

Meaning: decorous, proper, becoming, fitting, suitable, apt

Definition: conforming to accepted notions of propriety or good taste; decorous

Usage: I felt it was not seemly to observe too closely.

876. Shrew

Meaning: virago, dragon, vixen, cat, fishwife, witch, hellcat, she-devil

Definition: a bad-tempered or aggressively assertive woman.

Usage: The girls became shrews and harridans

877. Hegemony

Meaning: Leadership, dominance, dominion, supremacy, ascendancy, power, control, mastery

Definition: leadership or dominance, especially by one state or social group over others.

Usage: Germany was united under Prussian hegemony after 1871.

878. Sadistic

Meaning: callous, barbarous, bestial, vicious, brutal, cruel, savage, cold-blooded, inhuman, ruthless, heartless

Definition: deriving pleasure from inflicting pain, suffering, or humiliation on others

Usage: She took a sadistic pleasure in tormenting him.

879. Facile

Meaning: simplistic, superficial, over simple, schematic, black and white

Definition: ignoring the true complexities of an issue; superficial.

Usage: Facile generalizations.

880. Quack

Meaning: swindler, charlatan, rogue, villain, fraud, trickster

Definition: a person who dishonestly claims to have special knowledge and skill in some field, typically medicine.

Usage: A quack doctor.

881. Reckoning

Meaning: calculation, estimation, computation, working out, summation

Definition: the action or process of calculating or estimating something.

Usage: The sixth, or by another reckoning eleventh, Earl of Mar.

882. Preacher

Meaning: Minister (of religion), parson, clergyman, clergywoman, apostle, missionary, gospeller

Definition: a person who preaches, especially a minister of religion.

Usage: To preach the Truth to the face of Falsehood!

883. acquisition

Meaning: purchase, accession, addition, asset,

Definition: an asset or object bought or

obtained, typically by a library or museum.

Usage: The legacy will be used for new acquisitions

884. Anxiety

Meaning: worry, concern, apprehension, fear, tension, suspence

Definition: a feeling of worry, nervousness, or unease about something with an uncertain outcome

Usage: He felt a surge of anxiety.

885. Jeopardize

Meaning: threaten, endanger, imperil, menace, risk

Definition: put (someone or something) into a situation in which there is a danger of loss, harm, or failure

Usage: A devaluation of the dollar would jeopardize New York's position as a financial centre.

886. Oppressive

Meaning: Harsh, cruel, repressive, tyrannical, autocratic, dictational

Definition: inflicting harsh and authoritarian treatment.

Usage: An oppressive dictatorship.

887. Deplorable

Meaning: disgraceful, shameful, unpardonable, unforgivable

Definition: deserving strong condemnation; completely unacceptable.

Usage: Children living in deplorable conditions.

888. Contingent

Meaning: Chance, accidental, fortuitous, possible, unforeseen

Definition: subject to chance..

Usage: The contingent nature of the job.

889. Barricade

Meaning: Blockade, obstruct, closeup, bar, block off, fortify

Definition: block or defend with a barricade.

Usage: They barricaded the building and occupied it all night.

890. Reiterate

Meaning: repeat, say again, retell, iterate, harp on, dwell on

Definition: say something again or a number of times, typically for emphasis or clarity.

Usage: She reiterated that the government would remain steadfast in its support.

891. Authentic

Meaning: Genuine, original, real, actual, pukka, bona fide, ture, veritable

Definition: of undisputed origin and not a copy; genuine.

Usage: The letter is now accepted as an authentic document.

892. Predilection

Meaning: Liking, fondness, preference, partially, taste, penchant, weakness, leaning, bias, love

Definition: a preference or special liking for something; a bias in favour of something.

Usage: Your predilection for pretty girls.

893. Devout

Meaning: pious, religious, devoted, dedicated, reverent, believing, godly

Definition: having or showing deep religious feeling or commitment.

Usage: She was a devout Catholic

894. Inadvertently

Meaning: accidentally, by accident, unwittingly

Definition: without intention; accidentally

Usage: His name had been inadvertently omitted from the list.

895. Lunacy

Meaning: insanity, madness, mental illness, dementia, mania, frenzy

Definition: the state of being a lunatic; insanity (not in technical use).

Usage: It has been suggested that originality demands a degree of lunacy.

896. Reprimand

Meaning: rebuke, reproof, admonition, reproach, reproval, scolding

Definition: a formal expression of disapproval.

Usage: The golfer received a reprimand for a breach of rules.

897. Endeavour

Meaning: try, attempt, venture, undertake, aspire, aim

Definition: try hard to do or achieve something.

Usage: He is endeavouring to help the Third World.

898. Blunt

Meaning: Not sharp, unsharpened, dull, worn, edgeless

Definition: (of a cutting implement) not having a sharp edge or point.

Usage: A blunt knife.

899. Prerogative

Meaning: entitlement, right, privilege, advantage, due, birthright

Definition: a right or privilege exclusive to a particular individual or class.

Usage: In some countries, higher education is predominantly the prerogative of the rich.

900. Sycophant

Meaning: toady, creep, crawler, fawner, flatterer, flunkey, truckler, groveller, minion,

Definition: a person who acts obsequiously towards someone important in order to gain advantage.

Usage: My sister is a shallow sycophant who will flatter anyone for a free designer handbag.

901. Agile

Meaning: nimble, lithe, supple, light-footed, graceful

Definition: able to move quickly and easily.

Usage: Ruth was as agile as a monkey.

902. Bewilder

Meaning: Baffle, mystify, puzzle, confuse, confound, nonplus,

Definition: cause (someone) to become perplexed and confused.

Usage: She was bewildered by his sudden change of mood

903. Garner

Meaning: gather, collect , assemble

Definition: gather or collect (something, especially information or approval).

Usage: The police struggled to garner sufficient evidence

904. Remorse

Meaning: contrition, deep regret, repentance, penitence, guilt, feeling of guilt

Definition: deep regret or guilt for a wrong committed

Usage: They were filled with remorse and shame

905. Antsy

Meaning: Agitated, impatient, restless

Definition: the state of being restless or anxious

Usage: Being a complete introvert, Henry is shy and gets antsy when he has to speak to a girl.

906. Audacity

Meaning: daring, boldness, fearlessness, intrepidity, courage, heroism, pluck

Definition: a willingness to take bold risks.

Usage: He whistled at the sheer audacity of the plan.

907. Unceremonious

Meaning: abrupt, sudden, hasty, summary, rude, offhand

Definition: having or showing a lack of courtesy; rough or abrupt.

Usage: He was known for his strong views and unceremonious manners.

908. Complacent

Meaning: smug, self-satisfied, pleased with oneself, proud of oneself

Definition: showing smug or uncritical satisfaction with oneself or one's achievements

Usage: You can't afford to be complacent about security.

909. Expedite

Meaning: Speed up, accelerate, hurry, hasten, step up, quicken, rush

Definition: make (an action or process) happen sooner or be accomplished more quickly.

Usage: He promised to expedite economic reforms.

910. Superficial

Meaning: Surface, exterior, external, outer, outside, outermost, slight

Definition: existing or occurring at or on the surface.

Usage: The building suffered only superficial damage.

911. Anomaly

Meaning: Oddity, peculiarity, irregularity, inconsistency, incongruity, quirk

Definition: something that deviates from what is standard, normal, or expected

Usage: There are a number of anomalies in the present system

912. Equivocal

Meaning: hazy, foggy, vague, indefinite, inexplicit, nebulous, borderline

Definition: (of a person) using ambiguous or evasive language

Usage: The equivocal nature of her remarks

913. Lucid

Meaning: cogent, coherent, communicative, articulate, eloquent

Definition: expressed clearly; easy to understand

Usage: A lucid account

914. Precipitate

Meaning: bring about, cause, lead to, occasion, trigger, provoke, hasten

Definition: (cause (an event or situation, typically one that is undesirable) to happen suddenly, unexpectedly, or prematurely

Usage: The incident precipitated a political crisis

915. Assuage

Meaning: relieve, ease, alleviate, soothe, calm, reduce, lower, dilute

Definition: make (an unpleasant feeling) less intense

Usage: The letter assuaged the fears of most members

916. Erudite

Meaning: Learned, scholarly, well educated, well read, civilized

Definition: having or showing great knowledge or learning

Usage: Ken could turn any conversation into an erudite discussion

917. Antipathy

Meaning: hostility, antagonism, aversion, animus, opposition, enmity, hate, loathing

Definition: a deep-seated feeling of aversion

Usage: His fundamental antipathy to capitalism city council.

918. Opaque

Meaning: Non-transparent, cloudy, filmy, blurred, misty, dirty, dingy

Definition: not able to be seen through; not transparent

Usage: Bottles filled with a pale opaque liquid

919. Bolster

Meaning: Pillow, cushion, pad, support, rest

Definition: a long, thick pillow that is placed under other pillows for support

Usage: The fall in interest rates is starting to bolster confidence

920. Deride

Meaning: ridicule, mock, jeer at, scoff at, make fun of, pillory

Definition: express contempt for; ridicule

Usage: The decision was derided by environmentalists

921. Recede

Meaning: retreat, go back, move back, move away

Definition: go or move back or further away from a previous position

Usage: The floodwaters had receded.

922. Critical

Meaning: censorious, condemnatory, scathing, criticizing, disapproving, negative

Definition: expressing adverse or disapproving comments or judgements.

Usage: I was very critical of the previous regime.

923. Prominent

Meaning: Important, well known, leading, noted, public, foremost, big, top, great, famed

Definition: important; famous.

Usage: She was a prominent member of the

924. Gullible

Meaning: credulous, innocent, simple, unsceptical, unworldly, ignorant

Definition: easily persuaded to believe something; credulous.

Usage: An attempt to persuade a gullible public to spend their money.

925. Forgoing

Meaning: do without, go without, give up, surrender, eschew

Definition: go without (something desirable).

Usage: She wanted to forgo the tea and leave while they could.

926. Gauge

Meaning: measure, calculate, compute, work out, determine, ascertain

Definition: estimate or determine the amount, level, or volume of.

Usage: Astronomers can gauge the star's intrinsic brightness.

927. Incipient

Meaning: developing, impending, growing, emerging, emergent, dawning

Definition: (of a person) developing into a specified type or role.

Usage: We seemed more like friends than incipient lovers.

928. Malevolent

Meaning: malicious, spiteful, hostile, evil-minded, baleful, bitter

Definition: having or showing a wish to do evil to others.

Usage: The glint of dark, malevolent eyes.

929. Proposition

Meaning: theory, hypothesis, thesis, argument, premise, postulation, theorem, concept, idea, statement

Definition: a statement or assertion that expresses a judgement or opinion.

Usage: The proposition that high taxation is undesirable.

930. Soar

Meaning: fly up, wing, wing its way

Definition: fly or rise high in the air.

Usage: The bird spread its wings and soared into the air.

931. Jubilation

Meaning: Exultation, Joy, elation, glee, triumph

Definition: a feeling of great happiness and triumph.

Usage: Unbelievable scenes of jubilation.

932. Plummet

Meaning: Plunge, fall headlong, hurtle, dive, drop, crash, nosedive

Definition: fall or drop straight down at high speed.

Usage: A climber was killed when he plummeted 300 feet down an icy gully.

933. Unscrupulous

Meaning: unprincipled, unethical, immoral, amoral, sly, bad, improper, wicked, sinful,

Definition: having or showing no moral principles; not honest or fair

Usage: Unscrupulous landlords might be tempted to harass existing tenants.

934. Unpalatable

Meaning: disagreeable, unpleasant, displeasing, unattractive, regrettable, unwelcome, nasty, horrible

Definition: difficult to put up with or accept

Usage: The unpalatable fact that many of the world's people are starving.

935. Substantial

Meaning: Considerable, real, material, weighty, solid, sizeable, meaningful, Major, marked, useful

Definition: of considerable importance, size, or worth.

Usage: A substantial amount of cash.

936. Exacerbate

Meaning: Aggravate, make worse, worsen, inflame, compound

Definition: make (a problem, bad situation, or negative feeling) worse.

Usage: Rising inflation was exacerbated by the collapse of oil prices.

937. Empirical

Meaning: Observed, seen, factual, actual, real, firsthand

Definition: based on, concerned with, or verifiable by observation or experience rather than theory or pure logic.

Usage: They provided considerable empirical evidence to support their argument.

938. Rigour

Meaning: accuracy, correctness, exactitude, diligence, carefulness, exactness

Definition: the quality of being extremely thorough and careful.

Usage: His analysis is lacking in rigour.

939. Inexorable

Meaning: relentless, unstoppable, inevitable, inescapable

Definition: impossible to stop or prevent.

Usage: The seemingly inexorable march of new technology.

940. Lackluster

Meaning: Dry, flat, lifeless, tame, tired, colourless, dull

Definition: lacking in vitality, force, or

conviction; uninspired or uninspiring.

Usage: No excuses were made for the team's lackluster performance.

941. Leniency

Meaning: mercifulness, mercy, clemency, lenity, forgiveness

Definition: The fact or quality of being more merciful or tolerant than expected; clemency.

Usage: The court could show leniency.

942. Reluctant

Meaning: Unwilling, disinclined, grudging, resisting, opposed

Definition: unwilling and hesitant; disinclined.

Usage: She seemed reluctant to answer.

943. Curb

Meaning: Restraint, restriction, check, brake, rein, control, limit

Definition: a check or restraint on something.

Usage: Plans to introduce tougher curbs on insider dealing.

944. Frustrate

Meaning: defeat, foil, block, stop, counter, spoil, check, dash, crush

Definition: prevent (a plan or attempted action) from progressing, succeeding, or being fulfilled

Usage: The rescue attempt was frustrated by bad weather.

945. Enact

Meaning: make law, pass, approve, ratify, validate, sanction, authorize, accept

Definition: make (a bill or other proposal) law.

Usage: legislation was enacted to attract international companies.

946. Betray

Meaning: break one's promise to, be disloyal to, be unfaithful to, break faith with, play someone false, fail, let down

Definition: expose (one's country, a group, or a person) to danger by treacherously giving information to an enemy.

Usage: A double agent who betrayed some 400 British and French agents to the Germans.

947. Alleviate

Meaning: Reduce, quiet, relieve, dilute, modify, moderate

Definition: make (suffering, deficiency, or a problem) less severe.

Usage: He couldn't prevent her pain, only alleviate it.

948. Tangible

Meaning: touchable, palpable, tactile, material, physical, real, substantial

Definition: perceptible by touch.

Usage: the atmosphere of neglect and abandonment was almost tangible.

949. Demonstrate

Meaning: reveal, bespeak, indicate, signify, signal, denote, show, display

Definition: clearly show the existence or truth of (something) by giving proof or evidence.

Usage: Their shameful silence demonstrates their ineptitude.

950. Narrate

Meaning: tell, relate, report, relay, retail, detail, unfold

Definition: give a spoken or written account of.

Usage: The story is narrated by the heroine.

951. Recede

Meaning: retreat, go back, move back, move away

Definition: go or move back or further away from a previous position

Usage: The floodwaters had receded.

952. Critical

Meaning: censorious, condemnatory, scathing, criticizing, disapproving, negative

Definition: expressing adverse or disapproving comments or judgements.

Usage: I was very critical of the previous regime.

953. Prominent

Meaning: Important, well known, leading, noted, public, foremost, big, top, great, famed

Definition: important; famous.

Usage: She was a prominent member of the city council.

954. Gullible

Meaning: credulous, innocent, simple, unsceptical, unworldly, ignorant

Definition: easily persuaded to believe something; credulous.

Usage: An attempt to persuade a gullible public to spend their money.

955. Forgoing

Meaning: do without, go without, give up, surrender, eschew

Definition: go without (something desirable).

Usage: She wanted to forgo the tea and leave while they could.

956. Gauge

Meaning: measure, calculate, compute, work out, determine, ascertain

Definition: estimate or determine the amount, level, or volume of.

Usage: Astronomers can gauge the star's intrinsic brightness.

957. Incipient

Meaning: developing, impending, growing, emerging, emergent, dawning

Definition: (of a person) developing into a specified type or role.

Usage: We seemed more like friends than incipient lovers.

958. Malevolent

Meaning: malicious, spiteful, hostile, evil-minded, baleful, bitter

Definition: having or showing a wish to do evil to others.

Usage: The glint of dark, malevolent eyes.

959. Proposition

Meaning: theory, hypothesis, thesis, argument, premise, postulation, theorem, concept, idea, statement

Definition: a statement or assertion that expresses a judgement or opinion.

Usage: The proposition that high taxation is undesirable.

960. Soar

Meaning: fly up, wing, wing its way

Definition: fly or rise high in the air.

Usage: The bird spread its wings and soared into the air.

961. Brutalize

Meaning: attack, abuse, assault, beat, thump, pummel, pound

Definition: treat (someone) in a savage and violent way

Usage: They brutalize and torture persons in their custody.

962. Cantankerous

Meaning: irritable, cross, fraction, testy, touchy

Definition: bad-tempered, argumentative, and uncooperative.

Usage: He can be a cantankerous old fossil at times.

963. Obstacle

Meaning: Barrier, hurdle, stumbling block, bar, block, problem, deterrent, handicap

Definition: a thing that blocks one's way or

prevents or hinders progress.

Usage: The major obstacle to achieving that goal is money.

964. Trite

Meaning: hackneyed, banal, cliched, vapid, ordinary

Definition: (of a remark or idea) lacking originality or freshness; dull on account of overuse.

Usage: This point may now seem obvious and trite.

965. Derision

Meaning: Mockery, ridicule, jeering, sneers, scoffing

Definition: contemptuous ridicule or mockery.

Usage: My stories were greeted with derision and disbelief.

966. Meandering

Meaning: winding, windy, zigzag, turning, curving, twisting, snaky

Definition: following a winding course.

Usage: Meandering rivers flow at vastly different rates.

967. Fervent

Meaning: impassioned, intense, ardent, sincere, feeling, heartfelt

Definition: having or displaying a passionate intensity.

Usage: A fervent supporter of the revolution.

968. Florid

Meaning: ruby, red, rosy, red faced, pinkish

Definition: having a red or flushed complexion.

Usage: A stout man with a florid face.

969. Unanimity

Meaning: agreement, accord, concord, unity, union, solidarity

Definition: agreement by all people involved; consensus.

Usage: There is almost complete unanimity on this issue.

970. Vice

Meaning: immorality, wrong, badness, wickedness, evil, impurity

Definition: immoral or wicked behaviour.

Usage: An open sewer of vice and crime.

971. Disputable

Meaning: debatable, open to debate, Open to discussion, open to question, doubtful

Definition: not established as a fact, and so open to question or debate.

Usage: whether it can be described as art criticism may be disputable.

972. Reveal

Meaning: Open up, tell, bring out, disclose, release, leak

Definition: make (previously unknown or secret information) known to others.

Usage: Brenda was forced to reveal Robbie's whereabouts.

973. Deliberate

Meaning: Intentional, calculated, meant, prearranged, studied, done on purpose

Definition: done consciously and intentionally.

Usage: A deliberate attempt to provoke conflict.

974. Stimulate

Meaning: Tonic, restorative, bracing, refreshing

Definition: raise levels of physiological or nervous activity in (the body or any biological system).

Usage: The women are given fertility drugs to stimulate their ovaries.

975. Perilous

Meaning: Dangerous, hazardous, fraught with danger

Definition: full of danger or risk.

Usage: She a perilous journey south.

976. Jubilant

Meaning: Overjoyed, exultant, joyful, gleeful, thrilled

Definition: feeling or expressing great happiness and triumph.

Usage: A large number of jubilant fans ran on to the pitch.

977. Arraign

Meaning: Criticize, censure, attack, condemn, reprove, berate, find fault with

Definition: call or bring (someone) before a court to answer a criminal charge.

Usage: Her sister was arraigned on charges of attempted murder.

978. Accomplice

Meaning: Abettor, associate, collaborator

Definition: a person who helps another commit a crime.

Usage: An accomplice in the murder.

979. Meticulous

Meaning: careful, exacting, demanding, accurate, correct

Definition: showing great attention to detail; very careful and precise.

Usage: The designs are hand-glazed with meticulous care.

980. Accord

Meaning: Give, grant, tender, award, present, hand, yield

Definition: give or grant someone (power, status, or recognition).

Usage: The powers accorded to the head of state.

981. Ascent

Meaning: climb, scaling, scramble, clamber

Definition: a climb or walk to the summit of a mountain or hill.

Usage: The first ascent of the Matterhorn.

982. Eulogy

Meaning: Accolade, paean, tribute, compliment, commendation

Definition: a speech or piece of writing that praises someone or something highly, especially a tribute to someone who has just died.

Usage: A eulogy to the Queen Mother.

983. Hyperbole

Meaning: Overstatement, magnification, embroidery, excess, overkill, overplaying

Definition: exaggerated statements or claims not meant to be taken literally

Usage: He vowed revenge with oaths and hyperboles.

984. Mammoth

Meaning: Huge, enormous, giant, massive, towering, titanic, epic, massive, vast

Definition: huge

Usage: A mammoth corporation.

985. Amalgamate

Meaning: Combine, merge, unite, integrate, fuse, blend, mix, incorporate

Definition: combine or unite to form one organization or structure.

Usage: He amalgamated his company with another.

986. Influx

Meaning: in rush, rush, stream, flood, ingress

Definition: an arrival or entry of large numbers of people or things.

Usage: A massive influx of tourists.

987. Impeccable

Meaning: flawless, spotless, stainless, perfect, ideal, model

Definition: in accordance with the highest standards; faultless.

Usage: He had impeccable manners.

988. Zenith

Meaning: Highest point, crowning point, height, top, peak, climax, maximum, flower

Definition: the time at which something is most powerful or successful.

Usage: In **1977, punk was at its zenith.**

989. Orderly

Meaning: neat, trim, well kept, straight, tidy

Definition: neatly and methodically arranged.

Usage: An orderly arrangement of objects.

990. Endorse

Meaning: autograph, initial, superscribe, inscribe, countersign

Definition: declare one's public approval or support of.

Usage: The report was endorsed by the college.

991. Ailment

Meaning: illness, disease, sickness

Definition: an illness, typically a minor one.

Usage: We spend more on almost any article of bodily aliment than on our mental aliment.

992. Contaminated

Meaning: pollute, corrupt, infect

Definition: make (something) impure by exposure to or addition of a poisonous or polluting substance.

Usage: The site was found to be contaminated by radioactivity

993. Largesse

Meaning: liberality, bounty, generosity

Definition: Generosity in bestowing money or gifts upon others

Usage: Presumably public money is not dispensed with such largesse to anyone else

994. Flee

Meaning: run, escape, take off

Definition: Run away from a place or situation of danger

Usage: To escape the fighting, his family fled from their village

995. Outrage

Meaning: indignation, fury, anger

Definition: An extremely strong reaction of anger, shock, or indignation

Usage: Her voice trembled with outrage

996. Groom

Meaning: curry, brush, comb

Definition: Brush and clean the coat of (a horse, dog, or other animal)

Usage: The horses were groomed and taken to shows

997. Litigation

Meaning: case, legal proceeding, legal dispute

Definition: The process of taking legal action

Usage: The company wishes to avoid litigation

998. Trajectory

Meaning: course, route, path

Definition: The path followed by a projectile flying or an object moving under the action of given forces

Usage: The missile's trajectory was preset

999. Agitation

Meaning: anxiety, perturbation, disquiet, distress

Definition: A state of anxiety or nervous excitement

Usage: She was wringing her hands in agitation

1000. Premises

Meaning: property, site, place

Definition: A house or building, together with its land and outbuildings, occupied by a business or considered in an official context

Usage: The company has moved to new premises

UNIT 24

Idioms and Phrases with Hindi Meanings

24.1 A number of phrases and a single word substitute

1. To add insult to injury — To harm as well as humiliate (जले पर नमक छिड़कना) He has added insult to injury by writing this letter. (ऐसा पत्र लिखकर उसने जले पर नमक छिड़का है।)
2. At daggers drawn—On inimical terms (पारस्परिक शत्रुता) At one time Russia and America were at daggers drawn. (एक समय रूस और अमरीका एक-दूसरे के घोर शत्रु थे।)
3. Against the rainy day—Precaution against emergency (कठिन परिस्थितियों के लिये प्रबन्ध) You must save something every month against the rainy day. (तुम्हें आपातकाल के लिये कुछ बचत अवश्य करनी चाहिये।)
4. At a loss — To be confused (घबराजाना) He was at a loss to understand what to do against so much of opposition. (वह घबराहट में समझ नहीं सका कि इतने विरोध की स्थिति में वह क्या करे.)
5. At logger heads — Terms of hostility (शत्रुता की अवस्था) He is at logger heads with his own brother. (वह अपने ही भाई से शत्रुता रखता है.)
6. At an arm's length — To keep danger or evil at a distance (खतरे या बुराई को दूर रखना) Keep such rascals at an arm's length. (ऐसे दुष्टों को अपने से दूर ही रखो।)
7. At one's fingers' ends— To have full and ready knowledge (पूर्ण एवं तत्पर ज्ञान) A lawyer should have all the sections of the Act at his fingers' ends—(एक अच्छे वकील को कानून की सभी धाराओं को अँगुलियों पर रखना चाहिये।)
8. An apple of discord—Cause of quarrel (झगड़े की जड़) The Himalayan range is an apple of discord between India and China. (हिमालय पर्वत भारत और चीन के बीच झगड़े की जड़ है।)
9. An apple of one's eye—Very dear (आँख का तारा) Her only son is the apple of her eye—(उसका इकलौता बेटा उसकी आँख का तारा है।)
10. To add fuel to the fire — To aggravate some situation or matter (और अधिक भड़काने की कार्यवाही) His abusive language added fuel to the fire. (उसकी गाली वाली भाषा ने आग में घी डालने का काम किया।)
11. A bed of roses—An easy and comfortable situation (सरल और आराम की स्थिति) The post of the Prime Minister is not a bed of roses. (प्रधानमंत्री का पद गुलाब के फूलों की सैया नहीं है.)
12. Adam's ale Pure water (शुद्ध जल) In the dry districts people have to content themselves with Adam's ale. (शराब बन्दी वाले जिलों में लोगों को शुद्ध जल से ही संतोष करना पड़ता है।)
13. An axe to grind—Some personal motive (अपनी स्वार्थ सिद्धि) He flatters you so much perhaps he has some axe to grind. (वह तुम्हारी बड़ी खुशामद करता है, शायद वह अपना कोई स्वार्थ सिद्ध करना चाहता है।)
14. To beat about the bush — To stray from the main point (विषय से भटक जाना) A good student never beats about the bush in answering his questions—(एक अच्छा विद्यार्थी अपने उत्तर लिखने में विषय से भटकता नहीं है।)

15. To bear the brunt of — To endure the calamity or difficult situation (कठिनाई का हिम्मत से सामना करना) Maharana Pratap bore the brunt the Mughal invasions bravely. (महाराणा प्रताप ने मुगलों के सभी हमलों का बहादुरी से मुकाबला किया।)

16. To bring to light— To disclose (पता लगाना, छिपी बात को प्रकाश में लाना) The Enquiry Commission has brought many startling facts to light. (जाँच कमेटी ने बहुत सी सनसनीखेज बातों का रहस्योद्‌घाटन किया है।)

17. At sixes and sevens— In disorder (तितर-बितर) My young son has thrown my books at siÛes and sevens. (मेरे छोटे बेटे ने मेरी पुस्तकों को इधर-उधर बिखेर दिया है।)

18. At the eleventh hour — At the last moment (अंतिम क्षणों में) He reached the examination hall at the eleventh hour. (वह अंतिम क्षणों में परीक्षा भवन पहुँचा।)

19. At one's beck and call —At one's command (किसी के आदेश पर) I want my servants to be at my beck and call. (मैं चाहता हूँ कि मेरे नौकर मेरा आदेश मानने के लिये तत्पर रहें।)

20. At one's wits' end — To be confused (होश खो बैठना, घबरा जाना) At the sudden appearance of the police the suspect was at his wits' end. (पुलिस के अचानक आ जाने पर संदिग्ध अपराधी घबरा गया।)

21. To bear the palm — To be victorious (विजयी होना) Our team bore the palm in the final match. (अंतिम मैच में हमारी टीम ने विजय हासिल कर ली।)

22. Bosom friend—Intimate friend (घनिष्ट मित्र) Mohan is my bosom friend. (मोहन मेरा घनिष्ट मित्र है।)

23. Bag and baggage—With full luggage (सारे सामान सहित) He has left Agra bag and baggage- (उसने आगरा सारे सामान सहित छोड़ दिया है।)

24. To bury the hatchet—To end old enmity (पुरानी शत्रुता को भुला देना) Let us now bury the hatchet for ever and live like friends. (अब हमें अपनी शत्रुता हमेशा के लिये छोड कर मित्रों की तरह रहना चाहिये।)

25. By leaps and bounds—Very rapidly (बहुत तेजी से) India is progressing by leaps and bounds. (भारत बहुत तेजी से आगे बढ़ रहा है।)

26. To be in bad books of Out of favour (कृपा पात्र न होना) He is in bad books of his teachers. (वह अपने अध्यापकों की निगाह में अच्छा नहीं है।)

27. To be in good books of —To be in kind favour (कृपा पात्र होना) He is in good books of his teachers. (वह अपने अध्यापकों का कृपा पात्र है।)

28. To be in bad odour of— To be out of favour (किसी की बुरी राय में)। An dishonest servant is always in bad odour of his master. (एक बेईमान नौकर अपने मालिक की निगाह में गिरा रहता है।)

29. To be in good odour of—To be in good favour (किसी की अच्छी राय में) An honest servant is always in good odour of his master. (एक ईमानदार नौकर अपने मालिक की निगाह में चढ़ा रहता है।)

30. Bolt from the blue— A sudden calamity (अचानक आया हुआ संकट) The news of his father's death came as a bolt from the blue. (उसके पिता की मृत्यु का समाचार उसके लिये अप्रत्याशित संकट की तरह आया।)

31. Bad blood Enmity (शत्रुता) These two brothers have bad blood between them. (इन दोनों भाइयों में पारस्परिक शत्रुता है।)

32. Blue blood — To belong to an aristocratic family (उच्च घराने का होना) Lord Byron, the famous poet, was

very proud of his blue blood. (प्रसिद्ध) कवि लार्ड बायरन को अपने उच्च घराने का बड़ा गर्व था।)

33. To be born with a silver spoon in one's mouth—To be born in a rich family (समृद्ध परिवार में जन्म लेना) Jawaharlal Nehru was born with a silver spoon in his mouth. (जवाहरलाल नेहरू का जन्म एक अति समृद्ध परिवार में हुआ था।)

34. To burn the candle at both ends—To waste one's money or energy recklessly (अपनी शक्ति या धन व्यर्थ बरबाद करना) If you go on burning the candle at both ends, you will soon come to repentance. (यदि तुम अपनी क्षमता को इसी प्रकार बरबाद करते रहे तो तुम्हें शीघ्र ही पछताना पड़ेगा।)

35. Birds of the same feather— Persons of the same nature and taste (एक सी प्रकृति या पसंद के लोग) All the employees of this office are birds of the same feather. (इस दफ्तर के सभी कर्मचारी एक ही प्रकृति के हैं।)

36. Between Scylla and Charybdis (Between two great dangers) (दो कठिन परिस्थितियों के बीच) I am between Scylla and Charybdis; if I tell the truth my friend goes to the jail; if I do not] I betray my employer. (मैं बड़ी कठिन स्थिति में पड गया हूँ, यदि मैं सच बोलूँ तो मेरे मित्र को सजा हो जायेगी, और यदि सच न बोलूँ तो मेरे मालिक को धोखा देना होगा।)

37. Between the devil and the deep sea — To fall between two great difficulties (दो मुसीबतों के बीच फँस जाना) I have fallen between the devil and the deep sea; if I go to Kanpur, I lose the examination; if I don't my employer feels annoyed. (मैं एक विषम परिस्थिति में पड़ गया हूँ, यदि मैं कानपुर जाऊँ तो मेरी परीक्षा छूटती है, और यदि न जाऊँ तो मेरे मालिक नाराज होते हैं।)

38. To blow one's own trumpet —To praise one's ownself (अपनी ही शेखी बघारना) I hate those persons who blow their own trumpet (मैं ऐसे लोगों से घृणा करता हूँ जो अपनी ही शेखी बघारते रहते हैं।)

39. Bone of contention —The cause of quarrel (झगड़े का कारण) Kashmir is the bone of contention between India and Pakistan. (कश्मीर भारत और पाकिस्तान के बीच झगड़े की जड़ है।)

40. By fits and starts—Something done irregularly (किसी काम को रुक-रुक कर करना) You can never finish the work in time if you proceed by fits and starts. (यदि तुम रुक-रुक कर काम करोगे तो कभी काम पूरा नहीं कर पाओगे।)

41. Black sheep— An undesirable person (अनचाहा या धोखेबाज व्यक्ति) Many police officers proved black sheep in the Movement of 1942. (1942 के आन्दोलन में बहुत से पुलिस अधिकारी घोखेबाज सिद्ध हुए।)

42. By hook or by crook—By any means fair or foul (अच्छे या बुरे किसी भी प्रकार से) Some people are very clever in achieving their goal by hook or by crook. (कुछ लोग किसी न किसी प्रकार अपना उद्देश्य पूरा कर लेते हैं।)

43. To be hand and glove with Intimate friends (घनिष्ट मित्र होना) Ramesh and Mohan are hand and glove with each other. (रमेश और मोहन दोनों घनिष्ट मित्र हैं.)

44. Child's play— A very easy task (बच्चों का खेल) It is not a child's play to get first division. (प्रथम श्रेणी पाना बच्चों का खेल नहीं है।)

45. To count chickens before they are hatched—To anticipate profit beforehand (पहले से लाभ का विश्वास कर लेना) Do not make your plans so ambitious because it is no use counting chickens before they are hatched. (अपनी योजनायें इतनी महत्वाकांक्षी मत बनाओ, क्योंकि पहले से लाभ की आशा में रहना हितकर नहीं है।)

46. To cut the Gordian knot—(To solve a very difficult problem) The national leaders cut the Gordian knot by abolishing the native stetes (राज्यों को खत्म कर एक बहुत बड़ी समस्या हल कर ली।)

47. Cock and bull story — A fantastic story (मनगढ़ंत कहानी) The tale of his adventures is nothing but a cock and bull story. (उसके साहसिक कार्यों की कहानी एक मनगढ़ंत कहानी है।)

48. Cat and dog life — Quarrelsome life (झगड़ालू जीवन) Mohan and his wife live a cat and dog life. (मोहन और उसकी पत्नी झगड़ालू जीवन व्यतीत करते हैं।)

49. To call a spade a spade — To talk bluntly (मुँहफट बात करना) Dr. Johnson never hesitated in calling a spade a spade. (डाक्टर जोहन्सन साफ बात कहने में जरा भी नहीं झिझकते थे।)

50. Cry for the moon — An unattainable ambition (असंभव अभिलाषा) His hope of getting the Nobel Prize is a cry for the moon. (नोबेल प्राइज जीतने की उसकी अभिलाषा एक असंभव अभिलाषा है.)

51. Cry over spilt milk — To repent in vain after loss (हानि हो चुकने के बाद उस पर पश्चाताप करना) Be comforted my friend] it is no use crying over spilt milk. (मेरे मित्र धैर्य रखो, बिगड़े हुए काम के ऊपर रोना व्यर्थ है।)

52. A close shave — A narrow escape (बाल-बाल बचना) I had a close shave in a car accident. (कार दुर्घटना में मैं बाल-बाल बचा।)

53. Crocodile tears False show of grief (दिखावटी आँसू) He shed crocodile tears on the death of his step-mother. (अपनी सौतेली माँ की मृत्यु पर उसने घड़ियाली आँसू बहाये.)

54. Cold reception — No hearty welcome (दिखावटी स्वागत) The English cricket team was given a cold reception in India. (अँग्रेजों की क्रिकेट टीम का दिखावटी स्वागत किया गया.)

55. To be caught red—handed — To be caught while committing a crime (रँगे हाथ पकड़े जाना) The thief was caught red&handed. (चोर रंगे हाथ पकड़ा गया.)

56. Capital punishment — Death penalty (मौत की सजा) Capital punishment has been revived in many countries. (बहुत से देशों में मृत्युदंड फिर से लागू हो गया है.)

57. Corporal punishment—Bodily punishment (शारीरिक दड) Corporal punishment should not be given to young children. (छोटे बच्चों को शारीरिक दंड नहीं देना चाहिये.)

58. To carry coals to New Castle— Unnecessary and useless work (उल्टे बाँस बरेली) To export silk to China is like carrying coals to New Castle. (चीन को रेशम भेजना उल्टे बाँस बरेली भेजने की तरह है.)

59. To call names—To abuse (गाली देना) Calling names is a bad habit- (गाली देना बुरी आदत है.)

60. To cut one's coat according to one's cloth—To live within one's own means (अपनी आमदनी के अन्दर ही खर्च करना) It is always wise to cut one's coat according to one's cloth. (अपनी आमदनी के अन्दर खर्च करने में ही बुद्धिमानी है।)

61. Chip of the old block — The son resembling the father (जैसा बाप तैसा बेटा) Ram is a drunkard like his father. He is a chip of the old block—(राम अपने पिता की तरह शराबी है। जैसा बाप तैसा बैटा।)

62. To cut a sorry figure— To make a poor impression (अच्छा प्रभाव न डालना) When Gandhiji appeared in his first case, he cut a sorry figure in the court. (गांधी जी जब पहली बार न्यायालय में उपस्थित हुए तो उन्होंने बहुत ही घटिया प्रभाव डाला।)

63. To curry favour —To win favour by flattery (खुशामद करके कृपापात्र बनना) He has risen so high by currying favour of the Chairman of the factory. (वह फैक्टरी के चेयरमैन की खुशामद करके इतना ऊँचा उठ गया है।

64. To cast a slur— To bring disgrace (अपयश का कारण बनना) Your actions will cast a slur on the good name of your family. (तुम्हारे इस तरहं के कामों से तुम्हारे परिवार का अपयश होगा.)

65. A bull in a china shop— Heedless destroyer (विध्वंसकारी व्यक्ति) Nadir Shah proved to be a bull in a china shop. (नादिरशाह एक विध्वंसकारी व्यक्ति साबित हुआ.)

66. To put the cart before the horse—To do something in a wrong way (गलत ढंग से किसी कार्य को करना) Instead of calling the mechanic to the workshop, he took the whole machine to him. It was like putting the cart before the horse. (कारीगर को फैक्टरी में बुलाने के बजाय, वह मशीन को ही उसके पास ले गया यह गाड़ी को घोड़े के पास ले जाने जैसा था।)

67. To die in harness—To die while on duty (काम करते-करते मर जाना) Slaves die in harness. (काम करते-करते ही मर जाते हैं।)

68. A drop in the ocean—Very insignificant amount (अत्यन्त ही थोड़ी मात्रा) All your knowledge of science is only a drop in the ocean. (विज्ञान का तुम्हारा सारा ज्ञान सागर में एक बूँद के बराबर है।)

69. A dark horse—A person suddenly coming into prominence (अचानक ही प्रसिद्धि पाने वाला व्यक्ति) Mohan came out as a dark horse after the election. (चुनाव में जीतने के बाद मोहन अचानक ही प्रसिद्धि) पाने वाला व्यक्ति साबित हुआ।)

70. Drawn battle or Drawn match — A battle or match in which no party wins (बराबर की बाजी होना) The drawn cricket match was replayed in Calcutta yesterday. (बराबरी पर छूटा हुआ मैच कल कलकत्ते में फिर से खेला गया.)

71. Double dealing—Deceitful action (धोखेबाजी के कार्य) His double dealings are now exposed to the public. (उसके धोखाधड़ी के काम अब समाज में उजागर हो चुके हैं।)

72. To give the devil his due—Even the wicked man should be given the credit due to him (बुरे आदमी की भी उचित प्रशंसा करना) In spite of all his wickedness, he has helped you the devil should be given his due. (उसमें तमाम बुराइयों के होते हुए भी उसने तुम्हारी मदद की बदमाश को इतना श्रेय तो मिलना ही चाहिये।)

73. Dog in the manger—A selfish person (स्वार्थी व्यक्ति) He would rather keep his books locked than give them to you, because he is more or less a dog in the manger. (वह अपनी किताबों को ताले में भले ही बन्द रखे, परन्तु तुम्हें नहीं देगा. वह एक अति स्वार्थी व्यक्ति है।)

74. Sword of Damocles— An imminent danger (सिर पर लटकी तलवार) The aggressive policy of China is a sword of Damocles hanging over India. (चीन की आक्रामक नीति भारत के सिर पर लटकी तलवार है।)

75. To dance attendance upon—To flatter (चापलूसी करना) Officers in the present day want their subordinates to dance attendance upon them. (आज के अधिकारी चाहते हैं कि उनके मातहत उनकी चापलूसी में लगे रहें।)

76. On the horns of a dilemma — To face a difficult situation between two problems. (मुसीबत में फँसना, दो कठिन अवस्थाओं के बीच में) The new import policy has put many industries on the horns of a dilemma; they can neither run these industries nor close them down. (आयात की नई नीति ने बहुत सी नई औद्योगिक इकाइयों को मुसीबत में फँसा दिया है। वे न तो इन इकाइयों को आगे चला सकते हैं, न बन्द ही कर सकते हैं।)

77. To play ducks and drakes — To waste money (अपना धन बर्बाद करना) He is a reckless fellow playing ducks and drakes with his ancestral property. (वह बड़ा ही लापरवाह व्यक्ति है, उसने अपने पुरखों की जायदाद यों ही बर्बाद कर दी.)

78. A double-edged sword— Capable of causing harm to the other as to one's ownself (ऐसा कार्य जो दूसरे को और स्वंय को भी नुकसान पहुँचा सके) He has cheated many people with the help of his som but this may prove a double-edged sword one day. (उसने अपने बेटे की मदद से बहुत से लोगों को ठगा है।) लेकिन उसका यह कार्य एक दुधारी तलवार सिद्ध हो सकता है।)

79. A dog's life Very miserable life (कष्टदायक जीवन) People dwelling in the slums of great cities live a dog's life. (बड़े शहरों की गन्दी बस्तियों में रहने वाले कुत्तों का जीवन जीते हैं।)

80. A blessing in disguise—Something intrinsically good but having a bad appearamce (उपर से बुरी दिखने वाली पर वास्तव में अच्छी बात) His last year's failure was a blessing in disguise, because this year he has secured a first division. (उसका पिछली साल फेल होना एक वरदान सिद्ध हुआ, क्योंकि इस साल वह प्रथम श्रेणी में पास हुआ है।)

81. To end in smoke —To end in nothing (कोई फल न निकलना) The Summit Conference has ended in smoke. (उच्चस्तरीय कान्फ्रेंस निरर्थक सिद्ध हुई।)

82. Eye wash Ineffective remedy (आँसू पोंछना) The revised pay scale of the teachers is a mere eye- wash. अध्यापकों के नए वेतनमान केवल आँसू पोंछने के बराबर हैं।)

83. Every inch —Completely (पूरी तरह) Mohan is every inch a gentleman. (मोहन पूरी तरह एक भला आदमी है।)

84. Over head and ears —Beyond one's capacity (सामर्थ्य से बाहर) He is over head and ears in debt. (वह अपनी सामर्थ्य से अधिक कर्जे में फंसा है।)

85. Easy money Bribe or No officer who accepts easy money can sleep in peace. (कोई भी अधिकारी जो रिश्वत लेता है शान्ति से नहीं सो सकता है.)

86. Hush-money—Bribe given for concealing secrets (किसी रहस्य को छिपाने के लिये दी गई रिश्वत) He has given hush-money to the Editor of the daily newspaper for withholding the publication of this scandal. (उसने समाचार-पत्र के संपादक को रिश्वत दी है कि वह इस बदनामी की घटना को प्रकाशित न करे।)

87. To eat one's word /To break one's promise (वायदा खिलाफी करना) Whatever may happen I shall not eat my word. (चाहे कुछ भी हो, मैं वायदा खिलाफी नहीं करूँगा।)

88. To see eye to eye— To agree (सहमत होना) I do not see eye to eye with him on this issue. (मैं इस मामले में उससे सहमत नहीं हूँ।)

89. To take an exception to —To object to something (किसी बात का बुरा मानना) I take serious exception to this type of remark. (मैं इस तरह की बात का बहुत बुरा मानता हू।)

90. Enough and to spare Plentiful (प्रचुर मात्र में) Even the poorest man in America has enough and to spare. (अमरीका का गरीब से गरीब व्यक्ति भी प्रचुर मात्र में संसाधन रखता है।)

91. To make both ends meet— To live within one's income with difficulty (मुश्किल से गुजर-बसर करना) A school teacher hardly makes both ends meet. (एक स्कूल का अध्यापक मुश्किल से गुजर-बसर करता है।)

92. Elixir of life— Nectar of life (जीवन का अमृत) Contentment is the elixir of life. (संतोष जीवन का अमृत है।)

93. Foul play – Treachery (धोखाधड़ी) I suspect foul play in the dealings of this clever man. (इस चालाक आदमी से धोखाधड़ी का संशय है।)

94. Fool's paradise—Foolish ambition (मूर्खतापूर्ण अभिलाषायें) I pity the man; he is living in a fool's paradise. (मुझे उससे सहानुभूति है, वह मूर्खतापूर्ण अभिलाषायें रखता है.)

95. Fair weather friend—Selfish friends of prosperous days (अच्छे समय के स्वार्थी मित्र) As he was a fair-weather friend, he deserted me in my hard days. (वह मेरे अच्छे दिनों का मित्र (स्वार्थी) था; उसने मेरी मुसीबतों में मेरा साथ छोड़ दिया)

96. From hand to mouth—Bare existence (अत्यन्त गरीबी में रहना) The labouring class people in India live from hand to mouth. (भारत में मजदूर वर्ग के लोग मुश्किल से गुजारा करते हैं.)

97. Fair play Just dealing (ईमानदारी का बर्ताव) I expect nothing but fair play from you. (मैं तुमसे केवल ईमानदारी के बर्ताव की उम्मीद करता हूँ.)

98. Fall flat—To produce no effect (कोई प्रभाव न छोड़ना) The repeated warnings of the Government have fallen flat on the militants. (सरकार की बार-बार की चेतावनियों का आतंकवादियों पर कोई प्रभाव नहीं पड़ा।)

99. Follow suit— To follow the example (बड़ों के उदाहरण पर चलना) Gandhiji laid his life in the service of the poor; let us also follow suit. (गाँधीजी ने गरीबों की सेवा में अपना जीवन न्यौछावर कर दिया। हमें भी उनका अनुसरण करना चाहिये।)

100. To fish in troubled waters — To take advantage of the difficulties of others (दूसरों की परेशानी का लाभ उठाना) During epidemics many doctors fish in troubled waters (महामारियों के दिनों में डाक्टर जनता की मजबूरियों का फायदा उठाते हैं.)

101. To fan the flame—To aggravate (उत्तेजित करना) By writing this letter you will only be fanning the flame. (ऐसा पत्र लिख कर तुम आग को और भी प्रज्वलित करोगे।)

102. To show white feather—To betray cowardice (कायरता दिखाना) Maharana Pratap never showed the white feather. (महाराणा प्रताप ने कभी कायरता नहीं दिखाई।)

103. To fight to the finish —To fight to the end (आखिरी सीमा तक लड़ना) The Rajputs were pledged to fight to the finish. (राजपूतों ने अन्तिम सीमा तक लड़ने की प्रतिज्ञा की थी।)

104. To fly into a passion—To be enraged (क्रोधित होना) Weak men easily fly into a passion. (कमजोर लोगों को जल्दी गुस्सा आता है।)

105. To make a fortune—To grow rich (धनी बन जाना) He made a fortune in America. उसने अमरीका में बड़ा धन कमाया।)

106. To wear a long face—To look gloomy (उदास दिखाई देना) Do not wear a long face on this happy occasion. (ऐसे खुशी के मौके पर ऐसे उदास मत दिखो।)

107. Fair and square— Honest (ईमानदार) One must be fair and square in one's dealings. (हर किसी को अपने कार्यकलापों में ईमानदारी बरतनी चाहिए।)

108. To kill the fatted calf for—To arrange a lavish reception for somebody (किसी का धूमधाम से स्वागत

करना) Queen Elizabeth killed the fatted calf for the Commonwealth Prime Ministers' meet. (महारानी ऐलीजाबेथ ने राष्ट्रकुल के प्रधान मन्त्रियों के स्वागत के लिये जोरों से तैयारियाँ कर रखी हैं।)

109. To play the fool— To act foolishly (धोखा खाना) He played the fool in the hands of his clever friends. (वह अपने चालाक मित्रों के हाथ धोखा खा गया।)

110. From pillar to post — From one e'treme to another (एक स्थान से दूसरे तक दौड़धूप करना) Every young man has to run from pillar to post in search of a job. (हर नवयुवक को कोई धंधा ढूँढ़ने में इधर से उधर भटकना पड़ता है।)

111. From the bottom of one's heart—Very sincerely (अन्त:करण से) The beggar thanked me from the bottom of his heart. (भिखारी ने मुझे अन्त:करण से धन्यवाद दिया।)

112. To throw down the gauntlet — To give challenge (चुनौती देना) Mohan has thrown down the gauntlet to Ramesh. (मोहन ने रमेश को चुनौती दे रखी है।)

113. Gift of the gab — The skill of oratory (भाषण देने की कला) Dr. Radhakrishnan possessed a divine gift of the gab. (डा. राधाकृष्णन को दैवीप्रदत्त भाषण कला प्राप्त थी।)

114. To give a piece of one's mind —To scold a person (किसी को फटकारना) The teacher gave a piece of his mind to the mischievous boy—(अध्यापक ने शरारती लड़के को फटकार लगाई।)

115. To face the music — To face opposition (कठिनाई या विरोध का सामना करना) Every new teacher har to face the music on the first day in the class.(हर नये अध्यापक को कक्षा में पहले दिन विरोध का सामना करना पड़ता है।)

116. To give up the ghost — To die (मर जाना) The poor beggar gave up the ghost last night. (गरीब भिखारी ने कल रात दम तोड़ दिया।)

117. To get rid of—To escape from (छुटकारा पाना) I am trying my best to get rid of my quarrelsome neighbour at the earliest. (मैं अपने झगड़ालू पड़ौसी से जल्द से जल्द छुटकारा पाना चाहता हूं।)

118. To get the better of—To overcome (काबू पा लेना) At last he got the better of his adversary. (अंत में उसने अपने विरोधी के ऊपर काबू पा लिया।)

119. To go to the dogs — To be ruined (बरबाद हो जाना) This factory is gradually going to the dogs under the new management. (नए प्रबन्धतन्त्र के अन्तर्गत यह फैक्टरी बरबाद हो रही है।)

120. To gird up the loins—To be well prepared for some trying task (किसी कठिन कार्य को करने के लिये कमर कस कर तैयार होना) Let us all gird up the loins to eradicate the evil of untouchability from India. (हमें छुआछूत के अभिशाप को मिटाने के लिये कमर कस लेनी चाहिये।)

121. To grease the palm — To tip or bribe a person (किसी को रिश्वत देना) You will find easy access to the Governor if you grease the palm of his peon. (यदि आप चपरासी को कुछ देकर खुश कर लें तो आप गवर्नर से आसानी से मिल सकते हैं.)

122. A snake in the grass— Some hidden enemy (अज्ञात शत्रु) I could never expect that he would prove a snake in the grass. (मैं कभी यह उम्मीद नहीं करता था कि वह एक छिपा हुआ शत्रु सिद्ध होगा।)

123. For good Forever—(हमेशा के लिये) He has left Kolkatta for good. (उसने कलकत्ता हमेशा के लिये छोड़ दिया है।)

124. To hold one's ground—To stand firm (दृढ़ता से डटे रहना) The Rajputs held their ground to the end. (राजपूत दृढ़ता से अन्त तक अपने मोर्चे पर डटे रह।)

125. A golden opportunity—Very favourable opportunity or chance (स्वर्ण अवसर) You should not miss this golden opportunity. (तुम्हें यह स्वर्ण अवसर खोना नहीं चाहिये।)

126. To give vent to— To express one's thoughts or feelings (अपने विचारों या भावनाओं को प्रकट करना) Every individual is freely allowed to give vent to his feelings. (प्रत्येक व्यक्ति अपने विचारों को प्रकट करने के लिये स्वतन्त्र है।)

127. An hair-breadth escape—Very narrow escape (बाल-बाल बचना) I had an hair-breadth escape last evening in a car accident. (मैं कल एक कार दुर्घटना में बाल-बाल बचा।)

128. Harp on the same string—To keep on talking on the same topic (एक ही विषय पर बात करते रहना) Why do you unnecessarily harp on the same string? (तुम एक ही राग को व्यर्थ बार-बार क्यों अलापते रहते हो।)

129. Hang over one's head—Under danger (भय की आशंका में) Ever since the death of her husband, troubles have been hanging over her head. (उसके पति की मृत्यु होने के बाद बहुत सारी मुसीबतें उसके सिर पर मडराती रही हैं।)

130. To hang in balance— To remain undecided (अनिश्चय की स्थिति) I am hanging in balance whether I should accept this offer or not. (मैं अनिश्चय की स्थिति में हूँ कि मैं इस प्रस्ताव को स्वीकार करूँ या नहीं।)

131. To hang by a thread—Critical condition (नाजुक हालत) The life of a cancer patient hangs by a thread. (कैन्सर के मरीज की जिन्दगी एक धागे से लटकी रहती है।)

132. Heart and soul—In all sincerity (सच्चे दिल से) He is devoted to his studies heart and soul. (वह पूरे मनोयोग से अपने अध्ययन में लगा हुआ है।)

133. Hard and fast — Definite (निश्चित) There is no hard and fast rule for getting happiness in life. (जीवन में खुशी प्राप्त करने के कोई निश्चित नियम नहीं हैं।)

134. To hit below the belt— To take advantage by unfair means (अनुचित उपायों से लाभ उठाना) A Rajput warrior never hits below the belt. (एक राजपूत योद्धा कभी धोखे से वार नहीं करता।)

135. To hit the nail on the head—To act in the right way (ठीक निशाने पर चोट मारना) A good lawyer always hits the nail on the head in his arguments. (एक अच्छा वकील अपनी दलीलों में ठीक निशाने पर चोट मारता है।)

136. Hard nut to crack — A difficult problem to solve (कठिन समस्या का समाधान) The problem of unemployment is a hard nut to crack. (बेरोजगारी की समस्या का हल करना कठिन है.)

137. Hold water—To prove sound (ठीक सिद्ध होना) Your argument does not hold water in this case. (तुम्हारा तर्क इस केस में लागू नहीं होता है।)

138. Hold good—Valid; applicable (लागू, उचित ठहरना) This rule no longer holds good.

(यह नियम अब लागू नहीं है।)

139. A Himalayan blunder — A serious mistake (गंभीर गलती) We committed a Himalay trusting the assurances of America. (हमने अमरीका के वायदों पर विश्वास करके बड़ी गंभीर गलती की।)

140. To make head or tail of—To understand (समझना) The audience could make no head or tail of his learned lecture on mysticism (जनता उसके आध्यात्म के भाषण का कोई अर्थ नहीं समझ सकी।)

141. Heart to heart — Very frankly (पूरे दिल से, खुले रूप में) Let us have a heart to heart talk on this complicated issue. हमें इस उलझे हुए मामले पर दिल खोलकर बात करनी चाहिए।)

142. To take to one's heels—To run away (भाग जाना) As soon as the thief saw the police, he took to his heels. (चोर ने जैसे ही पुलिस को देखा, वह भाग खड़ा हुआ।)

143. To pick holes in — To find fault with (दूसरों में दोष निकालना) It is a bad habit always to try to pick holes in others. (दूसरों में दोष निकालना बुरी आदत है।)

144. To bring home—To explain (समझाना) Gandhiji brought home the fact that the heart of India lay in her villages. (गाँधीजी ने हमें बताया कि भारत का हृदय गावों में ही बसता है।)

145. Hot water — Troubles (परेशानियाँ) You will fall in hot water if you displease him. (यदि तुमने उसे नाराज कर दिया तो परेशानी में फँस जाओगे।)

146. Hue and cry—Noies and confusion (शोरगुल और परेशानी) ,When fire broke out in the village, there was much hue and cry. (जब गाँव में आग लग गई तो वहाँ बहुत शोर शराबा होने लगा।)

147. To break the ice—To break silence by speaking first (निस्तब्धता तोड़ना) The President broke the ice in the condolence meeting with a short speech. (शोक सभा में अध्यक्ष ने एक छोटे से भाषण से निस्तब्धता तोड़ी।)

148. Ill blood— Enmity (शत्रुता) There is no ill blood between Ram and Mohan. (राम और मोहन के बीच में कोई शत्रुता नहीं है।)

149. A man of iron — A strong man (दृढ व्यक्ति) Sardar Ballabh Bhai Patel was a man of iron. (सरदार बल्लभ भाई पटेल एक लौह-पुरुष थ।)

150. In cold blood — Very cruelly (निर्दयता के साथ) The dacoits killed the old man in cold blood. (डाकुओं ने उस वृद्ध को बड़ी निर्दयता के साथ मार डाला।)

151. In black and white —In writing (लिखित में) The agreement must be made in black and white. (राजीनामा लिखित में होना चाहिये।)

152. In the teeth of—Against strong opposition (कड़े विरोध में) The Finance Bill was passed in the teeth of strong opposition. (आर्थिक बिल कड़े विरोध के मध्य स्वीकृत किया गया।)

153. In full swing—In full glory (पूरे जोरों पर) The Kumbh Fair is in full swing these days. (कुंभ मेला इन दिनों पूरे जोर पर है।)

154. In the twinkling of an eye —In a moment, in no time (क्षण भर में) The flash of lightning disappears in the twinkling of an eye. (आकाशीय विद्युत की चमक क्षण मात्र में गायब हो जाती है।)

155. In a nut shell In brief (संक्षेप में) Please report the whole case in a nut shell.(कृपया पूरी बात संक्षेप में बताइये।)

156. In one's teens—Before attaining the age of twenty (बीस साल से कम उम्र) My eldest son is still in his teens. (मेरे सबसे बड़े लड़के की उम्र 20 साल से कम है।)

157. In a fix—In a difficult mental state (मानसिक उलझन में) I am in a fix ; I do not know what to do in this situation. (मैं बड़े असमंजस में हूँ; मैं समझ नहीं पा रहा हूँ कि इस स्थिति में क्या करूं।)

158. In the nick of time—Just in time (समय से ठीक पहले) I reached the station in the nick of time. मैं अंतिम क्षणों में स्टेशन पहुँचा।)

159. In embryo—Immature, in the making (अविकसित अवस्था) My scheme of sprung up a silk factory is still in embryo. (रेशम की फैक्टरी लगाने की मेरी योजना अभी प्रारम्भिक अवस्था में है।)

160. Intents and purposes For all practical purposes (पूर्ण व्यावहारिक दृष्टि से) He is the Managing Director for all intents and purposes. (हर व्यावहारिक दृष्टि से वह मैनेजिंग डाइरेक्टर है.)

161. Ins and outs —All details and secrets (सभी बातों का पूरा ज्ञान) I know all the ins and outs of this business. (मैं इस व्यापार की सभी बारीकियाँ जानता हूँ।)

162. In vogue — Popular (प्रचलित) Animal sacrifice is no longer in vogue in India. (पशु बलि प्रथा अब भारत में प्रचलित नहीं है।)

163. In the same boat— In the same condition (एक सी अवस्था में) Both these friends are sailing in the same boat. (ये दोनों मित्र एक सी अवस्था मे है।)

164. In no time – In a very short time (थोड़ी ही देर में) I can solve his question in no time.(मैं इस प्रश्न को थोड़ी ही देर मे हल कर सकता हूँ।)

165. Jack of all trades — A person knowing a little of many things (बहुत–सी बातों का थोड़ा बहुत ज्ञान रखने वाला) Ramesh is a Jack of all trades. (रमेश थोड़ा बहुत सब कामों के बारे में जानता है।)

166. Juda's kiss—False show of love (झूठा प्रेम) Who knows that his love is merely Juda's kiss ? (कौन जानता है उसका प्रेम केवल छल हो।)

167. To hold one's jaw—To stop talking (बोलने से बन्द होना) Kindly hold your jaw; it is enough. (अब कृपया चुप हो जाओ; अब बहुत हो गया।)

168. In the jaws of — In the grip of (दाँतों के बीच, किसी के कब्जे में (The patient is in the jaws of death- (अब बीमार मृत्यु के मुँह में है।)

169. To kill two birds with one stone—To serve two purposes at one time (एक तीर से दो शिकार, एक काम से दो बातें साधना) If you hold the meeting at Nainital in summer] you will be killing two birds with one stone. (यदि तुम गर्मियों में मीटिंग नैनीताल में करो, तो एक तीर से दो शिकार कर सकोगे।)

170. To kiss the dust—To be humiliated (अपमानित होना) In the wrestling bouts the boastful wrestler had to kiss the dust. (कुश्ती में घमंडी पहलवान को धूल चाटनी पड़ी।)

171. Kith and kin —Close relations (घनिष्ट सम्बन्धी) Who will not help his kith and kin. (अपने घनिष्ट जनों को कौन मदद नहीं करेगा?)

172. To knock against To collide with (टक्कर खाना) The truck knocked against the running train. (ट्रक चलती हुई रेलगाड़ी से टकरा गया।)

173. To keep up appearances To keep one's prestige (अपनी इज्जत बचाये रखना) He is somehow keeping up appearances in his old age.(वह किसी तरह से बुढ़ापे में अपनी इज्जत बचाये हुए है।)

174. To keep an eye To watch (निगाह रखना) The police keeps an eye on the vagabonds. (पुलिस आवारा लोगों पर निगाह रखती है।)

175. To keep at bay — To keep the enemy at a distance (दुश्मन को दूर रखना) It is not easy to keep the rebels at bay. (दुश्मन को दूर रखना आसान नहीं है।)

176. To keep the wolf from the door—To avoid starvation (भुखमरी से बचे रहना) He has to work day and night to keep the wolf from the door—(उसे भुखमरी से बचने के लिये दिन रात मेहनत करनी पड़ती है।)

177. To keep an open table—To entertain all comers (सबका स्वागत करना) He is very generous and always keeps an open table. (वह बड़ा दयालु है, और सबका स्वागत करने के लिये तैयार रहता है।)

178. The knock down price—Auction price (नीलाम में बोली गई कीमत) You will have to pay one—fourth of the knock down price just now. (तुम्हें नीलामी बोली का एक चौथाई बोली खत्म होते ही चुकाना पड़ेगा।)

179. To laugh in one's sleeves—To laugh secretly (चुपचाप हँसना) The lawyers laughed in their sleeves at the ignorance of the judge. (जज की अज्ञानता पर वकील लोग चुपचाप हँस रहे थे।)

180. To win laurels —To win honours (यश प्राप्त करना) Our athletes won laurels in the Olympic games. (ओलिम्पिक खेलों में हमारे खिलाड़ियों ने खूब यश प्राप्त किया।)

181. To lose the day To be defeated (हार जाना) Our team lost the day. (हमारी टीम हार गई।)

182. To lick the dust—To accept defeat (हार मान लेना) Be sure you will have to lick the dust in the end. (विश्वास करो, तुम्हें अंत में धूल चाटनी पड़ेगी।)

183. Leap in the dark Uncertainty about the outcome (अनिश्चित परिणाम) Marriage is a leap in the dark. (विवाह अँधेरे में छलाँग लगाने के समान है।)

184. To lay hands on—To seize (अधिकार जमा लेना) How can the government lay hands on my private property? (मेरी व्यक्तिगत सम्पति पर सरकार कैसे हाथ डाल सकती है?)

185. Lapped in luxury – Brought up in luxury (विलासिता में पलना) The princes are lapped in luxury. (राजघराने के राजकुमार विलासिता में डूबे रहते हैं।)

186. To lead by the nose—To wield undue influence (अनुचित अधिकार जमाना) She leads her husband by the nose. (वह अपने पति पर अनुचित दबाव रखती है।)

187. To lie in wait—To keep waiting for the victim (घात लगाये बैठे रहना) The robbers were lying in wait for the belated travellers. (लुटेरे देर से लौटने वाले मुसाफिरों के लिये घात लगाए बैठे थे।)

188. To turn over a new leaf , To start a new way of life (नया जीवन शुरू करना) He has turned a new leaf at sixty. (उसने साठ साल की उम्र पर नया जीवन शुरू किया है।)

189. To throw light on — To explain (प्रकाश डालना) The President threw light on the terms of agreement. (अध्यक्ष ने राजीनामा की शर्तों पर प्रकाश डाला।)

190. To wash dirty linen in public, To expose private affairs in public (व्यक्तिगत बातों को बाहर उछालना) There is no wisdom in washing dirty linen in public. (अपनी व्यक्तिगत बातों को बाहर फैलाना बुद्धिमानी की बात नहीं है।)

191. A man of letters — A learned man (विद्वान व्यक्ति) Dr. Radhakrishnan was a man of letters. (डॉ. राधाकृष्णन एक विद्वान व्यक्ति थे।)

192. A red letter day—A historic day (महत्वपूर्ण दिन) The 15th of August 1947 is a red letter day in the history of India. (भारत के इतिहास में 15 अगस्त, 1947 एक अति महत्वपूर्ण दिन है।)

193. A white lie—Clear falsehood (सफेद झूठ) He is telling a white lie. (वह सफेद झूठ बोल रहा है।)

194. To look down upon To hate a person (किसी व्यक्ति से घृणा करना) The rich should not look down upon the poor—(अमीरों को गरीबों से घृणा नहीं करनी चाहिये।)

195. On one's last legs—At the last stage of life (जीवन की अन्तिम अवस्था में) The patient is on his last legs. (रोगी जीवन के अन्तिम क्षणों में है।)

196. To lead to the altar— To marry (शादी करने जाना) I took the vow of life & long sincerity to my wife when I led her to the altar (मैंने अपनी पत्नी से शादी के समय जीवन भर निष्ठावान रहने की कसम खाई थी।)

197. Loaves and fishes—Material gains (भौतिक लाभ) Do not fall fron your ideals for loaves and fishes.) (छोटे से लाभ के लिये अपने आदर्शों से नीचे मत गिरो।)

198. To pull one's leg—To befool a person (किसी व्यक्ति की टाँग खिंचाई करना।) Prevent them from pulling the leg of the old man. (उन्हें उस वृद्ध की टाँग खिंचाई करने से रोको।)

199. Lion's share — The biggest share (सबसे बड़ा हिस्सा) The leader of the gang got the lion's share of the booty. (लुटेरों के सरदार को सबसे बड़ा हिस्सा मिला।।

200. To leave one in the lurch—To leave one in difficulties (किसी का कठिनाइयों में साथ छोड़ देना) My faithful friend, Mohan, will never leave me in the lurch. (मेरा पक्का मित्र मोहन मुझे कभी मुसीबतों में नहीं छोड़ेगा।)

201. Long and short— Brief substance (सारांश) Let me know the long and short of his speech. (मुझे उसके भाषण का सारांश बता दो।)

202. To leave no stone unturned leave no stone unturned to help — To make all possible efforts (कोई भी प्रयत्न बाकी न छोड़ना) I shall you. (मैं तुम्हारी मदद करने में कोई कमी न छोडूंगा।)

203. To let by gones be by gones— To forget old things (पुरानी बातों को भूल जाना) Let us start anew and let by—gones be by gones. (हमें पुरानी बातों को भुला कर नये सिरे से कार्य करना चाहिये।)

204. Man of parts—Talented man (बहुत से गुणों से सम्पन्न व्यक्ति) I can certify that he is a man of parts. (मैं प्रमाणित कर सकता हूँ कि वह एक गुण सम्पन्न व्यक्ति है।)

205. Mare's nest—Illusory discovery (धोखे की बात, झूठी अफवाह) The report of the discovery of gold mines proved to be a mare's nest. (सोने की खान मिलने की बात केवल झूठी अफवाह निकली।)

206. Move heaven and earth, To make every possible effort (हर प्रकार के प्रयत्न करना) He moved heaven and earth to find a job but it was all in vain. (उसने कोई काम पाने के लिये जमीन-आसमान मिला दिये, लेकिन वह असफल रहा।)

207. To make a clean breast of — To confess (खुले दिल से स्वीकार कर लेना) The dacoits made a clean breast of their crimes before Vinoba Bhave. (विनोवा भावे के सामने डाकुओं ने खुले दिल से अपने अपराध स्वीकार कर लिये।)

208. To make a mountain of a mole hill —To exaggerate small things (राई का पहाड़ बनाना) You are unnecessarily making a mountain of a mole&hill and quarrelling. (तुम व्यर्थ ही राई का पहाड़ बना कर लड़ रहे हो।)

209. To make after — To pursue or chase (पीछा करना) The police made after the thief and caught him. (पुलिस ने चोर का पीछा किया और उसे पकड़ लिया।)

210. By fair or foul means— By any means possible, right or wrong (सही या गलत किसी भी प्रकार से) He is very tactful and will succeed by fair or foul means. (वह बड़ा चालाक है और किसी न किसी तरह जीत जायेगा।)

211. To make up one's mind — To determine (निश्चय करना) He has made up his mind to appear at the examination this year. (उसने इस साल परीक्षा देने का निश्चय कर लिया है।)

212. To make much ado about nothing—To make much of little things (बात का बतंगड़ बनाना) You will only complicate the matter if you make much ado about nothing. (तुम यदि बात का बतंगड़ बनाओगे तो मामले को और भी उलझा दोगे।)

213. To throw mud at—To scandalise (बदनामी करना) Why do you throw mud at your colleagues? (तुम अपने साथियों पर कीचड़ क्यों उछालते हो?)

214. Upto the mark—Upto standard (उचित स्तर तक) Your answers are not upto the mark. (तुम्हारे उत्तर उचित स्तर के नहीं हैं।)

215. To make one's mark—To achieve distinction (अपना प्रभाव छोड़ना) India made its mark at the SAARC Summit meet. (भारत ने सार्क देशों के शिखर सम्मेलन में अपना गहरा प्रभाव छोड़ा।)

216. Milk of human kindness—Human compassion (मानवता से भरा हृदय।) The heat of Gandhi Ji overflowed with the milk of human kindness. (गांधीजी का हृदय मानवता के प्रति दया से भरा हुआ था।

217. To make amends , To compensate (हर्जाना देना, गलती के लिए माफी माँगना) You will have to make amends for causing so much harm to me. (तुम्हें मेरे प्रति किये गये अन्याय के लिये क्षति पूर्ति करनी पड़ेगी।)

218. To meet half-way— To be prepared for compromise (समझौते के लिये राजी होना)Gandhiji was always prepared to meet his adversaries half-way. (गांधीजी अपने विरोधियों से समझौता करने के लिये सदा तैयार रहते थे।)

219. To join the majority—To die (मर जाना) The poor beggar has joined the majority. (गरीब भिखारी मर गया।)

220. To make out—To understand (समझ लेना) I can hardly make out any meaning out of your speech. (मैं तुम्हारे भाषण को बिलकुल भी न समझ सका।)

221. Man in the street—Common man (साधारण व्यक्ति) The life of the man in the street is very hard. (साधारण व्यक्ति का जीवन बड़ा कठिन होता है।)

222. To nip in the bud— To destroy in the very beginning (आरम्भ में ही समाप्त कर डालना) All his hopes have been nipped in the bud. (उसकी सब आशायें आरम्भ में ही समाप्त हो गई।)

223. Null and void-Rendered invalid (बेकार सिद्ध कर देना) The court has declared these laws null and void. (न्यायालय ने इन कानूनों को अप्रभावी घोषित कर दिया है।)

224. Nook and corner — At every place (प्रत्येक स्थान पर) The police searched for the thief in every nook and corner. (पुलिस ने चोर को हर जगह तलाश किया।)

225. To set at naught—To ruin (खत्म कर देना) All my plans have been set at naught on the death of my father. (मेरे पिता की मृत्यु के कारण मेरे सारे उपाय व्यर्थ हो गये।)

226. Narrow circumstances—Hard days, poverty (गरीबी के दिन) He is living in narrow circumstances these days. (वह इन दिनों गरीबी के दिन जी रहा है।)

227. No love lost—Having no love (किसी प्रकार के प्रेम या मित्रता का न होना) There is no love lost between them. (उनमें किसी प्रकार की मित्रता नहीं है।)

228. Neither chick nor child No child (कोई बच्चा न होना) The unfortunate old man has neither chick nor child. (उस दुर्भाग्यशाली व्यक्ति के कोई बच्चा नहीं है।)

229. To strain every nerve—To make every possible effort (हर प्रकार का प्रयत्न करना)He will surely strain every nerve to get his work done. (वह निश्चय ही अपना काम निकालने के लिये हर संभव प्रयत्न करेगा।)

230. To feather one's own nest—To serve one's own purpose (अपना स्वार्थ सिद्ध करना) Many a so called social worker merely feathers his own nest. (बहुत से समाजसेवी कहे जाने वाले लोग केवल अपनी स्वार्थ सिद्धि करते हैं।)

231. Open secret Known to all (सर्वविदित) This is now an open secret. (यह बात अब सर्वविदित है।

232. Order of the day—Some popular thing of the age (कोई प्रचलित बात) Armament race is the order of the day. (हथियारों की दौड़ आज के युग में प्रचलित बात है।)

233. On the wrong side of—One's age being more than (किसी संख्या से अधिक उम्र का होना) He is on the wrong side of fifty. (उसकी उम्र पचास के ऊपर हो चुकी है।)

234. Out of sorts—Indisposed (तबियत खराब होना) I am out of sorts today. (मेरी तबियत आज कुछ खराब है।)

235. Old head on young shoulders — One over intelligent and experienced for one's age (अपनी उम्र से अधिक बुद्धिमान) My young son reads books of philosophy with interest; he has an old head on young shoulders. (मेरा छोटा बेटा दर्शनशास्त्र की पुस्तकें चाव से पढ़ता है। वह अपनी उम्र से अधिक बुद्धिमान दिखता है।)

236. To oil someone's hands—To bribe (रिश्वत देना) Oiling the hands of officials is an offence. (अधिकारियों को रिश्वत देना जुर्म है।)

237. To pay one back in one's own coin—Tit for tat (जैसे को तैसा) You have deceived Mohan and, therefore, take care that you may have to pay back in your own coin. (तुम मोहन को धोखा दिया है, सावधान रहो कहीं तुम्हें भी वैसा ही धोखा न खाना पड़े।)

238. To put the saddle on the right horse, To blame the really guilty person (सही अपराधी को पहचान लेना) By arresting Mohan the police have put the saddle on the right horse. (मोहन को गिरफ्तार कर पुलिस ने सही अपराधी को पकड़ा है।)

239. To put one's shoulder to the wheel, To do one's work with one's own efforts (अपने ही सहारे अपना कार्य करना) God helps those who put their shoulders to the wheel. (ईश्वर उनकी मदद करता है जो स्वंय प्रयत्न करते हैं।)

240. Pros and cons Points for and against/good or bad (किसी बात की अच्छाई बुराई समझ लेना) Let us consider all the pros and cons of the whole affair before we advance further. (आगे बढ़ने से पहले हमें मामले के सारे अच्छे-बुरे परिणाम सोच लेने चाहिये।)

241. To poke one's nose into— To interfere with the affairs of others (दूसरों की बातों में हस्तक्षेप करना) It is not wise to poke one's nose into the affairs of others. (दूसरों के मामलों में अपनी टाँग फँसाने में कोई बुद्धिमानी नहीं है।)

242. To pour oil on troubled waters—To pacify the anger of others (क्रोध को शान्त करने का प्रयत्न) He poured oil on troubled waters by his gentle and honest replies. (उसने अपने नम्र और सही उत्तरों से क्रोध को शांत करने का प्रयत्न किया।)

23. Pandora's Box—A source of evil powers (बुराइयों का भंडार) Greed opens Pandora's box. (लो बुराइयों का भंडार है।)

244. To play one's cards well—To play an intelligent role (समझदारी से काम करना।)good statesman always plays his cards well. (एक अच्छा राजनीतिज्ञ बड़ी समझदारी से काम करता है।)

245. To poison one's ears against—To set a person against another (किसी के विरु) कान भरना) He has poisoned the ears of my employer against me. (उसने मेरे विरुद्ध मेरे मालिक के कान भर दिये हैं।)

246. To set price on one's head—To offer reward for killing or helping in the arrest of a criminal (किसी अपराधी के मारने या पकड़वाने में मदद करने पर इनाम की घोषणा) The government have set a price of Rs. 50,000/- on the head of the rebel leader. (सरकार ने उपद्रवियों के सरगना को मारने या पकड़वाने के लिये पचास हजार रुपयों का इनाम घोषित किया है।)

247. Part and parcel—An essential part (आवश्यक अंग) A good laboratory is the part and parcel of the equipment of a scientist. (एक वैज्ञानिक के पास अच्छी प्रयोगशाला का होना अति आवश्यक है।)

248. To pester with—To be troubled with (किसी बात से परेशान होना) We are pestered with mosquitoes here. (हमें यहाँ मच्छरों ने परेशान कर डाला है।)

249. To take pains—To work hard (कठिन परिश्रम करना) Nothing can be gained without taking pains. (कठिन परिश्रम के बिना कुछ नहीं मिलता।)

250. To put up with —To tolerate (सहन करना) I cannot put up with this insult. (मैं इस अपमान को सहन नहीं कर सकता।)

251. To pull to pieces—To criticise adversely (कटु आलोचना करना) He has pulled my proposal to pieces. (उसने मेरे प्रस्तावों की कड़ी आलोचना की है।)

252. To put pen to paper, To begin writing (लिखना आरम्भ कर देना) I put my pen to paper at the first stroke of the bell. (मैं घंटा बजते ही लिखना आरम्भ कर देता हूँ।)

253. Pin prick—Small troubles (छोटी-मोटी परेशानियाँ) You should not lose your patience at such pin pricks. (तुम्हें इन छोटी-मोटी परेशानियों पर धैर्य नहीं खोना चाहिये।)

254. To play the second fiddle—To take a subordinate position (दूसरे स्थान पर काम करना) It is starange that your Principal plays the second fiddle to the Manager. (बड़े आश्चर्य की बात है कि तुम्हारे प्राचार्य अपने मैनेजर के पिछलग्गू हैं।)

255. To play a double game—To act dubiously (धोखाधड़ी करना) Take care, he is playing a double game with you. (सावधान रहो, वह तुम्हारे साथ धोखाधड़ी कर रहा है।)

256. To play fast and loose — To be unfaithful (विश्वासघात करना) You can never prosper if you play fast and loose with your own men. (यदि तुम अपने ही साथियों के साथ विश्वासघात करोगे तो कभी फलीभूत नहीं होगे।)

257. To play truant—To run away from the class (कक्षा से भाग जाना) He is in the habit of playing truant from the class. (उसे कक्षा से भाग जाने की आदत है।)

258. To play one false – To deceive (किसी को धोखा देना) You should not have played me false. (तुम्हें मुझे धोखा नहीं देना चाहिये था।)

259. Past master—An expert (किसी क्षेत्र का विशेषज्ञ) He is past master in acting on the stage. (वह स्टेज पर नाटक खेलने में दक्ष है।)

260. To put a spoke in one's wheel—To stand in the way of one's progress (किसी की उन्नति में बाघा डालना) My own brother is putting a spoke in my wheel. (मेरा खास भाई मेरी उन्नति में बाधा डाल रहा है।)

261. Pell mell In confusion (घबराहट में) People ran pell mell at the first tremor of the earthquake. (भूकंप के पहले झटके पर ही लोग घबराहट में भागने लगे।)

262. To pull the wire—To exercise secret influence (छिपे रूप से प्रभाव डालना। America is pulling the wire behind Pakistan's activities. (पाकिस्तान की कार्यवाही पर छिपे रूप में अमरीका का हाथ है।)

263. Point blank—Clearly (साफ तौर से) He has refused point blank to help me. (उसने मेरी मदद करने से साफ इनकार कर दिया है।)

264. Petticoat-Government—The undue influence of women (स्त्रियों का अनुचित दबाव) There is petticoat-government in most social organizations in France (फ्रांस के अधिकाश सामाजिक संगठनों पर महिलाओं का आधिपत्य है।)

265. To put to the sword—To kill (मार देना) Nadirshah put even children to the sword. (नादिरशाह ने बच्चों तक को मौत के घाट उतार दिया।)

266. Rank and file—Lower middle class people (साधारण श्रेणी के लोग) The learned speech of the great orator cannot be appreciated by the rank and file. (विद्वान वक्ता के भाषण को जनसाधारण लोग नहीं समझ सकते।)

267. To rain cats and dogs— To rain heavily (मूसलाधार बारिश) It is raining cats and dogs.(मूसलाधार बारिश हो रही है।)

268. To rise to the occasion—To come to help at the hour of need (समय पर सहायता के लिये तैयार रहना) My brother is there to rise to the occasion to help me. (मेरा भाई समय पर मेरी सहायता के लिये तैयार रहेगा।)

269. To run short—Not proving sufficient, shortage of something (किसी चीज की कमी)I am running short of money these days. (आजकल मेरे पास धन की कमी है।)

270. A rolling stone—A man not sticking to his job (अपने काम में न जमने वाला व्यक्ति) He will not prosper because he is a rolling stone. (वह कभी समृद्ध नहीं हो सकता, क्योंकि वह किसी काम में नहीं जमता है।)

271. Right-hand man— A very helpful person (अच्छा सहायक) My manager is my right & hand man. (मेरा मैनेजर मेरा अच्छा सहायक है।)

272. To read between the lines—To discover secret meaning (गुप्त अर्थ निकालना) It is a simple statement; why do you read between the lines? (यह एक साधारण कथन है, तुम इसमें गूढ़ अर्थ क्यों ढूँढ़ते हो?)

273. A broken reed—An unreliable person (अविश्वसनीय व्यक्ति) Every body knows that he is a broken reed; don't depend on him. (हर कोई जानता है कि वह अविश्वसनीय व्यक्ति है, उस पर भरोसा मत करो।)

274. Without rhyme or reason — Without any justification (अकारण) He has been criticising me without rhyme or reason. (वह अकारण ही मेरी बुराई करता फिरता है।)

275. To go to rack and ruin, To be completely ruined (पूर्णरूप से बरबाद हो जाना) His business has gone to rack and ruin. (उसका व्यापार पूर्णरूप से बरबाद हो चुका है।)

276. To rub shoulders with, To come in close contact with (किसी के निकट सम्पर्क में आना) I have rubbed shoulders with great scholars. (मैं बड़े-बड़े विद्वानों के सम्पर्क में आ चुका हूँ।)

277. To hold the scales even, To be impartial (निष्पक्ष रहना) A judge must hold the scales even (एक जज को निष्पक्ष रहना चाहिये।)

278. To scratch one's head, To be perplexed (परेशान हो जाना) When I saw the Mathematics paper, I just scratched my head. (जब मैंने गणित का पर्चा देखा तो परेशान होकर सिर खुजाने लगा।)

279. Storm in a tea-cup—Much hue and cry over a little matter (छोटी सी बात पर बहुत शोरगुल करना) You have unnecessarily raised storm in a tea-cup over this little matter. (तुमने व्यर्थ ही इस छोटी सी बात पर तूफान खड़ा कर दिया है।)

280. Stand in good stead , To be of great service (बहुत सहायक होना) Your upright character will always stand in good stead. (तुम्हारा सच्चरित्र हमेशा तुम्हारा सहायक रहेगा।)

281. Slip of the pen—A small unintentional mistake in writing (लिखने में भूल से जरा सी गलती) Please eÛcuse me for this slip of the pen. (लिखने की इस भूल के लिये मुझे क्षमा करें।)

282. Slip of the tongue—A slight mistake in speaking (बोलने में छोटी सी गलती) Do not give so much importance to his slip of the tongue. (बोलने में इस छोटी सी भूल को इतना महत्व न दें।)

283. Square meal—Full meal (पेट भर भोजन) Many people can hardly arrange even a square meal. (बहुत से लोग भरपेट खाना मुश्किल से जुटा पाते हैं।)

284. To save one's skin, To escape safely (जान छुड़ाना) I have somehow saved my skin from the scandal. (मैंने इस बदनामी से बड़ी मुश्किल से पीछा छुड़ाया है।)

285. To roll up one's sleeves, To be prepared for contest (मुकाबले के लिये तैयार रहना) When Mohan gave him the challenge, he rolled up his sleeves. (जब मोहन ने उसे ललकारा तो उसने भी अपनी बाहें चढ़ा ली।)

286. To give the cold shoulder, To discourage a person (निराश करना) I went to him for help] but he gave me the cold shoulder. (मैं उसके पास मदद माँगने गया, लेकिन उसने मुझे निराश कर दिया।)

287. At a stone's throw, At a little distance (थोड़ी दूर पर) My house is at a stone's throw from here. (मेरा घर यहाँ से थोड़ी ही दूरी पर है।)

288. To stand on one's own legs—To become independent (अपने पैरों पर खड़े होना) Now you are old enough to stand on your own legs. (अब तुम अपने पैरों पर खड़े होने लायक हो गये हो।)

289. Summer friends, Friends of prosperity (खुशहाली के मित्र) All my summer friends have deserted me in my adverse days. (मेरे सभी मतलबी मित्र मेरे बुरे दिनों में मेरा साथ छोड़ गये है।)

290. To screw up one's courage—To gather courage (साहस बढ़ाना) Do not be so disheartened; serew disheartenedi ge up your courage. (हिम्मत मत हारो अपना साहस बढ़ाओ।)

291. To see the light, To be born (जन्म लेना) His father died before he saw the light. (उसके पैदा होने से पहले ही उसके पिता मर चुके थे।)

292. Seal of love Kiss (चुम्बन) The mother bade him farewell by imprinting a seal of love on his forehead (उसकी माँ ने चुम्बन लेकर उसे विदा किया।)

293. The sheet of anchor— The place of protection or shelter (शरण पाने का स्थान) Her employer proved to be the sheet of anchor to her. (उसके मालिक में उसे शरण पाने का स्थान मिला।)

294. A thick-skinned person— Insensitive person (लज्जाहीन व्यक्ति) He is a very thick-skinned person. (वह बड़ा लज्जाहीन व्यक्ति है।)

295. Through thick and thin—Through all difficulties (सभी कठिनाइयों के बीच)She faithfully stood with her husband through thick and thin. (वह सभी परिस्थितियों में अपने पति के साथ खड़ी रही।)

296. To take into one's head—To think or to believe (किसी बात को सोचना या विश्वास कर लेना) Somehow he has taken into his head that he is the most intelligent boy. (किसी प्रकार उसके दिमाग में यह बात बैठ गई है कि वह सबसे बुद्धिमान लड़का है।)

297. A tool in the hands of Under the authority of another (दूसरे के हाथ में कठपुतली की भाँति) Pakistan is merely a tool in the hands of America. (पाकिस्तान अमरीका के हाथ की कठपुतली मात्र है।)

298. To take the bull by the horns—To face danger with courage (खतरे का हिम्मत से सामना करना) Be bold and take the bull by the horns. (बहादुर बनो और खतरों का हिम्मत से मुकाबला करो।)

299. To take time by the forelock, To do one's work in time (समय के अन्दर काम करना) You will never fail if you take time by the forelock. (यदि तुम समय के अन्दर काम करोगे तो कभी असफल नहीं होगे।)

300. True to one's salt—To be faithful to one's blood or character (अपने खून या चरित्र के प्रति कादार) The Rajputs were always true to their salt. (राजपूत लोग अपने खून के प्रति कादार रहते थे।)

301. To turn the tables, To change the situation completely (स्थिति को बिल्कुल बदल देना) In the last few minutes our captain turned the tables in our favour (अन्तिम कुछ मिनटों में हमारे कप्तान ने परिस्थितियों को हमारे पक्ष में बदल दिया।)

302. Tooth and nail—Contending with all force (पूरी शक्ति से विरोध करना) We shall oppose this move tooth and nail. (हम पूरी शक्ति से इस कदम का विरोध करेंगे।)

303. To turn a deaf ear —To pay no attention (कोई ध्यान न देना) My friend turned a deaf ear to my advice. (मेरे मित्र ने मेरी सलाह पर कोई ध्यान न दिया।)

304. Tall talk Boasting (शेखी मारना) He always indulges in tall talks, (वह हमेशा शेखी बघारता रहता है।)

305. To turn one's coat—To change one's party (पार्टी बदल लेना) He is an opportunist and has so often turned his coat. (वह अवसरवादी है और अपनी पार्टी बदलता रहता है।)

306. Under a cloud—Under suspicious conditions. (संदेहपूर्ण स्थितियों में) He is working under a cloud. (वह संदेहपूर्ण परिस्थितियों में कार्य करता है।)

307. Under the rose—Secretly (गुप्त रूप से) He is making love with her under the rose. (वह गुप्त रूप से उससे प्रेम करता है।)

308. Under one's nose—In the presence of (किसी के सामने) He accepted bribe under the nose of his senior officers. (उसने अपने अधिकारियों के सामने ही रिश्वत ली।)

309. Wild goose chase—Useless efforts (व्यर्थ का प्रयत्न) His efforts to marry the princess have proved a wild goose chase. (एक राजकुमारी से विवाह करने के उसके प्रयत्न व्यर्थ सिद्ध हुए।)

310. White elephant—A very expensive thing (बहुत खर्चीली वस्तु) A European wife is a white elephant for an Indian. (किसी भी भारतीय के लिये यूरोपीय पत्नी एक बहुत ही खर्चीली वस्तु सिद्ध होता है।)

311. Wolf in sheep's clothing—A deceitful man (बनावटी व्यक्ति) I don't trust him he is a wolf in sheep's clothing. (मैं उस पर विश्वास नहीं करता, वह भेड़ की खाल में भेड़िया है।)

312. Wash one's hands of To be free from (किसी बात से मुक्त हो जाना) I have washed my hands of her affairs. (मैंने उसके मामले से हाथ झाड़ लिये हैं।)

313. Much cry and little wool—Disappointing result (निराशाजनक परिणाम) After five years of studies abroad, he got a small post. It was much cry and little wool. (पाँच साल तक विदेश में पढ़ने के बाद उसे एक छोटा सा पद मिला है; यह बड़ा निराशाजनक परिणाम रहा।)

314. To bring to book— To punish (सजा देना) The offender should be brought to bool. (अपराधी को दंड अवश्य मिलना चाहिये।)

315. To show a clean pair of heels— To run away (भाग जाना) The thief showed a clean pair of heels to the police. (पुलिस को देखते ही चोर भाग खड़ा हुआ।)

316. To add a new feather in one's cap,To acquire a new honour or distinction (कोई नया सम्मान प्राप्त करना) His election to the Parliament has added a new feather in his cap. (संसद के चुनाव में जीतने से उसके सम्मान में एक पदक और जुड़ गया।)

317. To take a leaf out of another man's book—To imitate another person (दूसरों की नकल करना) He has no originality of thought; he is only taking a leaf out of another man's book. (उसके पास कोई मौलिक विचार नहीं है, वह दूसरों के विचारों की नकल किया करता है।)

318. Maiden speech First speech (किसी का पहला भाषण) His maiden speech was quite a success. (उसका पहला ही भाषण बहुत सफल रहा।)

319. Nine days' wonder—A short lived glory (थोड़ी देर का चमत्कार) The glory of Hitler was nine days wonder. (हिटलर का यश चार दिन की चाँदनी सिद्ध हुआ।)

320. To sow wild oats — Indulgence in youthful follies (युवावस्था की बेवकूफियाँ करना) It is the duty of the warden to see that his students do not sow wild oats. (व्यवस्थापक का यह कर्तव्य है कि वह देखे कि उसके विद्यार्थी युवावस्था के भ्रमों में न पड़ जायें।)

321. To pocket an insult—To bear insult (अपमान सहन कर लेना) The nationalists had to pocket much insult during their fight for independence. (राष्ट्रवादियों को स्वतन्त्रता के युद्ध में बहुत अपमान झेलने पड़े थे।)

322. A red rag to a bull—Something that irritates (उत्तेजित करने वाली बात) The fiery slogans against the police proved to be a red rag to a bull. (पुलिस के विरुद्ध लगाये गये नारों से पुलिसजन और भी भडक गये।)

323. Under the thumb of—Under the authority of someone (दूसरों के अधिकार में) The manager is under the thumb of the proprietor. (मैनेजर मालिक के अधिकार में है।

324. To get wind of— To know the secret (भेद जान लेना) Somehow the police got the wind of the conspiracy. (किसी तरह पुलिस को उस षडयन्त्र की भनक लग गई।)

325. To go a wool-gathering—To grow lunatic (पागल हो जाना) His wits have gone a wool-gathering. (वह पागल सा हो गया है।)

326. Over head and ears—Very deeply (सामर्थ्य से अधिक) He is in debt over head and ears. (वह अपनी सामर्थ्य से अधिक कर्जे में डूबा है।)

327. In the air—Spread as a rumour (बात फैल जाना) This news is very much in the air. (यह बात चारों ओर फैल चुकी है।)

328. Out of the wood —Out of difficulties (मुसीबत से छुटकारा) At last he came out of the wood. (आखिर उसे मुसीबतों से छुटकारा मिल गया।)

329. A royal road—An easy and popular way (आसान रास्ता) There is no royal road to success. (सफलता के लिये कोई भी रास्ता आसान नहीं है।)

330. To think lightly—Not to be serious about a thing (मजाक के रूप में लेना।) Please don't think lightly of my scheme. (कृपया मेरी योजना का मजाक न उड़ायें।)

331. To fight shy of—To be hesitant (डरते हुए कार्य करना) Face the problem boldly and don't fight shy of the situation. (समस्याओं का हिम्मत से मुकाबिला करो, परिस्थितियों से डरो मत।)

332. In the melting pot—In a confused state (अनिश्चित स्थिति) The whole affair is in the melting pot. (सारी स्थिति अनिश्चित है।)

333. By and large On the whole (अन्त में मोटे तौर पर) He is by and large a gentleman. (वह अधिकांशत: सज्जन व्यक्ति ह।)

334. Come across —Meet by chance (अचानक मुलाकात होना) Please give him my message if you come across him. (यदि उससे मुलाकात हो जाय तो उसे मेरा समाचार दे देना)

335. To make up — To make up the loss (क्षतिपूर्ति करना) I shall make up your loss. (मैं तुम्हारी क्षतिपूर्ति कर दूँगा।)

336. Run down — Reduced in health (स्वास्थ्य में गिरावट) He is very much run down these days. (आजकल उसके स्वास्थ्य में गिरावट आ गई है।)

337. A tower of strength— Chief support (शक्ति का स्तम्भ) Pt- Nehru was the tower of strength of the Congress Party. (जवाहरलाल नेहरू कांग्रेस के शक्ति स्तम्भ थे

319. Nine days' wonder— A short lived glory (थोड़ी देर का चमत्कार) The glory of Hitler was nine days wonder. (हिटलर का यश चार दिन की चाँदनी सिद्ध हुआ।)

320. To sow wild oats — Indulgence in youthful follies (युवावस्था की बेवकूफियाँ करना) It is the duty of the warden to see that his students do not sow wild oats. (व्यवस्थापक का यह कर्त्तव्य है कि वह देखे कि उसके विद्यार्थी युवावस्था के भ्रमों में न पड़ जायें।)

321. To pocket an insult — To bear insult (अपमान सहन कर लेना) The nationalists had to pocket much insult during their fight for independence. (राष्ट्रवादियों को स्वतन्त्रा के युवा) में बहुत अपमान झेलने पड़े थे।)

322. A red rag to a bull —Something that irritates (उत्तेजित करने वाली बात) The fiery slogans against the police proved to be a red rag to a bull. (पुलिस के विरुद्ध) लगाये गये नारों से पुलिसजन और भी भड़क गये।)

323. Under the thumb of —Under the authority of someone (दूसरों के अधिकार में) The manager is under the thumb of the proprietor. (मैनेजर मालिक के अधिकार में है।)

324. To get wind of— To know the secret (भेद जान लेना) Somehow the police got the wind of the conspiracy. (किसी तरह पुलिस को उस षडयन्त्र की भनक लग गई।)

325. To go a wool-gathering — To grow lunatic (पागल हो जाना) His wits have gone a wool and gathering. (वह पागल सा हो गया है।)

326. Over head and ears— Very deeply (सामर्थ्य से अधिक) He is in debt over head and ears. (वह अपनी सामर्थ्य से अधिक कर्जे में डूबा है।)

327. In the air—Spread as a rumour (बात फैल जाना) This news is very much in the air. (यह बात चारों ओर फैल चुकी है।)

328. Out of the wood —Out of difficulties (मुसीबत से छुटकारा) At last he came out of wood. (आखिर उसे मुसीबतों से छुटकारा मिल गया।)

329. A royal road —An easy and popular way (आसान रास्ता) There is no royal road to success. (सफलता के लिये कोई भी रास्ता आसान नहीं है।)

330. To think lightly—Not to be serious about a thing (मजाक के रूप में लेना) Please don't think lightly of my scheme. (कृपया मेरी योजना का मजाक न उड़ायें।)

331. To fight shy of —To be hesitant (डरते हुए कार्य करना) Face the problem boldly and don't fight shy of the situation. (समस्याओं का हिम्मत से मुकाबला करो, परिस्थितियों से डरो मत।)

332. In the melting pot—In a confused state (अनिश्चित स्थिति) The whole affair is in the melting pot. (सारी स्थिति अनिश्चित है।)

333. By and large — On the whole (अन्त में मोटे तौर पर) He is by and large a gentleman. (वह अधिकांशत: सज्जन व्यक्ति है।)

334. Come across —Meet by chance (अचानक मुलाकात होना) Please give him my message if you come across him. (यदि उससे मुलाकात हो जाय तो उसे मेरा समाचार दे देना।)

335. To make up—To make up the loss (क्षतिपूर्ति करना) I shall make up your loss. (मैं तुम्हारी क्षतिपूर्ति कर दूँगा।)

336. Run down—Reduced in health (स्वास्थ्य में गिरावट) He is very much run down these days. (आजकल उसके स्वास्थ्य में गिरावट आ गई है।

337. A tower of strength Chief support (शक्ति का स्तम्भ) Pt. Nehru was the tower of strength of the Congress Party. (जवाहरलाल नेहरू कांग्रेस के शक्ति स्तम्भ थे।)

338. Hold the fort—To stand firm on one's position (अपने स्थान पर डटे रहना) He held the fort against all odds. (वह सब विषम परिस्थितियों में अपने स्थान पर डटा रहा।)

339. To go back on—To withdraw (वायदा तोड़ देना) You should not go back on your word. (तुम्हें अपना वायदा नहीं तोड़ना चाहिये।)

340. Behind the scene—Secretly (छिपे रूप में) He is the governing power behind the scene. (वह पर्दे के पीछे से शक्ति प्रदान करता है।)

341. Once for all—Finally (अन्तिम रूप से) My reply is final once for all. (मेरा यह उत्तर अन्तिम है।)

342. On and on—To continue (जारी रखना) He went on and on with his scheme. (वह अपनी योजना को आगे बढ़ाता ही गया।)

343. Come true To prove true (सही सिद्ध होना) His warning has come true. (उसकी चेतावनी सही सिद्ध हुई।)

344. Put an end to To finish (समाप्त कर देना) He has put an end to his foolish schemes. (उसने अपनी बेवकूफी की योजनाओं को समाप्त कर दिया है।)

24. 2 Idiomatic Phrase (मुहावरेदार वाक्यांश)

(i) Noun Phrases

1. Cold war (पारस्परिक खराब सम्बन्ध) There should be no cold war between neighbouring countries. पड़ौसी देशों के पारस्परिक सम्बन्ध खराब नहीं होने चाहिये।

2. Dutch courage (शराब के नशे में पैदा हुआ साहस) His dutch courage will soon pass off. उसका नशे में पैदा हुआ जोश जल्दी उड़ जायेगा।

3. Fair play—(ईमानदारी के संबंध या कार्य) There is no fraud; it is a fair play. इसमें कोई धोखा नहीं है; यह ईमानदारी का कार्य है।

4. A fancy price—(ऊँची कीमत) His painting will fetch a fancy price. उसके चित्र की ऊँची कीमत मिलेगी।

5. Gala day—(खुशी का दिन) His birthday is a gala day for him. उसका जन्मदिन उसकी खुशी का दिन है।

6. The ins and outs—(पूर्ण जानकारी) Nobody can know the ins and outs of their secret service. उनकी गुप्त सेवा की पूर्ण जानकारी किसी को नहीं मिल सकती।

7. Red tapism—(अत्यधिक सरकारी औपचारिकतायें) Many projects are long held up on account of red tapism. सरकारी औपचारिकताओं के कारण बहुत सी योजनायें अधार में लटकी रहती हैं।

8. Sharp practice— (विधि कार्य में चालाकी) No lawyer can get success by resorting to sharp practice. चालाकी से कोई भी वकील सफल नहीं हो सकता।

9. A wet blanket—(हतोत्साहित करने वाली वस्तु या व्यक्ति) Too much seriousness acts as a wet blanket to cheerfulness. अत्यधिक गंभीरता खुशी को ठंडा कर देती है।

10. Hand and glove— (बहुत घनिष्ट) I am hand and glove with my friend. मैं अपने मित्र का बहुत घनिष्ट हूँ.

11. Forty winks— (दिन में थोड़ा सोना) I have forty winks every day after lunch. मैं दोपहर को खाने के बाद थोड़ा सोता हूँ।

12. A free lance—(स्वतन्त्र लेखक/राजनीतिज्ञ) He writes articles for the newspapers as a free lance. वह समाचार पत्रों में स्वतन्त्र लेखक की हैसियत से लेख लिखता है।

13. Iron will—(दृढ़ निश्चय वाला)। good statesman should be a man of iron will एक अच्छे राजनीतिज्ञ को दृढ़ निश्चयी होना चाहिये।

14. Fair sex—(नारी) This is the privilege of the fair sex. यह नारी जाति का विशेषाधिकार है।

15. A big gun— (महत्वपूर्ण व्यक्ति) He is a big gun. वह एक महत्वपूर्ण व्यक्ति है।

(ii) Adjective Phrases

16. With open arms —(उत्साहपूर्ण स्वागत) My friend received me with open arms. मेरे मित्र ने उत्साह से मेरा स्वागत किया।

17. Without reserve—(पूर्ण रूप से) We accept your terms without reserve. हम पूर्ण रूप से तुम्हारी शर्तों को स्वीकार करते हैं।

18. Beside himself—(परेशान) His heavy loss in business has thrown him beside himself. व्यापार में भारी नुकसान से वह होश हवाश खो बैठा है।

19. On the alert —(सावधान) The border areas should always be kept on the alert. सीमा क्षेत्रें में हमेशा सावधानी रखनी चाहिये।

20. Out of date—(पुरानी परिचलन के बाहर) Tight trousers have now become out of date. तंग पजामों का अब रिवाज नहीं रहा है।

21. Up-to- date—(आज की तारीख तक पूर्ण) He is up-to-date in his knowledge of political developments. राजनीतिक परिवर्तनों का उसे पूर्ण ज्ञान है।

22. In high spirits— (बहुत उत्साह व खुशी में) He is in high spirits today because of his grand success. वह अपनी महान सफलता के कारण आज बहुत उत्साहित है।

23. Out of spirits—(दु:खी एवं निराश) He is out of spirits today because of his failure in the examination. वह परीक्षा में फेल होने के कारण आज बड़ा निराश है।

24. Like wild fire—(तेजी से) The news of his murder spread like wild fire. उसके कत्ल का समाचार जंगल में आग की तरह फैल गया।

25. Out of gear — (बिगड़ी हुई हालत में) His business has gone out of gear these days. उसका व्यापार आज-कल बिगड़ी दशा में है।

26. At sea — (परेशान) I am at sea these days on account of all these problems coming together. इन सारी समस्याओं के एक साथ आने से मैं बहुत परेशान हूँ।

27. To the letter—(ठीक प्रकार से अक्षरश:) I have carried out his orders to the letter. मैंने उसके आदेश का अक्षरश: पालन किया है।

28. In the dark—(अंधकार में) don't keep your father in the dark अपने पिता को अंधकार में मत रखो।

29. At the first flush—(पहली ही बार देखने पर) You cannot appreciate this painting at the first flush. तुम पहली बार में इस चित्र को समझ नहीं सकते।

30. In the ascendant — (ऊँचे उठते हुए) His stars are in the ascendant these days. उसके सितारे आजकल बुलंदी पर है।

31. In hand — (नियन्त्रण में) Now the law and order situation is in hand. अब शान्ति व कानूनी स्थिति नियन्त्रण में है।

32. In the air—(चारों ओर फैला हुआ) The fear of an attack is in the air. आक्रमण का डर चारों ओर फैला हुआ है।

33. Out of the question—(असम्भव) His success in business is out of the question. व्यापार में उसका सफल होना असंभव है।

34. At a pinch—(कठिन परिस्थिति में) No friend of yours will come to your help at a pinch कठिन परिस्थिति में तुम्हारा कोई मित्र तुम्हारी मदद को नहीं आयेगा।

35. Ill at ease—(चिन्तित) He is ill at ease on account of his father's illness—वह अपने पिता की बीमारी के कारण चिन्तित है।

36. On his last legs—(अन्तिम स्थिति में) His grand father is on his last legs. उसके दादाजी जीवन की अन्तिम स्थिति मे हैं।

37. Head or tail—(कुछ भी अर्थ नहीं) We could make no head or tail of his long speech. हम उसके लम्बे भाषण का कोई अंश नहीं समझ सके।

38. With one voice—(सर्वसम्मति से) His proposal was accepted with one voice. उसका प्रस्ताव सर्वसम्मति से स्वीकार किया गया।

39. For good — (हमेशा के लिये) He has left Delhi for good. उसने दिल्ली हमेशा के लिये छोड़ दी है।

40. On the cards (शीघ्र होने वाली कोई बात) Now the elections are on the cards. अब चुनाव शीघ्र होने वाले हैं।

41. All the rage—(बहुत प्रचलित) Pop music is all the rage these days. इन दिनों पॉप म्यूजिक का बहुत प्रचलन है।

42. Under the wing—(सुरक्षा में) This port is under the wing of America. यह हवाई अड्डा अमेरिका की सुरक्षा में है।

43. In hot water—(परेशानी में) The journalist is in hot water due to his wrong reporting of Parlia mentary proceedings. यह पत्रकार संसद की गलत रिपोर्टिंग के कारण परेशानी में पड़ गया है।

(iii) Adverb Phrases

44. By degrees—(धीरे-धीरे) He is recovering from his heavy debts by degrees. वह धीरे-धीरे अपने कर्जे से उबर रहा है.

45. At times — (कभी-कभी) At times he behaves like a fool. कभी-कभी वह बेवकूफों सा व्यवहार करता है।

46. Once for all —(अन्तिम रूप से) You must take a decision once for all. तुम्हें अन्तिम निर्णय ले लेना चाहिये।

47. At random —(बिना किसी क्रम के) He gave me some suggestions at random which I could not accept—उसने मुझे बिना सोचे समझे कुछ परामर्श दिये जिन्हें मैं स्वीकार नहीं कर सका।

48. Of late—(अभी हाल में) Of late he has not seen me. हाल में वह मुझसे मिला नहीं है।

49. At best—(अधिक-से-अधिक) At best I can introduce you to him. अधिक-से-अधिक मैं उनसे तुम्हारा परिचय करा सकता हूँ.

50. Out and out — (पूरी तरह से) He is out and out a gentleman. वह पूरी तरह सज्जन व्यक्ति है।

51. Off and on—(कभी-कभी) Off and on he comes and stays with me. वह कभी-कभी मेरे पास आता है और ठहरता है।

52. Now and then—(कभी-कभी) Now and then he comes here. कभी-कभी वह यहाँ आता है।

53. Far and wide—(दूर-दूर तक) His fame has spread far and wide. उसका यश दूर-दूर तक फैल गया है।

54. Before long—(बहुत जल्दी) We are shifting to our new house before long- हम जल्दी ही अपने नये मकान में पहुँच रहे हैं।

55. At a stretch — (लगातार) I can drive my car for sixhours at a stretch. मैं अपनी कार को लगातार छ: घंटे तक चला सकता हूँ।

56. At the outset (प्रारम्भ मे) You must work very hard at the outset of your career. तुम्हें अपने व्यावसायिक जीवन के आरम्भ में कड़ी मेहनत करनी चाहिये।

57. At large— (भागा हुआ) The convict is still at large. अपराधी अभी भागा हुआ है।

58. At length — (पूर्ण विवरण के साथ) You should discuss your plan with me at length. तुम्हें अपनी योजना पूर्णरूप से मुझे बतानी चाहिये।

59. Of course—(नि:सन्देह) Of course he will never betray you. नि:सन्देह वह तुम्हें कभी धोखा नहीं देगा।

60. Time and again—(बार-बार) Please don't come to me for help time and again. कृपा करके बार-बार मेरे पास मदद के लिये मत आया करो।

61. By and by—(धीरे-धीरे) By and by he will adjust himself to the climatic conditions of this country. धीरे-धीरे वह इस देश की जलवायु का अभ्यस्त हो जायेगा।

62. Few and far between —(थोड़े से और एक-दूसरे से दूरी पर) In the desert the villages are few and far between. रेगिस्तान में गाँव थोड़े से और दूर-दूर होते हैं।

63. First and foremost (प्रथम और सबसे महत्वपूर्ण) Our first and foremost duty is to serve our country. हमारा प्रथम और सबसे महत्वपूर्ण कर्ततव्य है देश की सेवा करना।

64. For long — (बहुत समय तक) War cannot go for long. युद्ध बहुत दिनों तक नहीं चल सकता।

65. Over and above — (इस सबके अतिरिक्त) Over and above he is very hard working. इस सबके अतितिक्त वह बड़ा मेहनती व्यक्ति है।

66. To and fro — (आगे पीछे) He was pacing in the room to and fro वह अपने कमरे में इधर से उधर घूम रहा था।

67. Through and through — (पूरी तरह से) He is through and through a rogue. वह पूरी तरह से धूर्त है।

68. By all means—(हर प्रकार से) I will certainly help you by all means. मैं निश्चय ही हर तरह से तुम्हारी मदद करूँगा.

(iv) Prepositional Phrases

69. For the sake of—(की खातिर) A patriot would die for the sake of his country. एक देशभक्त अपने देश की खातिर अपने प्राण न्योछावर कर देता है।

70. In response to—(के उत्तर में) The public contributed liberally in response to an appeal by the Prime Minister. प्रधानमन्त्री की अपील के उत्तर में जनता ने दिल खोलकर सहायता की।

71. In regard to— (के सम्बन्ध में) The students met the Principal in regard to many of their problems. विद्यार्थी अपनी बहुत सी समस्याओं के सम्बन्ध में प्राचार्य से मिले।

72. In addition to—(के अतिरिक्त) We get gratuity in addition to our pension. हमें पेन्शन के अतिरिक्त ग्रेजुइटी भी मिलती है।

73. In accordance with—(के अनुसार) I have enclosed all the documents in accordance with the advertisement. मैंने विज्ञापन के अनुसार सभी सर्टीफिकेट लगा दिये हैं।

74. In proportion to—(के अनुपात मे) The workers are not paid in proportion to their work. कर्मचारियों को उनके परिश्रम के अनुसार पैसा नहीं मिलता है।

75. For want of (के अभाव में) I could not start my business for want of money. मैं धन की कमी के कारण अपना व्यवसाय शुरू नहीं कर सका।

76. In lieu of— (के बदले में) You can write an essay in lieu of translation. तुम अनुवाद के स्थान पर निबन्ध लिख सकते हो।

77. At the instance of (के सुझाव पर) I applied for this post at the instance of my father. मैंने पिताजी के कहने पर इस पद के लिये आवेदन किया।

78. In spite of— (के बावजूद भी) He failed in spite of hard labour. वह कड़ी मेहनत करते हुए भी फेल हो गया।

79. On account of— (के कारण) I could not go to office on account of heavy rains. मैं भारी वर्षा के कारण दफ्तर ना जा सका।

80. In view of—(के विचार से) In view of some disturbances in the city, the market was kept closed शहर में कुछ उपद्रवों के कारण बाजार बन्द रहे।

81. With a view to— (के उद्देश्य से) He has moved to Bombay with a view to setting up a factory the वह एक फैक्टरी डालने के उद्देश्य से बंबई चला गया है।

82. In the wake of— (किसी काम के एकदम बाद) The market has been closed in the wake of some disturbances. कुछ उपद्रव होने के कारण बाजार बन्द कर दिया गया है।

83. In a state of (की दशा में) He is lying in a state of coma. वह बेहोशी की दशा में पड़ा हुआ है।

84. By virtue of (के कारण) He secured first position by virtue of hard labour. उसने कड़ी मेहनत करने के कारण प्रथम स्थान पाया है।

85. In search of— (की तलाश में) He has come here in search of some job. वह यहाँ किसी धंधे की तलाश में आया है।

86. On the point of—(के बिन्दु पर) His factory is on the point of closure. उसकी फैक्टरी बन्द होने के बिन्दु पर है।

87. In order to—(के उद्देश्य से) He has appealed to the court in order to get some relief.उसने कुछ राहत पाने के लिये न्यायालय में अपील कर दी है.

88. In the act of (के मध्य में) He was caught in the act of cutting the road. वह सडक काटते हुए पकडा गया।

89. In the midst of—(के बीच में) He works in the midst of great difficulties. वह बड़ी कठिनाइयों के बीच काम करता है।

90. At the top of —(सबसे ऊपर) He shouted at the top of his voice. वह अपनी पूरी ताकत से चिल्लाया।

91. In consideration of (के विचार के कारण) I pardon you in consideration of your long service. मैं तुम्हारी लम्बी सेवा के कारण क्षमा करता हूँ।

92. By the way —(अचानक कोई बात कहना) By the way, are you Ram Mohan Roy ? क्षमा करें, क्या आप राम मोहन राय हैं?

(v) Verbal Phrases

93. Account for—(का कारण बनना) His cunningness accounts for his fall. उसके पतन का कारण उसकी चालाकी है।

94. Bear out — (गवाही देना) You will bear me out that I wanted to help her. तुम गवाह हो कि मैं उसकी मदद करना चाहता था।

95. Bear with —(बर्दाश्त करना) Please bear with me for some time more. कृपया थोड़े दिन और मुझे बर्दाश्त कर लो।

96. Break off — (अचानक रुक जाना) He suddenly broke off in the middle of his speech.वह अपने भाषण के बीच में अचानक रुक गया।

97. Break into — (जबरदस्ती घुसना, सेंध लगाना) The thieves broke into my shop last night. चोरों ने पिछली रात मेरी दुकान में सेंध लगा ली।

98. Bring about —(उत्पन्न करना) These measures will bring about prosperity in the country. इन उपायों से देश में समृद्धि आयेगी।

99. Bring in — (कमाना) He brings in five thousand rupees a month. वह पाँच हजार रुपये महीने कमाता है।

100. Bring out — (प्रकाश में लाना) The enquiry will bring out many startling facts. (जाँच समिति द्वारा बहुत से आश्चर्यजनक तथ्य प्रकाश में लाये जायेंगे।

101. Bring up — (लालन-पालन करना) He has a large family to bring up. उसे एक बड़े परिवार का पालन-पोषण करना है।

102. Back out—(वायदे से पीछे हटना) You can fully depend on him- He will never back out of his word. तुम उस पर विश्वास कर सकते हो। वह कभी अपने वायदे से पीछे नहीं हटेगा।

103. Bear up — (हिम्मत बनाए रखना) A strong man would bear up against all odds. एक दृढ़ संकल्प वाला व्यक्ति मुसीबतों में हिम्मत बनाये रखता है।

104. Blow out—(बुझा देना) Please blow out the lamp when you go out जब तुम बाहर जाओ, बत्ती बुझा देना।

105. Break with—(झगड़ा कर बैठना) Don't break with your old friends on such petty matters. ऐसी छोटी-छोटी बातों पर अपने मित्रों से झगड़ा मत करो।

106. Break out — (फैल जाना, आरंभ हो जाना) Cholera has broken out. War has broken out. हैजा फैल गया है। युद्ध शुरू हो गया है।

107. Break down — (बीच में ही रुक जाना, टूट जाना) He broke down in the middle of his speech. वह अपने भाषण के बीच में रुक गया।

108. Break up — (स्थगित हो जाना) The meeting has been broken up. मीटिंग स्थगित हो गई है।

109. Bring forth — (पैदा करना) They have brought forth a new variety of wheat. उन्होंने गेहूँ की एक नई किस्म पैदा की है।

110. Bring forward—(कोई नया तर्क देना) He has no new argument to bring forward. उनके पास कोई नया तर्क देने को नहीं है।

111. Bring out —(पुस्तक प्रकाशित करना) I have brought out a new book on Grammar. मैंने ग्रामर की एक नई किताब प्रकाशित की है।

112. Bring under — (दबा देना) It is your responsibility to bring under the rebellion उपद्रव को दवा देने की जिम्मेदारी तुम्हारी है।

113. To beggar description—(जिसका वर्णन न हो सके) Cleopatra's beauty beggard description— क्लियोपैट्रा की सुदंरता का वर्णन करना संभव नहीं था।

114. To bring home — (समझाना) The central idea of the poem was brought home to the students by the teacher. अध्यापक ने विद्यार्थियों को कविता का मुख्य भाव समझाया।

115. Call on —(किसी व्यक्ति से मिलने जाना) I shall call on you tomorrow morning. मैं कल सुबह तुमसे मिलने आऊँगा।

116. Call in — (बुलाना) Please call in my Secretary. कृपया मेरे सैक्रेटरी को अन्दर बुलाओ.

117. Carry out — (पालन करना) I cannot carry out your orders. मैं तुम्हारे आदेशों का पालन नहीं कर सकता।

118. Cast down (निराश)He feels much cast down owing to his failure. वह असफल होने के कारण कफी उदास है।

119. Cast away—(फेंक देना) He has cast away his old shoes. उसने अपने पुराने जूते फेंक दिये हैं।

120. Come across (किसी से अचानक मिलना) I came across my former boss yesterday. मैं कल अचानक अपने पुराने अधिकारी से मिल गया।

121. Come about — (होना) The change came about suddenly परिवर्तन अचानक हुआ।

122. Cry down — (आलोचना करना) Many people are in the habit of crying down their friends बहुत से लोगों में अपने मित्रें की आलोचना करने की आदत होती है।

123. Call names (गाली देना) He is in the habit of calling names. उसे गालियाँ देने की आदत है.

124. Call over — (नाम पुकारना) Please call over the names of the winners once again. कृपया विजेताओं के नाम दोबारा से पुकारिये।

125. Call off (समाप्त कर देना) The strike has been called off हड़ताल समाप्त कर दी गई है।

126. Call up — (पुरानी बात को याद करना) Please call up the promise you made to me. कृपया मुझसे किये अपने वायदे को याद करिये।

127. Call for—(स्पष्टीकरण माँगना) You must call for an explanation from him. तुम्हें उससे स्पष्टीकरण माँगना चाहिये।

128. Carry on— (सफलतापूर्वक चलाते रहना) He is carrying on his business successfully. वह सफलतापूर्वक अपना व्यापार कर रहा है।

129. Carry on with — (जारी रखना) You may carry on with your arguments. अपनी जिरह जारी रखो।

130. Come off — (होना, सम्पन्न होना) The function comes off next Sunday—समारोह अगले इतवार को होगा।

131. Come round — (बीमारी से मुक्त होना) He has come round his heart problem after a long treatment. उसे लम्बे इलाज के बाद अपने हृदय रोग से मुक्ति मिली है।

132. Come down upon (प्रताड़ना, सजा देना) Your boss will come down upon you for this negligence. तुम्हारा अधिकारी इस लापरवाही के लिये तुम्हें प्रताड़ित करेगा।

133. Cry up — (उत्साह बढ़ाना) Let us cry him up for this trial. हमें उसका इस संघर्ष में उत्साह वर्धन करना चाहिये।

134. Cut down— (खर्चा कम करना) You must cut down your expenditure on petrol. तुम्हें पैट्रोल पर अपना खर्चा कम करना चाहिये।

135. To come to grief — (दुःख की स्थिति में आना) If you don't mend yourself, you will come to grief. यदि तुम अपने को सुधारते नहीं हो, तो तुम्हें दुःख उठाना पड़ेगा।

136. Deal in—(व्यापार करना) He deals in silk. वह रेशम का व्यापार करता है।

137. Deal with—(निबटना) How will you deal with the rogues? तुम इन बदमाशों से कैसे निबटोगे?

138. Do away with (समाप्त करना, सम्बन्ध छोड़ देना) He has done away with all bad habits. उसने अपनी सारी बुरी आदतें छोड़ दी हैं।

139. Draw back — (वापस लौटना)The flood has drawn back. बाढ़ लौट गई है।

140. Fall out —(झगड़ा करना) These two brothers have fallen out. इन दोनों भाइयों में झगड़ा हो गया है।

141. Fall upon (आक्रमण करना) Our armies fell upon the enemy at midnight. हमारी सेना ने अर्द्ध रात्रि में दुश्मन पर हमला किया।

142. Fall through — (असफल होना) My scheme has fallen through for want of money. धन की कमी के कारण मेरी योजना असफल हो गई।

143. Get out of — (मुक्त होना) Try to get out of all your debts. अपने कर्जों से मुक्ति पाने की कोशिश करो।

144. Get through — (उत्तीर्ण होना) He will easily get through the examination. वह परीक्षा में आसानी से पास हो जायेगा।

145. Get up — (उठना) He gets up very early in the morning. वह सुबह जल्दी उठता है.

146. Give away —(पुरस्कार बाँटना) The Principal gave away the prizes. प्राचार्य ने पुरस्कार वितरित किये।

147. Give up — (छोड़ देना) I shall give up my claim. मैं अपना अधिकार छोड़ दूँगा।

148. Go through — (जाँच करना) Please go through my essay. कृपया मेरे निबंध को जाँच लें।

149. Go in for — (के पक्ष में) I shall go in for a new car. मैं एक नई कार लेने के पक्ष में हूँ।

150. Get on—(आगे बढ़ते रहना) You must get on with your scheme against all difficulties. तुम्हें सारी कठिनाइयों के होते हुए अपनी योजना में आगे बढ़ना चाहिये।

151. Get back — (वापस मिलना) It is not easy to get back your money from him. उससे रुपया वापस लेना आसान नहीं हैं।

152. Get off — (छूट कर निकल जाना) The convict got off from police custody. अपराधी पुलिस हिरासत से भाग गया।

153. Get over —(काबू में कर लेना) I have got over my greatest difficulty with his help. उसकी सहायता से मैंने अपनी सबसे बड़ी कठिनाई को पार कर लिया है।

154. Get on with— (सहमत होना, साथ-साथ रहना) I cannot get on with my treacherous friend any longer मैं अपने धोखेबाज मित्र के साथ अब और अधिक नहीं रह सकता।

155. Give over —(परिवर्तन, जिम्मेदारी सौंपना) He is giving over his charge on the last day of this month. वह इस महीने के अन्तिम दिन अपना कार्यभार छोड़ रहा है।

156. Give in—(झुक जाना, हथियार डाल देना) The militant gave in after a tough resistance. एक कड़े मुकाबिले के बाद आतंकी ने हथियार डाले।

157. Go off — (बारूद का फट जाना) The machine gun suddenly went off. मशीनगन अचानक चल गई।

158. Go out —(बुझ जाना) The candle has gone out. मोमबत्ती बुझ गई है।

159. Hold up—(रोक देना) The traffic has been held up by the agitators. आंदोलनकारियों ने रास्ता जाम कर दिया है।

160. Hold over —(स्थगित करना) Let us hold over this matter for the next meeting. हमें इस मामले को अगली मीटिंग के लिये स्थगित कर देना चाहिये।

161. Hold in—(काबू में रखना) He cannot hold in the untrained horse. वह अप्रशिक्षित घोड़े को काबू में नहीं रख सकता है।

162. Hold on—(जारी रखना, परिश्रम करते रहना) You must hold on with your efforts in all circumstances. तुम्हें हर परिस्थिति में अपने प्रयत्न जारी रखने चाहिये।

163 knock down—(गिरा देना) He was knocked down by a car. एक कार ने धक्का देकर उसे गिरा दिया।

164. Keep up — (बनाये रखना) He is creditably keeping up his reputation. वह प्रशंसनीय तरीके से अपनी इज्जत बनाये हुए है।

165. Lay down — (न्यौछावर करना) Many patriots would willingly lay down their life for their country. बहुत से देशभक्त देश के लिये खुशी से जान न्यौछावर कर देते हैं।

166. Lay by— (भविष्य के लिये बचाना) One should always lay by something for the rainy day. भविष्य की जरूरत के लिये कुछ बचत अवश्य करनी चाहिये।

167. Look after—(देखभाल करना) A mother looks after her children with selfless devotion. माँ अपने बच्चों की देखभाल निःस्वार्थ भाव से करती है।

168. Layout (जमा करना, व्यवसाय में रुपया लगाना) He is not in a position to lay out more than this amount वह ऐसी स्थिति में नहीं है कि अपने व्यवसाय में और रुपया लगा सके।

169. Leave out—(छूट जाना, छोड़ जाना) My name has been left out from the list. (मेरा नाम सूची में से छूट गया है।

170. Let off —(बिना सजा दिए हुए छोड़ देना) The police let the thief off पुलिस ने चोर को छोड़ दिया।

171. Look for—(तलाश करना) I am looking for a new house. मैं एक नये घर की तलाश में हूँ।

172. Look out for—(किसी की तलाश में लगे रहना) The police are looking out for unauthorized foreigners. पुलिस अनधिकृत विदेशियों को तलाश रही है।

173. Look through —(सरसरी निगाह से देख लेना) Please look through my essay. कृपया मेरे निबन्ध को सरसरी निगाह से देख लीजिये।

174. Look down upon —(घृणा की दृष्टि से देखना) It is bad to look down upon the poor. गरीबों को घृणा की दृष्टि से देखना बुरी बात है।

175. Look on—(किसी को किसी रूप में देखना) I look on him as a very respectable person.) मैं उसे बड़ा आदरणीय व्यक्ति समझता हूँ।

176. To lose ground — (आधार कमजोर पड़ना) Small political parties soon come to lose ground. छोटी-छोटी राजनीतिक पार्टियाँ जल्दी ही ताकत खो बैठती हैं।

177. Look forward to — (आशा करना) We look forward to meeting you very soon. हमें तुमसे जल्दी ही मिलने की आशा है।

178. Look into (जाँच करना) We shall look into your case very carefully. हम तुम्हारे मामले को बड़ी सावधानी से देखेंगे।

179. Make out (समझना) I could not make out anything from his letter. मैं उसके पत्र का कोई मतलब नहीं निकाल सका।

180. Make up —(क्षतिपूर्ति करना) You have to make up for the lost time. तुम्हें खोए हुए समय की क्षतिपूर्ति करनी होगी।

181. To make a mark (विशेषता प्राप्त करना) He has made a mark in the field of painting. उसने चित्रकला के क्षेत्र में विशेषता प्राप्त कर ली है।

182. Make good —(नुकसान की भरपाई करना) You have to make good my loss. तुम्हें मेरे नुकसान की पूर्ति करनी पड़ेगी।

183. Make up one's mind —(दृढ़ निश्चय कर लेना) I have made up my mind to resign from this post. मैंने इस पद से इस्तीफा देने का निश्चय कर लिया है।

184. Make away with —(छुटकारा पा लेना) I have made away with my treacherous friend. मैंने अपने धोखेबाज मित्र से पीछा छुड़ा लिया है।

185. Make off with — (लूट कर भाग जाना) The robbers made off with all our belongings. लुटेरे हमारा सारा सामान लूट कर भाग गये।

186. Put on— (घमंडी रूप या छद्म भेष धारण करना) He puts on much airs without any solid ground. वह बिना किसी आधार के ही बहुत दिखावा करता है।

187. Put down — (दबा देना, काबू में कर लेना) The rebellion has been put down with a strong hand. उपद्रव को कड़ी सख्ती से दबा दिया है।

188. Pass through — (गुजरना) India is passing through a difficult stage. भारत एक कठिन समय से गुजर रहा है।

189. Pull up —(डाँटना) The teacher pulled up the naughty boy. अध्यापक ने शरारती लड़के को डाँट लगाई।

190. Put out—(बुझाना) Don't put out the lamp, please. कृपया लैम्प को न बुझाइये।

191. Put off—(स्थगित करना) The meeting has been put off for tomorrow. मीटिंग कल के लिये स्थगित कर दी गई है।

192. Put up with — (सहना) It is very difficult to put up with a foolish friend. एक बेवकूफ मित्र को सहन करना बड़ा कठिन है।

193. To play false — (ठगना) One should not play false with friends. किसी को अपने मित्रों को दगा नहीं देना चाहिये।

194. Run after—(किसी वस्तु के पीछे भागते रहना) It is bad to run so much after money. रुपये के पीछे इस कदर भागना ठीक नहीं है।

195. Run into — (कर्जे में फँस जाना) He has run into heavy debts. वह बहुत कर्जे में फँस गया है।

196. Run out—(खत्म हो जाना) The stock of sugar has run out. चीनी का भंडार खत्म हो गया है।

197. Run down — (कमजोर पड़ जाना) He is very much run down owing to his long illness. वह लम्बी बीमारी के कारण बड़ा कमजोर हो गया है।

198. See through (गहराई से देख लेना) I can see through all his designs. मैं उसकी सारी चालाकियों को गहराई से देख सकता हूँ।

199. See off — (विदाई देना) We shall see him off at the airport. हम उसे हवाई अड्डे पर विदाई देंगे।

200. Set aside — (निरस्त कर देना) The court has set aside the orders of the Chairman. न्यायालय ने चेयरमैन के आदेश को निरस्त कर दिया है।

201. Set up— (स्थापित करना) He has set up a cement factory. उसने एक सीमेन्ट फैक्टरी स्थापित की है।

202. Set off (out) — (यात्रा पर जाना) He set off for America last night. वह कल अमेरिका के लिये रवाना हो गया।

203. Strike off — (काट देना, समाप्त कर देना) The teacher can strike off your name. अध्यापक तुम्हारा नाम काट सकते हैं।

204. Set forth — (यात्र पर जाना) He is setting forth to Delhi tomorrow morning. वह कल सुबह दिल्ली जा रहा है।

205. Set apart— (सुरक्षित बचाए रखना) You must set apart some money for paying the tax. तुम्हें कुछ रुपया टैक्स चुकाने के लिये सुरक्षित रखना चाहिये।

206. Set down—(लिखित रूप में रखना) Let us set down the terms of agreement. हमें राजीनामे की शर्तें लिख लेनी चाहिये।

207. Set in—(आरम्भ हो जाना) The rains have set in. वर्षा आरम्भ हो चुकी है।

208. Set off /out —(यात्रा पर चल पड़ना) He has set off out to Bombay just now. वह अभी बम्बई की यात्रा पर गया है।

209. Stand against— (विरोध में खड़े होना) He does not have the courage to stand against me. उसमें मेरे विरुद्ध खड़े होने की हिम्मत नहीं है।

210. Stand by—(सहायता करना) I shall always stand by you. मै हमेशा तुम्हारी सहायता करूंगा।

211. Taken in —(धोखा खा जाना) He was easily taken in by the cheat धोखेबाज ने उसे आसानी से धोखे में ले लिया।

212. Take off — (कपड़े उतार देना) It is very hot. Take off your coat. आज बहुत गर्मी है। अपना कोट उतार लो।

213. Take up —(किसी काम को हाथ में लेना) Now I will take up some new business. मैं अब कोई नया धंधा शुरू करूँगा।

214. Take over — (जिम्मेदारी का स्थान संभाल लेना) He has taken over as the Principal of the College. उसने कालेज के प्राचार्य का पद संभाल लिया है।

215. Take down—(लिख डालना) You must take down the important points. तुम्हें महत्वपूर्ण बिन्दुओं को लिख लेना चाहिये।

216. Turn out —(सिद्ध होना) He turned out to be a spy. वह एक जासूस निकला।

217. Turn out— (निकाल देना) He has been turned out of the university. उसे विश्वविद्यालय से निकाल दिया है।

218. Think over — (विचार करन) Please think over my proposal once again. कृपया मेरे प्रस्ताव पर पुनः विचार कर लीजिये।

219. Take after— (शक्ल मिलना) The girl strikingly takes after her mother. लड़की पूरे तौर पर अपनी माँ से मिलती है।

220. Tell upon (बुरा प्रभाव डालना) Smoking tells upon everyone's health. सिगरेट पीने से प्रत्येक के स्वास्थ्य पर बुरा असर पड़ता है।

221. Turn up — (आना, पर उपस्थित होना) He turned up at the last stroke of the bell वह घंटे की आखिरी आवाज

222. To take to heart — (गहराई से महसूस करना) She has taken her insult to heart. उसने अपने अपमान को दिल से महसूस किया है।

223. Work out (गणना करना) We should first work out the total expenditure on this project. तुम्हें पहले इस योजना पर होने वाले कुल खर्चे की गणना करनी चाहिये।

224. Wear out — (थक जाना, घिस जाना) The shoes of my young son wear out very soon. मेरे छोटे बेटे के जूते बड़ी जल्दी घिस जाते हैं।

225. Wait on— (किसी से मिलने जाना) We shall wait on the Chief Minister in this connection. हम इस सम्बन्ध में मुख्य मन्त्री से मिलेंगे।

226. Work up — (उत्तेजित कर देना) He worked up the mob against me. उसने भीड़ को मेरे विरुद्ध भड़काया।

(vi) Idiomatic Phrases in Pairs

227. Fits and starts—(अनियमित रूप से) He does his work by fits and starts. वह अपना काम अनियमित रूप से करता है।

228. Heart and soul —(पूरे मन से) I am devoted to my work heart and soul. मैं अपने काम में पूरी तरह से संलग्न हूँ।

229. Intents and purposes—(सभी अर्थों में) He is to all intents and purposes my real boss. वह सभी अर्थों में मेरा अधिकारी है।

230. Kith and kin —(सग-सम्बन्धी) I am really grateful to my kith and kin. मैं अपने सगे सम्बन्धियों के प्रति आभारी हूँ।

231. Leaps and bounds —(तीव्र गति से) His business is developing by leaps and bounds. उसका व्यापार तीव्र गति से बढ़ रहा है।

232. Odds and ends (इधर-उधर की चीजें) He filled his bag with odds and ends and ran away. उसने अपने थैले

को इधर-उधर की चीजों से भर लिया और भाग गया।

233. Part and parcel—(अभिन्न अंग) Kashmir is part and parcel of India. कश्मीर भारत का अभिन्न अंग है।

234. Rack and ruin—(सर्वनाश) His family has gone to rack and ruin owing to his reckless habits. उसकी फिजूलखर्ची की आदत के कारण उसका परिवार बरबाद हो गया है।

235. Time and tide (समय और अवसर) Don't miss this chance for time and tide wait for nobody. इस मौके को मत चूको, क्योंकि समय और अवसर किसी का इन्तजार नहीं करते।

236. Tooth and nail (पूरी ताकत से लड़ना) Let us fight casteism tooth and nail. हमें जाति प्रथा का डटकर विरोध करना चाहिये।

237. Wear and tear —(क्षय) There should be a separate fund for the wear and tear of machinery. मशीनों की घिसावट के लिये एक पृथक् कोष होना चाहिये।

238. All in all (सर्वेसर्वा) My uncle is all in all in my family. मेरे चाचाजी परिवार के सर्वेसर्वा हैं।

239. Black and white—(लिखित में) Let us make an agreement in black and white. हमें राजीनामा लिखित में करना चाहिये।

240. Hard and fast—(निश्चित) There can be no hard and fast rule for good conduct.अच्छे व्यवहार के लिये कोई ठोस नियम नहीं बनाये जा सकते।

241. Slow and steady (धीमी, पर नियमित गति से) The slow and steady wins the race. धीमी पर नियमित गति से विजय मिलती है।

242. Null and void —(निष्प्रभावी) This provision has been declared null and void by the Court. न्यायालय ने यह धारा निष्प्रभावी घोषित कर दी है।

243. Head and shoulders—(बहुत अधिक) He is head and shoulders above his friends in intelligence. वह बुद्धि में अपने मित्रों से बहुत ऊपर है।

244. Bread and butter — (खाना-पीना) There is no provision even for bread and butter in his family. परिवार में खाने पीने का भी प्रबन्ध नहीं है।

245. Fair and square— (ईमानदार, निष्पक्ष) I believe in fair and square dealings. मैं ईमानदारी के व्यवहार में विश्वास करता हूँ।

246. Rhyme and reason —(कारण) He is hostile to me without any rhyme or reason. वह बिना किसी कारण हमसे शत्रुता मानता है।

247. Cats and dogs—(मूसलाधार वर्षा) It is raining cats and dogs. मूसलाधार बारिश हो रही है।

248. Rank and file —(सर्व साधारण) You can never win against the wishes of rank and file. तुम सर्वसाधारण की इच्छा के विरुद्ध नहीं जीत सकते हो।

249. Root and branch — (पूरी तरह से) Let us do away with this evil custom root and branch. हमें इस कुप्रथा को जड़ से उखाड़ फेंकना चाहिये।

250. Long and short— (संक्षिप्त सार) Let me know the long and short of the whole episode. पूरी घटना का संक्षिप्त सार मुझे बताओ।

UNIT 25

Proverbs with their Meanings

We give below a list of Popular Proverbs—

1. A bad man is better than a bad name (बद अच्छा, बदनाम बुरा)
2. A bird in the hand is worth two in the bush (नौ नगद, न तेरह उधार)
3. A burnt child dreads the fire (दूध का जला छाछ को फूँक-फूक कर पीता है।)
4. A bad workman quarrels with his tools (नाच न जाने आँगन टेढ़ा)
5. A drowning man will catch at a straw (डूबते को तिनके का सहारा)
6. A figure among cyphers (अंधों में काना सरदार)
7. A guilty conscience needs no accuser (चोर की दाढ़ी में तिनका)
8. A prophet is not honoured in his own country (घर का जोगी जोगना आन गाँव का सिद्ध)
9. A little knowledge is a dangerous thing (नीम हकीम खतरे जान)
10. Penny wise and pound foolish (मोहरों की लूट, कोयलों पर छाप)
11. Save life save all (जान बची और लाखों पाये)
12. Might is right (जिसकी लाठी उसकी भैंस)
13. Rome was not built in a day (हथेली पर सरसों नहीं जमती)
14. Distance lends enchantment to the view (दूर के ढोल सुहावने)
15. An old dog learns no new tricks (बूढ़े तोते कुरान नहीं पढ़ते)
16. Where there is a will there is a way (जहाँ चाह, वहाँ राह)
17. Strike while the iron is hot (मौका न चूकना चाहिये।)
18. If the sky falls we shall बंजबी संतो (न नौ मन तेल होगा न राधा नाचेगी)
19. As you sow, so shall you reap (जैसी करनी वैसी भरनी)
20. To kill two birds with one stone (एक पंथ दो काज)
21. Self—praise is no recommendation (अपने मुँह मियाँ मिट्ठू)

22 While in Rome do as the Romans do (जैसा देश वैसा भेष)

23. It is hard to live in Rome and fight with the Pope (दरिया में रहकर मगर से बैर)
24. He who digs a pit for others falls into it himself (जो तोकूँ काँटा बुबै ताहि बोइ तू फूल, तोकूँ फूल के फूल हैं, बाकूँ हैं तिरशूल)

25. It is no use crying over spilt milk (अब पछताये होत क्या जब चिड़ियाँ चुग गई खेत)
26. Many hands make the burden light (सात-पाँच की लाकड़ी एक जने का बोझ)
27. All that glitters is not gold (हाथी के दाँत खाने के और दिखाने के और)
28. Coming events cast their shadows before (पूत के पाँव पालने में)
29. A good face needs no paint (लाल गुदड़ियों में नहीं छिपते)
30. Care kills the cat (चिन्ता बुरी बला है।)
31. At length the fox turns monk (नौसै चूहे खाइ बिल्ली हज को चली)
32. Cut your coat according to your cloth (तेते पाँव पसारिये जेती लम्बी सौर)
33. Do good and forget (नेकी कर दरिया में डाल)
34. Everybody's business is nobody's business (साझे की हड़िया चौराहे पर फूटती है।)
35. An empty mind is a devil's workshop (खाली दिमाग शैतान का घर)
36. Everything looks pale to the jaundiced eye (सावन के अंधे को हरा ही हरा दीखता है।)
37. Barking dogs seldom bite (गरजते हैं सो बरसते नहीं)
38. A rolling stone gathers no moss (डाँवाडोल की मिट्टी खराब)
39. Errors like straws over the surface flow, one who is in search of truth must dive below. (जिन खोजा तिन पाइयाँ गहरे पानी पैठ मैं बौरी बूढ़न डरी रही किनारे बैठ)
40. An empty vessel makes much noise (थोथा चना बाजे घना)
41. Christmas comes once a year (हर रोज दिवाली नहीं होती)
42. Half a loaf is better than no bread (घी न खाया कुप्पा ही बजाया)
43. All covet, all lose (आधी छोड़ साझी को धावै, आधी रहे न साझी पाव)
44. All's well that ends well (अन्त भला तो सब भला)
45. God's mill grinds slow but sure (भगवान के घर देर है, अन्धेर नहीं)
46. From a bad paymaster get what you can (भागते भूत की लँगोटी मली)
47. Birds of the same feather flock together (चोर-चोर मौसेरे भाई)
48. Better a tooth out than always aching (भाड़ में जाइ नथ तासे नाक कटे)
49. Even walls have ears (दीवारों के भी कान होते हैं।)
50. Death's day is doom's day (आप मरे जग प्रलय)
51. Diamond cuts diamond (लोहे को लोहा काटता है।
52. Every sable cloud has a silver lining (अँधेरे में भी आशा की किरण होती है।)
53. Deep rivers move in silent majesty, shallow brooks are noisy (अधजल गगरी छलकत जाय, भरी गगरिया चुप्पे जाय)
54. Haste makes waste (जल्दी का काम शैतान का)

55. Act in haste, repent at leisure (जल्दी करो, जीवन भर रोओ)

56. Kindness is lost upon an ungrateful man (साँप को दूध पिलाना)

57. Pride goes before a fall (घमंडी का सिर नीचा)

58. Prevention is better than cure (चिकित्सा से पथ्य उत्तम)

59. Little grief is loud, great griefs are silent (बिच्छू का काटा रोवे, साँप का काटा सोवे)

60. To have an old head on young shoulders (पेट में दाढ़ी)

61. Those who live in glass houses should not throw stones (काँच के घर में रहने वालों को पत्थर नहीं फेंकने चाहिये)

62. To swallow the whole ox and be choked with the tail (गुड़ खाय, गुलगुलों से परहेज)

63. He gives thrice who gives in a trice (तुरंत दान महा कल्यान)

64. Money makes the mare go (दाम सब कराता है।)

65. Necessity knows no law (आपत्ति काले मर्यादा नास्ति)

66. The nearer the church the farther from God (दिये तले अँधेरा)

67. It takes two to make a quarrel (एक हाथ से ताली नहीं बजती)

68. There is no rose without a thorn (जहाँ फूल तँह काँटा)

69. Out of the frying pan into the fire (चूल्हे से निकले भाड़ में गिरे)

70. A lie has no legs (चोर के पैर कहाँ)

71. Hunger is the best sauce (भूख में किवाड़ पापड़)

72. All your geese are swans (अपना गधा भी घोड़ा मालूम होता है)

73. Charity begins at home (अंधा बाँटे रेवड़ी, फिर-फिर घर को देइ)

74. See which way the wind blows (ऊँट किस करवट बैठता है।)

75. A nod to the wise and a rod to the foolish (चतुर को इशारा, मूर्ख की पिटाई)

76. A low- born man feels proud of his honours (कुत्ते को घी नहीं पचता)

77. Prosperity finds friends; adversity tries them (समृद्धि में पाओ, विपत्ति में परखों)

78. An unhappy man's cart is sure to tumble (कंगाली में आटा गीला)

79. Adversity is the touchstone of friendship (विपत्ति मित्रता की कसौटी है।)

80. Fortune favours the brave (पुरुष सिंह जो उद्यमी लक्ष्मी ताकी चेरी)

81. The wearer knows where the shoe pinches (जिसका दु:ख वही जाने)

82. Give an inch and he will take an ell (उँगली पकड़ के पहुँचा पकड़ना)

83. A good name is better than riches (लाख जाय पर साख न जाय)

84. Too many cooks spoil the broth (अनेक हकीम रोगी की मौत)

85. Welcome or not, I am still your guest (मान न मान मैं तेरा मेहमान)
86. You cannot sell the cow and have the milk too (चुपड़ी और दो-दो)
87. Heads I win, tails you lose (चित्त भी मेरी पट भी मेरी)
88. Time is a great healer (समय सब दु:ख भुला देता है।)
89. It is no use casting pearls before swine (भैंस के आगे बीन बजाना)
90. A blind man is no judge of colours (बन्दर क्या जाने अदरक का स्वाद)
91. An open door will tempt a saint (मुक्त की मदिरा काजी को भी हलाल)
92. Hope lasts with life (जब तक साँस तब तक आस)
93. I talk of chaff; he hears of cheese (कहे खेत की, सुने खलिहान की)
94. Practice makes a man perfect (काम सब सिखा देता है)
95. First deserve, then desire (यह मुँह और मसूर की दाल)
96. There are men and men (पाँचों उँगली बराबर नहीं होतीं)
97. Handsome is that handsome does (काम प्यारा है, चाम नहीं)
98. Blood is thicker than water (खून को खून पहचानता है।)
99. Ill got ill spent (पाप का धन मिट्टी में मिलता है।)
69. Out of the frying pan into the fire (चूल्हे से निकले भाड़ में गिरे)
70. A lie has no legs (चोर के पैर कहाँ)
71. Hunger is the best sauce (भूख में किवाड़ पापड़)
72. All your geese are swans (अपना गधा भी घोड़ा मालूम होता है)
73. Charity begins at home (अंधा बाँटे रेवड़ी, फिर-फिर घर को देइ)
74. See which way the wind blows (ऊँट किस करवट बैठता है)
75. A nod to the wise and a rod to the foolish (चतुर को इशारा, मूर्ख की पिटाई)
76. A low. born man feels proud of his honours (कुत्ते को घी नहीं पचता)
77. Prosperity finds friends; adversity tries them (समृद्धि में पाओ, विपत्ति में परखो)
78. An unhappy man's cart is sure to tumble (कंगाली में आटा गीला)
79. Adversity is the touchstone of friendship (विपत्ति मित्रा की कसौटी है।)
80. Fortune favours the brave (पुरुष सिंह जो उद्यमी लक्ष्मी ताकी चेरी)
81. The wearer knows where the shoe pinches (जिसका दु:ख वही जाने)
82. Give an inch and he will take an ell (उँगली पकड़ के पहुँचा पकड़ना)
83. A good name is better than riches (लाख जाय पर साख न जाय।)
84. Too many cooks spoil the broth (अनेक हकीम रोगी की मौत)

85. Welcome or not, I am still your guest (मान न मान मैं तेरा मेहमान)
86. You cannot sell the cow and have the milk too (चुपड़ी और दो-दो)
87. Heads I win, tails you lose (चित्त भी मेरी पट्ट भी मेरी)
88. Time is a great healer (समय सब दुःख भुला देता है।)
89. It is no use casting pearls before swine (भैंस के आगे बीन बजाना)
90. A blind man is no judge of colours (बन्दर क्या जाने अदरक का स्वाद)
91. An open door will tempt a saint (मुक्त की मदिरा काजी को भी हलाल)
92. Hope lasts with life (जब तक साँस तब तक आस)
93. I talk of chaff; he hears of cheese (कहे खेत की, सुने खलिहान की)
94. Practice makes a man perfect (काम सब सिखा देता है)
95. First deserve, then desire (यह मुँह और मसूर की दाल)
96. There are men and men (पाँचों उँगली बराबर नहीं होतीं।)
97. Handsome is that handsome does (काम प्यारा है, चाम नहीं)
98. Blood is thicker than water (खून को खून पहचानता है।)
99. Ill got ill spent (पाप का धन मिटी में मिलता है।)
100. A wise foe is better than a foolish friend (मूर्ख मित्र से चतुर शत्रु अच्छा)
101. An ass is an ass though laiden with gold (खर को कहा अरगजा लेपन)
102. As the crow is, so the eggs shall be (चूहे के बच्चे बिल ही खोदते हैं)
103. Close sits my shirt, but closer my skin (अपना अपना ही है और पराया पराया ही)
104. The cowl does not make a monk (गेरुए कपड़ों से कोई साधू नहीं होता)
105. His bread is buttered on both sides (पाँचों उँगलियाँ घी में)
106. Necessity is the mother of invention (आवश्यकता आविष्कारों की जननी है।)
107. Friend in need is a friend indeed (समय पर काम आने वाला दोस्त ही सच्चा दोस्त है।)
108. Face is not the index of the heart (हृदय की जाँच चेहरे से नहीं हो सकती)
109. Excess of everything is bad (अति हमेशा बुरी होती है।)
110. Time and tide wait for nobody (अवसर और समय किसी का इन्तजार नहीं करते)

Distinction between Similar Expressions एक से कथनों में अन्तर

कुछ Idiomatic Expressions एक से दिखाई पड़ते हैं, किन्तु उनके अर्थों में अन्तर होता है. ऐसे expressions अन्तर समझाते हुए उनकी लिस्ट नीचे दी जा रही है–

1. At no time – कभी नहीं

   In no time – बहुत जल्दी

2. In an hour – एक घंटा समाप्त होने तक

   Within an hour – एक घंटा समाप्त होने से पहले

3. Work in hand – जो काम इस समय हाथ में है

   Work on hand – जो काम अभी पूरा करने को बाकी है।

4. Go to the sea – समुद्री नौकरी करने के लिये, नाविक बनने के लिये जाना

   Go to sea – समुद्री यात्रा करने या घूमने के इरादे से जाना

5. Go to school – पढ़ने के लिये स्कूल जाना

   Go to the school – किसी दूसरे काम से स्कूल जाना

6. Go to market – खरीददारी के लिये बाजार जाना

   Go to the market – घूमने या अन्य किसी काम से बाजार जाना

7. Go to office – दफ्तर में काम करने के लिये जाना

   Go,to the office – दफ्तर किसी और काम के लिये जाना

8. Work hard – परिश्रम से काम करना

   Work hardly – बहुत कम काम करना

9. Come late – देर से आना

   Come lately अभी हाल ही में आना

10. Go direct – किसी स्थान को सीधे जाना

    Go directly – किसी जगह अभी जाना

11. Shoot a man – किसी आदमी को गोली से मार देना

    Shoot at a man – किसी की ओर गोली मारना

12. To search somebody – किसी की तलाशी लेना

    To search for somebody – किसी की तलाश करना

13. Believe a man – किसी की बात में विश्वास करना

    Believe in a man – किसी व्यक्ति की ईमानदारी में विश्वास करना

14. Meeta man– किसी आदमी से मिलना

    Meet with a man – किसी से अचानक भेंट हो जाना

UNIT 26 Examwise Idioms and Phrases

Given below are a number of phrases and a single word substitute for each of them

SN	Idioms/Phrases	Meaning
	SSC CGL 2020 Tier-2 [IDIOMS/PHRASES}	
1	To read between the lines	To understand the implied meaning
2	Full of hot air	Talking nonsense
3	To meet one's Waterloo	To experience defeat
4	Not make head or tail	not able to understand anything
5	Not mince words	To speak in a direct way
6	To take stock of	To assess
7	Read between the lines	Discern the hidden meaning in the text
8	Wear your heart on your sleeve	To show your true emotions
9	On tenterhooks	Anxious and tense
10	On cloud nine	Extremely happy and excited
11	Miss the boat	To lose an opportunity
12	Don't put all your eggs in the same basket	Don't concentrate all your resources in one place
13	To have an axe to grind	To have a selfish motive in doing something
14	A square deal	A fair and honest deal
15	Against one's grain	Against one's nature
16	To rise like a phoenix	To emerge with a new life
17	To turn the corner	To pass the critical stage
18	To hit below the belt	To attack in an unfair manner
19	Keep your head	To stay calm
	SSC CPO 2020 Tier-2 [IDIOMS/PHRASES}	
1	Fair-weather friend	A person whose friendship cannot be relied on in difficult times
2	Full of beans	Happy and energetic

SN	Idioms/Phrases	Meaning
3	To take pains	To make efforts
4	Fifth wheel	An unneeded person
5	Make head or tail of something	To figure out something
6	Fight tooth and nail	Fight very fiercely
7	Hue and cry	A noisy expression of anger
8	A hard nut to crack	A difficult person
9	Hold your horses	Be patient
10	Give and take	Obliging each other mutually
	SSC CGL 2021 10th Level [IDIOMS /PHRASES}	
1	Pain in the neck	Someone or something that is very annoying
2	Make a bee line	go straight to
3	Follow suit	do the same as others
4	Swim with the tide	Agree with the popular opinion
5	Come to blows	Start fighting after a disagreement
6	Cost (someone) dearly	To bring one suffering
7	A house of cards	An insecure situation
8	Take pains	Try hard
9	Lose count of	forget the accurate total
10	See the light of day	become publicly known
11	Have cold feet	Lose confidence
12	To be in hot water	To be in a difficult situation in which you can be criticised
13	To be ill at ease	to feel uncomfortable or worried in a situation
14	Bottom line	The most important fact
15	Be in someone's shoes	face the same situation as another person
16	All ears	To wait eagerly for some news
17	Flex one's muscles	give or make a show of one's strength
18	Full of hot air	Self-important
19	A piece of cake	To be easy
20	To raise a few eyebrows	To cause surprise or shock
21	In line with	In agreement
22	A hot potato	a controversial issue
23	Once for all	conclusively

SN	Idioms/Phrases	Meaning
24	Full of beans	Lively
25	On purpose	deliberately
26	The lion's share	The largest portion
27	Take a toll	To harm or damage
28	Learn the ropes	To learn how to do a job or activity
29	More or less	approximately
30	On the back burner	To temporarily not deal with some matter because it is not urgent
31	Fall out with someone	Stop being friendly after an argument
32	Eye wash	A deception
33	By and large	On the whole
34	No love lost	Persons who do not like each other at all
35	Spill the beans	To give away a secret
36	Have your back against the wall	To be in a desperate situation with very few options
SSC Selection Post 2021-12th Level [IDIOMS / PHRASES]		
1	Go back to the drawing board	Start planning all over again
2	Give someone the cold shoulder	Ignore someone
3	Be the devil's advocate	Present counter arguments
4	A stitch in time saves nine.	It is better to solve a problem straight away and not let it become bigger.
5	Go to the dogs	Be ruined or destroyed
6	Shed light on	To explain a situation
7	Hit a brick wall	Encounter an obstacle
8	Hold your horses	Be patient
9	Lock horns	Fight with someone
10	Get out of hand	Become difficult to control
11	Be off more more than you can chew	Take on more work than you can handle
12	Let the cat out of the bag	Reveal a secret
13	A dime a doren	Common and easily available
14	Raiming cats and dogs	Raining heavily
SSC Selection Post 2021 - Grade Level [IDIOMS / PHRASES]		
1	A wet blanket	A person who spoils other people's fun

SN	Idioms/Phrases	Meaning
2	Losing ground	Becoming less acceptable
3	Out of the blue	Completely unexpected
4	Keep one's head	Remain calm
5	To draw a blank	To get no results

SSC CGL 2021 Tier-1 [IDIOMS /PHRASES}		
1	Cake walk	Something easy
2	Rank and file	Ordinary people
3	Have bitten off more than I can chew.	To take on more than one can handle
4	Take into account	consider
5	Be hard up	Have very little money
6	In the same breath	Say two contradictory things at the same time
7	On the wane	On the decline
8	A long shot	Little chance of success
9	Money does not grow on trees	Money is hard earned and limited
10	Lie low	Try not to be noticed
11	To take after	To be similar in appearance
12	Foul play	Unfair or dishonest behaviour
13	Hold the key	To have control of something
14	Left no stone unturned	made every possible effort
15	A tight corner	A difficult situation
16	Nip in the bud	To destroy early
17	Dark horse	An unexpected winner
18	Stone's throw	Short distance
19	Easy money	Make money without much effort, maybe illegally
20	To bury the hatchet	To end a quarrel
21	To fight shy of	To try to avoid something
22	Keep someone at arm's length	Avoid being friendly with someone
23	Cool as a cucumber	Calm and composed
24	A hair in the butter	A challenging situation
25	To hold water	To be valid and reasonable
26	Play with fire	To do something dangerous

SN	Idioms/Phrases	Meaning
27	Blow your own trumpet	Boast about one's own qualities
28	A snake in the grass	A hidden enemy
29	A green horn	Inexperienced
30	Sticky fingers	An inclination to steal
31	Eat like a horse	eating excessively
32	Pay heed to	Listen carefully with attention
33	Back out	To withdraw
34	Have a change of heart	Change one's opinion
35	Smooth sailing	Easy progress
36	On purpose	Intentionally
37	Feast one's eyes on	Gaze at something with pleasure
38	Cold comfort	Very little satisfaction
39	Cat's paw	A person used as a tool by another
40	In the limelight	The centre of attraction
41	Hit a brick wall	Not able to make any progress
42	To sit on the fence	Avoid taking sides

SSC CHSL 2021 Tier-1 [IDIOMS/ PRASE]		
1	Hit the books	To study very hard
2	A piece of cake	An easy task
3	Crocodile tears	Pretended show of sorrow
4	To hold good	To remain valid
5	It's all Greek to me	I cannot understand anything
6	Pull a long face	To look sad
7	Bed of roses	Pleasant condition of life
8	fish out of water	Being uncomfortable and restless
9	Hobson's choice	A choice forced upon someone
10	Face up to	To accept a difficult situation
11	Running around in circles	To be very active but with few results
12	Hale and hearty	Strong and healthy
13	Strain every nerve	To try extremely hard to do something
14	Jump the gun	To do something too soon

SN	Idioms/Phrases	Meaning
15	Dark horse	An unexpected winner
16	Be like chalk and cheese	Be absolutely different
17	Green-eyed	jealous
18	Charley horse	Cramp
19	Carry the day	winning
20	White elephant	Costly but useless possession
21	To put someone's back up	To irritate someone
22	chip off the old block	Similar to one's parents in behaviour
23	High spirits	cheerful
24	Gear up for	Get ready for
25	Call upon	To order
26	Lose your touch	Not being as successful as previously
27	At one's elbow	Next to someone
28	Blow up	To destroy by an explosion
29	A fly on the wall	An unperceived observer
30	In the same boat	To be in the same difficult situation as some-one else
31	Hair's breadth	narrow margin
32	Grease someone's palm	Bribe someone
33	A storm in a tea cup	A lot of anger and worry about trivial things
34	Tell upon	To affect adversely
35	A snake in the grass	A deceitful person
36	Tit for tat	Counter attack
37	Win laurels	To gain honour
38	By the skin of one's teeth	Barely managed to escape
39	Safe pair of hands	A person who can be trusted to do something efficiently
40	Let down	To fail
41	Hard and fast	Strict
42	Catch 22	A difficult situation in which the solution to a problem is impossible
43	Knock down	To demolish
44	Eat like a horse	Eat a lot of food

SN	Idioms/Phrases	Meaning
45	Beat around the bush	To avoid talking about what is important
46	Red letter day	Memorable day
47	Read between the lines	Understand something that is not said outright
48	A kick in the teeth	Great disappointment
49	Donkey's years	Long time
50	Go to the wall	To fail
51	Under the weather	Feeling ill
52	By leaps and bounds	Very quickly
53	Have a long face	Look unhappy or disappointed
54	The best of both worlds	An advantageous situation from two different things at a time
55	Get away	To leave
56	Between Scylla and Charybdis	Between two dangers
57	Be at a loose end	To have nothing to do
58	Have a soft spot for someone	To like someone a lot
59	Pull the plug	End something
60	At loggerheads	Disagreeing with
61	Playing devil's advocate	One who argues against something just for the sake of arguing
62	Back out	To withdraw from
63	Comparing apples with oranges	Unequal comparisons
64	Lion's share	Largest share
65	Get the axe	Lose the job
66	Wipe the floor with someone	To defeat someone
67	To pay lip service	To express loyalty, respect, or support for something insincerely
68	Every dog has his day	Everyone has good luck or success at a point of time
69	Come about	To happen
70	Break a leg	Wish someone good luck
71	Miss the boat	Miss an opportunity
72	On cloud nine	Extremely happy
73	Sum and substance	Essence

SN	Idioms/Phrases	Meaning
74	Under duress	Under pressure
75	Apple of one's eye	Very dear
76	Up in arms	In rebellion
77	Cut straight to the chase	Avoid unnecessary introduction and go to the more important part
78	Make one's blood boil	to make someone very angry
79	Hard of hearing	partially deaf
80	Elbow grease	Hard physical efforts
81	Donkey's years	A very long time
82	make someone's flesh crawl/creep	to make someone feel disgusted, afraid, frightened
83	Start from scratch	Start entirely from the beginning
84	Chip off the old block	Someone who resembles their parent
85	To bite the bullet	Force oneself to do something unpleasant
86	Costs an arm and a leg	too expensive for us to buy
87	To bite the bullet	To be brave in a difficult situation
88	Call a spade a spade	talking too frankly
89	To draw a blank	To be unsuccessful at eliciting a response
90	Man of letters	Scholar
91	Jump the gun	Start something too soon or act hastily
92	In your birthday suit	Not wearing any clothes
93	Twist someone's arm	To try to force someone to do something
94	Cast aside	To reject
95	Tick all the boxes	To fulfil the required norms
96	Once in a blue moon	Very rarely
97	Child's play	An easy task
98	Apple-cart	Spoil careful plans
99	Pocket an insult	Tolerate insult without protest
100	Be under a cloud	To be untrustworthy
101	Hit the sack	Go to sleep
102	In queer street	In debt
103	Snail's pace	Very slow

SN	Idioms/Phrases	Meaning
104	The movers and shakers	People who have a lot of power and influence
105	Snake in the grass	Treacherous person
106	Get one's dander up	Lose one's temper
	SSC MTS 2021 [IDIOMS/PRASE]	
1	Raining cats and dogs	To rain very heavily
2	Ignorance is bliss	To remain ignorant of things that may cause stress
3	Stealing the thunder	Get praise for doing something before some-one
4	To smell a rat	To suspect something
5	Spill the beans	Give away a secret
6	On thin ice	In a risky situation
7	An iron hand	strict and harsh control
8	Come rain or shine	Whatever happens
9	Chase rainbows	To pursue unrealistic goals
10	Hold someone or something at bay	Prevent someone or something from moving closer
11	Have a whale of a time	Have an exceptionally fun or exciting experi-ence
12	Crocodile tears	False tears
13	To take with a grain of salt	To believe with some scepticism
14	Make a living	To earn enough money for things you need
15	Ring a bell	To sound familiar
16	Kick someone when they are down	To cause further trouble to someone already in a difficult situation
17	foaming at the mouth	To be enraged and show it
18	Back on one's feet	Well or successful again
19	Out of the blue	Completely unexpectedly
20	An iron hand	Strict control
21	In the heat of the moment	Saying or doing something without thinking due to anger
22	Let the cat out of the bag	To reveal a secret
23	To raise a dust	To cause disruption or confusion

SN	Idioms/Phrases	Meaning
24	Have an axe to grind	To have an ulterior motive
25	Keep an eye on	To watch over attentively
26	No spring chicken	A person who is no longer young
27	Move the goalposts	Unfairly alter the conditions or rules of a procedure during its course
28	Crying for the moon	To make an impractical or unreasonable request
29	That ship has sailed	Too late to do something
30	My mother is in raptures over her new stove.	extremely delighted
31	Once in a blue moon	Very rarely
32	Hit the nail on the head	To be exactly right about something
33	Flogging a dead horse	To waste time on useless things
34	Drop in the bucket	A very small part of something big or whole
35	Below the belt	Cruel and unfair
36	Keep body and soul together	Stay alive during hard times
37	A piece of cake	A very easy task

Idiomatic Phrases and their Usages

27.1. Idioms and Phrases (meaning and usage)

A phrase is a group of words without a verb, especially one that forms part of a sentence. In short, it is a group of words forming a short expression. An idiom is a phrase or group of words, the meaning of which is not clear from tin meaning of its individual words and which must be learnt as a whole unit.

Idioms and phrases are relative terms and both terms imply almost the same meaning. Idioms and phrases beautify and adorn a sentence.

1.	To back up (to support)	He *backed up* the ruling party to gain their favour.
2.	Blow over (pass off)	The present unfavourable tide wili soon *blow over*.
3.	To bear out (substantiate)	The police produced evidence *to bear out* the charge of murder.
4.	To dispose of (sell)	I am going to *dispose of* my furniture as soon as possible.
5.	To close with (accept)	I readily *closed with* his offer.
6.	To eat away (corrode)	Too many chocolates have *eaten away* my teeth completely.
7.	To grow upon (have stronger and stronger hold over)	The habit of smoking is steadily *growing upon* him.
8.	Hear someone out (to hear upto the end)	The teacher pleaded with the students to *hear him out*.
9.	To hit upon (to find)	She *hit upon* the perfect title for her new novel.
10.	To keep hanging about (loitering about)	Most of the students in our college *keep hanging about* the campus even after the completion of classes.
11.	Led up to (culminated in)	The continuous tension between the two groups finally *led up* to a communal war.
12.	To shake off (get rid of)	She has been trying to *shake off* some of her weight.
13.	Long for (desire)	Throughout his life, he has *longed for* a good friend in whom he could confide.
14.	Stave off (prevent, avert)	He is the only person who can *stave off* violent encounter between the two brothers.
15.	Trump up (concocted, fabricated)	The details of his various escapades seem *trumped up*.
16.	To be well of (in comfortable circumstances)	Despite her *being so well off*, she thinks twice before spending even a penny.
17.	Bore away (won)	The soldier *bore away* many prizes for bravery.

18.	To break into (enter by force)	The students *broke into* the Vice Chancellor's office and smashed all the windows.
19.	Break with (quarrel with)	I gave him no cause to *break with* me.
20.	Brought about (caused)	The income tax he paid, *brought about* his ruin.
21.	Brings in (yield as rent)	His agricultural output *brings in* at least a thousand rupees a month.
22.	Call off (withdraw)	The strike was finally *called off* after a month with everyone feeling contented.
23.	Come by (get)	How did he *come* by this book?
24.	Come to grief (suffer)	He will certainly *come to grief* if he does not mend his ways now.
25.	Done to death (murdered)	He was *done to death* by the dacoits.
26.	Draw over (win over)	The politician was trying to draw over the votes of the poor people.
27.	Get the better of (advantage over)	He *got the better of* his partner in that business.
28.	Give out (proclaim)	It was *given out* that the fort had been captured.
29.	Given to (addicted)	My uncle is *given to* drinking.
30.	Go in for (compete for)	Are you *going in for* the M.A. degree?
31.	Hold to (adhere to)	She always *holds* to her principle.
32.	Intrude on or upon (encroach upon)	Hope I am not *intruding upon* your privacy.
33.	Keep back (conceal)	She *keeps back* nothing from me.
34.	Look upon (regard)	We *look upon* her as our mother.
35.	Make over (transfer)	I want to *make over* my house to my daughter.
36.	Pull through (recover from illness)	The psychology of the patient helps him a lot to *pull through* his illness.
37.	Put by (save)	My grandmother always urged my mother to *put by* something for old age.
38.	Put off (postponed)	The marriage was *put off* owing to the sudden demise of a close relative.
39.	Run through (waste)	Do not *run through* your savings.
40.	See through (discern)	He was too innocent to see through any of her tricks.
41.	Set about (begin)	He *set about* his job assiduously.
42.	Set in (start)	Winter has begun to *set in*.
43.	Take after (resemble)	The baby has *taken after* her grandmother.
44.	Take down (note)	Please *take down* these points.
45.	Turn down (reject)	The officer *turned down* my request.

46.	Work on (influence)	We tempted him with many promises, but nothing would *work on* him.
47.	Work up (excite, agitate)	He gets extremely *worked up* if his daughter gets back late from college.
48.	Throw over (abandon or desert)	When he became rich, he *threw over* all his old friends.
49.	Set apart (reserved)	These seats are *set apart* for ladics.
50.	Run up (increased)	Recently, my expenses have *run up* considerably.
51.	Done for (ruined)	If this business venture fails, then I'm *done for*.
52.	A wild goose chase (fruitless task/ endeavour)	His trying to go abroad for studies is a *wild goose chase*.
53.	A red letter day (an important day)	It was a red letter day in the history of the nation.
54.	Kith and kin (relatives and friends)	I should look after my *kith and kin* whatever be the circumstances.
55.	A hard nut to crack (difficult thing/person to deal with)	Our principal is a *hard nut to crack* in matters concerning discipline.
56.	A cold reception (a welcome, lacking affection or warmth)	He was given *a cold reception* at the party.
57.	Black sheep (bad person)	He is the *black sheep* of our family.
58.	A bird's eye view (a general view)	I had *a bird's eye view* of the Himalayas recently, while I was flying to Sri nagar.
59.	A burning question (issue keenly discussed)	The budget presented recently, is a *burning question* now-a-days.
60.	A bed of roses (easy and comfortable)	Do not consider life *to be a bed of roses*.
61.	Bad blood (a feeling of enmity)	The cricket match ended up creating *bad blood* between the two teams.
62.	A bookworm (one who is always busy with his studies)	In spite of being a *bookworm*, he barely manages to pass.
63.	A fair weather friend (a friend only during the times of prosperity)	That *fair weather friend* of mine was not to be seen during my days of adversity.
64.	To add fuel to the fire (to aggravate the matter)	His blatant lies after stealing the money only *added fuel to the fire*.
65.	To be born with a silver spoon in one's mouth (to be born in a rich family)	Not many are privileged *to* be born with a silver spoon in their mouths.
66.	To blow one's own trumpet (to boast)	He keeps on *blowing his own trumpet* and in the process, makes a fool of himself.
67.	A bolt from the blue (an unexpected disaster)	The news of his brother's death was *a bolt from the blue* for him.

68.	To beat black and blue (to beat mercilessly)	The pickpocket when caught red-handed, was *beaten black arid blue* by the co-passengers.
69.	To cast an aspersion (bring discredit to)	The official's involvement in the corruption case has *cast an aspersion* on the integrity of his character.
70.	To change hands (to pass to a different owner)	Soon after the millionaire's death, his bungalow *changed hands*.
71.	To cry over spilt milk (to feel sorry for what has already happened)	Brooding after failing in the examination is like *crying over spilt milk.*
72.	To die hard (to change or disappear very slowly)	Old habits *die hard.*
73.	To end in smoke (fail)	All his proposals *ended in smoke* for want of popular support.
74.	To cut a sorry figure (to make a poor impression)	She *cut a sorry figure* when she could not speak correct English in front of her teachers.
75.	To go to the dogs (to be ruined)	The institution will *go to the dogs* if someone does not stop this corruption.
76.	To hang in the balance (to be undecided)	The fate of the accused will *hang in balance* till the court resumes its proceedings.
77.	To hit the nail on the head (to do the right thing at the right time)	By accepting this job, you have *hit the nail on the head.*
78.	To have the upper hand (to have more say or influence)	The English *had the upper hand* in everything while they ruled over India.
79.	To hold water (sound logical)	His explanation does not *hold water* any more.
80.	To leave no stone unturned (to try one's level-best)	He *left no stone* unturned to secure a seat for his son in one of the prestigious colleges.
81.	To live from hand to mouth (to have a scarce living)	Many families in India have *to live from hand to mouth* on account of economic backwardness.
82.	To lose heart (to be disheartened)	Do not *lose heart* because you have lost your job, you can always get another.
83.	To make up one's mind (decide)	She has *to make up her mind* about whom she wants to marry.
84.	To make both ends meet (to live within one's means)	He can hardly *make both ends meet* with his present income.
85.	To move heaven and earth (to go up to the extreme)	He *moved heaven and earth* to see his son married to the industrialist's daughter.
86.	To see eye to eye with (agree)	The manager and the accountant do not *see eye to eye at* the time when accounts are prepared.

87.	To play ducks and drakes (waste)	The young man *played ducks and drakes* with his inherited money.
88.	To put the cart before the horse (to do a thing in a wrong way)	Having a baby first and getting married afterwards, is like *putting the cart before the horse.*
89.	To have too many irons in the fire (to have too many things in hand)	Studying, working and looking after the house at the same time means she has *too many irons in the fire.*
90.	To kill two birds with one stone (to accomplish two tasks in one attempt)	If you are a little more tactful, you will hear more and make a better image of yourself, thereby *killing two birds with one stone.*
91.	To read between the lines (to try to understand the hidden meaning)	The letter is to be *read between* the lines.
92.	To turn over a new leaf (to change for the better)	After his defeat in the match, he has *turned over a new leaf.*
93.	To take the bull by the horns (to face difficulty boldly)	He is a young man of great courage and will *take the bull by the horns.*
94.	To win laurels (distinguish oneself)	Sunil Gavaskar has *won many laurels* as one of the greatest cricketers.
95.	A storm in a tea cup (used derisively to indicate a great fuss about a trifle)	A fight in the bus for a window seat, is like raising a *storm in a tea cup.*
96.	Not worth his salt (a good-for-nothing fellow)	He is *not worth his salt* if he fails at this juncture.
97.	To play up (to try to make something appear more important than it is)	She *played up* her past achievements just to impress us.
98.	To put a spoke in one's wheel (to obstruct progress, to prove a serious barrier or hindrance)	Brown was getting on well in business till Robinson opened a rival establishment, and that *put a spoke in Brown's wheel.*
99.	To set Thames on fire (to do something extraordinary or brilliant)	He is a steady worker, but never likely to *set Thames on fire.*
100.	To take people by storm (to captivate)	His singing *took the audience by storm.*
101.	To fight shy of (trying or attempting to avoid a person)	He tried to draw me into partnership with him in business, but I *fought shy of* him.
102.	To gild the pill (cover a disagreeable thing with something pleasant)	They demanded a large war indemnity from us and *gilded the pill* by offering us two warships.
103.	To nip in the bud (to destroy in early stages of growth, to kill in infancy)	Diphtheria is a disease which *nips many a life in the bud.*
104.	Other fish to fry (more important work to attend to)	Please be as brief as you can, I have *other fish to fry.*
105.	Go to roost (retire for the night)	I am in the habit of *going to roost* early.

106.	Pen and ink (in writing)	Unless you issue orders in *pen and ink*, no one is likely to follow them.
107.	Without fear and favour (impartially)	At your position, it is expected that you act *without fear and favour*.
108.	Judas kiss (false love)	His wife's love was after all a *judas kiss*.
109.	Is on the knees of gods (yet uncertain)	Success in examination is still *on the knees of gods*.
110.	Neck and crop (completely)	The earthquake has devastated the town *neck and crop*.
111.	Black ox (misfortune)	His failure in life can be attributed only to the *black ox*.
112.	To be at the zenith of (to be at the highest point of fame, glory, etc.)	Sunil Gavaskar has *been at the zenith* of his career for the past couple of years.
113.	All and sundry (everyone without distinction)	She invited *all and sundry* to the birthday party.
114.	At death's door (about to die)	Her grandfather is *at death's door*, so we must go and see him.
115.	Donkey's years (after a long time)	I have struggled for *donkey's years* to come to this position.
116.	Eagle-eyed (keen sighted)	You indeed are *eagle-eyed* to be able to spot Ramesh amidst the crowd.
117.	An old flame (sweetheart)	She was *an old flame* of my brother.
118.	Gate crasher (uninvited intruder)	Sorry for *gate crashing* like this, but we could not help it.
119.	Gift of the gab (power of talking)	It was only through his *gift of the gab* that he managed to win the elections.
120.	Heart to heart (frank and free)	It was only after a *heart to heart* talk with Leela that we were able to sort out our differences.
121.	Not cricket (unfair)	It is definitely *not cricket* to cheat in exams.
122.	To pick a quarrel (to seek fight)	I would rather not tell him about Arun's behaviour for he is quick *to pick a quarrel* with anyone.
123.	Penny wise pound foolish (to bother about small coins and to throw bundles of rupees carelessly)	Strange it is but nevertheless true that there should be *penny wise pound foolish* people in the world.
124.	Once in a blue moon (rarely)	One comes across a real good Hindi movie only *once in a blue moon*.
125.	Maiden speech (first speech of an individual)	Most people cut a sorry figure in their *maiden speech*.
126.	To while away (to spend time uselessly)	Those who *while away* time at the sowing season cannot hope to reap the harvest.

127.	Yearn for (to crave for)	The modern youth badly *yearns for* recognition, which certainly is not easy to get.
128.	Yeoman's service (excellent work done)	Lincoln certainly rendered *yeoman's service* to humanity by eradicating slavery from his country.
129.	To tax one's patience (to test one's patience)	Dull and long speeches *tax the patience* of the audience.
130.	Ups and downs (bad and good days)	Almost everyone must have seen *ups and downs* in life.
131.	Utopian scheme (unpracticable, unattainable ideal)	The scheme of Family Planning Ministry to check the population explosion in a year's time, appears *utopian.*
132.	To throw mud at (to accuse wrongly)	Pakistan always keeps on *throwing mud at* our country.
133.	To take french leave (to take leave without permission or information)	Gone are the days when the government servants *took french leave* very often.
134.	Through thick and thin (under all circumstances)	If you develop friendship with an individual, you must stand by him *through thick and thin.*
135.	Spick and span (neat and clean)	Do you expect a bachelor's flat to be *spick and span* ?.
136.	A square deal (justice)	The youth of the country must be given a *square deal* by the government.
137.	To save one's skin (to protect oneself)	Most of the invigilators do not check the students from using unfair means as they are only concerned *about saving their skin.*
138.	Small fry (ordinary)	Nobody in life cares for *small fries.*
139.	Scapegoat (one who is made to bear the blame)	When something goes wrong, everybody wants to make someone else the *scapegoat.*
140.	A stepping stone (source of advancement)	Your success in this examination should only be a *stepping stone* for your future plans.
141.	A thankless task (a job with no satisfaction or reward)	Many lecturers consider teaching to be *a thankless task.*
142.	Snake in the grass (a hidden enemy)	One must be cautious in life, as there are many *snakes in the grass* in this world.
143.	Lion's share (major part)	The Punjab wants a *lion's share* in the Beas river water.
144.	Lame excuse (false excuse)	The teachers are used to hearing *lame excuses* of the students.
145.	To keep abreast of (to keep in touch)	One must *keep oneself abreast of* the latest developments in the world.
146.	Losing ground (becoming less powerful or acceptable)	All the superstitious beliefs are *losing ground* with technological advancements.
147.	Jack of all trades (one who knows a little about many things)	In our world of specialisation, a *jack of all trades* cannot be successful.

148.	An iron will (strong determination)	Our Prime Minister has shown that he has *an iron will.*
149.	A herculean task (a work which needs tremendous efforts)	Checking population growth is really a *herculean task.*
150.	To hold one's tongue (to be quiet)	Many critics of the Prime Minister are *holding their tongues* out of fear.

27.2 Idioms and Phrases (Objectives Multiple Choice Type)

Below are given idios followed by four alternative meanings, marked (a), (b), (c) and (d). Tick (✓) the one which you think is the most appropriate.

1. **Fling away**
   (a) to have an affair
   (b) to flase up
   (c) to throw aside violently
   (d) to swing

2. **To plongh the sands**
   (a) to be extremely accompanied
   (b) to be resourceful
   (c) to be dejected
   (d) to busy oneself in an unprofitable position.

3. **Long in the tooth**
   (a) distant journey (b) rather old
   (c) ailment (d) young

4. **Knit one's brows**
   (a) to disappoint somebody
   (b) to from
   (c) to have a headache
   (d) to extress discontentment

5. **Elbow room**
   (a) opportunity for freedom of action
   (b) special room for the guest
   (c) to give enough space to move or work in
   (d) to add a new room to the house French leave

6. **French leave**
   (a) a person who does not take leave
   (b) leave without permission
   (c) to take long leave
   (d) to take a day off and have fun

7. **To call a spade a spade**
   (a) to play cards
   (b) to be arrogant
   (c) to speak plainly without mincing matters
   (d) to be confident about everything one does

8. **To commit to memory**
   (a) to learn by heart
   (b) to tax one's memory
   (c) to be forgetful
   (d) to commit oneself totally to a task

9. **To burn a hole in the pocket**
   (a) to steal from someone's pocket
   (b) to destroy other's belongings
   (c) to be very miserly
   (d) money that is spent quickly

10. **To bury the hatchet**
   (a) to have found a treasure
   (b) to make peace
   (c) to purchase something without discretion
   (d) to act in a suspicious manner

11. **To beggar description**
   (a) something of least importance
   (b) something beyond description
   (c) to describe a beggar
   (d) an accurate description

12. **To beat the air**
   (a) efforts that are vain, useless
   (b) to be satisfied with one's performance

(c) to be extremely relieved
(d) to be very happy

13. To provide against a rainy day
(a) to provide plentiful
(b) to provide for the whole family
(c) to store in case of any difficulty
(d) to store for the rainy season

14. A bone of contention
(a) area of agreement
(b) act of submission
(c) act of gratitude
(d) subject of dispute

15. To be all eyes
(a) to be cautious
(b) watching closely and attentively
(c) to be amazed
(d) to be non-plussed

16. Swollen headed
(a) to be suffering from illness
(b) to be conceited
(c) to be narrow-minded
(d) to be dumb

17. To be like a fish out of water
(a) to be face to face with death
(b) to be in a strange situation
(c) to be in want of a house
(d) to be determined to live

18. To stir up a hornet's nest
(a) to excite the hostility of people
(b) to do some social service
(c) to be totally at a loss in a situation
(d) to be bankrupt

19. My hands are full
(a) I am having a lot of things to carry
(b) I am having lots of money
(c) I am very busy
(d) I am anxious

20. To be at sea
(a) to be a sailor (b) to be a steward
(c) to be occupied (d) to be perplexed

21. No love lost between them
(a) to have a fight
(b) to dislike each other
(c) to be as friendly as ever
(d) to be upset

22. To be hand and glove with someone
(a) to be social (b) to be playful
(c) to be annoyed (d) to be intimate

23. To play fast and loose
(a) to deceive someone
(b) to be agile
(c) say one thing and do another
(d) to be efficient

24. To take stock of
(a) to imagine (b) to supply
(c) to survey (d) to attract

25. A man of straw
(a) a man of no substance
(b) a man without means
(c) a man of character
(d) a generous man

26. Wolf in sheep's clothing
(a) to act on the sly
(b) to be a good actor
(c) to be a hypocrite
(d) to be money-minded or materialistic

27. To cut someone short
(a) to oblige someone
(b) to assist someone
(c) to interrupt someone
(d) to insult someone

28. To stick to one's colours
(a) to refuse to yield (b) to be patriotic
(c) to be notorious (d) to be straightforward

29. An old head on young shoulders
(a) to be old before one's age
(b) to be wise beyond one's age
(c) to be youthful in spile of one's old age
(d) to maintain good health

30. To snap one's fingers at
(a) to honour someone
(b) to greet someone
(c) to beckon someone
(d) to defy

31. By fits and starts
(a) irregularly (b) mostly
(c) after a short time (d) regularly

32. Falling foul of
(a) quarrelling with
(b) becoming friends with
(c) being dishonest with
(d) being scared of

33. To show a clean pair of heels
(a) to admonish (b) to reject
(c) to announce (d) to run away

34. Harp on the same string
(a) to play music
(b) to dwell tediously on the same subject
(c) to beat someone
(d) to acknowledge

35. Keep a good table
(a) to have artistic taste
(b) to throw a party
(c) to provide luxurious food
(d) to be extravagant

36. Take up the cudgels
(a) to take notice
(b) to accept a present
(c) to defend someone vigorously
(d) to accept a challenge

37. Splitting hairs
(a) to be worried
(b) to be venturesome
(c) to trouble someone
(d) to dispute over petty points

38. A great hand at
(a) to be a good artist
(b) to be an expert
(c) to be a good player
(d) to be generous

39. To make a pile
(a) to make a fortune
(b) to make a mess
(c) to be absent-minded
(d) to be corrupt

40. Under someone's wing
(a) to work under someone
(b) to be under someone's protection
(c) to be alert
(d) to be in the army

41. To sow one's wild oats
(a) to swear
(b) to be at ease
(c) to engage in youthful excesses
(d) to till the land

42. An olive branch
(a) an offer of peace (b) an idea
(c) a lady (d) a wicked person

43. Not worth a rap
(a) worth nothing (b) very expensive
(c) worth a lot (d) modestly priced

44. In merry pin
(a) perplexed (b) merry making
(c) embarrassed (d) in a merry humour

45. To leap the pale
(a) to throw a bucket
(b) to get into debt, to spend more than one's income
(c) to have much of fear
(d) to become pale

46. To cut the gordian knot.
(a) to perform the opening ceremony
(b) to be present at the opening ceremony
(c) to solve a difficult problem
(d) to get a sharp cut

47. To sow the wind and reap the whirlwind
(a) to enjoy the fruits of hard work

(b) to be deprived of one's reward
(c) to act wisely
(d) to suffer for one's foolish conduct

48. To play possum
(a) to play hide and seek
(b) to feign ignorance
(c) to cheat somebody
(d) to play seriously

49. A grass widow
(a) a young widow
(b) widow who has illicit relations with men
(c) a woman whose husband is temporarily away from her
(d) a working old woman

50. Mad as a March hare
(a) sane
(b) intoxicated
(c) as mad as a hare in spring
(d) slightly touched in the brain

51. Halcyon days
(a) long days
(b) short days
(c) happy and peaceful days
(d) disturbed days

52. Mother wit
(a) to have an intelligent mother
(b) university
(c) silly
(d) commonsense

53. A blind date
(a) a cloudy day
(b) unknown future
(c) meeting with someone you do not know
(d) death-day

54. Much ado about nothing
(a) to take something seriously
(b) to play false
(c) to make fuss
(d) to add

55. Judas' kiss
(a) wooing
(b) a narrow escape
(c) hypocritical affection
(d) a religious person

56. To have no truck with
(a) have no means of conveyance
(b) scientifically backward
(c) to have no trade with
(d) to have no dealings with

57. To clean the Augean stables
(a) to purge the administration of its abuses
(b) to buy horses
(c) to sell horses
(d) to improve working conditions

58. A fly in the ointment
(a) to clean a thing
(b) to sterilise
(c) a problem in a situation
(d) an unsuccessful attempt

59. Of the deepest dye
(a) of the worst type
(b) of the best type
(c) of the most colourless type
(d) of the colourless type

60. To throw up the sponge
(a) to accept the challenge
(b) to forget the past offences
(c) to admit defeat
(d) to send message

61. To rule the roost
(a) to measure the height of something
(b) to measure the depth
(c) to strike with a stick
(d) to dominate

62. Bats in the belfry
(a) to be mad
(b) something needing cleanliness
(c) an impending danger
(d) to be deceived

63. To have a jaundice eye
(a) to have jaundice (b) to have fever
(c) to be prejudiced (d) to lose colour

64. To go leeward
(a) to make up for the lost time
(b) to move in the direction the wind blows
(c) to think that law is unnecessary
(d) to have a disregard for law and order and do as one likes

65. To egg on
(a) to egg on slowly
(b) to destroy slowly
(c) to give a walk over
(d) to instigate to proceed further

66. To haul over the coals
(a) to walk over the fire
(b) to burn
(c) to scold for something done wrong
(d) to throw into fire

67. To draw a bead on
(a) to say prayers (b) to count the beads
(c) to do one's best (d) to lake aim at

68. Fabian policy
(a) dictatorial policy
(b) democratic policy
(c) systematic policy
(d) policy of cautious persistence

69. At one's beck and call
(a) to climb the back
(b) to call from behind
(c) to be always at one's service or command
(d) not to care for anybody

70. To play to the gallery
(a) to try to get the appreciation from the least intelligent people
(b) to try to win appreciation of intelligent people
(c) to play in the gallery
(d) to disturb people sitting in the gallery

71. On the Greek calendars
(a) the old calendar of the Greeks
(b) the new calendar of the Greeks
(c) something within easy reach
(d) something which is impossible

72. Jog on
(a) to continue at a slow pace
(b) sleep
(c) to neglect duty
(d) to mishandle the case

73. To bite one's lips
(a) to feel sorry (b) to be angry
(c) laugh at others (d) to have doubt

74. Nail to the counter
(a) to expose publicly as false
(b) to be firm
(c) to be unsure
(d) to touch the exact point

75. To cool one's heels
(a) to give a cold treatment to somebody
(b) to be kept waiting for sometime
(c) a closed chapter
(d) a hot issue

76. Bag of bones
(a) a bag full of bones
(b) a dead person
(c) a person about to die
(d) an extremely weak person

77. All moonshine
(a) show (b) lighted only by moon
(c) false (d) far from reality

78. To shake the dust off one's feet
(a) to wash feet
(b) to walk fast
(c) to leave a place with a sense of resentment
(d) to rest after a long journey

79. To worm oneself into favour
(a) to win favour by flattery
(b) to win favour by bribery
(c) to win favour slowly and gradually

(d) to win favour fast .

80. A bird of passage
(a) a flying bird
(b) an unreliable person
(c) one who stays for a short time
(d) bad time

81. Thanks to
(a) be grateful
(b) as a result of
(c) ceremonially
(d) to wait for the benefactor

82. With a string
(a) not to give any aid
(b) to give unconditional aid
(c) gift or aid with condition
(d) to accept aid

83. To set stores by
(a) to value highly
(b) to hoard a large quantity of something
(c) to set up store
(d) fix a price

84. To draw the long bow
(a) to shoot (b) to exaggerate
(c) to criticize (d) to admire

85. To know the ropes
(a) to recognize the lost things
(b) to do rigging
(c) to know the procedure of doing a job
(d) to flog

86. To give the devil his due
(a) to be just to a person even though he does not deserve such treatment
(b) to surrender oneself willingly when one's mistake is detected
(c) to punish an innocent person
(d) to punish a guilty person

87. In the swim
(a) knowing latest current things
(b) to cross a river by a boat
(c) to cross a river by swimming
(d) to be in the river

88. To knuckle under
(a) to be in a crisis (b) to submit
(c) to take rest (d) to go to bed

89. To have a dig at
(a) to criticise someone
(b) to sow seeds
(c) to weed out
(d) to praise someone

90. All the go
(a) in fashion (b) fair
(c) smooth (d) total absence

91. Three R's
(a) radiogram, radiograph, radio telescope
(b) rabble, rattle, razzle
(c) reading, writing, arithmetic
(d) rail, radar, raft

92. A wild goose chase
(a) foolish and useless enterprise
(b) to hunt
(c) a violent chase
(d) to speak harshly

93. To rest on one's laurels
(a) to cease to strive for further glory
(b) to be lazy
(c) to be proud of one's victory
(d) to die

94. Raw deal
(a) unjust treatment
(b) unripe fruit
(c) early stage of business
(d) contract not yet finally decided

95. A forlorn hope
(a) a plan which has remote chances of success
(b) hope about unforeseeable future
(c) hope of a single person
(d) hope of a silly person

96. Printer's devil
(a) messenger boy in a printing office
(b) blunder
(c) low type of printed material

(d) delay in printing

97. To be on the carpet

(a) subject to criticism
(b) under consideration
(c) a heartfelt welcome
(d) on the ground

98. To bring the house down

(a) to appeal greatly to the audience
(b) to pull down a building
(c) to defame one's family
(d) to pass a bill unanimously

99. To have an edge on

(a) to cut with a knife
(b) to threaten to wound
(c) to be slightly better than
(d) to be in a dangerous situation

100. Sackcloth and ashes

(a) to cremate (b) penitence
(c) dirty clothes (d) cheap clothes

101. To put two and two together

(a) to progress steadily
(b) to compare the debit and credit
(c) to conclude keeping in view the merits and demerits
(d) to oppose as a last resort

102. To weather the storm

(a) to face a crisis
(b) to survive a crisis
(c) to be the victim of a crisis
(d) to create crisis

103. To grease the palm

(a) to bribe (b) to lubricate
(c) to cut down a tree (d) to fly in the sky

104. Lump in the throat

(a) to be hoarse
(b) a highly emotional state
(c) food of low type
(d) wind-pipe

105. To fight shy of

(a) to keep aloof from
(b) to fight social evils
(c) to be bold
(d) to fight and win

106. Hobson's choice

(a) lion's share
(b) the best choice
(c) option of taking the one offered or nothing
(d) the last chance

107. To hit it off

(a) to quarrel
(b) to be hostile
(c) to agree or be congenial
(d) to threaten

108. To whitewash

(a) to clean a place
(b) to work hard
(c) to retrieve damaged reputation
(d) to use cosmetics

109. Within an ace of

(a) very close
(b) within one's means
(c) within a narrow circle
(d) near centre

110. To keep an open mind

(a) to remember
(b) to forget
(c) to come to no decision on a subject of discussion
(d) to be clear-headed

111. Open question

(a) a question put to all
(b) a question without any generally agreed answer
(c) a permanent problem
(d) a clearly-written/expressed question

112. On one's mettle

(a) rouse to do one's best
(b) to put on an overcoat

(c) to safeguard against attack
(d) to use one's own money properly

113. To keep the pot boiling
(a) to maintain interest
(b) to heat
(c) to show anger
(d) to do experiments

114. Grist to one's mill
(a) grain to be ground
(b) useful for one's purpose
(c) income from will
(d) to work one's machine

115. Kangaroo court
(a) a group of kangaroos
(b) the young kangaroo
(c) unofficial court
(d) unofficial estimate

116. Wool gathering
(a) to become a shepherd
(b) to shear sheep
(c) to be absent-minded
(d) to live in the countryside

117. Between Scylla and Charybdis
(a) between two hills
(b) between two rivers
(c) between two enemies
(d) between two dangers

118. The heels of Achilles
(a) bare-foot
(b) to run fast
(c) to wait on somebody
(d) the weak point in a person

119. To know which side the bread is buttered on
(a) to know where one's interest lies
(b) to be a glutton
(c) to be fond of rich diet
(d) to know how to increase one's income

120. To eke out
(a) to subtract (b) to supplement
(c) to etch (d) to oust

121. To be in the doldrums
(a) to be in low spirits
(b) to be within doors
(c) to praise loudly
(d) to be in a crisis

122. Spick and span
(a) lean and thin (b) neat and clean
(c) honest and true (d) hale and hearty

123. Wild cat strike
(a) a furious attack
(b) strike not approved by the trade union
(c) a strike in which violence is committed
(d) to face a strong enemy

124. Blind alley
(a) blindness due to old age
(b) a dark room
(c) unprofitable action
(d) to continue to make efforts in spite of confusion

125. Tied to the apron strings of
(a) be independent (b) to be dependent on
(c) to live together (d) to fall in love with

126. Brown study
(a) to study sincerely (b) to study uselessly
(c) deep in thought (d) practical advantage

127. To see pink elephants
(a) to dream
(b) to anticipate luck
(c) to be afraid of
(d) to show courage

ANSWERS

1. (c)	2. (d)	3. (b)	4. (b)	5. (c)	6. (b)	7. (c)	8. (a)	9. (d)	10. (b)
11. (b)	12. (a)	13. (b)	14. (d)	15. (b)	16. (b)	17. (b)	18. (a)	19. (c)	20. (d)
21. (b)	22. (d)	23. (c)	24. (c)	25. (a)	26. (c)	27. (c)	28. (a)	29. (b)	30. (d)
31. (a)	32. (a)	33. (d)	34. (b)	35. (c)	36. (c)	37. (d)	38. (b)	39. (a)	40. (b)
41. (c)	42. (a)	43. (a)	44. (d)	45. (b)	46. (c)	47. (d)	48. (b)	49. (c)	50. (c)
51. (c)	52. (d)	53. (c)	54. (c)	55. (c)	56. (d)	57. (a)	58. (c)	59. (a)	60. (c)
61. (d)	62. (a)	63. (c)	64. (b)	65. (d)	66. (c)	67. (d)	68. (d)	69. (c)	70. (a)
71. (d)	72. (a)	73. (b)	74. (a)	75. (b)	76. (d)	77. (d)	78. (c)	79. (a)	80. (c)
81. (a)	82. (c)	83. (a)	84. (b)	85. (c)	86. (a)	87. (a)	88. (b)	89. (a)	90. (a)
91. (c)	92. (a)	93. (a)	94. (a)	95. (a)	96. (a)	97. (b)	98. (a)	99. (c)	100. (b)
101. (c)	102. (b)	103. (a)	104. (b)	105. (a)	106. (c)	107. (c)	108. (c)	109. (a)	110. (c)
111. (b)	112. (a)	113. (a)	114. (b)	115. (c)	116. (c)	117. (d)	118. (b)	119. (a)	120. (b)
121. (a)	122. (b)	123. (b)	124. (c)	125. (b)	126. (c)	127. (d)			

UNIT 28

Spellings asked in Competitive Exams

1. In the following question, four words are given out of which one word is correctly spelt. Select the correctly spelt word
(a) andulate (b) undulate
(c) undulete (d) andulete

2. In the following question, four words are given out of which one word is correctly spelt. Select the correctly spelt wor(d)
(a) revelars (b) rewellers
(c) revelers (d) rewelers

3. In the following question, four words are given out of which one word is incorrectly spelt. Find the incorrectly spelt word
(a) Hygeine (b) Fascist
(c) Career (d) Apparel

4. In the following question, four words are given out of which one word is incorrectly spelt. Find the incorrectly spelt word
(a) Reside (b) Revise
(c) Advise (d) Demice

5. In the following question, four words are given out of which one word is incorrectly spelt. Select the incorrectly spelt word
(a) Anxiety (b) Believe
(c) Height (d) Peity

6. In the following question, four words are given out of which one word is incorrectly spelt.
Select the incorrectly spelt word
(a) Admited (b) Benefited
(c) Married (d) Offered

7. In the following question, four words are given out of which one word is incorrectly spelt. Find the incorrectly spelt word
(a) Bulettin (b) Barrage
(c) Buoyant (d) Beginner

8. In the following question, four words are given out of which one word is incorrectly spelt. Find the incorrectly spelt word
(a) Guidance (b) Ambassador
(c) Handkercheif (d) Labourer

9. In the following question, four words are given out of which one word is correctly spelt. Select the correctly spelt wor(d)
(a) Mutiniers (b) Mutineers
(c) Muteniers (d) Muteneers

10. In the following question, four words are given out of which one word is correctly spelt. Select the correctly spelt word
(a) Obeisanse (b) Obeisance
(c) Obesance (d) Obesanse

11. In the following question, four words are given out of which one word is incorrectly spelt. Find the incorrectly spelt word
(a) Accurate (b) Business
(c) Sedentery (d) Jewellery

12. In the following question, four words are given out of which one word is incorrectly spelt. Find the incorrectly spelt word
(a) Chaufer (b) Committee
(c) Veterinary (d) Repentance

13. In the following question, four words are given out of which one word is incorrectly spelt. Find the incorrectly spelt word
(a) Entrepreneur (b) Remuneration
(c) Apprentice (d) Soveriegnity

14. In the following question, four words are given

out of which one word is incorrectly spelt. Find the incorrectly spelt word

(a) Tranquillity (b) Perseverence
(c) Resplendence (d) Accommodation

15. In the following question, out of the four alternatives, select the word similar in meaning to the word given.

(a) Solitary (b) Superficial
(c) Soothing (d) Brazier

16. In the following question, four words are given out of which one word is incorrectly spelt. Find the incorrectly spelt word

(a) Millionaire (b) Omission
(c) Foreign (d) Proprietry

17. In the following question, four words are given out of which one word is incorrectly spelt. Find the incorrectly spelt word

(a) Acquaintence (b) Appeasement
(c) Abnormality (d) Accentuate

18. Direction : In the following question, four words are given out of which one word is incorrectly spelt. Select the incorrectly spelt word

(a) Usable (b) Defense
(c) Inventor (d) Annaul

19. Direction : In the following question, four words are given out of which one word is incorrectly spelt. Select the incorrectly spelt word

(a) Changeable (b) Inedible
(c) Tracable (d) Valuable

20. In the following question, four words are given out of which one word is incorrectly spelt. Find the incorrectly spelt word

(a) Pertinacious (b) Demarcation
(c) Temperament (d) Sureptitious

21. In the following question, four words are given out of which one word is incorrectly spelt. Find the incorrectly spelt word

(a) Treachery (b) Refrendum
(c) Suppression (d) Resemblance

22. In the following question, four words are given out of which one word is correctly spelt. Select the correctly spelt word

(a) Perverted (b) Pervirted
(c) Parverted (d) Parvirted

23. In the following question, four words are given out of which one word is correctly spelt. Select the correctly spelt word

(a) Blandnes (b) Blandeness
(c) Blandenes (d) Blandness

24. In the following question, four words are given out of which one word is incorrectly spelt. Find the incorrectly spelt word

(a) Forfeit (b) Gorilla
(c) Blissfull (d) Corrupt

25. In the following question, four words are given out of which one word is incorrectly spelt. Find the incorrectly spelt word

(a) Afforestation (b) Translusent
(c) Foreigner (d) Achievement

26. In the following question, four words are given out of which one word is incorrectly spelt. Select the incorrectly spelt word

(a) Autumn (b) Desperate
(c) Reciept (d) Traffic

27. In the following question, four words are given out of which one word is incorrectly spelt. Select the incorrectly spelt word

(a) Century (b) Finance
(c) Remember (d) Sponser

28. In the following question, four words are given out of which one word is incorrectly spelt. Find the incorrectly spelt word

(a) Impression (b) Personnal
(c) Terrorism (d) Illiterate

29. In the following question, four words are given out of which one word is incorrectly spelt. Find the incorrectly spelt word

(a) Stupefaction (b) Preferential
(c) Surveillence (d) Detrimental

30. In the following question, four words are given out of which one word is incorrectly spelt. Select the incorrectly spelt word
(a) Colonel (b) Hypocracy
(c) Offence (d) Strength

31. In the following question, four words are given out of which one word is incorrectly spelt. Select the incorrectly spelt word
(a) Preceed (b) Proceed
(c) Recede (d) Succeed

32. In the following question, four words are given out of which one word is incorrectly spelt. Select the incorrectly spelt word
(a) Acquiescence (b) Alienate
(c) Belligerent (d) Sabbotage

33. In the following question, four words are given out of which one word is incorrectly spelt. Select the incorrectly spelt word
(a) Alluminium (b) Cemetery
(c) Recommend (d) Satellite

34. In the following question, four words are given out of which one word is incorrectly spelt. Select the incorrectly spelt word
(a) Ecstasy (b) Profecient
(c) Sacrifice (d) Temporary

35. In the following question, four words are given out of which one word is incorrectly spelt. Select the incorrectly spelt word
(a) Familiar (b) Grammer
(c) Narrator (d) Operator

36. In the following question, four words are given out of which one word is incorrectly spelt. Select the incorrectly spelt word
(a) Continuous (b) Glamoros
(c) Meticulous (d) Vicious

37. In the following question, four words are given out of which one word is incorrectly spelt. Select the incorrectly spelt word
(a) Secondary (b) Sizable
(c) Succumb (d) Sustanence

38. In the following question, four words are given out of which one word is incorrectly spelt. Find the incorrectly spelt word
(a) Literary (b) Leakeage
(c) Laudable (d) Loafer

39. In the following question, four words are given out of which one word is incorrectly spelt. Find the incorrectly spelt word
(a) Anasthetic (b) Obliterate
(c) Concurrence (d) Blithesome

40. In the following question, four words are given out of which one word is incorrectly spelt. Select the incorrectly spelt word
(a) Pedestrain (b) Plaintiff
(c) Potatoes (d) Potassium

41. In the following question, four words are given out of which one word is incorrectly spelt. Select the incorrectly spelt word
(a) Fabulous (b) Gorgeous
(c) Heterogeneous (d) Inocuous

42. In the following question, four words are given out of which one word is incorrectly spelt. Find the incorrectly spelt word
(a) Tomorrow (b) Occurence
(c) Temperature (d) Preferable

43. In the following question, four words are given out of which one word is incorrectly spelt. Find the incorrectly spelt word
(a) Receeding (b) Cemetery
(c) Parallelogram (d) Rehearsal

44. In the following question, four words are given out of which one word is correctly spelt. Select the correctly spelt word
(a) Ditheering (b) Dethering
(c) Dithering (d) Detheering

45. In the following question, four words are given out of which one word is correctly spelt. Select the correctly spelt word
(a) Throtled (b) Throttlede
(c) Throtlede (d) Throttled

46. In the following question, some part of the sentence may have errors. Find out which part of the sentence has an error and select the appropriate option. If a sentence is free from error, select 'No Error'. She was so (A)/ near to (B)/ achieving her goal. (C)/No Error (D)
(a) A (b) B
(c) C (d) D

47. In the following question, some part of the sentence may have errors. Find out which part of the sentence has an error and select the appropriate option. If a sentence is free from error, select 'No Error'. He watched as fights (A)/ broke out (B)/ along the city. (C)/No Error (D)
(a) A (b) B
(c) C (d) D

48. In the following question, four words are given out of which one word is correctly spelt. Select the correctly spelt wor(d)
(a) Litegants (b) Litigents
(c) Litigants (d) Litegents

49. In the following question, four words are given out of which one word is correctly spelt. Select the correctly spelt wor(d)
(a) Stoically (b) Stoicaly
(c) Stoecally (d) Stoecaly

50. In the following question, four words are given out of which one word is correctly spelt. Select the correctly spelt wor(d)
(a) Threashing (b) Thrasheing
(c) Threasheing (d) Thrashing

51. In the following question, four words are given out of which one word is correctly spelt. Select the correctly spelt wor(d)
(a) Conssensus (b) Consenssus
(c) Consensus (d) Conssenssus

52. In the following question, some part of the sentence may have errors. Find out which part of the sentence has an error and select the appropriate option. If a sentence is free from error, select 'No Error'. They did nothing (A)/ that was down the (B)/ dignity of princes. (C)/ No Error (D)
(a) A (b) B
(c) C (d) D

53. In the following question, some part of the sentence may have errors. Find out which part of the sentence has an error and select the appropriate option. If a sentence is free from error, select 'No Error'. What are (A)/ you doing (B)/ by here? (C)/No Error (D)
(a) A (b) B
(c) C (d) D

54. In the following question, four words are given out of which one word is correctly spelt. Select the correctly spelt wor(d)
(a) Composure (b) Cumposure
(c) Composore (d) Cumposore

55. In the following question, four words are given out of which one word is correctly spelt. Select the correctly spelt wor(d)
(a) Alliviate (b) Aleviate
(c) Alleviate (d) Aliviate

56. In the following question, four words are given out of which one word is correctly spelt. Select the correctly spelt wor(d)
(a) Scriptare (b) Screpture
(c) Scripture (d) Screptare

57. In the following question, four words are given out of which one word is correctly spelt. Select the correctly spelt wor(d)
(a) Anoyance (b) Annoyanse
(c) Anoyanse (d) Annoyance

58. In the following question, four words are given out of which one word is correctly spelt. Select the correctly spelt wor(d)
(a) Threashing (b) Thrasheing
(c) Threasheing (d) Thrashing

59. In the following question, four words are given out of which one word is correctly spelt. Select

the correctly spelt wor(d)
(a) Conssensus (b) Consenssus
(c) Consensus (d) Conssenssus

60. In the following question, four words are given out of which one word is correctly spelt. Select the correctly spelt wor(d)
(a) Reterate (b) Reiterate
(c) Reiterete (d) Reterete

61. In the following question, four words are given out of which one word is correctly spelt. Select the correctly spelt wor(d)
(a) Extrution (b) Extrusion
(c) Extrosion (d) Extrotion

62. In the following question, four words are given out of which one word is correctly spelt. Select the correctly spelt wor(d)
(a) Contusion (b) Contution
(c) Cuntusion (d) Cuntution

63. In the following question, four words are given out of which one word is correctly spelt. Select the correctly spelt wor(d)
(a) cemitars (b) Scimitars
(c) Scimetars (d) Scemetars

64. In the following question, four words are given out of which one word is correctly spelt. Select the correctly spelt wor(d)
(a) consenses (b) concensus
(c) concenssus (d) consensus

65. In the following question, four words are given out of which one word is correctly spelt. Select the correctly spelt wor(d)
(a) presedents (b) pricedents
(c) precedents (d) prisedents

66. In the following question, four words are given out of which one word is correctly spelt. Select the correctly spelt wor(d)
(a) castegated (b) castigatad
(c) castigated (d) casttigated

67. In the following question, four words are given out of which one word is correctly spelt. Select the correctly spelt wor(d)
(a) poseses (b) posesses
(c) possesses (d) posseses

68. In the following question, four words are given out of which one word is correctly spelt. Select the correctly spelt wor(d)
(a) palatable (b) palateble
(c) pallateble (d) pallatable

69. In the following question, four words are given out of which one word is correctly spelt. Select the correctly spelt wor(d)
(a) unnerving (b) unnerveing
(c) unerving (d) unerveing

70. In the following question, four words are given out of which one word is correctly spelt. Select the correctly spelt wor(d)
(a) possesses (b) posseses
(c) posesses (d) poseses

71. In the following question, four words are given out of which one word is correctly spelt. Select the correctly spelt wor(d)
(a) murmuring (b) murmurring
(c) murrmuring (d) murrmurring

72. In the following question, four words are given out of which one word is correctly spelt. Select the correctly spelt wor(d)
(a) illecitly (b) illicitly
(c) ilicitly (d) illicitley

73. In the following question, four words are given out of which one word is correctly spelt. Select the correctly spelt wor(d)
(a) brutalety (b) brutality
(c) bruttality (d) bruttalety

74. In the following question, four words are given out of which one word is correctly spelt. Select the correctly spelt wor(d)
(a) atrocias (b) atrocious
(c) atroceous (d) atroacious

75. In the following question, four words are given out of which one word is correctly spelt. Select the correctly spelt wor(d)
(a) curvacias (b) curvaceous
(c) curvaceuse (d) curveaceous

76. In the following question, four words are given out of which one word is correctly spelt. Select the correctly spelt wor(d)
(a) jukstapose (b) jaxtapuse
(c) juxtapose (d) jaxtapose

77. In the following question, four words are given out of which one word is correctly spelt. Select the correctly spelt wor(d)
(a) amusemant (b) ammusement
(c) ammusemant (d) amusement

78. In the following question, four words are given out of which one word is correctly spelt. Select the correctly spelt wor(d)
(a) analoges (b) analogese
(c) analogues (d) analoguese

79. In the following question, four words are given out of which one word is correctly spelt. Select the correctly spelt wor(d)
(a) unraffled (b) unruffled
(c) unrufled (d) unrafled

80. In the following question, four words are given out of which one word is correctly spelt. Select the correctly spelt wor(d)
(a) bereaving (b) bereaveing
(c) bereving (d) bireaving

81. In the following question, four words are given out of which one word is correctly spelt. Select the correctly spelt wor(d)
(a) deligence (b) diligence
(c) delegence (d) dilegence

82. In the following question, four words are given out of which one word is incorrectly spelt. Select the incorrectly spelt wor(d)
(a) Dictionory (b) Irrelevant
(c) Perishable (d) Tangible

83. n the following question, four words are given out of which one word is incorrectly spelt. Select the incorrectly spelt wor(d)
(a) Conceive (b) Leisure
(c) Neice (d) Reign

84. In the following question, four words are given out of which one word is correctly spelt. Select the correctly spelt wor(d)
(a) bereving (b) bereaving
(c) bareaving (d) bareving

85. In the following question, four words are given out of which one word is correctly spelt. Select the correctly spelt wor(d)
(a) frothyiest (b) frotheist
(c) frothyeist (d) frothiest

86. In the following question, four words are given out of which one word is correctly spelt. Select the correctly spelt wor(d)
(a) loopholes (b) lupholes
(c) looppholes (d) luppholes

87. In the following question, four words are given out of which one word is correctly spelt. Select the correctly spelt wor(d)
(a) wherefor (b) wharefore
(c) wharefor (d) wherefore

88. In the following question, four words are given out of which one word is incorrectly spelt. Select the incorrectly spelt wor(d)
(a) Gaurantee (b) Itinerary
(c) Magnificent (d) Writing

89. In the following question, four words are given out of which one word is incorrectly spelt. Select the incorrectly spelt wor(d)
(a) Etiquete (b) Exquisite
(c) Restaurant (d) Scavenger

90. In the following question, four words are given out of which one word is correctly spelt. Select the correctly spelt wor(d)
(a) hypnotyst (b) hipnotyst
(c) hipnotist (d) hypnotist

91. In the following question, four words are given out of which one word is correctly spelt. Select the correctly spelt wor(d)
(a) theurise (b) theoris
(c) theuris (d) theories

SOLUTION

5. Piety is the correct word and its meaning is the quality of being religious.

6. Admitted is the correct word and it means confess to be true.

9. Mutiny is to revolt. Mutineers are the person who revolt. 'Mutineers' is the right way to spell the wor(d)

10. Obeisance is the right way to spell the word whose meaning is to respect.

ANSWER KEY

1. (b)	**2.** (c)	**3.** (a)	**4.** (d)	**5.** (d)	**6.** (a)	**7.** (a)	**8.** (c)	**9.** (b)	**10.** (b)
11. (c)	**12.** (a)	**13.** (d)	**14.** (b)	**15.** (d)	**16.** (d)	**17.** (a)	**18.** (d)	**19.** (c)	**20.** (d)
21. (b)	**22.** (a)	**23.** (d)	**24.** (c)	**25.** (b)	**26.** (c)	**27.** (d)	**28.** (b)	**29.** (c)	**30.** (b)
31. (a)	**32.** (d)	**33.** (a)	**34.** (b)	**35.** (b)	**36.** (b)	**37.** (d)	**38.** (b)	**39.** (a)	**40.** (a)
41. (b)	**42.** (b)	**43.** (a)	**44.** (c)	**45.** (d)	**46.** (b)	**47.** (c)	**48.** (c)	**49.** (a)	**50.** (d)
51. (c)	**52.** (b)	**53.** (c)	**54.** (a)	**55.** (c)	**56.** (c)	**57.** (d)	**58.** (d)	**59.** (c)	**60.** (b)
61. (b)	**62.** (a)	**63.** (b)	**64.** (d)	**65.** (c)	**66.** (c)	**67.** (c)	**68.** (a)	**69.** (a)	**70.** (a)
71. (a)	**72.** (b)	**73.** (b)	**74.** (b)	**75.** (b)	**76.** (c)	**77.** (d)	**78.** (c)	**79.** (b)	**80.** (a)
81. (b)	**82.** (a)	**83.** (c)	**84.** (b)	**85.** (d)	**86.** (a)	**87.** (d)	**88.** (a)	**89.** (a)	**90.** (d)
91. (d)									

PRACTICE SET

DIRECTIONS: (Qs. 1-143) Choose the correct spelling of the given word.

1. (a) Efflorascence (b) Efflorescence
(c) Efflorescence (d) Eflorescence

2. (a) Aliennate (b) Allienate
(c) Alienate (d) Alienatte

3. (a) Forefiet (b) Forefeit
(c) Forfeit (d) Forfiet

4. (a) Comemorate (b) Commemmorate
(c) Momemmorate (d) Commemorate

5. (a) Exampli (b) Exampel
(c) Example (d) Exampal

6. (a) Psychology (b) Sycology
(c) Psykology (d) Sychology

7. (a) Accessible (b) Accesibel
(c) Accessible (d) Acessible

8. (a) Tresspass (b) Trespass
(c) Tresspas (d) Trespas

9. (a) Argumant (b) Arguemant
(c) Argument (d) Arguement

10. (a) Aproched (b) Aproached
(c) Appraoched (d) Approached

11. (a) Comentry (b) Commentry
(c) Commentery (d) Commentary

12. (a) Coimmision (b) Comision
(c) Comission (d) Commision

13. (a) Guerila (b) Gurilla
(c) Gorila (d) Gorilla

14. (a) Pasanger (b) Pessenger
(c) Pesanger (d) Passenger

15. (a) Tariff (b) Tarriff
(c) Tarif (d) Tarrif

16. (a) Jewelery (b) Jewellry
(c) Jwellry (d) Jewellery

17. (a) Grametic (b) Grammetic
(c) Grammatic (d) Gramatic

18. (a) Blisfull (b) Blissful
(c) Blisful (d) Blissfull

19. (a) Embarasment (b) Embarassment
(c) Embarrasment (d) Embarrassment

20. (a) Sattellite (b) Satellite
(c) Sattelite (d) Satelite

21. (a) Ocasion (b) Ocassion
(c) Occasion (d) Occassion

22. (a) Posesion (b) Possession
(c) Posession (d) Possesion

23. (a) Greivance (b) Greievance
(c) Griveance (d) Grievance

24. (a) Beligrent (b) Beligerent
(c) Belligrent (d) Belligerent

25. (a) Coruppt (b) Curropt
(c) Corrupt (d) Currupt

26. (a) Dielectic (b) Deallectic
(c) Dilectic (d) Dialectic

27. (a) Achievment (b) Acheivment
(c) Achievement (d) Achevement

28. (a) Coreander (b) Coriander
(c) Coriandar (d) Coreandor

29. (a) Bouquete (b) Bouquet
(c) Boquet (d) Bouquette

30. (a) Translucent (b) Translusent
(c) Transluscent (d) Tranclucent

31. (a) Hetrogenous (b) Hetrogeneous
(c) Heterogenous (d) Heterogeneous

32. (a) Foreigner (b) Forienor
(c) Foriegnor (d) Foreiner

33. (a) Addultration (b) Adultration
(c) Addulteration (d) Adulteration

34. (a) Gorgette (b) Georgette
(c) Gorgete (d) Georget

35. (a) Examplary (b) Exemplary
(c) Examplery (d) Exemplery

36. (a) Sobotage (b) Sobbotage
(c) Sobotaze (d) Sabatage

37. (a) Colaboration (b) Collaberation
(c) Colaberation (d) Collaboration

38. (a) Exagerate (b) Exadgerate
(c) Exaggerate (d) Exeggerate

39. (a) Acurrate (b) Accurate
(c) Acurate (d) Accuratte

40. (a) Buisness (b) Bussiness
(c) Business (d) Buisiness

41. (a) Forecast (b) Forcaust
(c) Forcast (d) Forecaste

42. (a) Liesure (b) Leisure
(c) Leasure (d) Lesiure

43. (a) Colliberation (b) Calliberation
(c) Callibration (d) Calibration

44. (a) Adviceable (b) Advisable
(c) Advicable (d) Adviseable

45. (a) Interegnum (b) Intrenum
(c) Interregnum (d) Interregnim

46. (a) Aforstation (b) Aforestation
(c) Afforstation (d) Afforestation

47. (a) Entreprenuer (b) Entrepraneur
(c) Entrapreneur (d) Entrepreneur

48. (a) Harasment (b) Harassment
(c) Harrassment (d) Harrasment

49. (a) Perseverance (b) Preservarance
(c) Preseverence (d) Preserverence

50. (a) Sovereignty (b) Soveriegnty
(c) Sovereignity (d) Soveriegnity

51. (a) Receding (b) Receeding
(c) Reeceding (d) Recedeing

52. (a) Illusteous (b) Illistrious
(c) Ilustrious (d) Ilustrious

53. (a) Skillful (b) Skillfull
(c) Skilful (d) Skilfull

54. (a) Septaganarian (b) Septagenarian
(c) Septuaganarian (d) Septuagenarian

55. (a) Pitiaeble (b) Pitiable
(c) Pitiaable (d) Pitiabale

56. (a) Incumbent (b) Incumbant
(c) Incambant (d) Incambent

57. (a) Budgetary (b) Budgetry
(c) Budgetery (d) Bugetary

58. (a) Paralelled (b) Parallelled
(c) Paralleled (d) Parralleled

59. (a) Arangement (b) Arrangement
(c) Arrangment (d) Arangement

60. (a) Cemetry (b) Cemetery
(c) Cemetary (d) Cemmetery

61. (a) Vetniary (b) Vetarinary
(c) Veteninary (d) Veterinary

62. (a) Lauriate (b) Laureat
(c) Laureate (d) Lauriat

63. (a) Comander (b) Commander
(c) Commandor (d) Comandar

64. (a) Tranquillity (b) Trenquillity
(c) Trenquility (d) Tranquility

65. (a) Alitration (b) Alliteration
(c) Alitration (d) Aliteration

66. (a) Chaufer (b) Chauffer
(c) Chaufeur (d) Chauffeur

67. (a) Remunaration (b) Ramunration
(c) Remeuneration (d) Remuneration

68. (a) Coitment (b) Comittment
(c) Committment (d) Commitment

69. (a) Fullfil (b) Fulfil
(c) Fulfill (d) Fullfill

70. (a) Genelogy (b) Genealogy
(c) Geneology (d) Genalogy

71. (a) Defendant (b) Defendent
(c) Defandent (d) Defandant

72. (a) Recommand (b) Recommend
(c) Reccomend (d) Recomend

73. (a) Varstile (b) Verstile
(c) Versatile (d) Vorstyle

74. (a) Correspondant (b) Corraspondent
(c) Corraspondant (d) Correspondent

75. (a) Finnancer (b) Financier
(c) Financer (d) Financeir

76. (a) Etiquete (b) Etiquette
(c) Ettiquete (d) Ettiquette

77. (a) Overlapped (b) Overlaped
(c) Overleped (d) Overelaped

78. (a) Necessary (b) Necesarry
(c) Necesary (d) Neccessary

79. (a) Inocculate (b) Inoculate
(c) Innoculate (d) Innocculate

80. (a) Benefeted (b) Benifited
(c) Benefitted (d) Benifitted

81. (a) Supreintendent (b) Superintendent
(c) Suprintendent (d) Supereintendent

82. (a) Temparament (b) Temprament
    (c) Temperament (d) Temperamant

83. (a) Homeopathy (b) Homoepathy
    (c) Homiopathy (d) Homoeopathy

84. (a) Numrator (b) Numerator
    (c) Numerater (d) Numrater

85. (a) Ommission (b) Omision
    (c) Omission (d) Ommision

86. (a) Mountaineous (b) Mountaneous
    (c) Mountainous (d) Mountanous

87. (a) Giraf (b) Gerraffe
    (c) Geraff (d) Giraffe

88. (a) Legendary (b) Legendery
    (c) Legendry (d) Legandery

89. (a) Aquaintence (b) Acquaintance
    (c) Aquaintance (d) Acquaintence

90. (a) Arodrome (b) Airodrome
    (c) Aerodrom (d) Aerodrome

91. (a) Forein (b) Fariegn
    (c) Foriegn (d) Foreign

92. (a) Aprentic (b) Aperentic
    (c) Apprentic (d) Apperentice

93. (a) Indigenous (b) Indigenuous
    (c) Indiginous (d) Indeginuous

94. (a) Coleagu (b) Colleagu
    (c) Coleague (d) Colleague

95. (a) Lieutinant (b) Lieutenant
    (c) Leutenant (d) Liutenant

96. (a) Paralelogram (b) Paralellogram
    (c) Parallelogram (d) Parallellogram

97. (a) Corigendum (b) Coridgendum
    (c) Corrigendum (d) Corridgendum

98. (a) Prevalent (b) Prevalent
    (c) Prevelant (d) Prevelent

99. (a) Milennium (b) Millenium
    (c) Millennium (d) Milenium

100. (a) Acomodation (b) Accomodation
    (c) Acommodation (d) Accommodation

101. (a) Inimitable (b) Innimatible
    (c) Inimitible (d) Inimmitable

102. (a) Refrigerator (b) Refriderater
    (c) Refridgerator (d) Referigerator

103. (a) Apallation (b) Appellation
    (c) Appelation (d) Appallation

104. (a) Catlogg (b) Catlog
    (c) Catlogue (d) Catalogue

105. (a) Obssesion (b) Obssession
    (c) Obsession (d) Obsessien

106. (a) Alottee (b) Allotee
    (c) Alotte (d) Allottee

107. (a) Seperable (b) Separable
    (c) Saperable (d) Saparable

108. (a) Hindrence (b) Hindrance
    (c) Hinderence (d) Hinderance

109. (a) Proprietry (b) Propriatory
    (c) Proprietary (d) Proprietory

110. (a) Strategam (b) Strategem
    (c) Stratagem (d) Stratagam

111. (a) Reharsal (b) Rehersal
    (c) Rehearsal (d) Rehearsel

112. (a) Cancelation (b) Cancelletion
    (c) Cancellation (d) Cancellasion

113. (a) Assasination (b) Asasination
    (c) Assassination (d) Asassination

114. (a) Millonare (b) Millionaire
    (c) Millionare (d) Millonaire

115. (a) Draut (b) Drout
    (c) Drougt (d) Drought

116. (a) Fabullous (b) Fablous
    (c) Fabulous (d) Fabuleous

117. (a) Accomplish (b) Ackmplesh
    (c) Accompalish (d) Acomplush

118. (a) Simaltanious (b) Simultaneous
(c) Simultanious (d) Simaltaneous

119. (a) Turnament (b) Tournamant
(c) Tournament (d) Turnamant

120. (a) Tomarow (b) Tomarrow
(c) Tomorrow (d) Tommorow

121. (a) Neighbur (b) Neighber
(c) Neighbour (d) Neibur

122. (a) Fasist (b) Facict
(c) Facist (d) Fascist

123. (a) Occurrance (b) Occurrence
(c) Occurance (d) Occurence

124. (a) Gaurantee (b) Guarantee
(c) Garuntee (d) Guaruntee

125. (a) Parlamentary (b) Parliamentary
(c) Parlimentary (d) Parliamentery

126. (a) Tentaitive (b) Tentative
(c) Tentitive (d) Tantitive

127. (a) Surveilance (b) Survellance
(c) Surveillance (d) Survaillance

128. (a) Careir (b) Career
(c) Caireer (d) Carreer

129. (a) Resteraunt (b) Restaurent
(c) Rastaurent (d) Restaurant

130. (a) Damage (b) Dammage
(c) Damaige (d) Dammege

131. (a) Farenheit (b) Fahrenhiet
(c) Farenhiet (d) Fahrenheit

132. (a) Recommandation (b) Recomandation
(c) Recommendation (d) Recomendation

133. (a) Accessible (b) Accissible
(c) Acessible (d) Aceesible

134. (a) Tempereture (b) Tempearature
(c) Temperature (d) Tamperature

135. (a) Rennaisance (b) Rennaissance
(c) Renaissance (d) Renaisance

136. (a) Milennium (b) Millenium
(c) Milleneum (d) Millennium

137. (a) Ocassion (b) Occassion
(c) Occasion (d) Occation

138. (a) Garulous (b) Garrulous
(c) Garullous (d) Garrullous

139. (a) Marquee (b) Markue
(c) Marquei (d) Marquie

140. (a) Puissant (b) Puiscant
(c) Puiscent (d) Puissent

141. (a) Disconncerting (b) Disconserting
(c) Discuncerting (d) Disconcerting

142. (a) Exilarate (b) Exhilerate
(c) Exsilarate (d) Exhilarate

143. (a) Plebeian (b) Plibeian
(c) Plebian (d) Plebiean

DIRECTIONS (Qs. 144-220) : Choose the mis-spelt word out of given options.

144. (a) Designation (b) Amature
(c) Controversy (d) Burglar

145. (a) Deceive (b) Conneive
(c) Perceive (d) Acheive

146. (a) Penance (b) Menace
(c) Tendancy (d) Governance

147. (a) Prejudicial (b) Affectionate
(c) Indispensible (d) Assiduous

148. (a) Kitten (b) Cumulative
(c) Justified (d) Inediable

149. (a) Hillock (b) Vilify
(c) Mileage (d) Hillarious

150. (a) Predilection (b) Discipline
(c) Indigenous (d) Preferrable

151. (a) Suicide (b) Suiteable
(c) Summarize (d) Superficial

152. (a) Neice (b) Neither
(c) Neigh (d) Rein

153. (a) Light (b) Fight
(c) Hight (d) Might

154. (a) Control (b) Confusion
(c) Confrence (d) Committee

155. (a) Instantanious (b) Intermediate
(c) Intermittent (d) Interference

156. (a) Breakage (b) Brevity
(c) Breathless (d) Briliance

157. (a) Nuptial (b) Nickers
(c) Nephew (d) Nuisance

158. (a) Explaination (b) Extermination
(c) Exaggeration (d) Expectation

159. (a) Covetous (b) Coherent
(c) Consice (d) Consent

160. (a) Plateau (b) Plebian
(c) Plaedge (d) Pollinate

161. (a) Cruelly (b) Truly
(c) Verbally (d) Rudely

162. (a) Oversear (b) Oscillate
(c) Ossicle (d) Obnscure

163. (a) Cruise (b) Deduse
(c) Truce (d) Bruise

164. (a) Democracy (b) Aristocracy
(c) Advocacy (d) Courtecy

165. (a) Hyphen (b) Hygene
(c) Hurdle (d) Haphazard

166. (a) Believe (b) Relieve
(c) Drieve (d) Decieve

167. (a) Juice (b) Jersy
(c) Jaggery (d) Japanese

168. (a) Envelope (b) Enthuse
(c) Eratic (d) Emigrant

169. (a) Freshner (b) Forlorn
(c) Foreign (d) Fruity

170. (a) Democracy (b) Beaureaucracy
(c) Prophecy (d) Aristocracy

171. (a) Spurious (b) Studious
(c) Subsidary (d) Sensible

172. (a) Charade (b) Studious
(c) Cartrige (d) Sensible

173. (a) Ballistic (b) Baloon
(c) Bulletin (d) Bullock

174. (a) Winner (b) Winning
(c) Writer (d) Writting

175. (a) Bataliion (b) Believe
(c) Bewilder (d) Bogie

176. (a) Asterisk (b) Audience
(c) Acrue (d) Almighty

177. (a) Bearer (b) Governor
(c) Conquerer (d) Admirer

178. (a) Ceremony (b) Agression
(c) Schedule (d) Knowledge

179. (a) Parasology (b) Possibility
(c) Potassium (d) Preamble

180. (a) Careful (b) Untill
(c) Fulfil (d) Final

181. (a) Essential (b) Rehabilitation
(c) Appreciation (d) Concomitant

182. (a) Knack (b) Knee
(c) Kneed (d) Kneel

183. (a) Amend (b) Commend
(c) Assend (d) Comprehend

184. (a) Monotonous (b) Monastry
(c) Monitor (d) Moraine

185. (a) Adultration (b) Adulation
(c) Advancement (d) Admittance

186. (a) Soothe (b) Sponser
(c) Stepney (d) Struggle

187. (a) Resembelance (b) Recuperate
(c) Recommend (d) Resource

188. (a) Rapport (b) Substance
(c) Gravyard (d) Resistible

189. (a) Hack (b) Hawl
(c) Halve (d) Hark

190. (a) Deep (b) Heap
(c) Sleep (d) Weap

191. (a) Semester (b) Senesent
(c) Sensory (d) Salacious

192. (a) Solution (b) Tuition
(c) Circutous (d) Fruition

193. (a) Stolen (b) Eaten
(c) Beaten (d) Writen

194. (a) Device (b) Demice
(c) Revise (d) Advice

195. (a) Illegal (b) Illitrate
(c) Illegitimate (d) Illegible

196. (a) Concession (b) Reconciliation
(c) Humilliation (d) Polliation

197. (a) Anxiety (b) Ankel
(c) Accommodation (d) Allergy

198. (a) Anaemia (b) Attitude
(c) Admiralty (d) Acquarium

199. (a) Nemesis (b) Necessary
(c) Nectar (d) Nieghbour

200. (a) Trachaea (b) Tragedy
(c) Trajectory (d) Training

201. (a) Chancellor (b) Trailor
(c) Traitor (d) Inheritor

202. (a) Handicapped (b) Hankerchief
(c) Handiwork (d) Handicraft

203. (a) Auspicious (b) Available
(c) Attainable (d) Auxilliary

204. (a) Butcher (b) Burrow
(c) Buoyant (d) Buletin

205. (a) Procession (b) Profession
(c) Possession (d) Occassion

206. (a) Enterance (b) Elementary
(c) Endeavour (d) Eccentricity

207. (a) Mischeif (b) Belief
(c) Thief (d) Grief

208. (a) Vacuum (b) Vaccinate
(c) Vacilate (d) Varnish

209. (a) Jeopardy (b) Jealosy
(c) Jaundice (d) Javelin

210. (a) Curiculum (b) Contingency
(c) Cauliflower (d) Cooperate

211. (a) Despair (b) Desperate
(c) Maintain (d) Maintainance

212. (a) Photostate (b) Palmistry
(c) Posthumous (d) Polytechnic

213. (a) Termination (b) Culmination
(c) Determination (d) Defination

214. (a) Voluntary (b) Vomitting
(c) Vaocabulary (d) Vicisitude

215. (a) Mortgaze (b) Manicure
(c) Miraculous (d) Mesmeric

216. (a) Pellicle (b) Pilgrimage
(c) Portrait (d) Parepet

217. (a) Sceptic (b) Agnostic
(c) Prolific (d) Assetic

218. (a) Miscelleneous (b) Mathematics
(c) Cautiously (d) Competition

219. (a) Soldier (b) Beautiful
(c) Infinite (d) Clearify

220. (a) Sandwitch (b) Sculpture
(c) Secrecy (d) Sovereign

ANSWER KEY

1. (b)	**2.** (c)	**3.** (c)	**4.** (d)	**5.** (c)	**6.** (a)	**7.** (c)	**8.** (b)	**9.** (c)	**10.** (d)
11. (d)	**12.** (d)	**13.** (d)	**14.** (d)	**15.** (a)	**16.** (d)	**17.** (c)	**18.** (b)	**19.** (d)	**20.** (b)
21. (c)	**22.** (b)	**23.** (b)	**24.** (d)	**25.** (c)	**26.** (d)	**27.** (c)	**28.** (b)	**29.** (b)	**30.** (a)
31. (d)	**32.** (a)	**33.** (d)	**34.** (b)	**35.** (b)	**36.** (a)	**37.** (d)	**38.** (c)	**39.** (b)	**40.** (b)
41. (a)	**42.** (b)	**43.** (d)	**44.** (b)	**45.** (c)	**46.** (d)	**47.** (d)	**48.** (b)	**49.** (a)	**50.** (a)
51. (a)	**52.** (d)	**53.** (c)	**54.** (d)	**55.** (b)	**56.** (a)	**57.** (a)	**58.** (c)	**59.** (b)	**60.** (b)
61. (b)	**62.** (c)	**63.** (b)	**64.** (a)	**65.** (b)	**66.** (d)	**67.** (d)	**68.** (d)	**69.** (c)	**70.** (b)
71. (a)	**72.** (b)	**73.** (c)	**74.** (d)	**75.** (b)	**76.** (b)	**77.** (a)	**78.** (a)	**79.** (b)	**80.** (c)
81. (b)	**82.** (c)	**83.** (d)	**84.** (b)	**85.** (c)	**86.** (c)	**87.** (d)	**88.** (a)	**89.** (b)	**90.** (d)
91. (d)	**92.** (d)	**93.** (a)	**94.** (d)	**95.** (b)	**96.** (c)	**97.** (c)	**98.** (b)	**99.** (c)	**100.** (d)
101. (a)	**102.** (a)	**103.** (b)	**104.** (d)	**105.** (c)	**106.** (d)	**107.** (b)	**108.** (b)	**109.** (c)	**110.** (c)
111. (c)	**112.** (c)	**113.** (c)	**114.** (b)	**115.** (d)	**116.** (c)	**117.** (a)	**118.** (b)	**119.** (c)	**120.** (c)
121. (c)	**122.** (d)	**123.** (b)	**124.** (b)	**125.** (b)	**126.** (b)	**127.** (c)	**128.** (b)	**129.** (d)	**130.** (a)
131. (d)	**132.** (c)	**133.** (a)	**134.** (c)	**135.** (c)	**136.** (d)	**137.** (c)	**138.** (b)	**139.** (a)	**140.** (a)
141. (d)	**142.** (d)	**143.** (b)	**144.** (b)	**145.** (d)	**146.** (c)	**147.** (c)	**148.** (d)	**149.** (d)	**150.** (d)
151. (b)	**152.** (a)	**153.** (c)	**154.** (c)	**155.** (a)	**156.** (d)	**157.** (b)	**158.** (a)	**159.** (c)	**160.** (b)
161. (b)	**162.** (a)	**163.** (b)	**164.** (d)	**165.** (b)	**166.** (d)	**167.** (b)	**168.** (c)	**169.** (a)	**170.** (b)
171. (c)	**172.** (c)	**173.** (b)	**174.** (d)	**175.** (a)	**176.** (c)	**177.** (c)	**178.** (b)	**179.** (a)	**180.** (b)
181. (d)	**182.** (c)	**183.** (c)	**184.** (b)	**185.** (a)	**186.** (b)	**187.** (a)	**188.** (c)	**189.** (b)	**190.** (d)
191. (b)	**192.** (c)	**193.** (d)	**194.** (b)	**195.** (b)	**196.** (c)	**197.** (b)	**198.** (d)	**199.** (d)	**200.** (a)
201. (b)	**202.** (b)	**203.** (d)	**204.** (d)	**205.** (d)	**206.** (a)	**207.** (a)	**208.** (c)	**209.** (b)	**210.** (a)
211. (d)	**212.** (a)	**213.** (d)	**214.** (d)	**215.** (a)	**216.** (d)	**217.** (d)	**218.** (a)	**219.** (d)	**220.** (a)

UNIT 29 Root Words

Given below are a number of important prefixes, suffixes and root words.

Root words	Meanings	Examples
a	without	**Abyss** - without bottom (a very deep hole that seems to have no bottom) **Achromatic** - without color **Anhydrous** - without water , containing no water. **Amoral** - without moral sense **Anexual** - without sexual feelings or associations
a	on	Afire - on fire Ashore - on the shore, onto the land from the sea, a river, etc. Aside - on the side
ab	not	Abnormal - not normal Absent - not present Aberration - a departure from normal Abstinence - not indulging in alcohol or sex
acro	height, tip, beginning	Acrobat - a high walker Acronym - a word formed from the first (capital) letters of a word Acrophobia - fear of height Acropolis - a citadel in ancient greek city built on a hill
aer/o	air	Aerate to let air reach something Aerial - relating to the air Aerospace the air space Aeronaut - someone who operates an aircraft Aerodynamics- the branch of mechanics that deals with the motion of gases (especially air) and their effects on bodies in the flow

Root words	Meanings	Examples
Agog	leading	Demagogue - an orator who appeals to the passions and prejudices of his audience Pedagogue - someone who educates young people Pedagogy - the activities of educating or instructing Synagogue- the place of worship for a jewish congregation
agr/i/o	farming	Agriculture management of the land Agribusiness-making money by utilizing land Agrarian - relating to the management of land
aholic/oholic	obsession for	Workaholic - obsession for work Shopaholic - obsession for shopping Alcoholic - obsession for alcohol
alg/o	pain	Neuralgia - pain caused by a nerve Analgesic - a drug that makes one pain free Nostalgia - aching for the familiar
ambi, amphi	both, on both sides, around	Ambidextrous - able to use both hands equally Ambient - completely enveloping Ambiguous - having more than one meaning Ambivalence - conflicting or opposite feelings toward a person or thing
ambul	walk, move	Amble - to walk in a slow relaxed manner Ambulant - walking or moving around Ambulance - a vehicle that moves a patient
ami/o	love	Amiable - friendly and lovable Amity - friendly and peaceful relations Amorous - showing romantic love

Root words	Meanings	Examples
andr/o	man, male	Androgynous - being both male and female Android - resembling a human Misandry - hatred towards men
anim	life, spirit	Animal- a living organism Animate - to make alive Equanimity - of balanced spirit
ann/enn	year	Anniversary- a date observed once a year Annual - happening once a year Millennium- 1,000 years
ante	before, in front	Antecede - to come before something in time Antemeridian - before noon Anteroom- a small room before the main room
anthrop/o	human	Anthropology - the study of mankind. Anthropomorphism - giving human form to non-human things Philanthropy - the love to mankind
anti	opposite of , against	Antibody - a substance that destroys micro-organisms Antiseptic - preventing infection. Antisocial - opposing social norm
aqu/a	water	Aquarium - a water container for fish Aquatic - relating to water Aqueduct - a pipeline for water
arbor	tree	Arborist - someone working with trees Arbor - a shady area formed by trees Arborous - having many trees

Root words	Meanings	Examples
arch/i	most important, rule, chief	Archbishop - the highest ranking bishop Archenemy - chief or worst enemy Matriarch - a female who rules a group Patriarch - a male who rules a group Monarch - a king or queen
arch/a/i	ancient, primitive	Archaeology - the study of ancient cultures Archaic - belonging to an earlier period Archive - a collection of historical materials
arthr/o	joint	Arthroscope - a tool to see inside a joint Arthritis - inflammation of a joint Arthropod - invertebrates
art	skill	Artifact - object made by a person's skill Artisan - a person skilled in a craft - Artist - a person who creates skillfully
astro, aster	star, stars, outer space	Astronaut - a person traveling to the stars Astronomer - someone who studies the stars A star-shaped sign used as a reference tool star-shaped sign used as a reference tool
aud/i/io	hear	Audible - loud enough to be heard Audience - people who listen to a program Audiovisual - relating to sound and vision
auto	self, same, one	Autocrat - a person who governs with absolute power Autograph - a person's own signature Automatic - moving by itself
avi/a	bird	Aviary - a large enclosure for birds Aviatrix - a female airplane pilot Aviation - the art of designing or operating aircraft

Root words	Meanings	Examples
bar/o	pressure, weight	Baric - pertaining to pressure, esp. of the atmosphere Millibar - metric unit, equal to 1/1000th of a bar Baryon - heavy elementary particle
bell/i	war	Bellicose - warlike Belligerent - hostile, ready to fight Rebel - person who opposes and fights
bene	good, well	Benefactor - person who gives money to a cause Beneficial - producing a good effect Benevolent - showing kindness or goodwill
bi/n	two, twice, once in every two	Biannual - happening twice a year Binoculars - optical device with two lenses Bilateral - of or involving two sides
bibili/o	book	Bibliography - a list of books used as sources Bibliomania - an extreme love of books Bibliophile - a person who loves books
bio	life, living things	Biography- a life story written by another person Biology - the science of life Biosphere - earth's surface inhabited by living things
cand	glowing, iridescent	Candid-free from bias, prejudice, or malice Candle- something that gives light Incandescent- white, glowing, or luminous with intense heat
cardi/o	heart	Cardiac - relating to the heart Cardiogenic - resulting from heart disease Cardiologist - a heart doctor
carn/i	flesh	Carnivorous - flesh eating Carnal - pertaining to the body or flesh Incarnate - given bodily form

Root words	Meanings	Examples
cata	intensive	Cataclysm - a flood or other disaster Catalog - a complete listing Catastrophe - turning for the worst, a substantial disaster
caust, caut	to burn	Cauterize - to burn with a hot instrument Caustic - capable of burning or eating away Holocaust - total devastation, especially by fire
cede, ceed, cess	go, yield	Exceed - to go beyond the limits Recede - to go back Accessible - easily entered, approached, or obtained
cent/i	hundred	Centennial - the 100th anniversary Centimeter - 1/100 of a meter Century - 100 years
centr/o/i	centre	Egocentric - self-centered, selfish Eccentric - not having a common center Centrifugal - moving outward from a center
cerebro/o	brain	Cerebral - pertaining to the brain Cerebrate - to use the brain Cerebrospinal - pertaining to the brain and the spinal cord
chrom/o,chromat/o, chros	colour, pigment	Achromatic - without color Chromium - a blue-white metallic chemical element Chromatics - the study of color
chron/o	time	Chronic - lasting for a long time Chronological - arranging events in time order Synchronize - happening at the same time
cide, cise	cut, kill	Homicide - murder Insecticide - a chemical used to kill insects Incisor - a sharp tooth for cutting food

Root words	Meanings	Examples
circum, circle	around, about	Circumnavigate - to sail around Circumscribe - to draw around Circumspect - looking around
co	with, together, joint	Coauthor - writer who collaborates with another author Coeducation - educating males and females together Cohousing - planning your neighborhood in an intentional neighborly fashion
col	together, jointly	Collaborate - to work together Collision - smashing together Colloquial - words formed by everday interaction
com	together, common	Commemorate - to memorize together Composition - an arrangement or putting together of parts Commune - living together while owning things in common
cogn/i	know	Cognition - process of acquiring knowledge Incognito - disguised so no one knows you Recognize - to discover that one knows
con	with, jointly	Concur - to agree with someone Contemporary - of the same time period as others Convention - a gathering of people with a common interest
contra/o	against, opposite	Contradict - to argue against Contrary - not in agreement Controversy - disagreement
corp/o	body	Corporation - a company recognized by law as a single body Corpse - a dead body Corporal - pertaining to the body

Root words	Meanings	Examples
cosm/o	universe	Cosmonaut - a russian astronaut Cosmos - the universe Microcosm - a miniature universe
counter	opposite, contrary, opposing	Counteract - to oppose the effects of an action Countermand - to cancel a previous order Counteroffensive - attack against an attack
cracy	rule, government, power	Aristocracy - government by nobility Bureaucracy - government by state officials Theocracy - government by gods
cranio	skull	Craniology - the study of skull characteristics Cranium - skull of vertebrates Cranial - pertaining to the skull
cred	believe	Credence - belief that something is true or valid Credulous - believing things too easily Incredible - unbelievable
crypto	hidden, secret	Cryptic of hidden meaning Cryptography - science of secret codes Encrypt - encode into secret code
de	reduce, away, down, remove	Decelerate - to slow down Dethrone - to remove from power Debug - to remove bugs
dec/a, deka	ten	Decade - 10 years Decathlon - athletic contest that includes 10 disciplines in which each participant competes December - formerly the 10th month of the roman calendar

Root words	Meanings	Examples
deci	one tenth	Deciliter - a tenth of a liter Decimate - reduce dramatically Decibel - one tenth of the sound volume unit bel
dem/o	people	Democracy - government of the people Demographic - the study of people Epidemic - spreading among people in a region
demi	half, less than	Demitasse - a small cup of coffee Demimonde - someone of little respected life style Demi god - half god
dendro/o/i	tree	Philodendron - a climbing plant that grows on trees Dendrochronology - dating events by studying growth rings in trees Dendriform - in the shape of a tree
dent, don't	tooth	Dental - relating to teeth Dentist - a doctor for the teeth Dentures - a set of false teeth
derm/a	skin	Dermatologist - a doctor for the skin Pachyderm - a class of animals with very thick skin Dermatitis - inflammation of the skin
di/plo	two, twice	Dichromatic - displaying two colors Diploma - a certificate, literally "a letter folded double" Dilemma - a situation that requires a choice between two alternative
domin	master	Dominate - to be the master of; domineering Domineering - excessively controlling Predominate - to have more power than others

Root words	Meanings	Examples
du/o	two, twice	Duplicate - make an identical copy Duet - a musical composition for two voices or instruments Duo - a pair normally thought of as being together
dys	abnormal, bad	Dyspepsia - abnormal digestion Dystopia - an imaginary place of total misery Dyslexia - impairment of the ability to handle words
ectiomy	surgical removal of	Appendectomy - a surgical operation to remove the appendix Hysterectomy - a surgical operation to remove all or part of the uterus
ego	self	Egoistic - self-centered Alter ego - a higher aspect of oneself Egomania - excessive preoccupation with oneself
endo	within, inside	Endotherm - a creature that can keep its inside temperature fairly constant Endocrine- relating to glands that secrete directly into the blood or lymph Endogamy - the custom to marry within one's clan, tribe etc.
enn/i, anni	years	Bicentennial - of or relating to an age or period of 200 years Centennial - of or relating to an age or period of 100 years Perennial -lasting through many years
ep/i	on, upon, over, at, after,	Epidemic - the rapid spread of something negative Epilogue - a short speech delivered after a play Epicenter - the center of an earthquake

Root words	Meanings	Examples
equ/i	equal, equally	Equidistant - an equal distance from two points Equanimity - calm temperament, evenness of temper Equation - a statement of equality.
erg/o	work	Ergonomics - study of the working environment Energy - the power to accomplish work Energetics -science that looks at energy and its transformation.
esth/aesth	feeling, sensation, beauty	Esthetician - someone who beautifies Aesthetic - pertaining to a sense of beauty Kinesthesia - the sensation of bodily movement.
ethno	race, people	Ethnic - pertaining to a defined group of people Ethnocentric - focusing on the ethnicity of people Ethnology - the science of people and races.
eu	good, well	Euphemism - replacing an offensive word with an inoffensive one Euphonious - having a pleasant sound Euphoria - feeling of well-being.
ex	from, out,	Excavate - to dig out Exhale - to breathe out Extract - to pull out.
extra, extro	outside, beyond	Extraordinary- beyond ordinary Extraterrestrial - outside the earth Extrovert - an outgoing person.
fid	faith	Confide - place trust in someone Fiduciary - a trustee Fidelity - faithfulness

Root words	Meanings	Examples
flor/a, fleur	flower	Florist - someone working with flowers Floral - flowerlike Flora - the plant life of a particular time or area
fore	in front of, previous, earlier	Forebear - ancestor Forebode - to give an advance warning of something bad Forecast - a preview of events to be.
gamy	marriage, union	Monogamy - the practice of marrying one person at a time Polygamy - the practice or custom of having more than one wife or husband at the same time
gastro/o	stomach	Gastric - pertaining to the stomach Gastronomy - serving the stomach by providing good food Gastritis - inflammation of the stomach.
gen/o/e/	birth,	Genealogy - the study of the history of a family Generation - all the people in a family, group who were born at about the same time.
geo	earth, soil, global	Geography - study of the earth's surface Geology - study of the structure of the earth Geoponics - soil based agriculture.
ger	old age	Geriatrics - medicine pertaining to the elderly Gerontocracy - the rule of the elders Gerontology - the science of aging.
giga	a billion	Gigabyte - unit of computer storage space Gigahertz - unit of frequency (one billion hz/sec) Gigawatt - unit of electric power (one billion watts)
gon	angle	Decagon - a polygon with 10 angles Diagonal - a slanting line running across a space Octagon - a geometrical figure with 8 angles.

Root words	Meanings	Examples
gram	letter, written	Diagram - a simple drawing Grammar - rules of how to write words in sentences Telegram - a message sent by telegraph.
graph/y	writing, recording, written	Graphology - the study of handwritings Autograph - written with one's own hand Seismograph - a machine noting strength and duration of earthquakes
gyn/o/e	woman, female	Gynecology- the science of female reproductive health Gynephobia - fear of women Gynecoid - resembling a woman,
gress, grade/e/i	to step, to go	Digression - a departure from the main issue, subject, etc. Progress - movement forward or onward Gradual - step by step.
hect/o, hecat	hundred	Hectoliter - 100 liters Hectare - metric unit equaling 100 ares or 10,000 square meters Hectometer - 100 meters.
helic/o	spiral, circular	Helicopter - an aircraft with horizontal rotating wing Helix - a spiral form Helicon - a circular tuba.
heli/o	sun	Heliotropism - movement or growth in relating to the sun Heliograph - apparatus used to send message with the help of sunlight Helianthus - genus of plants including sunflowers.
hemi	half, partial	Hemicycle - a semicircular structure Hemisphere - one half of the earth Hemistich - half a line of poetry.

Root words	Meanings	Examples
hem/o/a	blood	Hemorrhage - clotting of the blood Hemorrhoids - swelling of the blood vessels Hemoglobin - red blood particle.
hepa	liver	Hepatitis - inflammation of the liver Hepatoma - a tumor of the liver Hepatotoxic - toxic and damaging to the liver.
hept/a	seven	Heptagon - a shape with seven angles and seven sides Heptateuch - the first seven books of the old testament Heptameter - a line of verse consisting of seven metrical feet.
herbi	grass, plant	Herbicide - any chemical used to kill unwanted plants, etc. Herbivorous - plant-eating Herbal - relating to plants.
hetero	different, other	Heterogeneous - made up of unrelated parts Heteronyms - words with same spelling but different meanings Heterodox - not conforming to traditional beliefs.
hex/a	six	Hexagon - a shape with six angles/sides Hexameter - a verse measured in six Hexapod - having six legs.
homo, homeo	like, alike, same	Homogeneous - of the same nature or kind Homonym - sounding alike Homeopath - a therapy that is based on treating "same with same"
hydro/o	liquid, water	Hydrate - to add water to Hydrophobia - intense fear of water Hydroponics - growing plants in liquid nutrient solution Hydraulic - operated by force created by a liquid.

Root words	Meanings	Examples
hyper	too much, over, excessive, beyond	Hyperactive - very restless Hypercritical - too critical Hypertension - above normal pressure.
hyp/o	under	Hypoglycemia - an abnormally low level of sugar in the blood Hypothermia - abnormally low body temperature Hypothesis - a theory that is unproven but used under the assumption that it is true.
intr/o	medical care	Geriatrics - medical care of the elderly Pediatrician - a doctor who treats children Podiatry - medical care for feet.
icon/o	image	Icon - an (often religious) image, in modern usage a simplified graphic of high symbolic content Iconology - science of symbols and icons Iconoclast - someone who destroys religious images and traditional beliefs.
idio	peculiar, personal, distinct	Idiomatic - peculiar to a particular language Idiosyncracy - a physical or mental characteristic typical or a particular person Idiot - someone who is distinctly foolish or stupid.
il, im, in	not, without	Illegal - not legal Impossible - not possible Inappropriate - not appropriate
image	likeness	Image - a likeness of someone Imaginative - able to think up new ideas or images Imagine - to form a picture or likeness in the mind.
infra	beneath, below	Infrastructure - underlying framework of a system Infrared - below the regular light spectrum.

Root words	Meanings	Examples
inter	between, among, jointly	International - involving two or more countries Intersection - place where roads come together Intercept - to stop or interrupt the course of.
intra, intro	within, inside	Intrastate - existing in one state Intravenous - inside or into a vein Introvert - shy person who keeps within him/herself.
ir	not	Irredeemable - not redeemable Irreformable - not reformable Irrational - not rational.
iso	equal	Isobar – a line one a map connecting points of equal barometric pressure Isometric – having equality of measure Isothermal – having equal or constant temperature.
ject	throw	Eject – to throw someone/something out Interject – to throw a remark into a discussion Project – to cost or throw something.
jud	law	Judgment - a decision of a court of law Judicial - having to do with judges or courts of law Judiciary - a system of courts of law. Disjunction - a disconnection Junction - a place where two things join.
juven	young	Juvenile - youthful or childish Rejuvenate - to bring back to youthful strength or appearance.
killo	thousand	Kilometer - 1,000 meters Kilograms - 1,000 grams.

Root words	Meanings	Examples
kine/t/mat	motion, division	Psychokinesis or telekinesis - the ability to move objects with your mind Cinematography - motion picture making.
lab	work	Collaborate - to work with a person Elaborate - to work out the details Laborious - requiring a lot of hard work.
lact/o	milk	Lactate - to give milk, nurse Lactose - the sugar contained in milk Lactic - acid.
liber	free	Liberate - to set free Libertine - a person with a free, wild lifestyle Liberty - freedom.
lingu	language, tongue	Linguist - one who studies languages Multilingual - able to communicate in multiple languages Linguine - long, flat "tongue-shaped" pasta.
lip/o	fat	Liposuction - the mechanical removal of fat reserves in the tissue Lipase - enzyme that breaks down fat Lipoid - resembling fat.
loc	place	Dislocate - to put something out of its usual place Location - a place Relocate - to move to a new place.
log/o	word, doctrine, discourse	Logic - correct reasoning Monologue - a long speech by one speaker Analogy - similarity, especially between things otherwise dissimilar.

Root words	Meanings	Examples
loqu, locu	speak	Eloquent - speaking beautifully and forcefully Loquacious - very talkative Elocution - art of public speaking.
lumin	light	Illuminate - to fill with light Lumen - unit measuring light.
lun/a/i	moon	Lunar - relating to the moon Lunarscape - the surface of the moon Lunatic - insane (as if driven mad by the moon).
macro	large, great	Macroevolution - large scale evolution Macromolecule - a large molecule Macroeconomics - study of the overall forces of economy.
magn/a/i	great, large	Magnify - make larger Magnificent - grand Magnate - a powerful person, especially in business or industry.
mal/e	bad, ill, wrong	Malcontent - wrong content Malaria - "bad air", infectious disease thought to originate from the "bad air" of the swamps, but caused by the bite of an infected mosquito Malicious - showing strong ill will.
man/i/u	hand	Maneuver - to move by hand Manual - done with the hands Manuscript - a book written by hand.
mania	madness, insanity, excessive desire	Bibliomania - a crazy love of books Egomania - a mad love of oneself Maniac - an insane person.

Root words	Meanings	Examples
mar/i	sea	Marina - a harbor for pleasure boats Maritime - relating to the sea Submarine - an undersea boat Aquamarine - color of sea water.
mater, matr/i	mother	Maternal - relating to motherhood Maternity - the state of being a mother Matriarch - a woman head of a household.
max	greatest	Maximal - the best or greatest possible Maximize - to make as great as possible Maximum - the greatest amount.
medi	middle	Medieval - pertaining to the middle ages Medium - in the middle Mediocre - only of medium (inferior) quality.
mega	great, large, million	Megalopolis - an area with many nearby cities Megaphone - a device that projects a loud voice Megastructure - huge building or other structure.
mealan/o	black	Melancholy - a state of dark emotions Melanoma - malignant dark tumor of the skin Melodrama - a dark, pathetic drama.
memor/i	remember	Commemorate - to honor the memory of, as by a ceremony Memorial - related to remembering a person or event Memory - an ability to retain knowledge or an individual's stock of retained knowledge
meta	change, after, beyond, between	Metaphysics - study of nature and reality Metamorphosis - a complete change of form Metastasis - the transmission of disease to other parts of the body.

Root words	Meanings	Examples
meter, metr/y	measure	Audiometer - an instrument that measures hearing acuteness Chronometer- an instrument that measures time Metric - measured.
micro	very small, short, minute	Microbe - a very small living thing Microchip - a tiny wafer with an integrated circuit Microscope - a device to see very small things.
mid	middle	Midriff - the area between the chest and the waist Midterm - middle of a term in school Midway - halfway between.
migr	move	Immigrant - a person who moves to a new country to settle Migrant - person who moves from place to place Migration - the process of moving.
milli	onethousandth	Millimeter - one thousandth of a meter Millibar - one thousandth of a bar Milliliter - one thousandth of a liter.
min/i	small, less	Mini - something that is very small Minuscule - extremely tiny Minutiae - very small or trivial details.
miss/o	bad, badly, wrong, wrongly, to hate	Misbehave - to behave badly Misprint - an error in printing Misnomer - an error in naming a person or thing.
miss, mit	send, let go	Dismiss - to send someone away Missile - a weapon sent into the air Emit - to send something out Admittance - entry.

Root words	Meanings	Examples
mob	move	Immobilize - to stop from moving Mobile - able to move freely Mobility - the quality of being able to move.
mom/o	one, single, alone	Monochromat - having one color Monologue - a speech spoken by one person Monotheism - belief in one god.
mot, mov	move	Motion - the act of moving Motivate - to move someone to action Promote - to move someone forward Removable - able to be taken or carried away.
morph/o	form	Metamorphosis - complete change of form Endorphins - chemical in the brain able to transform pain Amorphous - without distinct shape or form.
mort	death	Immortal - living forever, unable to die Mortal - certain to die Mortician - an undertaker.
multi	many, more than one or two	Multicolored - having many colors Multimedia - using a range of media Multitasking - doing many things at once.
mut	change	Immutable - not changing Mutant - an organism that has undergone change Mutate - to undergo a change.
my/o	muscle	Myocardium - the middle muscle of the heart Myasthenia - muscle fatigue or weakness Myosin - common protein in muscle tissue.

Root words	Meanings	Examples
narr	tell	Narrate - to tell a story Narrative - a story Narrator - a person who tells a story.
nat	born	Innate - included since birth Natal - relating to birth Natural - gotten at birth, not afterward.
nav	ship	Circumnavigate - to sail around a place Naval - relating to a navy or warships Navigate - to sail a ship through a place.
necr/o	dead, death	Necrophil- loving death Necrosis - the death of tissue due to disease or injury Necrology - a list of persons who have recently died.
neg	no	Negate - to say it didn't happen Negative - meaning "no" Renege - to go back on a promise.
neo	new,recent	Neoclassic - a revival of classic form, neocolonialism - the indirect ("new") economical and political control of a region by a more powerful foreign power Neonatal - a newborn child, especially the first few weeks.
nephr/o	kidney	Nephritis - inflammation of the kidneys Nephrotomy - surgical incision of a kidney Nephron - a single, excretory unit in the kidney.
neur/o	nerve	Neuralgia - pain along a nerve Neurologist - doctor specializing in the nerves Neurotic - mental disorder that usually does not include an impaired perception of reality.

Root words	Meanings	Examples
nom/in	name	Misnomer - an error in naming a person or thing Nominal - being something in name only but not in reality Nominate - to name for election or appointment, to designate.
non	no,not,without	Nondescript - with no special characteristics Nonfiction - true, real, not made-up Nonsense - without sense.
noun,nunc	declare	Announce - to declare in public Denounce - to proclaim harsh criticism Enunciate - to speak or declare something clearly.
nov	new	Innovate - to introduce a new way Novelty - something new Novice - a person who is new at a job Renovate - to make something like new again.
numer	number	Enumerate - to name a number of items on a list Numerology - the study of magical uses of numbers Numerous - a large number.
ob,op	in the way, against	Object - to be against something Obscure - hard to understand Opposition - the act of resistance or action against.
oct/a/o	eight	Octagon - a figure with 8 sides and 8 angles Octogenarian - person in his or her 80s Octopus- sea animal with 8 arms.
ocu	eye	Binoculars - lens device for seeing distances Monocula - relating to one eye Oculist - an eye doctor.

Root words	Meanings	Examples
odor	smell, scent	Deodorant - a substance that helps prevent body odor Malodorous - having a terribly bad smell Odoriferous- something that bears or diffuses a scent
ology	study of, science of	Anthropology - the study of human societies and cultures and their development Archaeology - the study of human history and prehistory through the excavation of sites Biology - the study of living organisms
omni	all	Omnipotent - with all the power Omniscient - knowing all things Omnivorous - eating all foods
ortho	straight	Orthodontist - a dentist that straightens teeth Orthopedic - a doctor concerned with the proper alignment of the bones Orthography - the correct way of writing.
osteo	bone	Osteoarthritis - inflammation caused by degeneration of the joints Osteopathy- therapy that uses among others manipulation of the skeleton to restore health Osteology - the study of bones.
over	excessive	Overconfident - more confident than is appropriate Overstock - more supplies than is desirable Overexcited - more excited than one should be.
pale/o	ancient	Paleontology - study of ancient fossils Paleography - the study of ancient forms of writing Paleolithic - period of the stone age.

Root words	Meanings	Examples
pan	all, any, everyone	Panacea - a cure for all diseases or problems Panorama - an all-around view Pantheism - the worship of all gods Pandemic - affecting all.
para	beside, beyond, abnormal, assistant	Parasite - an organism that lives on and off another living being Parallel - alongside and always an equal distance apart Paragraph - a portion of a written document that presents a distinct idea.
pater, patr/i	father	Paternal- relating to fathers Paternity - fatherhood Patriarch - a man who rules a group.
path	feeling, emotion	Antipathy - a feeling of great dislike Apathy - a lack of feeling or interest Empathy - ability to understand another's feelings.
ped/i/e	foot, feet	Pedal - a lever pushed by the foot Pedestrian - one who walks Pedicure - cosmetic treatment of feet and toes.
pent/a	five	Pentagon - shape having 5 angles and 5 sides, pentagram a five-pointed star formerly used as a symbolic figure in magic Pentathlon - an athletic contest that includes five events.
pept,peps	digestion	Dyspepsia - abnormal digestion Peptic - aiding digestion Pepsin - a digestive enzyme.
per	through, throughout	Permanent - lasting throughout all time Permeate - to spread throughout Persist - to continue for a long time Perennial - lasting through many years.

Root words	Meanings	Examples
peri	around, enclosing	Periodontal - pertaining to bone and tissue around a tooth Peripheral - lying outside of the center Perimeter - the outer boundary of an area.
phag/e	to eat	Esophagus - muscular tube that carries food to the stomach Anthropophagy or sarcophagy - cannibalism Xylophagous-feeding on wood.
phil/o	love, friend	Philanthropist - one who loves humanity Philology - the love of words Philosophy - the love of wisdom Bibliophil - loving books. Pyrophile - the love of fire or fireworks Audiophile - the love of high-fidelity sound reproduction
phobia	abnormal fear of	Acrophobia - abnormal fear of heights Claustrophobia - abnormal fear of closed or narrow spaces Xenophobia - abnormal fear of against people from other countries
phon/o/e/y	sound	Cacophony - loud, unpleasant sounds Microphone - a device that records and amplifies sound Phonetic - relating to human speech sounds.
phot/o	light	Photogenic - caused by light Photograph - image made on light-sensitive film Photon - the smallest possible unit of light.
phyll/o	leaf	Chlorophyll - a group of green pigments found in leaves Phyllotaxis - the arrangement of leaves on a stem Phyllite - a rock that forms sheets, similar to slate.

Root words	Meanings	Examples
phys	nature, medicine, the body	Physical - relating to the body Physician - a doctor Physique - nature and shape of one's body.
phyt/o/e	plant, to grow	Epiphyte- a plant growing independently on the surface of another Hydrophyte - a plant that grows only in water Neophyte - a beginner, especially a person recently converted to a new belief.
pneum/o	breathing, lung, air, spirit	Pneumonia - inflammation of the lungs Pneumatic - using the force of air Dyspnea - difficulty in breathing.
pod/e	foot	Podiatrist - a doctor for the feet Podium - a small platform to stand on Tripod - a stand or frame with 3 legs.
poly	many, more than one	Polychrome - with many colors - Polyglot - a person fluent in many languages Polygon - shape with 3 or more straight sides.
pop	people	Popular - appealing to a lot of people Population - all of the people who live in a particular area Populist - a supporter of the rights of people.
port	carry	Export - to carry goods out of a place to another Portable - able to be carried Porter - a person who carries luggage.
post	after, behind	Posthumous - after someone's death Postpone - to delay something Postscript - an addition to an place where someone is.

Root words	Meanings	Examples
pre	earlier, before, in front of	Preamble - a part in front of a formal document Prepare - to get ready in advance Prediction - a statement foretelling the future.
pro	before, in front of, for, forward	Prognosis - a prediction of what will happen Prologue - a passage before the main part Prophet - a person who foretells the future.
prot/o	primitive, first, chief	Prototype - the first of a kind Proton - on of the very basic parts of an atom Protocol - a first draft from which a document is prepared.
pseud/o	wrong, false	Pseudonym - a fictitious name Pseudoscience - theories presumed without proof of a scientific nature Pseudopregnancy - a false pregnancy.
psych/o	mind,mental	Psyche - the human spirit or soul Psychic - relating to the human mind or someone who has supernatural mental abilities Psychology- the study of the mind.
pugn/,pung	to fight	Pugnacious - having a quarrelsome or aggressive nature Repugnant - distasteful, offensive or revolting Pungent - piercing.
pul	urge	Compulsion - a very strong urge Expulsion - to someone out Impulsive - having a spontaneous urge to do something.
purg	clean	Purge - remove anything undesirable Purgatory - according to roman catholics a place where souls must clean themselves of sin Expurgate - remove objectionable passages from a publication.

Root words	Meanings	Examples
pyr/o	fire, heat	Pyrotechnics - the art of making fireworks Pyrometer - a thermometer for measuring high temperature Pyretic - relating to or producing fever.
quad/r/ri	four	Quadrant - open space with buildings on 4 sides Quadrennium - period of 4 years Quadruped - a 4-footed animal.
quart	fourth	Quarter - one fourth Quart - a fourth of a gallon Quartet - a musical composition or group involving 4 voices or instruments.
quin/t	five, fifth	Quintett - a composition for 5 voices or instruments Quintessence - pure essence, based on the ancient philosophy that there was a fifth element that was present in all things Quintuple - fivefold.
radic,radix	root	Eradicate - pull out at the roots Radical - fundamental, looking at things from a drastic point of view Radish - an edible root of the mustard family.
radio	radiation, ray	Radioactive - emitting radiation Radiologist - someone diagnosing or treating via radiation.
ram/i	branch	Ramification - the resulting consequence of a decision Ramify - to spread or branch out Ramus - a branchlike part.

Root words	Meanings	Examples
re	again, back, backward	Rebound - to spring back again Rewind - to wind something backward Reaction - a response Recognize - to identify someone or something seen before
retro	backward, back	Retroactive - relating to something in the past Retrogress - to go back to an earlier condition Retrospect - the remembering of past events.
rhin/o	nose	Rhinoceros - a species of animals with a big horn on the snout Rhinoplasty - surgery of the nose Rhinovirus - viruses that are causing the common cold.
rhod/o	red	Rhododendron - a flower with red/pink flowers Rhodium - an element which produces a red solution Rhodopsin - a purple pigment in the retina that is needed for vision.
rupt	break, burst	Bankrupt - unable to pay because you're "broke" Interrupt - to break into a conversation or event, to disturb Rupture - a break in something.
san	health	Sane - mentally healthy Sanitary - relating to cleanliness and health Sanitation - maintenance of public health and cleanliness.
scend	climb, go	Ascend - to climb upward Crescendo - a climbing up of the volume of music Descend - to go or climb down.
sci	know	Conscience - sense of knowing right from wrong Conscious - knowing what is happening Omniscient - knowing everything.

Root words	Meanings	Examples
scop/e/y	see, examine, observe	Microscope - a device used to see tiny things Periscope - a seeing instrument on a submarine Telescope - a device used to see over a distance.
scrib,script	write, written	Inscribe - to write letters or words on a surface Scribe - a person who writes out documents Describe - to represent with words or pictures.
se	apart	Secede - to formally break away from Seclude - to keep away from Serum - a liquid isolated out of another.
sect	cut	Dissect - to cut apart piece by piece Intersection - the place or point where two things cross each other Bisect - to cut into two equal parts.
semi	half, partial	Semiannual - every half year Semicircle - half a circle Semiconscious - partly conscious Semiannual - every half of a year.
sept/i	seven	September - this used to be the seventh month in the roman calendar Septet - a group of seven musicians Septuagenarian - a person in his/her seventies.
sol	alone	Desolate - lonely, dismal, gloomy Solitary - done alone, by yourself Solo - a performance done by one person alone.
sol	sun	Solar - involving the sun Parasol - umbrella protecting from the sun Solarium - a room where one is exposed to sun light.

Root words	Meanings	Examples
somn/I	sleep	Insomnia - inability to fall asleep Somniloquy - talking in your sleep Somnolent - feeling sleepy.
son	sound	Consonant - a speech sound Sonorous - producing loud, full, rich sounds Supersonic - faster than sound Unison - as one voice.
soph	wise	Philosopher - a wise person Sophisticated - wise about the ways of the world Sophism - a clever but misleading argument.
spec/t, spic	see, look	Circumspect - cautious, looking all around Retrospective - a looking back at past things Spectator - a person who sees an event.
spir	breathe	Inspire - to stimulate or animate Transpire - to give of vapor with waste product through the skin or a membrane Spirit - invisible life force.
sta	stand	Stable - standing steady and firm Stagnant - standing still, not moving Stationary - at a standstill, fixed.
stell	star	Constellation - a group of stars that forms a pattern Interstellar - between the stars Stellar - relating to stars.
struck	build	Construct to build Destruction - the act of destroying something that was built Structure - something built Infrastructure - underlying framework of a system.

Root words	Meanings	Examples
sub	under, lower than, inferior to	Submarine - an underwater boat Submerge - to put underwater Substandard - inferior to accepted standards.
sum	highest	Sum - the combined total of everything Summation - the total, highest amount game Summit - the highest point or top
super	higher in quality or quantity	Super bowl - the final annual football Superior - above average, better in quality Supersonic - faster than the speed of sound.
tact, tang	touch	Contact - a state in which two things touch Tactile - relating to the sense of touch Tangible - able to be touched Intact - with nothing missing.
tel/e/o	far, distant, complete	Telephone - a device to talk to a distant person Telescope - a device to view distant objects Television - a device to receive pictures from afar Telecommuting - working remotely, bridging the distance via virtual devices.
temp/or	time	Contemporary - existing at the same time Temporal - relating to time Temporary - lasting for a limited time.
ter,trit	rub	Attrition- the act of rubbing together or wearing down Detritus- a product of disintegration or wearing away Trite- used or occurring so often as to have lost interest, freshness, or force
term/ina	end, limit	Determine - to find something out at the end of an investigation Terminate - to end Exterminate - to destroy or get rid of completely.

Root words	Meanings	Examples
tarr/a/i	land, earth	Extraterrestrial - existing outside the earth Terrain - ground or land Territory - an area of land.
tetra	four	Tetrapod - having 4 legs Tetrarchy - government by 4 rulers Tetrose - a monosaccharide with four carbon atoms.
the/o	god	Monotheism - belief in one god Polytheism - worshiping more than one god Theology - the study of religion, god, etc.
therm/o	heat	Thermal - relating to heat Thermos - an insulated jar that keeps heat in Thermostat - a device that controls heat.
tort	twist	Contortion - a twisted shape or position Distort - to alter the shape or condition of Retort - reply in a manner that is supposed to change the effect of something previously said.
tox	poison	Detoxification - the process of removing poisons Toxic - poisonous Toxicology - the study of poisons Intoxicated - influenced by drugs.
tract	pull, drag	Attract - to pull objects nearer Distract - to drag attention away from something Tractor - a motor vehicle that pulls things.
trans	across, beyond, through	Transcontinental - across the continent Transfer - to move from one place to another Transport - to carry something across a space.

Root words	Meanings	Examples
tri	three, once in every three, third	Triangle - a figure with 3 sides and 3 angles Triathlon - an athletic contest with 3 events Tricycle - a 3-wheel vehicle with pedals.
ultra	beyond, extreme, more than	Ultrahigh - extremely high Ultramodern - more modern than anything else Ultrasonic - sound waves beyond human hearing.
un	not,opposite of, lacking	Unabridged - not shortened Unfair - opposite of fair Unfriendly - lacking friendliness.
uni	one, single	Unicycle - a vehicle with one wheel Unilateral - decided by only one person or nation Unique - the only one of its kind Unison - as one voice.
urb	city	Suburb - residential area on the edge of a city Urban - relating to a city Urbanology - the study of city life.
vac	empty	Evacuate - to empty a dangerous place Vacant - empty, not occupied Vacation - a time without work.
ven/t	come	Circumvent - to go around or bypass restrictions Convention - a gathering or assembly of people with a common interest Intervene - to come between.
ver/I	truth	Veracious - truthful, honest Veracity - the truth Verify - to make sure that something is true.

Root words	Meanings	Examples
verb	word	Verbalize - to put into words Adverb - a word relating to a verb Proverb - a short saying that expresses a well-known truth.
vers, vert	turn	Reverse - to turn around Introvert - being turned towards the inside Version - a variation of an original Controversy - a conversation in which positions are turned against each other.
vince,vic	conquer	Convince - to win someone over Invincible - not able to be conquered Victory - the conquest of an enemy.
viv,vit	live, life	Revival - the act of bringing back to life Vital - pertaining to live Vivacious - high-spirited and full of life.
voc/i	voice, call	Advocate - to speak in favor of Equivocate - to use misleading language that could be interpreted two different ways Vocalize - to produce with your voice.
vor,vour	eat	Carnivorous - meat-eating Voracious - desiring or eating food in great quantities Devour - to eat quickly.
xen/o	foreign	Xenophobic - afraid of foreigners Xenogenesis - the creation of offspring that is completely different from either parent Xenophile - attracted to foreigners.
xer/o/I	dry	Xerophyte - a plant that grows in dry climate Xerography - a dry photocopying process Xeric - requiring small amounts of moisture.

Notes:

Notes: